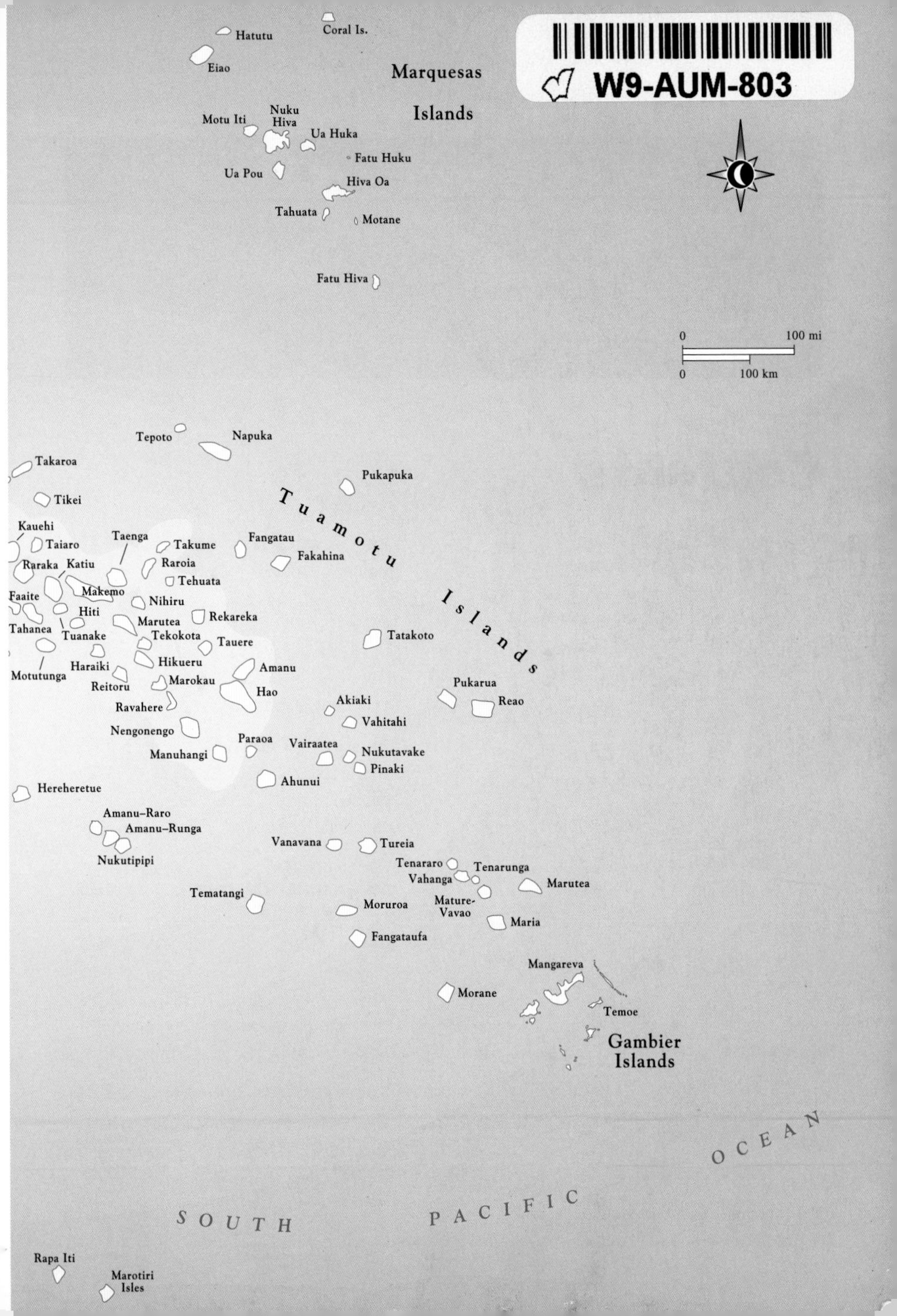

Hatutu
Coral Is.
Eiao
Marquesas Islands
Motu Iti
Nuku Hiva
Ua Huka
Fatu Huku
Ua Pou
Hiva Oa
Tahuata
Motane
Fatu Hiva

0 100 mi
0 100 km

Tepoto
Napuka
Takaroa
Pukapuka
Tikei
Tuamotu Islands
Kauehi
Taiaro
Taenga
Takume
Fangatau
Raraka
Katiu
Raroia
Fakahina
Tehuata
Makemo
Faaite
Nihiru
Hiti
Rekareka
Marutea
Tahanea
Tuanake
Tekokota
Tatakoto
Tauere
Hikueru
Motutunga
Haraiki
Amanu
Marokau
Reitoru
Hao
Pukarua
Ravahere
Akiaki
Reao
Vahitahi
Nengonengo
Paraoa
Vairaatea
Nukutavake
Manuhangi
Pinaki
Ahunui
Hereheretue
Amanu-Raro
Amanu-Runga
Nukutipipi
Vanavana
Tureia
Tenararo
Tenarunga
Vahanga
Marutea
Tematangi
Mature-Vavao
Moruroa
Maria
Fangataufa
Mangareva
Morane
Temoe
Gambier Islands

SOUTH PACIFIC OCEAN

Rapa Iti
Marotiri Isles

Contents

Discover Tahiti and French Polynesia

French Polynesia embraces a vast ocean area strewn with faraway outer islands, each with a mystique of its own. The 118 islands and atolls are scattered over an expanse of water 18 times the size of California, though in dry-land terms the territory is only slightly larger than Rhode Island.

Every oceanic island type is represented. The coral atolls of the Tuamotus are so low they're threatened by rising sea levels, while volcanic Tahiti soars to 2,241 meters. Bora Bora and Maupiti, also high volcanic islands, rise from the lagoons of what would otherwise be atolls.

Marine life flourishes wherever the ocean and lagoon meet. The passes into the lagoons are teeming with dolphins, barracuda, rays, and sharks, while myriad tropical fish populate the brilliant reefs. Flowers blossom along palm-fringed shores throughout the islands. Even the climate is dramatic, switching from brilliant sunshine to pelting rain and back in a matter of minutes.

These detached corners of the world were reached by Polynesian voyagers two millennia ago. Over time, a sophisticated civilization emerged in harmony with nature. Eighteenth-century explorers Wallis, Bougainville, and Cook told of a land of spellbinding beauty and enchantment. Legendary Tahiti became known as the isle of love or "la Nouvelle Cythère," the earthly paradise.

For the modern traveler, a visit to French Polynesia is guaranteed to

be full of adventure: scuba diving, snorkeling, surfing, kayaking, sailing, and fishing. Lagoon tours deposit you in natural aquariums, or you can cruise in search of dolphins and whales. It's not uncommon to snorkel with rays or to dive among feeding sharks.

Back on land, the adventures continue. There are sightseeing tours along the coasts and jeep safaris into the interiors. Hedonistic visitors can wallow in a Polynesian spa or experience a Tahitian massage. See and be seen on flashy resort beaches or be the first of the day to leave footprints on the white sands of an outer island.

French Polynesia is a fascinating mélange of French taste and Polynesian warmth. The friendly, easygoing manner of many people isn't just a cliché. Despite over a century and a half of French colonialism, the Tahitians retain many of their age-old ways, be it in personal dress, Polynesian dancing, or outrigger canoe racing. Relax, smile, and say *bonjour* to strangers – you'll almost always get a warm response.

Welcome to paradise!

Planning Your Trip

▸ WHERE TO GO

Tahiti

Tahiti is French Polynesia's largest island, the site of its only international airport. The capital, Papeete, will entertain you for a day with its stylish waterfront, markets, restaurants, shops, buildings, parks, and colonial monuments. Then take a ride around Tahiti for the diverse scenery, beaches, historical relics, and museums. There are also jeep safaris across the center of the island for the adventurous.

Moorea

A high-speed catamaran ferry links Moorea to Tahiti. The island's stunning Opunohu Valley is replete with splendid mountain scenery, lush vegetation, and fascinating archaeological sites. Moorea is a favorite of beach lovers, aquatic enthusiasts, and hikers. At Hauru you can snorkel with huge manta rays or join a quest for wild spinner dolphins. Half a dozen scuba operators are based on Moorea, and snorkeling, parasailing, deep-sea fishing, surfing, sailing, and horseback riding are all on the menu.

The Leeward Islands

The enchanting island of Huahine has the greatest concentration of old Polynesian temples

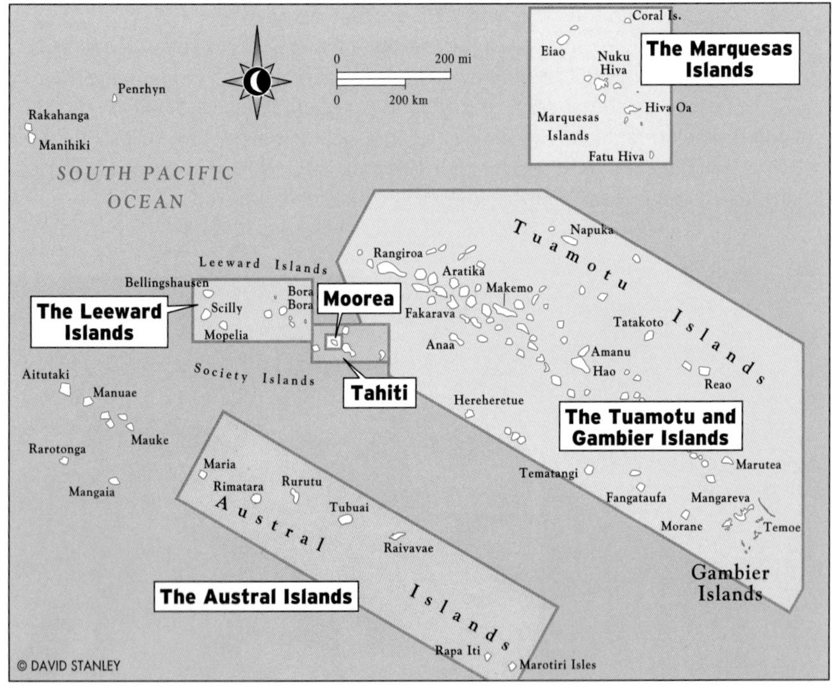

IF YOU HAVE . . .

- **ONE WEEK:** Visit Bora Bora or Huahine plus Moorea and Tahiti.
- **TWO WEEKS:** Add two Leeward islands and an extra day on Tahiti.
- **THREE WEEKS:** Add a week in the Tuamotu or Marquesas islands by air.
- **FOUR WEEKS:** For the third and fourth weeks, take a two-week cruise in the Marquesas on the *Aranui*.

a passage into the Bora Bora lagoon

in French Polynesia, and the little port town of Fare is among the most picturesque in the territory. Neighboring Raiatea and Taha'a are off the beaten track, though French Polynesia's most important yacht harbor is on Raiatea. Bora Bora is a chic resort island with a sheer volcanic plug plunging into a brilliant lagoon. To see a comparable isle still untouched by tourism one must travel farther west to Maupiti.

The Austral Islands

The remote Austral Islands south of Tahiti are noticeably cooler. Those who make it this far can enjoy excellent hiking on scenic Rurutu and wonderful swimming and snorkeling in the broad Tubuai lagoon. Raivavae is a mystery island far off the beaten track with massive stone tikis. Remote little Rapa is the southernmost island in the South Pacific, accessible only by boat.

The Tuamotu and Gambier Islands

Rangiroa, Tikehau, Manihi, and Fakarava are mainly for the scuba diver or ardent beachcomber. Polynesia's most spectacular atoll may be Rangiroa, where the Avatoru and Tiputa Passes are world-renowned for tidal-drift diving. The marine life here is outstanding, and it's even better at lesser-known Fakarava. The other 74 Tuamotu atolls have most of French Polynesia's black pearl farms. The far-removed Gambier Islands are best known for massive churches erected under the orders of a fanatical Catholic priest.

The Marquesas Islands

The passenger-carrying freighter *Aranui* cruises the remote Marquesas group 15 times a year—the easiest way to go. Islands such as Nuku Hiva and Hiva Oa harbor many archaeological and scenic wonders. Taiohae on Nuku Hiva is the capital of the Marquesas, and many huge Polynesian stone tikis are just across the island. The impressionist painter Paul Gauguin lived and died at Atuona on Hiva Oa.

Hatiheu Bay of the north shore of Nuku Hiva, Marquesas Islands

WHEN TO GO

The seasonal climatic variations in French Polynesia are not extreme. There's a hotter, more humid season from November to April and a cooler, drier time from May to October. On Tahiti, December–February are the wettest months, and July–September are the driest. These contrasts are more pronounced in areas closer to the equator, such as the Marquesas, and less noticeable in the Austral Islands. Hurricanes can come during the "rainy" season but such storms only last a few days a year.

The southeast trade winds sweep the South Pacific from May to October, the cruising season for yachts. Cooler and drier, these are the ideal months for travel in French Polynesia. For the scuba diver, the best diving conditions are during the dry season, with the marine life most profuse from July to November. May–October is the best time for mountain climbing, sailing, and bicycling, and July–September is the peak surfing season. Whale-watchers will need to come July–October.

a traveler's tree in front of the post office in Fare, Huahine

BEFORE YOU GO

Visas and Officialdom

Most visitors do not require a visa to enter French Polynesia, although a passport and a ticket to leave are mandatory. Citizens of the United States, Canada, Japan, New Zealand, and a dozen other countries get one month upon arrival, while citizens of the European Union countries, Australia, Norway, and Switzerland get three months. Extensions of stay are available in Papeete.

Getting There

Direct flights to Papeete arrive from Auckland, Honolulu, Los Angeles, Nouméa, Paris, Rarotonga, Santiago, and Tokyo. Seven international airlines fly here or have code-share agreements.

Getting Around

The domestic carrier Air Tahiti has regular flights to all parts of French Polynesia from their hubs on Tahiti, Bora Bora, and Rangiroa.

High-speed catamarans glide between Papeete and Moorea every couple of hours, but the ferry service between Tahiti, Huahine, Raiatea, and Bora Bora was not operating at the time of going to press.

Frequent bus service is available on Tahiti. On Moorea, public buses meet most ferries. Public transportation on the other islands is poor to nonexistent, and you may need to rent a bicycle or car. Group tours are an alternative.

Explore Tahiti and French Polynesia

▸ THE BEST OF FRENCH POLYNESIA

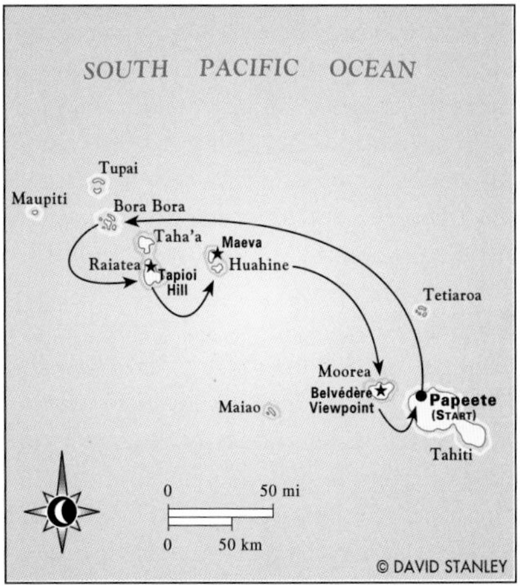

Two weeks of serious traveling will allow you to experience all the main attractions of the Society Islands. Air Tahiti sells a Bora Bora Pass which can be extended to the Austral, Tuamotu, and Marquesas Islands at the time of purchase.

Alternatively, you could skip the pass and fly one-way to Bora Bora, returning to Papeete by a combination of boat and air. The high-speed ferry *Maupiti Express 2* cruises between Bora Bora and Raiatea four times a week and Moorea is easily accessible by catamaran. Ferry service between Raiatea, Huahine, and Tahiti was in flux at press time, so verify the current situation at the time of travel.

Day 1

If your international flight to Papeete arrives early enough in the day, change a good chunk of money at the airport bank and catch a connecting flight to Bora Bora. Upon arrival, you'll be transferred to Vaitape on a free ferry. On the main island, most accommodations are at Matira Point, about six kilometers from Vaitape Wharf. The more upscale hotels on the *motu* meet their guests at Bora Bora Airport itself and ferry them directly to their resorts. Once you're settled, spend the rest of your day snorkeling and enjoying the beach.

Day 2

Today you should rent a bicycle and pedal around Bora Bora, stopping at the viewpoints and archaeological sites. You can circumnavigate the island in about three hours; scooters and cars are also available, if you prefer. Don't overlook the upscale resorts as free sightseeing attractions. All of them will let you walk in. If you're going to Raiatea by ferry, book your ticket while in Vaitape.

Day 3

A lagoon tour by motorized outrigger canoe is probably the best way to experience Bora Bora, and many companies offer them. You'll get to snorkel with reef sharks and manta rays and enjoy a picnic lunch on a deserted beach. Otherwise, go scuba diving, or just chill on the beach.

Day 4

Catch a ferry or flight from Bora Bora to Raiatea, where the pension owners usually pick up prebooked guests from the airport or wharf. Otherwise, rent a car. That's a good idea anyway, as public transportation on Raiatea is minimal. Depending on where you're staying and how energetic you are, you could climb Tapioi Hill for the view or just explore the vicinity of Uturoa.

Day 5

If you've rented a car, you'll want to drive around Raiatea. There are some archaeological sites to see, but the main thing is just to enjoy the scenery, so don't speed. The yacht harbor at Apooiti Bay is always worth a stop. Alternatively, you could ask your host to help you arrange an outrigger canoe tour around Taha'a or south to Marae Taputapuatea.

Day 6

Continue to Huahine today by ferry or flight. The ferry service from Raiatea to Huahine and Tahiti was in a state of change at the time of going to press, so check locally. At Huahine, the boats tie up at Fare Wharf within walking distance of several places to stay. If you arrived on the morning flight, you'll have most of the day to explore Fare and enjoy the beach.

Day 7

Once again, public transportation is almost nonexistent here, so you'll need to rent a bicycle, scooter, or car if you really want to see Huahine. Begin with the intriguing archaeological remains of Maeva, then cross the spine of Hauhine-iti from Faie to Maroe Bay. A drive around Huahine-iti will fill the rest of your day. By bicycle it would be too much, so plan accordingly.

Day 8

A number of excellent outrigger canoe lagoon tours are offered from Fare. Otherwise you could go scuba diving, take a jeep safari, or go sailing. Also consider taking the shuttle boat from Fare to the Te Tiare Beach Resort for lunch and a day at the beach.

Day 9

A daily flight links Huahine to Moorea. Be

performance by a traditional dance troupe during the Heiva i Tahiti Festival in Papeete

a sunset over Huahine, Leeward Islands

sure to buy a ticket for the bus transfer on Moorea as you're checking in at Huahine, as transfer tickets are not sold at Moorea Airport and you'll be stuck with expensive taxi fare. You'll have the rest of the day on Moorea to enjoy the beach and the vicinity of wherever you're staying.

If you want to try to return to Tahiti by boat, verify the schedule locally and be prepared for delays as ferry services to/from Huahine are currently in a state of change. Upon arrival in Papeete, connect with the catamaran to Moorea as soon as you can and save Tahiti for later.

Day 10

Rent a bicycle or car and ride around Moorea today. The trip up to the Belvédère viewpoint is obligatory; you'll pass the Marae Titiroa archaeological site on the way. Aside from the usual tourist attractions, it's fun to drop into the Sofitel, Pearl Resort, Hilton, and InterContinental resorts for a look around; ask about their Polynesian dance shows. If you don't care to drive, several companies offer half-day bus tours around the island.

Day 11

Today is the day for a lagoon trip by motorized outrigger canoe, either to swim with the sharks and rays at Hauru or to search for wild spinner dolphins. Scuba diving is also easily arranged.

Day 12

Catch a flight or ferry back to Tahiti this morning. Even if you have a plane ticket, you might want to use the high-speed catamaran instead for the experience. The ferry will drop you right in town within walking distance of a few hotels. Spend the rest of the day exploring Papeete, beginning with the market.

waterfall plunging over a volcanic cliff

Day 13

Travel around Tahiti today, either by public bus, rental car, or organized bus tour. There are waterfalls, beaches, museums, and gardens to visit. If going by public bus, get an early start on a weekday and go clockwise. You might end up having to hitchhike back to Papeete along the south coast, but that's very easy to do. Otherwise, take one of the jeep safaris across the center of Tahiti via Relais de la Maroto.

Day 14

If you're leaving Tahiti later today, store your bags at your hotel or at the airport left-luggage office. Depending on your flight time, you might be able to get in another half-day tour, or spend some more time in Papeete. Just don't go scuba diving on your departure day, as it could lead to a case of the bends.

▸ UNDERWATER IN THE TUAMOTU ISLANDS

While the Society Islands can be visited on a reasonable budget, you'll need to invest considerably more money to see the other island groups of French Polynesia. Your best bet is to buy one of the Air Tahiti passes, which cover the Austral, Tuamotu, and Marquesas Islands. These passes are valid for 28 days travel in total, so you could build on *The Best of French Polynesia* itinerary. Frankly, that's the only practical way to go, as point-to-point airfares are prohibitive and boat travel is basic and irregular.

To combine the Tuamotu Islands with the Society Islands, you'll need to buy Air Tahiti's Bora Bora–Tuamotu Pass and do the itinerary above in reverse, proceeding Tahiti–Moorea–Huahine–Raiatea–Bora Bora. For those who want to visit the Tuamotus only, Air Tahiti has a Lagoon Pass that includes Ahe, Fakarava, Manihi, Rangiroa, and Tikehau.

Day 1

The flight from Bora Bora to Tikehau operates four days a week, usually via Rangiroa. From Tahiti to Tikehau, the flights are daily.

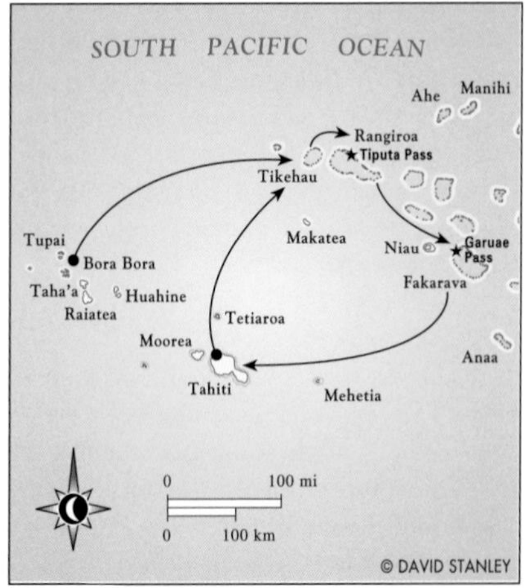

THE LIFE AQUATIC

Sports and recreation are well developed in French Polynesia. Water sports are offered at all the resorts, but it's sometimes less expensive to deal with independent operators beyond the hotel gates. Scuba diving is the most popular sport among visitors, but while diving quickly absorbs large amounts of money, snorkeling is free and you can do it as often as you like. Surfing, ocean kayaking, sailing, and fishing are also popular activities.

SCUBA DIVING

Well-established dive shops exist in resort areas throughout French Polynesia. **Drift dives** and swimming with sharks, rays, eels, dolphins, and even whales are offered. **Lagoon diving** is recommended for beginners; those with more experience will find that the reef drop-offs and passes into the lagoons nurture the most marine life.

Best Dive Sites

- **The Spring, Tahiti:** An outer reef location off Punaauia where fresh spring water rises eerily to the surface from the reef.
- **The Canyon, Moorea:** Beyond the reef opposite the Hilton, this site is visited mostly for shark and eel feeding.
- **Avapeihi Pass, Huahine:** Large schools of barracuda and other fish are seen here, plus reef sharks in their natural habitat (no feeding).
- **Teavapiti Pass, Raiatea:** Reef and pelagic fish are seen in great numbers as you drift along a coral ridge.
- **Tapu, Bora Bora:** At this ocean site opposite Motu Tapu, blacktip and lemon sharks are fed by hand.
- **Sharks Cave, Rangiroa:** Several dozen gray reef sharks will greet you on this dive, which culminates in a drift through the Tiputa Pass.
- **Garuae Pass, Fakarava:** Huge schools of fish and many kinds of sharks are seen on this drift dive into the lagoon.

SNORKELING

Even if you aren't interested in scuba diving, you should definitely investigate the many snorkeling possibilities. A few scuba operators will take snorkelers out on their regular trips, although many dive sites are too deep for worthwhile snorkeling.

Snorkeling with manta rays is possible at Bora Bora.

Best Snorkeling Sites

- **The Aquarium, Tahiti:** Fish feeding has been practiced in the lagoon off the InterContinental Resort Tahiti for many years. It's a good place to photograph colorful reef fish.
- **Stingray World, Moorea:** The shallow lagoon just off the InterContinental Resort Moorea's beach is home to many meter-wide stingrays that glide past you in search of food.
- **Avea Beach, Huahine:** The clear lagoon waters off southern Huahine-iti host numerous small fish between the coral heads.
- **Anau, Bora Bora:** This site off Fitiiu Point is frequented by manta rays up to four meters across. Blacktip reef sharks and moray eels may also be seen here.
- **Tiputa Pass, Rangiroa:** The lagoon water inside Tiputa Pass is teeming with reef fish that have been fed by humans.
- **Tumakohua Pass, Fakarava:** From the boat, you drift in through the pass past a huge variety of colorful fish and hundreds of sharks.
- **The Pygmy Orcas, Nuku Hiva:** When the sea is calm, a boat can drop you among hundreds of melon-headed whales.

the Blue Lagoon at Rangiroa Atoll, Tuamotu Islands

Tikehau is a typical Tuamotu atoll. Once you've found a room at one of the island's half dozen small pensions, go for a swim and a stroll along the beach.

Day 2

Ask your host on Tikehau to help you arrange a motorized canoe trip today, or else go scuba diving.

Day 3

Enjoy another day relaxing or diving on Tikehau.

Day 4

Flights from Tikehau to Rangiroa operate five times a week. You'll notice right away that Rangiroa is more developed than Tikehau. Go for a swim and explore the vicinity of your hotel.

Day 5

Many people come to Rangiroa specifically to drift dive the Tiputa Pass, and it should be your first priority if you're certified. Otherwise, ask your host to arrange a guided snorkel trip through the pass.

Day 6

Take a lagoon excursion today to the Blue Lagoon, Île aux Récifs, Sables Roses, or Motu Paio. Or go scuba diving again.

Day 7

The flight from Rangiroa to Fakarava is four times a week, and from Fakarava to Rangiroa

A diver enjoys the view of an impressive Napoleon wrasse, found among the marine life of Tiputa Pass.

twice weekly. Fakarava is similar to Rangiroa but less developed. Luckily, there's a good selection of places to stay. Find a room, then go for a walk through the village.

Day 8

If you're a certified diver, a drift dive through Fakarava's Garuae Pass will be your first choice. Even if you're not certified, visit the dive shop anyway to ask if they have any boat trips for you. Your host may be able to set up a motorized canoe trip across the lagoon.

Day 9

A snorkeling trip to the Tumakohua Pass at the south end of Fakarava would be ideal. Or just go diving again.

Day 10

There are daily flights from Fakarava back to Tahiti.

ROMANCE ON THE SOUTH SEAS

The legendary beauty and sensual pleasures of French Polynesia have made it a sought-after honeymoon destination. The upscale resorts do their best to deliver the dream with over-water bungalows, luxury spas, couples massage, gourmet beach dinners, bottles of champagne, fruit baskets, canoe breakfasts, bouquets, and beds of flowers. Honeymooners should advise their resorts beforehand and bring along their wedding certificate, as some provide special dinners, champagne, and other gifts for couples who can prove they really are on honeymoon.

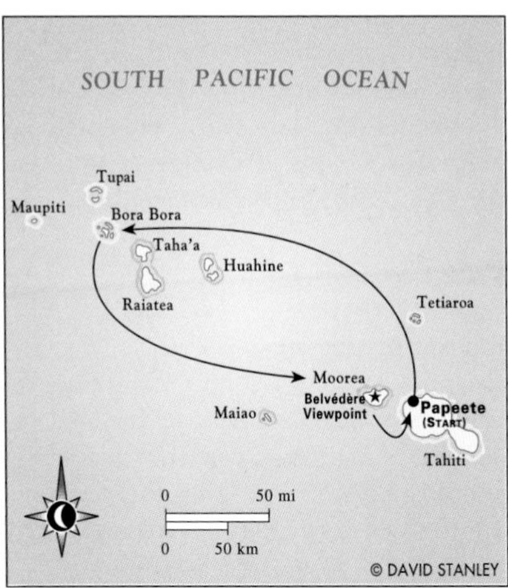

In 2009 the 30-day residency period for couples wishing to get legally married in French Polynesia was scrapped.

Where to go? No South Seas island offers a greater choice of luxurious honeymoons than Bora Bora. However, Bora Bora's resorts don't come cheap, and do-it-yourself honeymooners are better served on Moorea. The Tiki Theater Village on Moorea stages nonbinding Tahitian royal weddings for a romantic reaffirmation of vows. On Tahiti, the Papeete waterfront is perfect for an evening stroll to round out your Polynesian honeymoon.

Day 1

Upon arrival, catch a connecting flight to Bora Bora and your private over-water bungalow at a *motu* resort. Go for a swim in the ocean or pool, followed by a visit to the resort's spa. Enjoy the sunset from your lagoon-view dinner table, then go for a stroll along the beach.

Day 2

Order breakfast from room service, delivered by canoe if possible. Many resorts offer catamaran cruises for two with a gourmet lunch on a private beach. Take a lagoon tour

Mount Mouaroa, Moorea

that includes swimming with sharks and rays if you can, but lather up to avoid sunburn! If your resort is staging a Polynesian dance show tonight, you're in luck. A sunset dinner cruise is another possibility.

Day 3

After a morning of relaxation, catch the boat shuttle from your resort to the main island and take a circle island tour. Bora Bora has many fancy boutiques selling black pearl jewelry, and there are plenty more on Tahiti and Moorea. If you have reservations, cap you day off with intimate fine dining at seven-table Villa Mahana. Otherwise, the Kaina Hut Bistro and Bloody Mary's accept walk-ins and offer free transportation back to the wharf. Be sure to verify the exact times of the resort shuttle before setting out.

Day 4

After a morning swim and another spa visit, catch the midday flight from Bora Bora to Moorea. All four large resorts on Moorea have spas with special packages for couples. Take a dip in the pool or beach and sign up for a sunset cruise.

Day 5

A snorkeling trip with sharks and rays should be your first priority today, or a boat ride in search of Moorea's famous spinner dolphins. Tonight dine out at one of the many small restaurants around the island. Most offer free hotel pickup if you call ahead.

Day 6

Today you should explore Moorea by bicycle, rental car, tour bus, or four-wheel-drive vehicle, according to your taste. Don't miss the Belvédère viewpoint in the center of the island, and drop into one of the numerous black pearl shops. If you enjoyed eating out last night, do it again at another place.

Day 7

Catch a ferry or flight back to Papeete. If you have another night in French Polynesia, the InterContinental Resort Tahiti can provide over-water bungalows, a spa, and romantic dining. Otherwise, the new Hôtel Tahiti Nui is within walking distance of the colorful downtown waterfront and night market.

▸ TIKIS AND TREKS IN THE MARQUESAS

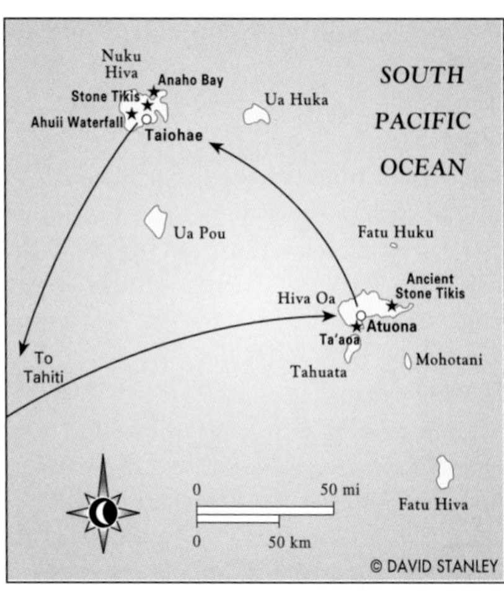

The magnificent Marquesas Islands offer some of the most evocative archaeological sites in French Polynesia. Air Tahiti's Marquesas Extension sold in combination with its other air passes is expensive, but you'll get to visit two of the most spectacular islands in the South Pacific. Be aware that the airports on both Hiva Oa and Nuku Hiva are far from the hotels, and transfer costs can be high. Fortunately, the accommodations are more affordable.

A far better way to go is on a two-week cruise from Papeete to the Marquesas Islands aboard the passenger-carrying freighter *Aranui,* offered 15 times a year. This ship not only visits all six inhabited islands of the Marquesas but stops at a couple of the Tuamotu atolls en route. However, the itinerary below should be less expensive and you'll still get a taste of the island group.

Day 1

The flights from Tahiti to Atuona on Hiva Oa are daily, sometimes via Nuku Hiva. If you arrive early enough, you'll have time for a walk around the village with the possibility of a visit to the graves of Paul Gauguin and Jacques Brel. Visit the Cultural Center and Museum if it's open.

Day 2

Rent a car and drive across the island to Puama'u to visit the ancient stone tikis

tiki at Puama'u, Hiva Oa

just behind the village. If you have time to spare on the way back to Atuona, take a few of the side roads to remote villages on scenic bays.

the grave of French painter Paul Gauguin at Atuona, Hiva Oa

Day 3

Hike south from Atuona to Ta'aoa with its black beach, *me'ae* (temple) platforms, and tiki. If you're back early, spend the rest of the day poking around Atuona. Otherwise, go scuba diving.

Day 4

There's a daily flight from Atuona to Nuku Hiva. Upon arrival, you're looking at a 2.5-hour Land Cruiser ride to Taiohae. After checking into your hotel, go for a stroll along Taiohae's waterfront, taking in the sights.

Day 5

Either rent a car or arrange to be driven across Nuku Hiva to Hatiheu. There's one large collection of stone tikis near Taipivai and another at Hatiheu. If you have time, hike across the pass from Hatiheu to lovely Anaho Bay.

Day 6

Ask Jocelyne Henua Enana Tours to arrange a boat trip to Hakaui to visit the Ahuii Waterfall. Otherwise you could hike over to Haaotupa Bay for a swim.

Day 7

With airport transfers, the nonstop flight from Nuku Hiva back to Tahiti will fill this day.

In the tropics, shallow ponds in coastal areas are often covered by lilies.

▸ ANCIENT TEMPLES AND SACRED SITES

The first archaeological survey of French Polynesia was undertaken in 1925 by Professor Kenneth P. Emory of Honolulu's Bernice P. Bishop Museum. Emory's successor, Professor Yosihiko Sinoto of the same museum, has carried out extensive excavations and restorations in the area since 1960. In 1962, at a 9th-century graveyard on Maupiti's Motu Pae'ao, Emory and Sinoto uncovered artifacts perfectly matching those of the first New Zealand Maoris. A few years later, at Ua Huka in the Marquesas, Sinoto discovered a coastal village site dating from A.D. 300, the oldest yet found in Eastern Polynesia. Sinoto was responsible for the restoration of the Maeva *marae* (temples) on Huahine and many historical *marae* on Tahiti, Moorea, Raiatea, and Bora Bora. During construction of the former Bali Hai Hôtel on Huahine in 1973–1977, Sinoto's student diggers found 10 flat hand clubs of the *patu* model, previously thought to exist only in New Zealand, plus some planks of a 1,000-year-old sewn double canoe. Contemporary visitors can connect with old Polynesia at the territory's numerous archaeological sites.

Tahiti

Two impressive *marae* are easily visited on a trip around the island. The pyramidical Marae of Mahaiatea at Papara is in ruins but still impressive. Marae Arahurahu at Paea has been restored and is used for occasional historical reenactments. Marae Fare Hape and nearby sites in the center of Tahiti illustrate how Polynesian communities were often located inland before Protestant missionaries moved them to the coasts. The Museum of Tahiti and the Islands at Punaauia outlines Polynesia's ancient history in detail.

Moorea

Moorea's most striking ancient temples are also in the center of the island. Marae Titiroa,

marae along the shore of Lake Fauna at Maeva, Huahine

yachts at anchor off Fare, Huahine

Marae Ahu o Mahine, and Marae Afareaito are part of a well-restored complex just below the Belvédère viewpoint. The remains of a few smaller temples such as Marae Nuurua at Haapiti are found along the coast.

Huahine

Huahine has the largest ancient temple complex in French Polynesia at Maeva. Several dozen temples in various states of preservation are on Matairea Hill, and just across Lake Fauna is Marae Manunu with its massive stone wall. Marae Anini at Parea on the southeast side of Huahine-iti is similar to Marae Manunu but smaller.

Raiatea

Raiatea hosts the most sacred pagan site in French Polynesia, Marae Taputapuatea at Opoa. Great festivals featuring recreated catamaran canoes or tattooing have been held here in recent years, and devotees still come to meditate or pray on the vast stone platforms. Marae Tainuu at Tevaitoa is far less important.

Bora Bora

A number of restored temples are near the road around Bora Bora. Marae Aehautai near the island's eastern point offers excellent views. Marae Fare Opu, Marae Taianapa, and Marae Marotetini all face Faanui Bay.

Nuku Hiva

The ancient sites of the Marquesas Islands are less visited and perhaps even more evocative for that reason. Near Taipivai are a huge *tohua* (ceremonial plaza) and the Pa'eke Me'ae with 11 massive stone tikis. The restored Hikoku'a Tohua is closer to Hatiheu, and nearby is the Te I'ipoka Me'ae, site of cannibal feasts.

Hiva Oa

A number of restored *tohua* with several *me'ae* (temple) platforms are at deserted Ta'aoa southwest of Atuona. However, Hiva Oa's greatest ancient site is the Me'ae Iipona at Puama'u, with the largest ancient tiki yet found in French Polynesia, plus many other intriguing stone statues.

BACK TO NATURE

While the rain forests of the sea—the coral reefs—are top attractions, the island interiors are seldom visited. Yet all of the high volcanic islands have hiking trails leading up their valleys, along their ridges, and toward their highest peaks. Not only do you get to see the vegetation close up, but many hikes culminate in fabulous views. The following is only a sampling of what's out there.

Tahiti

Papeete's water supply originates in the Fautaua Valley behind the city, and hiking to a lovely waterfall is allowed with a permit from the Hôtel de Ville. A beaten trail leads up the island's second highest mountain, Aorai, and there are huts along the ridge. The Thousand Springs Trail below Orohena, Tahiti's highest mountain, is easy enough, although Orohena itself is only for experts. The island's finest coastal hike is around the wild Te Pari Coast between Teahupoo and Tautira.

Moorea

It's possible to hike up and across Moorea from near the Vaiare ferry terminal to Paopao in half a day. Several good hikes are possible in the Opunohu Valley, including the Three Coconut Trees Trail to a ridge overlooking both coasts. A more challenging trail follows the ridge up Mount Rotui.

Raiatea

Any reasonably fit person can climb Tapioi Hill behind Uturoa for a view of four islands. The Temehani Plateau, accessible from the west coast, is best explored with a guide, especially if you wish to find the sacred white flower, the *Tiare apetahi.*

Bora Bora and Maupiti

On Bora Bora, Mount Pahia, overlooking Vaitape, can be climbed with a guide, but tombstone-shaped Otemanu is impossible to climb. Maupiti's highest peak, Mount Teurafaatiu, can be climbed from Farauru village on the east side of the island.

Austral Islands

There are many tracks and trails across the Tetuanui Plateau on Rurutu. It's easy to hike from the cross-island road to the TV tower on Manureva, continuing to nearby Taatioe, Rurutu's highest peak. On Tubuai, Mount

SURFING TAHITI

Polynesia's greatest gift to the world of sport is surfing. In 1771, Captain Cook saw Tahitians surfing in a canoe; board surfing was first observed off Hawaii in 1779. Surfing was revived at Waikiki, Hawaii, at the beginning of the 20th century, and it's now the most popular sport among young Tahitians.

Famous surfing spots include Tahiti's **Papara Beach** and **Teahupoo,** Moorea's **Matauvau Passage,** Huahine's **Fare Reef,** and Raiatea's **Teavapiti Passage.** The top surfing season is generally April-September (winter), when the trade winds push the Antarctic swells onto the south shores. During the hurricane season, October-March (summer), tropical storms can generate some spectacular waves on the north shores.

The summer swells are the same ones that hit Hawaii three or four days earlier. The reef breaks off the north shore of Moorea work better than Tahiti's beach breaks. The most powerful, hollow waves are in winter. The reef breaks in the passes are a lot longer paddle than those off the beaches (where you can expect lots of company). To avoid bad vibes, make a serious effort to introduce yourself to the local surfers.

Maupiti's rugged interior as seen from the airport across the lagoon

Taitaa is easily climbed from the road between Mataura and the south coast.

Marquesas Islands

Nuku Hiva is perfect for hiking, with its open landscapes and spectacular views. The two-hour hike up the valley from Hakaui to the Ahuii or Vaipo Waterfall is usually done after a boat ride from Taiohae to Hakaui. However, it's also possible to reach Hakaui on an old bridle path from Taiohae. Another great Nuku Hiva hike is across the Toovii Plateau to a viewpoint over Aakapa Bay. All of the other islands of the Marquesas have unforgettable hiking possibilities as well.

TAHITI

Tahiti, largest of the Societies, is an island of legend and song lying in the eye of Polynesia. Though only one of 118, this lush island of around 178,000 inhabitants is paradise itself to most people. Here you'll find an exciting city, big hotels, restaurants, nightclubs, things to see and do, valleys, mountains, reefs, trails, and history, plus transportation to everywhere. Since the days of Wallis, Bougainville, Cook, and Bligh, Tahiti has been the eastern gateway to the South Pacific.

In 1891 Paul Gauguin arrived at Papeete after a 63-day sea voyage from France. He immediately felt that Papeete "was Europe—the Europe which I had thought to shake off…it was the Tahiti of former times which I loved. That of the present filled me with horror." So Gauguin left the town and rented a native-style bamboo hut in Mataiea on the south coast, where he found happiness in the company of a 14-year-old Tahitian *vahine* (woman) whose "face flooded the interior of our hut and the landscape round about with joy and light." Somerset Maugham's *The Moon and Sixpence* is a fictional tale of Gauguin's life on the island.

Legends created by the early explorers, amplified in Jean-Jacques Rousseau's "noble savage" and taken up by the travel industry, make it difficult to write objectively about Tahiti. Though the Lafayette Nightclub is gone from Arue and Quinn's Tahitian Hut no longer graces Papeete's waterfront, Tahiti remains a delightful, enchanting place. In the late afternoon, as Tahitian crews practice canoe racing in the lagoon and Moorea

HIGHLIGHTS

Papeete Market: Papeete's central market is a great place to enjoy the local scene. The city's best curio shopping is on the balcony upstairs, overlooking a busy main floor where vendors sell everything from fish to baked goods to shell necklaces (page 32).

Tahua Vaiete: The nightly open-air food market on Papeete's waterfront is another nice place for people-watching while enjoying a tasty dinner. On weekends, a local band plays live music (page 33).

Point Venus: Tahiti's northernmost point has a good beach, a picturesque lighthouse, and great views of the island's central mountains. Many famous explorers spent time here, as several monuments in the park attest (page 69).

Gauguin Museum: The life and work of the most famous painter to work in the South Pacific is showcased here. The region's largest botanical garden is next door (page 74).

Museum of Tahiti and the Islands: This is one of the finest historical museums in the South Pacific, with four exhibition halls. Outside, you can sit on the seawall and watch the surfers just offshore (page 76).

The Interior of Tahiti: The mountains and valleys of Tahiti's uninhabited interior are best seen on the 37-kilometer safari tour across the island (page 80).

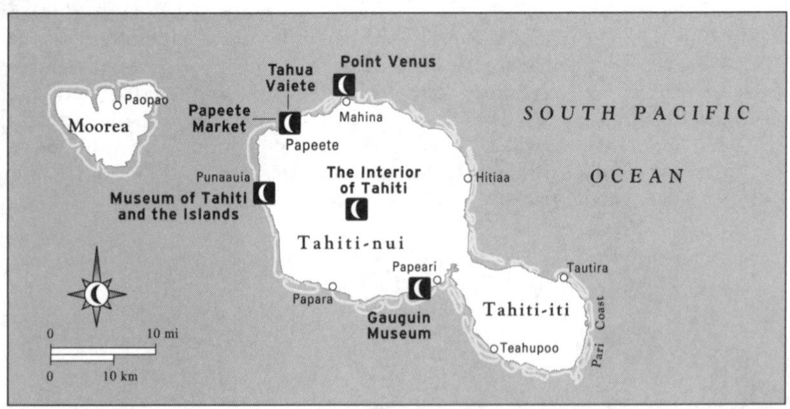

LOOK FOR ☾ TO FIND RECOMMENDED SIGHTS, ACTIVITIES, DINING, AND LODGING.

gains a pink hue in the distance, the romance resurfaces.

If you steer clear of the traffic jams and congestion in commercial Papeete, you'll get a taste of the magic that Gauguin experienced. Whether you love or hate the capital, keep in mind that it's only on the outer islands, away from the motorists and military complexes, that the full flavor of old Polynesia endures.

The island of Tahiti (1,045 square kilometers) accounts for almost a third of the land area of French Polynesia. Like Hawaii's Maui, Tahiti was formed more than 1 million years ago by two or three shield volcanoes joined at the isthmus of Taravao. These peaks once stood 3,000 meters above the sea, or 12,700 meters high counting from the seabed. Today the rounded, verdant summits of Orohena (2,241 meters) and Aorai (2,066 meters) rise

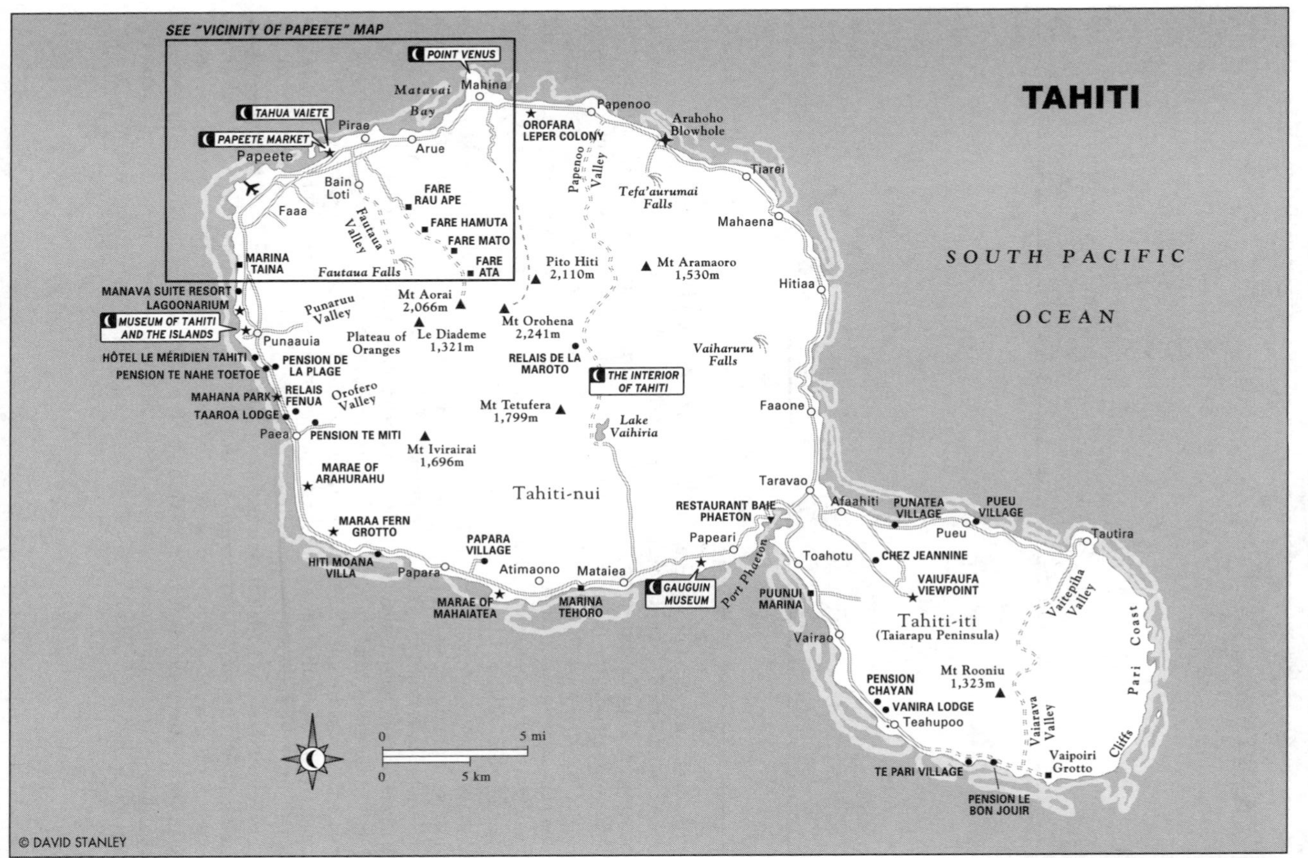
TAHITI
SOUTH PACIFIC
OCEAN
SEE "VICINITY OF PAPEETE" MAP
POINT VENUS
Matavai Bay
Mahina
TAHUA VAIETE
PAPEETE MARKET
Pirae
Arue
Papeete
Bain Loti
Faaa
Fautaua Valley
Fautaua Falls
FARE RAU APE
FARE HAMUTA
FARE MATO
FARE ATA
MARINA TAINA
MANAVA SUITE RESORT
LAGOONARIUM
MUSEUM OF TAHITI AND THE ISLANDS
Punaauia
HÔTEL LE MÉRIDIEN TAHITI
PENSION TE NAHE TOETOE
PENSION DE LA PLAGE
MAHANA PARK
RELAIS FENUA
TAAROA LODGE
Paea
PENSION TE MITI
Punaruu Valley
Plateau of Oranges
Orofero Valley
Mt Aorai 2,066m
Le Diademe 1,321m
Mt Orohena 2,241m
Pito Hiti 2,110m
RELAIS DE LA MAROTO
OROFARA LEPER COLONY
Papenoo
Papenoo Valley
Arahoho Blowhole
Tefa'aurumai Falls
Tiarei
Mahaena
Mt Aramaoro 1,530m
Hitiaa
Vaiharuru Falls
THE INTERIOR OF TAHITI
Mt Tetufera 1,799m
Lake Vaihiria
Faaone
Mt Iviraírai 1,696m
MARAE OF ARAHURAHU
Tahiti-nui
Taravao
MARAA FERN GROTTO
HITI MOANA VILLA
Papara
PAPARA VILLAGE
Atimaono
MARAE OF MAHAIATEA
Mataiea
MARINA TEHORO
GAUGUIN MUSEUM
Papeari
RESTAURANT BAIE PHAETON
Port Phaeton
Afaahiti
PUNATEA VILLAGE
PUEU VILLAGE
Pueu
Tautira
Toahotu
CHEZ JEANNINE
VAIUFAUFA VIEWPOINT
PUUNUI MARINA
Tahiti-iti (Taiarapu Peninsula)
Vaitepiha Valley
Pari Coast
Vairao
Mt Rooniu 1,323m
PENSION CHAYAN
VANIRA LODGE
Teahupoo
Vaiarava Valley
Cliffs
Vaipoiri Grotto
TE PARI VILLAGE
PENSION LE BON JOUIR
0 5 mi
0 5 km

TAHITI

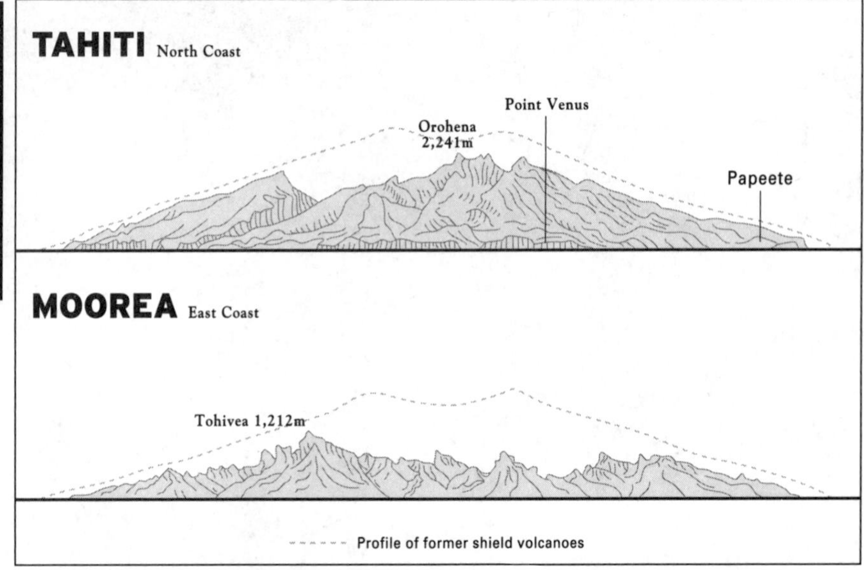

in the center of Tahiti-nui, and deep valleys radiate in all directions from these central peaks. Steep slopes drop abruptly from the high plateaus to coastal plains. The northeast coast is rugged and rocky, without a barrier reef, and thus exposed to intense pounding surf; villages lie on a narrow strip between mountains and ocean. The south coast is broad and gentle with large gardens and coconut groves; a barrier reef shields it from the sea's fury.

Tahiti-iti (also called the Taiarapu Peninsula) is a peninsula with no road around it. It's a few hundred thousand years younger than Tahiti-nui, and Mount Rooniu (1,323 meters) forms its heart. The populations of big *(nui)* and small *(iti)* Tahiti are concentrated along the coast; the interiors of both Tahitis are almost uninhabited. Contrary to the popular stereotype, mostly brown/black beaches of volcanic sand fringe this turtle-shaped island. To find the white/golden sands of the travel brochures, you must cross over to Moorea.

PLANNING YOUR TIME

Almost everyone arrives at Faa'a International Airport, five kilometers west of Papeete, the capital and main tourist center of French Polynesia. East of Papeete are Pirae, Arue, and Mahina, with a smattering of hotels and things to see, while south of Faa'a lie the commuter communities Punaauia, Paea, and Papara. On the narrow neck of Tahiti is Taravao, a refueling stop on your 117-kilometer way around Tahiti-nui. Tahiti-iti is a backwater, with dead-end roads on both sides.

You can see the main sights of Papeete in a day and travel around the island in another day. However, if you can afford the time and expense, it's worthwhile to rent a car for three days and explore Tahiti at your leisure. A good selection of accommodations is available all around the island. Boulevard Pomare curves around Papeete's harbor to the Office du Tourisme near the market—that's where to begin. Moorea is clearly visible to the northwest.

Papeete

Papeete (pa-pay-EH-tay) means "water basket." The most likely explanation for this name is that islanders originally used calabashes enclosed in baskets to fetch water at a spring behind the present Territorial Assembly. Papeete was founded as a mission station by the Reverend William Crook in 1818, and whalers began frequenting Papeete's port in the 1820s, as it offered better shelter than Matavai Bay. It became the seat of government when young Queen Pomare IV settled here in 1827. The French governors who "protected" the island from 1842 onward also used Papeete as their headquarters.

Today Papeete is the political, cultural, economic, and communications hub of French Polynesia. More than 80,000 people live in this cosmopolitan city, crowded between the mountains and the sea, and its satellite towns, Faa'a, Pirae, and Arue—constituting almost half the people on the island. "Greater Papeete" extends for 32 kilometers from Paea to Mahina. The French Naval facilities in the harbor area were constructed in the 1960s to support nuclear testing in the Tuamotus.

Since the opening of Faa'a International Airport in 1961, Papeete has blossomed with large hotels, expensive restaurants, bars with wild dancing, radio towers, skyscrapers, and rock bands pulsing their jet-age beats. Where a nail or red feather may once have satisfied a Tahitian, VCRs and Renaults are now in demand. Tens of thousands of registered vehicles jam Tahiti's 200 kilometers of roads. Noisy automobiles, trucks, and buses clog Papeete's downtown and roar along boulevards Pomare and Prince Hinoï, buffeting pedestrians with pollution and noise.

Yet along the waterfront the yachts rock luxuriously in their Mediterranean moorings (anchor out and stern lines ashore). There's no need to "tour" Papeete—instead, simply

Papeete, with Tahiti's second highest mountain, Aorai, rising in the background

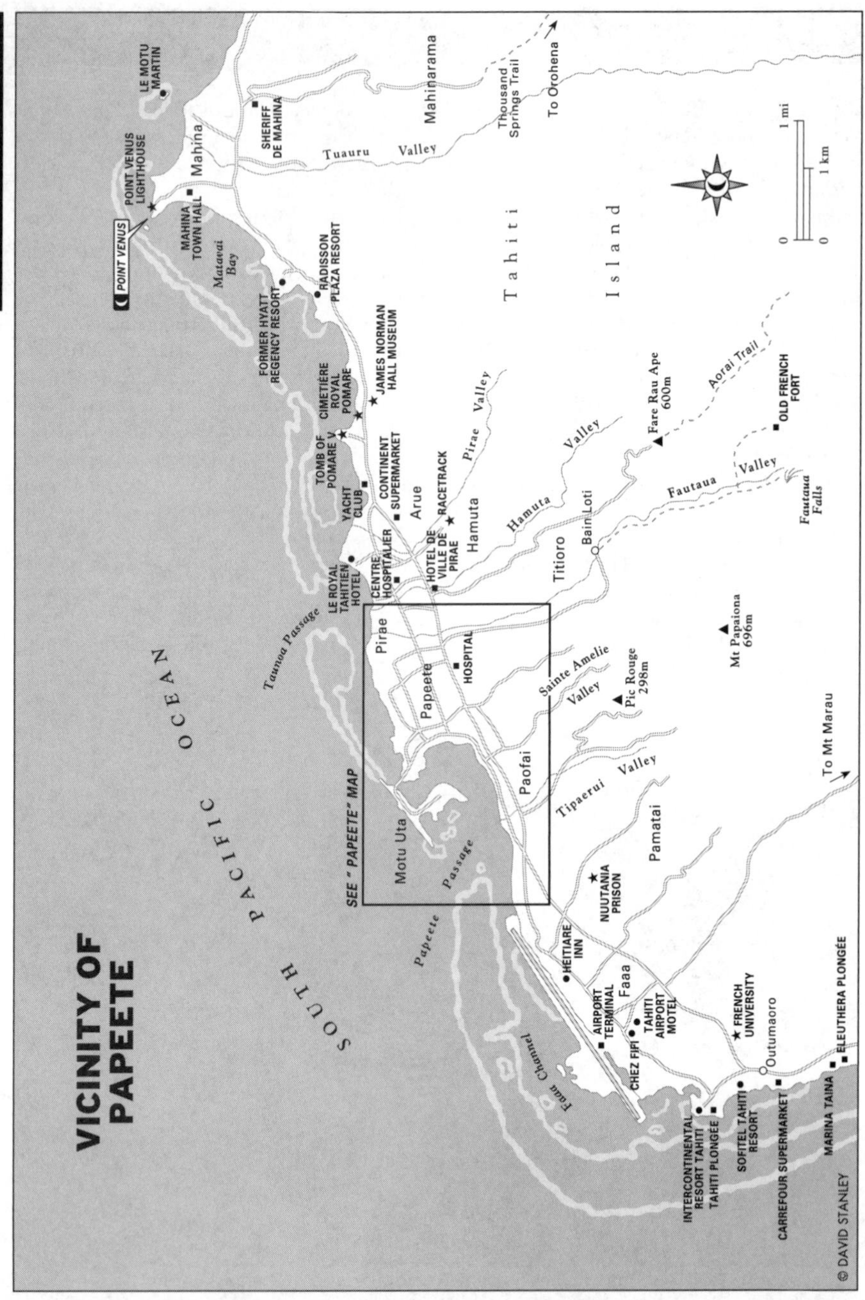
VICINITY OF PAPEETE
SOUTH PACIFIC OCEAN
POINT VENUS
POINT VENUS LIGHTHOUSE
LE MOTU MARTIN
Mahina
MAHINA TOWN HALL
SHERIFF DE MAHINA
Mahinarama
Tuauru Valley
Thousand Springs Trail
To Orohena
Matavai Bay
FORMER HYATT REGENCY RESORT
RADISSON PLAZA RESORT
Tahiti Island
CIMETIÈRE ROYAL POMARE
JAMES NORMAN HALL MUSEUM
TOMB OF POMARE V
YACHT CLUB
CONTINENT SUPERMARKET
Arue
Pirae Valley
RACETRACK
Hamuta
Hamuta Valley
Fare Rau Ape 600m
Aorai Trail
OLD FRENCH FORT
Fautaua Valley
Fautaua Falls
Bain Loti
Titioro
LE ROYAL TAHITIEN HOTEL
CENTRE HOSPITALIER
HOTEL DE VILLE DE PIRAE
Taunoa Passage
Pirae
HOSPITAL
Papeete
Sainte Amelie Valley
Pic Rouge 298m
Mt Papaiona 696m
SEE "PAPEETE" MAP
Paofai
Tipaerui Valley
To Mt Marau
Motu Uta
Passage
Pamatai
NUUTANIA PRISON
Papeete
HEITIARE INN
Faaa
AIRPORT TERMINAL
TAHITI AIRPORT MOTEL
CHEZ FIFI
FRENCH UNIVERSITY
Outumaoro
Faaa Channel
INTERCONTINENTAL RESORT TAHITI
TAHITI PLONGÉE
SOFITEL TAHITI RESORT
CARREFOUR SUPERMARKET
MARINA TAINA
ELEUTHERA PLONGÉE
0 1 mi
0 1 km
© DAVID STANLEY

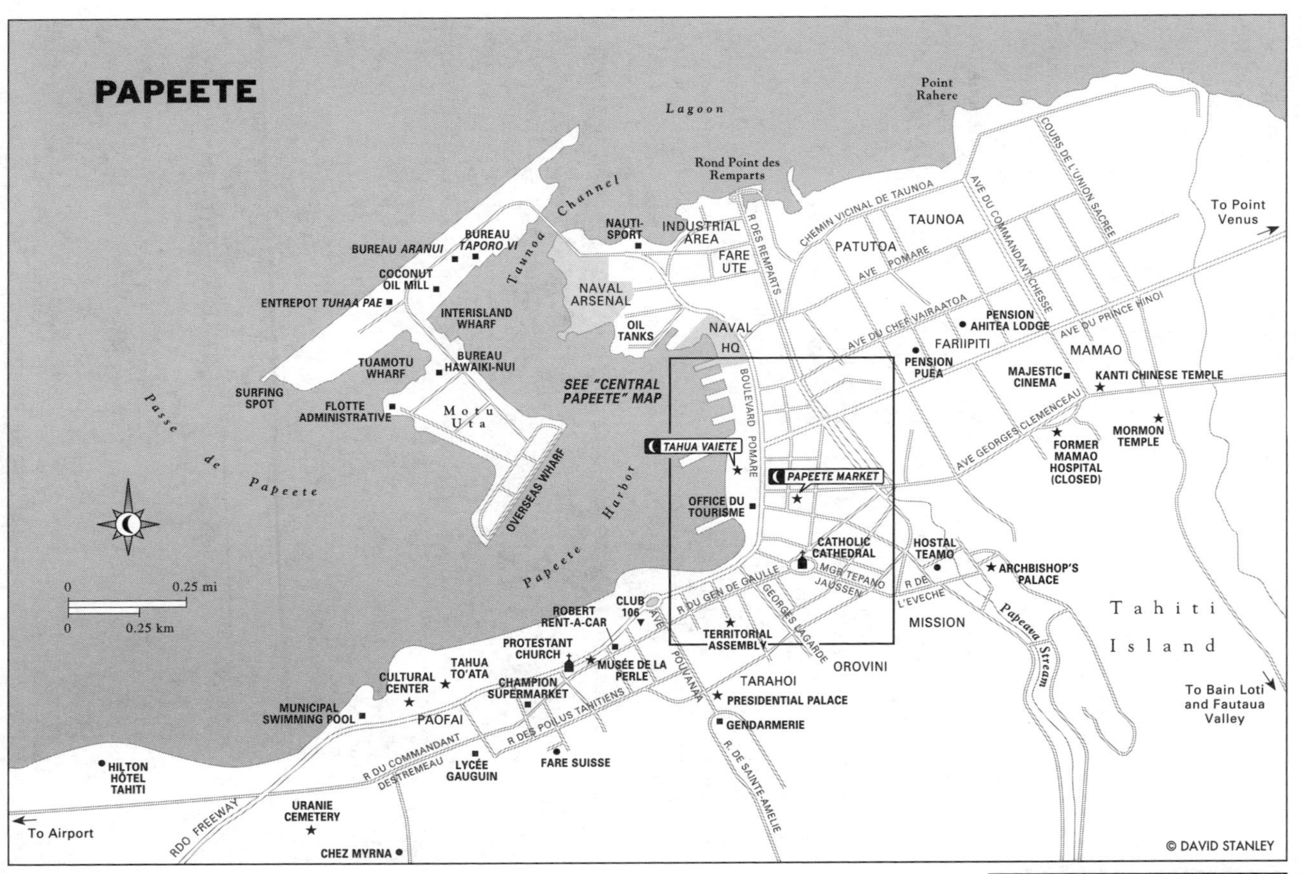
PAPEETE
Lagoon
Point Rahere
Rond Point des Remparts
To Point Venus
Tauona Channel
BUREAU TAPORO VI
BUREAU ARANUI
COCONUT OIL MILL
ENTREPOT TUHAA PAE
INTERISLAND WHARF
NAUTI-SPORT
INDUSTRIAL AREA
FARE UTE
NAVAL ARSENAL
OIL TANKS
NAVAL HQ
R DES REMPARTS
CHEMIN VICINAL DE TAUNOA
TAUNOA
PATUTOA
AVE POMARE
AVE DU CHEF VAIRAATOA
AVE DU COMMANDANT CHESSE
COURS DE L'UNION SACREE
AVE DU PRINCE HINOI
PENSION AHITEA LODGE
FARIIPITI
PENSION PUEA
MAMAO
MAJESTIC CINEMA
KANTI CHINESE TEMPLE
MORMON TEMPLE
FORMER MAMAO HOSPITAL (CLOSED)
AVE GEORGES CLEMENCEAU
TUAMOTU WHARF
BUREAU HAWAIKI-NUI
SURFING SPOT
FLOTTE ADMINISTRATIVE
Motu Uta
SEE "CENTRAL PAPEETE" MAP
Passe de Papeete
OVERSEAS WHARF
Papeete Harbor
TAHUA VAIETE
BOULEVARD POMARE
PAPEETE MARKET
OFFICE DU TOURISME
CATHOLIC CATHEDRAL
MGR TEPANO JAUSSEN
HOSTAL TEAMO
ARCHBISHOP'S PALACE
R DE L'EVECHE
MISSION
Papeava Stream
Tahiti Island
To Bain Loti and Fautaua Valley
0 0.25 mi
0 0.25 km
CLUB 106
ROBERT RENT-A-CAR
R DU GEN DE GAULLE
GEORGES LAGARDE
TERRITORIAL ASSEMBLY
OROVINI
PROTESTANT CHURCH
MUSÉE DE LA PERLE
AVE POUVANAA
TARAHOI
PRESIDENTIAL PALACE
GENDARMERIE
TAHUA TO'ATA
CULTURAL CENTER
CHAMPION SUPERMARKET
MUNICIPAL SWIMMING POOL
PAOFAI
R DES POILUS TAHITIENS
R. DE SAINTE-AMELIE
R DU COMMANDANT DESTREMEAU
LYCÉE GAUGUIN
FARE SUISSE
HILTON HÔTEL TAHITI
URANIE CEMETERY
To Airport
RDO FREEWAY
CHEZ MYRNA
© DAVID STANLEY

wander around without any set goal. Visit the highly specialized French boutiques, the Chinese stores trying to sell everything, and the Tahitians clustered in the market. Avoid the capital on weekends, when life washes out into the countryside; on Sunday afternoons it's a ghost town. Explore Papeete, but make it your starting point—not a final destination.

Orientation

Thanks to airline schedules, you'll probably arrive at the crack of dawn. Change money at the airport bank and take a bus to Papeete market. The helpful Office du Tourisme on the waterfront opens early, as do the banks nearby. You can buy a special pass for discounted local flights at the Air Tahiti office behind the market. Most of the other places you'll have to get to around town are easily accessible on foot.

A trip around the island will fill a day if you're waiting for plane or boat connections, and Papeete itself can be fun. Fare Ute, north of French naval headquarters, was reclaimed with material dredged from the harbor in 1963. West across a bridge is Motu Uta, where you can jump aboard a passenger-carrying freighter. The Moorea ferries leave from the new Gare Maritime near the Office du Tourisme downtown.

There are no public beaches right in Papeete. To go for a swim, take a bus marked Outumaoro (CFP 130) past the airport and get off when it turns around near Marina Taina. Walk 500 meters south, and directly behind McDonald's you'll find **Plage Publique Taina** (daily 0600–2000) with a freshwater shower. Point Venus is another good choice for a day at the beach.

SIGHTS

Papeete Market

Papeete's teeming central market, a block away from the waterfront, was completely rebuilt in 1987 on the site of an older market building. Downstairs on the main floor you'll see Tahitians selling fish, fruit, root crops, and breadfruit; Chinese gardeners with their

© DAVID STANLEY

The produce of the islands is for sale at Papeete Market.

© DAVID STANLEY

Since 1977 the Vaima Center has been a Papeete landmark. Many fine shops and restaurants are here.

tomatoes, lettuce, and other vegetables; and French or Chinese offering fish, meat, and bakery products. Several stalls selling shell necklaces are also here, plus snack and coffee vendors to one side. The territory's largest handicrafts market is upstairs on the balcony, with pareu, Marquesas wood carvings, and every kind of curio. Surprisingly, it's often cheaper to buy handicrafts here than on the outer islands where they are made! There's also a large cafeteria upstairs where you can get a self-service meal and listen to local musicians at lunchtime. It's great fun taking photos of the fish and vegetable vendors below from the balcony. The flower displays outside the market also make great photos, and everyone is quite friendly. The biggest market of the week begins around 0500 Sunday morning and is over by 0800.

Tahua Vaiete

Take a stroll in the evening along the Papeete waterfront past the dozens of gaily lit vans known as *les roulottes,* which form a colorful night food market at Tahua Vaiete by the Quai d'honneur. As the city lights wink gently across the harbor, sailors promenade with their *vahine,* adding a touch of romance and glamour. The food and atmosphere are excellent, and even if you're not dining, it's a scene not to miss. On Friday and Saturday nights a live band plays in the bandstand. It all happens nightly 1800–0200.

Central Papeete

The streets to the north of the market are lined with two-story Chinese stores built after the great fire of 1884. The **Hôtel de Ville** on rue Paul Gauguin was inaugurated in 1990 on the site of a smaller colonial building demolished to make way. The architect designed the three-story city hall building to resemble the palace of Queen Pomare IV that once stood on Place Tarahoi near the present post office. A contemporary Marquesan stone tiki stands beside a pond in front of the building.

Notre Dame Catholic Cathedral (1875) is on rue du Général de Gaulle, a block and

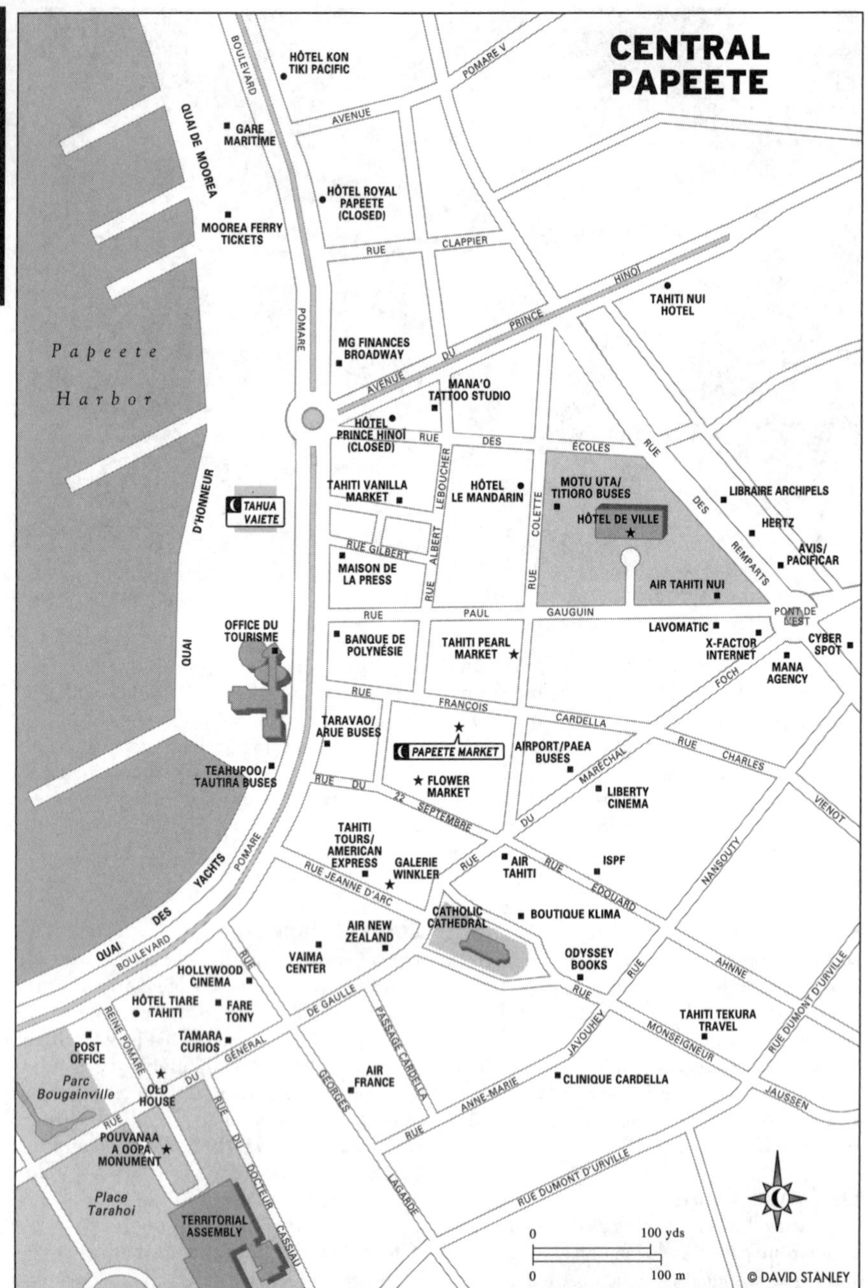
CENTRAL PAPEETE
Papeete Harbor
HÔTEL KON TIKI PACIFIC
GARE MARITIME
HÔTEL ROYAL PAPEETE (CLOSED)
MOOREA FERRY TICKETS
TAHITI NUI HOTEL
MG FINANCES BROADWAY
MANA'O TATTOO STUDIO
HÔTEL PRINCE HINOÏ (CLOSED)
TAHITI VANILLA MARKET
HÔTEL LE MANDARIN
MOTU UTA/ TITIORO BUSES
HÔTEL DE VILLE
LIBRAIRE ARCHIPELS
HERTZ
AVIS/ PACIFICAR
AIR TAHITI NUI
TAHUA VAIETE
MAISON DE LA PRESS
OFFICE DU TOURISME
BANQUE DE POLYNÉSIE
TAHITI PEARL MARKET
LAVOMATIC
X-FACTOR INTERNET
CYBER SPOT
MANA AGENCY
PONT DE L'EST
TARAVAO/ ARUE BUSES
PAPEETE MARKET
AIRPORT/PAEA BUSES
TEAHUPOO/ TAUTIRA BUSES
FLOWER MARKET
LIBERTY CINEMA
TAHITI TOURS/ AMERICAN EXPRESS
GALERIE WINKLER
AIR TAHITI
ISPF
CATHOLIC CATHEDRAL
BOUTIQUE KLIMA
AIR NEW ZEALAND
VAIMA CENTER
ODYSSEY BOOKS
HOLLYWOOD CINEMA
HÔTEL TIARE TAHITI
FARE TONY
TAHITI TEKURA TRAVEL
POST OFFICE
TAMARA CURIOS
Parc Bougainville
OLD HOUSE
AIR FRANCE
CLINIQUE CARDELLA
POUVANAA A OOPA MONUMENT
Place Tarahoi
TERRITORIAL ASSEMBLY
BOULEVARD POMARE
AVENUE POMARE V
QUAI DE MOOREA
RUE CLAPPIER
AVENUE DU PRINCE HINOÏ
RUE DES ÉCOLES
RUE LEBOUCHER
RUE ALBERT
RUE GILBERT
RUE COLETTE
RUE DES REMPARTS
RUE PAUL GAUGUIN
QUAI D'HONNEUR
RUE FRANÇOIS CARDELLA
FOCH
RUE CHARLES VIENOT
RUE DU MARÉCHAL
RUE DU 22 SEPTEMBRE
QUAI DES YACHTS
RUE JEANNE D'ARC
RUE EDOUARD AHNNE
NANSOUTY
RUE DUMONT D'URVILLE
RUE MONSEIGNEUR JAUSSEN
RUE JAVOUHEY
RUE DU GÉNÉRAL DE GAULLE
PASSAGE CARDELLA
GEORGES LAGARDE
RUE ANNE-MARIE
REINE POMARE
RUE DU DOCTEUR CASSIAU
0 100 yds
0 100 m
© DAVID STANLEY

THE STREETS OF PAPEETE

Papeete's streets bear the names of an odd assortment of French politicians, officials, military leaders, missionaries, and explorers, many of them unfamiliar to English speakers. The city's principal coastal boulevard is named for the Pomare dynasty, which ruled during the implantation of French colonialism. Similarly, Prince Hinoï (1869-1916), who succeeded the puppet king Pomare V, lent his name to the main avenue leading east from the harbor. Papeete's most prominent park bears the name of French explorer Louis-Antoine de Bougainville (1729-1811), whereas Captain Samuel Wallis, who arrived a year earlier, is not remembered, and Captain Cook merits only a small side street west of the center. In contrast, an important bypass behind downtown celebrates Dumont d'Urville (1790-1842), a French explorer who visited Tahiti 55 years after Wallis.

Admiral Abel Dupetit-Thouars, who declared a French protectorate over Tahiti in 1842, is acclaimed by a street near the residence of the present French High Commissioner. Until the pro-independence Temaru government took office in 2005, avenue Pouvanaa a Oopa was called avenue Bruat, named for the protectorate's first governor, Admiral Armand Bruat, who set up a military camp here in 1843. A busy east-west thoroughfare passing here bears the names of four prominent Frenchmen: Commandant Maxime Destremeau, who defended Papeete against German cruisers in 1914; General De Gaulle (1890-1970), who initiated nuclear testing in Polynesia in 1966; Maréchal Foch (1851-1929), the Allied military commander during the closing months of World War I; and Georges Clémenceau (1841-1929), the French premier during and after World War I.

Less known are the church leaders whose names have been attached to streets around Papeete's Catholic cathedral. Rue Monseigneur Tepano Jaussen, the road leading to the bishop's palace, recalls Florentin Étienne Jaussen (1815-1891), who was appointed vicar apostolic in 1851. This road crosses a street that commemorates Venerable Anne-Marie Javouhey (1779-1851), who founded the Sisters of St. Joseph of Cluny, which did Catholic missionary work in the French colonies. A road between Papeete's city hall and the market honors Gilles Colette, the free-thinking parish priest of Papeete in the late 19th century. Protestants have been awarded a nearby backstreet named for Huguenot missionary Charles Viénot, who promoted Protestant education on Tahiti around the beginning of the previous century. The street between rues Viénot and Jaussen recalls Edouard Ahnne, the director of Catholic boys schools on Tahiti in the early 20th century and leader of the campaign to recognize the Free French forces at the beginning of World War II.

The street in front of the Catholic cathedral recognizes Jeanne d'Arc (1412-1431), the national hero of France who was burned at the stake for heresy after helping to save France from the English. Rue des Poilus Tahitiens, in front of the war memorial on avenue Pouvanaa a Oopa, memorializes the Tahitian volunteers who fought for France in World War I. Rue de la Canonnière Zélée nearby salutes the French warship sunk at Papeete by German cruisers in 1914. And last but not least, rue Paul Gauguin passes in front of Papeete city hall, a bastion of minor officialdom, the very class so despised by the painter during his lifetime.

a half southeast of the market. Inside, notice the Polynesian faces and the mélange of Tahitian and Roman dress on the striking series of Gauguin-influenced paintings of the crucifixion.

Diagonally across the street from the cathedral is the **Vaima Center,** Papeete's finest window-shopping venue, erected in 1977.

Official Papeete

A few blocks west along rue du Général de Gaulle is Place Tarahoi. The **Territorial Assembly** on the left occupies the site of the former royal palace, demolished in 1966. You're allowed to freely wander around the picturesque grounds and observe the proceedings if the assembly happens to be meeting. Be sure

© DAVID STANLEY

Official Papeete is found along avenue Pouvanaa a Oopa with the high commissioner, president, ministries, courts, and both police forces based here.

to continue to the very back of the compound, where there's a botanical garden with many of the trees and plants labeled—just the place to escape the bustle of the capital. A lovely lily pond separates these gardens from those of the adjacent French high commissioner's residence (which cannot be visited). The **Bassin de la Reine,** the royal bathing pond of Queen Pomare IV, is the rectangular pool with large goldfish below a huge banyan tree at the very back of the gardens.

In front of the Territorial Assembly's entrance gate is a monument erected in 1982 to **Pouvanaa a Oopa** (1895–1977), a Tahitian World War I hero who struggled all his life for the independence of his country. In July 1995 nearly a third of the adult population of Tahiti gathered here to protest French nuclear testing in the Tuamotus.

Across the busy avenue from Place Tarahoi, notice the old wooden house with a red roof to the right of the post office. This is the former residence of Queen Marau, wife of King Pomare V. The house is full of 19th-century furniture, but it's still occupied by the former royal family and cannot be visited. On the other side of the post office is **Parc Bougainville.** A monument to Bougainville himself, who sailed around the world 1766–1769, is flanked by two old naval guns. One, stamped "Fried Krupp 1899," is from Count Felix von Luckner's famous raider *Seeadler,* which ended up on the Maupihaa reef in 1917; the other is off the French gunboat *Zélée,* sunk in Papeete harbor by German cruisers in 1914. Parc Bougainville is a ManaSPOT Wi-Fi hotspot.

Much of the bureaucracy works just west along avenue Pouvanaa a Oopa, a gracious tree-lined French provincial avenue. You may observe French justice in action at the **Palais de Justice** (avenue Pouvanaa a Oopa, weekdays 0800–1200). The public gallery is up the stairway and straight ahead. Just past the police station farther up avenue Pouvanaa a Oopa is the War Memorial.

In 1999 the Caserne Brioche, a military barracks dating to 1886, was demolished to make way for the **Palais Présidentiel de Papeete,**

POUVANAA A OOPA

Pouvanaa a Oopa was born at Maeva on Huahine in 1895, and during World War I he served in France. In 1942 he denounced war profiteers and was placed under arrest on Huahine. A year later he managed to escape with another man by canoe to Bora Bora in the hope of obtaining American help, but he was arrested and returned to Huahine three days later. After the war Pouvanaa continued to oppose the colonial administration and to advocate a freer political alliance with France. He was elected a deputy to the French parliament in 1949, 1952, and 1956 on an autonomy program. In 1957 he became vice president of the local administration and campaigned for independence in the 1958 referendum, but the "no" side got only 35 percent of the vote throughout the territory. Later that year he was falsely accused of trying to set Papeete aflame and was sentenced to 15 years' imprisonment. Finally pardoned in 1968, Pouvanaa was elected a senator in the French parliament two years later, a post he held until his death in 1977. Known to the Tahitians as *metua* (spiritual father), Pouvanaa a Oopa remains a symbol of the Polynesian struggle for independence.

official residence of the president of French Polynesia. This elegant neocolonial structure near the gendarmerie at the top of avenue Pouvanaa a Oopa was built intentionally more impressive than the nearby French high commissioner's residence—a proud symbol of Tahiti Nui. Free guided tours of the building are offered on Tuesday and Thursday 0900–1600. Inquire at the Protocol Office (rue Dumont d'Urville, tel. 47-21-31, www.presidence.pf) at the entrance to the underground parking around the side of the building. Only 30 visitors a day are accepted, and the tours are often fully booked by local groups. However, the staff will usually make space available for foreigners who drop by the day before.

Along Boulevard Pomare

Facing the waterfront a few blocks west of avenue Pouvanaa a Oopa is the headquarters of the **Evangelical Church** in French Polynesia, with a church dating from 1875 but rebuilt in 1981. It was here that the London Missionary Society established Paofai Mission in 1818. From 1837 to 1958 the British consulate occupied the site of the six-story Paofai girl's hostel opposite the church, and George Pritchard, an early British consul, had his office here.

Behind the church is the **Musée de la Perle** (boulevard Pomare, tel. 46-15-55, Mon.–Sat. 0900–1700, admission free) which introduces Polynesia's famous black pearls. The center is owned by a pioneer of the black pearl industry, Robert Wan, who operates nine farms in the Gambier and Tuamotu groups. You can purchase the output on Wan's farms at the Tahiti Perles store in the center of the museum.

Continue west along the bay past the outrigger racing canoes to the **Tahua To'ata,** a striking open-air venue created in 2000 for the annual Heiva i Tahiti festival held in July.

Adjacent is the neo-Polynesian **Cultural Center** (1973) or Te Fare Tauhiti Nui, which houses a public library, notice boards, and auditoriums set among pleasant grounds. This complex is run by the Office Territorial d'Action Culturelle (www.maisondelaculture.pf), which organizes the annual Heiva Festival and many other events.

The **municipal swimming pool** is on the coast beyond the Cultural Center (go upstairs for a view). Return to the center of town along the waterfront.

Archbishop's Palace

Another walk takes you east from downtown to the Catholic Archbishop's Palace (1869), a lonely remnant of the Papeete that Gauguin saw. To get there, take rue Jaussen behind the Catholic cathedral, keep straight, and ask for the *archevêché catholique.* Without doubt, this is the finest extant piece of colonial architecture in a territory of fast-disappearing historic buildings. The park grounds, planted in citrus, and the modern open-air church nearby (to

© DAVID STANLEY

Outrigger racing canoes line the beach beside the Evangelical Church in Papeete.

the right) also merit a look. The huge mango trees here were planted in 1855 by Tahiti's first bishop, Monseigneur Tepano Jaussen.

Fautaua Valley

If you'd like to make a short trip out of the city, go to the Hôtel de Ville and take a Mamao–Titioro bus (CFP 130) to the **Bain Loti,** three kilometers up the Fautaua Valley from the Mormon Temple. A bust of writer Pierre Loti marks the spot where he had a love affair he later described in *The Marriage of Loti.* Today the local kids swim in a pool in the river here, but it's unlikely you'll want to join them as the area is a bit messy.

A dirt road continues three kilometers farther up the Fautaua Valley but because it's part of a water catchment, private cars are prohibited, so you must walk. From the end of the road, a trail straight ahead leads directly to **Fautaua Falls,** 30 minutes' walk with several river crossings. Back a bit on the left, just before the end of the road, is a wooden footbridge across the river. Here begins a steep one-hour trail up to a 19th-century French fort at the top of the falls. The fort controlled the main trail into Tahiti's interior, and it's still an excellent hiking area. Take your bathing suit as swimming is allowed at the falls. Take a picnic too and lots of water.

To hike in the Fautaua Valley, a permit must be obtained in Papeete from the "Régie des Recettes" office on the back side of the Hôtel de Ville (rue des Écoles, tel. 41-58-36, weekdays 0730–1430) at a cost of CFP 600 for adults or CFP 150 for teenagers 12–17 (under age 12 free). You may be denied entry to the valley if you don't have one. The only good thing about having to obtain this bureaucratic permission is that the bus to Mamao–Titioro leaves from rue Colette just around the corner. The valley itself is open daily 0730–1530.

Back on avenue Georges Clemenceau near the Mormon Temple is the impressive **Kanti Chinese Temple,** built in 1987, which is usually open mornings until noon.

Arue

Another easy side trip is east to Arue (a-roo-AY). Begin by taking an Arue or Mahina bus

KING POMARE V

© TAHITI TOURISME

the mausoleum of King Pomare V at Arue on Tahiti

Pomare V's mother died in 1877 after reigning for 50 troubled years, during which she was exhorted to accept a French protectorate over her Polynesian kingdom. A less heroic figure than his mother, King Pomare V, the fifth and last of his name to hold the throne, took over a luckless dynasty and also took to drink. He was particularly fond of Bénédictine liqueur, and although the distinctive symbol enshrined forever atop his pylon-shaped mausoleum at Arue appears to be a massive Bénédictine bottle, it is actually a Grecian vase. He died in 1891 an unhappy man.

(CFP 250) from boulevard Pomare opposite the Office du Tourisme to the colonial-style **Mairie de Arue** at PK 5.6. Built by businessman Victor Raoulx in 1892, the building became the town hall of Arue in 1978. There has always been a degree of rivalry between Arue, heartland of the old Tahitian royal family, and neighboring Pirae, a power base of pro-French politicians.

From Arue town hall, walk back a few minutes in the direction of Papeete to the **James Norman Hall Museum** (tel. 50-01-60, www.jamesnormanhallhome.pf, Tues.–Sat. 0900–1600, admission CFP 600 includes a guided tour) at PK 5.5 on the inland side of the road. Hall achieved fame during the 1930s as co-author of the **Bounty Trilogy** with Charles Nordhoff. He moved to Tahiti in 1920 and had this building erected in 1925. After his death in 1951, the house deteriorated to the point where it had to be completely rebuilt in 1991. The museum opened in 2002, and all captions on the exhibits are in English, French, and Tahitian. About 3,000 books from Hall's personal library are on display, and there's a comfortable lounge where you can sit and read excerpts from Hall's works.

Cross the highway from the museum and

walk another 200 meters west toward Papeete to the École Maternelle Ahutoru at PK 5.4, Arue. Adjacent to this school is the little-known **Cimetière Royal Pomare** with the tombs of Pomare I, II, III, and IV. A map next to the cemetery clearly identifies the many Pomare graves, including that of Pomare V's successor Prince Hinoï. The most elevated tomb here belongs to Princess Elvina Pomare Buillard, who died in 1999. The Reverend Henry Nott (1774–1884), who translated the Bible into Tahitian, is buried directly behind the school (go around behind the building to see the ornate tomb). Nott arrived on the ship *Duff* in 1796 and served with the London Missionary Society for 18 years.

At PK 4.7, Arue, less than 10 minutes west of the Pomare cemetery on foot, is the **Tomb of King Pomare V,** down a side road to a point of land on the lagoon. The mausoleum, surmounted by a Grecian urn, was built in 1879 for Queen Pomare IV, but her remains were subsequently removed to make room for her son, Pomare V, who died of drink in 1891 at the age of 52 (Paul Gauguin witnessed the funeral). A century earlier, on February 13, 1791, his grandfather, Pomare II, then age nine, was made first king of Tahiti on the great *marae* that once stood on this spot. Pomare II became the first Christian convert and built a 215-meter-long version of King Solomon's Temple here, but nothing remains of either temple.

There's an excellent view of **Matavai Bay** from the Evangelical Church compound surrounding Pomare V's tomb. In 1767 Captain Samuel Wallis anchored in this bay after having "discovered" Tahiti, and most of the early English explorers (including Fletcher Christian and Captain Bligh) also came ashore here. The eighth Nuclear Free and Independent Pacific Conference was held in the church compound in 1999.

To return to Papeete, simply walk back to the main highway and flag down the first westbound bus.

ENTERTAINMENT AND EVENTS

Five Papeete cinemas show French films and American films dubbed into French (admission CFP 950). The Concorde is in the Vaima Center; Hollywood I and II are on rue Georges Lagarde beside the Vaima Center; Liberty Cinema is on rue du Maréchal Foch near the market; and the Majestic Cinema is near Mamao Hospital.

Nightlife

After dark, local carousers and French sailors take over the little bars crowding the streets around rue des Écoles and east on boulevard Pomare. Yet for the glitzy capital of a leading French resort island, the nightlife is surprisingly down-market.

The places with live music or a show generally impose a CFP 1,000–2,000 cover charge on men, which includes one drink (women can usually enter for free). The dress code for men is no shorts or sandals. Nothing much gets going before 2200, and by 0100 everything is very informal (many bars stay open until 0400). Visitors should ensure they've got their steps right before inviting any locals onto the floor—or face immediate rejection.

French soldiers and sailors out of uniform patronize the bars along boulevard Pomare opposite the Maritime Terminal, including **Bar Le Chaplin** (tel. 42-73-05), next door to Paradise Night Club, and **Bar Le Taina Kaina** (301 boulevard Pomare at rue Clappier, tel. 42-64-40, daily 0900–0100).

Metropolis Night Club (boulevard Pomare and avenue Pomare V, tel. 42-35-42, metropolistahiti.skyrock.com) charges CFP 1,500 admission on weekends. Around midnight Friday and Saturday, the dance floor is jammed with strobe lights flashing and go-go girls gyrating on stage.

Paradise Night Club (boulevard Pomare, tel. 42-73-05, www.paradisenight.pf, Sun.–Thurs. 2200–0300, Fri.–Sat. 1930–0400), opposite the Maritime Terminal, caters to all ages with West African and reggae music. Friday–Saturday after 2200, admission is CFP 2,000 per person, including one drink. A dress code applies.

Le Manhattan Discotheque (271 boulevard Pomare, tel. 42-63-65, Thurs.–Sat.

2200–0300, CFP 1,500 cover charge Fri.–Sat.), below Hôtel Kon Tiki, is similar to Paradise Night Club. The street level bar here (open daily) is the most colorful in Papeete and also has ManaSPOT Wi-Fi Internet access.

Mana Rock Café (boulevard Pomare at rue des Écoles, tel. 50-02-40), in front of Hôtel Prince Hinoï, is a popular meeting place. There's a European-style disco upstairs with dancing Thursday–Saturday 2200–0300 (CFP 2,000 admission includes a drink for males Fri.–Sat. nights).

The **Piano Bar** (rue des Écoles, tel. 42-88-24, Tues.–Sat. 2200–0300, spicy cabaret show Fri.–Sat. 0130), beside Hôtel Prince Hinoï, is the most notorious of Papeete's *mahu* (transvestite) discos. Directly above the Piano Bar, check out **Restaurant Lounge Bar Dao** (tel. 82-08-08). Many of the people dressed in sexy miniskirts along rue des Écoles are not exactly what they appear to be. Notice the "ladies" beckoning from upstairs windows.

Café de l'Amour, across rue des Écoles from the Piano Bar, has beer on tap. A lively crowd patronizes this colorful establishment, where a seasoned Tahitian band plays on weekends.

Bar Royal Kikiriri (rue Colette at rue des Écoles, tel. 43-58-64, Wed.–Sat. 2200–0300) is another Tahitian disco. Entry costs CFP 1,500 Friday and Saturday and includes one drink.

Club 106 (483 boulevard Pomare, tel. 42-72-92, Thurs.–Sat. 2200–0400), just west of avenue Pouvanaa a Oopa, caters to a slightly older crowd than the other places. It has a different DJ every night, and admission for men is CFP 2,000, which includes a drink.

Cultural Shows for Visitors

A Tahitian dance show takes place in the Bougainville Restaurant, downstairs at the **Sofitel Tahiti Maeva Beach Resort** (PK 7.5, Punaauia, tel. 86-66-00, Fri. 2000). If you're not interested in having dinner, a drink at the Bar Moorea by the pool will put you in position to see the action (no cover charge). On Sunday this hotel presents a full Tahitian feast at 1200, complete with an earth oven *(ahimaa)*

Buskers play for passersby on a Papeete street.

© DAVID STANLEY

a dancer at the Sunday afternoon show at the Sofitel Tahiti Maeva Beach Resort

and dancing at 1300. Since it's daytime, taking pictures is easier, and you can watch the show for the price of a drink.

The **Radisson Plaza Resort Tahiti** (PK 7, Arue, tel. 48-88-88) has a Polynesian show Saturday nights at 1900.

The Tiare Restaurant at the **Inter-Continental Resort Tahiti** (PK 7, Faa'a, tel. 86-51-10) stages one of the top Tahitian dance shows on the island; attend for the price of a drink at the bar near the pool (no cover charge). The Grand Ballet de Tahiti (Lorenzo) performs here on Friday and Saturday at 2030 with another troupe appearing on Wednesday at 2030.

Hôtel Le Méridien Tahiti (PK 15, Punaauia, tel. 47-07-07) presents Tahitian dancing on Friday nights.

There's Tahitian dancing by the O Tahiti E troupe in the **Captain Bligh Restaurant** (tel. 43-62-90) at the Punaauia Lagoonarium (PK 11.4) on Friday and Saturday nights at 2030. The buffet here is CFP 5,000, but you can also simply order a few drinks.

Be sure to check these times and days before going out of your way, as things change. If you want dinner, do reserve.

SHOPPING

Normal shopping hours in Papeete are weekdays 0730–1130 and 1330–1730, Saturday 0730–1200. Papeete's largest shopping complex is the **Vaima Center,** where numerous shops sell black pearls, designer clothes, souvenirs, and books. It's certainly worth a look; then branch out into the surrounding streets. **Galerie Winkler** (17 rue Jeanne d'Arc, tel. 42-81-77), beside American Express, sells contemporary paintings of Polynesia. **Galerie Antipodes** (tel. 54-05-05, www.galerieantipodes.com), in Fare Tony, has several new shows a month.

Galerie des Tropiques (boulevard Pomare opposite Place To'ata, tel. 41-05-00, www.galeriedestropiques.com, weekdays 0900–1200 and 1400–1800, Sat. 0900–1200) has prints of paintings by famous local artists, plus many high-quality originals.

Don't overlook the local fashions. Several shops along rue Paul Gauguin sell very chic island clothing.

If you want to look like a surfer, check **Kelly Surf** (Fare Tony behind Patachoux, tel. 45-44-00), near the market.

Nauti-Sport (tel. 50-59-59, weekdays 0730–1200 and 1300–1630, Sat. 0800–1200) in Fare Ute carries a good selection of quality snorkeling or dive masks at reasonable prices.

Tahiti Vanilla Market (tel. 83-74-83) in the Quartier du Commerce behind the Banque de Polynésie on boulevard Pomare sells an amazing range of products made with vanilla: extract, honey, incense, lotion, perfume, rum, soap, syrup, tea, and vinegar, as well as vanilla beans.

The **Centre Philatelique** (boulevard Pomare, tel. 54-18-00, www.tahitiphilatelie.com) downstairs at the main post office sells the stamps and first-day covers of all the French Pacific territories. Some are quite beautiful and inexpensive.

Souvenirs

The best handicraft shopping is upstairs in

© DAVID STANLEY

a basket merchant at Papeete Market

Papeete Market. The pareu are outstanding. Surprisingly, handicrafts are often cheaper in Papeete than on their island of origin.

Tamara Curios (rue du Général de Gaulle, tel. 42-54-42), opposite McDonald's, is a large craft shop with mass-produced objects.

Serious collectors should visit **Galerie Ganesha** (tel. 43-04-18, www.ganeshatahiti.com) in the Vaima Center. The top-quality handicrafts here include Fatu Hiva tapa, tikis, bowls, Marquesas nose flutes, and carved mother of pearl. There are also objects from other areas, such as Fiji. Prices are high but fair.

Tahiti Music (5 rue du Maréchal Foch, tel. 42-74-83), opposite the cathedral, has a selection of compact discs of Tahitian music. You can use headphones to listen to the music.

Pearls

Several dozen jewelers around Papeete, including **Vaima Perles** (tel. 42-55-57, www.vaimaperles.com) in the Vaima Center and **Tahiti Perles** (tel. 46-15-15, www.perlesdetahiti.net) at the Musée de la Perle, sell the famous black pearls, and it's wise to visit several before making such an important purchase. **Frédéric Missir Joaillier** (boulevard Pomare just west of the Vaima Center, tel. 50-78-78) displays many original creations. **Tahiti Pearl Market** (25 rue Colette, tel. 54-30-60, www.tahitipearlmarket.com) shows a 12-minute film on pearl farming upon request. At all the black pearl outlets, remember to ask for a discount on the sticker price.

Tattoo Shops

Many visitors leave Tahiti with a fresh Polynesian tattoo on their hide, and you can too. The tattoo shops both in Tahiti and on the other islands have albums illustrating their designs, and the proprietors usually speak English. Inquire about sanitary precautions, including clean razors and disposable needles—a listing here is no guarantee. Buy the antiseptic cream they'll tell you to buy, and don't expose your tattoo to salt water or the sun until it has healed.

Mana'o Tattoo Shop (43 rue Leboucher, tel. 42-45-00, www.manaotattoo.pf, Tues.–Sat. 1000–1800), directly behind Hôtel Prince

Hinoï, does tattoos. Established in 1980, Mana'o was the first professional tattoo shop in French Polynesia, and tourists are its main clientele.

MOUNTAIN CLIMBING

Aorai

Tahiti's finest climb is to the summit of Aorai (2,066 meters), second-ranking peak on the island. (Some writers claim 2,110-meter Piti Hiti is the second-highest peak on Tahiti, but it's actually a shoulder of Orohena.) A beaten 10-kilometer track all the way to the top of Aorai makes a guide unnecessary, but food, water, flashlight, and long pants *are* required, plus a sleeping bag and warm sweater if you plan to spend the night up there. At last report the refuges at Fare Mato (1,400 meters) and Fare Ata (1,800 meters) were in good shape, with drinking water available and splendid sunset views. Each refuge sleeps about 10 people on the floor at no charge.

The road toward the summit begins beside the **Hôtel de Ville de Pirae,** an outlandish mock-colonial building surrounded by 66 massive Doric columns constructed in 2002 at a cost of over 1 billion Pacific francs. It could be called "Gaston's folly" for ex-mayor Gaston Flosse, who pushed the project through. Just inland from this building, take the first turn on the right and head up the hill to the access road on the left (if in doubt, ask). The trailhead is at Fare Rau Ape (600 meters) near **Le Belvédère** (tel. 42-73-44), a touted French restaurant seven kilometers up the narrow paved road from Pirae. Taxis want CFP 5,000 for the trip from Papeete, and few people live up there, so hitching would be a case of finding tourists headed for the restaurant, and weekends are best for this. You could rent a small car at the kilometer rate, but parking near the restaurant is limited.

The restaurant does provide its clients with free transportation in a traditional *truck* from most Papeete hotels, and this is the easiest way to get there. You can reserve the Belvédère *truck* at the Hôtel Tiare Tahiti reception and most other hotels in Papeete. Of course, in order to use it you'll be required to buy a complete meal for CFP 5,600, including salad, main course,

The best view of Le Diadème in the center of Tahiti is obtained on the Aorai hike.

dessert, coffee, and wine. The specialty is fondue bourguignon, a meat fondue, but you can substitute mahimahi, steak, or shish kebab. The food is OK but definitely not gourmet. The *truck* departs most Papeete hotels at 1130 and 1630, leaving the restaurant for the return trip to Papeete at 1430 and 2000.

To make a day of it, catch the 1130 *truck* up to the restaurant on the understanding that you'll be eating dinner and returning to town on the 2000 *truck* (make sure all of this is clearly understood before you pay—Tina Brichet at Le Belvédère speaks good English). This would give you all afternoon to cover part of the trail, although it's unlikely you'd have time to reach the top (even if you only get as far as Fare Mato, it's still well worth the effort). Take along a sandwich for lunch. You should be able to leave some clean clothes at the restaurant to change into for dinner, and be sure to bring your bathing suit and a towel so you'll be able to take a dip in the swimming pool after the hike. If you can do all of this, the CFP 5,600 per person price becomes reasonable.

A large signboard outside the restaurant maps out the hike. Just above the restaurant is the French Army's Centre d'Instruction de Montagne, where you can sign a register. From Fare Rau Ape to the summit takes seven hours: 1.5 hours to Hamuta, another two to Fare Mato (good view of Le Diadème, not visible from Papeete), then 2.5 hours to Fare Ata, where most hikers spend the first night in order to cover the last 40 minutes to the summit the following morning. Just above Fare Mato, cables have been fixed along the section of trail with the steepest drops on both sides. The hut at Fare Ata is in a low depression 100 meters beyond an open shelter.

The view from Aorai is magnificent, with Papeete and many of the empty interior valleys in full view. To the north is Tetiaroa atoll, while Moorea's jagged outline fills the west. Even on a cloudy day the massive green hulk of neighboring Orohena (2,241 meters) often towers above the clouds like Mount Olympus. A bonus is the chance to see some of the original native vegetation of Tahiti, which survives better at high altitudes and in isolated gullies. In good weather Aorai is exhausting but superb; in the rain it's a disaster. Very few people do the climb, and if you go in the middle of the week you can expect to have the mountain to yourself.

Thousand Springs Trail

A much easier hike with better parking at the trailhead leads along the side of Aorai's neighbor Orohena. Turn off the coastal highway at the office of the Sheriff de Mahina, behind the Poissonnerie de Mahina (PK 11), and follow the paved road five kilometers straight up through Mahinarama subdivision. At the top of the ridge at about 600 meters elevation the road ends. Park here—the trail is straight ahead. Anyone at Mahinarama will be able to direct you to the "Route des Mille Sources."

A jeep track built into the slope in 1975 follows the contour six kilometers up the Tuauru River valley to the Thousand Springs at 900 meters elevation. The trail to the 2,241-meter summit of Orohena itself begins at the Thousand Springs and climbs steeply to Pito Iti, where hikers spend the night before ascending Orohena the following morning. The Orohena climb involves considerable risks, and a guide is required, but almost anyone can do the Thousand Springs hike on his or her own, enjoying the good views of the rounded peaks of Orohena to the left and Aorai's long ridge to the right. Since your car does most of the climbing, this is certainly the easiest way to see the island's unspoiled interior. There's nothing special to see at the Thousand Springs, so turn back whenever you like.

Mount Marau

The road inland from directly opposite Faa'a Airport goes under the RDO (Route de Dégagement Ouest) bypass road and up the side of the island to an excellent viewpoint over northwestern Tahiti. It's a rough 10-kilometer drive, which should be attempted only by four-wheel drive in dry weather. You must drive through a horrendous municipal dump on the way. From the TV tower at the end of the track it's only 30 minutes on foot to the summit of Mount Marau (1,493 meters). From here you'll get another incredible view down into the Plateau of Oranges to the south, up the Fautaua Valley to the north, and along the ridge to Le Diadème and Aorai to the east. Several tour companies offer half-day four-wheel-drive trips up here, the easiest way to go.

Guided Hikes

Numerous hikes around Tahiti are organized by Vincent Dubousquet of **Polynesian Adventure** (tel. 43-25-95 or 77-24-37, www.polynesianadventure.fr.st). A couple of times a month, he takes visitors on an easy walk up the Fautaua Valley near Papeete. Vincent's hikes to the lava tubes at Hitiaa, the Vaipoiri Cave or Te Pari Coast at Teahupoo, and the Three Coconut Trees on Moorea have a minimum group size of four people. Call or email to find out which hikes are scheduled during your stay. Prices range CFP 5,400–17,700 per person.

Tahiti Evasion (tel. 56-48-77, www.tahitievasion.com) does day trips to Fautaua Falls or the Orofero Valley at CFP 8,900/6,900/5,200 per person for two/three/four people. A three-day trek along the Pari Coast is CFP 23,500/18,000/15,500 on foot or CFP 32,500/24,000/20,000 by outrigger canoe. To climb Aorai in a day, it charges CFP 7,500 per person (minimum of two people) including the shuttle and a picnic lunch. Tahiti Evasion also offers several excellent hikes on Moorea.

Tahiti Reva Trek (tel. 74-77-20, www.tahitirevatrek.com) specializes in day hikes on Tahiti and Moorea or overnight camping trips. A half-day hike to the Fautaua Valley or Mount Marau is CFP 4,500, otherwise a full-day trek to the lava tubes, Plateau of the Oranges, or Moorea is CFP 5,900. Overnight trips around the Pari Coast at the east end of Tahiti-iti or to Aorai are CFP 12,000 per person. Check their website for the monthly program.

Randonnées Pacifique (tel. 70-56-18, www.randopacific.com) organizes canyoneering at the lava tubes (CFP 12,000) and other locations around Tahiti.

OTHER SPORTS AND RECREATION

Surfers often stay at Pension Te Miti or Taaroa Lodge in Paea on Tahiti-nui's west coast, or at Pension Le Bon Jouir or Te Pari Village at Teahupoo on Tahiti-iti.

The **École de Surf Tura'i Mataare** (tel. 41-91-37, www.tahitisurfschool.info) teaches surfing and body surfing to people aged eight and up. A half-day "discovery" package is CFP 4,800 per person, including a board, insurance, and transportation. A 10-lesson pass is CFP 27,000. For more advanced surfers, there are five-day group lessons that include video analysis, personal advice, and trips to the best spots (CFP 23,000). Surfboard and bodyboard rentals are also offered. Most activities require a minimum of three participants.

The **Ski Nautique Club de Tahiti** (on the waterfront at PK 7.5, Punaauia, tel. 77-22-62, www.tahitiwakeboard.com, Tues.–Fri. 1200–1800, weekends 0900–1800) offers waterskiing at CFP 320 per minute or CFP 18,000 per hour. Training sessions can be arranged.

Papeete's **municipal swimming pool** (boulevard Pomare, tel. 42-89-24, Tues.–Fri. 1145–1645, Sat.–Sun. 0730–1645, admission CFP 400) is open to the public. Most evenings after 1800 **soccer** is practiced in the sports field opposite the municipal swimming pool.

Scuba Diving

Tahiti is best known for its steep drop-offs. Sharks are seen year-round, whales July–November only. The wrecks of a wooden interisland ship and a Catalina seaplane are in the lagoon near the airport runway. Most of the dive sites regularly visited are off Punaauia and Vairao. The companies listed below will usually take along snorkelers upon request.

Scuba Tek Tahiti (at the yacht club at PK 4, Arue, tel. 42-23-55, www.scubatek-tahiti.com, Tues.–Sat. 0900 and 1400, Sun. 0900) organizes outings to offshore *faille* (faults). Dolphin-watching is CFP 3,500 per person (minimum of four people). Whale-watching (CFP 6,000) is offered August–November.

Tahiti Charter Island (PK 5, Arue, tel.

41-38-33, www.tciplongees.com), in the Centre de détente de Moana, offers diving at rates far below those of most other operators (CFP 3,400/15,500/28,000 for 1/5/10 dives). However, one must pay a membership fee of CFP 30,000 a year per family, so it's only useful if you're planning a long stay.

On the other side of Papeete, **Bathys Diving** (PK 7, Faa'a, tel. 53-34-96, www.bathys-diving.com), at the InterContinental Resort Tahiti, offers scuba diving three times a day at 0800, 1030, and 1400. It's one of French Polynesia's best-equipped dive shops, charging CFP 7,900/14,000 for a one/two-tank dive or CFP 11,400 for night diving (at 1800). A three-day open-water scuba certification course with pool training runs CFP 59,000. They also organize two-hour guided snorkeling trips by boat at CFP 5,500 per person (at 1030 and 1400). Bathys can organize free pick-ups anywhere between Papeete and Hotel Le Méridien.

Tahiti Plongée (PK 7.5, Punaauia, tel. 41-00-62, www.tahitiplongee.pf), also known as "Club Corail-Sub," offers scuba diving several times daily. The charge is CFP 7,500 per dive, all-inclusive. You can ocean dive Tuesday–Sunday at 0800 and on Wednesday and Saturday at 1400; lagoon diving is daily at 1000 and weekdays at 1400 (no diving on Monday). Dive master Henri Pouliquen was one of the first to teach scuba diving to children. The youngest person Henri has dived with was two-and-a-half years old; the oldest was a woman of 72 on her first dive. Since 1979 Tahiti Plongée has arranged more than 10,000 dives with children, certainly a unique achievement. Another specialty is diving with people with disabilities. A fish-filled site called the **Aquarium** near its base is safe for all divers.

Eleuthera Plongée (PK 9, Punaauia, tel. 42-49-29, www.dive-tahiti.com), at the Marina Taina beside McDonald's, charges CFP 6,900/13,200/23,500 for one/two/five dives. Exploration dives are at 0900 and 1400 daily. Their introductory dive is at 1100 daily. They offer whale-watching in season (Aug.–Nov.).

Nearby at the Marina Taina are **Fluid Dive Center** (tel. 85-41-46, www.fluidtahiti.com), near the Casa Bianca Restaurant, offering scuba diving, PADI courses, and whale- and dolphin-watching; and **La Vie en Bleu** (tel. 77-90-99, www.tahiti-whales.com), with more whale-watching and some exceptional snorkeling trips.

If you want to set out on your own, **Nauti-Sport** (tel. 50-59-59, weekdays 0730–1200 and 1300–1630, Sat. 0800–1200) in Fare Ute sells every type of scuba gear and also rents tanks.

Day Cruises

Many of the yachts and catamarans tied up at the Quai des Yachts along boulevard Pomare opposite the Vaima Center offer excursions to Tetiaroa, deep-sea fishing, scuba diving, yacht charters, etc. Departures are often announced on notice boards, and a stroll along the waterfront will yield current information.

Croisieres L'Escapade (tel. 72-85-31, www.escapade-voile.pf), on the waterfront opposite the Hôtel Tiare Tahiti, does Tetiaroa day trips on a 14-meter yacht at CFP 13,000 per person including breakfast, lunch, and drinks. Weekend cruises (Fri. afternoon–Sun. night) are also possible. The catamaran *Vehia,* tied up nearby, does this same trip on Wednesday, Saturday, and Sunday 0700–2000. Only nine passengers are accepted per trip, so book early.

ACCOMMODATIONS

Many of the places to stay are in the congested Punaauia-to-Mahina strip engulfing Faa'a International Airport and Papeete, and they offer poorer value for money than comparable accommodations on Moorea. The hotel listings that follow are arranged clockwise around Faa'a and Papeete in each category. In recent years a number of medium-priced places have sprung up on the Tahiti-iti peninsula and the south side of Tahiti, offering the chance to break up your trip around the island.

US$50-100

Chez Fifi (tel. 82-63-30), aka Pension Dahl, is directly across the street from the airport terminal (the fourth house on the left up the hill beside Blanchisserie Pressing Mea Ma), a three-minute walk. It offers four basic rooms without lockable doors at CFP 5,000/6,700 single/double, plus several open four- and five-bed dormitories at CFP 2,300 per person. Breakfast is included, but only if you ask for it. Communal cooking and bathing facilities are available, but bring insect repellent. Check out time is 1000. The location is noisy because of the nearby industrial laundry and airport, but a bed at Chez Fiji beats sitting up all night in the airport.

Family-style **Chez Myrna** (106 Chemin vicinal de Tipaerui, tel. 42-64-11, dammeyer.family@mail.pf) is almost opposite Limonaderie Singapour, two kilometers southwest of central Papeete. Myrna offers one small shared-bath room at CFP 4,450/6,150 single/double and one room with private bath at CFP 6,100/7,855 (minimum stay two nights). Breakfast and barnyard sounds are included. The dormitory is CFP 2,050 per person without breakfast. Her husband, Walter, is a German expat who has been on Tahiti for decades. Book this one far in advance.

Many backpackers head for **Teamo Hostel** (8 rue du Pont Neuf, Quartier Mission, tel. 42-47-26, www.teamoguesthouse.com), a century-old house hidden behind a four-story building near the Archbishop's Palace, just a short walk east of downtown. If the door is locked when you arrive, look for the owner at No. 3 across the street. To get there from the market, head inland on rue François Cardella, which soon becomes rue Charles Vienot. It's a little hard to find the first time, but convenient once you know it. Dormitory-style accommodations are CFP 2,500 per person in six-bed dorms. The four rooms with shared bath are CFP 7,500 double, while the one with private bath is CFP 8,000. Bring your own towel. The shared cooking facilities can be used only 1800–2000. A grocery store is nearby, and there's a veranda with French TV. A CFP 1,000 key deposit is required (and don't forget to ask for it back, as they may not remind you). Checkout time is 1000, at which time you'll be asked to vacate the premises, although the receptionist will hold your luggage for CFP 300 per day. If you arrive before 1000, the full fee for the previous night will be payable. It's all rather basic, but Teamo remains the choice of those in search of the cheapest possible option.

Pension Puea (87 rue du Pasteur Octave Moreau, tel. 85-43-43, www.pensionpuea.com) is off avenue du Prince Hinoï, 500 meters east of the Gare Maritime. The six rooms with shared bath in this two-story building are CFP 6,990 double or CFP 9,550 for a studio, breakfast included. A shared microwave and fridge are available, but no alcohol is allowed on the premises. Polynesians from the outer islands often stay here.

US$100-150

The **Heitiare Inn** (PK 4.3, Faa'a, tel. 83-33-52, sylvie.faafatua@mail.pf) near the Mairie de Faa'a, one kilometer east of the airport, has 12 rooms at CFP 7,500/8,500 single/double without air-conditioning or CFP 8,500/9,500 with air-conditioning. Communal cooking facilities are provided, and the location isn't great. Free airport transfers are provided if you call.

Fare Suisse (tel. 42-00-30, www.fare-suisse.com) is in Quartier Buillard, off rue Venus just up from rue des Poilus Tahitiens, three blocks inland from the harbor—very convenient to town. From Champion Supermarket on rue du Commandant Destremeau, go inland on the street beside the building marked "Vaimoanatea" and continue up the hill on a smaller street, turning right at the first lane. Beni, Fare Suisse's friendly manager, will collect you from Faa'a International Airport at no additional charge provided you book ahead through his website. The four clean rooms at Fare Suisse start at CFP 9,500 double (CFP 15,000 triple for a family room with cooking facilities). If you're willing to share your room with another traveler, the price is CFP 5,000 per person. Breakfast is extra, but you can easily prepare your own in the communal kitchen. There's also a lounge where you get to meet other travelers. In case you don't have a chance to book online, Beni asks that you call ahead because Quartier Buillard (where Fare Suisse is located) is a gated community, and you'll need to know the security code to enter.

In 2010 three large hotels in this price category on boulevard Pomare near the new Marine Terminal were closed. The fates of the six-story **Hôtel Prince Hinoï** and the timeworn **Hôtel Royal Papeete** are still unknown, but the 36-room **Hôtel Kon Tiki Pacific** may have reopened under new management by the time you get here. If it does and you decide to stay there, don't accept one of the noisy rooms near the elevator, which are always offered first, and avoid rooms on the lower floors, which are subjected to disco noise. Instead, get one with a balcony on the upper front side of the building. You'll have an excellent view straight into the adjacent French naval base.

On a back street a block behind Pension Puea and under the same ownership, **Pension Ahitea Lodge** (avenue Vairaatoa, tel. 53-13-53, www.ahitea-lodge.com) is similar but nicer. This two-story pension opened in 2005, and the manager is quite friendly. There are four rooms at CFP 8,500 single or double, six rooms at CFP 9,500, one family room at CFP 10,800, and two rooms at CFP 11,600. Some rooms have shared bath, so ask to see a few and compare. Air-conditioning costs extra, but a continental breakfast is included. Facilities include a nice swimming pool (open 0630–1900 only), a microwave and fridge, and left luggage (CFP 500 per day or for free if you'll be staying here again). Pension Ahitea Lodge is in a residential area, so be prepared for rooster noise in the early morning, and bring insect repellent. The streets leading here are inadequately lit at night, with dogs roaming freely. Five-star it's not, but it is good value if you're on a budget.

US$150-250

The seven-story **Sofitel Tahiti Maeva Beach Resort** (PK 7.5, Punaauia, tel. 86-66-00, www.sofitel.com) was built by UTA French Airlines in 1969. The 216 air-conditioned rooms in this pyramidal high-rise cost CFP 15,286 single or double mountain view, CFP 17,429 lagoon view, CFP 31,000 superior suite, plus 14 percent tax (children under 12 free). Discounts can be obtained by booking through the Sofitel website. Although the rooms are reasonably priced for a large hotel, the meal package isn't worth it, and you'll do better ordering à la carte or eating out (several good restaurants are just down the road). The service at the hotel restaurants and bars leaves much to be desired. The Sofitel faces an artificial white beach, but with pollution on the increase in the adjacent Punaauia Lagoon, most swimmers stick to the hotel pool. Tennis courts are available. The rooms at the Maeva Beach are small and rather dated, so if you're at all fussy, you should spend a little more and stay at the InterContinental.

Tahiti Airport Motel (tel. 50-40-00, www.tahitiairportmotel.com), a large five-story building on the hillside above the airport, opened in 2006. It's clearly visible directly across the highway from the terminal, a short if steep climb away. By car, head inland from the airport on the road that goes below an underpass and turn right up the side road marked Cite de l'Air. Taxi drivers clip you for CFP 2,000 for the short drive here. The 46 spacious rooms with TVs and fridges start at CFP 13,398 single or double, tax included. All of the rooms are nonsmoking, but the air-conditioners are inadequate. There's no restaurant, but pizza delivery can be arranged, and there's a popular Chinese restaurant by the underpass down the hill. This somewhat overpriced motel will suffice for your first or last night in French Polynesia.

Opened in 1997, the six-story **Hôtel Tiare Tahiti** (417 boulevard Pomare, tel. 50-01-00, www.hoteltiaretahiti.info) is the best downtown hotel in its price range. It's right on the waterfront, and while the rooms on the side facing the post office are the quietest, those on the upper floors in front have the best views. The 38 air-conditioned rooms with TVs begin at CFP 12,620/14,338 double/triple, including tax. The rooms are large enough but not spotless. An ice machine in the corridor compensates for the lack of refrigerators. Coffee makers are also missing. Still, for Papeete, the Tiare Tahiti is value for money.

© DAVID STANLEY

The flashy Hôtel Tahiti Nui opened near downtown Papeete in 2008.

The six-story **Hôtel Le Mandarin** (51 rue Colette, tel. 50-33-50, www.hotelmandarin.com), in the heart of the market area, dates from 1988. The 37 air-conditioned rooms, costing CFP 12,354/14,312 single/double (children under 12 CFP 1,000 each), have TVs and minibars but no coffee-making facilities. The levels of service and cleanliness at Le Mandarin leave much to be desired. Friday to Sunday there's live music in the restaurant downstairs (get a room on one of the top floors to be well away from it). Travel agents often book their clients here because it's easy for them to do.

Papeete's finest downtown hotel is currently the three-star **Hôtel Tahiti Nui** (avenue du Prince Hinoï, tel. 46-38-99, www.hoteltahitinui.com), just east of rue des Remparts. This sleek, modern, seven-story hotel under the same ownership as Hôtel Le Mandarin opened in 2008. The 45 standard rooms are CFP 18,380/21,920 double/triple, the 40 junior suites CFP 21,205/24,745/28,285 double/triple/quad, and the six executive suites CFP 25,160/28,700/32,240. All rooms have air-conditioning, TVs, minibars, and balconies. None of the rooms has much of a view, so ask for one on the back side of the building to be away from the noisy traffic. Continental breakfast is CFP 2,040 per person. Two swimming pools, a gym, La Velvet Restaurant, and the Chocco Latte Lounge Bar are on the premises.

US$250 and Up

The **InterContinental Resort Tahiti** (west of the airport at PK 7, Faa'a, tel. 86-51-10, www.tahitiresorts.intercontinental.com) is a former Travelodge built in 1974. This smart international hotel with a Polynesian flair is the largest resort in French Polynesia. The 270 air-conditioned rooms in the eight main buildings begin at CFP 27,941 single or double; it's about double that for one of the 32 over-water bungalows. Children under age 15 sharing the room with their parents stay for free, so this resort is a favorite with families. A breakfast and dinner meal plan is CFP 11,300 per person extra (half price for children under age 12). The InterContinental's over-water Le Lotus Restaurant is reputed to be among

© DAVID STANLEY

over-water bungalows at the InterContinental Resort Tahiti

the best on the island. Tahitian dancing and crafts demonstrations are regular features at the Tiare Restaurant. The lunch buffet there is overpriced, and room service is a viable alternative. A huge Carrefour supermarket is only a 15-minute walk away, and you can save a bundle by stocking your minibar with snacks and drinks. The InterContinental's beach is artificial, but the swim-up bar is fun (the mixed drinks tend to be warm and weak). Stingrays and colorful fish swim freely in a saltwater "lagoonarium" directly below the main pool at the InterContinental (fish feeding at 0900 and 1500). The hotel pools are reserved for guests. The InterContinental has a Deep Nature Spa by Algotherm. Paid activities include waterskiing, snorkeling trips, and scuba diving with **Bathys Diving** (tel. 53-34-96, www.bathys-diving.com).

The former **Hilton Hôtel Tahiti** (PK 2.6 between Papeete and the airport) opened in 1999 after being completely redeveloped by Louis Wane, brother of pearl baron Robert Wan. This site was once the residence of Princess Pomare, daughter of the last king of Tahiti, and from 1961 to 1996 a historic colonial-style hotel stood here. Outrigger Hotels of Hawaii managed the property initially but withdrew in 2000 after disagreements with Wane. Sheraton then assumed management, only to be replaced by Hilton in 2009. In March 2010 the Hilton Hôtel Tahiti closed due to a slump in tourism, and it was reported that the building would be converted into a private clinic. If so, clinic patients will find the 200 air-conditioned rooms in a series of four-story American-style buildings functional but not luxurious. The property features a large beachside freshwater swimming pool with a whirlpool tub on the knoll just above the waterfall, a spa, a 500-seat banquet hall, and an over-water restaurant with splendid sunset views of Moorea. **TOPdive** (www.topdive.com) handled scuba diving at the Hilton, but they've now moved to the InterContinental and merged with Bathys Diving. The former Hilton is just west of Papeete, and you can walk into town along the waterfront in half an hour. The frequent Outumaoro buses pass the Hilton, InterContinental, and Sofitel until 2000.

Hôtel Le Royal Tahitien (off avenue du Prince Hinoï at PK 3.5, Pirae, tel. 50-40-40, www.hotelroyaltahitien.com) is a peaceful two-story building facing beautifully kept grounds on a litter-strewn black-sand beach. You're unlikely to see anyone swimming here, as the water is murky with no coral, but the windsurfing is good. The hotel does have a pool with a drippy waterfall. The 40 air-conditioned rooms are CFP 20,644 single or double, plus 14 percent tax. The rooms and furnishings are showing their age (one-channel TV, tired air-conditioners, faulty plumbing, etc). On the plus side, ManaSPOT wireless Internet access is available at this hotel. Breakfast and dinner are served on the attractive terrace overlooking the lagoon (in general, the food prices here are exorbitant). Seats in the restaurant become scarce after 1930 on Wednesday, Friday, and Saturday, when the live music begins. It's a long, boring walk into town dodging cars parked on the sidewalk (and no public transport back after 1700)—you'll get better-value beach accommodations on Moorea for this kind of money.

In late 2004 the **Radisson Plaza Resort Tahiti** (PK 7, Arue, tel. 48-88-88, www.radisson.com/aruefrp) opened on the black sands of Lafayette Beach facing Matavai Bay, seven kilometers east of central Papeete. This resort is just east of Arue, at the foot of the hill bearing the former Hotel Tahara'a. The 86 ocean-view rooms, 53 suites, and 26 duplex suites in seven blocks start at CFP 26,800 single or double, plus 14 percent tax. You can get a better price if you book ahead through the Radisson website (there are often special deals for families). Food, drink, and activities here are expensive. The core of the resort is a huge lagoon swimming pool with a sloping beach entry and waterfall edge. Be aware of the waves and currents here if you swim in the sea. All the facilities of a resort hotel are provided, including a spa and health club. Smoking is not allowed anywhere on resort property. In terms of public transportation, it's not as convenient as the resorts west of Papeete, as bus service ends at 1700 and is always sporadic on weekends.

FOOD

Tahua Vaiete

Portable food vans called *les roulottes* set up on **Tahua Vaiete** between the Gare Maritime and the Office du Tourisme nightly from 1800–0200. Here you'll find everything from couscous, pizza, waffles, crepes, and *brouchettes* (shish kebab) to steak with real *pommes frites*. There's no better place to sample *poisson cru*. The most crowded *roulottes* generally have the best food, but you may have to wait, as lots of people bring large bowls to be filled and taken home. **Ah Léon** is notable for its Chinese dishes and shish kebab, while **La Crêperie de la Boule Rouge** is famous for its crepes and *galettes au sarrasin* (buckwheat wafers). Meals cost CFP 1,100–1,600 per plate. The biggest drawback is that beer is not available.

Tahua To'ata

At Tahua To'ata, a 15-minute walk west along the waterfront, a similar atmosphere prevails. Here a row of outdoor terrace restaurants, including **Snack Vaimiti, Chez Jimmy, Snack Moeata, Chez Mado,** and **Toa Sushi,** are always crowded with local residents. Pick the one that is most crowded. Opening hours vary, but there are usually a couples of places serving lunch from 1100–1400 and dinner from 1800–2200. Expect to pay CFP 1,000 and up per plate. Alcohol is not served here, but this area is a ManaSPOT Wi-Fi hotspot.

Snack Bars

To sample the cuisine of the people, check out the Chinese/Tahitian eateries on rue Cardella right beside the market. Try *ma'a tinito,* a mélange of red beans, pork, macaroni, and vegetables on rice (CFP 1,250).

Upstairs in the market under a thatched awning, **La Cafétéria de Marché** (tel. 42-25-37, Mon.–Sat. 0500–1600) serves a typical Tahitian lunch at CFP 1,000–1,500, accompanied by a local trio. *Ma'a Tahiti* (CFP 2,000 complete) is available at noon on Fridays. Starting at 0400, you can get coffee at stalls downstairs in the market for CFP 100.

Snack Julienne (rues Clappier and

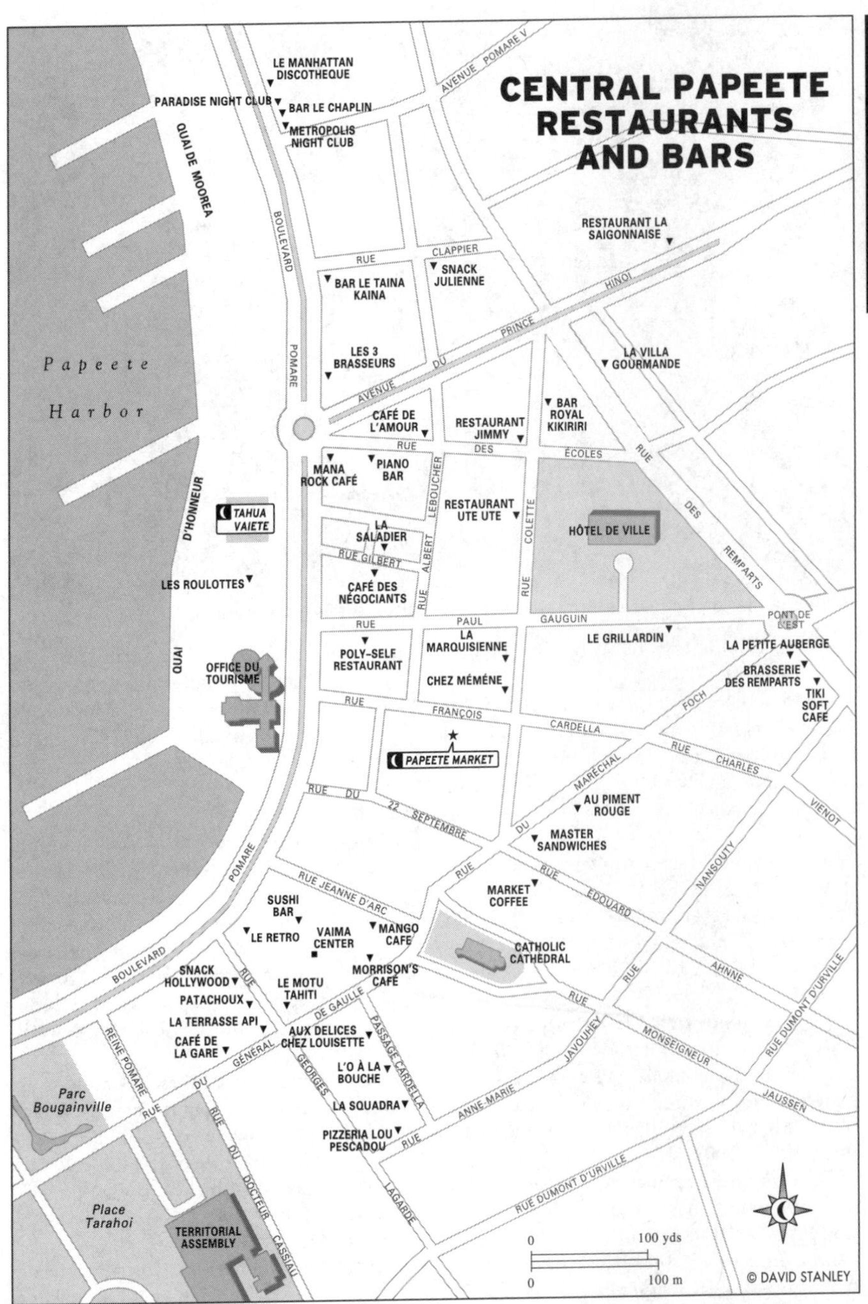
CENTRAL PAPEETE RESTAURANTS AND BARS
LE MANHATTAN DISCOTHEQUE
PARADISE NIGHT CLUB
BAR LE CHAPLIN
METROPOLIS NIGHT CLUB
AVENUE POMARE V
QUAI DE MOOREA
BOULEVARD POMARE
RESTAURANT LA SAIGONNAISE
RUE CLAPPIER
BAR LE TAINA KAINA
SNACK JULIENNE
AVENUE DU PRINCE HINOI
Papeete Harbor
LES 3 BRASSEURS
LA VILLA GOURMANDE
CAFÉ DE L'AMOUR
RESTAURANT JIMMY
BAR ROYAL KIKIRIRI
RUE DES ÉCOLES
RUE DES REMPARTS
MANA ROCK CAFÉ
PIANO BAR
QUAI D'HONNEUR
TAHUA VAIETE
RESTAURANT UTE UTE
HÔTEL DE VILLE
LA SALADIER
RUE GILBERT
RUE ALBERT LEBOUCHER
RUE COLETTE
LES ROULOTTES
CAFÉ DES NÉGOCIANTS
RUE PAUL GAUGUIN
PONT DE L'EST
LE GRILLARDIN
LA MARQUISIENNE
LA PETITE AUBERGE
POLY-SELF RESTAURANT
OFFICE DU TOURISME
CHEZ MÉMÉNE
BRASSERIE DES REMPARTS
TIKI SOFT CAFE
RUE FRANÇOIS CARDELLA
RUE MARÉCHAL FOCH
PAPEETE MARKET
RUE CHARLES VIENOT
RUE DU 22 SEPTEMBRE
AU PIMENT ROUGE
MASTER SANDWICHES
RUE NANSOUTY
RUE JEANNE D'ARC
MARKET COFFEE
RUE EDOUARD AHNNE
SUSHI BAR
LE RETRO
VAIMA CENTER
MANGO CAFE
CATHOLIC CATHEDRAL
SNACK HOLLYWOOD
LE MOTU TAHITI
MORRISON'S CAFE
PATACHOUX
LA TERRASSE API
RUE DU GÉNÉRAL DE GAULLE
RUE MONSEIGNEUR JAUSSEN
RUE DUMONT D'URVILLE
CAFÉ DE LA GARE
AUX DELICES CHEZ LOUISETTE
RUE REINE POMARE
RUE GEORGES LAGARDE
PASSAGE CARDELLA
L'O À LA BOUCHE
RUE JAVOUHEY
Parc Bougainville
LA SQUADRA
RUE ANNE-MARIE
PIZZERIA LOU PESCADOU
RUE DU DOCTEUR CASSIAU
Place Tarahoi
TERRITORIAL ASSEMBLY
0 100 yds
0 100 m
© DAVID STANLEY

© TAHITI TOURISME

Having dinner on Papeete's Tahua Vaiete is a not-to-be-missed experience.

Leboucher, tel. 42-86-49, Mon.–Fri. 0500–1700, Sat.–Sun. 0500–1100) is an unpretentious local place with some of the best prices in town. Its morning café au lait with bread and butter is CFP 350, while the cooked lunch plates go for CFP 800–1,050. The large *casse-croûtes* (baguette sandwiches) can't be beat.

Some of the freshest baguette sandwiches in town (around CFP 300) are sold over the counter at **Master Sandwiches** (26 rue du Maréchal Foch, tel. 43-03-43), near the market. It has a CFP 100 coffee machine in back.

A more trendy, upscale lunch place is **La Saladière** (9 rue Gilbert, Mon.–Sat. 0600–1700), behind Maison de la Presse and opposite Café des Négociants, with sandwiches (CFP 300–500), paninis (CFP 450–500), and salads (CFP 700–1,200).

For fruit juices, sandwiches, crepes, waffles, and ice cream cones, search no further than **Le Motu Tahiti** (corner of rue du Général de Gaulle and rue Georges Lagarde, tel. 41-33-59, Mon.–Sat.), behind the Vaima Center. The stand-up tables on the corner are very Parisian. **Vitamine Saladerie** (tel. 43-37-70, Mon.–Sat.), just upstairs from Le Motu, has a happy combination of salads (CFP 950–1,350) and draft beer.

Asian

Poly-Self Restaurant (8 rue Gauguin, tel. 43-75-32, weekdays 0500–1330), behind the Banque de Polynésie, dispenses unpretentious, filling Chinese-style plate lunches at less than CFP 1,000. Beer is CFP 300, cold water and bread are free. Most of the food is gone by 1300. Poly-Self is always jammed with locals at lunchtime, but additional seating is available upstairs.

Other inexpensive Chinese restaurants are along rue Colette east from the market. **Snack Méméne** (27 rue Colette, tel. 43-09-26, Mon.–Sat. 0500–1700) is a nice open-air locale with *poisson cru,* sashimi, chicken, beef, and chow mein priced CFP 1,000–1,400. Wash it down with draft beer.

Restaurant Jimmy (rue Colette at rue des Écoles, tel. 43-63-32, Mon.–Sat.), near Hôtel

© DAVID STANLEY

Le Motu Tahiti and Vitamine Saladerie at the entrance to the Vaima Center are among Papeete's most popular snack bars.

Le Mandarin, features a clean, simple dining room with specialties such as Thai curries, Vietnamese rice, Chinese plates, Chinese seafood, and filet mignon. Lobster is available at the market price. The extensive menu is posted outside, and most dishes are under CFP 2,000.

Restaurant La Saigonnaise (67 avenue du Prince Hinoï, tel. 42-05-35, Tues.–Sat. 1130–1330 and 1930–2130) has moderately expensive but fresh Vietnamese food served in a quiet setting. The Saigonese soup (CFP 1,450) makes a good lunch. The surly service is hard to explain, and the air-conditioning is turned up too high. There's live music the last Friday of the month.

Finally Papeete has its own **Sushi Bar** (tel. 45-35-25, Mon.–Tues. and Sat. 1100–1400, Wed.–Fri. 1100–1400 and 1900–2000) near the Qantas office in the Vaima Center. You choose from the typical Japanese specialties floating in wooden bowls in a trough along the bar, and you're charged per dish depending on the color of the bowl (CFP 400–800 each). What better place to have sashimi?

French

For the aspiring gourmet, Papeete has much to offer. For example, **Café des Négociants** (10 rue Gilbert, tel. 48-08-48, www.cafedesnegociants.pf, Mon.–Thurs. 0530–2200, Fri. 0530–midnight, Sat. 0600–midnight), in the Quartier du Commerce behind La Maison de la Presse, is a Parisian bistro offering a huge selection of beers and French and Tahitian dishes on a pleasant outdoor terrace. There are seafood dishes (CFP 2,100–2,800), meats (CFP 2,200–2,800), and *poisson cru* (CFP 1,850). The plat du jour is CFP 2,000. There's live Tahitian music beginning at 1800 weekdays and 1600 on Saturday and continuing until closing.

La Villa Gourmande (rue des Remparts, tel. 42-23-42, Mon. 1200–1430, Tues.–Fri. 1200–1430 and 1800–2230, Sat. 1800–2230) has an elegant colonial-style dining room featuring French cuisine: salads (CFP 1,800), fish (CFP 2,500–2,900), meat (CFP 2,000–3,200), and the plat du jour (CFP 1,950). There's live music here every Thursday 1730–2100.

Le Grillardin (rue Paul Gauguin, tel. 43-09-90, Mon.–Sat.), opposite the Air Tahiti Nui office, offers fine French cuisine in a traditional country inn. Fish dishes are CFP 2,700–4,500, meat CFP 2,600–4,500.

La Petite Auberge (Pont de l'Est, tel. 42-86-13, Mon.–Sat.) is a fancy French country inn with linen tablecloths. The menu includes seafood, grilled meats, and traditional house specialties priced CFP 2,450–3,400.

Restaurant Au Piment Rouge (30 rue du Maréchal Foch, tel. 85-64-64, Tues.–Fri. lunch, Fri. lunch and dinner) serves specialties from southwestern France in the CFP 2,100–2,850 range. It's always crowded with French football fans who come to eat, drink, and be merry. Try the Basque lamb stew *(txilindron)* at CFP 2,400, and be sure to ask for a small dish of ground-up peppers. They only open for lunch, and reservations are recommended.

The **Mango Café** (rue Jeanne d'Arc, tel. 43-25-55, Mon.–Tues. 1100–1500, Wed.–Fri. 1100–1500 and 1730–2300, Sat. 1730–2300), below the Vaima Center, features white walls with mirrors all around and bright new furnishings. The huge glass atrium façade on rue Jeanne d'Arc is strikingly modern. The French gourmet dishes with local ingredients served up by owner-operator Patrick Brunel are among the most original you'll find in Papeete. Be prepared; a three-course meal with wine will set you back around CFP 4,000 if you order carefully, but all reports to date say the food and service are well worth the money. Fish mains are CFP 2,500–2,600, meat CFP 2,400–3,600. The Mango Café is also one of the only Papeete restaurants where smoking is not allowed at the tables (smoking is allowed at the bar). There's a DJ with disco dancing Thursday and Friday nights at 2000.

Restaurant L'O à la Bouche (tel. 45-29-76, weekdays 1130–1400 and 1915–2130, Sat. 1915–2130), up passage Cardella opposite Air New Zealand, is an elegant French restaurant with funky blue decor. The nouvelle cuisine includes mouthwatering seafood and meat at CFP 3,300–3,950. Specialties include lamb

The chic Mango Café serves original French gourmet dishes with local ingredients.

brains, duck in honey, and mahimahi in passion fruit sauce. It's popular with trendy young French locals.

Restaurant La Romana (3 rue de Commandant Destremeau, tel. 41-33-64, Mon. and Wed.–Fri. 1130–1500 and 1830–2200, Tues. 1130–1500, Sat. 1830–2200) is an elegant air-conditioned restaurant popular with bureaucrats from nearby government offices. It has meat dishes priced CFP 2,550–2,800 and seafood at CFP 2,500–2,800. Italian and French cuisine is served.

La Corbeille d'Eau (571 boulevard Pomare, tel. 43-77-14, weekdays 1200–1330 and 1900–2130, Sat. 1900–2130), west of the center a block beyond the Protestant church, is an elegant French restaurant with main plates costing CFP 2,700–3,900.

Italian

For a taste of the Mediterranean, **Pizzeria Lou Pescadou** (rue Anne-Marie Javouhey a long block back from the Vaima Center, tel. 43-74-26, Mon.–Sat. 1100–1430 and 1830–2200) is friendly, unpretentious, breezy, inexpensive, and fun. The pizza *pescatore* (CFP 980) makes a good lunch, and a big pitcher of ice water is included in the price. Owner Mario Vitulli may be from Marseilles, but you won't complain about his spaghetti—a huge meal for about CFP 1,000. And where else will you get unpitted olives on a pizza? Nonalcoholic drinks are on the house while you stand and wait for a table. The service is lively, and Lou Pescadou is very popular among local French—a high recommendation.

La Squadra Café (tel. 41-32-14, Mon.–Tues. 1100–1400, Wed.–Sat. 1100–1400 and 1900–2200, Sun. 1900–2200), on Passage Cardella around the corner from Lou Pescadou, is a sports bar–style restaurant. The menu includes meat dishes (CFP 1,950–3,150), Italian dishes (CFP 1,800–2,400), and seafood (CFP 1,900–2,500).

L'api'zzeria (44 rue de Commandant Destremeau, tel. 42-98-30, Mon.–Sat.

Les 3 Brasseurs, a microbrewery on boulevard Pomare facing Papeete's waterfront, is an inexpensive and fun place to eat and drink.

1130–2200), near the Protestant church, also prepares real pizza in a brick oven. This garden restaurant is a bit more expensive than Lou Pescadou (spaghetti CFP 830–1,650, pizzas CFP 990–1,950, fish CFP 1,950–2,850), but still a very good value. Draft beer is available.

Pub Food

Les 3 Brasseurs (boulevard Pomare near avenue Prince Hinoï, tel. 50-60-25, www.3brasseurs-pacific.com, daily 0700–midnight), with a fashionable sidewalk terrace overlooking the Gare Maritime, is very popular. This northeastern French-style microbrewery, which produces its own unpasteurized pure malt beer, specializes in *flammekueche* (like a pizza made with unleavened bread and no tomato sauce). The "classique" with onions and ham is CFP 1,200 with a small beer. A hamburger is CFP 700–850, *poisson cru* is CFP 1,650. It's all spelled out in a menu resembling a French newspaper. There's often live music on Thursday–Saturday nights from 2000. It's always jammed with hip young locals drinking beer until late.

Brasserie des Remparts (Pont de l'est, tel. 42-80-00, weekdays 0630–2200, Sat. 1000–1500), on rue des Remparts between La Petit Auberge and Tiki Soft Café, is a Belgian-style pub. The meals range CFP 1,950–2,990. It's very popular with local French expats at lunchtime. Wireless Internet is available here.

La Terrasse API (rue du Général de Gaulle and rue Georges Lagarde, tel. 43-01-98, Mon.–Fri. 0500–1800, Sat. 0630–1600) is a world better than the McDonald's across the street. The plat du jour here is CFP 1,980, and if it's sold out, you can get hamburgers (CFP 960) or grilled meats. It's a good place to enjoy an afternoon beer as the world walks by, and ManaSPOT wireless Internet is available. A Tahitian orchestra is often here Fridays 1600–2000.

Café de la Gare (rue du Général de Gaulle, tel. 42-75-95, Mon.–Wed. 0900–2200, Thurs.–Fri. 0900–0100), opposite McDonald's, is a typical French pub with draft beer. The only meal served here is lunch (CFP 2,100).

Other Restaurants

Market Coffee (rue Edouard Ahnne, tel. 45-60-70, Mon.–Sat. 0530–1430), behind Air Tahiti, is a lively unpretentious place with dancing on Friday night. A full breakfast here will cost CFP 1,200. Also try the salads.

Café Restaurant Ute Ute (45 rue Colette, tel. 53-46-46, Mon.–Fri. 1100–0100, Sat. 1800–0100), opposite the City Hall, is a swanky place serving meals on an outdoor terrace at CFP 1,800–2,900. There's live music here some nights, and the Jack Daniels Road bar is upstairs. **Bar and Restaurant Gaia** (tel. 53-15-00), two doors down, is similar.

The Papeete equivalent of a Hard Rock Cafe is **Morrison's Café** (tel. 42-78-61, http://myspace.com/morrisonscafe, Mon.–Tues. 1100–1430, Wed.–Fri. 1100–1430 and 1800–0100, Sat. 1800–0100), upstairs in the Vaima Center. Use the elevator on the side of the building just outside Air New Zealand. Morrison's offers grilled dishes or a plat du jour on a breezy rooftop terrace with a view of Tahiti. Some readers have reported that the lunch is of variable quality. There's an extensive wine list, a happy hour from 1630–1830, and live music Thursday and Friday from 1700 and on Saturday from 2200.

Moana Iti Le Bistro (boulevard Pomare, tel. 82-26-00, www.moanaiti.com, Mon.–Sat. 0930–2300), a trendy new wine bar next to Club 106, has club sandwiches at CFP 1,100–1,800 and other mains at CFP 1,850–2,850. A tapas buffet is available weekdays 1800–1900. There's live jazz some nights.

Cafés

Le Retro (tel. 42-86-83, Sun.–Tues. 0500–2000, Wed.–Sat. 0500–2300) on the boulevard Pomare side of the Vaima Center is *the* place to sit and sip a drink while watching the passing parade. The fruit-flavored ice cream is intense, and for yachties, a banana split after a long sailing trip can be heavenly.

Cheaper meals and drinks are available at **Snack Hollywood** (on pedestrians-only rue Georges Lagarde, tel. 54-59-51, weekdays 0600–1900, Sat. 0630–2030, Sun.

© DAVID STANLEY

Snack Hollywood and adjacent Patachoux give you a taste of Paris with your café au lait.

1000–1900), around the corner from Le Retro. The menu includes fruit salads (CFP 400), *poisson cru* (CFP 1,000), omelet sandwich (CFP 320), grilled cheese (CFP 280), chicken and chips (CFP 800), and *steak frites* (CFP 1,100). Coffee, tea, and chocolate are CFP 220. It's a good bet on Sunday when many other places are closed.

Next door to Hollywood on rue Georges Lagarde is **Patachoux** (tel. 83-72-82, weekdays 0600–1730, Sat. 0600–1600), owned by the same people as the more upscale Mango Café. The grilled fish or chicken plat du jour is good value at CFP 1,750, and the menu also features salads (CFP 1,080–1,640), quiche (CFP 545–610), sandwiches, *poisson cru,* tacos, fajitas, pizza, and desserts. Their coffee and *tarte normande* (CFP 390) are superb.

Aux Delices Chez Louisette (passage Cardella, tel. 45-46-46, weekdays 0600–1600), on the narrow street running inland almost opposite Air New Zealand, is good for ice cream, pastries, quiche, and coffee. It's clean and chic with most items displayed in the window and nothing over CFP 1,500.

When the heat gets to you, **Pâtisserie La Marquisienne** (29 rue Colette, tel. 42-83-52, weekdays 0500–1700, Sat. 0500–1200, Sun. 0500–1000) offers coffee and pastries in air-conditioned comfort. It's popular among French expats.

Tiki Soft Café (rue des Remparts at rue du Maréchal Foch, tel. 88-93-98, weekdays 1100–0100) is a venue for local French gays, especially on Friday nights. ManaSPOT wireless Internet is available.

Le Manava Café or "MC" (avenue Pouvanaa a Oopa at Commandant Destremeau, tel. 42-02-91, weekdays 05300–1800, Sat. 0630–1100) has a nice open-air sidewalk terrace ideal for a coffee and a bar perfect for a draft beer.

Groceries

Downtown there's **Champion** (rue du Commandant Destremeau, tel. 54-29-29, Mon.–Sat. 0700–1930, Sun. 0630–1200), a large supermarket. Get whole barbecued chickens and chow mein in the deli section.

Just south of the junction of the auto route to Papeete is the **Centre Commercial**

Moana Nui (PK 8.3, Punaauia), Tahiti's first enclosed shopping mall, which opened in 1986. Some of the cheapest groceries on the island are available at the large adjoining **Carrefour** supermarket (tel. 46-08-08, Mon.–Sat. 0800–1950, Sun. 0800–1150). The deli section has a good selection of takeout items, including barbecued chicken, and there's also a fancy snack bar on the mall. The supermarket doesn't sell only groceries but also clothing and mass-produced souvenirs at the best prices on the island. Carrefour is easily accessible from Papeete on the frequent Outumaoro bus, which finishes its route across the highway.

Other big supermarkets around the island include **Supermarche Venustar** (PK 10, tel. 48-10-13, Mon.–Sat. 0630–1930, Sun. 0600–1130), at the turnoff to Point Venus on the circle island highway, and **Champion** (tel. 57-36-36, Mon.–Sat. 0600–1900, Sun. 0600–1200) in Taravao. All of these are good places to pick up picnic supplies.

INFORMATION

The **Office du Tourisme** (tel. 50-57-12, weekdays 0730–1730, Sat. 0800–1600) is at Fare Manihini, a neo-Polynesian building between boulevard Pomare and the Quai d'honneur where the cruise ships tie up. The staff can answer simple questions and supply a free map of Papeete, but they don't make phone calls or reservations on behalf of visitors.

The **Institut de la Statistique de la Polynésie Française** (1st floor, Immeuble Uupa, rue Edouard Ahnne, tel. 47-34-34, www.ispf.pf, Mon.–Thurs. 0730–1330, Fri. 0730–1200), next to Honolulu, puts out a useful annual abstract titled *La Polynésie en Bref.*

Bookstores

You'll find Papeete's biggest selection of books in English at **Libraire Archipels** (68 rue des Remparts, tel. 42-47-30). It has a good Pacific section.

The **Libraire du Vaima** (tel. 45-57-44) in the Vaima Center carries antiquarian books

The Office du Tourisme on the Papeete waterfront is a good first stop before setting out to explore the city.

about the South Pacific, topographical maps, and posters.

Papeete's largest bookstore is **Odyssey** (rue Jaussen behind the Catholic cathedral, tel. 54-25-25), although most of the books are in French.

There's a news kiosk (tel. 41-02-89) with magazines in English in front of the Vaima Center by the taxi stand on boulevard Pomare.

Maps

Topographical maps (CFP 1,500 per sheet) of many islands are available from the Section Topographie of the **Service de l'Urbanisme** (4th floor, Administrative Center, 11 rue du Commandant Destremeau, tel. 46-80-33).

La Boutique Klima (13 rue Jaussen, tel. 42-00-63), behind the cathedral, sells nautical charts (CFP 3,350) and many interesting French books on Polynesia.

Nauti-Sport (tel. 50-59-59) in Fare Ute also retails the same French nautical charts of Polynesia at CFP 3,450 per sheet.

Library

A public library (646 boulevard Pomare, tel. 54-45-44, www.maisondelaculture.pf, Mon.–Thurs. 0800–1700, Fri. 0800–1600) is in the Cultural Center. Visitors cannot take books out, but you're welcome to sit and read. The padded chairs in the air-conditioned reading room are great for relaxing.

Airline Offices

Reconfirm your international flight at your airline's Papeete office. Many of the airline offices are in the Vaima Center: **Air New Zealand** (tel. 54-07-47), **LanChile** (tel. 50-30-10), and **Qantas** (tel. 46-42-80). **Air Tahiti Nui** (61 rue Gauguin, tel. 46-03-03) is near the Hôtel de Ville. **Air France** (tel. 47-47-47) is on rue Georges Lagarde inland from the Vaima Center. **Aircalin** (tel. 85-09-04) has an office upstairs above the international check-in counters at the airport, while **Hawaiian Airlines** (tel. 86-60-00) is next to the Banque de Polynésie at the airport. If the clerk tells you it's not necessary to reconfirm, check your seat assignment and leave a local contact phone number to ensure that your booking is still in the system.

SERVICES

Money

MG Finances Broadway (boulevard Pomare, tel. 42-34-39, Mon.–Thurs. 0700–2200, Fri.–Sat. 0700–0100, Sun. 0800–2200), adjacent to Les 3 Brasseurs, changes cash at odd hours without commission. They'll also change traveler's checks, but only in the morning when the cashier is present. MG Finances is good if you're changing a small amount; otherwise the banks give a better rate that you must line up to receive. It's an excellent place to change excess CFP back into euros at the fixed official rate (the bank at the airport may be out of euros).

The **Banque de Polynésie** (355 boulevard Pomare, tel. 46-66-66, Mon.–Thurs. 0745–1530, Fri. 0745–1430), directly across from the Office du Tourisme, takes CFP 474

© DAVID STANLEY

an automatic banknote changing machine in Papeete

commission. This branch has an Automatic Currency Exchange machine outside their office that changes the banknotes of six countries for the usual commission. The **Banque de Tahiti** (boulevard Pomare west of the Vaima Center, tel. 41-70-00, weekdays 0800–1145 and 1330–1630, Sat. 0800–1130) charges a whopping CFP 1,306 commission.

Several banks around town have ATMs where you can get cash if the machine's software recognizes your card. **Banque Socredo** (411 boulevard Pomare, tel. 41-51-23), on the waterfront just east of the post office, has an ATM accessible 24 hours a day. There have been numerous complaints about Tahiti ATMs that didn't work, so using one of these machines at a time when the bank itself is closed is not recommended. The ATM at the Banque de Polynésie opposite the back side of the Vaima Center seems to take most cards. If you need to have money wired to you, the Banque de Polynésie has a connection with Western Union.

Post and Telecommunications

The main **post office** (weekdays 0730–1700, Sat. 0730–1100) on boulevard Pomare next to Parc Bougainville is usually packed with locals paying bills. Rather than waiting an eternity to buy your stamps at the counters upstairs, try getting them at the Philatelic Bureau downstairs, where there will be no line. Pick up poste restante (general delivery) mail downstairs, with a collection fee per piece. Around Tahiti, small branch post offices with public telephones are found in Arue, Faa'a Airport, Mahina, Mataiea, Paea, Papara, Papeari, Pirae, Punaauia, and Taravao.

If you have an American Express card, you can have your mail sent c/o Tahiti Tours, B.P. 627, 98713 Papeete, French Polynesia. Its office (15 rue Jeanne d'Arc, tel. 54-02-50, www.americanexpress.pf, Mon. 1330–1600, Tues.–Fri. 1230–1600) is next to the Vaima Center.

Courier Services

The **DHL Worldwide Express** agent (tel. 83-

© DAVID STANLEY

Papeete has many Internet cafés, but they're hard to use due to the prevalence of French keyboards.

73-73, Mon.–Thurs. 0730–1600, Fri. 0730–1500) is near Faa'a Airport, just up the road running inland from the coastal highway.

Cowan et Fils (tel. 80-37-37), upstairs above the Air Tahiti freight office in the airport itself, is the **United Parcel Service** agent.

Internet Access

La Maison de la Press (343 boulevard Pomare, tel. 50-93-93, Mon.–Thurs. 0800–1900, Fri.–Sat. 0800–2000, Sun. 0830–1200 and 1630–2000), opposite Tahua Vaiete, has a nine-computer Internet café upstairs (CFP 16 per minute). Ask for a machine with an English keyboard.

Tiki Copy (run Jeanne d'Arc, tel. 85-54-55, Mon.–Thurs. 0800–1700, Fri. 0800–1600, Sat. 0800–1200), opposite the Vaima Center, offers cheap Internet access at CFP 12 per minute, but they only have confusing French keyboards.

Cyber Esp@ce Cibernesia (tel. 85-43-67, www.cybernesia.pf, weekdays 0800–1700, Sat. 0900–1300), in the Vaima Center, also charges CFP 12 per minute.

X-Factor Internet (avenue de Marechal Foch, Mon.–Sat. 0800–2000, Sun. 0900–1900), just off Pont de l'Est, offers the cheapest Internet access in Papeete at CFP 10 per minute, but all of their computers have French keyboards. **Cyber Spot** (48 rue des Remparts, tel. 45-16-61, daily 0800–2000), around the corner, is also CFP 10 per minute and also has French keyboards only.

The **Mana Agency** (9 avenue de Marechal Foch, Pont de l'Est, tel. 47-99-99) sells the MiPASS for dial-up Internet access and the Carte ManaSPOT for Wi-Fi access. These cards can also be purchased at most post offices and ManaSPOT wireless hotspots.

Immigration Office

If you arrived by air, visa extensions are handled by the **Police Aux Frontières** (tel. 80-06-00, weekdays 0730–1200 and 1330–1700) at the airport (up the stairs beside the snack bar). Drop by at least a week before your current visa will expire. Yachties are handled by the **Bureau des Yachts** (tel. 42-40-74) at the new Gare Maritime in the center of town. If you wish to extend a three-month visa, ask the Office du Tourisme where you need to go to apply. Be patient and courteous with the officials if you want good service.

For those uninitiated in the French administrative system, the **police station** (in emergencies tel. 17) opposite the War Memorial on avenue Pouvanaa a Oopa deals with Papeete matters, while the **gendarmerie** (tel. 46-73-73) at the head of avenue Pouvanaa a Oopa is concerned with the rest of the island. The locally recruited Papeete police wear blue uniforms, while the paramilitary French-import gendarmes are dressed in khaki.

Consulates

The **Consular Agency of the United States** (tel. 42-65-35, www.usconsul.pf, Tues. 1000–1200 or by appointment) is upstairs in the Centre Tamanu Iti near the US Info computer store and not far from Hôtel Le Méridien Tahiti in Punaauia. This office does not issue U.S. visas.

Other countries with honorary consuls in Papeete are **Australia and Canada** (tel. 46-88-53), **Austria** (tel. 43-91-14), **Belgium** (tel. 50-65-65), **Chile** (tel. 43-89-19), **China** (tel. 45-61-79), **Denmark** (tel. 54-04-54), **Finland** (tel. 46-76-58), **Germany** (tel. 42-99-94), **Israel** (tel. 42-41-00), **Italy** (tel. 43-45-01), **Japan** (tel. 45-45-45), **Korea** (tel. 43-64-75), **Netherlands** (tel. 42-49-37), **Norway** (tel. 42-89-72), **Spain** (tel. 77-85-40), **Sweden** (tel. 47-54-75), and the **United Kingdom** (tel. 70-63-82). New Zealand is not represented here.

Launderettes

Lavomatic du Pont de l'Est (64 rue Gauguin, tel. 43-71-59, Mon.–Fri. 0700–1730, Sat. 0700–1200) charges CFP 2,500 to wash and dry seven kilograms.

Laverie Automatique Majamat (303 boulevard Pomare, tel. 41-26-65, weekdays 0700–1500), opposite the Gare Maritime, charges CFP 1,200 to wash and dry two kilograms.

Public Toilets

Public toilets are found on Tahua Vaiete near

© DAVID STANLEY

The public toilets on the waterfront at Tahua Vaiete are convenient and clean.

the Office du Tourisme, beside the Flower Market, at the bus stop on rue Colette beside the city hall, and at the Tahua To'ata west along the waterfront. Bring your own toilet paper. Restaurants and bars often have toilets available to patrons, though you might have to request the key.

Yachting Facilities

Yachts pay a daily fee to anchor at the **Marina Taina** (PK 9, Punaauia, tel. 41-02-25), accessible via the Faa'a Channel without exiting the lagoon. Otherwise visiting boats can use one of the anchor buoys at the **Yacht Club of Tahiti** (PK 4, Arue, tel. 42-78-03) for a monthly fee. Another popular anchorage is **Port Phaeton** at Taravao. Tahiti's sunny west and south coasts are excellent cruising grounds, while there are few good anchorages on the windward, rainy, and often dangerous east and north coasts.

Health

In early 2010 Mamao Territorial Hospital on avenue Georges Clemenceau was closed and all of its facilities were moved to the new **Centre Hospitalier de Polynésie Française** (tel. 46-62-62) in Pirae, just east of Papeete. As was the case in the old hospital, the state-of-the-art Centre Hospitalier is always crowded with locals awaiting subsidized treatment, and unless you've been taken to the **recompression chamber** *(caisson hyperbare)* located there or it's an emergency, you're better off attending a private clinic.

At the **Clinique Paofai** (boulevard Pomare, tel. 46-18-18) you can see a doctor anytime in the emergencies *(urgences)* department on the first floor (brief consultations CFP 3,600 0700–1700, CFP 7,600 1700–0700). The facilities and care are excellent.

In case of emergencies around Papeete, call **S.O.S. Médecins** at tel. 42-34-56. To call an ambulance, dial 15.

A dentist, Dr. Michel Ligerot (415 boulevard Pomare, tel. 43-32-24), is on the second floor of the building next to the Hôtel Tiare Tahiti.

The **Pharmacie de la Cathedrale** (tel. 42-02-24, weekdays 0700–1830, Sat. 0700–1230) is across the street from the Catholic cathedral. There are many other pharmacies around Papeete.

GETTING THERE AND AROUND

For information on air and sea services from Papeete to the other islands, see *Getting Around* in the *Essentials* chapter.

Bus

You can go almost anywhere on Tahiti by bus. RTC (Reseau de Transport Collectif) buses to Arue, Mahina, Papenoo, Taravao, Tautira, and Teahupoo leave from both sides of boulevard Pomare near the Office du Tourisme. Those to the airport, Outumaoro, Punaauia, Paea, and Papara are found in front of the Banque de Tahiti on rue du Maréchal Foch. Local services to Motu Uta (infrequent), Mission, Titioro, and Tipaeriu depart from rue Colette near the Hôtel de Ville.

Buses marked "Outumaoro" run from Papeete to Faa'a International Airport and the traffic circle near Marina Taina daily every few minutes 0400–2000. Weekdays, the last trip from Papeete to Mahina, Paea, and points beyond is around 1700, with reduced frequency on Saturday and no buses on Sunday.

Buses to Teahupoo and Tautira, both via Paea, leave from boulevard Pomare on the same side of the street as the Office du Tourisme. They depart Papeete weekdays about every hour 0630–1730 and less frequently on Saturday. The bus to Taravao via Papenoo leaves from across the street from the Office du Tourisme weekdays almost hourly 0515–1800 but on Saturday only at 0930, 1130, and 1430. There are no buses to the southeast side of Tahiti on Sunday.

Destinations and fares are posted on the side of the vehicles: CFP 130 to the airport (CFP 200 after 1800), CFP 200 to Punaauia or Paea, CFP 250 to Arue, CFP 280 to Mahina, CFP 300 to Papenoo, CFP 250 to Papara, CFP 400 to Taravao, Teahupoo, and Tautira. After dark, all bus fares increase. Outside Papeete some buses will stop anywhere if you wave, but others only stop at marked bus stops.

Air-conditioned buses link Papeete to the east end of the island several times a day.

Taxis

Taxis in Papeete are extremely expensive, and it's important not to get in unless there's a meter that works or you've agreed to a flat fare beforehand. The basic fare is CFP 1,000 during the day (0600–2000) or CFP 1,200 at night (2000–0600). Add to that the per-kilometer fee of CFP 120 by day or CFP 240 at night. The flat rate per hour is CFP 4,000 during the day or CFP 6,000 at night. Waiting time is CFP 2,000 per hour by day, CFP 3,000 at night. Baggage is CFP 50–100 per piece.

During the day, expect to spend at least CFP 1,000 for a short trip within Papeete, CFP 1,500 to the airport, or CFP 1,700 to the InterContinental or Sofitel. A trip around the island costs CFP 16,000. Taxi stands are found at the Vaima Center (tel. 43-72-47), Mana Rock Café, and airport (tel. 86-60-66). Official set fares are listed on a board at the Vaima Center taxi stand. If you feel cheated by a taxi driver, take down the license number and complain to the Office du Tourisme, although what you consider a rip off may be the correct amount. We've received numerous complaints about Papeete taxi drivers, and they're best avoided if at all possible.

Car Rentals

If you want to whiz around the island, packing in as many side trips as you can in a day, an unlimited-mileage car rental is for you, and with a few people sharing, it becomes affordable. Don't rent on a per-kilometer basis unless you plan to keep the car for at least three days and intend to use it only for short hops. Most agencies impose a 50-kilometer daily minimum on their per-kilometer rentals to prevent you from traveling *too* slowly; most rentals are for a minimum of 24 hours. Almost all the car rental companies have kiosks inside Faa'a Airport, and most offer clients a free pickup and drop-off service to the hotels and airport. An additional CFP 700 tax is charged on car rentals at the airport instead of a downtown location.

Check the car as carefully as they check you; be sure to comment on dents, scratches, flat tires, etc. All the car rental agencies include third-party public liability insurance in the basic price, but collision damage waiver (CDW) varies CFP 1,000–3,500 extra per day with CFP 50,000 and up deductible (called the *franchise* in French). Most agencies charge the client for stolen accessories and damage to the tires, insurance or no insurance, and Tahiti insurance may not be valid if you take the car to Moorea by ferry (ask). You'll also pay for towing if you are judged responsible. On Tahiti the car comes full of gas, and you'll see Mobil and Total gas stations all around the island.

Avis/Pacificar (56 rue des Remparts, tel. 54-10-10, www.avis-tahiti.com, Mon.–Sat. 0730–1700, Sun. 0730–1200) is on pont de l'Est, at the east end of rue Paul Gauguin. It also has a desk at the airport. Avis/Pacificar has unlimited-kilometer cars from CFP 9,600/17,659/26,489 for one/two/three days, including insurance. You're responsible for the first CFP 88,000 in damages. Insurance to eliminate that risk is CFP 2,200 a day.

Hertz (tel. 42-04-71) is on rue des Remparts next to Avis and at the airport (tel. 82-55-86). Its cars begin at CFP 2,240 per day, plus CFP 44 per kilometer, plus CFP 1,500 insurance. Otherwise it's CFP 9,520/17,890/23,800 for one/two/three days with unlimited mileage. Hertz has an attractive price for two weeks, and you can take the car to Moorea.

Europcar (tel. 86-61-96, www.europcarpolynesie.com) is in the Vaima Center and at the airport. Its cars start at CFP 6,750 and include 50 kilometers, plus CFP 44 per additional kilometer. With unlimited kilometers and insurance it's CFP 9,450/26,700 for one/three days. The minimum age is 21, but the insurance coverage is limited for those under 25. All clients are responsible for the first CFP 55,000 in damages to the car.

Location de Voitures Daniel (tel. 81-96-32, daniel.location@mail.pf) at the airport terminal begins at CFP 2,200 per day, plus CFP 41 per kilometer (50 km minimum), plus CFP 951 insurance. With unlimited mileage it's CFP 8,467/13,938/19,745 for one/two/three days. Drivers aged 21 and up are accepted.

The starting price at **Tahiti Rent a Car** (tel. 81-94-00), also known as Location de Voitures Pierrot et Jacqueline, is CFP 2,200 per day, plus CFP 41 per kilometer and CFP 1,308 insurance. With unlimited kilometers it's CFP 9,200/16,680/21,000 for one/two/three days, insurance included. This company will allow you to take the car to Moorea if you ask beforehand, but the insurance won't be valid over there. The minimum age to rent is 21, but drivers under 25 are responsible for the first CFP 150,000 in damages to the car. This company has an office at the airport.

Robert Rent-a-Car (rue du Commandant Destremeau, tel. 42-97-20, ets.robert@mail.pf) has the least expensive cars, starting at CFP 7,900 per day including unlimited kilometers and insurance. For two/three days it's CFP 6,800/6,000 per day.

© DAVID STANLEY

Those who manage to find on-street parking in downtown Papeete must feed parking machines or face fines.

Parking

The street parking in Papeete is chaotic, with double parking and parking on the sidewalk commonplace. Blue European-style parking-fee machines bearing the letter "P" are now in operation on some streets. You must place a receipt obtained from the coin-operated machine face up on your dash; otherwise the car rental company will collect any outstanding parking fines when you turn in the car. The parking machines must be used weekdays 0800–1700, Saturday 0800–1200, and cost CFP 100 per hour (two hours maximum).

There's underground parking at the Hôtel de Ville (weekdays 0600–1800, Fri. 1800–Sun. 0900), accessible from rue Colette opposite Hôtel Le Mandarin, and costs CFP 120 for the first hour, CFP 60 for each subsequent hour. Parking du Centre Vaima (tel. 42-46-30, Mon.–Sat. 0700–1900), entrance from rue Georges Lagarde off rue du Général de Gaulle in front of Hollywood Cinema, charges CFP 150 for the first hour, CFP 200 for each subsequent hour.

The cheapest parking in Papeete is in the big lot (weekdays 0600–1730, Sat. 0630–1200) next to McDonald's in front of the Territorial Assembly. The first hour costs CFP 100, each additional hour CFP 50, or CFP 750 per day. It's free on Saturday.

Bicycle

Unfortunately the fast and furious traffic on Tahiti's main highways makes cycling dangerous and unpleasant, and motor-scooter rentals have been discontinued after fatal accidents.

Garage Bambou (avenue Georges Clemenceau, tel. 42-80-09), near the Chinese temple, sells new bicycles from CFP 46,500 and does repairs.

Local Tours

Tahiti Safari Expédition (tel. 42-14-15, www.tahiti-safari.com) offers four-wheel-drive jeep tours to Mount Marau, the Papenoo Valley, and Lake Vaihiria. The highly recommended day trip across Tahiti via the Relais de la Maroto (CFP 10,200 with lunch) not only provides a rare glimpse of the interior but a good introduction to the flora and fauna of the island. Most hotel receptions (including the Hôtel Tiare Tahiti) will book this tour.

Natura Exploration (tel. 43-03-83, natura .explo@mail.pf) does the same trip across the island for CFP 8,000 with a picnic lunch. Natura does a half-day Mount Marau four-wheel-drive trip for CFP 5,500 per person. **Patrick Adventure** (tel. 83-29-29) also does cross-island tours.

Marama Tours (tel. 50-74-74, www.marama tours.com), at the Sofitel, does six-hour circle-island tours for CFP 4,900 (admission fees extra). It also sells the four-wheel-drive tours for CFP 10,200 that include a picnic lunch. **Tahiti Nui Travel** (tel. 46-42-00, www .tahitinuitravel.com), at the Vaima Center and various hotels, offers a full-day circle-island tour on Sunday for CFP 4,900 per person, excluding lunch and entry fees (four-person minimum).

Getting Away

The **Air Tahiti** booking office (corner of rue du Maréchal Foch and rue Edouard Ahnne, tel. 47-44-00, weekdays 0800–1700, Sat. 0800–1100) is just inland from the market. **Air Moorea** (tel. 86-41-41) is at Faa'a International Airport.

The ferries to Moorea depart from the new Gare Maritime near the Office du Tourisme downtown. Most other interisland ships, including the cargo vessels *Taporo VI* and *Hawaiki-Nui,* leave from the Tuamotu wharf or Quai des Caboteurs in Motu Uta, across the harbor from downtown Papeete. You can catch a bus directly to Motu Uta from the Hôtel de Ville, if you're lucky (it's very infrequent). The ticket offices of some of the vessels are in Fare Ute just north of downtown, while others are at Motu Uta.

Around Tahiti

A 117-kilometer Route de Ceinture (Belt Road) runs right around Tahiti-nui, the larger part of this hourglass-shaped island. Construction began in the 1820s as a form of punishment imposed on the Tahitians by Protestant missionaries for their "sins." For orientation, you'll see red-and-white kilometer stones, called PK *(pointe kilométrique),* along the inland side of the road. These are numbered in each direction from the Catholic cathedral in Papeete, meeting at Taravao.

Go clockwise to get over the most difficult stretch first; also, you'll be riding on the inside lane of traffic and less likely to go over a cliff in case of an accident (an average of 55 people a year are killed and 700 injured in accidents on this island). Southern Tahiti is much quieter than the northwest, whereas from Paea to Mahina it's hard even to slow down as tailgating motorists roar behind you.

You can easily drive a rental car around Tahiti in a day, and if you're adventurous, it's possible to do a circle-island tour by public bus, provided you get an early start and go clockwise with no stop until Taravao. The buses don't run right around the island, although some go as far as Tautira and Teahupoo on Tahiti-iti. The buses to Tautira and Teahupoo go via the south coast, so if you want to do a full-circle trip, you'll need to begin by going to Taravao via Papenoo.

Large buses to Taravao via Papenoo (1.5 hours, CFP 400) leave Papeete from the opposite side of boulevard Pomare as the Office du Tourisme weekdays at 0515, 0615, 0830, 0930, 1100, 1215, 1330, 1430, 1530, 1640, and 1800, and Saturdays at 0930, 1130, and 1430. Once at Taravao, look for a bus coming from Tautira or Teahupoo to take you back to Papeete along the south coast. The last return bus to Papeete leaves Tautira at 1330 weekdays and 1200 Saturdays. The last bus back from Teahupoo is at 1430 weekdays and 1400 Saturday. Service is reduced on Saturday, and there are no buses at all on Sunday, so go on a weekday. The buses often leave a little early and they're not 100 percent reliable. It is comforting to know that if you get stuck anywhere along the way, hitchhiking *(l'autostop)* is fairly easy and relatively safe on Tahiti. There's abundant traffic along

© DAVID STANLEY

Pointe kilométrique (PK) markers mark distances on the road around Tahiti.

the south coast highway all day, and it's almost certain you'll get a ride.

After Paea, the frequency of bus service increases, so ask the driver to let you out at the Marae Arahurahu (PK 22.5). The last Paea for Papeete leaves at 1630 Monday to Saturday, so you're OK until then. Your next stop could easily be the Marina Taina as bus service from nearby Outumaoro is every few minutes until 2000. The huge Carrefour supermarket opposite the Outumaoro bus terminus is always fun to look around.

TOWARD POINT VENUS

East of Arue, the highway climbs sharply to the **Point de View du Tahara'a** on One Tree Hill (PK 8), where there's a splendid view across Matavai Bay to Papeete and Moorea. Adjacent to the viewpoint is the entrance to the former Hôtel Tahara'a, erected by Pan American Airways in 1968. From 1988 to 1997 this was a Hyatt Regency, and then it became the Hôtel Royal Matavai Bay before closing for good in 1998. If the main gate is open, it's worth going in to get a closer look at this 190-room structure, built on a spectacular series of terraces down the hillside to conform to a local regulation that no building should be more than two-thirds the height of a coconut tree. There's another glorious view from the Governor's Bench on the knoll beyond the swimming pool above the entrance to the building.

Point Venus

Continue east to Mahina (PK 10) and turn left beside Supermarche Venustar to Point Venus. Captain Cook camped on this point between the river and the lagoon during his visit to observe the transit of the planet Venus across the sun on June 3, 1769. Captain Bligh also occupied Point Venus for two months in 1788 while collecting breadfruit shoots for transportation to the West Indies. And on March 5, 1797, the first members of the London Missionary Society landed here. From Tahiti, Protestantism spread throughout Polynesia and as far as Vanuatu.

Today there's a park on the point, with a 25-meter-high lighthouse (1867) among the palms and ironwood trees. Across from the monument to Captain Cook, with a large ball behind an iron railing, is a newer monument to the *Bounty* mutineers, erected by their descendents in 2006. The faces on the large volcanic stone are those of Fletcher Christian and his Tahitian *vahine*. Yet another monument in the park recalls the landing of the first missionaries.

The view of Tahiti across Matavai Bay from Point Venus is superb, and twin-humped Orohena, the highest peak on the island, is in view (you can't see it from Papeete itself). Weekdays, Point Venus is a peaceful place, the perfect choice if you'd like to get away from the rat race in Papeete and spend some time at the beach, but on weekends it gets crowded. Any Mahina bus (CFP 280) will bring you here.

Accommodations

Le Motu Martin (tel. 77-63-71, www.motu-martin.com) is on a tiny coral island just east of Point Venus. You can stay in one of four simple thatched bungalows with shared bath for CFP 5,000 per person. Each solar-powered bungalow has 10 beds, and you're expected to bring along a sleeping bag and towel. Otherwise, pitch your own tent for CFP 4,000 per person. Included are boat transfers from the fishing dock at Point Venus at 0800 with the return trip at 1600 (transfers outside these hours are CFP 3,000). You must bring your own food and cutlery. Also bring a cooler for perishables, as no refrigeration is available on the island. Kayaks and snorkeling gear are loaned free. For surfers, there's a lefthander on the reef just 150 meters from shore, and the winds here are perfect for kite surfing. On weekends the island gets crowded as local groups come over for picnics.

THE NORTHEAST COAST

The coast is very rugged all along the northeast side of Tahiti, with no barrier reef at many points between Point Venus and Mahaena. The **leper colony** at Orofara (PK 13.2) was founded in 1914. Previously the colony was on Reao atoll in the Tuamotus, but this proved too remote to service. Although leprosy is now a thing of the past, about 50 of the former patients' children who grew up there remain at Orofara, along with a couple of older leprosy patients.

From November to March, surfers ride the waves at Chinaman's Bay, Papenoo (PK 16), one of the best river-mouth beach breaks on the north side of the island. The bridge over the broad **Papenoo River** (PK 17.9) allows a view up the largest valley on Tahiti. A paved road leads a few kilometers up the valley before becoming a rough track across the island. (See *The Interior of Tahiti* in this chapter for a description of this route.)

At the **Arahoho Blowhole** (PK 22), jets of water shoot up through holes in the lava rock beside the highway at high tide. It's dangerous to get too close to the blowhole, as a sudden surge could toss you out to sea. A nice picnic area is provided here. Just a little beyond the blowhole, a road to the right leads 1.3 kilometers up to the three **Tefa'aurumai Falls** (admission free), also known as the Faarumai Falls. Vaimahuta Falls is accessible on foot five minutes along the easy path to the right across the bridge. The 30-minute trail to the left leads to two more waterfalls, Haamaremare Iti and Haamaremare Rahi. The farthest waterfall has a pool deep enough for swimming. Bring insect repellent and carefully lock your rental car before heading off to see the falls (the same applies at the blowhole).

At **Mahaena** (PK 32.5) is the battleground where 441 well-armed French troops defeated a dug-in Tahitian force twice their size on April 17, 1844, in the last fixed confrontation of the French-Tahitian War. The Tahitians carried on a guerrilla campaign for another two years until the French captured their main mountain stronghold. No monument commemorates the 100 Tahitians who died combating the foreign invaders here.

The French ships *La Boudeuse* and *L'Étoile,* carrying explorer Louis-Antoine de Bougainville, anchored by the southernmost of two islets off **Hitiaa** (PK 37.6) on April 6, 1768. Unaware that an Englishman had visited Tahiti a year before, Bougainville christened the island "New Cythera," after the Greek isle where love goddess Aphrodite rose from the sea. A plaque near the bridge recalls the event. A clever Tahitian recognized a member of Bougainville's crew as a woman disguised as a man, and an embarrassed Jeanne Baret entered history as the first woman to sail around the world. (Bougainville lost six large anchors during his nine days at this dangerous windward anchorage.)

From the bridge over the Faatautia River at PK 41.8, **Vaiharuru Falls** are visible in the distance. The American filmmaker John Huston intended to make a movie of Herman Melville's *Typee* here in 1957, but when Huston's other Melville film, *Moby Dick,* became a box-office flop, the idea was dropped.

TARAVAO

At Taravao (PK 53), on the strategic isthmus joining the two Tahitis where the PKs meet, is an **old fort** built by the French in 1844 to

THE FIRST WOMAN TO CIRCUMNAVIGATE THE GLOBE

In late 1766, Louis-Antoine de Bougainville set sail from France aboard the frigate *Boudeuse* on a voyage of discovery that would last 28 months. The expedition's second vessel, the *Etoile,* carried the king's botanist, Philibert Commerson. The ships spent more than a year off the east coast of South America on various missions. In Brazil, Commerson collected a violet flowering climber that he named *bougainvillea* for his captain.

After rounding Cape Horn, Bougainville and crew reached Tahiti in April 1768. Commerson's passion for native plants was shared by his hardworking assistant, Bonnefoy. There had been speculation aboard the *Etoile* that the fresh-faced boy dressed in baggy clothes might be a female, and all doubt was removed when "Bonnefoy" stepped ashore at Hitiaa. Tahitians immediately surrounded the youth, crying *vahine, vahine* (woman, woman) and offering to do her *les honneurs de l'isle* (the honors of the island). Jeanne Baret had to beat a hasty retreat to the ship.

Years later Bougainville described the situation in his *Journal:*

> *With tears in her eyes Baret acknowledged that she was a girl, that she had misled her master (Commerson) by dressing in men's clothes, that she was an orphan from Burgundy, that a lawsuit had reduced her to poverty, and that news of a voyage around the world had piqued her interest. I considered her case unique and admired her courage and wisdom. I took measures to ensure that nothing unpleasant happened to her. The royal court, I believe, will forgive this infringement of the rules. She was neither plain nor pretty and hardly 25 years old.*

When the expedition reached the French colony of Mauritius in the Indian Ocean, Commerson and Baret disembarked. There Commerson named the *baretia,* a plant species with flowers of cryptic sexuality, for this "valiant young woman who, adopting the dress and temperament of a man, had the curiosity and audacity to traverse the whole world, by land and sea, accompanying us without ourselves knowing anything."

Through the centuries Commerson has been largely forgotten because of his decision not to return directly to Europe with Bougainville. Though his work at Mauritius, Madagascar, and Réunion was important, many of his specimens and reports have been lost. After Commerson's death at Réunion in 1773, it became apparent that the only way Jeanne could return to France was by marrying a soldier, which she did. In 1785 Jeanne Baret, now Madame Dubernat, a widow living in Burgundy, was granted a naval pension at Bougainville's request. She died quietly in 1807.

cut off the Tahitians who had retreated to Tahiti-iti after the battle mentioned above. Germans were interned here during World War II, and the fort is still occupied today by the 1st Company of the Régiment d'Infanterie de Marine du Pacifique.

The assortment of supermarkets, banks, a post office, gas stations, and restaurants at Taravao make it a good place to break up your trip around the island.

Food

For lunch, consider **Restaurant L'Escale** (PK 60, Taravao, tel. 57-07-16, Mon.–Sat. 1100–1500 and 1830–2100, Sun. 1100–1500), an atmospheric old French country inn on the highway near the Total gas station. The plat du jour is indicated on a blackboard outside; otherwise order a seafood dish from the menu (mains from CFP 1,500). L'Escale has Moroccan dishes. Another good choice is **Restaurant Baie de Phaeton** (PK 58.9, tel. 57-08-96, Wed.–Sat. 0900–1400 and 1700–2100, Sun. 0900–1400), between Taravao and the Gauguin Museum. The Chinese and French entrées are reasonably priced, and there's a lovely terrace overlooking the bay; on weekends there's often live music here.

TAUTIRA

If you have your own transportation, three roads are explorable on rugged Tahiti-iti. An excellent 18-kilometer highway runs east from Taravao to quaint little **Tautira.** You'll get a good view up the Vaitepiha River valley from the black-sand beach on the west side of town. Two Spanish priests from Peru attempted to establish a Catholic mission here in 1774, but it lasted for only one year. Scottish author Robert Louis Stevenson stayed at Tautira for two months in 1888 and called it "the most beautiful spot, and its people the most amiable, I have ever found." The road peters out a few kilometers beyond Tautira, but you can continue walking 12 kilometers southeast to the Vaiote River, where there are petroglyphs, sacred rocks, and *marae.* These are difficult to find without a guide, and a few kilometers beyond are the high cliffs that make it almost impractical to try hiking around the Pari Coast to Teahupoo. Intrepid sea kayakers have been known to paddle the 30 kilometers around, although there's a wild four-kilometer stretch not protected by reefs. Most visitors go by speedboat.

Accommodations

Punatea Village (PK 4.6, tel. 57-71-00, www.punatea.com) is between Taravao and Pueu on the road to Tautira. The four bungalows with private bath facing a black pebble beach are CFP 9,450 double, while the five rooms with shared bath in a long thatched building cost CFP 5,830. The units are fan-cooled (no air-conditioning). Meals are available (cooking facilities not provided). There's a small swimming pool and garden.

Adjacent to the Punatea Village is **Pension Fare Maïthé** (tel. 57-18-24, www.chez-maithe.com), with two rooms with shared kitchen facilities and TV at CFP 7,000/7,500 single/double. It's in a quiet area near the sea with lush tropical vegetation.

Flotahia Chambres d'Hôtes (PK 5.6, tel. 57-97-38, http://chez.mana.pf/~heitaa.flo), a bit closer to Tautira, offers three rooms with shared bath at CFP 5,500/8,000/10,000 single/double/triple. Meals can be ordered, and there's a swimming pool.

Pueu Village (PK 9.8, Pueu, tel. 57-57-87, www.pueuvillage.com) has four waterside bungalows from CFP 10,000 double. A swimming pool and pontoon are provided.

TARAVAO PLATEAU

Another paved nine-kilometer road climbs straight up the Taravao Plateau from just before the hospital in Taravao, 600 meters down the Tautira road from Champion supermarket. Turn right, then left on the second road (no sign). If you have a car and time to take in only one of Tahiti-iti's three roads, this should be your choice. At the 600-meter level on top is the **Vaiufaufa Viewpoint,** with a breathtaking view of both Tahitis. You'll witness spectacular sunsets from here, and the herds of cows grazing peacefully among the grassy meadows give this upland an almost Swiss air. A rough side road near the viewpoint cuts down to rejoin the Tautira road near the PK 3 marker.

Accommodations

Pension Chez Jeannine (tel. 57-07-49, pensionchezjeannine@mail.pf), also known as "L'Eurasienne," is on the Route de Plateau five kilometers above Taravao. You'll need a rental car to stay here, as it's way up on the road to the Vaiufaufa Viewpoint and the buses don't pass anywhere nearby. The four two-story bungalows with cooking facilities and wicker furniture are CFP 10,000 double, while the three rooms above the restaurant are CFP 7,000 double. Have a look at the room before accepting it and verify all prices carefully. The cool breezes and good views are complemented by a swimming pool, but this place can feel deserted at night. Jeannine's restaurant (Fri.–Wed.) features Vietnamese dishes and seafood.

TEAHUPOO

The third road on Tahiti-iti runs 18 kilometers along the south coast to Teahupoo. Seven kilometers east of Taravao is a **marina** with an artificial beach (PK 7). American pulp Western writer Zane Grey had his fishing camp near here in the 1930s. Just east of the marina is **Maui Beach,** a long stretch of natural white sand beside the road where you'll see fishermen spearing by torchlight on the opposite reef in the evening. In the afternoon it's a great picnic spot. The two huge moorings near the shore were used by ocean liners before Papeete harbor was developed in the 1960s, as this is the finest natural deep-water harbor on Tahiti. Some of Tahiti's best reef-break surfing is possible out there in the Tapuaeraha Pass, but you'll need a boat. The 2009 IMAX movie *The Untimate Wave 3D* was filmed at the Teahupoo surfing site. Yachts can tie up to a pier near the *mairie* in **Vairao.** An oceanographic research station studying shrimp breeding is nearby.

The **Teahupoo** road ends abruptly at a river crossed by a narrow footbridge. There's an excellent mountain view from this bridge; walk east along the beach to get a glimpse of Polynesian village life. After a couple of kilometers the going becomes difficult because of yelping dogs, seawalls built into the lagoon, fences, fallen trees, and *tapu* (keep out) signs. Beyond is the onetime domain of the "nature men" who tried to escape civilization by living alone with nature almost a century ago.

Accommodations

Pension Chayan (PK 14, Vairao, tel. 57-46-00, www.pensionchayantahiti.pf) has four sturdy self-catering bungalows at CFP 14,150 double. The peaceful garden setting is nice with a few small waterfalls and paths among the luxuriant vegetation. A long pier stretches out from their private beach, and kayaks are loaned free. On a clear night, the sky is truly amazing from the end of the pier. From April to October you'll probably find surfers staying here as shuttles to all the main surfing sites are easily arranged. Vaipori Cave excursions are also offered.

Vanira Lodge (PK 15.6, Teahupoo, tel. 57-70-18, www.vaniralodge.com) has seven sizable thatched bungalows for rent at CFP 12,500/16,000 double/quad. Each stylish unit has cooking facilities and a covered terrace overlooking the sea. Bicycles and kayaks are loaned free. Surfers often stay here.

Tauhanihani Village Lodge (PK 16, Teahupoo, tel. 57-23-23, www.lavaguebleue.net), or "the Blue Wave," has five bungalows with bath and TV at CFP 14,000/16,000 garden/beach for two adults and two children. Lunch and dinner cost CFP 2,800 each, but kayaks and outrigger canoes are loaned free.

PARI COAST

Three hours on foot from the end of the road is **Vaipoiri Grotto,** a large water-filled cave best reached by boat. Try hiring a motorized canoe or hitch a ride with someone at the end of the road. Beyond this the 300-meter-high cliffs of the Pari Coast terminate all foot traffic along the shore; the only way to pass is by boat. All the land east of Teahupoo is well fenced off, so finding a campsite would involve getting someone's permission.

Teahupoo Excursion Taxi-Boat (tel. 75-11-98, http://web.me.com/teahupooexcursion) does surf shuttles plus excursions along the Pari Coast.

Accommodations

On the Pari Coast beyond the end of the road at Teahupoo is **Pension Le Bon Jouir** (tel. 57-02-15, www.bonjouir.com). The six bungalows start at CFP 9,500 double; otherwise the four rooms with baths are CFP 7,000 (two-night minimum). There's also a dormitory at CFP 2,500 per person. You can cook for yourself or order breakfast and dinner at CFP 3,500 per person per day. Return boat transfers (at 1300 and 1700) are CFP 2,000 per person, and it costs CFP 500 per day for parking at the wharf in Teahupoo. Le Bon Jouir is in a verdant location backed by hills, and it makes a great base for exploring this area. It's opposite the famous Teahupoo surfing break.

On the same coast but a bit closer to Teahupoo than Le Bon Jouir is **Te Pari Village** (tel. 42-59-12, www.tahiti1.com/tepari). There is no direct phone at the guesthouse but you can call tel. 42-59-12 in Papeete for information. The three rather basic huts are CFP 20,900 double, including all meals (two-night minimum stay). Boat transfers and kayaks are free. Unless you're a surfer or hiker, you won't get much out of this simple place. The wharf where both these establishments pick up their guests is at PK 17.1, a kilometer back from the end of the road.

THE PAINTER PAUL GAUGUIN

Onetime Paris stockbroker Paul Gauguin arrived at Papeete in June 1891 at age 43 in search of the roots of "primitive" art. He lived at Mataiea with his 14-year-old mistress, Teha'amana, for a year and a half, joyfully painting. In August 1893 he returned to France with 66 paintings and about a dozen wood carvings, which were to establish his reputation. Unfortunately, his exhibition flopped, and in August 1895 Gauguin returned to Tahiti, impoverished and infected with VD, settling at Punaauia. After an unsuccessful suicide attempt, he recovered somewhat, and in 1901 a Paris art dealer named Vollard signed a contract with Gauguin, assuring him a monthly payment of 350 francs and a purchase price of 250 francs per picture. His financial problems alleviated, the painter left for Hiva Oa in the Marquesas Islands to find an environment uncontaminated by Western influences. During the last two years of his life, at Atuona, Gauguin's eccentricities put him on the wrong side of the ecclesiastical and official hierarchies. He died in May 1903 at age 53, a near outcast among his countrymen on the islands, yet today a Papeete street and school are named after him.

PAPEARI

Port Phaeton on the southwest side of the Taravao Isthmus is a natural "hurricane hole," with excellent holding for yachts in the muddy bottom and easy access to Taravao from the head of the bay. (The entire south coast of Tahiti is a paradise for yachties, with many fine protected anchorages.) Timeless oral traditions relate that the first Polynesians to reach Tahiti settled at Papeari (PK 56—measured now from the west). In precontact times the chiefly family of this district was among the most prestigious on the island.

Gauguin Museum

The Gauguin Museum (PK 51.7, tel. 57-73-24, daily 0900–1700, CFP 600) is in Papeari District, 12 kilometers southwest of Taravao. The museum opened in 1965 thanks to a grant from the Singer Foundation (of sewing machine fame), and a couple of minor Gauguin prints, small wood carvings, and other objects associated with the painter are in the collection. These are displayed in the air-conditioned "Salle Henri Bing" to the left of the entrance, but unfortunately the captions are in French only and it's hard to distinguish the originals from the copies (most of the copies are marked "Facsimilé" in small letters). The other three exhibition rooms provide haphazard English translations. The display on the tormented life of Gauguin is well presented with numerous illustrations and explanations in English. Strangely, Gauguin's Tahitian mistresses receive little attention, and his clashes with the colonial authorities are swept under the carpet. A hall at the back of the museum contains a model of Gauguin's "Maison de Jouîr" in Atuona, Hiva Oa, plus bronze replicas of his wood carvings. The final room deals with Gauguin's influences and influences on Gauguin. Even with the museum's limitations, it is still well worth a visit. This is the place to learn about the world-famous painter and his connection to Tahiti.

The surroundings of the museum compete with Gauguin for attention. Two huge stone tikis are in the garden outside. The one closest to the beach stands 272 centimeters tall, the largest ancient stone statue in Polynesia outside of Easter Island. It's said to be imbued with a sacred *tapu* spell, and Tahitians believe this tiki, carved on the island of Raivavae hundreds of years ago, still lives. The three Tahitians who moved it here from Papeete in 1965 all died mysterious deaths within a few weeks. A curse is still said to befall all who touch the tiki.

A **botanical garden** rich in exotic species is part of the Gauguin Museum complex (CFP 600 additional admission). This 137-hectare garden was created 1919–1921 by the American botanist Harrison Smith (1872–1947), who introduced more than 200 new species to the island, among them the sweet grapefruit (pomelo), mangosteen, rambutan, and durian. Unfortunately, few native Tahitian plants are to be seen here. Two large Galapagos tortoises traipse through the east side of the gardens, the last of several such animals given to the children of writer Charles Nordhoff back in the 1930s. Yachts can enter the lagoon through Temarauri Pass and anchor just west of the point here.

THE SOUTH COAST

At PK 49 is the **Jardin Public Vaipahi** (admission free), with a lovely waterfall minutes from the road. It's a good substitute if you missed the botanical garden. A few hundred meters west of Vaipahi is the **Bain du Vaima,** a strong freshwater spring with several deep swimming pools. This is one of the favorite free picnic spots on the island, and on weekends it's crowded with locals. Yachts can anchor offshore.

In 1891–1893 Gauguin lived near the Oriental-style church at **Mataiea** (PK 46.5).

The **Olivier Breaud International Golf Course** (PK 41, Atimaono, tel. 57-43-41, skiptahiti@yahoo.com or egat@mail.pf, daily 0800–1700) stretches up to the mountainside on the site of Terre Eugenie, a cotton and sugar plantation established by Scotsman William Stewart at the time of the U.S. Civil War (1863). Many of today's Tahitian Chinese are descended from Chinese laborers imported to do the work, and a novel by A. T'Serstevens, *The Great Plantation,* was set here. The present 5,405-meter, 18-hole course was laid out by Californian Bob Baldock in 1970 with a par 72 for men, par 73 for women. If you'd like to play a round, greens fees are CFP 5,500 per person. Since 1981 the Tahiti Open in July has attracted golf professionals from around the Pacific. The course restaurant (daily 1130–1445) is said to be good and has ManaSPOT wireless Internet access.

The **Marae of Mahaiatea** (PK 39) at Papara was once the most hallowed temple on Tahiti, dedicated to the sea god Ruahatu. After a visit in 1769, Captain Cook's botanist, Joseph Banks, wrote, "It is almost beyond belief that Indians could raise so large a structure without the assistance of iron tools." Less than a century later, planter William Stewart raided the *marae* for building materials, and storms did the rest. All that's left of the 11-story pyramid today is a rough heap of stones. Still, it's worth visiting for its aura and setting, and you can swim off the beach next to the *marae* if you pay attention to the currents. The unmarked turnoff to the *marae* is 100 meters west of Magasin Maruia Junior (large Coca-Cola sign), then straight down to the beach. From April to October surfers often take the waves at black-colored **Taharuu Beach** on nearby Popoti Bay (PK 38.5), one of the top beach-break sites on southern Tahiti.

Beside Temple Zion at **Papara** (PK 36) is the grave of Dorence Atwater (1845–1910), U.S. consul to Tahiti 1871–1888. During the American Civil War, Atwater recorded the names of 13,000 dead Union prisoners at Andersonville Prison, Georgia, from lists the Confederates had been withholding. Himself a Union prisoner, Atwater escaped with his list in March 1865. His tombstone provides details.

Maraa Fern Grotto (PK 28.5) is by the road just across the Paea border. An optical illusion, the grotto at first appears small but is quite deep, and some Tahitians believe *varua ino* (evil spirits) lurk in the shadowy depths. Others say that if you follow an underground river back from the grotto, you'll emerge at a wonderful valley in the spirit world. Paul Gauguin wrote of a swim he took across the small lake in the cave. You're welcome to jump in the blue-gray water. Fill your water bottle with fresh mineral water from eight spouts next to the parking lot.

Maraa Pass is almost opposite the grotto, and yachts can anchor in the bay.

Accommodations

Papara Village (PK 38.5, Papara, tel. 57-41-41, paparavillage@mail.pf) is up on a hill one kilometer off the south coast highway. The three solid bungalows with private baths, fridges, TVs, and kitchens are CFP 10,000 single or double (minimum two-night stay). A swimming pool is on the premises.

Hiriata Chambres d'Hôtes (PK 34.2, Papara, tel. 77-78-49, pensionhiriata@mail.pf) has four self-contained motel-style rooms with cooking facilities and fridge at CFP 6,500 single or double, breakfast included.

Hiti Moana Villa (PK 32, tel. 57-93-93, www.papeete.com/moanavilla) is right on the lagoon between Papara and Paea. The four fan-cooled bungalows with kitchens, living rooms, TVs, terraces, private baths, and doors that cannot be locked are CFP 12,500 for four people. Four additional units without kitchens are CFP 10,000 double (CFP 1,000 surcharge for one night). Bring insect repellent. There is no beach, but there are a swimming pool and a pontoon, and the manager has a boat and motor for rent. This place is often full—especially on weekends—and advance bookings are recommended. Credit cards are not accepted here.

THE WEST COAST

Paea

The **Marae Arahurahu** (PK 22.5, Paea, open daily, admission free) is easily the island's most beautiful archaeological site. It's up the road inland from Magasin Laut—take care, the sign faces Papeete, and so it's not visible if you're traveling clockwise. This temple, lying in a tranquil verdant spot under high cliffs, is perhaps Tahiti's only remaining pagan mystery. The ancient open altars built from thousands of cut stones were carefully restored in 1954, the first such restoration in French Polynesia.

Mahana Park (PK 18.3, Papehue, admission free) is a territorial beach park. It's not as affected by pollution as the beaches closer to Papeete and is a good place to stop for an afternoon swim or even a sunset over Moorea.

HINANO BEER

The Brasserie de Tahiti was launched in 1914, and over the next 39 years the denizens of Polynesia were able to quench their thirst with a brew known as Aorai. The operation underwent a major modernization in 1955, and the hearty Hinano of today was born, to the delight of beer drinkers. Since 1976 the brewery has received technical support from the Dutch brewer Heineken, whose beer is bottled on Tahiti under license. A nonalcoholic beer called Vaitia was first produced in 1982, and in 1992 the Hei-Lager light beer was added to the line. Hei-Lager Gold followed in 1994, then Tabu lager in 2003. The computer-controlled cannery that opened at Punaruu on Tahiti in 1986 was expanded in 1991, making it possible to export canned Hinano to beer connoisseurs around the world. At present the company produces more than 30 million liters of Hinano per year and can fill 32,000 bottles and 22,000 cans per hour. It's one of the world's great beers.

Museum of Tahiti and the Islands

The Museum of Tahiti and the Islands (Pointe des Pêcheurs, Punaauia, tel. 54-84-35, Tues.–Sun. 0930–1730, CFP 600, groups CFP 500, students and children free) opened in 1977. In a large air-conditioned complex on Punaauia Bay, about 600 meters down a narrow road from PK 14.7, this museum has four halls devoted to the natural environment and settlement, Polynesian material culture, the social and religious life, and the history of Polynesia. The museum's collections include almost 1,700 seashells gathered from various sources, some 13,000 plant specimens dating back as far as 1847, and around 1,300 carvings from pre-European times to the present day. Several hours can be spent studying the exhibits, although a much faster walk through will also be educational and entertaining. Outside is an anchor Captain Cook lost at Tautira in 1773. Despite the stiff admission fee, only some of the captions are in English, and many of those are abbreviated from the French version. Nonflash, noncommercial photography is allowed.

If it's too late for any more sightseeing on your circle-island trip, don't worry—the museum makes an excellent half-day excursion from Papeete by public bus. Any of the Paea or Papara buses on rue du Maréchal Foch near Papeete market will bring you to the turnoff in 30 minutes. The road to the museum begins beside a Total gas station, 100 meters south of the large bridge over the Punaruu River just beyond a major traffic circle (ask). Go in the morning, as the last bus back to town is at 1630.

When the waves are right, you can sit on the seawall behind the museum and watch the Tahitian surfers bob and ride, with the outline of Moorea beyond. It's a nice picnic spot. Many of the trees in the park are labeled. On your way back to the main highway from the museum, look up to the top of the hill at an **old fort** used by the French to subjugate the Tahitians in the 1840s. The crown-shaped pinnacles of **Le Diadème** (1,321 meters) are also visible from this road.

Punaauia

Punaauia and Paea are Tahiti's sheltered "Gold Coast," with old colonial homes hidden behind trees along the lagoon side and nouveau riche villas dotting the hillside above. From 1896 to 1901 Gauguin had his studio at Punaauia, but nothing remains of it; his *Two Tahitian Women* was painted there. The view of Moorea is excellent all along the coast here.

At the traffic circle just north of the bridge near the Museum of Tahiti and the Islands turnoff, you have a choice of taking a fast bypass highway straight back to Papeete or continuing on the older coastal road to the Lagoonarium; the coastal road is the second, smaller exit from the circle. The **Lagoonarium** (PK 11.4, Punaauia, tel. 43-62-90, daily

the road around the island at Outumaoro on Tahiti's west coast

© DAVID STANLEY

the Outumaoro Bus Station at Punaauia on Tahiti's west coast

0900–1700, CFP 500 adults, CFP 300 children under 12), below the lagoon behind Captain Bligh Restaurant, provides a vision of the underwater marine life of Polynesia safely behind glass. The big tank full of black-tip sharks is a feature; the shark feeding takes place Tuesday–Saturday around noon. Straight out from the Lagoonarium is the Taapuna Pass, the southern entrance to the Punaauia Lagoon and another popular surfing venue.

To continue north, you must briefly rejoin the bypass. At PK 8, Outumaoro, just past the huge Carrefour shopping center, is the turn-off for the RDO autoroute to Papeete, Tahiti's superhighway. Follow the "Université" signs from here up to the ultramodern campus of the **Université de la Polynésie Française** (tel. 80-38-03, www.upf.pf) with its fantastic hilltop view of Moorea. The academic year for the 2,500 students runs mid-September–mid-May.

On the old airport road just north are two of Tahiti's biggest hotels, the **Sofitel Tahiti Maeva Beach Resort** (PK 7.5) and the **InterContinental Resort Tahiti** (PK 7), each worth a sightseeing stop. Pollution is a problem all around northeastern Tahiti, and one should ask at a resort reception before swimming in the sea. From the point where the InterContinental is today, the souls of deceased Tahitians once leapt on their journey to the spirit world. A sunset from either of these hotels, behind Moorea's jagged peaks across the Sea of the Moon, would make a spectacular finale to a circle-island tour. The **Mairie de Faa'a** (PK 5), just east of the airport, was erected in the traditional Maohi style in 1989.

Accommodations

One of the best low-budget places on Tahiti is **Pension Te Miti** (PK 18.5, Paea, tel. 58-48-61, www.pensiontemiti.com) in Papehue village, 450 meters up off the main road. The six rooms in two adjacent houses cost CFP 6,500–7,500 double depending on the size of the room. Backpackers and surfers often choose one of the four beds available in each of the two dorms at CFP 2,500 per person. Breakfast is included. Amenities include a communal fridge, cooking facilities, a TV corner, luggage storage, bicycles, and Internet access. The young French couple running this place is kind and helpful. Airport transfers are CFP 1,500 per person, but it's fairly easy to get there on the Paea bus during the day. Mahana Park and various shops and restaurants are nearby.

Taaroa Lodge (PK 18.1, Paea, tel. 58-39-21, www.taaroalodge.com), a large house right on a rocky beach behind Restaurant Snack PK 18, offers a 10-mattress dorm at CFP 2,500 per person, one room at CFP 6,000 single, and two bungalows at CFP 10,000 for up to three persons (two-night minimum stay). There's a common kitchen. Surfers are the main clientele, and several surf breaks, including Sapinus Reef, are nearby. The atmosphere is good, the company congenial, the managers friendly, and the sunsets great. Needless to say, it's often full.

Directly across the highway from the Taaroa Lodge access road is **Relais Fenua** (PK 18, Paea, tel. 45-01-98, www.relaisfenua.com) with three rooms on each side of a V-shaped building facing a small pool. Rates are from CFP 8,900/9,340 single/double. Some but not all of the rooms have kitchens and air-conditioning. The buffet breakfast is CFP 1,000 per person.

Pension Otaha (PK 17.3, tel. 58-24-52, www.otaha-lodge.com) is right on a sandy beach facing Moorea. Six self-catering bungalows and rooms are available at CFP 11,760 double or CFP 16,000 for four people (minimum stay two nights). Kayaks and snorkeling gear are loaned for free, and a washing machine is available.

Pension Te Nahe Toetoe (PK 15.4, Punaauia, tel. 58-42-43, www.pensionarmelle.com), also known as Chez Armelle (almost opposite a large Mobil service station), has eight rooms at CFP 5,980/7,620 single/double, plus five percent tax. A bungalow is CFP 9,120 triple. Air-conditioning is CFP 2,000 extra. Breakfast is included in all rates, and dinner is available at CFP 1,500 per person. The minimum stay is two nights. There's a pleasant snack bar facing the beach, but the rooms are ensconced in the complex. No parking space is provided, and rental cars must be left overnight at a public beach park next door. Snorkeling gear, canoes, kayaks, and bicycles are available. At night, airport transfers are CFP 1,500 per person each way. This pension caters more to French migrants who pay by the week or month, but it's still worth a look.

Pension de la Plage (PK 15.4, Punaauia, tel. 45-56-12, www.pensiondelaplage.com), across the highway from Pension Te Nahe Toetoe, has two long motel-style blocks of six rooms each at CFP 7,900/8,800 single/double (CFP 9,100/10,300 with kitchenette). The rooms face a small pool, and beach access through Toaroto Beach Park is across the street. Parking space is provided.

The **Hôtel Le Méridien Tahiti** (PK 15, Punaauia, tel. 47-07-07, www.tahiti.lemeridien.com), which opened in 1998 about nine kilometers southwest of the airport, is currently managed by Starwood Hotels. The 138 air-conditioned rooms in the four-story main building begin at CFP 35,000 single or double, while the 12 over-water bungalows are CFP 69,000 single or double, plus 14 percent tax. The over-water bungalows have no direct access to the water and are best avoided. The breakfast and dinner plan is CFP 7,186 plus 14 percent tax per person. The service in the dining room is poor, but several less expensive restaurants are only a short walk away. The Polynesian night with a show and a buffet is CFP 7,143. There's a huge sand-bottomed swimming pool linked to the rather poor beach as well as a 500-seat conference center. French families account for many of the guests. The Museum of Tahiti and the Islands is just a 10-minute walk away, and the sunsets over Moorea are superb.

In March 2009 Pearl Resorts launched the **Manava Suite Resort Tahiti** (PK 10.5, Punaauia, tel. 50-84-45, www.manavasuiteresorttahiti.blogspot.com). Many of the 121 units in five four-story buildings have kitchens. The rooms come in nine different categories, beginning with 20 garden suites at CFP 18,500 and culminating in the six-person, three-bedroom suite at CFP 45,000, all plus

14 percent tax. Children under 15 stay and eat free. Facilities include a fitness center and Manea Spa, two bars, a restaurant, and meeting rooms. On the beach are a real infinity swimming pool looking across to Moorea and a small offshore island with deck chairs. Food is expensive, but several outside restaurants are within walking distance.

Food

Le Coco's (PK 13.3, Punaauia, tel. 58-21-08, daily 1145–1345 and 1845–2145, CFP 3,000–4,000) has long been regarded as one of the finest seafood restaurants in French Polynesia, although it seems to have lost its way of late. The view of Moorea from the garden is still splendid, especially at sunset.

The **Western Grill** (PK 12.6, Punaauia, tel. 41-30-56, www.westerngrill-tahiti.com, daily, CFP 1,500–3,000) offers steaks and Tex-Mex specialties. There's live country music here Friday and Saturday evenings.

Le Blue Banana (PK 11.1, Punaauia, tel. 41-22-24, www.bluebanana-tahiti.com, Tues.–Sun. 1130–1400 and 1830–2200) is a family-oriented waterfront restaurant with excellent sunset views. They specialize in fresh fish (CFP 1,850–2,600) and pizza (CFP 1,250–1,850), and on Sunday you can order "ma'a Tahiti." Yachties can dinghy up to the dock.

La Casa Bianca (PK 9, Punaauia, tel. 43-91-35, www.casabianca-tahiti.com, daily 1000–2230) at the Marina Taina serves pizza (CFP 1,200–1,900), pastas (CFP 1,500–2,000), and seafood (CFP 1,550–2,200). There's often live jazz music here or in the adjacent Le Dinghy Bar.

The **Pink Coconut Bistro** (PK 9, Punaauia, tel. 41-22-23, www.pinkcoconuttahiti.com, Mon.–Sat.), on the other side of Marina Taina, is more upscale with seafood at CFP 2,450–3,450 and meats CFP 2,400–3,250. Happy hour is 1700–1830, and they present live music or a DJ Thursday–Saturday 1900–2330.

THE INTERIOR OF TAHITI

Most of Tahiti's coast is well traveled, but the interior is still largely uninhabited. There's no better way to get a sense of the natural environment of this high volcanic island than to visit the interior. A dirt track across the center of Tahiti begins next to the bridge over the Papenoo River (PK 17.9) on the north coast. In the dry season, you could drive a rental car 15 kilometers up the track to the suspension bridge across the Vaitamanu River and perhaps another kilometer to the Vaituoru Dam. Beyond that, only a four-wheel-drive vehicle could proceed, as a large sign proclaims. If you wish to go farther, you'll have to park at the bridge or dam and continue on foot. In the rainy season use your own judgment as to how far you wish to drive.

From coast to coast it's a four-hour, 37-kilometer trip by four-wheel-drive jeep, or two days on foot. The easiest (and probably best) way to do this trip is with one of the adventure tour operators that leave their brochures at the Office du Tourisme. Expect to pay CFP 10,000 per person, including a reasonable lunch, from one of these Papeete-based operators: **Tahiti Safari Expédition** (tel. 42-14-15, www.tahiti-safari.com); **Natura Exploration** (tel. 43-03-83, natura.explo@mail.pf); **Patrick Adventure** (tel. 83-29-29); and **Marama Tours** (tel. 50-74-74, www.maramatours.com).

The Papenoo Valley is the caldera of Tahiti-nui's great extinct volcano, considered by the ancient Tahitians to be the realm of the gods. On the slopes of Mount Orohena (2,241 meters), 10 kilometers south of Papenoo, is the entrance to the **Parc Naturel Te Faaiti,** Tahiti's first (and as yet undeveloped) territorial park. On the east side of the Papenoo Valley stands Mount Aramaoro (1,530 meters). Since 1980 the rivers here have been harnessed for hydroelectricity, and they now supply more than a third of Tahiti's electric requirements.

Up a steep incline two kilometers south of the Vaituoru Dam, a side road to the right leads to **Marae Fare Hape,** a well-restored archaeological site with an archery platform, a *marae* with stone backrests, and the outlines of other buildings. A large dam, the Barrage Tahinu, is a couple of kilometers west of Marae Fare Hape. A primitive campsite exists next to Marae Fare Hape.

The tour groups stop for lunch at the **Relais**

de la Maroto (tel. 57-90-29, maroto@mail.pf), at 217 meters elevation above the junction of the Vaituoru and Vainavenave Rivers. It's only one kilometer from Marae Fare Hape, 18 kilometers from Papenoo. This cluster of solid concrete buildings was built to house workers during construction of the hydroelectric installations. The 10 rooms in a long block beside the parking lot rent for CFP 7,500 single or double, while the three bungalows on the ridge are CFP 10,500 for up to three persons. Breakfast costs CFP 1,300 continental, CFP 1,700 American, and other meals range from hamburgers at CFP 950 to beef, fish, or shrimp dishes at CFP 2,500. If you wish to stay, call ahead to make sure the Relais is open and has a room for you, especially on weekends.

South of the Relais de la Maroto, the track climbs five kilometers to 780 meters elevation, where the 110-meter Urufau Tunnel (opened in 1989) cuts through to the south coast watershed. The track then winds down to Lake Vaihiria, Tahiti's only lake, at 473 meters elevation, 25 kilometers south of Papenoo. Sheer cliffs and spectacular waterfalls squeeze in around this spring-fed lake. Native floppy-eared eels, known as *puhi taria,* up to 1.8 meters long, live in these cold waters, as do prawns and trout. With its luxuriant vegetation, this rain-drenched spot is one of the most evocative on the island.

Just south of the lake, a concrete track with a 37-degree incline drops to a dam and upper power station. Four kilometers beyond this is a smaller dam and lower power station, then it's seven kilometers on a rough dirt track to PK 47.6 on the south coast highway near Mataiea.

Other Windward Islands

MAIAO

Maiao, or Tapuaemanu, 70 kilometers southwest of Moorea, is a low coral island with an elongated 154-meter-high hill at the center. On each side of this hill is a large greenish-blue lake. Around Maiao is a barrier reef with a pass on the south side accessible only to small boats. About 300 people live in a small village on the south side of 8.3-square-kilometer Maiao, all of them Polynesians. Problems with an Englishman, Eric Trower, who attempted to gain control of Maiao for phosphate mining in the 1930s, have resulted in a ban on Europeans and Chinese living on the island. Most of the thatch used in touristic constructions on Moorea and Tahiti originates on Maiao.

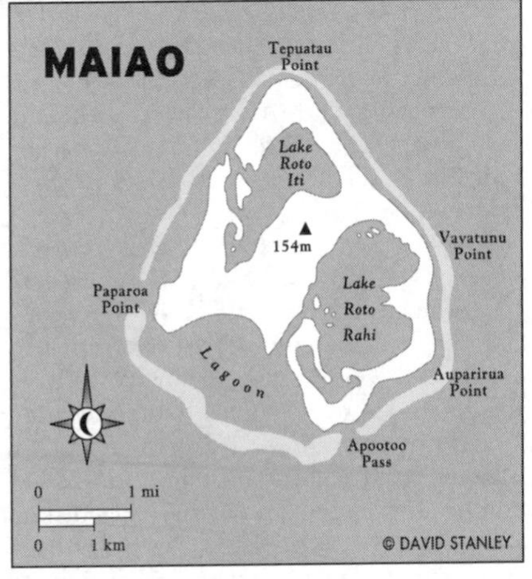

There are no tourist accommodations on Maiao, and an invitation from a resident is required to visit. Proposals to develop the island for tourism have been rejected by the inhabitants, and there's no airstrip.

MEHETIA

Mehetia is an uninhabited volcanic island about 100 kilometers east of Tahiti. Although Mehetia is less than two kilometers across, Mount Fareura reaches 435 meters. There's no lagoon, and anchorage is untenable. Landing is possible on a black beach on the northwest side of the island, but it's difficult. Anglers from the south coast of Tahiti visit Mehetia occasionally.

© TAHITI TOURISME

an aerial view of Tetiaroa Atoll north of Tahiti

TETIAROA

Tetiaroa, 55 kilometers north of Tahiti, is a low coral atoll with a turquoise lagoon and 13 deep-green coconut-covered islets totaling 490 hectares. Only small boats can enter the lagoon. Tahuna Iti has been designated a seabird refuge (it's fenced off), and the lagoon is a marine reserve. Three-kilometer-long Rimatuu islet served as a retreat for Tahitian royalty, and the remains of Polynesian *marae* and giant *tuu* trees may be seen.

In 1904 the Pomare family gave Tetiaroa, once a Tahitian royal retreat, to a Canadian dentist named Walter J. Williams to pay their bills. Dr. Williams, who served as British consul from 1916 until his death in 1937, had a daughter who sold Tetiaroa to actor Marlon Brando in 1966. Brando came to Tahiti in 1960 to play Fletcher Christian in the MGM film *Mutiny on the Bounty,* and he ended up marrying his leading lady, Tarita Teriipaia (who played Mameetee, the chief's daughter). From 1973 to 2004, she and her family ran a 14-bungalow resort called the Hôtel Tetiaroa Village on Motu Onetahi, where there's a small airstrip. Tarita and Marlon had two children: son Teihotu, born in 1965, and daughter Cheyenne, born in 1970.

The gunshot death of Dag Drollet, Cheyenne's ex-boyfriend and father of her son, Tuki, at the Brando residence in Los Angeles in 1990, resulted in a 10-year prison sentence for Cheyenne's half-brother, Christian Brando, on an involuntary manslaughter plea bargain. On Easter Sunday 1995, Cheyenne committed suicide, and she was buried next to Dag in the Drollet family crypt at Papeete's Uranie Cemetery. After this tragedy, Brando never visited Tetiaroa again, and the original

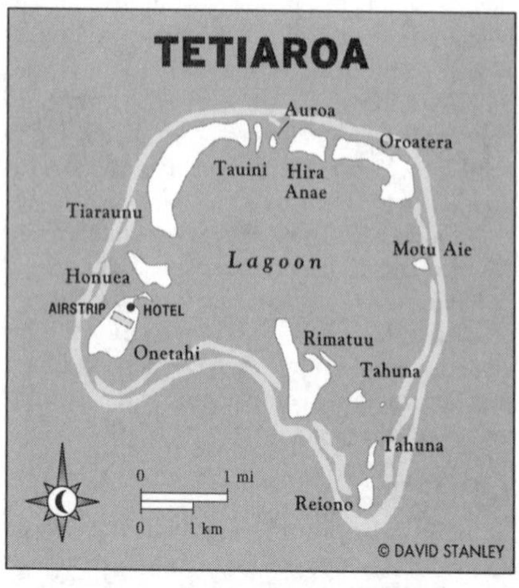

resort closed shortly before his death in 2004. Brando's will stipulated that any subsequent development could only be on Motu Onetahi.

In 2009 construction began on a 47-bungalow ecotourism resort called **The Brando** (www.thebrando.com), built by Tahiti-based resort developer Richard Bailey's Tahiti Beachcomber SA. Scheduled to open in late 2011, the InterContinental chain is expected to manage the property. Each bungalow will have a private plunge pool, and rates should be in the US$1,500 per night range. Tetiaroa's airstrip has been extended.

Getting There

Yachts and catamarans tied up opposite the Vaima Center in Papeete offer day trips to Tetiaroa, and their departure times and rates are posted. Prices vary according to the quality of the boat and whether lunch is included. (See *Day Cruises* in the *Papeete* section in this chapter for listings of visits to Tetiaroa.) On all of the boat trips from Papeete, be aware that up to three hours will be spent traveling each way, and on a day trip you'll have only about four hours on the atoll. The boat trip tends to be rough, and many people throw up their fancy lunch on the way back to Papeete. (In 1995 Marlon Brando won a lawsuit to prohibit "floating hotels" in the Tetiaroa lagoon, so overnight trips are not possible.)

Cruising yachts with careless captains sometimes make an unscheduled stop at low-lying Tetiaroa, as it's directly on the approach to Papeete from Hawaii. Several good boats have ended their days here.

MOOREA

Moorea, Tahiti's heart-shaped sister island, is clearly visible across the Sea of the Moon, just 21 kilometers northwest of Papeete. This enticing island offers the white-sand beaches rare on Tahiti, plus long deep bays, lush volcanic peaks, and a broad blue-green lagoon. Much more than Tahiti, Moorea is the laid-back South Sea isle of the travel brochures. And while Bora Bora has a reputation as Polynesia's most beautiful island, easily accessible Moorea seems more worthy of the distinction (and it's less expensive too). When Papeete starts to get to you, Moorea is only a hop away.

With a population of just 16,000, Moorea lives a quiet, relaxed lifestyle; coconut, pineapple, and vanilla plantations alternate with pleasant resorts and the vegetation-draped dwellings of the inhabitants. Tourism is concentrated along the north coast around Paopao and Hauru; many of the locals live in the more spacious south. Traffic roars along the north coastal road all day, and like Bora Bora, Moorea is in danger of becoming overdeveloped. The choicest sections of shoreline have been barricaded by restaurants and resorts. On the plus side, most of the hotels are clusters of thatched bungalows, and you won't find many of the monstrous steel, glass, and cement edifices that scream at you in Hawaii.

This triangular 125-square-kilometer island is actually the surviving southern rim of a shield volcano once 3,000 meters high. Moorea is twice as old as its Windward partner, Tahiti, and weathering is noticeably advanced. Two spectacular bays cut into the north coast on each side of Mt. Rotui (899 meters), once

HIGHLIGHTS

Cook's Bay: This is Moorea's scenic highlight, combining the best views, restaurants, and shopping. The beaches here aren't the best, but it's a required stop on trips around the island (page 89).

Opunohu Valley: This very special place combines excellent scenery, Moorea's finest viewpoint, hiking trails, and the island's largest archaeological site (page 91).

Stingray World: Few visitors will want to miss the chance to snorkel or scuba dive with stingrays. You can snorkel out from shore at the InterContinental Resort Moorea, or join an organized boat trip to the best ray-viewing spots (page 95).

Tiki Village Theater: Catch a sunset show or guided tour of this recreated Tahitian village where French Polynesia's largest traditional dance troupe performs (page 97).

Dolphin-Watching: Watching a pod of several dozen spinner dolphins performing their acrobatics around your boat is an unforgettable experience (page 100).

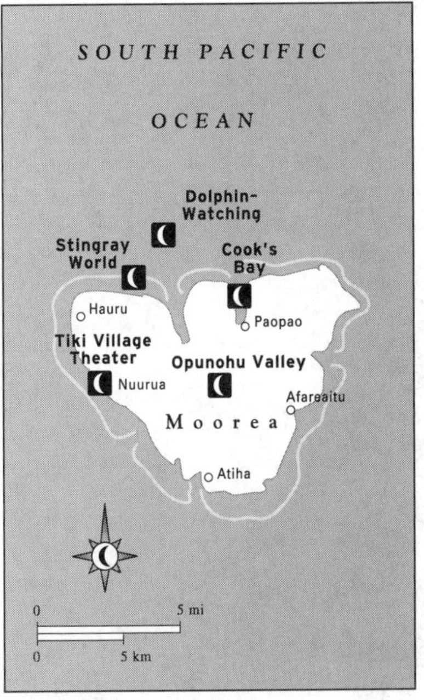

LOOK FOR ☾ TO FIND RECOMMENDED SIGHTS, ACTIVITIES, DINING, AND LODGING.

Moorea's core. The crescent of jagged peaks facing these long northern bays is scenically superb.

Shark tooth–shaped Mt. Mouaroa (880 meters) is a visual triumph, but Mt. Tohivea (1,207 meters) is higher. Polynesian chiefs were once buried in caves along the cliffs. Moorea's peaks protect the north and northwest coasts from the rain-bearing southeast trades; the drier climate and scenic beauty explain the profusion of hotels along this side of the island. Moorea is surrounded by a coral ring with several passes into the lagoon. Three *motu* enhance the lagoon, one off Afareaitu and two off Hauru.

Moorea's interior valley slopes are unusually rich, with large fruit and vegetable plantations and human habitation. At one time or another, coconuts, sugarcane, cotton, vanilla, coffee, rice, and pineapples have all been grown in the rich soil of Moorea's plantations. Stock farming and fishing are other occupations. Vegetables such as taro, cucumbers, pumpkins, and lettuce along with fruit such as bananas, oranges, grapefruit, papaya, star apples, rambutans, avocados, tomatoes, mangoes, limes, tangerines, and breadfruit make Moorea a veritable Garden of Eden.

PLANNING YOUR TIME

The accommodations are plentiful and good, and weekly and monthly rentals make even extended stays possible. You'll need a minimum of two nights to see the best of Moorea, one day for a trip around the island with a side

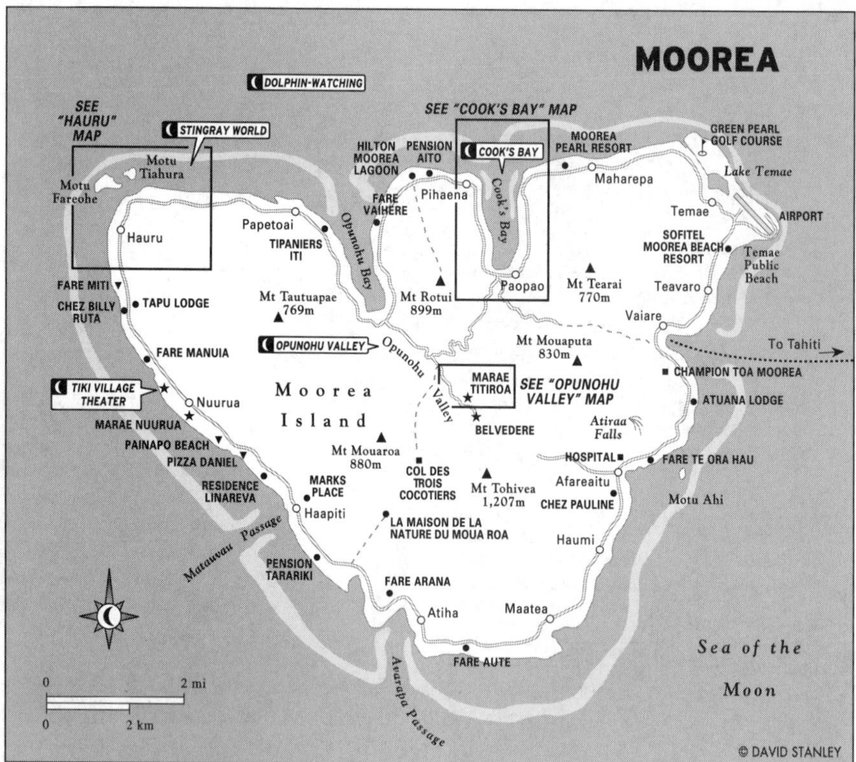

trip to the Belvédère viewpoint, another for a lagoon trip. Don't try to see Moorea as a day trip from Tahiti: this is a place to relax! And unless you're on a prepaid package tour, flying between Tahiti and Moorea is also not recommended because going over by ferry is a big part of the experience. Do bring insect or mosquito repellent, however.

Orientation

If you arrive by ferry, you'll get off at Vaiare, four kilometers south of Temae Airport. Your hotel may be at Maharepa (Moorea Pearl Resort), Paopao (Club Bali Hai, Motel Albert), Pihaena (Hilton), or Hauru (InterContinental, Les Tipaniers, Hibiscus, the campgrounds), all on the north coast. The Paopao hotels enjoy better scenery, but the beach is far superior at Hauru. Add a CFP 150 per person per day municipal services tax to the hotel accommodations prices quoted (CFP 50 at pensions and campgrounds).

The PKs (kilometer stones) on Moorea are measured in both directions from PK 0 at the access road to Temae Airport. They're numbered up to PK 35 along the north coast via Hauru and up to PK 24 along the south coast via Afareaitu, meeting at Haapiti halfway around the island.

Our circle-island tour and the accommodations and restaurant listings begin at Vaiare Wharf and go counterclockwise around the island in each category.

HISTORY

Legend claims that Aimeho (or "Eimeo," as Captain Cook spelled it) was formed from the second dorsal fin of the fish that became

MONOÏ OIL

The Maohi women produce *monoï* by squeezing coconut pulp to liberate the oil, which is then allowed to cure for several weeks. Blossoms of the *tiare Tahiti*, a white-petaled flower often used as a symbol of Tahiti, are added to the oil to give it a special fragrance. *Monoï* is judged by its fluidity and purity, and it's primarily a skin conditioner used as a moisturizer after showers or in traditional Polynesian massage. On Tahiti, newborn babies are bathed in *monoï* rather than water during their first month of life. *Monoï* is also a sure remedy for dry hair. It doesn't prevent sunburn and can even magnify the sun's rays, but it does provide instant relief for sunburned skin.

Tahiti. The present name, Moorea, means "yellow" *(rea)* "lizard" *(moo)* for a yellow lizard that appeared to a high priest in a dream. It has also been called Fe'e or "octopus" for the eight ridges that divide the island into eight segments. A hole right through the summit of Mt. Mouaputa (830 meters) is said to have been made by the spear of the demigod Pai, who tossed it across from Tahiti to prevent Mt. Rotui from being carried off to Raiatea by Hiro, the god of thieves.

Captain Samuel Wallis was the European discoverer of the Windward Islands in 1767. After leaving Tahiti, he passed along the north coast of Moorea without landing. He named it Duke of York's Island. The first European visitors were botanist Joseph Banks, Lieutenant Gore, the surgeon William Monkhouse, and Herman Sporie. Captain Cook anchored in Opunohu Bay for one week in 1777. His visit was uncharacteristically brutal, as he smashed the islanders' canoes and burned their homes when they refused to return a stolen goat.

In 1792 Pomare I conquered Moorea using arms obtained from the *Bounty* mutineers. Moorea had long been a traditional place of refuge for defeated Tahitian warriors, thus in 1808 Pomare II fled into exile here after his

The only addresses on Moorea are the kilometer stones (PK) placed around the island.

bid to bring all Tahiti under his control failed. A party of English missionaries established themselves at Papetoai in 1811, and Moorea soon earned a special place in the history of Christianity: Here in 1812 the missionaries finally managed to convert Pomare II after 15 years of trying. On February 14, 1815, Patii, high priest of Oro, publicly accepted Protestantism and burned the old heathen idols at Papetoai, where the octagonal church is today. Shortly afterward the whole population followed Patii's example. The *marae* of Moorea were then abandoned, and the Opunohu Valley depopulated. The first Tahitian translation of part of the Bible was printed on Moorea in 1817. From this island Protestantism spread throughout the South Pacific.

After Pomare II finally managed to reconquer Tahiti in 1815 with missionary help (the main reason for his "conversion"), Moorea again became a backwater. American novelist Herman Melville visited Moorea in 1842 and worked with other beachcombers on a sweet-potato farm in Maatea. His book *Omoo* contains a marvelous description of his tour of the island. Cotton and coconut plantations were created on Moorea in the 19th century, followed by vanilla and coffee in the 20th and pineapples in the 21st, but only with the advent of the travel industry has Moorea become more than a beautiful backdrop for Tahiti.

Sights

NORTHEAST MOOREA

You'll probably arrive on Moorea at **Vaiare Wharf,** which is officially PK 4 on the 59-kilometer road around the island. To the north is the **Sofitel Moorea la Ora Beach Resort** (PK 1.3), built in the mid-1970s. If you have your own transport, stop for a swim and a look around the resort. It's also enjoyable to walk north along the beach from this hotel or even to go snorkeling. At PK 1 on the main road, high above the Sofitel, is the fine **Toatea Lookout** over the deep passage, romantically named the Sea of the Moon, between Tahiti and Moorea.

One of the only public beach parks on Moorea is on Nuarei Bay at **Temae,** about a kilometer down a gravel road to the right a bit before you reach the airport access road. The Temae area is a former *motu* now linked to the main island, and surfers will find an excellent long right wave around the point next to the airstrip. There's good snorkeling here, and the view across to Tahiti is fine.

The 18-hole, par-70 Jack Nicklaus **Moorea Green Pearl Golf Course** (PK 1.5, tel. 56-27-32, www.mooreagolf-resort.com, daily 0730–1700) wraps around the west end of Temae Lake near the interisland airport. The course opened in 2008, and in 2010 the 154-room Warwick Moorea Golf and Spa Resort went up between the clubhouse and the sea. The pro shop is below the large restaurant at the entrance. Greens fees are CFP 6,000/10,000 for 9/18 holes. Other fees include CFP 3,000/4,000 for 9/18 holes cart rental, and CFP 3,000/4,000 to rent a half/full set of clubs. To practice on the putting and chipping green is CFP 500. The Hilton and Sofitel both have special golf packages. The Temae course is the first major golf course to be built in French Polynesia in 35 years (the Olivier Breaud golf course on the south side of Tahiti was laid out in 1970). Golf course and resort development is a controversial issue in French Polynesia. A 1991 attempt to construct an 18-hole golf course and Sheraton resort on territorial land in Moorea's Opunohu Valley was defeated by referendum voters.

Four kilometers west, just past the Moorea Pearl Resort, is **La Maison Blanche** (PK 5.4, tel. 56-13-26, Mon.–Sat. 0900–1800, Sun. 0900–1400), on the mountain side of the road. This stately mansion of a former vanilla plantation is now a pareu salesroom. The **Shopping Center Maharepa** (PK 5.5) just beyond contains a useful assortment of banks, shops, a post office, restaurants, and cafés.

COOK'S BAY

Ironically, Captain James Cook never visited the bay that today bears his name. Cook's Bay is easily Moorea's scenic highlight, offering an unobstructed view into the island's interior. Rectangular Mt. Tohivea overlooks the south end of the bay, and as you approach Paopao, Mouaroa, or "Shark Tooth," pierces the sky. To the west, Mt. Rotui overlooks the bay.

At the entrance to Cook's Bay is **Ron Hall's Island Fashion Black Pearls** (PK 6.7, tel. 56-11-06, Mon.–Sat. 0900–1800), with a nice selection of tropical beachwear and black pearl jewelry, all clearly priced. The **Galerie Aad Van der Heyde** (PK 7, tel. 56-14-22) is as much a museum as a gallery. Aad's paintings hang outside in the flower-filled courtyard; inside you'll find his black-pearl jewelry, a large collection of Marquesan sculpture, and more paintings. The narrated soundtrack of *The Stonecutter,* an 85-minute movie based on a fairy tale Aad wrote for his granddaughter, is available on compact disc at the Galerie.

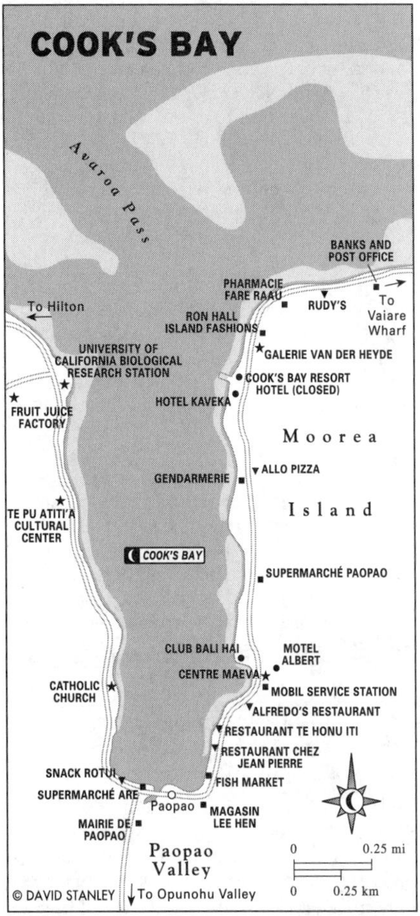

The mock-colonial **Cook's Bay Resort Hôtel** (PK 7.2) has been closed for years, but there's an excellent view of Cook's Bay from the public wharf just behind the hotel. It's a good place to go for a swim (public toilets face the parking lot). **Hôtel Kaveka** nearby offers another spectacular view of Cook's Bay and the corals from its long wooden wharf beyond the restaurant.

The **Centre Maeva** beside the Mobil Service Station opposite Club Bali Hai has a small **museum** (PK 8.6, Mon.–Fri. 1000–1700, Sun. 0900–1200, CFP 300 includes a guided tour) with reproductions of old artifacts.

Paopao is the capital of Moorea, with the gendarmerie, *mairie,* and several supermarkets serving the island community. The **Fish Market** (PK 9.3, Paopao) is worth a stop to admire the large wall painting of a market scene by François Ravello.

A rough four-kilometer dirt road up to the paved Belvédère viewpoint road, locally known as the "Pineapple Road," begins just west of the bridge at Paopao (PK 9.6), and it's nice to hike up past the pineapple plantations. This is a good shortcut to the Opunohu Valley, easily covered by rental car or worth the walk.

On the west side of Cook's Bay, one kilometer farther along the north coast highway, is a new **Catholic church** (PK 10). In the older St. Joseph's Church next door is an interesting altar painting with Polynesian angels done by the Swedish artist Peter Heyman in 1948. Unfortunately, this building is usually closed.

Te Pu Atiti'a Cultural Center (tel. 56-13-74), standing on the hillside at PK 11.5, opened in 2009. It features a garden with

CAPTAIN JAMES COOK

The extraordinary achievements of James Cook (1728-1779) on his three voyages in the ships *Endeavor, Resolution, Adventure,* and *Discovery* left his successors with little to do but marvel over them. A product of the Age of Enlightenment, Cook was a mathematician, astronomer, practical physician, and master navigator. Son of a Yorkshire laborer, he learned seamanship on small coastal traders plying England's east coast. He joined the British Navy in 1755 and soon made a name for himself in Canada, where he surveyed the St. Lawrence River, greatly contributing to the capture of Quebec City in 1759. Later he charted the coast of Newfoundland. Chosen to command the *Endeavor* in 1768 though only a warrant officer, Cook was the first captain to eliminate scurvy from his crew (with sauerkraut).

The scientists of his time needed accurate observations of the transit of Venus, for if the passage of Venus across the face of the sun were measured from points on opposite sides of the earth, then the size of the solar system could be determined for the first time. In turn, this would make possible accurate predictions of the movements of the planets, vital for navigation at sea. Thus Cook was dispatched to Tahiti, and Father Hell (a Viennese astronomer of Hungarian origin) to Vardo, Norway.

So as not to alarm the French and Spanish, the British admiralty claimed Cook's first voyage (1768-1771) was primarily to take these measurements. His real purpose, however, was to further explore the region, in particular to find *terra australis incognita.* After three months on Tahiti, he sailed west and spent six months exploring and mapping New Zealand and the whole east coast of Australia, nearly tearing the bottom off his ship, the *Endeavor,* on the Great Barrier Reef in the process. Nine months after returning to England, Cook embarked on his second expedition (1772-1775), resolving to settle the matter of *terra australis incognita* conclusively. In the *Resolution* and *Adventure,* he sailed entirely around the bottom of the world, becoming the first to cross the Antarctic Circle and return to tell about it.

In 1773 John Harrison won the greater part of a £20,000 reward offered by Queen Anne in 1714 "for such Person or Persons as shall discover the Longitude at Sea." Harrison won it with the first marine chronometer (1759), which accompanied Cook on his second and third voyages. Also on these voyages was Omai, a native of Tahiti who sailed to England with Cook in 1774. Omai immediately became the talk of London, the epitome of the "noble savage," but to those who knew him he was simply a sophisticated man with a culture of his own.

In 1776 Cook set forth from England for a third voyage, supposedly to repatriate Omai but really to find the Northwest Passage from the Pacific to the Atlantic. He rounded Cape Horn and headed due north, encountering Kauai in the Hawaiian Islands on January 18, 1778. After two weeks on Hawaii, Cook continued north via the west coast of North America but was forced back by ice in the Bering Strait. With winter coming, he returned to Hawaiian waters and found the two biggest islands of the group, Maui and Hawaii. On February 14, 1779, in a short, unexpected, petty skirmish with the Hawaiians, Cook was killed. Today he remains the giant of Pacific exploration.

medicinal plants, canoe building exhibitions, and a thatched *fare pote'e* or traditional meeting house. Folkloric shows are presented in an amphitheater here on special occasions.

It's possible to visit the Distillerie de Moorea **fruit-juice factory** (PK 12, tel. 55-20-00, www.manuteatahiti.com), 300 meters up off the main road. Aside from the excellent papaya, grapefruit, and pineapple juices made from local fruits, the factory produces apple, orange, and passion fruit juices from imported concentrate, with no preservatives added. It also makes 40-proof brandies (carambola or "star fruit," ginger, grapefruit, mango, orange, and pineapple flavors) and 25-proof liqueurs (coconut, ginger, and pineapple varieties). These are for sale, and if the staff thinks you might buy a bottle, they'll invite you to sample the brews (no free samples for obvious backpackers). The sales room is open weekdays 0830–1630, but the factory is open 0800–1400 only.

OPUNOHU BAY TO BELVÉDÈRE

The Hilton Moorea Lagoon Resort (PK 14) is the only large hotel between Paopao and Hauru. A trail up **Mount Rotui** (899 meters) begins opposite the "Faimano Village" accommodations nearby. Rotui is Moorea's second-highest peak and it will take most of the day to climb up and down. Go up the driveway directly opposite Faimano Village and turn right before the house on the hill. A red arrow painted on a coconut tree points the way, but you may have to contend with the local dogs as you start up the hill. Once up behind the house the trail swings right and onto the ridge, which you follow to the summit. The land at the trailhead belongs to the Faimano Village's owner, and he doesn't mind climbers, but you should ask permission to proceed from anyone you happen to meet near the house. From on top you'll have a sweeping view of the entire north coast. It's better not to go alone as there are vertical drops from the narrow ridgeline and steep rocks in places, and after rains the trail could be dangerous. This is not a climb to be undertaken lightly.

A famous yacht anchorage called Robinson's Cove is off the east side of Opunohu Bay. Moorea residents have had to fight a running battle with developers to keep Opunohu Bay the way it is, and from the unspoiled surroundings it's easy to understand why the 1984 remake of *The Bounty* was filmed here.

Opunohu Valley

The Opunohu Valley is another of Moorea's visual feasts. Freshwater shrimp are bred in large basins at the head of Opunohu Bay (PK 18). From here a paved five-kilometer side road runs up the largely uninhabited valley to the Belvédère viewpoint. After two kilometers you reach the junction with the dirt connecting road from

MOOREA

Mount Rotui between Cook's and Opunohu Bays can be climbed from the Moorea Hilton.

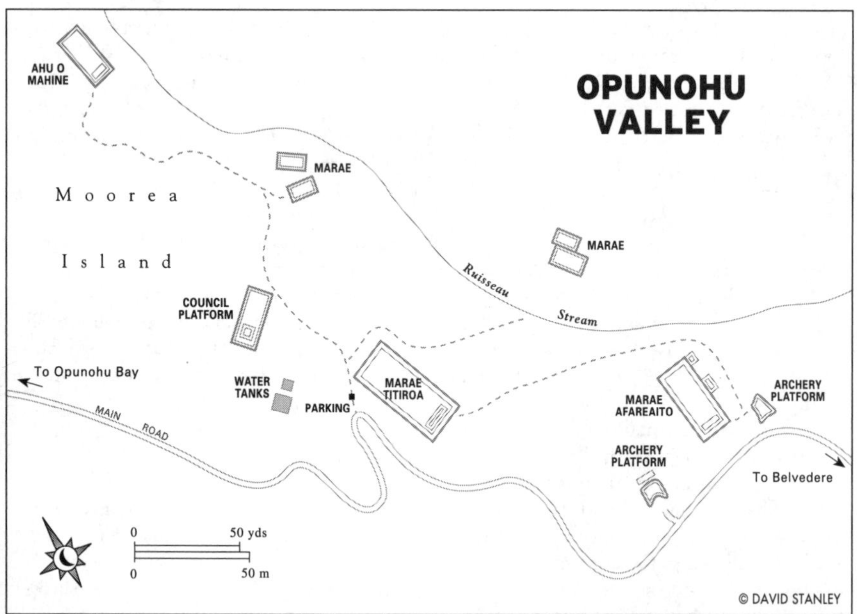

Cook's Bay, then another kilometer up and on the right is the **Lycée Professionnel Agricole,** Moorea's agricultural high school. This worthy institution, with students from all the islands of French Polynesia, has hundreds of hectares planted in pineapples, vanilla, coffee, fruit trees, decorative flowers, and native vegetables on land seized from a German company in 1914.

Another kilometer above this is **Marae Titiroa,** largest of a group of Polynesian temples restored in 1969 by Professor Y. H. Sinoto of Honolulu. The small platform, or *ahu,* at the end of this *marae* was a sacred area reserved for the gods, and stone backrests for chiefs and priests are also seen. Here the people offered gifts of tubers, fish, dogs, and pigs, and prayed to their gods, many of whom were deified ancestors. Near the water tanks just 50 meters northwest of Marae Titiroa is a long council platform, and 50 meters farther are two smaller *marae* surrounded by towering Tahitian chestnut trees *(mape).* The most evocative of the group is four-tiered **Marae Ahu o Mahine,** about 250 meters down the trail.

About 500 ancient structures have been identified in this area, and if you're very keen, you should be able to find a few in the forest across the stream, evidence of a large population with a highly developed social system. Following the acceptance of Christianity in the early 19th century, the Opunohu Valley's importance declined sharply. Today lots of side trails lead nowhere in particular, but you'll discover many crumbling *marae* walls. Naturalists will enjoy the vegetation.

Continue up the main road from Marae Titiroa about 200 meters and watch for some stone **archery platforms** on the left. Here kneeling nobles once competed to see who could shoot an arrow the farthest. The bows and arrows employed in these contests were never used in warfare. Just up on the left is access to another archery platform and **Marae Afareaito.** The stone slabs you see sticking up in the middle of the *marae* were backrests for participants of honor.

From the archaeological area the winding road climbs steeply another kilometer to the

Belvédère, or Roto Nui, a viewpoint high up near the geographical center of the island. Much of northern Moorea is visible from here, and it's easy to visualize the great volcano that once existed. Mt. Rotui (899 meters) in front of you was once the central core of an island more than three times as high as the present. The north part is now missing, but the semicircular arch of the southern half is plain to see. (An ice cream from the *roulotte* in the parking lot may be a welcome treat.)

Although most easily toured by rental car or bus, this intriguing area can also be explored on foot. If you're staying anywhere around Cook's Bay, begin by hiking up the four-kilometer dirt "Pineapple Road" from the bridge in Paopao. If staying at Hauru, take the ferry bus to Cook's Bay to get started. After "doing" the *marae* and Belvédère, walk down the Opunohu Valley road if you're returning to Hauru. For experienced hikers, a trail to Paopao through the bush begins at the rear left corner of the Belvédère parking lot. (Don't take a left turn near three pine trees, as this branch only returns to the *marae.*) Carry lots of water and a picnic lunch and make a day of it.

PAPETOAI TO HAURU

Back down on the coastal highway, continue west along Opunohu Bay. **Papetoai** (PK 22) is the oldest village on Moorea, where all the early explorers and missionaries initially came. The octagonal Protestant church behind the post office was built on the site of the temple of the god Oro in 1822. Despite having been rebuilt several times, the church is known as "the oldest European building still in use in the South Pacific."

At **Hauru** the road begins to curve around the northwest corner of Moorea, passing a number of large resorts, including the InterContinental (PK 24.5) and the former Club Med (PK 26.5).

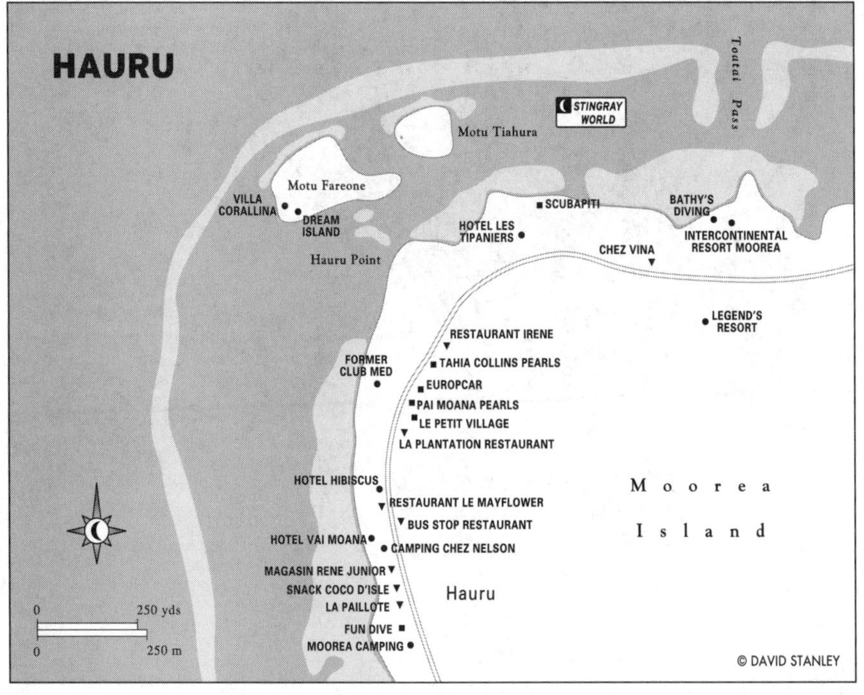

BUYING A BLACK PEARL

The relative newness of this gemstone is reflected in varying prices. A radiant, perfectly round, smooth, and flawless pearl with a good depth of metallic green or blue can sell for many times more than a similar pearl with only one or two defects. The luster is more important than the color. Size can vary 8–20 millimeters, with the larger pearls that much more expensive. Black pearls are in fashion in Paris, so don't expect any bargains. A first-class necklace can cost as much as US$50,000, and individual pearls of high quality cost US$1,000 and up, but slightly flawed pearls are much cheaper (beginning at US$100). The "baroque" pearls still make exquisite jewelry when mounted in gold and platinum. In recent years, prices have even come down as production begins to exceed demand.

Consider buying a loose pearl and having it mounted back home. If you think you might do this, check with your local jeweler before leaving for Tahiti. Half the fun is in the shopping, so be in no hurry to decide, and don't let yourself be influenced by a driver or guide who may only be after a commission. If no guide is involved, the shop should pay the commission to you in the form of a discount (ask). It's preferable to buy pearls at a specialized shop rather than somewhere that also sells pareu and souvenirs (and never buy a pearl from a person on the street). A reputable dealer will always give you an invoice or certificate verifying the authenticity of your pearl. If you've made an expensive choice, ask the dealer to make a fresh X-ray right in front of you in order to be sure of the quality.

Pai Moana Pearls at Hauru is one of many black pearl shops found around Moorea.

There's excellent reef-break surfing in Taotai Pass off the InterContinental. **Moorea Black Pearl** (www.mooreablackpearl.com), opposite the entrance to the InterContinental, has pearls set by jeweler William Haring, and they're open to bargaining.

Unfortunately, there is no public beach access at Hauru. You can always walk through Hôtel Les Tipaniers (PK 25.9) to their beach, but use the large parking lot across the highway as parking on the hotel side of the road is for staff only. The beach at Hauru looks nice, but the water is rather shallow unless you go far out. The scuba operators and recreation people at the resorts will ferry you over to much better snorkeling areas off small islands such as Tarahu and Tiahuru for a fee. For example, Scubapiti at Hôtel Les Tipaniers charges CFP 700 per person round-trip for *motu* transfers, leaving at 0830, 1200, 1400, and 1630.

In early 2002 the 350-bungalow Club Méditerranée closed after having problems renewing its lease. **Le Petit Village** shopping mall, across the street from the former Club Med, has a bank, grocery store, snack bar, gas station, and lots of expensive little shops patronized by people on circle-island bus tours. **Sibani Pearls** has a store in Le Petit Village. A half dozen other black pearl shops are along the road just north of Le Petit Village. Drop into **Pai Moana Pearls** (PK 26.2, tel. 56-25-25) near Le Petit Village and ask for a free copy of owner Rick Steger's excellent brochure on pricing pearls. **Tahia Collins** (PK 26.2, tel. 55-05-00, www.tahiacollins.com) produces some uniquely artistic settings not seen elsewhere, and their jeweler is often at work in the shop.

Most of the restaurants and hotels south of Le Petit Village actively discourage beach access through their properties.

Stingray World

One of French Polynesia's most unforgettable snorkeling spots is the lagoon off the InterContinental Resort Moorea. The stingrays here are fed regularly by excursion boat operators, and they fearlessly approach snorkelers in the hope of receiving a piece of fish. As many as a dozen meter-wide rays can be seen in waters less than shoulder deep within swimming distance from the resort's beach. As the huge animals glide past just above the lagoon's floor, snorkelers are able to stroke the beasts. Half a dozen blacktip reef sharks will also cruise in when the feeding begins. There have been no incidents as yet involving the barbed stinger on the rays' long tails, but it would be tempting fate to touch the animal's tail or ride a stingray, and encounters with the wild always involve some risk. The safest way to get there is on one of the numerous excursion boats that offer shark and ray viewing. It would also be possible for a strong swimmer to snorkel across the channel to the anchored boats from the beach at the InterContinental. The greatest dangers here are not being attacked by the inoffensive sharks but getting hit by a speedboat or being swept away by the current.

SOUTHERN MOOREA

The south coast of Moorea is residential and much quieter than the north. You'll drive for kilometers through the open coconut plantations past unspoiled villages and scenic vistas. Good beaches are few and far between on this side of the island. At PK 31 is **Tiki Village Theater,** the only one of its kind in the territory. Just past the Fire Department (PK 31.5, Haapiti) is **Marae Nuurua,** on the beach across the soccer field. This three-tiered *marae* was restored in 1991 and bears a petroglyph of a turtle. Beyond is the much higher rubble heap of an unrestored *marae.* It's on private property, so you have to look at it over a barbed wire fence.

At PK 33 you can have your photo taken in front of a huge concrete Tahitian warrior roadside at the Painapo Beach Paradise restaurant (www.painapo.com). To swim here, you must buy a CFP 2,000 day pass. You might also stop at **Résidence Linareva** (PK 34.5, tel. 55-05-65) where colorful reef fish swim around the dock, which also affords an excellent mountain view.

At PK 35/24, Haapiti, the kilometer numbering begins its descent to Temae Airport.

The twin-towered **Église de la Sainte Famille** (1891) at Haapiti was once the head church of the Catholic mission on the island. There's good anchorage here for yachts entering Matauvau Pass and a tall left-hander for the surfers out there.

Afareaitu (PK 9) is the administrative center of southern Moorea. After Papetoai, this was the second center of missionary activity on Moorea, and on June 30, 1817, at the printing works at Afareaitu, King Pomare II ceremonially printed the first page of the first book ever published on a South Pacific island, a Tahitian translation of the Gospel of St. Luke. Before the press was moved to Huahine a year later, more than 9,000 books totaling more than a half million pages had been printed at Afareaitu. After 1821 the London Missionary Society established its Academy of the South Seas here to instruct the children of the missionaries and the Tahitian chiefs.

From opposite the old Protestant church (1912) in Afareaitu, a one-hour walk on the road between Magasin Ah Sing and a school leads up the **Afareaitu Valley** to a high waterfall, which cascades down a sheer cliff into a pool. You can cut your walking time in half by driving a car two-thirds of the way up the valley. Park at the point where a normal car would have problems and hike on up the road to the right. When this road begins to climb steeply, look for a well-beaten footpath on the right, which will take you directly to the falls. You'll need a bit of intuition to find the unmarked way on your own.

You get a good view of **Mt. Mouaputa,** the peak pierced by Pai's spear, from the hospital just north of Afareaitu. The first road inland north of the hospital leads to a different waterfall, **Atiraa Falls.** The access road is very rough, so park just before a small concrete bridge and continue the 30-minute hike on foot.

ACROSS THE ISLAND

An excellent day hike involves taking a morning bus to Vaiare Wharf, then hiking over the mountains to Paopao. From there you can

The three-hour hike across Moorea from Vaiare to Paopao rewards the adventurous visitor.

MOOREA

catch another bus back to your accommodations, or try hitching. The shaded three-hour trail, partly marked by red, white, and green paint dabbed on tree and rock, does demand attention and perseverance, however. There are a few steep ascents and descents, and after rains it can be muddy and slippery.

Take the road inland beside Magasin du Quai, about 50 meters south of the first bridge south of the Vaiare ferry wharf. As you follow the dirt road up the valley, you'll take two forks to the right. Don't cross the stream after the second fork but go left and walk past some houses, just beyond which is an old Polynesian *marae* on the left. Farther along you'll cross the stream and continue past a number of local gardens. The trail to Paopao leads off to the left near the last garden, and once you're on it, it's fairly easy to follow if you keep your eyes open. When you see an old stone stairway on the left five minutes after leaving the gardens, you'll know you're on the correct trail. All of the locals know about this trail, and if you say "Paopao?" to them in a questioning way, they'll point you in the right direction.

When you reach the divide, go a short distance south along the ridge to a super viewpoint. On a clear day the rounded double peak of Orohena, Tahiti's highest, will be visible, plus the whole interior of Moorea. On the way down the other side, avoid taking the wrong turn at a bamboo grove. You'll come out among the pineapple plantations of central Moorea behind Paopao. It's not possible to do this hike eastbound from Paopao to Vaiare without a guide, but westbound an experienced hiker should have no difficulty, and it's worth going simply to see a good cross section of the vegetation. Take water and wear sturdy shoes.

Entertainment

CULTURAL SHOWS FOR VISITORS

See Tahitian dancing in the restaurant of the **Sofitel Moorea la Ora Beach Resort** (PK 1.3, tel. 55-12-00) Monday–Saturday at 1930. The **Moorea Pearl Resort** (PK 5.3, tel. 55-17-50) has Polynesian shows Wednesday and Saturday nights at 2000. At **Club Bali Hai** (PK 8.5, tel. 56-16-25) there's Polynesian dancing Wednesday at 1800. The **Hilton Moorea Lagoon Resort** (PK 14, tel. 55-11-11) has Polynesian dancing Tuesdays and Saturdays. The Tahitian shows at the **InterContinental Resort Moorea** (PK 24.5, tel. 55-19-19) are on Wednesdays and Saturdays. These times often change, so check. The Tahitian feasts that come with the shows are pricey, but you can often observe the action from the bar for the price of a drink. It's well worth going.

Restaurant Le Miki Miki (PK 1.5, tel. 56-26-70, Tues.–Sun.), at the Moorea Green Pearl Golf Course, has a musical evening Friday nights (CFP 1,000) with a live orchestra 2100–0100. Happy hour is Wednesday–Saturday 1730–1830.

Tiki Village Theater

Since 1986 Moorea has had its own instant culture village, the Tiki Village Theater (PK 31, Haapiti, tel. 55-02-50, www.tikivillage.pf, Tues.–Sat. 1100–1500). A charge of CFP 1,500 includes a visit to the village and pearl farm as well as the small dance show at 1300. The guided tour of the recreated Tahitian village is informative, and the 32 dancers and other staff members who live in the village year-round are enthusiastic, but sometimes they're a little disorganized, so you might obtain some details about the showtime before parting with your francs. Lunch is available in the à la carte restaurant, but the food could be better. On Tuesday, Wednesday, Friday, and Saturday beginning at 1800 there's a big sunset show with dancing and drumming by the full troupe, accompanied by a *tamaaraa* (underground oven) buffet (CFP 6,700, reservations required).

The full Polynesian show with 60 performers starts at 2045 (CFP 4,500 for the show alone). Transportation is CFP 1,250 per person round-trip, if required. If you've got CFP 150,000 to spare, a "royal" Tahitian wedding can be arranged at the village (bring your own partner; same-sex couples welcome). The ceremony lasts two hours, from 1600 to sunset. The bridegroom arrives by canoe and the newlyweds are carried around in a procession by four "warriors." Otherwise there's the less extravagant "princely" wedding for CFP 120,000, photos included. Yes, it's kinda tacky, but that's showbiz. (Such weddings are not legally binding.)

Sports and Recreation

SCUBA DIVING

The shark and ray viewing at Moorea is good year-round. Some, but not all, Moorea dive shops offer shark feeding. It's still unknown if this activity will eventually attract larger sharks into the Moorea lagoon. At sites such as The Tiki, the swarm of fish sometimes becomes so thick the guide is lost from sight, yet as the resident shark scatters the mass of fish to steal the bait, the dive master is seen again patting *le requin* as it passes. Large schools of tuna, sea perch, and jackfish are encountered year-round, but humpback whales are only here from July to October. Most diving is off the north coast, where the corals were devastated by Hurricane Ollie in February 2010.

Ia Ora Diving (tel. 77-86-44, www.iaoradiving.com) at the Sofitel charges CFP 7,200/12,400 for one/two tanks or CFP 9,800 for night diving. They'll take out snorkelers for CFP 4,800.

Moorea Blue Diving (tel. 55-17-04, www.mooreabluediving.com), at the Moorea Pearl Resort, does one/two tank dives for CFP

© DAVID STANLEY

Scubapiti nautical activities kiosk on the beach at Hôtel Les Tipaniers, Hauru

6,300/12,300, introductory dives for CFP 6,900, and a PADI scuba certification course with pool training for CFP 41,000. Japanese-speaking instructors are available here.

TOPdive Moorea (tel. 56-17-32, www.topdive.com) handles diving at the Hilton Moorea Lagoon Resort.

Bathys Diving (tel. 56-31-44, www.bathys-diving.com), at the InterContinental Resort Moorea, offers two-tank scuba diving for CFP 14,000, including gear. Book directly at their own office behind the resort activities kiosk; otherwise you'll pay CFP 500 more. This is the only PADI five-star facility in the territory, a classy and genuinely helpful outfit. Bathys does underwater fish, eel, ray, and shark feeding.

Scubapiti (Daniel Cailleux, tel. 56-20-38, www.scubapiti.com), on the beach at Hôtel Les Tipaniers at Hauru, offers scuba diving daily at 0800 (CFP 6,020/11,800 one/two tanks). Instead of putting on a show, Daniel keeps things natural on his cave, canyon, and drift dives. Shark feeding and other gimmicks are not offered. Diving lessons are at 1330, and Daniel offers PADI or CMAS scuba certification courses (CFP 47,000). Free hotel transfers are provided from anywhere in northwestern Moorea.

Moorea Fun Dive (tel. 56-40-38, www.moorea-fundive.com) is based next to Moorea Camping in Hauru. It's CFP 6,400/11,980 for one/two dives, or CFP 32,700 for six dives, including all gear (except a wetsuit). Ocean dives are at 0830, and hotel pickups are available from almost anywhere on northern Moorea. Diving instruction is at 1430.

SNORKELING

On Moorea, you don't need to be a scuba diver to see spectacular marine life and coral. You could see dolphins, whales, and human surfers on the snorkeling trips offered by any number of operators. The unexpected highlight of these trips is the chance to swim alongside groups of rays and blacktip sharks in the lagoon just off the InterContinental. Some snorkeling trips visit "Le Monde de Mu," an underwater sculpture garden in the lagoon off Papetoai, with 10 large tikis created in 1998 by the renowned Tahitian stone carver Tihoti. The tikis represent the old Tahitian mythology cast off after the acceptance of Christianity.

Unfortunately, the shark-feeding event included in some of these trips has become just a bit too popular, especially when four boats carrying 10 tourists each arrive at the same time. The guides throw a few pieces of tuna to three or four well-fed sharks, which sniff disinterestedly at the bait. This has been going on for years, and no incidents have been reported, so don't hesitate to swim with the sharks!

Miki Miki Excursions operates an outstanding three-hour shark and stingray feeding tour from Moorea Camping and Camping Chez Nelson at Hauru daily at 0900 for CFP 3,500 per person (four-person minimum). This trip visits the Maiau Beach Garden on Motu Tiahura, where Bill Gates once celebrated his birthday.

Albert Activities (tel. 55-21-10, www.albert-transport.net) runs a six-hour motorized aluminum canoe ride around Moorea with a stop for snorkeling (gear provided), departing Tuesday, Wednesday, Friday, and Sunday at 0900 (CFP 7,000 per person includes lunch, minimum of four persons). For free pickup, inquire at one of the Albert Activities centers opposite the Pearl Resort and the InterContinental.

Other companies such as **Moorea Boat Tours** (tel. 56-28-44, www.mooreaboattours.com) run a variety of trips, such as a *motu* excursion by outrigger or a *motu* picnic party. On many of these, the canoes are without radios, life jackets, or flotation devices, and they can be frightening if you're not a good swimmer. The snorkeling itself is great.

DAY CRUISES

At 0930 and 1400 daily the **InterContinental Resort Moorea** (PK 24.5, tel. 55-19-19) offers a four-hour cruise on the catamaran *Manu* for CFP 9,405 per person. The 1.5-hour sunset cruise is CFP 7,110, including drinks.

Tahiti Cruise (tel. 72-23-45, www.tahiticruise.pf) operates Moorea sailing cruises aboard a 13-meter catamaran based at Cook's Bay. You have a choice of three hours of lagoon sailing and snorkeling or a two-hour sunset cruise.

From the Moorea Pearl Resort, **Moorea Jet Ski Tours** (tel. 77-02-19, www.tahiti-jetski.com) runs two-hour tours that visit sharks, rays, and dolphins. Departures are at 0900 and 1400 and cost CFP 24,000 for two adults sharing one Jet Ski.

SWIMMING WITH DOLPHINS

The **Moorea Dolphin Center** (tel. 55-19-48, www.mooreadolphincenter.com) at the InterContinental Resort Moorea gives tourists the opportunity to pay CFP 20,000 each to spend time wading around a shallow lagoon enclosure with four captive dolphins (touching and even kissing the penned mammals is allowed). These activities begin at 0900, 1330, and 1445. It's possible to don a mask and snorkel in a deeper part of the enclosure and grasp the animal's pectoral or dorsal fins to be taken for a ride (CFP 36,000). The InterContinental tacks on a CFP 1,000 surcharge if you're not a hotel guest, and photos are charged extra. To see the dolphin enclosure, cross the bridge to the over-water bungalows on the opposite side of the reception from the swimming pool and turn left. This whole business has environmental and moral implications; the dolphins held here were flown in from Hawaii and San Diego after the native dolphins proved impossible to tame and kept trying to escape. The operators claim their dolphins crave the touch of humans and enjoy such interactions, yet the dolphin's smiling face could have more to do with the shape of the animal's jawline, as dolphins smile even in death. It's clear that somebody is making a lot of money by exploiting these highly intelligent animals as a tourist attraction.

DOLPHIN-WATCHING

A quite different type of dolphin encounter is offered by Dr. Michael Poole of **Dolphin and Whale Watching Expeditions** (tel. 56-23-22 or 77-50-07, dwwe@mail.pf, www.drmichaelpoole.com). Dr. Poole has been on Moorea researching dolphins and whales since 1987 and is a founding member of the South Pacific Whale Research Consortium. He's now in charge of the Marine Mammal Research Program at CRIOBE (Centre de Recherches Insulaires et Observatoire de l'Environnement), a French biological research station on Moorea that provides material and financial support for research projects by master's and PhD students from around the world. In May 2002 French Polynesia's government declared its entire exclusive economic zone a whale and dolphin sanctuary, protecting these animals in more than 5 million square kilometers of ocean. Dr. Poole was the author of this proposition, working 10 years to bring it to fruition, and he wrote the original guidelines that were used as a basis for the legislation.

On his trips, small groups are taken out in boats to see acrobatic spinner dolphins—the only dolphins to spin vertically in the air like tops or ballerinas—in the wild. Dr. Poole claims a 95 percent success rate in finding spinner dolphins year-round. You may also observe dolphins surfing, and from July to October humpback whales are seen nine times out of 10.

These ecotours of 3–4 hours go out early on Monday and Thursday mornings and cost CFP 7,800 per person, with half-price reductions for children 12 and under. Included in the price are bus or boat pickups at all hotels between the Sofitel and Hauru. Space is sometimes limited, so reserve well ahead through one of the Moorea Activities offices, a hotel tour desk, or by calling the numbers above. Be sure to state clearly that you want "Dr. Poole's boat," as several unscientific imitators are trying to do the same thing with varying degrees of success. The activities desks at resorts such as the Hilton push the captive dolphin show at the InterContinental for the commissions they earn, and may claim not to know of Dr. Poole's ecotour.

Dolphin Lagoonarium (tel. 56-38-75, www.dolphinlagoonarium.com) offers dolphin watching from a covered speedboat with

© DAVID STANLEY

boats for rent at Hôtel Les Tipaniers on Moorea's north coast

a stop at Motu Moea (CFP 7,500/4,500 for adults/children).

SURFING

Surfing is possible in most of the passes around the island or off the beach next to the airstrip, but it's not quite as good as on Tahiti or Huahine. A boat or a long paddle is required to reach the reef breaks. Surfers often stay at Pension Tarariki Village on the south side of the island.

DEEP-SEA FISHING

Game fishing is offered by **Tea Nui Charters** (tel. 56-15-08 or 72-81-82, teanuiservices@mail.pf), based at the InterContinental, at CFP 17,600 per person for a half day (four-person minimum). The captain keeps the catch.

Halfon VIP Tours (tel. 77-02-19, www.halfon-vip-tours.com) also offers half-day fishing trips at CFP 18,000 per person (four-person minimum).

OTHER NAUTICAL ACTIVITIES

The "Activities Nautiques" kiosk on the wharf at the **InterContinental Resort Moorea** (PK 24.5, tel. 55-19-19) offers parasailing (CFP 7,550).

AquaBlue Exploration (PK 24.5, tel. 56-53-53) at the InterContinental offers the experience of walking on the seabed while wearing a yellow Jules Verne–style helmet for CFP 7,500.

Moorea Loca Boat (PK 25.9, tel. 78-13-39), on the beach at Hôtel Les Tipaniers, rents small aluminum outboard motorboats at CFP 7,000/9,000/15,000 for two/four/eight hours, gas included. No license is required. Pedal boats are CFP 1,500/2,500/3,500 for one/two/three hours. **Kite Surf Rental** (tel. 77-09-71, www.mooreakiteboarder.com) next door rents kite boards and gives lessons.

HORSEBACK RIDING

Ranch Opunohu Valley (tel. 78-42-47, Tues.–Sun.), on the dirt road from the Belvédère road to Paopao, offers two hours of horseback riding at 0830 and 1415 (CFP 6,000 per ride includes hotel pickups). Only six people are taken out at a time. Readers who've gone say it's definitely worth it.

Accommodations

US$25-50

One of the South Pacific's nicest campgrounds is **Camping Chez Nelson** (PK 27, Hauru, tel. 56-15-18, www.camping-nelson.pf), near the Hôtel Hibiscus. It's beautifully set in a coconut grove right on the beach. The camping charge is CFP 1,400/1,500 garden/beach per person, with toilets, showers, a refrigerator, and communal cooking facilities provided. No tents are for rent, but the 10 two-bed "dormitory" rooms go for CFP 1,800 per person (CFP 2,200 for one night). The three cabins are CFP 4,900 single or double (CFP 5,400 for one night); four larger rooms with shared bath in a long building near the office are CFP 4,500 single or double (CFP 5,000 for one night). The sunset cabin near the beach is CFP 6,300 (CFP 6,900 for one night). Snorkeling gear, kayaks, and bicycles are for rent. The campground office is open Monday–Saturday 0800–1200 and 1300–1800, Sunday 0900–1200 and 1300–1800. This place is clean, quiet, breezy, spacious, and well equipped, but don't leave valuables unattended or within reach of an open window at night.

A second campground is just a little south of Chez Nelson. Friendly **Moorea Camping** (PK 27.5, tel. 56-14-47) faces the same white-sand beach. It has three-bed dorms at CFP 1,200 per person (CFP 1,800 for one night), plus another eight double rooms in a long building at CFP 2,500 single or double (CFP 3,800 for one night). The five beachfront bungalows are CFP 4,800 single or double (CFP 5,800 for one night). All rooms at both campgrounds have shared baths only, and those at Moorea Camping are extremely basic, as you might expect from the price. Camping is CFP 1,100 per person (CFP 1,500 for one night). The camping area behind the kitchen is much smaller than the one at Chez Nelson, but there's more shade. Official quiet hours start

© DAVID STANLEY

Camping Chez Nelson offers beachside accommodations and tent space on Moorea's west coast.

© DAVID STANLEY

Moorea Camping is the least expensive place to stay on the island.

at 2200. If you were planning an early morning departure, have your shower the night before, as there may not be any water in the morning. Communal kitchen and washing facilities are provided, but you must pay a deposit for cooking utensils. A grocery store (with cold beer) is between the two campgrounds, and many restaurants are nearby. One-person kayaks are loaned free. The reception is open 0800–1200 and 1330–1700 Monday–Saturday and 0800–1200 Sunday. Young French residents of Papeete often book all of the bungalows and rooms on weekends. Moorea Camping is great for young low-budget travelers and other adventurers—you'll meet some wonderful people—just don't expect luxuries of any kind as this is one of the last true backpacker camps in French Polynesia.

US$50-100

Motel Albert (PK 8.5, tel. 56-12-76, www.motelalbert.pro.tm), on the slope opposite Club Bali Hai at Paopao, catches splendid views across Cook's Bay. The four older apartments with one double bed, a kitchen, and a private bath are CFP 6,500 single or double, while four larger apartments with two double beds, a kitchen, and a private bath are CFP 7,520 double or triple (two-night minimum stay). The 10 two-bedroom bungalows with kitchen and private bath are CFP 9,740 for up to four people. The larger apartments are often taken by monthly rentals at CFP 120,000. The minimum stay is three nights. Each unit has cooking facilities, fridge, and hot water in a garden setting on spacious grounds. Several stores are nearby, and the Mobil service station next door sells bread and groceries.

Chez Dina (PK 12.5, Pihaena, tel. 56-10-39, www.pensiondinamoorea.pf) is on the inland side of the road one kilometer east of the Hilton. The three thatched bungalows are CFP 7,500 triple, CFP 8,500 for up to four people (minimum of two nights, discounts for weekly stays). Cooking facilities are provided.

Pension Aito (PK 13.1, Pihaena, tel. 56-45-52, www.aitomoorea.com), on the beach, has five thatched units starting at CFP 6,500 double, or CFP 7,500 with cooking facilities. Snorkeling gear is loaned free. Aito

© DAVID STANLEY

Pension Aito, near the Hilton, is better known for its over-water restaurant than its rooms.

has an attractive over-water restaurant (Wed.–Mon.) serving Corsican specialties (fish from CFP 2,100, meat CFP 2,200–2,800, lobster CFP 4,200). The food and service in the restaurant are variable, but you'll enjoy the live Hawaiian and country music on Monday and Friday nights.

Chez Francine (PK 14.5, Pihaena, tel. 56-13-24) doesn't have a sign, but look for three buildings with red tile roofs between the highway and the shore. A two-room house is CFP 9,500 double with kitchenette or CFP 7,500 double without kitchenette. The beach and view are excellent.

Chez Billy Ruta (PK 28.3, Hauru, tel. 56-12-54) consists of nine thatched A-frame bungalows lined up along the beach. The one without a kitchenette is CFP 5,000 double, while the other seven with kitchens are CFP 7,000 double. These units have been around for a while, but they're conveniently located and the price is right. They're rented by the month (CFP 65,000) and are often full.

Pension Tarariki (PK 21.5, Haapiti, tel. 55-21-05, pensiontarariki@mail.pf) has four bungalows with private baths at CFP 7,500 single or double and two rooms with shared bath at CFP 4,500 single or double. The minimum stay is two nights, and you'll need insect repellent. There's a secluded beach below the pension's large tree house, and it's only a couple of kilometers to the pass for surfing. May–October the owner provides boat transfers to Haapiti Pass for surfers. A grocery store is nearby, and you must cook as meals are not available.

Chez Pauline (PK 9, Afareaitu, tel. 56-11-26) is between the two stores near the church. It's a lovely old colonial house with five rooms with double beds and shared bath at CFP 4,500/6,500 single/double, including breakfast. A picturesque restaurant with tikis on display rounds out this establishment, which has great atmosphere. Dinner must be ordered in advance.

US$100-150

The **Hôtel Kaveka** (PK 7.4, tel. 56-50-50, www.hotelkaveka.com), at the east entrance to Cook's Bay, has 24 wooden bungalows with fridges at CFP 13,500–26,500 double, including tax. Children under 11 can share their parents' room at a reduced rate. The cheapest units are not air-conditioned, and you'll need to burn a mosquito coil at night. The consumption of food in the rooms is not allowed, and the fridge is for drinks only. On the plus side, the Kaveka's thatched over-water restaurant is reasonable if you order carefully, and other restaurants are nearby. The snorkeling off the small artificial beach is fine, and there's a great view of Cook's Bay from the wharf. All in all, the Kaveka is good value if you're willing to forgo luxuries like satellite TV and designer decor.

Next door to Pension Aito, **Pension Motu Iti** (PK 13.2, Pihaena, tel. 55-05-20, www.pensionmotuiti.com) has two garden bungalows for CFP 10,500 and three beach bungalows for CFP 12,000 double. There's also a 20-bed dormitory at CFP 1,700 per person, but it's open to the elements and best avoided. The fan-cooled rooms are nice but not bug-free. Check-in time is noon. The restaurant facing the lagoon serves pizza (CFP 1,050–1,300), fish (CFP 1,100–2,150), and meat (CFP 1,700–1,950). The nearest grocery store is at Cook's Bay. There's no beach here, but the snorkeling is good.

Fare Nani (PK 14.1, Pihaena, tel. 56-19-99), on the west side of the Hilton, has three thatched bungalows with kitchenettes for CFP 10,000 single or double.

The signposted **Faimano Village** (PK 14.1, tel. 56-10-20, www.levillagefaimano.com), right next to Fare Nani, has seven lovely thatched *fare* with cooking facilities for CFP 14,700 for up to four people or CFP 10,500/12,075 double garden/beach (two-night minimum stay). Faimano Village has an easygoing atmosphere and a nice garden setting facing the beach, but single women should avoid it, as there have been reports of prowlers. The doors and windows cannot be properly locked.

Long-stay visitors to Moorea often choose **Hôtel Tipaniers Iti** (PK 21, Papetoai, tel. 56-12-67, www.lestipaniers.com) on the west side of Opunohu Bay. It's a low-key place with five tin-roofed self-catering bungalows in a garden setting at CFP 8,200 plus 14 percent tax for up to three people. Weekly rates are available. There's no beach, but the long wooden deck offers a great view of the bay. The reception is open 0900–1300 daily.

Hôtel Les Tipaniers (PK 25.9, Hauru, tel. 56-12-67, www.lestipaniers.com) is cramped around the reception but spacious and attractive as you approach the beach. The 22 bungalows (13 of them with kitchens) start at CFP 14,250 single or double, plus 14 percent tax. Children under 10 can share their parents' bungalow for free. Four small garden rooms are CFP 7,500 double (often full). The units are without air-conditioning, but they do have ceiling fans, and you can borrow a table fan by leaving a deposit at the reception. Still, insects could be a problem. Les Tipaniers' well-known restaurant offers very good Italian and seafood dishes. The hotel will lend you a bicycle or outrigger canoe at no charge, but snorkeling gear is extra. This hotel has a good reputation, and there's a resident dive master and many other nautical activities at reasonable prices.

Near the south end of the west coast strip is **Fare Manuia** (PK 30, Hauru, tel. 56-26-17, faremanuia@gmail.com) with six *fare* with cooking facilities at CFP 12,000 for up to four people, CFP 15,000 for up to six people, or CFP 18,000 on the beach. The minimum stay is two nights. It's a little isolated from the restaurants and other facilities at Hauru.

In 2003 **Marks Place** (PK 23.5, Haapiti, tel. 56-43-02, www.marksplacemoorea.com) opened inland from the Catholic church on the south side of the island. The location is peaceful, but there's no beach. The seven good-quality self-catering bungalows are CFP 10,000/12,500 double/quad. The minimum stay is two nights. Bicycles, kayaks, and snorkeling gear are for rent. The campsite and dormitory here have closed, and the owner, Mark Walker, is working hard to make his place more upscale. It's buzzing with surfers during the May–August Haapiti surfing season, as some of the best waves on the island are nearby.

Haapiti Surf Lodge (PK 22.5, Haapiti, tel.

© DAVID STANLEY

A pier points out into the lagoon at Hôtel Les Tipaniers on Moorea's north coast.

56-40-36, haapitisurf@mail.pf) is new place with four self-catering bungalows at CFP 8,500/10,000 single/double, including breakfast. Like Marks Place and Pension Tarariki nearby, surfers are the target clientele.

La Maison de la Nature du Mou'a Roa (PK 21, Haapiti, tel. 56-58-62, www.lamaisondelanature.com), off the south coast road, is used mainly to accommodate school groups of children aged 5–16. This large colonial mansion has eight four-bed dorms at CFP 10,500 per person, including an organic breakfast, lunch, and dinner (children under 12 half price). This hiking base camp is in the Vaianee Valley, a 45-minute walk up a rough jeep track that begins next to a Mormon church. Guests are not allowed to drive in and must arrive on foot. A hiking trail to the Three Coconut Trees with its spectacular view of the north coast begins here.

US$150-250

Club Bali Hai (PK 8.5, Paopao, tel. 56-13-68, www.clubbalihai.com) has one of the most scenic locations on Moorea with a spectacular view of Cook's Bay. The 20 rooms in the main two-story building start at CFP 14,000 single or double, plus 19 beachfront or over-water bungalows at CFP 16,000–18,000. A third person pays CFP 1,200, and the 14 percent tax is extra (you may be quoted higher prices in U.S. dollars here). The more expensive rooms have kitchenettes. Check the website for specials. To stay afloat, the company has sold many units to Americans on a time-share basis, with each owner getting two weeks per year at the Club. Nonguests are welcome to use the club's swimming pool by the bay, provided they order lunch (hamburger and fries CFP 880, *poisson cru* CFP 1,650) at L'Ananas Blue Snack Bar (daily 0700–1400). The artificial beach is small, and there isn't much for snorkelers. This is the last survivor of the famous Bali Hai hotel chain, which once stretched clear across the Society Islands. It's not a polished resort like the Hilton or InterContinental, but it has a more personal atmosphere. During happy hour, Thursday–Tuesday at 1700, you can meet Muk McCallum, one of the original Bali Hai Boys, by the pool for a yarn about the good old days. Avis has a desk at Club Bali Hai.

Fare Vaihere (PK 15.5, tel. 56-19-19, www.farevaihere.com), on peaceful Opunohu Bay, has five bungalows at CFP 17,800 single or double. You can order an excellent dinner for CFP 3,500, and a large communal kitchen and lounge are available in the main building. A long pier leads out to the edge of the reef.

The aging **Hôtel Hibiscus** (PK 27, Hauru, tel. 56-12-20, www.hotel-hibiscus.pf), on the beach right next to the defunct Club Med, offers 29 thatched bungalows beneath the coconut palms at CFP 15,400 triple in the garden or CFP 18,000 on the beach, plus 14 percent tax. A fourth person is CFP 1,900 extra. The 12 air-conditioned rooms are CFP 17,000 double. There's a discount on a weekly basis. Don't expect luxury, bring insect repellent, and be prepared for nocturnal dog and rooster noise. The breakfast and dinner plan is CFP 5,250 per person, but all units have simple kitchenettes and a fridge, and there is a large supermarket nearby. A swimming pool is provided.

Fare Vaimoana (PK 27.1, Hauru, tel. 56-17-14, www.fare-vaimoana.com) is next to a large restaurant overlooking a small beach adjacent to Camping Chez Nelson. The 13 attractive thatched bungalows are CFP 14,000 double in the garden or CFP 18,000 facing the beach, tax included. Half board is CFP 7,500 per person. There's live music Saturday from 1830. This place is very French, and English speakers may feel more comfortable at the nearby Hôtel Hibiscus or Les Tipaniers.

Moorea Fare Miti (PK 27.7, Hauru, tel. 56-57-42, www.mooreafaremiti.com) has a row of eight self-catering bungalows at CFP 13,000 for up to four people. The beachfront unit is CFP 2,000 more, and a fifth person is another CFP 2,000. The simple units have table fans, but insect repellent or coils will be required, as is usual in thatched bungalows of this kind. There's no restaurant, but the friendly managers will deliver a fresh baguette to your door in the morning and help you order takeout food from a nearby *roulotte* in the afternoon. Kayaks are loaned free, but bring your own snorkeling gear. Fare Miti will suit families and anyone looking for a do-it-yourself beach holiday.

Tapu Lodge (PK 28.3, Hauru, tel. 55-20-55, www.tapulodge.com) is on the hillside. The four smaller bungalows are CFP 13,780 for up to four people, while the two houses capable of accommodating six are CFP 24,380. Each unit has cooking facilities, and the whole place is clean and new. There's a two-night minimum stay. Sometimes you'll be offered a free lagoon excursion if you stay here. Beach access is through Chez Billy Ruta across the street.

Fare Edith (PK 32.5, Haapiti, tel. 56-35-34, www.fareedith.com) has four self-catering beach bungalows for rent, starting at CFP 8,000/11,500 single/double or CFP 13,000–15,000 for the two larger units. Mosquito nets are provided. The setting is nice, although the units are rather closely spaced.

Résidence Linareva (PK 34.5, tel. 55-05-65, www.linareva.com) sits amid splendid mountain scenery on the wild side of the island. Prices begin at CFP 14,500 single or double and increase to CFP 25,500, with 10 percent weekly discounts. Each of the eight units is unique, with TVs, fans, and full cooking facilities. Bicycles, masks and snorkels, kayaks, and an outrigger canoe are loaned free. Many of the guests here are from Germany.

On a hilltop, **Fare Arana** (PK 19.5, Atiha, tel. 56-44-03, www.farearana.com) offers an excellent view of Avarapa Passage from the swimming pool. The three thatched, air-conditioned bungalows are CFP 11,900 double. The kitchen, lounge, and bathroom are downstairs, the bedroom in a loft upstairs. If you cook, you can dine on your own terrace. Check the door lock on your unit. You'll need to rent a car if you stay here.

Fare Aute (PK 16.4, Atiha, tel. 56-45-19, www.pensionaute.com) is on a white beach 12 kilometers southwest of the ferry terminal. The four spacious self-catering bungalows are CFP 11,700/13,000 single or double garden/beach, or CFP 24,000 for a six-person garden unit (minimum stay two nights). Bicycles, kayaks, and canoes are free. The manager speaks English.

Fare Te Ora Hau (PK 8.2, Afareaitu, tel. 77-48-22, www.teorahau.com) is on the beach opposite Motu Ahi. The three attractive bungalows with kitchens are CFP 13,500 double or CFP 22,000 for up to six people. Kayaks are loaned free.

The closest accommodations to the ferry terminal is **Atuana Lodge** (PK 6.3, Afareaitu, tel. 56-36-03, www.atuanalodge.com). The self-catering bungalow and two rooms with private baths are CFP 16,000 double (two-night minimum stay). Meals can be ordered.

US$250 AND UP

The **Sofitel Moorea Ia Ora Beach Resort** (PK 1.3, tel. 55-12-12, www.sofitel-frenchpolynesia.com), between Vaiare and the airport, sits on one of the finest beaches on the island with a splendid view of Tahiti (but poor snorkeling). There is also a small swimming pool. The 114 tastefully furnished thatched bungalows begin at CFP 44,286 single or double, plus 14 percent tax. The 19 over-water bungalows with steps down into the water start at CFP 77,857. You should be able to get a discount by booking through the Sofitel website. Check-in time is 1400. The breakfast and dinner plan here is very expensive at CFP 11,914 per person extra. Because the Sofitel is rather isolated, some of the Maharepa restaurants won't pick up diners here, and no alternative restaurants are within walking distance. This is OK if you're willing to stay put and enjoy the resort, but look elsewhere if you're on any kind of a budget. A dive shop is on the premises, and there's an Avis desk in the lobby. In 2006 a seven-room spa was added.

In 2002 the **Moorea Pearl Resort and Spa** (PK 5.3, Maharepa, tel. 55-17-50, www.pearlresorts.com) was erected on the site of the former Hôtel Bali Hai, dating to 1961. The new resort features 30 rooms and suites in a long two-story concrete block with a thatched roof starting at CFP 32,770 double, 37 garden and beach bungalows from CFP 44,070, and 28 over-water bungalows on reinforced concrete piles beginning at CFP 66,670 (third person CFP 7,345, children under 15 sleep and eat

The mountains of central Moorea rise above the Moorea Pearl Resort and Spa.

free). Add 14 percent tax to these rates. You might as well take one of the cheaper garden rooms, as most of the over-water bungalows have poor views. The restaurant is pretty fancy with breakfast at CFP 3,110. Don't prepay any meals, as half a dozen good restaurants are nearby. The resort's Manea Spa (www.maneaspa.com) uses techniques based on ancient Tahitian traditions such as volcanic stone massage, coconut oil scrubs, pineapple oil massage, and synchronized four-hands duo massage. The beach isn't large and the snorkeling is poor, but there's an infinity pool. Moorea Blue Diving is based here, and Avis has a desk at the resort. Many banks, shops, and cafés are only a short walk away. The Albert Tours kiosk across the highway from the Pearl Resort arranges tours and rental cars at prices lower than those available inside.

The **Hilton Moorea Lagoon Resort and Spa** (PK 14, Pihaena, tel. 55-11-11, www.hiltonworldresorts.com), formerly the Hôtel Sheraton Moorea Lagoon, has 52 garden and beach bungalows from CFP 41,000 double, plus 52 over-water bungalows beginning at CFP 74,000, plus 14 percent tax. The air-conditioned rooms are well equipped, but the TVs only show local French stations, and the entire resort is crowded for the site. Rather than take all your meals here, seek out the atmospheric Aito Restaurant (tel. 56-45-52, Wed.–Mon.) one kilometer east. There aren't many other shopping or dining possibilities nearby, and the activities desk tacks a 10 percent surcharge onto anything booked through it. There's excellent snorkeling offshore, a swimming pool, and a Mandara Spa. TOPdive is based here.

The 147-room **InterContinental Resort Moorea** (PK 24.5, tel. 55-19-19, www.tahitiresorts.intercontinental.com) has a friendly, welcoming atmosphere. The 48 standard air-conditioned rooms in the main building, erected in 1987, start at CFP 37,347 single or double, tax included, but it's better value to pay CFP 51,607 for one of the 16 garden bungalows. The 28 beach bungalows are CFP 61,483. For one of the 50 over-water bungalows, have

© DAVID STANLEY

the beach at the InterContinental Resort Moorea on the island's north coast

© DAVID STANLEY

Legends Resort Moorea offers spectacular views of the island's north coast.

your CFP 85,247 ready. A third person pays CFP 9,040 for an uncomfortable extra bed, but children under 15 are free (this resort has a comprehensive children's activities program at additional cost). The breakfast and dinner plan is CFP 10,266 per person (half price for kids under 12). The service in the restaurant is often laughable, and alternative eateries are quite a walk away (a good supermarket is across the street). Honeymooners can request a romantic dinner on their bungalow's terrace, complete with a wedding cake and bottle of champagne. The InterContinental's Hélène Spa (www.spa-tahiti.com) offers a traditional coconut milk massage for couples. This spacious resort has a large swimming pool, and abundant paid sporting activities are available (kayaks, outrigger canoes, tennis, and snorkeling gear are free for guests). Rays swim freely off the resort's artificial beach and can be visited with a mask and snorkel. The hotel's captive Hawaiian dolphins are a far more controversial attraction. A Turtles Clinic at the resort shelters sick or wounded sea turtles or those seized by the authorities for eventual release back into the wild. You can book tours and rental cars at Moorea Tours, on the highway just outside the resort gate, at much lower prices than those offered inside.

Legends Resort Moorea (PK 24.5, tel. 55-15-15, www.legendsresortvillas.com), on a hillside directly across the street from the InterContinental, offers spectacular lagoon views. The 22 two-bedroom thatched wooden villas (up to four people) start at CFP 45,000 double, and 24 three-bedrooms (up to six people) are from CFP 74,000. Additional guests after the first two are CFP 10,000 each (children under 14 free). Each elegant villa has a full kitchen, living room, and deck with a Jacuzzi. A swimming pool, tennis courts, and fitness room are on the premises, and there's a golf cart shuttle. Legends is far from the beach, but they do provide a free boat ride over to a *motu*. The grocery store at the bottom of the hill sells supplies, and you can book rental cars and tours at an adjacent kiosk.

Dream Island (tel. 77-84-70, www.dream-island.com) sits on idyllic Motu Fareone off Moorea, accessible by boat from

Hauru. The four lovely thatched bungalows begin at CFP 240,000 per week for up to five people with cooking facilities, a terrace, and TVs. Meals can be ordered if you don't want to cook.

Also on Motu Fareone, **Villa Corallina Moorea** (tel. 77-05-90, www.villacorallina.com) is a luxury villa for rent at CFP 53,700/71,600/89,500 double/triple/quad. The villa contains almost everything you need, including mosquito netting. The snorkeling is very good here.

Food

MAHAREPA

Restaurant Le Mahogany (PK 4, tel. 56-39-73, Thurs.–Tues. 1100–1500 and 1800–2200, CFP 1,500–3,000), one kilometer east of the Pearl Resort, offers French and Chinese dishes. Nearby **Chez Luciano** (tel. 56-15-20, http://moorea.name/chezluciano, Mon.–Thurs. 1100–1330 and 1730–2030, Fri.–Sat. 1100–1400 and 1700–2200, Sun. 1700–2200, CFP 2,000) is a pizza restaurant. A bit west is the popular **Restaurant Le Cocotier** (PK 4.5, tel. 56-12-10, Wed.–Mon. 1130–1430 and 1830–2130) with meat dishes at CFP 2,450–3,250 and fish at CFP 2,250–2,850. There's a menu at the entrance.

The French ☾ **Pâtisserie Caraméline** (PK 5.5, tel. 56-15-88, daily 0700–1700), next to the post office in the Shopping Center Maharepa, has a nice terrace and fast service—perfect for breakfast or lunch. It's also good for pastries, sandwiches, and crepes. Be sure to try the coconut ice cream. Of course, the coffee here is *magnifique*.

Le Sud Restaurant (PK 5.6, Maharepa, tel. 56-42-95, Tues.–Sat. 1100–1400 and 1800–2100, Sun. 1800–2100), on the main road near

Rudy's is a popular new surf and turf restaurant at Maharepa.

the banks at Maharepa, has pizza in the CFP 1,550–1,800 range.

Rudy's (PK 6, Maharepa, tel. 56-58-00, Mon.–Tues. 1730–2130, Wed.–Sun. 1130–1330 and 1730–2130), a bit west of the Maharepa Shopping Center, is a new place with Santa Fe hacienda decor. They specialize in steaks (CFP 2,950) and seafood (CFP 2,200–4,250). Try the parrot fish stuffed with crab or the beef bourguignon. Rudy is the son of Syd Pollock, an American who has been operating restaurants, hotels, and nightclubs on Moorea for over 40 years. You'll probably meet father and son if you dine here.

PAOPAO

The over-water **Kaveka Restaurant** (PK 7.4, tel. 56-50-50) at the Hôtel Kaveka serves chicken in pineapple sauce (CFP 1,850), fish in curry sauce (CFP 2,450), and Chinese food (CFP 1,000–2,000). The view from the terrace is superb, and there's even a beach. Musicians entertain Tuesday, Friday, and Saturday nights.

Allo Pizza (PK 7.8, tel. 56-18-22, Mon. 1700–2100, Tues.–Sat. 1100–1400 and 1700–2100), opposite the gendarmerie, bakes 38 kinds of thin-crust wood-fired pizzas costing CFP 1,300–1,900. It's the best pizza on Moorea.

Alfredo's Restaurante (PK 8.7, tel. 56-17-71), on the inland side of the road a few hundred meters south of Club Bali Hai, has pizza (CFP 1,750) plus fish and meat dishes (CFP 2,450–3,250). There's occasionally live music here on Thursday and Sunday nights. We've received mixed reports about Alfredo's and can't recommend it.

Over-water **Restaurant Te Honu Iti** (PK 9.1, tel. 56-19-84, www.restaurant-te-honu-iti.com, Mon.–Tues. and Thurs.–Sat. 1130–1400 and 1830–2100, Sun. 1830–2100) has seafood at CFP 3,200–3,500, meat at CFP 2,600–3,500, and lobster at CFP 4,000. Chef Roger and his two sons have worked hard to garner a reputation for the finest French cuisine available on Moorea. After dinner, they feed the rays from

© DAVID STANLEY

Restaurant Te Honu Iti at Paopao on Cook's Bay combines colonial charm with fine French cuisine.

their panoramic deck—watch the action from your table. Call ahead for the free shuttle.

Restaurant Chez Jean Pierre (PK 9.2, tel. 56-18-51, Mon. 1100–1430, Tues. and Thurs.–Sat. 1100–1430 and 1800–2130, Sun. 1800–2130), close to the Fish Market, is one of the less expensive places to eat, but the food can be bland and tasteless. The specialty is roast suckling pig in oyster sauce (CFP 1,980) served on Saturday night, but there's also chicken (CFP 1,750–1,850), duck (CFP 1,750), and seafood (CFP 1,950–2,450), plus Chinese dishes.

The outdoor **Roulotte Jules et Claudine** (PK 9.3, tel. 56-25-31, Mon.–Sat. 1800–2100) at the Fish Market serves meals priced CFP 1,200–1,800.

Snack Rotui (PK 9.8, tel. 56-18-16, Tues.–Sun. 0700–1600), just west of the bridge at Paopao, could be the cheapest place on the island, with sandwiches (CFP 200), chicken wings, French fries, cake, egg rolls, and ice cream cones. The terrace overlooks Cook's Bay, it's friendly, and English is spoken.

HAURU

Sunday at 1230 **Restaurant Chez Vina** (PK 25.2, tel. 56-13-17), formerly known as "Chez Serge," between Hôtel Les Tipaniers and the InterContinental, serves a *ma'a Tahiti* buffet lunch (CFP 3,800) of local foods that includes pork, fish, chicken, and other delicacies cooked in an underground oven.

Hôtel Les Tipaniers (PK 25.9, tel. 56-12-67) has an excellent Italian restaurant on the highway serving dinner daily 1830–2115 and a classy snack bar on the beach with lunch served daily 1200–1415. At the main restaurant, the mahimahi with vanilla sauce (CFP 1,800) and *tartare de thon* (CFP 1,680) are excellent, and don't miss the homemade desserts, especially the crème brûlée (CFP 800). Les Tipaniers's beachside snack bar is an excellent choice for lunch (the *poisson cru* at CFP 1,150 is very good).

Irène Restaurant (PK 26, tel. 56-15-93, Tues.–Sun.), a few hundred meters north of Le Petit Village, has fish for CFP 1,700 and

MOOREA

© DAVID STANLEY

Roulotte a L'Heure du Sud at Hauru is a popular lunch spot for the surfing crowd.

seafood specialties like shrimp and octopus at CFP 2,600. You can eat outside on the terrace. Irène is a good ukulele player as well as a good cook.

Le Motu (PK 26.2, tel. 56-16-70, Tues.–Fri. 1100–1430 and 1700–2000, Sat. 1100–2000), just north of Le Petit Village, serves pizza priced CFP 1,150–1,400 on their open patio. A large beer is CFP 600.

The **Iguane Rock Café** (PK 26.5, tel. 56-17-16) at Le Petit Village in Hauru has pizza for CFP 1,300–1,600.

Roulotte a L'Heure du Sud (Thurs.–Tues. 1000–1600) between Le Petit Village and Restaurant La Plantation sells takeaway lunches (CFP 500–1,000). The *casse-croûte* sandwich, consisting of chicken or tuna stuffed inside a baguette, is a filling treat.

Restaurant La Plantation (PK 26.7, tel. 56-45-10, www.laplantationmoorea.com, Wed.–Mon.) is a large colonial-style terrace restaurant just south of Le Petit Village, with French cuisine priced CFP 2,500–3,500. There's live music or a DJ some evenings.

Good pizza and pasta (CFP 1,500–1,550) and ocean views are available at the beachfront **Le Sunset Pizzeria** (PK 26.8, tel. 56-26-00, daily 1100–1430 and 1800–2130) at the Hôtel Hibiscus. There's also fish (CFP 2,100–2,950), but avoid the salads.

Restaurant Le Mayflower (tel. 56-53-59, www.restaurantmayflower.com, Sun. and Tues.–Fri. 1130–1430 and 1830–2100, Sat. 1130–1430), next to Hôtel Hibiscus, has dishes such as lobster ravioli (CFP 2,650), sashimi (CFP 1,850), and mahimahi with béarnaise sauce (CFP 2,300). It's good value. **Pâtisserie La Polynesienne** (tel. 56-20-45) next door is a breakfast place.

A bright yellow sign almost opposite Hôtel Hibiscus announces the new **Bus-Stop Restaurant** (tel. 56-41-19, Thurs.–Tues.). They serve fish or seafood at CFP 1,450–2,450 and meats for CFP 1,750–2,450. Try the seared red tuna with a creamy vanilla sauce at CFP 1,950. A choice of six desserts is CFP 950 each, and there's a children's menu priced at CFP 1,000. Outdoor seating is provided.

The Bus-Stop Restaurant at Hauru is famous for its seared red tuna with a creamy vanilla sauce.

Snack Coco d'Isle (PK 27.3, tel. 56-59-07), between the two campgrounds, has lunch specials such as mahimahi in vanilla sauce or swordfish for CFP 2,300. Its *poisson cru* is CFP 1,850. There's sometimes live music on Friday and Saturday nights.

PKO Restaurant (PK 27.3, tel. 56-55-46, www.pkomoorea.com, Mon.–Tues. and Thurs.–Sat.), adjacent to Coco d'Isle at Hauru, features Thai dishes (CFP 1,400–2,100), sushi (CFP 1,800–2,450), and fish (CFP 1,950–2,100). They have live music Thursday nights.

La Paillote (PK 27.3, tel. 27-29-34, Wed.–Mon. 1130–1400 and 1730–2030), adjacent to the PKO Restaurant, is less expensive than its neighbors and has tasty fish dishes at CFP 1,300–1,800 and meat dishes CFP 1,200–1,400. Their specialty is barbecued chicken (CFP 1,200 for a half). You eat in an open thatched pavilion. Takeaway chickens are CFP 1,300/700 for a whole/half (Moorea Camping is nearby). No alcohol is served.

Jean-Claude Snack (PK 28, tel. 56-10-08, Mon. and Wed.–Sat. 1130–1400 and 1730–2100, Sun. 1730–2100), south of Moorea Camping, serves *poisson cru,* Chinese dishes, hamburgers, and *steak frites* on an outdoor deck by the highway.

Pizza Daniel (PK 34, Haapiti, tel. 56-39-95, Fri.–Wed. 1100–2100), just west of Résidence Linareva at Haapiti, is famous for its thin crust seafood pizzas (CFP 1,500).

GROCERIES

Many grocery stores are spread around Moorea. The largest and cheapest is **Champion Toa Moorea** (PK 4.8, tel. 56-18-89, Mon.–Sat. 0800–1900, Sun. 0600–1200), a kilometer south of the Vaiare ferry wharf.

Magasin Remy (PK 4.5, Maharepa, tel. 56-35-39, Mon.–Sat. 0545–1200 and 1430–1900, Sun. 0500–0800) is a kilometer east of the Moorea Pearl Resort. **Supermarché Maharepa** (PK 5.5, tel. 56-35-90) is almost opposite the Banque de Tahiti in Maharepa.

Supermarché Pao Pao (PK 8.1, Mon.–Sat. 0530–1200 and 1430–1800, Sun. 0500–0900) is 150 meters north of Club Bali Hai. At the head of Cook's Bay you have a choice of **Magasin Lee Hen** (PK 9.4, tel. 56-15-02) and **Supermarché Are** (PK 9.7, tel. 56-10-28) just west of the bridge nearby. Lee Hen and some of the others sell local take-out snacks.

Moorea Market (PK 24.5, daily 0600–1900), across the highway from the entrance to the InterContinental, sells groceries and drinks.

ABC Store (PK 26.5, Mon.–Sat. 0700–1900 and Sun. 0700–1300) is at the back of Le Petit Village. **Magasin Rene Junior** (PK 27.2, tel. 56-28-53, Mon.–Sat. 0630–1200 and 1430–1830) is between the campgrounds at Hauru.

All that you're likely to find in the **municipal market** at Paopao is a limited selection of fish. Fresh produce is much harder to obtain on Moorea than it is on Tahiti, so buy things when you see them and plan your grocery shopping carefully. Ask the stores what time the bread arrives, then be there promptly. The hybrid lime-grapefruit grown on Moorea has a thick green skin and a unique taste.

Information and Services

INFORMATION

The currently defunct **Moorea Visitors Bureau** (tel. 75-01-01, www.gomoorea.com) is next to the gas station in front of Le Petit Village; it may reopen at some point.

Kina Maharepa (PK 5.5, Maharepa, tel. 56-22-44), next to the post office, sells books and magazines in French. There's also a newsstand in Le Petit Village.

SERVICES

The Banque Socredo, Banque de Polynésie, and Banque de Tahiti are all in the Shopping Center Maharepa near the Moorea Pearl Resort. Banque Socredo has an ATM opposite Vaiare Wharf. The Banque de Polynésie branch in Le Petit Village shopping mall does not change money. None of these banks are open on Saturday, but most have ATMs accessible 24 hours.

The main **post office** (PK 5.5, tel. 56-27-00, Mon.–Thurs. 0730–1200 and 1330–1600, Fri. 0730–1200 and 1330–1500, Sat. 0730–0930) is near the banks at Maharepa. A branch post office (PK 22, tel. 56-16-76) is found at Papetoai.

The **Iguane Rock Café** (PK 26.5, tel. 56-17-16) at Le Petit Village in Hauru provides Internet access at CFP 500 for 30 minutes. Tiki@Net nearby charges only CFP 300 for 30 minutes. ManaSPOT wireless internet access is available at Vaiare Wharf and at both post offices on Moorea.

The **gendarmerie** (PK 7.8, Paopao, tel. 55-25-05) is just south of the Hôtel Kaveka.

HEALTH

The island's hospital (PK 8.5, tel. 55-24-24) is at Afareaitu, on the opposite side of the island from most of the resorts. If you need to, it's much easier to see a private doctor or dentist.

Dr. Frédéric Foucher works out of the Cabinet Medical (PK 5.5, Maharepa, tel. 56-32-32, Mon.–Tues. and Thurs.–Fri. 0700–1200 and 1400–1730, Wed. and Sat. 0700–1100 only), behind the Banque de Polynésie, a short walk from the Moorea Pearl Resort. In the same building is Dr. Frédéric Avet's Cabinet Dentaire (tel. 56-32-44, Mon.–Fri. 0800–1130 and 1500–1800, Sat. 0800–1130).

Dr. Dominique Barraille (PK 27, tel. 56-27-07) has an office next to Camping Chez Nelson. A dental office is near Camping Chez Nelson and opposite Magasin Rene Junior at PK 27, Hauru.

Pharmacie Tran Thai Thanh (PK 6.5, tel. 55-20-92, weekdays 0730–1200 and 1400–1800, Sat. 0800–1200 and 1430–1630, Sun. 0800–1000) is between Maharepa and Paopao. There's also **Pharmacie de Haapiti** (PK 30.5, Haapiti, tel. 56-38-37, weekdays 0900–1200 and 1600–1830, Sun. 0900–1100), a bit west of Tiki Village Theater.

Don't drink the water on Moorea without first boiling it, as there have been cases of salmonella.

Getting There and Around

Flights to Moorea

Air Moorea and Air Tahiti (both tel. 55-06-01) are based at Moorea Temae Airport. **Air Tahiti** has direct 10-minute flights from Moorea to Huahine (CFP 13,900), Raiatea (CFP 13,900), and Bora Bora (CFP 19,500).

An Air Tahiti subsidiary, **Air Moorea** (tel. 86-41-41) has flights between Tahiti and Moorea (CFP 3,900 one-way) leaving Papeete almost hourly 0600–1800. The Air Moorea terminal on Tahiti is in a separate building at the east end of Faa'a Airport. The free baggage allowance is 10 kilograms (excess CFP 66 per kilogram). The transfer service from

© DAVID STANLEY

Moorea's small airport terminal receives flights from Tahiti and the Leeward Islands.

Temae Airport to any point on Moorea is CFP 700 per person if booked while checking in at Tahiti. In August 2007 an Air Moorea flight crashed into the ocean shortly after takeoff from Moorea, killing all 20 people aboard.

Moorea Airport

Moorea Temae Airport (MOZ) is in the northeast corner of the island. The airport transfer service is only for people on prebooked tours, so unless you rent a car, you'll be stuck with a rip-off taxi fare in addition to the airfare: CFP 1,500 to the Moorea Pearl Resort, CFP 2,600 to the Hilton, and CFP 4,000 to the InterContinental.

Thanks to intimidation from the taxi drivers, none of the hotels are allowed to offer airport pickups. The bright yellow Moorea Explorer transfer buses at the airport are allowed to carry passengers with vouchers only. As you're checking in for your flight to Moorea at Papeete Airport, you can buy a transfer voucher to any hotel on Moorea for CFP 700 per person. If you fail to do so and ask at the transfer desk inside the Moorea terminal for a voucher, you'll be told to take a taxi. Your hotel reception should be able to book your return trip to the airport on these buses.

Avis and Europcar have counters at the airport, but it's essential to reserve beforehand. Otherwise they may not have a car for you, and you'll be subjected to the taxi scam just mentioned.

Considering all this, you should seriously consider using the ferry to and from Moorea. At a third of the price of flying (CFP 1,365 compared to CFP 3,900), the scenic 30-minute catamaran ride to or from Tahiti may end up being one of the highlights of your visit. It's mostly tourists on prepaid packages who arrive by air—those traveling independently usually take the ferry. If you do fly, try to sit on the left side of the aircraft on the way to Moorea and on the right on the way to Papeete.

Ferries to Moorea

The Moorea ferries carry about two million passengers and 250,000 motor vehicles a year, making Papeete the third-largest port under the French flag (after Calais and Cherbourg) as far

© DAVID STANLEY

The *Aremiti Ferry* makes four or five trips a day between Tahiti and Moorea.

as passenger movement goes. Two types of ferries do this trip: fast catamarans carrying mostly walk-on commuters (30 minutes), and large car ferries with capacity for 400 foot-passengers and 80 vehicles (one hour). Departure times are posted at the Maritime Terminal on the Papeete waterfront. Ferries are punctual, and reservations are not required: You just buy your ticket before you board. The first departure from Papeete is at 0600 weekdays, 0645 weekends.

All of the ferries go to Vaiare Wharf on the east side of Moorea. Local buses meet the ferries at Vaiare and carry passengers to any part of Moorea for a flat CFP 300 fare. Don't be too slow boarding, as the buses do fill up at times and they don't wait around.

The high-speed catamarans *Aremiti V* (tel. 56-31-10, www.aremiti.net) and *Moorea Express* (tel. 56-43-43, www.mooreaferry.pf) make 5–6 trips a day between Tahiti and Vaiare (CFP 1,365 one-way, children under 14 CFP 850, cars CFP 2,900, scooters CFP 845, bicycles CFP 212). Check the times and prices of the smaller *Moorea Express* first as it's often cheaper than the *Aremiti V.* On the Moorea cats you're allowed to sit or stand outside on the roof to get an all-round view, which makes them fun.

The large car ferries *Moorea Ferry* and *Aremiti Ferry* also shuttle 4–5 times a day between Papeete and Vaiare. Their fares are the same as the faster catamarans.

Public Transportation

Buses await the ferries from Tahiti at Vaiare Wharf. Although they don't go around the island, the northern and southern bus routes meet at Le Petit Village opposite the former Club Med, so you could theoretically effect a circumnavigation by changing buses there, provided you caught the last service back to Vaiare from Le Petit Village. You should have no problem catching a bus when you arrive on Moorea from Tahiti by ferry, but be quick to jump aboard (except on Sunday, when service is limited).

Be aware that the bright yellow "Moorea Explorer" buses at the wharf are for tourists on prearranged package tours only. The public buses the locals use charge CFP 300, and the fare is the same to anywhere on the island.

Buses leave Le Petit Village for the ferry weekdays at 0400, 0530, 0630, 0930, 1330, and 1530; Saturday 0400, 0630, 0930, 1330, and 1530; and Sunday and holidays at 0400, 0630, 1330, and 1430.

© DAVID STANLEY

Island buses await ferry passengers disembarking at Moorea's Vaiare Wharf.

From Vaiare Wharf, the buses leave Monday–Thursday at 0635, 0800, 0945, 1230, 1630, and 1800; Friday at 0635, 0800, 0945, 1230, 1500, 1630, and 1800; Saturday 0800, 0945, 1245, and 1630; Sunday and holidays 0800, 0945, 1600, and 1720.

If you have to catch a bus somewhere along its route, add the appropriate traveling time and ask advice of anyone you can. Some of the buses run 30 minutes early or late, and the times quoted above are only an indication. Sometimes the bus doesn't show up at Le Petit Village at all. Buses marked "uta ra a tamarii" are for school children only.

A taxi on Moorea is actually a minibus with a white letter **T** inside a red circle. Taxi fares are exorbitant for everyone. Hitching is possible, and if you really need the ride, you'll probably get it; just be prepared to do some walking.

Car Rentals

To get around Moorea you really do have to rent a car, scooter, or bicycle, or take a bus tour. The public buses serving the wharf are unreliable. There are usually no sidewalks, and the cars roaring up and down the road around the island make walking hot and unpleasant. There's only one choice: Join them.

Europcar (tel. 56-34-00, www.europcarpolynesie.com) has a main office near Le Petit Village and branches at Vaiare Wharf, the airport, and opposite the InterContinental. Unlimited-mileage cars begin at CFP 9,450/17,600/26,750 for one/two/three days. Bicycles are CFP 1,900/3,630 for one/two days. Despite these prices, Europcar's vehicles are sometimes in bad shape. Clients are responsible for the first CFP 55,000 in damages to the vehicle.

Avis (tel. 56-32-68, www.avis-tahiti.com) at Vaiare wharf, the airport, Club Bali Hai, and the Sofitel has cars from CFP 8,000/15,000 for one/two days including unlimited kilometers. These cheaper cars are often unavailable, and you may find yourself being quoted considerably more. In fact, Avis prices on Moorea vary according to where you are staying, and everyone pays a different price.

Rental cars and bicycles are also obtained at **Albert Car & Scooter Rental** (tel. 55-21-10, www.albert-transport.net, daily 0800–1700), with locations opposite the Pearl Resort (PK 5.3), Club Bali Hai (PK 8.5), and the InterContinental (PK 24.5). Unlimited-mileage cars begin at CFP

7,500/8,500/15,000 for 8/24/48 hours, including liability insurance. Some of the vehicles are of the "rent a wreck" variety, so look the car over before signing the credit card voucher and insist on a replacement or a discount if it's a high-mileage bomb. Scooters are CFP 5,500/6,000/11,000 for 8/24/48 hours.

If your time is limited, it's best to reserve an Avis or Europcar vehicle a day or two ahead at one of their offices in Papeete, as all cars on Moorea are sometimes taken. If you're coming on a package tour, you might be able to reserve a car for a cheaper price. There are five gasoline stations around Moorea: Mobil is beside Champion one kilometer south of Vaiare Wharf, Shell is opposite Vaiare Wharf, Total is at the airport access road, another Mobil is near Motel Albert at Paopao, and another Total is at Le Petit Village. The maximum speed limit is 60 kilometers per hour.

Scooter and Bicycle Rentals

Upon arrival you can rent a scooter from **Tehotu Location de Scooters** (PK 4, tel. 56-52-96) at Vaiare Wharf. If you do rent a scooter, beware of sudden attacks by dogs and keep to the center of the road. Tehotu Location also rents two-person road buggies at CFP 12,000/16,000 for four/eight hours.

Rent a Bike (tel. 71-11-09, rentabike@ifrance.com), between Le Petit Village and Roulotte a L'Heure du Sud, rents motor scooters at CFP 4,500–5,500 a day.

Photo Magic (tel. 56-59-59, Mon.–Sat. 0800–1830, Sun. 0800–1200), next to Restaurant La Plantation at Hauru, rents bicycles at CFP 1,000/1,200/1,500 for 4/8/24 hours. Magic Photo, the Total Service Station at Le Petit Village, and Rent a Bike all rent bicycles for the same price, so compare for quality.

Local Tours

Moorea Explorer (tel. 56-12-86) at the airport operates island tours (CFP 3,300/4,500 per person by bus/4WD) at 0800 and 1300. Its bright yellow buses are newer than those of the other companies, but the tours tend to be rushed, with fewer stops and little flexibility.

The tours offered by **Albert Activities** (tel. 55-21-10, www.albert-transport.net), at the airport and opposite the Pearl Resort and InterContinental, are much more personal than those of Moorea Explorer, and the guides are generally more receptive to individual requests. If you get one of the Haring brothers as your guide, you'll definitely enjoy it. Daily at 0900 Albert does a four-hour circle-island bus tour, including a visit to the Belvédère and lots of shopping, at CFP 3,300 (lunch not included). Albert's four-hour four-wheel-drive jeep safari with less shopping is CFP 4,500 per person (do it in the morning).

Moorea Mahana Tours (tel. 56-20-44, www.mooreamahanatours.com), based at the Hilton and InterContinental, offers a wide variety of tours and activities.

Hiro's Tours (tel. 56-57-66, www.hirotour.com) at Club Bali Hai does a four-hour four-wheel-drive island tour at CFP 4,400 daily and a 5.5-hour shark show and ray-feeding tour at CFP 5,500/6,500 without/with a picnic lunch four times a week. Hiro is the son of Hugh Kelley, one of the legendary Bali Hai Boys and an interesting character to meet.

Several other companies offer much the same. Whichever circle-island tour you choose, be prepared for a stop at the black pearl showroom that pays the guides the highest commission.

Tahiti Evasion (tel. 56-48-77, www.tahitievasion.com) at Hôtel Les Tipaniers specializes in hiking and mountain climbing with a half-day trip to the Three Coconuts Pass (CFP 4,500) and full-day hikes to Pierced Mountain and Rotui (CFP 8,000). They'll schedule a trip if two people want to go.

Inner Island Safari Tour (tel. 56-20-09) offers an exhilarating four-wheel-drive tour to various viewpoints and around Moorea. The four-hour morning Roto Nui Tour to the Opunohu Valley is CFP 5,500 per person, while the 3.5-hour afternoon Mana Tour to the same area is CFP 5,000.

THE LEEWARD ISLANDS

After Tahiti and Moorea, the Leeward Islands are the most visited part of French Polynesia, especially legendary Bora Bora. The scenery is superb, with winding coastlines and verdant volcanic peaks above the waterline and brilliant coral gardens and exotic marine life in the lagoons. The laid-back Polynesian lifestyle of Huahine, Raiatea, Taha'a, and Maupiti is very relaxing, and traditional customs are better preserved here than in Papeete. Every visitor should attend at least one Island Night at a fancy Bora Bora resort for the wild *tamure* dancing and drumming. These happen several times a week, and it's often possible to avoid the high cost of the buffet by settling for a drink at the bar.

Tourism is highly developed on Bora Bora, less so on the other islands. For the traveler, there's no getting around the fact that travel here is expensive. Bora Bora is easily the most upscale tourist destination in the South Pacific, with 15 resorts charging more than US$250 double per night without meals. Yet it's also true that you can greatly reduce your costs if you book your top-end hotel rooms as part of a package tour. Another option is to stay in small, locally operated pensions. Bora Bora has seven hostels and pensions in the US$50–100 range, and you can also camp at a few of the pensions. The other islands have fewer swanky resorts and more family-run pensions.

Most visitors get around the islands by air, and you can save money by purchasing one of Air Tahiti's 28-day air passes through your travel agent. A Society Islands air pass will cost around US$450, or US$650 if you add

HIGHLIGHTS

Maeva: Huahine boasts one of the largest archaeological sites in the South Pacific, with several dozen stone platforms along the shores of Lake Fauna Nui and on the adjacent hill (page 134).

Tapioi Hill: Climb this distinctive hill behind Uturoa on Raiatea in a couple of hours for a magnificent view of four islands (page 144).

Marae Taputapuatea: This temple complex on the southeast side of Raiatea was the most sacred site in the Society Islands during pre-European times (page 148).

Bora Bora's Landscape: This mythical island rising from a turquoise lagoon is among the most memorable sights of the South Pacific (page 154).

Manta Ray Ballet: A feature of the Bora Bora day cruises is a chance to snorkel with huge manta rays, harmless reef sharks, and other marine fauna. These trips also allow you to admire the island's spectacular scenery from the water, and most include a picnic lunch (page 161).

LOOK FOR TO FIND RECOMMENDED SIGHTS, ACTIVITIES, DINING, AND LODGING.

on the Tuamotu Islands. Passenger-carrying cargo boats do ply from Tahiti to Bora Bora several times a week, but they're basic and the overnight trip northbound can be rough. If you want to experience the boat trip one way, you're better off flying from Tahiti to Bora Bora and then returning to Tahiti by boat. Southbound, the boats sail during daylight hours, and you can island-hop between Maupiti and Raiatea by fast ferry.

Car rentals cost over US$100 a day—ouch! An alternative is to rent a bicycle instead of a car. It's easy to ride a bicycle around Bora Bora in a day, and you can walk around Maupiti. Four-wheel-drive safari tours are offered on all the main islands, and these are cheaper than renting a car. There are also sightseeing tours by outrigger canoe with unlimited snorkeling included.

PLANNING YOUR TIME

When to go? May–October is the cooler, less humid time, although prolonged rainfall is possible year-round. An optimum time to be there is for the Heiva festival on Huahine and Bora Bora in early July. Whenever you go, it's worth trying to visit several of the islands, as they are all very different. Bora Bora and

© DAVID STANLEY

a white beach next to the former Sofitel Heiva resort, Huahine

Maupiti have similar environments, but one is three decades ahead of the other in tourism development. Huahine has good facilities without the golden hordes often encountered on Bora Bora. Raiatea and Taha'a have larger local populations and are less dependent on tourism. Each of the five islands is well worth a couple of days of your time.

Just over a week is enough time to see the best of these islands, even if you decide to do part of your interisland traveling by ferry. Three nights on Bora Bora will give you enough time for a trip around the island and a lagoon tour to see the sharks and rays. If you have the time, you can make a two-night side trip from Bora Bora to unspoiled Maupiti on a fast ferry, which operates three times a week.

Raiatea is worth a couple of nights to explore the island by rental car and to do a day trip to Taha'a by motorized outrigger canoe. The fast ferry between Bora Bora and Raiatea makes it practical to do this leg by boat as well. A few cargo boats (and maybe a faster ferry) cross from Raiatea to Huahine, another jewel of the Leeward Islands. Huahine has the largest archaeological site in French Polynesia, plus an easygoing main town. The island is interesting to drive around, with a pearl farm, botanical garden, hiking trails, and a nice snorkeling beach along the way. Two nights are the minimum you'll want to spend on Huahine.

HISTORY

The Leeward Islands were settled by Polynesians around 850. The Dutch explorer Roggeveen, coming from Makatea in the Tuamotus, sighted (but did not land on) Bora Bora and Maupiti on June 6, 1722. Captain Cook "discovered" the other Leeward Islands in July 1769, which was quite easy since the Tahitians knew them well. In fact, Cook had the Raiatean priest Tupaia on board the *Endeavour* as a pilot. Cook wrote, "To these six islands, as they lie contiguous to each other, I gave the names of Society Islands." Later the name was extended to the Windward Islands. In 1773 a man named Omai from Raiatea sailed to England with Cook's colleague, Captain Furneaux, aboard the *Adventure.* He returned with Cook in 1777 and was dropped off on Huahine.

During the 19th century, American whalers spent their winters away from the Antarctic in places such as Huahine, refurbishing their supplies with local products such as sugar, vegetables, oranges, salted pork, and *aito,* or ironwood. These visits enriched the island economy, and the New England sailors presented the islanders with foreign plants as tokens of appreciation for the hospitality received. English missionaries arrived in 1808, and later Pomare II extended his power to the Leeward Islands, abolishing the traditional religion. In 1822 missionary law was imposed. Among the missionaries was William Ellis, whose book *Polynesian Researches,* published in London in 1829, has left us a detailed picture of the island at that time.

Though Tahiti and Moorea fell under French control in 1842, the Leeward Islands remained a British protectorate until 1887, when these islands were traded for fishing rights off Newfoundland and a British interest in what was then New Hebrides (today Vanuatu). Marines from the French warship *Uranie* had attacked Huahine in 1846, but they were defeated at Maeva. A year later France promised Britain that it would not annex the Leeward Islands, yet in 1887 it proceeded to do so. The local chiefs refused to sign the annexation treaty until 1895, and resistance to France, especially on Raiatea, was overcome only by force in 1897. The French then expelled the English missionary group that had been there for 88 years; nonetheless, today 80 percent of the population of the Leewards remains Protestant.

In 1918 the Spanish influenza pandemic wiped out a fifth of the population, including the last queen, Tehaapapa III. Only in 1945 was missionary law finally abolished and French citizenship extended to the inhabitants. In the 1958 referendum, 76 percent of the population of Huahine voted in favor of independence.

GETTING THERE

Air Tahiti flies nonstop from Papeete and Moorea to Huahine, Raiatea, and Bora Bora, and from Papeete, Raiatea, and Bora Bora to Maupiti. Direct flights from Bora Bora to Fakarava, Manihi, Rangiroa, and Tikehau allow tourists to easily combine the Leeward and Tuamotu Islands.

By Boat

In mid-2010 the fast ferry service between Papeete and the Leeward Islands was canceled after a taxation dispute between the shipping company Raromatai Ferry and the Government of French Polynesia. Despite high demand for inexpensive ferry services to these islands, no news of a replacement service was available at press time. Something may materialize eventually, so check back at the time of travel. Meanwhile, foreign and local passengers alike will have little choice other than to accept Air Tahiti's high fares and baggage restrictions.

Both of the older cargo ships to the Leeward Islands depart Motu Uta wharf, a 20-minute walk from downtown Papeete. Northbound, the MV *Taporo VI* leaves Papeete Tuesday and Thursday at 1600; southbound it leaves Bora Bora Wednesday and Friday at 0900. The MV *Hawaiki-Nui* also departs Papeete for Huahine, Raiatea, and Bora Bora on Tuesday and Thursday at 1600. Southbound, the *Hawaiki-Nui* leaves Bora Bora Wednesday at 1300 and Friday at 1200.

The timing on the cargo ships is more civilized if you stay on the boat right through to Bora Bora northbound: You get to see sunset over Moorea, go to bed, and when you awake you'll be treated to a scenic cruise past Taha'a and into the Bora Bora lagoon. Getting off at Huahine in the middle of the night is no fun. Southbound between Bora Bora, Raiatea, and Huahine you travel during daylight hours. Southbound you board at Huahine at dusk, and there are no disturbances before Tahiti (where you may be asked to disembark in the middle of the night). If you plan to fly one-way, fly out and take the boat back.

Although the ships do make an effort to stick to their timetables, the times are approximate—ask at the company offices. They're more likely to be running late on the return trip from Bora Bora to Tahiti. Expect variations if there's a public holiday or major festival that week. In Papeete, board the ship at least an hour before departure to be sure of a reasonable place to sleep (mark your place with a beach mat). If you've got some time to kill before your ship leaves Papeete, have a look around the government-owned coconut-oil mill next to the wharf.

You can try to buy a deck ticket at the *Taporo VI* office (tel. 67-68-68, Mon.–Fri. 0730–1100 and 1330–1700, Sat. 0700–1100), facing the wharf at Motu Uta, and at the *Hawaiki-Nui* office (tel. 54-99-54, www.stim.pf), beyond the parking lot at the port entrance. Both ships accept only 12 deck passengers, and they're often fully booked weeks in advance. Interisland travel between Hauhine and Raiatea and returning to Papeete by boat is often easier. In the Leeward Islands, buy a ticket from the agent at their office as far in advance as possible. The consumption of alcohol aboard ship is prohibited.

One-way fares from Papeete to any of the islands are CFP 2,000 deck on the *Hawaiki-Nui* or CFP 1,911 from Papeete on the *Taporo VI.* On the *Hawaiki-Nui* couchettes are CFP 5,400 for one bed. Interisland fares within the Leeward Islands are CFP 800–1,601.

If you can't get on any of the above ships, try the Flotille Administrative (tel. 50-66-75) at the west end of Motu Uta. They operate the red-colored government supply ship *Tahiti Nui VI* from Papeete to Maupiti every Wednesday or Thursday around noon. Again, only 12 passengers are accepted, but since there aren't as many people going to Maupiti, it's much easier to find a place. Deck passage is CFP 2,500 one way. The *Tahiti Nui VI* reaches Maupiti around 0600 and leaves again for Papeete at 0800.

Interisland Ferry

The 20-meter fast ferry *Maupiti Express 2* (tel. 67-66-69 on Bora Bora, tel. 66-37-81 on Raiatea, www.maupitiexpress.com) shuttles between Bora Bora and Maupiti, Taha'a, and Raiatea three or four times a week. The boat leaves Bora Bora for Taha'a (80 minutes) and Raiatea (95 minutes) Monday, Wednesday, and Friday at 0700, departing Raiatea for the return at 1600. On Sunday it leaves Bora Bora at 1500 and Raiatea at 1800. The ferry leaves Bora Bora for Maupiti Tuesday, Thursday, and Saturday at 0830, departing Maupiti to return at 1600. The fare between Bora Bora and Taha'a, Raiatea, or Maupiti is CFP 4,000/5,000 one-way/round-trip. It's possible to buy a through ticket from Raiatea to Maupiti for CFP 5,000/7,000, although one night must be spent on Bora Bora. The 140 passengers have a choice of sitting in an air-conditioned salon or standing on the open upper deck.

Huahine

Huahine, the first Leeward island encountered on the boat trip from Tahiti, is a friendly, inviting island 175 kilometers northwest of Papeete. In many ways, lush, mountainous Huahine (74 square kilometers) has more to offer than overcrowded Bora Bora. The variety of scenery, splendid beaches, deep bays, exuberant vegetation, archaeological remains, and charming main town all invite you to visit. Huahine is a well-known surfing locale, with consistently excellent lefts and rights in the two passes off Fare (try to befriend the local surfers before entering their space). Schools of dolphins sometimes greet ships arriving through Avapeihi Pass. Huahine's mosquito population is also surprisingly large.

It's claimed the island got its name because, when viewed from the sea, Huahine has the shape of a reclining woman—very appropriate for such a fertile, enchanting place. *Hua* means "phallus" (from a rock on Huahine-iti) while *hine* comes from *vahine* (woman). A narrow

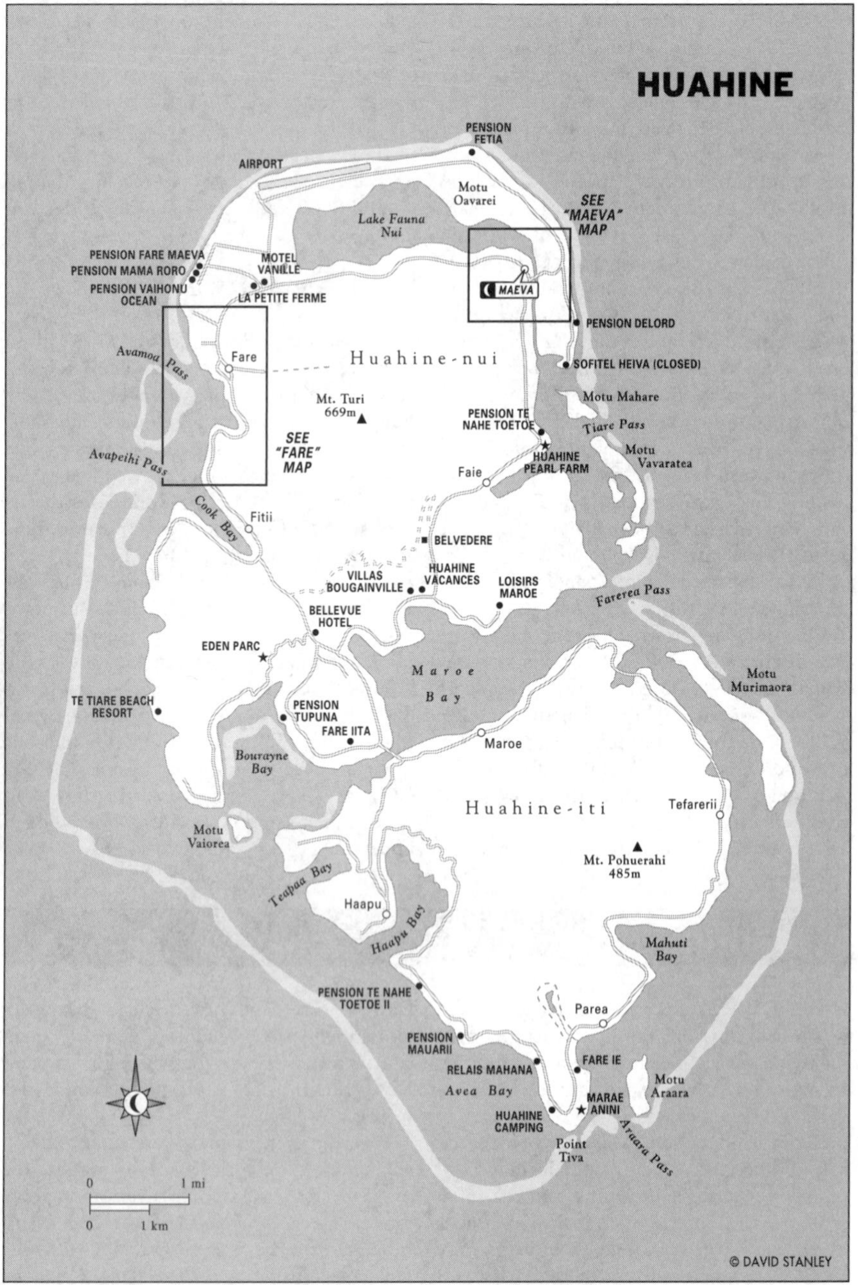
HUAHINE
PENSION FETIA
AIRPORT
Motu Oavarei
SEE "MAEVA" MAP
Lake Fauna Nui
PENSION FARE MAEVA
PENSION MAMA RORO
PENSION VAIHONU OCEAN
MOTEL VANILLE
LA PETITE FERME
MAEVA
PENSION DELORD
Avamoa Pass
Fare
Huahine-nui
SOFITEL HEIVA (CLOSED)
Motu Mahare
Mt. Turi 669m
PENSION TE NAHE TOETOE
Tiare Pass
HUAHINE PEARL FARM
Motu Vavaratea
Avapeihi Pass
SEE "FARE" MAP
Faie
Cook Bay
Fitii
BELVEDERE
VILLAS BOUGAINVILLE
HUAHINE VACANCES
LOISIRS MAROE
Farerea Pass
BELLEVUE HOTEL
EDEN PARC
Maroe Bay
Motu Murimaora
TE TIARE BEACH RESORT
PENSION TUPUNA
FARE IITA
Maroe
Bourayne Bay
Huahine-iti
Tefarerii
Motu Vaiorea
Mt. Pohuerahi 485m
Teapaa Bay
Haapu
Haapu Bay
Mahuti Bay
PENSION TE NAHE TOETOE II
Parea
PENSION MAUARII
RELAIS MAHANA
FARE IE
Motu Araara
Avea Bay
MARAE ANINI
HUAHINE CAMPING
Point Tiva
Araara Pass
0
1 mi
0
1 km
© DAVID STANLEY

channel crossed by a concrete bridge slices Huahine into Huahine-nui and Huahine-iti (Great and Little Huahine, respectively). The story goes that the demigod Hiro's canoe cut this strait.

The almost entirely Polynesian population numbers only 6,000, yet some of the greatest leaders in the struggle for the independence of Polynesia, Pouvanaa a Oopa among them, have come from this idyllic spot. The artist Bobby Holcomb and the poet Henri Hiro are also well remembered.

In recent years Huahine has been discovered by international tourism, and small pensions and bungalow-style developments are now found in different parts of the island. Luckily Huahine has been able to absorb this influx fairly painlessly, as it's a much larger island than Bora Bora, and the resorts are well scattered and constructed in the traditional Tahitian style. It's an oasis of peace after Papeete. The island has also become a major port of call for the yachts that rock at anchor off Fare. Tourism began in 1973 with the building of the airstrip. Today, the accommodations on Huahine are mostly in small pensions; large hotels have a history of going broke here.

Archaeology

Archaeologists have found that human habitation on Huahine goes back at least 1,300 years; Maeva village was occupied as early as A.D. 850. In 1925 Dr. Kenneth P. Emory of Hawaii's Bishop Museum recorded 54 *marae* on Huahine, most of them built after the 16th century. In 1968 Professor Yosihiko H. Sinoto found another 40. Huahine-nui was divided into 10 districts, with Huahine-iti as a dependency. As a centralized government complex for a whole island, Maeva, on the south shore of Lake Fauna Nui, is unique in French Polynesia. Here all the district chiefs on Huahine-nui lived side by side and worshiped their ancestors at their respective *marae,* 28 of which are recorded here.

Since 1967 about 16 *marae* have been restored, and they can be easily visited today. The great communal *marae* at Maeva and Parea have two-stepped platforms *(ahu)* that served as raised seats for the gods. Like those of Raiatea and Bora Bora, the Huahine *marae* are constructed of large coral slabs, whereas comparable structures on Tahiti and Moorea are made of round basalt stones. During construction of the defunct Hôtel Bali Hai just north of Fare in 1972, a *patu* hand club was uncovered, suggesting that New Zealand's Maoris originated in this area.

FARE

The unpretentious little town of Fare, with its tree-lined boulevard along the quay, is joyfully peaceful after the roar of Papeete. A beach runs along the west side of the main street, and local life unfolds without being overwhelmed by tourism. From here Bora Bora is visible in the distance to the left while the small twin peaks of Taha'a are to the right. The seven other villages on Huahine are linked to Fare by winding, photogenic roads. The snorkeling offshore north of town is good, but despite the easygoing atmosphere, it's unwise to leave valuables unattended on the beach (and beware of unperceived currents).

Sights

Colorful fish are visible from the wharf at Fare. A reasonable beach is directly opposite Pension Guynette with public showers. There's better swimming at the site of the former Hôtel Bali Hai, a five-minute walk north along the shore from New Te Marara Snack.

The **Handicraft Market** (daily 0730–1700), at the south end of the waterfront, has necklaces from shells and seeds, pareu, and baskets for sale.

After you've explored the Fare waterfront, visit the beautiful *mape* (chestnut) forest up the Faahia Valley. Walk inland 15 minutes along the road that begins two houses south of the Total service station. You'll pass banana, pineapple, breadfruit, taro, and coconut plantations, then the road becomes a jungle trail that you can easily follow another 15 minutes up a small stream into a tropical forest laced with vanilla vines and the sweet smell

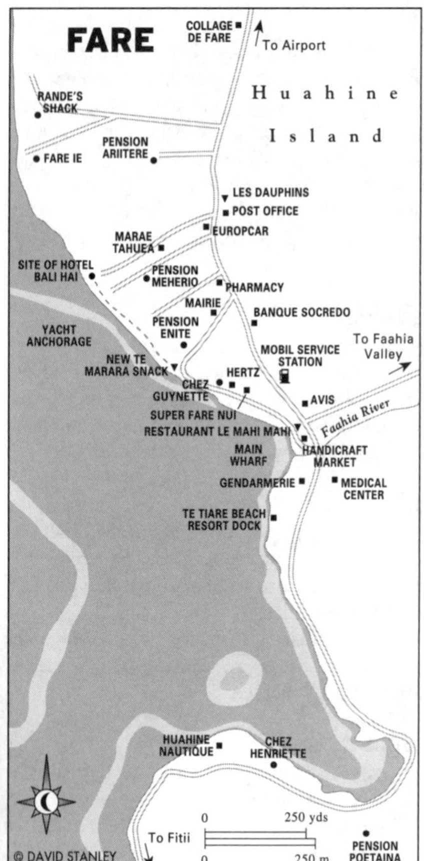

of fermenting fruit. By the stream is a long bedlike rock known as Ofaitere, or "Traveling Rock," but you'd need to have someone point it out to you. A guide will certainly be required to continue to the summit of Huahine's highest peak, Mount Turi (669 meters), in about three hours, as it's rough going.

Entertainment and Events

Bar Restaurant Les Dauphins (tel. 68-89-01), beside the post office north of town, offers disco dancing to local Tahitian groups on Friday and Saturday nights from 2100. It's also open for lunch Tuesday–Saturday.

In July, Huahine also has a Heiva Festival similar to the better-known ones on Tahiti and Bora Bora, with an artisans village, fishing tournaments, canoe races, a parade, *pétanque* competitions, fruit-bearer races, and dance and song contests between Huahine's villages.

Sports and Recreation

Pacific Blue Adventure (tel. 68-87-21, www.divehuahine.com), based at Fare since 1990, offers scuba diving at CFP 6,200/23,200 for one/four dives. Trips to sites such as Avapeihi Pass, Fa'a Miti, Coral City, and Yellow Valley leave at 0900 and 1400, depending on demand. Pacific Blue picks up at hotels around Fare.

Annie Brunet's **Mahana Dive** (tel. 73-07-17, www.mahanadive.com) shares an office with Huahine Lagoon on the Fare waterfront. It goes out at 0900 daily, charging CFP 5,900/21,600 for one/four dives. Leopard rays, barracuda, moray eels, and sharks are seen year-round.

La Petite Ferme (tel. 68-82-98, http://la-petite-ferme-forever.skyrock.com), between Fare and the airport, offers riding on 15 small, robust Marquesan horses. A two-hour ride along the beach at 0900 or 1500 is CFP 3,800 per person. They also offer a full day of riding for CFP 8,800, including a picnic lunch. Beginning at 0900, you ride east to Maeva and the Sofitel, have a swim, and return via the *motu*. Call the day before to let them know you're coming. Novice riders and children eight and over are welcome, but those weighing over 100 kilograms cannot be accommodated. This is the number-one horseback-riding operation in French Polynesia and is recommended.

Huahine Sport Fishing (tel. 68-84-02, www.huahine.com/ruau) has an 11-meter boat, the *Ruau II,* based at the Te Tiare Beach Hotel dock in Fare.

Accommodations

US$50–100

Pension Chez Guynette (tel. 68-83-75, http://huahineisland.com/guynette), also known as "Club Bed," is on the waterfront to the left as you get off the ship. It's one of the best value places to stay in French Polynesia. The

© DAVID STANLEY

the sleepy waterfront at Fare, Huahine

seven rooms, each with the name of a different Society island, are CFP 4,900/5,900/6,900 single/double/triple, including tax, with fans and private baths. The eight-bed dorm facing the kitchen at the back of the building is CFP 1,750 per person. A CFP 300 surcharge is payable if you only stay one night. You can cook your own food in the communal kitchen, and everyone walks through the dorm to get there. It's lights out in the kitchen and dorm at 2200. On departure day the rooms must be vacated by 1000, but you can leave your bags in the dorm until 1800 if you're catching a late ferry. Arrivals before 0700 pay the full tariff for the previous night.

The oldest pension on the island is **Pension Enite** (tel. 68-82-37, martial.enite@mail.pf), an eight-room boardinghouse at the west end of the Fare waterfront beyond the snack bar (no sign). The eight rooms with shared bath are CFP 9,500/17,000 single/double with half board (two-night minimum stay, no singles). The meals are served in a thatched cookhouse on the beach, and the food is good. It's mostly French expats who stay here.

Pension Ariitere (tel. 68-82-09, www.pensionariitere.com) is a new place on a street running toward the beach just north of Fare. The four self-contained, self-catering bungalows are CFP 7,500 double, while two rooms with private baths in the main house go for CFP 6,200/7,000 without/with air-conditioning (minimum stay two nights). Breakfast is included, a small circular pool is provided, and bicycles and airport transfers are free.

Chez Ella (tel. 68-73-07, chezellahuahine@yahoo.fr), next to Motel Vanille at the airport turnoff, has two good-quality houses at CFP 8,050 single or double, plus one larger house at CFP 10,800 for up to four persons. Breakfast is included. Each bungalow has a kitchen, fridge, and TV, and you can ask to use the washing machine. The use of bicycles is free.

Pension Fare Maeva (tel. 68-75-53, www.fare-maeva.com) is on a rocky shore, 900 meters down an unpaved access road that begins between Le Petite Ferme and the fire hall. It's two kilometers from the airport or three kilometers from Fare. The 10 self-catering bungalows are CFP 12,705 single or double, while the 10 motel-style rooms go for CFP 7,420. Inquire about the price of having a car included with the bungalow. The swimming pool and restaurant face the beach, but the rooms are back across the street. Airport transfers are CFP 800 return.

Pension Mama Roro (tel. 68-84-82), between Pension Vaihonu and Pension Fare Maeva, has two large self-catering bungalows at CFP 7,500 single or double, plus CFP 1,500 per additional person up to four maximum. Airport transfers are free.

Pension Vaihonu (tel. 68-87-33, www.vaihonu.com), just south of Pension Fare Maeva on the coast north of Fare, is a popular backpacker hangout. It has a seven-bed dorm at CFP 1,800, three simple *fare* with shared bath at CFP 3,500/5,000 single/double, and two self-catering duplex apartments with private baths at CFP 8,000 double. Camping is possible. Six percent tax is extra, and there's a surcharge of CFP 300/600/1,000 dorm/*fare*/duplex if you stay only one night. A communal kitchen is provided, and airport transfers are free. Guests get discounts on Huahine Explorer four-wheel-drive island tours.

Chez Henriette (tel. 68-83-71) is a pleasant 15-minute walk south of Fare, beside the lagoon a few hundred meters beyond Pension Poetaina. The six thatched *fare* all have basic cooking facilities. The two smaller units with double beds, mosquito nets, fridges, hot plates, and shared bath are CFP 5,000 double, while the four larger *fare* with two double beds and private baths are CFP 7,675 for up to four people—OK for a family with two children. It's sort of like staying in a local village while retaining a measure of privacy.

US$100-150

Pension Meherio (tel. 60-61-35, meherio.huahine@mail.pf), on the road toward the beach from near the Europcar office, has three duplex units at CFP 8,400–10,500 double, including breakfast. Two of the units are disabled-friendly, and there are deals for families with children under 12. Kayaks, snorkeling gear, a TV room, and airport transfers are provided.

Rande's Shack (tel. 68-86-27, randesshack@mail.pf), by the beach between Fare and the airport, is run by an American named Rande Vetterli. It has two screened self-catering houses at CFP 10,000/15,000 for one/two bedrooms (three-night minimum stay). Bicycles, kayaks, snorkeling gear, and a Polynesian canoe are lent free. It's one heck of a deal.

La Petite Ferme (tel. 68-82-98, http://la-petite-ferme-forever.skyrock.com), between Fare and the airport, has a very nice self-catering bungalow at CFP 12,000 for up to five people (two-night minimum stay). The six-bed dormitory is CFP 1,650 per person, and one basic room with shared bath attached to the dorm is CFP 3,900 double. Breakfast is included in all rates, and dinner can be ordered for CFP 1,650. Airport transfers are free. It's a great place to stay if you're at all interested in horseback riding.

In a valley one kilometer south of Fare (inland from the second bridge) is **Pension Poetaina** (tel. 60-60-06, www.poetaina.com), a large two-story building with spacious balconies and a lounge. The four rooms with shared bath are CFP 8,480 single or double, while two larger rooms with private baths are CFP 11,130 (two-night minimum stay). Communal cooking facilities are provided, and there's a pool. Boat trips around Huahine are arranged at CFP 9,000 per person, including lunch and snorkeling. It's a bit overpriced.

US$150-250

Fare Ie (tel. 60-63-77, www.tahitisafari.com), adjacent to Rande's Shack, consists of two furnished safari tents standing on a deck facing the beach. Each has a private bathroom and a common kitchen, costing CFP 16,500 double, plus CFP 1,900 for a third and fourth person. A good breakfast is included. Bicycles, kayaks, and snorkeling gear are loaned for free. Fare Ie provides the luxury of camping by the ocean without having to sacrifice creature comforts.

Motel Vanille (tel. 68-71-77, www.motelvanille.com) is on the corner of the airport access road and the road from Fare to Maeva. The five thatched bungalows positioned around the swimming pool are CFP 11,814/15,871 single/double with breakfast, bicycles, and airport transfers included (two-night minimum stay). Dinner can be ordered. It's one kilometer from the beach.

Food

A half dozen **food trailers,** or *roulottes,* park at Fare Wharf at different times of the day, selling spring rolls, pastries, and long French sandwiches. At night you can get *steak frites,* pizza, chicken and chips, or *poisson cru* for around CFP 1,000. Look for the trailer that parks next to a row of telephone booths, as it has excellent fish brochettes.

Snack Ida (weekdays 0600–1300), facing the Total Service Station on the waterfront, serves a good breakfast of bread and butter with coffee for CFP 300, sandwiches CFP 250–350, and omelets CFP 550–650. You eat seated on a stool at the counter. It's popular with the locals.

Pension Guynette (tel. 68-83-75) serves an inexpensive breakfast and lunch on its popular waterfront terrace bar; it's also a good choice for just coffee and a snack. There's nowhere better to sit and watch the sunset while meeting old and new friends.

New Te Marara Snack Bar (tel. 68-70-81, Mon.–Sat.), at the west end of the waterfront, has a nice terrace built overlooking the lagoon. Main courses are CFP 1,500–2,100 and hamburgers CFP 900. It's fine for a sunset beer.

Restaurant Le Mahi Mahi (tel. 68-70-55), at the south end of the waterfront, is a French-owned restaurant with lobster dinners at CFP 4,000. The *poisson cru* is perfect for lunch, and for breakfast you can get excellent croissants and *pains au chocolat.* A *roulotte* serving crepes and waffles parks across the street.

Super Fare-Nui (tel. 68-84-68, Mon.–Thurs. 0600–1830, Fri.–Sat. 0600–1900, Sun. and holidays 0530–1100), on the Fare waterfront, sells groceries and cold beer.

The tap water on Huahine can be clouded after heavy rains.

Roulottes parked along the waterfront at Fare, Huahine, provide tasty, inexpensive meals.

Information

The **Manava Huahine Visitors Bureau** (tel. 68-78-81, weekdays 0730–1130) is next to Chez Guynette on the main street.

Houses available for long-term rental on Huahine are advertised on handwritten notices taped up at the Mobil and Total gas stations in Fare.

Services

ATMs are outside the **Banque de Tahiti** (tel. 68-82-46, weekdays 0745–1145 and 1330–1630), on the Fare waterfront, and the **Banque Socredo** (tel. 47-00-00, weekdays 0730–1130 and 1330–1600), on the first street back from the waterfront.

The **post office** (tel. 68-86-35, Mon.–Thurs. 0700–1500, Fri. 0700–1400) is on the road between the airport and Fare. The gendarmerie (tel. 60-62-05) is opposite the hospital over the bridge at the south end of town.

Ao Api New World (tel. 68-70-99, Mon.–Sat. 0830–1200 and 1700–2000, Sun. and holidays 1700–2000) Internet café, next to Pension Chez Guynette and upstairs, charges CFP 15 per minute.

Public toilets and washbasins are in one of the yellow buildings on the waterfront opposite Pension Guynette (if open).

Health

A **Gabinet Medical-Dentaire** (tel. 68-82-20, Mon.–Fri. 0730–1200 and 1400–1600) is next to the Mobil Service Station on the next street back from the wharf.

La Pharmacie de Huahine (tel. 60-61-41, weekdays 0730–1130 and 1430–1700, Sat. 0800–1200) is across the street from the Mormon church just north of town on the way to the post office.

Getting There

Air Tahiti (tel. 68-77-02) has one office at the airport and another (Mon.–Fri. 0730–1145 and 1330–1630, Sat. 0730–1130) next to Super Fare Nui in Fare. Air Tahiti's direct flight between Huahine and Moorea would be great if it didn't cost CFP 13,900 when the flight to or from Papeete is only CFP 11,400.

The airport (HUH) is three kilometers north of Fare. Make arrangements for the regular airport minibus (CFP 600 pp) at Pension Enite.

the airport terminal just north of Fare, Huahine

The Papeete **ferries** tie up to the wharf in the center of town. Northbound, the *Taporo VI* calls at Huahine on Wednesday and Friday at 0100; southbound on Wednesday and Friday at 1700. Deck fares from Huahine are CFP 800 to Raiatea or CFP 1,911 to Papeete. The *Hawaiki-Nui* also passes once a week, northbound Wednesday at 0200 and southbound Friday at 1830. If you arrive in the middle of the night on a cargo ship, you can sleep in an open pavilion until dawn.

Tickets for the *Taporo VI* are sold at its office in the yellow warehouse on the wharf beginning the day before the sailing. The *Hawaiki-Nui* office (tel. 68-78-03) is nearby.

Getting Around

Getting around Huahine is not easy unless you rent a car. Weekdays only, a few *trucks* leave outlying villages for Fare in the early morning, returning to the villages around 1000. They don't come back again until the next day. Check this with the drivers of any *trucks* you see parked along the waterfront. Otherwise, the locals are fairly good about giving lifts. The only sure way of getting around is to rent something, although the four-wheel-drive excursions are a good alternative.

Moe Taxi (tel. 68-79-50), based at Pension Guynette, charges CFP 500 per person for airport transfers to or from Fare, or CFP 1,000 one way from Fare to Maeva.

Europcar (tel. 68-82-59, www.europcarpolynesie.com) is opposite the post office, with branch offices at the airport, Relais Mahana, and Te Tiare Beach Resort. Its smallest car is CFP 9,400/17,400 for one/two days with unlimited kilometers. Bicycles/scooters are CFP 2,000/6,200 a day. All prices include tax.

Avis (tel. 68-73-34, www.avis-tahiti.com) is at the airport and next to the Mobil Service Station a block back from the waterfront. Its cars start at CFP 12,600 including mileage.

Huahine Locations/Hertz (tel. 68-76-85, huahinelocation@mail.pf), facing the waterfront between Super Fare Nui and Chez Guynette, has the best deals on rental cars at CFP 8,900 all-inclusive for 24 hours. They also have bicycles at CFP 2,000 for 24 hours.

Huahine has only two gas stations, both in Fare and open weekdays 0630–1100 and 1330–1600, Saturday 0630–1100 and 1300–1500, Sunday and holidays 0630–0800. They both sometimes close early.

Huahine Lagoon (tel. 68-70-00), next to New Te Marara Snack Bar at the north end of the Fare waterfront, rents small aluminum boats with outboard motors at CFP 5,000/7,000/10,000 for two/four/eight hours (gas not included). Masks, snorkels, life jackets, an anchor, oars, and an ice chest come with the boat. Bicycles and kayaks are also for rent.

Local Tours

Island Eco Tours (tel. 68-79-67, islandecotours@mail.pf) offers four-hour four-wheel-drive tours of Huahine twice daily at CFP 5,000. What sets these trips apart from the usual photo-op affairs is the emphasis on archaeology and natural history. It also schedules hiking tours of the Maeva ruins upon request. Owner Paul Atallah is a former student of Professor Yosihiko H. Sinoto, who restored many of the territory's ancient *marae,* and he's the only guide on Huahine who has conducted scientific research on the sites he now shows his clients.

Huahine Explorer (tel. 68-87-33, h-explorer@mail.pf), based at Pension Vaihonu, offers a four-hour four-wheel-drive tour (CFP 5,000 per person) twice a day as well as a daily combined boat and four-wheel-drive tour (CFP 12,000, 7.5 hours). Experienced guides introduce the land and flora.

Huahine Land (tel. 68-89-21) also offers 3.5-hour four-wheel-drive safaris at CFP 5,000 per person—a good alternative to renting a car.

Sailing Huahine (tel. 68-72-49, www.sailing-huahine.com) offers snorkeling cruises on the 15-meter yacht *Eden Martin.* A half/full day costs CFP 7,200/12,500 per person, including lunch or refreshments (minimum of four people). It's also possible to charter the yacht for one-week cruises within the Society Islands at CFP 69,000 per day, including the skipper and fuel (meals are extra). The same to the Tuamotu Islands is CFP 86,250 a day.

Huahine Nautique (tel. 68-83-15, www.huahine-nautique.com) offers a circle-island boat tour (CFP 8,500 per person) with fish feeding, a picnic lunch, and drinks served on a *motu.* It also rents two-person Jet Skis at CFP 23,000 with a minimum rental of two Jet Skis at a time. Hotel pickups are free.

Nonguests can take the shuttle boat from Fare to the Te Tiare Beach Resort for CFP 500 per person. The shuttle operates hourly from 0730 to 1800, and even though you're expected to order lunch at the resort, it's a reasonable way to spend the day.

HUAHINE-NUI

Huahine-nui, or Great Huahine, has more to offer than just Fare. The *marae,* or temple platforms, of Maeva on Lake Fauna should not be missed. Many of the platforms are right next to the road, but the most intriguing *marae* are on the hillside up a narrow jungle path. Near Maeva, there's a beach at the former Sofitel Heiva where you can swim and snorkel. You'll also want to drive south to Faie with its pearl farm and river eels. The many deep bays and winding roads make this mountainous island highly picturesque.

Maeva

At Maeva, six kilometers east of Fare, you'll encounter that rare combination of an easily accessible archaeological site in a spectacular setting. Here each of the 10 district chiefs of Huahine-nui had his own *marae,* and huge stone walls were erected to defend Maeva against invaders from Bora Bora (and later France). The plentiful small fish in Lake Fauna Nui supported large chiefly and priestly classes (ancient stone fish traps can still be seen near the bridge at the east end of the village). In the 1970s Professor Yosihiko H. Sinoto of Hawaii restored many of the structures strewn along the lakeshore and in the nearby hills.

There's an **archaeological museum** (no phone, Mon.–Fri. 0900–1600, CFP 500) in round-ended Fare Pote'e, a replica of an old communal meeting house on the shores of the lake. **Marae Rauhuru,** next to Fare Pote'e,

Marae Rauhuru next to Lake Fauna at Maeva, Huahine

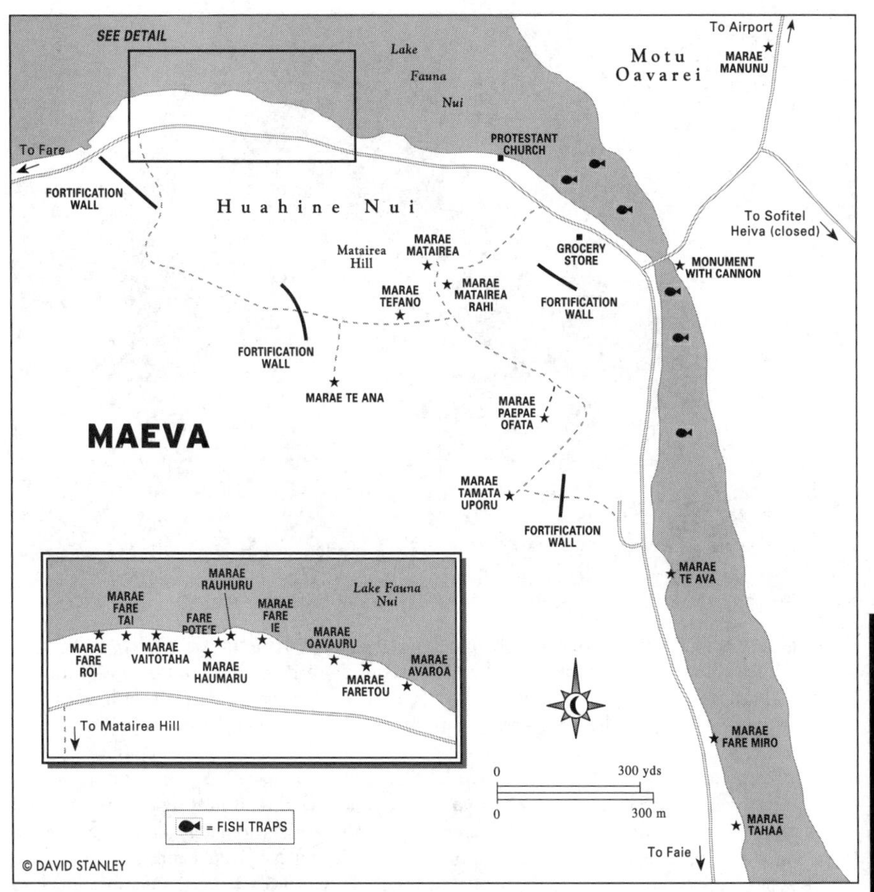

bears petroglyphs of turtles. Explanatory signboards in French, English, and Tahitian are provided in this area.

From Fare Pote'e, walk back along the road toward Fare about 100 meters to a **fortification wall** on the left, built in 1846 with stones from the *marae* to defend the area against the French. Follow this inland to an ancient well at the foot of the hill, then turn right and continue around the base of the hill to the trail up onto Matairea Hill (opposite a stone platform). Twenty meters beyond, a second, older fortification wall along the hillside is the access to **Marae Te Ana** on the right. The terraces of this residential area for chiefly families, excavated in 1986, mount the hillside.

Return to the main trail and continue straight up to the ruins of **Marae Tefano,** which are engulfed by an immense banyan tree. **Marae Matairea Rahi,** farther along and to the left, was the most sacred place on Huahine, dedicated to Tane, the principal god of Huahine associated with warfare and canoe building. The backrests of Huahine's principal chiefs are in the southernmost compound of the *marae,* where the most important religious ceremonies took place. Backtrack a bit and keep straight, then head up the fern-covered hill to

© DAVID STANLEY

Marae Tefano before a large banyan tree on Matairea Hill, Maeva, Huahine

the right to **Marae Paepae Ofata,** which gives a magnificent view over the whole northeast coast of Huahine.

Continue southeast on the main trail past several more *marae* and you'll eventually cross another fortification wall and meet a dirt road down to the main highway near **Marae Te Ava.** Throughout this easy two-hour, 2.5-kilometer hike, watch for stakes planted with vanilla by the present villagers (and don't touch them).

When you get back down to the main road, walk south a bit to see photogenic **Marae Fare Miro,** then backtrack to the bridge, across which is a **monument** guarded by seven cannons. Beneath it are buried French troops killed in the Battle of Maeva (1846), when the islanders successfully defended their independence against marauding French marines sent to annex the island. The ancient **fish traps** in the lagoon, recently repaired, are still being used. Fish enter the stone traps with the incoming and outgoing tides.

Seven hundred meters farther along toward the ocean and to the left is two-tiered **Marae Manunu,** the community *marae* of Huahine-nui, dedicated to the gods Oro and Tane. According to a local legend, Princess Hutuhiva arrived at this spot from Raiatea hidden in a drum. In the base of the *marae* is the grave of Raiti, the last great priest of Huahine. When he died in 1915 a huge stone fell from the *marae.*

The unpaved road passing Marae Manunu runs another six kilometers along the elevated barrier reef north of Lake Fauna Nui directly to Huahine Airport, an alternative route back to Fare. White beaches line this cantaloupe- and watermelon-rich north shore.

Otherwise, take the side road between Marae Manunu and the bridge southeast toward the former Sofitel Heiva Huahine. Melanie at **Galerie Umatatea** (tel. 68-70-79, www.polynesiapaintings.com), halfway down this road, sells prints and original paintings of local scenes. From 1989 to 2005, the **Sofitel Heiva Huahine** accommodated guests in a coconut grove two kilometers southeast of Maeva, but the resort is currently closed. Unspoiled white beaches stretch all along this section of the lagoon, and there's passable snorkeling off the ocean-side beach. If you'd care to swim, park

BOBBY HOLCOMB

Dancer, choreographer, musician, composer, singer, and painter, Bobby Holcomb (1947-1991) personified the all-round artist. He was born in Honolulu, child of a half-Hawaiian, half-Portuguese prostitute and an American sailor. Later he traveled widely, with periods as a rock musician in France and an actor in Venice. From Salvador Dalí he absorbed surrealism. In 1976 Holcomb arrived at Huahine aboard a friend's yacht, and there he established his studio at Maeva. Prints of his colorful paintings of Polynesian mythology and legends are widely available in the islands, as are recordings of his joyful Tahitian music. With his dreadlocks and tattoos on his arms and legs, Holcomb personified living theater. He's buried near Marae Fare Miro at Maeva.

just outside the resort's gate and walk over to the beach.

Faie

Just before Faie, four kilometers south of Maeva, is the **Huahine Pearl Farm** (tel. 78-30-20, daily 1000–1500), which offers a free boat tour of its operation in the hope that you'll buy a pearl or some local pottery. You should tip the boatman.

Below the bridge in the center of Faie is a river populated by sacred blue-eyed eels. Legend holds that it was huge eels that brought fresh water to the village. You can buy fish to feed them at the red kiosk.

From Faie the very steep Route Traversiere crosses the mountains to Maroe Bay (2.5 kilometers), making a complete circuit of Huahine-nui possible. If continuing south by bicycle, don't begin coasting too fast on the other side, as you may not be able to stop.

A side road from Hôtel Bellevue, six kilometers south of Fare, leads one kilometer west to **Eden Parc** (tel. 68-86-58, www.edenparc.org). At last report, this commercial botanical garden north of Bourayne Bay was closed, but it may eventually reopen. If so, you'll be able to learn about French Polynesia's medicinal plants, orchids, and flowers while following the park trail winding through the luxuriant vegetation and get a view of the center of the island from Three Bays Rock.

Accommodations

Pension Fetia (tel. 72-09-50, pension-fetia@caramail.com) is on an unswimmable ocean beach three kilometers east of the airport via the unpaved road around the north side of Lake Fauna Nui. There are four nice little bungalows with basic cooking facilities and crushed coral floors from CFP 7,000 single or double. It's a little isolated but fine if you've rented a car.

On the road to the former Sofitel Heiva Huahine, one kilometer from the bridge at Maeva, is **Pension Delord** (tel. 68-89-51) with small thatched *fare* on a rocky beach at CFP 3,000/5,000 single/double, including breakfast, and other meals can be ordered. This place is also known as Camping Vanaa, and it's cheaper to pitch your own tent. Your generous hosts try to make you feel at home, and it's a shady spot, conveniently located for exploring the *marae.* Bring insect repellent.

Pension Te Nahe Toetoe (tel. 68-71-43, www.pension-tenahetoetoe.net), next to the landing for the Huahine Pearl Farm at the entrance to Faie Bay, has three rooms with shared bath at CFP 3,000/4,200 single/double. A small bungalow is CFP 5,300, and camping is CFP 1,500 per person. Breakfast/dinner can be ordered at CFP 500/1,500, or you can cook your own food. There's a common sitting room, and bicycles and outrigger canoes are loaned for free. This colorful place is associated with a pension of the same name on Tahiti and is very popular with young French travelers, so call ahead. Ask about their Parea branch on a much better beach at Avea Bay (camping CFP 1,500 per person, bungalow CFP 7,500 double). Ask about room and rental car packages.

Across the road from Maroe Bay, **Huahine Vacances** (tel. 68-73-63, www.huahinevacances.com) has three large villas for rent at

CFP 17,500/20,500 single/double, including a car and a boat. For a group of up to seven people, it's CFP 27,500. A similar property, **Villas Bougainville** (tel. 60-60-30, www.villas-bougainville.com), with rates from CFP 20,500–32,500, is just to the west of here.

The **Hôtel Bellevue** (tel. 68-82-76, http://chez.mana.pf/hotelbellevue/accueil_ta.htm), six kilometers south of Fare, offers 10 bungalows with cooking facilities at CFP 6,000/7,000 single/double. Otherwise, it's CFP 70,000 per month. The poor lighting makes it hard to read in the evening. The Bellevue has an abandoned look to it, but contrary to what's written in some guidebooks, it's still open and a reasonable value for the money. There's a lovely view of Maroe Bay from the figure-eight shaped swimming pool.

Fare Iita (tel. 68-70-21, www.fare-iita.net), down the road to Bourayne Bay from the bridge joining the islands, has three rooms in a "papaya house" on the hillside. It's CFP 7,500/9,500 single/double, including breakfast. Christine serves dinner at CFP 3,000 per person, while Daniel organizes four-wheel-drive adventures.

Further along the same way, **Pension Tupuna** (tel. 68-70-36, www.pensiontupuna.com) has four rustic bungalows next to Bourayne Bay at CFP 12,000 double. Breakfast is included, and a good dinner is CFP 3,000 per person, accompanied by a noisy generator. The shoreline is muddy, but the scenery is superb, and you can borrow kayaks and snorkeling gear.

In 1999 the **Te Tiare Beach Resort** (tel. 60-60-50, www.tetiarebeachresort.com) opened on the west side of Huahine-nui. Initially part of the Pearl Resorts Group and later run by the Hawaii-based Outrigger hotel chain, it's now independent. The 10 garden bungalows, nine deluxe garden bungalows, six beach bungalows, and five lagoon bungalows start at CFP 41,000 double, while the 11 over-water bungalows with whirlpool baths and large decks are CFP 70,000, plus 14 percent tax. Half board is CFP 8,500 per person, served in an over-water restaurant. This is not a five-star luxury resort, although the prices may suggest it. The food at the resort's Ari'i Restaurant is good and the grounds are immaculate, but the spacious rooms are not impeccable, although the decks do offer memorable sunset views. The small freshwater swimming pool is OK, but the snorkeling off the resort is poor. Sign up for one of the memorable drift snorkeling tours instead. To enhance the sense of isolation, this resort is accessible only by a frequent shuttle boat. Airport transfers are CFP 6,000 per person round-trip.

Getting Around

Other than the minibus from the airport to Fare, there's no public transportation to speak of on Huahine-nui. Most people rent a car, but it's just as easy to peddle a bicycle to Maeva. If you decide to cycle across the high ridge between Faie and Maroe Bay, beware of going down the other side too quickly, as the brakes on your rental bicycle may not be able to stop you.

HUAHINE-ITI

Huahine-iti, or Little Huahine, has some of Huahine's best beaches and beach resorts. The swimming and snorkeling on Avea Bay on the southwest side of Huahine-iti is superb, and there's another old *marae* to visit. There's an easy hiking trail up a valley at Parea. You can easily see it all in a day on the 30-kilometer drive around Huahine-iti.

Sights

Haapu village was originally built entirely over the water for lack of sufficient shoreline to house it. One of the best established grocery stores on Huahine-iti is at Haapu. As you approach the southern end of the island, there's a wide white beach along **Avea Bay,** with good swimming right beside the road. Yachts can follow a protected channel inside the barrier reef down the west coast of Huahine to the wonderful (if occasionally rough) anchorage at Avea Bay, but shallows at Point Tiva force sailboats to return to Fare.

On another white beach on the east side of Point Tiva, one kilometer south of Parea, is **Marae Anini,** the community *marae* of Huahine-iti. It was built by an ancestor of Hiro sometime between 1325 and 1400 as an offshoot of Marae Taputapuatea on Raiatea. Look for petroglyphs on this two-tiered structure, dedicated to the god of war Oro, where human sacrifices once took place. Surfing is possible in Araara Pass, beside the *motu* just off Marae Anini. If snorkeling here, beware of an outbound current in the pass.

It's a pleasant one-hour walk inland around a small creek on a track that begins at the bridge at Parea, one hour on foot. You can also do it in 10 minutes by car.

Accommodations

The places to stay near Parea cater to both ends of the market. Funky ☾ **Pension Mauarii** (tel. 68-86-49, www.mauarii.com), 20 kilometers south of Fare, sits on Avea Bay's lovely shaded white sand beach. Some of the finest snorkeling in French Polynesia is available along here. Rooms in the main building with shared bath and thin walls are CFP 5,500/8,300 single/double, or CFP 10,000 in the mezzanine. The two new beach rooms with baths are CFP 14,000. The three garden bungalows are CFP 15,000 double. A beach bungalow is CFP 21,000. No cooking facilities are provided but a breakfast and dinner plan is available at CFP 4,500 per person. The seafood restaurant is open daily 1200–1400 and 1800–2100 and is slightly overpriced with uneven service. The sports center here arranges Hobie catamaran sailing, windsurfing, boat rentals, and a snorkeling trip, and Heremiti Dive offers scuba diving. Hertz has a desk at Pension Mauarii. Chez Tara (tel. 68-78-45), just up the beach from Pension Mauarii, serves a delicious *ma'a Tahiti* lunch at their Tahitian-style restaurant every Sunday.

Relais Mahana (tel. 60-60-40, www.relaismahana.com) is on the same long white beach as Pension Mauarii, a little more than two kilometers west of Parea. It's a step up in luxury and price from Pension Mauarii, but some of the personal touches are replaced by a touch of Parisian snobbery. The 32 fan-cooled units with mini-fridges and TVs are CFP 22,950 single or double for a garden bungalow, CFP 3,000 more for a beach bungalow, plus 14 percent tax. Add another CFP 2,138 per person for the buffet breakfast. There are no cooking

the beach at Relais Mahana on Avea Bay, Huahine-iti, Huahine

facilities for guests, and a notice asks you not to eat in your room. Bicycles, kayaks, and snorkeling gear are lent for free. Recreational activities as well as the pool and beach are strictly for hotel guests only, but the restaurant-bar is open to all, with variable meals in the CFP 2,500–4,500 range. The Tahitian dance show here some weekend nights is CFP 5,804 (no additional charge for guests on meal plans). You can see colorful fish and corals from Relais Mahana's dock, and there's good snorkeling. Airport transfers are CFP 3,780 per person round-trip. Europcar has a desk here.

Huahine Camping (tel. 68-85-20), also known as Ariiura Camping, 22 kilometers south of Fare and 1.4 kilometers from Parea, shares the same lovely white beach with Relais Mahana, 800 meters northwest. There are six small open *fare,* each with a double bed, mosquito net, and no lock on the door, at CFP 6,000 double (minimum stay two nights). A small grocery store is nearby. Camping is CFP 1,800 per person per day, and a communal kitchen and pleasant eating area overlook the turquoise lagoon. Bring insect repellent and coils. Bicycles and kayaks are for rent. The snorkeling and surfing here are superb. Transfers from the airport or wharf are CFP 1,500 per person one-way.

Fare Ie (tel. 60-63-77, www.tahitisafari.com), between Marae Anini and Parea, offers accommodations in four deluxe safari tents starting at CFP 16,500 double. A larger beach tent is CFP 26,500, breakfast included. The accommodations and cooking facilities at Fare Ie are good, but it's open to the trade winds (which do blow away the mosquitoes). The beach is nicer at Relais Mahana, where it's calmer and better protected from the wind. Bicycles and snorkeling gear are free.

Getting There and Around

Though the concrete "July Bridge" joins the two islands, Huahine-iti is far less accessible than Huahine-nui. It's 24 kilometers from Fare to Parea via Haapu, and another 16 kilometers from Parea back to the bridge via Maroe. You can rent a car in Fare and tour Huahine-iti in one day, or arrange a transfer to one of the accommodations and stay awhile.

You can rent a furnished safari tent at Fare Ie, at Parea, Huahine-iti, Huahine.

Raiatea

At 171 square kilometers, Raiatea is the second-largest island of French Polynesia. Its main town and port, Uturoa, is the business, educational, and administrative center of the Leeward Islands, or Îles Sous-le-Vent (islands under the wind). The balance of Raiatea's population of about 12,000 lives in eight flower-filled villages around the island: Avera, Opoa, Puohine, Fetuna, Vaiaau, Tehurui, Tevaitoa, and Tuu Fenua. The west coast of Raiatea south of Tevaitoa is old Polynesia through and through.

Raiatea is traditionally the ancient Havai'i, the "sacred isle" from which all of eastern Polynesia was colonized. It may at one time have been reached by migrants from the west, as the ancient name for Taha'a, Uporu, corresponds to Upolu, just as Havai'i relates to Savai'i, the largest islands of the Samoan chain. A legend tells how Raiatea's first king, Hiro, built a great canoe he used to sail to Rarotonga. Today Raiatea and Taha'a are mostly worth visiting if you want to get off the beaten tourist track. Though public transportation is scarce, the island offers good possibilities for scuba diving, charter yachting, and hiking, and the varied scenery is worth a stop.

The Landscape

Raiatea, 229 kilometers northwest of Tahiti, shares a protected lagoon with Taha'a three kilometers away. Legend tells how the two islands were cut apart by a mythical eel. About 30 kilometers of steel-blue sea separates Raiatea from both Huahine and Bora Bora. The highest mountain is Toomaru (1,017 meters), and some of the coastlines are rugged and narrow. All of the people live on a coastal plain planted in coconuts where cattle also graze.

According to Polynesian mythology, the god Oro was born from the molten rage of Mount Temehani (772 meters), the cloud-covered plateau that dominates the northern end of the island. *Tiare apetahi,* a sacred white flower that exists nowhere else on earth and resists transplantation, grows above the 400-meter level on the slopes around the summit. The fragile one-sided blossom represents the five fingers of a beautiful Polynesian girl who fell in love with the handsome son of a high chief but was unable to marry him because of her lowly birth. The petals pop open forcefully enough at dawn to make a sound, and local residents sometimes spend the night on the mountain to be there to hear it. These flowers are protected, and there's a minimum CFP 50,000 fine for picking one. Small pink orchids also grow here.

No beaches are found on big, hulking Raiatea itself. Instead, picnickers are taken to a picture-postcard *motu* in the lagoon. Surfing is possible at the 10 passes that open onto the Raiatea-Taha'a lagoon, and windsurfers are active. The Leeward Islands are the most popular sailing area in French Polynesia, and most of the charter boats are based at Raiatea. Many pearl farms dot the lagoon around Raiatea and Taha'a.

History

Originally called Havai'i, legend holds that the island was rechristened by Queen Rainuiatea in honor of her parents: Rai, a warrior from Tahiti, and Atea, queen of Opoa. Before European encroachment, Raiatea was the religious, cultural, and political center of what is now French Polynesia. Tradition maintains that the great Polynesian voyages to Hawaii and New Zealand departed from these shores.

Raiatea was Captain Cook's favorite island; he visited three times. During his first voyage in 1769 he called first at Opoa July 20–24. After having surveyed Bora Bora from the sea, he anchored for a week in the Rautoanui Pass on the northwest coast of Raiatea, near the village of Tuu Fenua. During his second voyage Cook lay at anchor twice, first September 8–17, 1773, and again May 25–June 4, 1774, both times at Rautoanui. His third visit was November 3–December 7, 1777, again at Rautoanui. It can

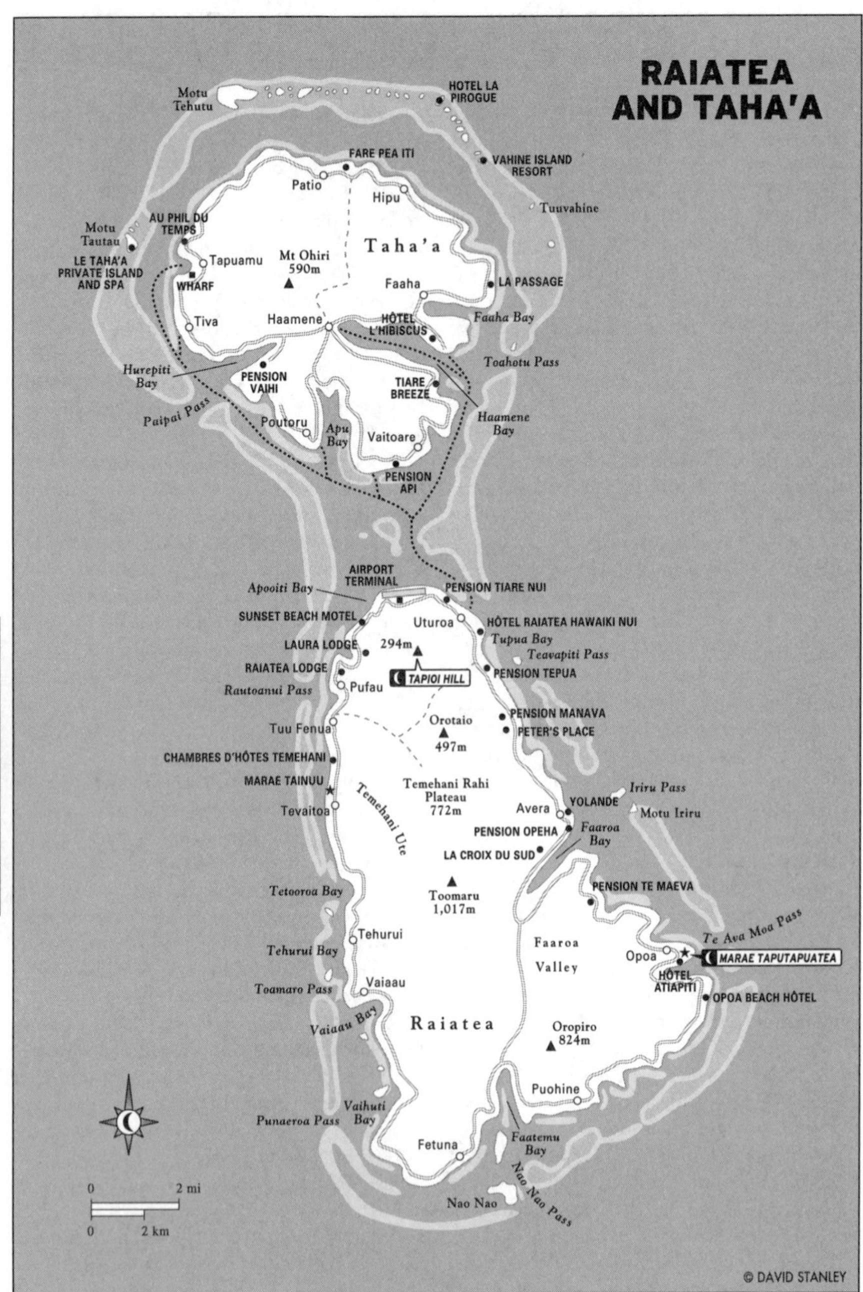

THE LEEWARD ISLANDS

therefore be said that Rautoanui (which he calls "Haamanino Harbour" in his journals) was one of Cook's favorite anchorages.

These islands accepted Christianity soon after the Tahitians were converted. The noted Protestant missionary John Williams arrived in 1818, as recalled by a monument in the form of a black basalt pillar standing in front of the Protestant church just north of Uturoa. From Raiatea, Williams carried the gospel to Rarotonga in 1823 and Samoa in 1830. Later Queen Pomare IV spent the years 1844–1847 in exile on Raiatea. When France annexed the island in 1887, Chief Teraupoo launched a resistance campaign that lasted until 1897, when French troops and warships conquered the island. Teraupoo was captured after six weeks of fighting and deported to New Caledonia, where he remained until 1905. The Queen of Raiatea and 136 of her followers were exiled to remote Eiao Island in the Marquesas.

UTUROA

Uturoa (pop. 4,000) is the territory's second city and the first stop on any exploration of the island. It's an easy place to find your way around, with a row of Chinese stores along a

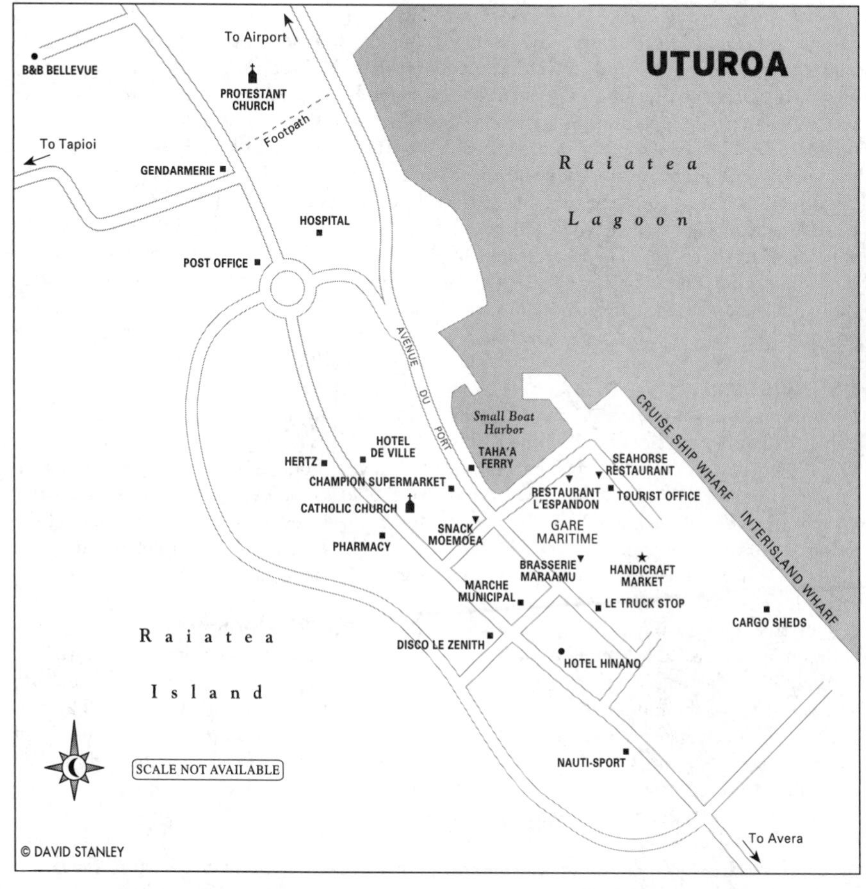

main drag opening onto the Gare Maritime. In 2001 the Uturoa waterfront was entirely redeveloped with a new cruise ship terminal, information offices, restaurants, and shops, plus a traditional-style handicraft market. The ferry plying between Tahiti and Bora Bora calls here, and there's a frequent shuttle to Taha'a. The island's airport is three kilometers west of town with the main yacht charter base, Marina Apooiti, one kilometer beyond that.

Large cruise ships call here several times a week, flooding the little town with visitors. If you'd like to be able to sit at a waterfront café in peace or have the undivided attention of shop clerks, try to find out when love boats such as the *Paul Gauguin* and *Tahitian Princess* will be in port and avoid Uturoa those days. Rental cars will be in high demand, so reserve well ahead. If you're a cruise ship passenger yourself, be aware that the various excursions sold on board are highly inflated by multiple commissions. You'll probably save money by dealing directly with the tour operators inside the Gare Maritime right on the wharf, although you could also miss out. The large groups on rushed tours don't have the same experience as those who take the time to spend a few days on these islands.

Tapioi Hill

For a spectacular view of four islands (Raiatea, Taha'a, Huahine, and Bora Bora), climb Tapioi Hill (294 meters), the peak topped by a television relay antenna behind Uturoa. As you stand on the rocky hilltop facing Taha'a, Bora Bora will be at 10 o'clock on your left and Huahine directly right. It's one of the easiest and most satisfying climbs in French Polynesia, an excellent free activity if you're traveling with children. You'll probably even have the hill to yourself. Take the road beside the gendarmerie and you'll reach the foot of the hill in a few minutes. This is private property, and although the owners allow visitors to climb Tapioi on foot, they've posted a sign just before the cattle grid at the bottom of the hill asking that private cars not be used, and this request should be respected. The fastest time on record for climbing the 3.5 kilometers up Tapioi is 17 minutes, but it's best to allow two or three hours to hike up and down. Take sufficient water along with you and wear comfortable shoes.

Entertainment

Discothèque Le Zénith (tel. 66-27-49, Fri.–Sat. from 2100) is above Super Marché Léogite opposite Banque Socredo. Men pay CFP 1,500 admission, but women get in for free.

Sports and Recreation

The coral at Raiatea is rather poor, but there's ample marine life, including gray sharks, moray eels, humphead wrasses, barracudas, manta rays, and countless tropical fish in places such as **Teavapiti Pass.** Just off the Raiatea Hawaiki Nui is the century-old wreck of a 50-meter Dutch coal boat, the *Nordby,* the top of which is 18 meters down.

Hémisphère Sub (tel. 66-12-49, VHF channel 68, www.raiatea-diving.com), at the Marina Apooiti and Raiatea Hawaiki Nui, offers scuba diving at CFP 6,000 per dive (10 dives CFP 54,300). It offers free pickups.

Diving is also offered by **Te Mara Nui Plongée** (tel. 66-11-88, www.temaranui.pf) at the marina just north of Uturoa. It's CFP 6,000/26,500 for one/five dives.

Nauti-Sports (tel. 66-35-83), next to the Kuomintang building at the south end of Uturoa, sells quality snorkeling gear.

There's good swimming in a large pool open to the sea at the **Centre Nautique** *(la piscine)* on the coast just north of Uturoa, beyond the new yacht harbor. The local Polynesians keep their long racing canoes here.

Accommodations

Most of the places to stay are on the northeast side of Raiatea, and they're arranged here from north to south in each price category. The proprietors often pick up guests who call ahead for reservations at the airport or harbor. The transfers are often free, but ask.

UNDER US$25

You can camp free on **Motu Iriru,** a tiny island

on the south side of Iriru Pass off Avera. It's owned by the territory and serves as a public park, with picnic tables, barbecue pits, outdoor showers, and flush toilets. A caretaker keeps the island clean. Permission to picnic or camp here is not required. Bring food and drinking water. To get here contact West Coast Charters (tel. 79-28-78 or 66-45-39, www.raiatea-tours.com) in the Gare Maritime d'Uturoa, or ask about water taxi services.

US$25-50

The backpacker's number-one choice on Raiatea is **Peter's Place** (tel. 66-20-01) at Hamoa, six kilometers south of Uturoa and just beyond Pension Manava. The eight neat double rooms in a long block are CFP 1,600 per person, or you can pitch a tent in the large grassy area facing the rooms for CFP 1,000 per person. A large open pavilion is used for communal cooking, but there are no grocery stores nearby, so bring food. The pavilion doubles as a traveler's library with good lighting, and it's very pleasant to sit there on a rainy night as torrents of water beat on the tin roof. Bicycles are for rent. Ask the managers about hikes up the valley to a picturesque waterfall with swimming in the river, fish feeding, and a tour of a vanilla plantation for a negotiable group price. Transfers are CFP 600 per person round-trip.

US$50-100

Pension Tiare Nui (tel. 66-34-06, www.raiatea.com/tiarenui) has four small bungalows with private bath for rent behind the Europcar office between the airport and Uturoa. It's CFP 5,700/6,250/6,800 single/double/triple, or pay CFP 11,750 double for a bungalow and an unlimited-mileage car. It's a deal worth checking out if you were planning to rent a car anyway, but cooking facilities are not provided. At the airport, ask Europcar.

Bed and Breakfast Bellevue (tel. 66-15-15, www.raiateabellevue-tahiti.com) has five attractive rooms facing a swimming pool at CFP 7,250/7,990 single/double, including breakfast. Each includes a private bath, fridge, and TV, but no cooking facilities. It's on the north side of Uturoa, 700 meters up the hill from the Lycée des Îles Sous-le-Vent. Airport transfers are CFP 1,000 per person.

The **Hôtel Hinano** (tel. 66-13-13, www.hotel-hinano-tahiti.com), conveniently situated on the main street in the center of Uturoa, has 10 basic rooms with baths at CFP 6,500/7,850 single/double (CFP 1,000 extra for one of the four air-conditioned rooms). Cooking facilities are not available.

Pension Tepua (tel. 66-33-00, www.pension-tepua.com) is by the lagoon just beyond a small grocery store, 2.5 kilometers south of Uturoa. Three bungalows with kitchens and TVs are CFP 10,000 single or double in the garden or CFP 13,000 facing the lagoon. There's also a dormitory with 12 beds (CFP 2,500 per person) and three rooms with shared bath at CFP 5,000/7,500 single/double. A supplement of up to CFP 1,000 is charged if you stay only one night, and checkout time is 1000. Meals must be ordered a day in advance, but common cooking facilities are provided, and there's a bar. Bicycles, kayaks, and a washing machine are for rent, and there's sometimes hot water. Boat trips are arranged. Pension Tepua has a swimming pool, but there's no beach and no snorkeling. The lagoon off Pension Tepua is good for windsurfing, and there's surfing off Taoru Island in nearby Teavapiti Pass. ManaSPOT wireless Internet is available. Airport transfers are CFP 1,000 per person round-trip.

Pension Manava (PK 6, Avera, tel. 66-28-26, www.manavapension.com), right next door to Kaoha Nui Ranch, is run by Andrew and Roselyne Brotherson. This warm, sympathetic couple has four Polynesian-style bungalows with cooking facilities, private baths, and fans at CFP 8,500 single or double, depending on the unit (plus CFP 1,000 per additional person or for one-night stays). Two rooms in a separate building are CFP 5,000 single or double with shared kitchen and bath. A half-day boat trip to southern Raiatea is CFP 4,900 per person, and they also do a full-day boat trip right around Taha'a at CFP 7,800, including lunch (six-person minimum)—these trips are also open to nonguests. *Motu* transfers are CFP 1,500 per person (four-person minimum). Bicycles are for rent. Ask Roselyne to show you how she paints Tahitian pareu. Call for a free airport and harbor pickup.

Pension Yolande (PK 10, Avera, tel. 66-35-28) is in an attractive location facing the lagoon. The four rooms are CFP 6,000/8,000 single/double with private baths. Cooking facilities are provided, but you may be asked to take half pension (CFP 3,500 per person). You'll like the family atmosphere.

US$100-150

Pension Opeha (PK 10.5, Avera, tel. 66-19-48, www.pensionopeha.pf) has five new air-conditioned bungalows with kitchens and TVs at CFP 10,000 double, including a good breakfast. This place is beside the lagoon, and although there's no beach, you can swim off a pontoon or paddle a kayak out to a *motu*. There isn't much to see along the road nearby but boat trips (CFP 5,500) are easily arranged. Airport transfers are provided.

Vini Beach Lodge (PK 12, Avera, tel. 60-22-45, www.raiatea.com/vinibeach) is right on Faaroa Bay near the yacht charter base. The seven self-catering duplex bungalows are CFP 10,920/15,850 double garden/lagoon. Weekly and monthly rates are available. A swimming pool and restaurant with a view are by the bay. Airport transfers cost CFP 1,220 return.

On the hillside above the Faaroa Bay yacht charter base is **Pension La Croix du Sud** (PK 12, Avera, tel. 66-27-55). The two rooms with bath are CFP 7,700/8,700 single/double, including breakfast. Cooking facilities are not provided but meals can be ordered. Facilities include a swimming pool and bicycles. Airport transfers are CFP 3,000 per person.

US$250 AND UP

The 28-unit **Hôtel Raiatea Hawaiki Nui** (tel. 60-05-00, www.hawaikinui.pf), just 1.5 kilometers south of Uturoa, is Raiatea's only luxury hotel. From 1998 to 2009 the Hawaiki Nui was part of the Pearl Resorts chain, but it now operates independently. This is the former Raiatea Bali Hai where French Polynesia's very first over-water bungalow was erected in 1968. The layout is attractive, with a small swimming pool overlooking the lagoon. There's no beach, but you can snorkel off the end of the pier or borrow a kayak and paddle out to a *motu*. The rates are CFP 26,000 double for one of the eight garden rooms or eight thatched garden bungalows, CFP 29,000 for one of the three lagoon bungalows, or CFP 33,000 for the six over-water bungalows, plus 14 percent tax. The fan-cooled rooms are beginning to show their age. You can walk into Uturoa for dinner in about 15 minutes. There's a Polynesian dance show at the Hawaiki Nui Fridays at 2000; otherwise, organized activities are minimal. A Europcar desk and Hémisphère Sub dive shop are here.

Food

Brasserie Maraamu (tel. 66-46-64, weekdays 0700–2100, Sat. 1000–1400) is in the corner of the new Gare Maritime facing town. This is a good place to come for an inexpensive coffee, baguette, and butter breakfast. The lunch menu tilts toward Chinese food with ample main plates CFP 1,000–1,800. There's also excellent *poisson cru,* and Hinano is on tap.

Restaurant L'Espadon (tel. 66-30-81, Mon.–Fri. 1000–2200, Sat. 1800–2200), on the side of the Gare Maritime facing the small boat harbor, offers a nice view from its terrace. The menu includes *poisson cru* and other dishes priced CFP 1,400 and up. Ice cream cones are sold from a window facing the harbor. L'Espadon presents live jazz early Friday and Saturday nights.

The trendy **Sea Horse Restaurant** (tel. 66-16-34, Mon.–Sat. 1000–1330 and 1800–2130), on the side of the Gare Maritime facing the cruise ship wharf, serves Chinese dishes at CFP 1,200–1,800 and seafood at CFP 1,500–2,100.

Snack Moemoea (tel. 66-39-84, weekdays 0600–1700, Sat. 0600–1400), on the small boat harbor, serves hamburgers (CFP 800) and a range of French and Chinese dishes on its terrace. Despite the name, it's rather upscale, with meat, fish, or Chinese dishes at CFP 1,500–1,900.

The largest supermarket is **Champion** (tel. 66-45-45, Mon.–Sat. 0730–1830), facing the small boat harbor. Consider getting a whole barbecued chicken and having a picnic. The **Marché Municipal de Uturoa** (Mon.–Sat. all day and Sun. early morning) is in the center of town.

Most of the stores in Uturoa close for lunch 1200–1330, and it's a ghost town after 1030 on Sunday.

Information and Services

In the Gare Maritime opposite the cruise ship wharf is a **tourist office** (tel. 60-07-77, raiatea-info@tahiti-tourisme.pf, Mon.–Fri. 0800–1600).

None of Uturoa's **banks** is open on Saturday, but ATMs accessible 24 hours are outside the Banque Socredo and Banque de Tahiti.

The large modern **post office** (tel. 66-35-50, Mon.–Thurs. 0730–1500, Fri. 0700–1400, Sat. 0800–1000) is opposite the new hospital just north of town, with the **gendarmerie** (tel. 66-31-07) about 50 meters beyond on the left.

For Internet access, there's **ITS Multimédia** (tel. 60-25-25, www.its.pf) in the Gare Maritime.

There are free **public toilets** *(sanitaires publics)* in the Gare Maritime facing the main wharf, not far from the tourist office. They're hard to find, so ask.

One kilometer west of the Sunset Beach Motel is **Raiatea Carenage Services** (tel. 60-05-45, www.raiatea.com/carenage), a repair facility often used by cruising yachts. The only easily accessible slip facilities in French Polynesia are here (maximum 120 tonnes).

Health

Uturoa's public hospital (tel. 60-08-00) is on the north side of town.

Several private doctors have offices above the pharmacy opposite the Catholic church in central Uturoa. Among them are Dr. Alain Repiton-Préneuf and Dr. Bruno Bataillon, general practitioners.

Pharmacie de Raiatea Leroi (tel. 66-34-44, weekdays 0730–1200 and 1330–1730, Sat. 0730–1200, Sun. 0930–1030) is opposite the Catholic church.

Getting There

The **Air Tahiti** office (tel. 60-04-44) is at the airport in a separate building adjacent to the main terminal. Air Tahiti flies from Papeete to Raiatea (CFP 13,000) several times per day. There's a direct connection from Moorea to Raiatea (CFP 13,900) five times a week. Flights from Raiatea to Maupiti (CFP 7,400) operate three times a week.

The **airport** (RFP) is three kilometers northwest of Uturoa. A taxi from the Uturoa market taxi stand to the airport is CFP 1,300 (double tariff late at night). Europcar has a car rental desk inside the terminal.

The Tourist Board information kiosk at the airport is open at flight times only. The airport restaurant offers a good plat du jour at lunchtime.

Otherwise, you can catch the cargo vessels *Taporo VI* and *Hawaiki-Nui* to Papeete on Wednesday and Friday. The *Hawaiki-Nui* office (tel. 66-42-10, weekdays 0800–1100) is at the south end of the main wharf. If it's sold out, ask who is selling tickets for the *Taporo VI.* Book as far ahead as possible.

The yellow and blue *Maupiti Express 2* (tel. 66-37-81, www.maupitiexpress.com), a fast ferry with 140 airline-type seats, charges CFP 4,000/5,000 one-way/round-trip between Raiatea and Bora Bora, departing Uturoa for Bora Bora Monday, Wednesday, Friday, and Sunday afternoons. It's not possible to go directly from Raiatea to Maupiti on this vessel—you must overnight on Bora Bora—although you can buy a through ticket for CFP 5,000/7,000.

The fast ferries *(navettes)* of **Enota Transport Maritime** (tel. 65-61-33) shuttle between Raiatea and Taha'a at CFP 1,000 per person each way (bicycles CFP 600). The fleet consists of two 57-seat ferries, the *Tehaere Maru IV* and *Tehaere Maru V.* A ferry for Taha'a's east coast (Haamene) leaves Uturoa weekdays at 1030 and 1630, departing Haamene for Uturoa at 0630 and 1200. To the west coast (Poutoru, Patio, Tapuamu), the ferry leaves Uturoa weekdays at 1630 and leaves Tapuamu at 0530 and 1030. On Saturdays there's only one trip, leaving Tapuamu at 0545 and leaving Uturoa at 1030. Ask about bus connections to Patio. There's no schedule at all on Sunday and holidays.

The 66-passenger ferry *Tamarii Taha'a I* (tel. 65-65-29) also leaves Uturoa for the west coast of Taha'a (Poutoru, Tiva, Tapuamu, Patio) at 1000 and 1600 weekdays, and at 1000 on Saturdays (CFP 1,000 one-way). The *Tamarii Taha'a II* leaves Uturoa for Haamene at 1000 and 1600 weekdays and at 1000 on Saturdays.

Getting Around

Getting around Raiatea by *le truck* isn't easy. You should be able to use it to get into town in the morning, and the people where you're staying will know at what time you have to be waiting. In Uturoa the *trucks* usually park behind Hôtel Bajoga Hinano, and the drivers themselves are the only reliable source of departure information. In theory they leave Uturoa for Opoa at 1015 and 1515 and for Fetuna at 0930 and 1530 on weekdays only.

Raiatea Location Europcar (tel. 66-34-06, www.europcarpolynesie.com), between the airport and Uturoa, is the main car rental operator on Raiatea. The cars begin around CFP 9,700 per day, including mileage and insurance (minimum age 18). Ask about the package that gives you a bungalow behind the main office and a small car at CFP 11,750 double. Bicycles are CFP 1,800/2,400/3,500 for 4/8/24 hours, which is expensive. Apart from cars and bikes, Raiatea Location rents a four-meter boat with a six-horsepower motor at CFP 7,700/9,800 for four/eight hours. Scooter rentals are generally unavailable.

Moana Rent a Car (tel. 75-08-30, www.moanarentacar.com), near the airport, has cars at CFP 9,200 per day.

Hertz (tel. 66-44-88) is at Raiatea Motors opposite the Hotel de Ville in Uturoa.

Local Tours

Many of the hotels and pensions run circle-island bus tours and boat trips to a *motu* or Taha'a. Whenever a cruise ship is in port all activities will be fully booked. On Sundays, everything is closed.

West Coast Charters (tel. 66-45-39, www.raiatea-tours.com), in the Gare Maritime, offers a full-day boat tour around Taha'a or Raiatea (CFP 9,000 per person, including lunch, minimum six people) and a half-day Faaroa River tour (CFP 5,000 per person, minimum four people).

Raiatea 4x4 (tel. 66-24-16), run by Gérard Duvos, offers safari expeditions to the island's interior at CFP 4,500 per person.

AROUND RAIATEA

It takes the better part of a day to ride a bicycle the 150 kilometers around Raiatea; by car you can take anywhere from a couple of hours to a leisurely day.

The East Coast

The road down the east coast circles fjord-like **Faaroa Bay,** associated with the legends of Polynesian migration. Stardust Marine has a yacht charter base on the north side of the bay, and from the anchorage there's a fine view of Toomaru, the highest peak in the Leeward Islands. Boat trips are offered up the Apoomau River, which drains the Faaroa Valley. It's navigable for about one kilometer, and if you're on a yacht, you could explore it with your dingy. Yellow hibiscus flourishes along the river's banks.

Marae Taputapuatea

Instead of crossing the island from Faaroa Bay, keep left and follow the coast around to a point of land just beyond Opoa, 32 kilometers from Uturoa. Here stands Marae Taputapuatea, one of the largest and best-preserved temples in Polynesia, its mighty *ahu* measuring 43 meters long, 7.3 meters wide, and 2–3 meters high. Before it is a rectangular courtyard paved with black volcanic rocks. A small platform in the middle of the *ahu* once bore the image of

Oro, god of fertility and war (now represented by a reproduction); backrests still mark the seats of high chiefs on the courtyard. Marae Taputapuatea is directly opposite Te Ava Moa Pass, and fires on the *marae* may once have been beacons to ancient navigators.

Several of the temple platforms have been restored. **Hauvivi** was the welcoming *marae,* where guests would have been received as they disembarked from their canoes. They would then have proceeded to Marae Taputapuatea, the main temple, where rituals were performed. Meals were served on **Hiti Tai,** a temple platform on the north side of the complex. **Papa Ofeoro** was the place of sacrifice (about 5,000 skulls were discovered during excavations at the site). **Opu Teina** near the beach was the temple platform where visitors would say their farewells. Departing chiefs would often take a stone from this *marae* to be planted in new *marae* elsewhere, which would also receive the name Marae Taputapuatea.

In 1995 a fleet of traditional Polynesian voyaging canoes, including three from Hawaii and two each from Cook Islands and Tahiti, plus an Easter Island raft, gathered at Taputapuatea to lift a 650-year-old curse and rededicate the *marae.* The seven canoes then left for the Marquesas, navigating by the stars and swells. Some carried on to Hawaii and the west coast of the United States in an amazing demonstration of the current revival of this aspect of traditional culture. In April 2000 a tattoo festival took place at Marae Taputapuatea. During important events, fire-walking is practiced at a site across the road from the main temples.

ACCOMMODATIONS

Pension Te Maeva (PK 23.5 East, tel. 66-37-28, www.temaeva.com), toward Opoa, has two self-catering bungalows on the hillside at CFP 7,800/8,800 single/double, including breakfast. There's a swimming pool and free bicycles. Airport transfers are CFP 5,000.

The **Hôtel Atiapiti** (PK 31 East, Opoa, tel. 66-16-65, www.atiapiti.com), on the beach just south of Marae Taputapuatea, has six self-catering beach bungalows and one garden bungalow from CFP 14,500 double, plus CFP 2,500 per additional person up to five. Half board is CFP 4,000 per person, or you can order à la carte in the hotel's own restaurant (they have lobster!). The managers organize excursions to a *motu* and around the island, and there's great snorkeling off their wharf. The view of Huahine from here is excellent. The hotel's biggest drawback (or advantage) is its isolation, but someone will pick you up at the port or airport if you call ahead (CFP 3,900 per person round-trip). It's good for a couple of days of relaxation.

In June 2009 the **Opoa Beach Hôtel** (PK 37 East, Opoa, tel. 60-05-10, www.opoabeach.com) opened six kilometers down the coast from Hôtel Atiapiti. The nine luxury bungalows with minibars and TVs start at CFP 22,000 single or double, plus 14 percent tax. Add CFP 7,500 for half board (the food is excellent). Canoes, kayaks, and snorkeling gear are loaned free. The beach is artificial, but there's a swimming pool. Airport transfers with a guided tour en route are CFP 4,500 per person return. There's no shuttle into town, but the friendly owners will take you along if they have to go to the airport and there's space in the minibus.

The West Coast

The only places to buy food in the southern part of Raiatea are the two Chinese grocery stores at **Fetuna** and at **Vaiaau,** on the west side of Raiatea. Vaiaau Bay marks the end of the protected inner channel from Uturoa around Raiatea clockwise, and yachts must exit the lagoon through Toamaro Pass in order to continue northward. At Rautoanui Pass sailboats can come back in behind the barrier reef to continue the circumnavigation, with the possibility of a side trip south to Tevaitoa.

Behind Tevaitoa church is **Marae Tainuu,** dedicated to the ancient god Taaroa. Petroglyphs on a broken stone by the road at the entrance to the church show a turtle and some other indistinguishable figure. At Tevaitoa Chief Teraupo and his people fought their last battles against the French invaders in early 1897.

The territory's largest yacht charter base is the **Marina Apooiti,** which opened in 1982 one kilometer west of the airport. Aside from The Moorings and Tahiti Yacht Charter, there's a large restaurant-bar here and a dive shop. ManaSPOT wireless Internet access is available at the Tahiti Yacht Charter office.

ACCOMMODATIONS

Chambres d'Hôtes Temehani (PK11.3, Tevaitoa, tel. 66-12-88, www.vacances-tahiti.com) rents three rooms with shared bath in a colonial-style bungalow from CFP 9,000 double. Dinner is CFP 2,800.

The **Raiatea Lodge Hôtel** (PK 9.8, Pufau, tel. 60-01-00, www.raiateahotel.com), formerly known as Hôtel Miri Miri and Hôtel Tenape before that, opened on the west coast in 1999. The 15 air-conditioned rooms in this long, two-story colonial-style building start at CFP 13,560/16,950 single/double, plus 14 percent in taxes and service charges (two-night minimum stay). The rectangular swimming pool substitutes for a beach. You'll have to patronize the pleasant restaurant-bar as no alternatives are nearby (late-night parties are common, so ask for a room well away from the bar).

Laura Lodge (PK 8.5, Tumaraa, tel. 66-15-57, www.lauralodgeraiatea.com), facing Miri Miri Pass, rents one fully-equipped self-catering beach bungalow at CFP 12,000 single or double (CFP 14,000 for one night). There's a swimming pool.

The friendly **Sunset Beach Motel** (Apooiti, tel. 66-33-47, www.sunset-raiatea.pf) is in a coconut grove five kilometers west of Uturoa. It's on the point across the bay from Marina Apooiti, about 2.5 kilometers west of the airport. The 22 comfortable, well-spaced bungalows with cooking facilities and private baths (with hot water) are CFP 11,000/12,000/13,000/14,000 single/double/triple/quad—good value for families (children under age 13 are CFP 500 each, under age three free). Camping is CFP 1,100 per person, and there's a large communal kitchen. Discounts of 10 percent per fortnight and 20 percent per month are available, but there's a CFP 1,000 surcharge if you stay only one night. Bicycles and pedal boats are for rent, and hitching into Uturoa is easy. It's one of the nicest places to stay in the islands, and the managers speak English. Call for free airport transfers.

Taha'a

Raiatea's 90-square-kilometer lagoon mate, Taha'a, is shaped like a hibiscus flower with four long bays cutting into its rugged south side. Mount Ohiri (590 meters), the highest point on the island, got its name from Hiro, god of thieves, who was born here. Taha'a is known as the "vanilla island" for its plantations that produce 70 percent of the territory's "black gold." The Taha'a Festival in late October includes stone fishing, with a line of people in canoes herding the fish into a cove by beating stones on the surface of the lagoon. In November the Hawaiki Nui Outrigger Canoe Race passes Taha'a on its way from Huahine to Bora Bora.

It's a quiet island, with little traffic and few tourists. Most families use speedboats to commute to their gardens on the reef islets or to fishing spots, or to zip over to Raiatea on shopping trips, so they don't really need cars. Beaches are scarce on the main island, but the string of *motu* off the northeast side of Taha'a has fine white-sand beaches. The pension owners and tour operators arrange picnics on a few of these, and pearl farms have been established on some. This is the only Society Island you can sail a yacht or cruise ship right around inside the barrier reef, and the many anchorages and central location between Raiatea, Huahine, and Bora Bora make Taha'a a favorite of both cruisers and charterers.

There aren't many specific attractions on

Taha'a, and a dearth of inexpensive places to stay and lack of public transportation has kept this island off the beaten track. The easy way to visit Taha'a is still an all-day outrigger canoe tour from Raiatea. This could change, but meanwhile the isolation has made the 5,000 Taha'a islanders rather wary of outsiders.

Orientation

The administrative center is at Patio (or Iripau) on the north coast, where the post office and *mairie* share a compound. A second post office and the gendarmerie (tel. 60-81-05) are at Haamene, where four roads meet. The ship from Papeete ties up to a wharf at Tapuamu, and there's a large covered area at the terminal where you could spread a sleeping bag in a pinch.

The 67-kilometer coral road around the main part of the island passes six of the eight villages; the other two are south of Haamene. A scenic road goes over the 141-meter Col Taira between Haamene and Tiva. There are ferries from Raiatea to Tapuamu and Haamene but no regular public transportation.

VANILLA

Vanilla, a vine belonging to the orchid family, is grown on small family plantations. Brought to Tahiti from Manila in 1848, the aromatic *Vanilla tahitiensis* type, which has a worldwide reputation, originated from a mutation of *Vanilla fragrans*. The plants must be hand-pollinated, then harvested between April and June. The pods are then put out to dry for a couple of months – an exceptionally time-consuming process. Vanilla is used in cooking, perfumes, and cosmetics. It's one of the world's most expensive spices, and most of the vanilla currently used in the United States and Japan is actually synthetic. Between 1915 and 1933 Tahiti produced 50-150 tonnes of real vanilla per year, peaking in 1949 at 200 tonnes. Production remained high until 1966, when a steady decline began because the producers were leaving for paid employment in Papeete related to nuclear testing. By 1990 production had fallen to only 39 tonnes, and in 2008 just nine tonnes were exported, two-thirds of it to Europe.

SIGHTS

Several pearl and vanilla farms around the island can be visited. The mountain pass between Haamene and Tiva offers excellent views of Hurepiti and Haamene Bays, two of the four deep fjords cutting into the southern side of the island. You could also follow the rough track from Haamene up to the Col Vaitoetoe for an even better view. This track continues north, coming out near the hospital in Patio.

Rarahu, the girl immortalized in Pierre Loti's 1880 novel *The Marriage of Loti,* is buried near Vaitoare village at the south end of Taha'a, east of the Taha'a Marina Resort.

RECREATION

Taha'a Blue Nui Dive Center (tel. 65-67-78, www.bluenui.com) is based at Le Taha'a Private Island and Spa.

Taha'a Diving (tel. 65-78-37, www.tahaa-diving.com) on Haamene Bay visits more than 20 diving spots around Raiatea and Taha'a islands.

ACCOMMODATIONS

US$50-100

The least expensive place to stay is **Pension Chez Pascal** (tel. 65-60-42). From the Tapuamu ferry wharf you'll see a small bridge at the head of the bay. Turn left as you leave the dock and head for this. Chez Pascal is the first house north of the bridge on the inland side. The rate for the four bungalows and two rooms is CFP 5,000 per person for bed, breakfast, and dinner, or CFP 3,000 per person with breakfast only. Boat trips to a *motu* and the loan of the family bicycle are possible.

Pension Vaihi (tel. 65-62-02) on Hurepiti Bay has three *fare* at CFP 6,000/8,000/10,000 single/double/triple. Breakfast and dinner are CFP 3,700 per person.

Pension Api (tel. 65-69-88, jjwatlp@mail.pf), just east of the south tip of Taha'a, has two thatched bungalows in a garden setting at CFP 8,000 single or double, plus CFP 4,000 per person for breakfast and dinner.

US$100-150

Hôtel L'Hibiscus (tel. 65-61-06, www.hibiscustahaa.com) on the northeast side of Haamene Bay gets mixed reviews. The seven bungalows are CFP 10,556 single or double, plus CFP 4,900/7,000 per person for half/full board. Cooking facilities and common drinking water are not supplied (bring bottled water). Frankly, L'Hibiscus can be unpleasant at times and it is not recommended.

US$150-250

Pension Au Phil de Temps (tel. 65-64-19, www.pension-au-phil-du-temps.com) at Tapuamu has two *fare* at CFP 13,000/17,500 single/double with half board. The private bathrooms are in a separate block. Bicycles and canoes are loaned free. The sunsets over Bora Bora can be superb.

Le Passage (tel. 65-66-75, www.hotel-tahaa.com) faces the lagoon at Faaaha, 10 kilometers east of Haamene. The three small air-conditioned bungalows on the hillside are CFP 18,000 per person including breakfast, dinner, and an island tour. Le Passage is on a vanilla and pineapple plantation featuring an ancient lava flow and fine lagoon views. There's a miniature swimming pool and pontoon. Car rentals, boat trips, and scuba diving can be arranged. Direct boat transfers from Raiatea Airport are CFP 8,000 per person round-trip.

US$250 and Up

In 2002 the overtly luxurious **Le Taha'a Private Island and Spa** (tel. 60-84-00, www.letahaa.com) opened on Motu Tautau opposite the shipping wharf at Tapuamu. It's part of the Relais and Châteaux chain and overpriced for what you get. The 12 beach villas with private swimming pools start at CFP 115,000 double, while the 48 thatched over-water suites are from CFP 125,000, plus 14 percent tax. The two royal beach suites are CFP 290,000. Full board (and poor service) is another CFP 14,300 per person. Bring bottled water to drink in your room as prices here are exorbitant. Le Taha'a even charges extra if you use the coffeemaker in your room! The resort's Manea Spa is open 1500–1930. Le Taha'a looks lovely at first, but the snorkeling is nonexistent, and a couple of nights here would be enough. Scuba diving is with Taha'a Blue Nui. Verify the cost of boat or helicopter transfers beforehand as they vary (nothing about this place is cheap).

Hôtel La Pirogue (tel. 60-81-45, www.hotel-la-pirogue.com) is on Motu Porou off Hipu village in northwestern Taha'a. The eight simple open bungalows are priced CFP 26,000 double in the garden or CFP 30,000 on the beach (plus 14 percent tax). Half board is CFP 7,500 per person extra, and the food is very good. Canoes, kayaks, and snorkeling gear are free. Airport transfers are CFP 7,000 per person. Unlike Le Taha'a, which gets mostly Americans, most of the guests at La Pirogue are French.

Vahine Island Resort (tel. 65-67-38, www.vahine-island.com), on Motu Tuuvahine off the northeast side of the island, has six seafront bungalows from CFP 52,000 single or double, plus three over-water units at CFP 65,000, plus 14 percent tax. Half board is CFP 9,900 per person. For airport transfers you'll pay CFP 8,000 per person round-trip. Outrigger canoes, kayaks, windsurfing, snorkeling, and fishing gear are lent for free, and moorings are provided for yachts.

Fare Pea Iti (tel. 60-81-11, www.farepeaiti.pf) at Patio has three tastefully-decorated thatched bungalows at CFP 30,000/36,000 single/double. Add CFP 7,400 per person for a fancy breakfast and dinner. A long wharf stretches out from their white sand beach. There's a swimming pool and fitness room. Boat trips (CFP 6,400), island tours (CFP 5,500), and car rentals are easily arranged. Although there isn't much to see around Fare Pea Iti, at least you're not trapped, as you are on a *motu*. ManaSPOT wireless Internet is available here. Transfers from Raiatea Airport are CFP 8,400 per person.

Tiare Breeze (tel. 65-62-26, www.tiare

breeze.com) on Haamene Bay has one luxury self-catering bungalow on the hillside at CFP 35,000, including breakfast. An over-water pontoon pavilion, bicycles, and snorkeling gear are included.

OTHER PRACTICALITIES

Food

Village stores are at Tapuamu, Tiva, Haamene, and Patio. Grocery trucks circle the island daily except Sunday, and any resident will know when to watch for them. Most of the accommodations serve meals, and several other small places to eat are at Haamene. **Snack Mac China 99** (tel. 65-67-81, Mon.–Sat. 0700–2000), opposite the post office in Haamene, has Chinese seafood and poultry dishes. **Restaurant Taha'a Maitai** (tel. 65-70-85, CFP 1,500–3,000) is more upscale, with French cuisine served on an open terrace on Haamene Bay. They bake their own pastries.

Services

Post offices are found at Patio (tel. 65-64-70) and Haamene (tel. 65-60-11). The Banque Socredo (tel. 60-80-10) is at Patio, while the Banque de Tahiti (tel. 65-63-14) is at Haamene. There's a medical center (tel. 65-63-31) at Haamene. Dr. Régis Rouveyrol (tel. 65-60-60) is at Haamene.

GETTING THERE

There's no airport on Taha'a. Large ships and ferries call at Tapuamu Wharf on the west side of Taha'a just behind the Total service station. There's a telephone booth on the wharf that you can use to call your hotel to have someone pick you up.

The *Taporo VI* departs Taha'a for Raiatea, Huahine, and Papeete Wednesday and Friday at 1100. The *Hawaiki-Nui* (tel. 65-61-59) visits Taha'a southbound Wednesday and Friday at 1430. Try to buy you ticket well in advance.

The high-speed ferry *Maupiti Express 2* (www.maupitiexpress.com) leaves Taha'a for Bora Bora Monday, Wednesday, Friday, and Sunday afternoons (CFP 4,000/5,000 one-way/round-trip).

Enota Transport (tel. 65-61-33) fast ferries leave Taha'a for Raiatea weekdays at 0515 and 1030 from Tapuamu, and at 0630 and 1200 from Haamene. On Saturdays there's only one departure, at 0545 from Tapuamu (CFP 1,000 per person each way, bicycles CFP 600). The *Tamarii Taha'a I* (tel. 65-65-29) leaves Patio for Raiatea at 0514 and 1125 weekdays and 0515 on Saturday with stops at Tapuamu, Tiva, and Poutoru (CFP 1,000 one-way). The *Tamarii Taha'a II* leaves Haamene for Raiatea weekdays at 0520 and 1020, Saturdays at 0520.

GETTING AROUND

Trucks on Taha'a are for transporting schoolchildren only, so you may have to hitch to get around. It's not that hard to hitch a ride down the west coast from Patio to Haamene, but there's little traffic along the east coast.

Rental cars are available from **Monique Location** (tel. 65-62-48) at Haamene, **Taha'a Location Voitures** (tel. 65-66-75) at Résidence Le Passage east of Haamene, and **Taha'a Car Services** (tel. 65-68-99). It's smart to book ahead if you want to be sure of a car.

LOCAL TOURS

Several companies offer full-day outrigger canoe trips right around Taha'a at CFP 10,000 per person, such as **l'excursion bleue** (tel. 66-10-90, www.tahaa.net). Lunch, snorkeling, a visit to a pearl farm and vanilla plantation, and transfers on Raiatea are included. Bruno Fabre of l'excursion bleue takes his guests to the best snorkeling spots around Taha'a, not just the convenient but less spectacular "coral gardens" off eastern Taha'a, which the quickie tours from Raiatea prefer to visit. He doesn't cater to large groups or cruise ships and may be available when all of the other activities operators are booked out.

Vanilla Tours (tel. 65-62-46, vanilla.tours@mail.pf) has a half-day, ethnobotanical tour by four-wheel drive that departs at 0800 whenever four people have booked (CFP 5,500 per person without lunch). Alain is very knowledgeable about the island's botany and speaks good English.

Bora Bora

Bora Bora, 260 kilometers northwest of Papeete, is everyone's idea of a South Pacific island. Dramatic basalt peaks soar 700 meters above a gorgeous multicolored lagoon. Slopes and valleys blossom with hibiscus. Some of the most perfect beaches you'll ever see are here, replete with topless sunbathers. Not only are the beaches good, but there's also plenty to see and do. The local population of 9,000 lives in three villages, Anau, Faanui, and Vaitape. Many are skilled dancers. To see them practicing in the evening, follow the beat of village drums back to their source. Tourism is the main business here: Resorts ring the island, and Jet Skis churn the lagoon.

The Landscape

Seven-million-year-old Bora Bora (29 square kilometers) is made up of a 10-kilometer-long main island, a few smaller high islands in the lagoon, and a long ring of *motu* on the barrier reef. Pofai Bay marks the center of the island's collapsed crater with Toopua and Toopuaiti as its eroded west wall. Mount Pahia's gray basalt mass rises 649 meters behind Vaitape, and above it soar the sheer cliffs of Otemanu's mighty volcanic plug (727 meters). The wide-angle scenery of the main island is complemented by the surrounding coral reef and numerous *motu,* one of which bears the airport. Motu Tapu of the travel brochures was featured in F. W. Murnau's classic 1931 silent movie *Tabu,* about two young lovers who escape to this tiny island. Te Ava Nui Pass is the only entry through the barrier reef.

History

The sound "b" doesn't exist in Tahitian, so Bora Bora is actually Pora Pora, meaning "first born," since this was the first island created after Raiatea. The island's traditional name, Vava'u, suggests Tongan voyagers may have reached here centuries ago. It's believed Bora Bora has been inhabited since the year 900, and 42 *marae* ruins can still be found around the island. The Bora Borans of yesteryear were indomitable warriors who often raided Maupiti, Taha'a, and Raiatea.

"Discovered" by Roggeveen in 1722, Bora Bora was visited by Captain James Cook in 1769 and 1777. The first European to live on the island was James O'Connor, a survivor of the British whaler *Matilda,* wrecked at Moruroa atoll in 1793. O'Connor made his way to Tahiti, where he married into the Pomare family and eventually ended up living in a little grass shack on "Matilda Point," later corrupted to Matira Point. In 1895 the island was annexed by France.

In February 1942 the Americans hastily set up a refueling and regrouping base, code-named "Bobcat," on the island to serve shipping between the U.S. West Coast or Panama Canal and Australia and New Zealand. You can still see remains from this time, including eight huge naval guns placed here to defend the island against a surprise Japanese attack that never materialized. The big lagoon with only

STONE FISHING

This traditional method of fishing is now practiced only on very special occasions in the Leeward Islands. Coconut fronds are tied end to end until a line a half kilometer long is ready. Several dozen outrigger canoes form a semicircle. Advancing slowly together, men in the canoes beat the water with stones tied to ropes. The frightened fish are driven toward a beach. When the water is shallow enough, the men leap from their canoes, push the leaf vine before them, yell, and beat the water with their hands. In this way the fish are literally forced ashore into an open bamboo fence, where they are caught. A famous scene in the Marlon Brando version of *Mutiny on the Bounty* depicts stone fishing at Bora Bora.

one pass offered secure anchorage for as many as 100 U.S. Navy transports at a time. The Americans built Farepiti Wharf, and a cable was stretched across Faanui Bay. Ships would hock onto the cable instead of dropping anchor. A road was built around the island, and by April 1943 the present airfield on Motu Mute had been constructed. The 4,400 American army troops also left behind 130 half-caste babies, 40 percent of whom died of starvation when the base closed in June 1946 and the abandoned infants were forced to switch from their accustomed American baby formulas to island food. The survivors are now approaching retirement age. Novelist James A. Michener, a young naval officer at the time, left perhaps the most enduring legacy by modeling his Bali Hai on this "enchanted island," Bora Bora.

Orientation

You can arrive at Motu Mute airport and be carried to Vaitape Wharf by catamaran, or disembark from a ship at Farepiti Wharf, three kilometers north of Vaitape. Most of the stores,

© TAHITI TOURISME

Tombstone-shaped Mount Otemanu is Bora Bora's highest peak.

banks, and offices are near Vaitape Wharf (and free public toilets are provided in the souvenir shop on the wharf itself). The finest beaches are at Matira Point at the island's southern tip.

SIGHTS

Vaitape

Behind the Banque de Tahiti at Vaitape Wharf is the **monument to Alain Gerbault,** who sailed his yacht, the *Firecrest,* solo around the world 1923–1929—the first Frenchman to do so. Gerbault's first visit to Bora Bora was in 1926. He returned to Polynesia in 1933 and stayed until 1940. A supporter of the Pétain regime in France, he left Bora Bora when the colony declared its support for General de Gaulle, and died at Timor a year later while trying to return to Vichy France.

To get an idea of how the Bora Borans live, take a stroll through Vaitape village; go up the road that begins just south of the Protestant church.

Southern Bora Bora

The largely paved and level 32-kilometer road around the island makes it easy to see Bora Bora by rented bicycle. At the head of **Pofai Bay** notice the odd assortment of looted war wreckage across the road from Alain et Linda Galerie d'Art. Surrounded by a barbed wire fence are a seven-inch American gun dragged here from Tereia Point in 1982 as well as two huge anchors. The locations of seven other MK II naval guns that have thus far escaped desecration are given below.

Stop at **Bloody Mary's Restaurant** to scan the goofy displays outside the gate, but more importantly to get the classic view of the island's soaring peaks across Pofai Bay as it appears in countless brochures. For an even better view, go inland on the unmarked road that begins at a double electricity pole 100 meters north of Bloody Mary's. This leads to a jeep route with two concrete tracks up the 139-meter-high hill to a **radio tower,** a 10-minute hike. From the tower you get a superb view of the south end of the island.

The finest beach on the island stretches east from Hôtel Bora Bora to Matira Point. Some of the best **snorkeling,** with a varied multitude of colorful tropical fish, is off the small point at Hôtel Bora Bora. Enter from east of the hotel grounds (such as via the Bora Diving Center or the beach beyond) and let the current pull you toward the hotel jetty, as the hotel staff doesn't appreciate strangers who use their property to access the beach. From the way they approach you, the small fish are quite obviously accustomed to being fed here. Stay on the east side of the point, away from the over-water bungalows. For a more natural scene you could also snorkel due south to the northern edge of the barrier reef. Just beware of getting run over by a boat.

Two **naval guns** sit on the ridge above Hôtel Matira's restaurant, accessible via a trail along the eastern side of some bungalows.

Bora Bora's most popular public beach is **Matira Beach Park** in front of the huge open thatched pavilion directly across the street from the InterContinental Le Moana Resort on Matira Point. Don't leave valuables unattended here. At low tide you can wade from the end of **Matira Point** right out to the reef. These same shallows prevent yachts from sailing around the island inside the barrier reef. Northwest of the point is **Motu Piti uu Uta** with the Private Island component of the Sofitel Bora Bora Marara Beach and Private Island and more great snorkeling (if you swim over, don't enter the Private Island grounds, as you won't be welcome).

Proceed north to the **Sofitel Bora Bora Marara Beach,** a good place for a sightseeing stop. The road climbs over a hill to avoid the former Club Med. The two general stores at **Anau** can supply a cold drink or a snack.

Northern Bora Bora

On the north side of Vairou Bay the road begins to ascend a ridge. Halfway up the slope, look down to the right and by the shore you'll see the *ahu* of **Marae Aehautai,** the most intact of the three *marae* in this area. From the *marae* there's a stupendous view of Otemanu, and you should be able to pick out Te Ana Opea cave far up on the side of the mountain. To visit the two American **seven-inch guns** on Fitiiu Point, follow the rough jeep track to the right at the top of the ridge a few hundred meters east (on foot) to a huge black rock from which you can see the guns. The steep unpaved road on the other side of this ridge can be dangerous on a bicycle, so slow down or get off and walk. There's a municipal dump in this area, and you might catch the stench of burning garbage.

Just before Taihi Point at the north end of the main island is **Musée de la Marine** (tel. 67-75-24, donations accepted) on the right, which is usually closed. Just beyond Taihi Point you'll notice a concrete trestle running right up the side of the hill from the ruins of a group of platforms meant to be the over-water bungalows. This is all that remains of an undercapitalized **Hyatt Regency hotel** project that went broke in the early 1980s. Actor Jack Nicholson is reputed to be among the owners of the over-water condominiums nearby.

One American **naval gun** remains on the hillside above the rectangular concrete water tank with a transformer pole alongside at Tereia Point. The housing of a second gun, vandalized in 1982, is nearby. The remains of several American concrete wharves can be seen along the north shore of **Faanui Bay.** Most of the American wartime occupation force was billeted around here, and a few Quonset huts linger in the bush. Just beyond the small boat harbor (a former American submarine base) is **Marae Fare Opu,** notable for the petroglyphs of turtles carved into the stones of the *ahu.* Turtles, a favorite food of the gods, were often offered to them on the *marae.* (Guides sometimes highlight the turtles in chalk for the benefit of tourist cameras, unaware of how disrespectful it is.)

Western Bora Bora

Between Faanui and Farepiti Wharf, just east of the Brasserie de Tahiti depot and the electricity-generating plant, is **Marae Taianapa;** its long *ahu,* restored in 1963, is visible on the hillside from the road. The most important *marae* on Bora Bora was **Marae Marotetini,** on the point near Farepiti Wharf—west of the wharf and accessible along the shore at low tide. The great stone *ahu,* 25 meters long and up to 1.5 meters high, was restored by Professor Yosihiko Sinoto in 1968 and can be seen from approaching ships.

The last two **American guns** are a 10-minute scramble up the ridge from the main road between Farepiti Wharf and Vaitape. Go straight up the concrete road a bit before you reach Otemanu Tours (where you see several *trucks* parked). At the end of the ridge there's a good view of Te Ava Nui Pass, which the guns were meant to defend, and Maupiti is farther out on the horizon. This is private property so ask permission to proceed from anyone you meet.

FRENCH POLYNESIA ON THE SILVER SCREEN

Since the days of silent movies, Hollywood has shared the fascination with Polynesia felt by poets and novelists. In fact, many of the best films about the region are based on books by Charles Nordhoff, James Norman Hall, Somerset Maugham, and James A. Michener. And like the printed works, most of the films are about Europeans in the islands rather than the islanders themselves. The clash between the simplicity of paradise and the complexity of civilization is a recurrent theme.

In 1932 Robert Flaherty teamed up with F. W. Murnau to create one of the classics of the silent movie era, *Tabu,* the story of two lovers who flee to a tiny island on Bora Bora's barrier reef. Also in 1932, Douglas Fairbanks Sr. and Maria Alba traveled to the Society Islands by private yacht for the filming of *Mr. Robinson Crusoe.*

Three generations of filmmakers have used the *Bounty* saga popularized by American novelists Charles Nordhoff and James Norman Hall as their way of presenting paradise. In 1935 Frank Lloyd's *Mutiny on the Bounty* won the Oscar for Best Picture, with Charles Laughton starring as the cruel Captain Bligh and Clark Gable as gallant Fletcher Christian. Lloyd portrayed the affair as a simplistic struggle between good and evil, but the two subsequent remakes were more historically accurate.

The extravagant MGM production of *Mutiny on the Bounty* (1962) starring Trevor Howard as Captain Bligh and Marlon Brando as Fletcher Christian is well remembered in Tahiti because of Brando's ongoing ownership of Tetiaroa atoll. Unlike the 1935 *Bounty* movie filmed on Catalina Island in California, MGM captured the glorious color of Tahiti and Bora Bora in what may be the most spectacular movie ever made in the South Pacific. The salaries paid to the 6,000 extras used in the film had a real economic impact on Tahiti at the time.

The Bounty (1984), with Sir Anthony Hopkins as a purposeful Bligh and Mel Gibson portraying an ambiguous Christian, comes closer to reality than the other two *Bounty* films, and the views of Moorea are stunning.

The theme of the despot is picked up by director John Ford, who adapted Nordhoff and Hall's story of a young couple fleeing the haughty governor of tropical Manikoora in *The Hurricane* (1937). Surprisingly, this black-and-white movie remains an audiovisual feast, and the climactic storm is not soon to be forgotten. Dorothy Lamour stars in Ford's film. In 1978 Dino de Laurentiis remade *Hurricane* on Bora Bora with Mia Farrow and Trevor Howard in the starring roles.

The Moon and Sixpence, Albert Lewin's 1943 film version of Somerset Maugham's novel about the life of Paul Gauguin in Polynesia, appeals to the mind as much as to the senses. It's the dissonance between the main character's private mission and his social obligations that gives this movie depth.

In 2009 Universal Studios released *Couples Retreat,* which follows four couples vacationing on a tropical isle (Bora Bora). Three of the couples are at the resort to play while the fourth is trying to work out marital problems. They soon discover that participation in the resort's couples therapy is not optional.

Videos and DVDs of all of these films can be ordered through www.southpacific.org/films.html.

ENTERTAINMENT AND EVENTS

Disco

Le Récife Bar (tel. 67-76-83, Fri.–Sat. from 2230), between Vaitape and Farepiti Wharf, is Bora Bora's after-hours club. Disco dancing continues almost until dawn, but expect loud, heavy-on-the-beat music with few patrons. Steer clear of the local drunks hanging around outside.

Otherwise, the evening activity on Bora Bora is geared toward honeymooners and romance-focused couples. Singles looking for some fun or an authentic island scene could leave a little disappointed.

Cultural Shows for Visitors

Tahitian dancing occurs after dinner Tuesday and Saturday nights at 2000 at the **InterContinental Le Moana Resort** (tel. 60-49-00). You can watch it for the price of a drink. **Hôtel Le Maitai Polynesia** (tel. 60-30-00) has Tahitian dancing in the restaurant Wednesday at 2000. Here too it's possible to watch the show from the bar for the price of a drink. Another Tahitian dance show takes place at the **Sofitel Bora Bora Marara Beach Resort** (tel. 60-55-00) every Saturday night. Unless you're taking the pricey buffet, you may have to pay a cover charge (which includes one drink) to see the show here.

Of the offshore island resorts, the **Bora Bora Pearl Beach Resort and Spa** (tel. 60-52-00) and the **InterContinental Bora Bora Resort and Thalasso Spa** (tel. 60-76-00) both have shows Monday and Friday nights. The **Bora Bora Lagoon Resort** (tel. 60-40-00) and the **Hilton Bora Bora Nui Resort and Spa** (tel. 60-33-00) have shows on Tuesday nights. The **Hôtel Le Méridien Bora Bora** (tel. 60-51-51) has their show Tuesday and Friday at 2115.

Events

The **Festivites du Heiva,** or "Fêtes de Juillet," are celebrated at Bora Bora with special fervor during the first two weeks of July. During the day there are canoe races by sail and paddle, javelin throwing, coconut husking, and other sports (football, Ping-Pong, *pétanque,* basketball, foot races, volleyball, tennis, etc.). The Maohi Triathlon involves a canoe race, fruit carrying, and coconut milk preparation. One evening is devoted to a floral carriage contest, and traditional singing and dancing competitions run for 10 nights from 2000 until 0300. Try to participate in the marathon to prove that all tourists aren't lazy, but don't take the prizes away from the locals. If you win, be sure to give the money back to them for partying. You'll make good friends that way and have more fun dancing in the evening. The stands are beautiful because the top decorations win prizes too.

SHOPPING

Plenty of small boutiques around Vaitape sell black coral jewelry, pearls, pareu, T-shirts, designer beachwear, etc. The **Centre Artisanal** near Vaitape Wharf is a good place to buy a shell necklace or a pareu directly from the locals. **Tahia Collins** (tel. 60-37-00, www.tahiacollins.com) has a pearl shop near the wharf in Vaitape.

A cluster of shops on Pofai Bay offers some of Bora Bora's best tourist shopping. **Boutique Gauguin** (tel. 67-76-67) has tropical clothing, T-shirts, souvenirs, and jewelry.

Near Boutique Gauguin is the gallery of neoimpressionist Basque painter and sculptor **Garrick Yrondi** (tel. 60-57-15, www.yrondi.pf), who has spent most of his life in French Polynesia. These shops surround a small garden called *Le Jardin Gauguin,* with a series of tacky plaster sculptures depicting scenes from Gauguin's paintings.

A little south on Pofai Bay is **Tahiti Pearl Market** (tel. 60-38-60, www.tahitipearlmarket.com, daily 0900–1730) with black pearls on display. A full pearl necklace will cost US$9,000–15,000—the gift of a lifetime.

Matira Pearls (tel. 67-79-14, www.matirapearls.com), between the InterContinental Le Moana Resort and Hôtel Le Maitai Polynesia, has island fashions as well as black pearls.

The Farm (tel. 70-06-75, www.borapearl.com), just north of Hôtel Bora Bora, specializes in top quality black pearl products, with some of the jewelry made on the premises. Books and postcards by photographer Erwin Christian (www.tahitibooks.com) are also available.

SPORTS AND RECREATION

Scuba Diving

The **Bora Diving Center** (tel. 67-71-84, www.boradiving.com), just east of Hôtel Bora Bora, offers scuba diving daily at CFP 8,000/14,500 for one/two tanks, CFP 40,000 for a six-dive package, or CFP 9,500 for night dives. Ten different sites are visited (those around Toopua Island are recommended for snorkelers). Hotel pickups are available to divers who have booked ahead. The **Nemo World Diving Center** (tel. 67-77-85), by the road near the Sofitel Bora Bora Marara Beach, is part of the same company and charges the same rates.

Bathys Diving (tel. 60-50-50, www.bathys-diving.com), formerly TOPdive, just north of Vaitape, is the best-positioned operation for dives outside the reef where the visibility is better and the schools of fish (especially sharks) are larger. It charges CFP 8,500 for one tank or CFP 70,000 for 10 tanks, with free pickups.

The Pearl Beach, InterContinental, and other island resorts have specialized dive shops of their own. Since it's a long way around to the single pass, most scuba diving from the resorts on the east side of the island is within the lagoon, and visibility is limited January–April.

THE LEEWARD ISLANDS

Mountain Climbing

If you're experienced and determined, it's possible to climb **Mount Pahia** in about four hours of rough going. Take the road inland just south of the Protestant church in Vaitape and go up the depression past a series of mango trees, veering slightly left. Circle the cliffs near the top on the left side, and come up the back of Snoopy's head and along his toes. (These directions will take on meaning when you study Pahia from the end of Vaitape's wharf.) The trail is not maintained, and a local guide would be a big help. Avoid rainy weather, when the way will be muddy and slippery. **Otemanu Tours** (tel. 67-70-49) and some other tour operators can organize an all-day Mount Pahia hiking tour in the dry season.

Despite what some tourist publications claim, slab-sided **Otemanu,** the high rectangular peak next to pointed Pahia, has *never* been climbed. It's possible to climb up to the shoulders of the mountain, but the sheer cliffs of the main peak are inaccessible because clamps pull right out of the vertical, crumbly cliff face. Helicopters can land on the summit, but that doesn't count. Otemanu's name means "it's a bird."

Day Cruises

Bora Bora is famous for its lagoon trips. Prices vary depending on whether lunch is included, the length of the trip, the luxury of the boat, and so on, so check around. A seafood picnic lunch on a *motu,* reef walking, and snorkeling gear are usually included, and you get a chance to see giant clams, manta rays, and shark feeding. For the latter you don a mask and snorkel, jump into the shark-infested waters, and grasp a line as your guide shoves chunks of fish at a school of generally innocuous reef sharks in a feeding frenzy. It's an encounter with the wild you'll never forget. A boat tour around the island by **Pension Chez Nono** (across from the InterContinental Le Moana Resort, tel. 67-71-38, www.cheznonobora.com) includes shark feeding (0930–1600, CFP 8,600 with lunch); **Chez Robert et Tina** (tel. 67-63-55, pension robertettina@mail.pf), on Matira Point, offers lagoon trips at CFP 9,000 per person.

Motorized canoe trips around Bora Bora are also offered. An excursion of this kind is an essential part of the Bora Bora experience, so splurge on this one. Otherwise, rent or borrow a kayak and organize your own free lagoon tour.

Moana Adventure Tours (tel. 67-61-41, www.moanatours.com), between the Kaina Hut and Bloody Mary's on Pofai Bay, does a shark and ray safari (CFP 6,600 per person) several times a week, departing around 1300. A half-day deep-sea fishing charter is CFP 40,500 for two people.

Matira Tours (tel. 67-70-97), on Matira

Point near Chez Robert et Tina, does lagoon tours 0930–1500 at CFP 9,000, including lunch (minimum of six people). **Shark Boy of Bora Bora** (tel. 67-60-93, sharkboy@mail.pf), **Moanareva Tours** (tel. 71-87-39), and **Teiva Tours** (tel. 67-64-26) also offer these trips.

Three-hour tours to the **Bora Lagoonarium** (tel. 67-71-34, http://boraboraisland.com/lagoonarium, Sun.–Fri., admission CFP 7,250), near Hôtel Le Méridien on a *motu* off the main island, occur daily except Saturday at 0845 and 1300. The price is reduced slightly if you book directly at the Lagoonarium office at Anau. You'll see more colorful fish than you ever thought existed. Call for a free hotel pickup.

Reef Discovery (www.reefdiscovery.pf) offers groups of up to six a private 3.5-hour circle island boat tour every morning and afternoon with stops at a snorkeling site called the Aquarium, an ocean beach, and some coral gardens. Book it through your hotel.

Bora Bora Voile (tel. 67-64-30, www.boraboraexcursion.com) offers a half-day cruise around Bora Bora on the catamaran *Taaroa III* at CFP 8,000 per person, including snorkeling (children under 12 half price). Their sunset cruise is CFP 6,000 per person.

Roa Yachting (tel. 71-83-86, www.roa-yachting.com) can accommodate eight to 12 passengers on the 24-meter luxury motor yacht *Roa.* Day outings around Bora Bora or six-night all-inclusive cruises of the Leeward Islands are possible. Celebrities and millionaires take note!

La Plage Boat Rental (tel. 67-68-75, laplage.bora@hotmail.com) at Matira rents small motorized boats from CFP 10,000 for four hours or CFP 16,000 per day, including gasoline. A license is not required with the 6 hp boats, and a VHF radio and ladder are on board. You get in a lot of snorkeling this way, but avoid the shallow "coral gardens" where it's hard to avoid getting scraped. If there are a few of you, consider hiring a larger boat with a guide. A four-seat open speedboat and driver-guide will be CFP 29,000 for three hours, while a six-seat boat is CFP 33,000 for three hours. Transfers from anywhere on the main island are included. *Motu* boat transfers are CFP 3,500 per person return.

On **Bora Bora Submarine** (tel. 74-99-99 or 67-55-55, www.submarineborabora.com) you aren't tied to the surface. This vessel can descend to depths of 35 meters outside the lagoon to observe sharks and other marine life. The six passengers each pay CFP 18,000 for their 30-minute ride, including hotel transfers.

Manta Ray Ballet

Most of the scuba diving and lagoon tour operators just mentioned take their clients to a site called Anau, where huge manta rays are on patrol. It's within the lagoon just east of Fitiiu Point in waters of three meters to well over 20 meters in depth. The animals use this sandy pass to commute between their feeding areas, and as many as a dozen manta rays up to three meters across may be seen with a mask and snorkel. It's important to remain calm as the mantas glide toward you since sudden movements will drive them away. Aside from the mantas, you may encounter blacktip reef sharks, barracuda, remora, Napoleons, and other fish, though you won't see much coral, as it's mostly dead in this area. The visibility is variable. Access is by boat; it's too far to swim from shore.

Other Activities

A half/full-day charter with **Bora Bora Sport Fishing** (tel. 72-95-85, www.boraborasportfishing.com) on the *Luna Sea,* a Black Watch 34 fishing boat, costs CFP 99,000/132,000 plus tax for up to six people.

Aqua Safari (tel. 67-61-98, www.aquasafaribora.com) offers an activity during which you walk along the shallow lagoon floor wearing a diving helmet connected to the boat for CFP 8,000, scuba certification not required! Their office is near the Kaina Hut Restaurant at Povai Bay.

Matira Jet Tours (tel. 67-62-73, www.boraborawaverunner.com) operates Jet Ski tours to a *motu* where you board an ATV for a two-kilometer ride around the sandy islet. You must remain in line with the others while on your personal Jet Ski. It's a bit cheaper if you're willing to share your Jet Ski and ATV with another rider instead of riding alone.

ACCOMMODATIONS

Be prepared for some of the highest room rates in the South Pacific. In all categories you'll pay about 50 percent more than you would for the same thing on Moorea. However, most guests at the top hotels arrive on prepaid packages and pay considerably less than the prices quoted here. Some tour operators engaged in packaging Bora Bora are listed in this guide's *Essentials* chapter, and you should also compare prices on the resort's own website before booking. The places charging less than US$150 seldom discount their rooms.

That said, there's a good choice of places to stay, and only at holiday times—especially during the July festivities—does everything fill up. When things are slow, the budget hotel owners meet the airport ferry and interisland ships in search of guests. If someone from the hotel of your choice isn't on the dock when you arrive, get on the blue *truck* marked Vaitape-Anau and ask to be taken wherever you want to go. This should cost CFP 500 per person, plus CFP 100 for luggage. However, if you're staying at a luxury resort, you could be charged as much as CFP 5,000 per person return for airport transfers (be sure to ask).

Despite a desalination plant that opened in 2001, Bora Bora still suffers from water shortages, so use it sparingly, and protect yourself against theft by carefully locking your room when you go out. A daily CFP 50–150 per person municipal services tax is collected at all accommodations.

US$50-100

Pension Moon (tel. 67-74-36), next to Galerie d'Art Alain et Linda on Pofai Bay, has two well-constructed bungalows with fans and fridges at CFP 7,350 double (or CFP 5,250 for stays longer than two nights). This place opened in 2001.

Pension Chez Rosina (tel. 67-70-91, chez_rosina@mail.pf), on Pofai Bay, has five rooms in the house at CFP 5,350/6,460 single/double with shared bath and CFP 5,880/8,050 with private bath. Communal cooking facilities are provided, and transfers are included. Rosina is friendly, but there's no beach.

On the Matira Point peninsula are two excellent alternatives to the upmarket hotels. **Pension Chez Nono** (tel. 67-71-38, www.cheznonobora.com) faces a public beach across from the InterContinental Le Moana Resort. It has two large bungalows (CFP 13,015 double), two smaller bungalows with private baths (CFP 9,813), and an old six-room thatched guesthouse with shared bathrooms and kitchen at CFP 6,350/7,450 single/double per room. The breakfast isn't worth it. Good communal cooking facilities are provided. Ventilation spaces between the ceilings and walls mean you hear *everything* in the other rooms, but the atmosphere is amiable and all guests soon become good friends (though a few of the staff seem rather jaded). Tahitians from other islands and local French often stay here. The garden is a pleasant place to sit, but the bungalows occasionally experience noise from beach parties. The solar hot-water heating only works when the sun is shining. Bring mosquito coils and toilet paper. A boat tour around the island 0930–1600 includes shark feeding (CFP 8,600 with lunch). Kayaks are loaned free.

Also good is **Chez Robert et Tina** (tel. 67-63-55, pensionrobertettina@mail.pf), down the road from Chez Nono at the tip of Matira Point, with 11 rooms with shared bath in three European-style houses at CFP 8,100 single or double (plus CFP 1,000 for only one night). Three fully-equipped kitchens are provided. Robert offers lagoon trips at CFP 9,000 per person. You'll enjoy it more if you know a little French. The beachfront location between two snorkeling locales can't be beat.

An outstanding choice for backpackers is **Chez Maeva** (tel. 67-72-04) on a small beach between the InterContinental Le Moana and Le Maitai Polynesia at Matira. This five-room guesthouse charges CFP 6,610 single or double or CFP 3,700 per person in an open four-bed dormitory. Add a CFP 1,000 surcharge for one-night stays. A communal kitchen is provided. This place is owned by Rosine Temauri-Masson, widow of noted painter Jean Masson.

Pension Chez Henriette (tel. 67-71-32) is beside the lagoon toward Pension Lagoonarium at Anau. It's CFP 2,500 per person to stay in the four-bed dormitory. Camping is possible (with your own tent). Ask for Stellio's *truck* at the wharf and you'll get a ride here for free if you're staying at least two nights.

The **Pension Lagoonarium** (tel. 67-71-34, lagonarium@mail.pf) at Anau has four rooms with shared bath at CFP 6,000 double, three bungalows with bath at CFP 8,000, and beds in a 10-bed dorm at CFP 3,000 per person. Communal cooking facilities are provided. It's right on the lagoon, but there's no beach.

US$150-250

Rohotu Fare Lodge (tel. 70-77-99, www.rohotufarelodge.com) is set on a hillside at Nunue, 200 meters above Pofai Bay. The three traditional thatched *fare* are CFP 18,900 single or double and include bicycles, taxes, and transfers. Children under 10 can share their parents' bungalow for free. Each unit, built of teak and mahogany, has cooking facilities, a huge bathroom with marble flooring, a four-poster bed with mosquito netting, an outdoor shower, and a private garden. It's three kilometers from the beach and four from Vaitape.

Hôtel Matira (tel. 67-70-51, www.hotel-matira.com) sits on the fine white public beach opposite the InterContinental Le Moana Resort. The 14 cubical bungalows with fridge are CFP 14,500/17,500/20,000/22,000 standard/garden/lagoon/beach, single or double, including transfers from the wharf and tax. Prices vary with the season, and you should ask about specials such as three nights for the price of two. Hôtel Matira is a fair value for Bora Bora, but the fan-cooled units can be rather hot. The hotel's beachfront restaurant is 500 meters down the road toward Vaitape, and you're better off booking a package without meals.

Village Temanuata (tel. 67-75-61, www.temanuata.com), just north of the InterContinental Le Moana Resort at Matira, has two thatched beachfront bungalows at CFP 18,070 double, seven garden bungalows at CFP 15,950, and two garden bungalows with kitchens at CFP 20,910. In 2004 four self-catering beach bungalows costing CFP 19,130 opened at "Temanuata Iti" 800 meters away on Matira Beach. The "Iti" units come with bicycles. There's no restaurant.

US$250 and Up

Hôtel Bora Bora (tel. 60-44-60, www.amanresorts.com), which opened on a spectacular point in 1961, was the island's first large hotel. It grew into one of the most exclusive millionaire's playgrounds in the South Pacific, with actors Pierce Brosnan and Eddy Murphy as regulars. In October 2008 the 54-unit hotel closed for complete reconstruction. The smaller and even more luxurious rebuilt resort is expected to reopen in 2011 for its 50th anniversary. Amanresorts will manage the property.

The **InterContinental Le Moana Resort** (tel. 60-49-00, www.tahitiresorts.intercontinental.com), formerly known as the Beachcomber, opened in 1987 on a superb white-sand beach at Matira Point. There's also a swimming pool. One of the 14 beachfront bungalows here will set you back CFP 74,669 single or double, plus 14 percent tax; the 50 over-water bungalows start at CFP 83,531 (children under 15 free). It's CFP 11,839 per person extra for breakfast and dinner (you can ask to have breakfast delivered to your room by outrigger canoe). There's a free shuttle over to the larger and more upscale InterContinental Resort and Thalasso Spa on Motu Pitiaau, and you can even take your breakfast there if you're on a meal plan. You could also skip the pricey meal plan as many good restaurants are within easily walking distance of Le Moana.

Hôtel Le Maitai Polynesia (tel. 60-30-00, www.hotelmaitai.com) at Matira is owned and managed by Tahiti Beachcomber SA, which also owns French Polynesia's four InterContinental resorts. It's Bora Bora's most affordable large hotel. Until 1997 there was a campground here, but this real estate was far too valuable for backpackers, and in 1998 a deluxe two-story hotel was built. The 48 air-conditioned rooms in the main building start at CFP 24,790 single or double, plus 14 percent tax. Across the road, the seven beach bungalows go for CFP 44,167, while the 19 over-water bungalows are CFP 60,376. Internet specials can reduce these rates. Transfers from Vaitape Wharf are CFP 2,500 round-trip. If you're on a budget, don't bother taking the meal plan as there are lots of outside restaurants in the vicinity. You can also arrange your rentals and activities at lower cost just down the road.

The three-star **Antipodes Club Resort Bora Bora** (tel. 60-59-50, www.antipodes-group.com) was known as the Novotel Bora Bora Beach Resort until the property was sold in early 2010. The plans of the new owners were still unknown at press time, and it's possible the 80 air-conditioned rooms in 10 thatched buildings will be sold as timeshares. This resort is well situated near the Sofitel Bora Bora Marara Beach Resort, and no over-water bungalows clutter its beach. If operating, expect to pay around CFP 20,500 single or double, plus 14 percent tax.

The **Sofitel Bora Bora Marara Beach and Private Island** (tel. 60-55-00, www.sofitel.com), near the north end of the Matira hotel strip, was built in 1978 to house the crew filming Dino de Laurentiis's *Hurricane* with Mia Farrow and Trevor Howard. The film flopped, but the hotel has been going strong ever since. In July 2006 it reopened after a US$15 million renovation. The 32 garden bungalows are CFP 41,429 single or double, the 11 beach bungalows CFP 50,000, and the 21 larger over-water units from CFP 57,143, plus 14 percent tax. The "over-water" units are much closer to shore than those at the other resorts. If the food in the restaurant isn't to your liking, there are lots of other restaurants nearby (think twice before buying the meal plan). An infinity-edge swimming pool, spa, and water-sports center are provided. The service here has rough edges. In 2009 the former Sofitel Motu, which opened in 1999 on Motu Piti uu Uta off the east side of the Matira peninsula, was annexed to become the Private Island component of the main resort. The 30 island/over-water bungalows are CFP 52,857/62,857 double, plus 14 percent tax. Breakfast is served on the island, but you must take a boat to the main resort for other meals. There's an artificial waterfall off the Private Island lobby and the views of Bora Bora are unforgettable. Compulsory transfers from Vaitape Wharf to either part of the resort are CFP 4,456 per person round-trip (children 11 and under CFP 1,136).

In February 2009 the 150-bungalow **Club Méditerranée** on the southeast side of Bora Bora was closed after suffering financial losses. Built in 1993 to replace an earlier Club Med north of Vaitape, this US$30 million resort was the largest on the island. It may eventually reopen, but at last report the rooms were being used to accommodate staff from other hotels.

Offshore Resorts

Most new developments around Bora Bora are on the long sandy *motu* surrounding the main island. The offshore resorts have wonderful beaches and excellent views of the mountainous interior. All of them offer the romantic over-water bungalows featured in the brochures, but some are too close together, and you hear *everything* your neighbors are doing. If you select one of the properties listed below, you'll need to buy a meal plan, as there are few opportunities to eat out. You'll also be obliged to purchase all of your optional activities from your resort's tour desk, while those staying on the main island can shop around for better prices. All of the *motu* resorts have regular shuttles to the main island, but some are problematic and not all are free.

Pension Le Paradis (tel. 67-75-53, pensionleparadis@mail.pf) on Motu Paahi, near the airport, offers two large self-catering bungalows with private baths at CFP 18,020 double and five smaller thatched bungalows with shared bath at CFP 10,600. Compulsory meals cost CFP 1,060/2,650 per person for breakfast/dinner. Fresh fish and lobster are available in abundance here. It's your chance to experience life on a *motu* without blowing your budget. The snorkeling in the nearby lagoon is so good that other (much more expensive) resorts bring their guests here to snorkel. The sunsets are awesome at Le Paradis. Airport transfers are CFP 1,060 and trips to the main island are easily arranged.

Also on Motu Paahi, **Blue Heaven Island** (tel. 72-42-11, www.blueheavenisland.com) is similar to Le Paradis with five simple thatched bungalows at CFP 24,000 single or double. Breakfast and dinner are compulsory at CFP 4,500 per person extra, served at a common table. A thatched pavilion with armchairs faces the small dock. Kayaks for exploring the lagoon are free. It's idyllic provided you can live without air-conditioning, swimming pools, and large groups.

Mai Moana Island (Stan Wisnieswski, tel. 67-62-45, www.mai-moana-island.com), on a tiny *motu* between the Pearl Beach Resort and the airport, has three thatched bungalows at CFP 34,800/39,800 double with half/full board. It's possible to rent the entire island for two people at CFP 45,000 without meals—less than you'd pay for a single room at most of the other large island resorts. The owner is a retired Polish filmmaker, and show business personalities sometimes choose his place for a secluded getaway. Round-trip transfers from the airport/Vaitape are CFP 3,000/4,500 for one/two people. Island tours and scuba diving can be arranged.

The **Bora Bora Pearl Beach Resort and Spa** (tel. 60-52-00, www.bora-bora-resort.org), on Teveiroa Island between the airport and Vaitape, has 20 garden suites with private pools at CFP 55,000 double, 10 beach suites with whirlpool baths at CFP 69,000, and 50 over-water bungalows starting at CFP 78,000, plus 14 percent tax. Half/full pension is an extra CFP 8,750/12,000 per person, and the meals are good though not exceptional considering the price (there is Polynesian dancing with dinner Monday and Friday nights). There is a swimming pool, a large Manea Spa (www.maneaspa.com), a Blue Nui Dive Center (tel. 67-79-07, www.bluenui.com), and a full range of activities, including a free shuttle to Farepiti Wharf (airport transfers CFP 5,500 per person plus tax).

The **Bora Bora Lagoon Resort** (tel. 60-40-00, www.boraboralagoon.com) is perched at the north end of Toopua Island opposite Vaitape. Opened in 1993, it's owned by Orient Express Hotels, which has been trying to unload this money-loser since 2007. The Lagoon Resort does offer wonderful views of Mount Pahia, and the large swimming pool compensates for the average beach and shallow lagoon. The 120 gloomy units vary between garden bungalows at CFP 57,279 double, beach bungalows at CFP 72,195, over-water bungalows at CFP 84,725, and pontoon bungalows at CFP 101,431, plus 14 percent tax. An overbooked Maru Spa is on the premises. Meals are extra, and it's forbidden to bring your own food and drink into the resort. Free activities include tennis, sailing, windsurfing, canoeing, a fitness center, and the hourly launch to Vaitape. Paid activities have hidden commissions tacked on, and airport transfers cost extra. Check-in time is 1500, not earlier, even if the place is almost empty.

In 2002 the 120-unit **Hilton Bora Bora Nui Resort and Spa** (tel. 60-33-00, www.boraboranui.com) opened at the south end of Toopua Island. Formerly part of the Starwood Chain's "Luxury Collection," this resort joined the Hilton chain in 2009 (although it's actually managed by a local company). The 16 lagoon-view suites begin at CFP 62,500 double and increase to a whopping CFP 284,600 for the two "over-water royal horizon suite bungalows." Meals are extra and average for the money. Of course, few pay these outlandish prices, as the vast majority of guests at all of Bora Bora's deluxe resorts arrive on special packages. At the Hilton you don't get the fabulous views available at the other Bora Bora resorts because the main beach faces the over-water reception and bungalows. The Mandara Spa on a hilltop above the resort is worth visiting for its 360-degree view of Bora Bora alone. Bring along a couple of DVDs to watch on your TV, as there's not much to do in the evening.

Three resorts are on 10-kilometer-long Motu Pitiaau on the east side of Bora Bora. At these, the resort launches go to Anau rather than Vaitape, a disadvantage if you want to go shopping. The St. Regis and Four Seasons are on Motu Tofari to the north of Motu Pitiaau toward the airport.

The **Bora Bora Eden Beach Resort** (tel. 67-50-97, www.boraborahotel.com), dating from 2001, prides itself on being one of the only "green" hotels in French Polynesia, with solar energy, water conservation, and recycling. Whether this is true or not is questionable. The eight garden bungalows are CFP 35,000 double and the four beach bungalows CFP 45,000, plus 14 percent tax. Food is extra, and airport transfers are CFP 3,000 per person each way. Unless you take the scheduled boat to Anau, transfers to the main island are CFP 700–900 each way. The beach looks great, but the snorkeling isn't. The owner warns guests against walking to the InterContinental because of "wild dogs," but the Eden Beach provides free kayaks that you can easily paddle there.

In 2006 Bora Bora got its second InterContinental resort, the **InterContinental Resort and Thalasso Spa Bora Bora** (tel. 60-76-00, www.tahitiresorts.intercontinental.com) to the north of the Eden Beach. The 80 spacious over-water villas are connected by crab-claw wharves reaching into the lagoon. These luxurious units start at CFP 108,663 single or double, plus 14 percent tax (four-night minimum stay). A good breakfast and dinner cost another CFP 11,839 per person, and mandatory airport transfers are CFP 4,362 per person. The InterContinental's spa proposes water massage, seaweed body wraps, mud treatments, and custom massage. The resort can organize a private picnic barbecue on a *motu* with the table in the water. There's a free shuttle to the InterContinental Le Moana Resort on the main island, but it isn't frequent. Interestingly, this resort is cooled by ocean water pumped up from the depths. Bathys Diving (www.bathys-diving.com) has a dive shop here.

In 1998 **Hôtel Le Méridien Bora Bora** (tel. 60-51-51, www.lemeridien-borabora.com) was built at the north end of Motu Pitiaau, a bit beyond the InterContinental Resort and Thalasso Spa Bora Bora. Its 82 thatched over-water bungalows start at CFP 93,000 single or double, while the 18 beach bungalows are CFP 86,000. Lagoon bungalows cost CFP 66,000, all plus 14 percent tax (children under 16 free). Add CFP 8,850/13,009 plus tax per person for two/three meals. Polynesian dancing comes with the buffets on Tuesday and Friday nights. All the usual sporting activities are offered, including scuba diving. Other features include an infinity-edge swimming pool, over-water wedding chapel, sea turtle sanctuary, flat-screen TVs, and wireless Internet. This resort tries hard to cater to families with young children, and Japanese honeymooners love it. Airport transfers are CFP 5,000 per person. Le Méridien Bora Bora is managed by Starwood Hotels and Resorts.

Not far from Le Méridien but across an open channel, the overhyped **St. Regis Resort Bora Bora** (tel. 60-78-98, www.stregis.com/borabora) on Motu Tofare opened in 2006. The 100 luxurious units in a Y-shaped formation offer slightly more privacy than those at the InterContinental and Méridien. This is one of the most expensive places to stay in French Polynesia, starting at CFP 103,000 for a standard over-water bungalow and increasing to an incredible CFP 449,000 for a royal villa, plus 14 percent tax. Despite these prices, the St. Regis is poorly managed by Starwood Hotels and Resorts, the staff are disorganized, the food is variable, and the vaunted St. Regis "butler service" is just a joke. Of the two main swimming pools, one has a swim-up bar, while the other is an adult pool with private daybed cabanas. The resort's Miri Miri Spa and fitness center are on a separate islet. The snorkeling here is poor. The St. Regis promises free bicycles, but there aren't enough to go around. Return airport transfers are CFP 7,500 per person, and the shuttle to the main island is unreliable. Hollywood stars such as Nicole Kidman have stayed at the St. Regis, and in October 2008 Universal Studios filmed the comedy *Couples Retreat,* starring Vince Vaughn, here. Even so, this place just isn't worth over US$1,000 a night.

Around the corner on Motu Tofare (aka Motu Tehotu), the **Four Seasons Resort Bora Bora** (tel. 60-31-30, www.fourseasons.com/borabora) opened in 2008. The 100 small over-water bungalows on four long piers and seven larger beachfront villas with pools start at CFP 130,000/134,000 single/double, plus 20 percent in taxes, charges, and fees. Half board is another CFP 10,500 per person plus 15 percent (drinks not included). The resort has two restaurants, two bars, two tennis courts, two pools, and a fitness center. The scent of native vanilla leads to a cathedral-like spa. A boat shuttle from the Four Seasons to Vaitape is available four times a day at CFP 1,500 per person each way (the shuttle to the main island is free at most of the other offshore resorts). Everyone raves about this place.

FOOD

Vaitape

Snack Bora Bora Burger (no phone, Mon.–Sat. 0800–1700), on the main road just south of the Banque de Polynésie near the wharf, serves hamburgers, French fries, and baguette sandwiches for under CFP 1,000.

Aloe Cafe (tel. 67-78-88, Mon.–Sat. 0600–1800), at the back of the Centre Commercial La Pahia opposite the Protestant church just north of the wharf, offers things such as crepes, hot sandwiches (CFP 500–900), ice cream, cakes, coffee, and beer. At lunchtime the plat du jour is around CFP 1,950. Internet access is available weekdays 0900–1300 and 1600–1800, Saturday 0900–1300, at CFP 40 per minute.

Restaurant Le St James (tel. 74-56-25, www.stjamesborabora.com, Mon.–Sat. 1130–1400 and 1830–2130, main dishes CFP 2,500), in the Helen's Bay Center at the north end of Vaitape village, serves French cuisine based on local products. Their deck has a wonderful lagoon view, especially at sunset. Le St James offers a free pickup for dinner.

Pofai Bay

Sunset Boulevard Restaurant Bar (tel. 67-57-67, www.enjoyborabora.com, Tues.–Sun., CFP 2,000–3,000), between Vaitape and Pofai Bay, serves Japanese-style seafood, including sushi. There's a DJ on Friday nights.

Villa Mahana (tel. 67-50-63, www.villamahana.com) is a fancy French restaurant in a Mediterranean-style villa behind Boutique Gauguin on Pofai Bay. Works by local artist Garrick Yrondi decorate this seven-table establishment, and romantic music plays in the background. The food and service are truly exceptional, but a couple should budget US$300 and up depending on your choice of wine. The set menu is CFP 11,000–15,000 per person. Advance reservations are essential.

At the **Kaina Hut Bistro** (tel. 67-54-06, Wed.–Mon. 1130–1400 and 1800–2130), under a thatched roof and shell chandelier on Pofai Bay, barefoot waitresses glide gracefully over a sandy floor. In fact, this is one of Bora Bora's most highly rated restaurants, with local seafood and grilled meats at CFP 1,600–2,800). Don't miss the breadfruit gnocchi. A couple should be able to dine here for under US$100. There's live music on Saturday nights. The Kaina Hut arranges free transportation to and from most resorts for diners who reserve.

Bloody Mary's (tel. 67-72-86, Mon.–Sat. 1130–1500 and 1800–2100), on Pofai Bay one kilometer south of Le Jardin Gauguin, is the longest established nonhotel restaurant on the island, with a tradition dating to 1979. A board outside lists "famous guests," including Jane Fonda and Baron George Von Dangel. The lunch menu includes teriyaki, fish kabob, and *poisson cru,* though when things are slow it doesn't bother dishing out lunch at all. At dinner you choose from the fresh seafood (CFP 2,700–3,200) laid out on ice in front of you. The drinks are reasonable here, and the souvenir T-shirts are popular. For ambience, menu, service, and staff it's hard to beat, although the food itself is only so-so. Don't miss the zany toilets. Bloody Mary's is large enough that reservations can be considered optional. Free hotel pickups for diners are available at 1830 if you call ahead.

Matira

Ben's Snack (daily 0900–1700), between Hôtel Bora Bora and Hôtel Matira's restaurant, turns out pizza (CFP 850–1,600), lasagna, pasta, steaks, and omelets, but it's open irregularly. One reader said that her hamburger was reminiscent of a "where's the beef?" commercial.

Le Matira Beach Restaurant (tel. 67-77-32, Fri.–Wed.), across the street and a bit east of Ben's, is the best place around for a leisurely budget lunch. The menu includes hamburgers, mahimahi with *frites, steak frites,* pizza, *poisson cru,* and big *casse-croûte* sandwiches. The food is good, but no beer is available on the nice beachfront terrace. Lunch is under CFP 2,000, but main courses on the dinner menu start at CFP 3,000.

Snack Moi Here (tel. 67-56-46, daily 0630–2200), right on Matira Beach, is good for the large *casse-croûte* sandwiches and mahimahi with fries. Other meals are in the CFP 1,100–2,600 range. Its agreeable terrace overlooks the beach.

Restaurant Fare Manuia (tel. 67-68-08, Mon. 1800–2200, Tues.–Sat. 1130–1400 and 1800–2200), a.k.a. "Lucky House," near the turnoff to the InterContinental Le Moana Resort, offers good but rather expensive Chinese dishes and French specialties. Local seafood dishes are in the CFP 2,600–3,900 range, meat CFP 2,300–4,000. Try the prawns breaded with coconut, steak with mushrooms, *poisson cru,* or lobster. It fills up quickly in the evening.

Restaurant La Bounty (tel. 67-70-43, Tues.–Sun. 1130–1400 and 1830–2100), near Tiare Market just north of Le Maitai Polynesia, has an open-air terrace under a thatched roof. Its lunch plates and American-style pizzas are CFP 1,500–1,650, dinner CFP 1,500–3,000. Try the lobster ravioli, *poisson cru,* or seafood curry. The reasonably priced menu is only in French. The largely local clientele doesn't seem to mind the slow service—order a couple of beers and relax. After 1900, you can avoid having to wait for a table by reserving in advance.

Groceries

Bora Bora's best established supermarket is **Magasin Chin Lee** (tel. 67-73-86, Mon.–Sat. 0500–1900, Sun. 0500–1100), opposite the island's Mobil gas station north of Vaitape Wharf. Notice the takeaway meals at the checkout counters. **Super To'a Amok** and the Total service station are farther north.

Tiare Market (tel. 67-61-38, Mon.–Sat. 0630–1900, Sun. 0630–1300 and 1500–1830), between Le Maitai Polynesia and the Sofitel Marara at Matira, is very well stocked with a good wine section and even some fresh vegetables. It's always crowded with tourists from the upmarket hotels.

Other places to buy groceries are the two general stores (Mon.–Sat.) at Anau, halfway around the island, and a small grocery store at the head of Pofai Bay. A grocery truck passes Matira around noon and 1600 daily except Sunday.

INFORMATION AND SERVICES

A **Visitors Bureau** (tel. 67-76-36, info-bora-bora@mail.pf, weekdays 0900–1600) is in the Centre Artisanal next to Vaitape Wharf. **Boutique "3 Tiki"** (Hinano Marraud, tel. 21-69-36, hinanoborabora.com), across the street from the Centre Artisanal, acts as an activities booking center.

The three main **banks** all have offices near Vaitape Wharf, but they're open only weekdays 0745–1130 and 1330–1600. Many yachties "check out" of French Polynesia at Bora Bora and reclaim their bond, or *caution,* at these banks. It's wise to check with the Banque Socredo (tel. 47-00-00) a few days ahead to make sure it'll have your cash or traveler's checks ready. At last report, such refunds were available only on Tuesday and Thursday.

The **post office** (tel. 67-70-24, Mon. 0800–1500, Tues.–Fri. 0730–1500, Sat. 0800–1000), gendarmerie (tel. 60-59-05), and health clinic *(Santé Publique)* are within a stone's throw of Vaitape Wharf.

Richard Guenett, manager of **Bloody Mary's Restaurant** (tel. 67-72-86, rick.bmarys@mail.pf), provides free moorings, water, ice (first bag only), and trash disposal to cruising yachties who patronize the restaurant and bar. Mooring reservations are not accepted, and it's strictly first come, first served. Beware of theft from yachts anywhere around this island.

Health

The private **Cabinet Médical** (tel. 67-70-62,

weekdays 0700–1200 and 1500–1800, Sat. 0700–1200) is behind Mom's Boutique in Vaitape.

Dr. François Macouin's **Cabinet Dentaire** (tel. 67-70-55, weekdays 0730–1800, Sat. 0730–1200) is in the Centre Commercial Le Pahia opposite Magasin Chin Lee and the large Protestant church. Another Vaitape dentist is Dr. Emmanuel Zona (tel. 67-69-42, weekdays 0730–1200 and 1430–1730, Sat. 0730–1200).

Pharmacie Thomas (tel. 67-70-30, weekdays 0800–1200 and 1530–1800, Sat. 0800–1200 and 1700–1800, Sun. 0900–0930) is north of the wharf.

GETTING THERE AND AROUND

Getting There

Air Tahiti (tel. 60-53-53, weekdays 0730–1130 and 1330–1630) is beside the Banque de Tahiti on Vaitape Wharf. There are flights from Papeete to Bora Bora (CFP 15,400) several times per day, and there's a direct connection from Moorea to Bora Bora (CFP 19,500) five times a week. Air Tahiti has useful transversal services direct from Bora Bora to Rangiroa and Tikehau (both CFP 24,400) 4–5 times per week. Bora Bora to Fakarava and Manihi (both CFP 27,500) operates 3–4 times per week.

Bora Bora's **airport** (BOB) on Motu Mute north of the main island was built by the Americans during World War II. The first commercial flight from Paris to French Polynesia landed here in October 1958, and until March 1961 all international flights used this airstrip; passengers were then transferred to Papeete by Catalina amphibious or Bermuda flying boat seaplanes. Today, a 25-minute catamaran ride brings arriving air passengers to Vaitape Wharf (included in the plane ticket). Make sure your luggage is loaded on or off the boat at the airport. Returning to the airport, you must board the ferry one hour and 15 minutes before your flight time.

When the catamaran from the airport arrives at Vaitape Wharf, all of the luxury hotels will have guest transportation waiting, but the budget places don't always meet the flights (the deluxe places don't bother meeting the interisland boats). As you arrive at the wharf, shout out the name of your hotel and you'll be directed to the right *truck* (they don't have destination signs). At the airport the resorts use color-coded flower leis to sort out their guests.

If you're flying from Papeete to Bora Bora, go early in the morning and sit on the left side of the aircraft for spectacular views—it's only from the air that Bora Bora is the most beautiful island in the world.

Ships from Raiatea and Papeete tie up at Farepiti Wharf, three kilometers north of Vaitape. For the cargo boats, contact the shipping company representatives on Bora Bora for exact departure times. Drivers of the *trucks* are also likely to know. Try to buy your ticket in advance. Officially the *Taporo VI* departs Bora Bora for Raiatea, Huahine, and Papeete Wednesday and Friday at 0830 (CFP 1,911 deck to Papeete). The *Hawaiki-Nui* (tel. 67-72-39) leaves here on Wednesday and Friday around noon. Obtaining accurate information about these services is difficult, and you should be wary of early departures.

A fast yellow-and-blue passenger ferry, the *Maupiti Express 2* (tel. 67-66-69, www.maupitiexpress.com), departs Vaitape Wharf for Maupiti, Taha'a, and Raiatea. It leaves for Maupiti on Tuesday, Thursday, and Saturday at 0830, for Taha'a and Raiatea on Monday, Wednesday, and Friday at 0700, and Sunday at 1500. Tickets (CFP 4,000/5,000 one way/round-trip) are sold on board.

Getting Around

Getting around is a bit of a headache, as *le truck* service is irregular, and at lunchtime everything stops. Public *trucks* usually meet the boats, but many of the *trucks* you see around town are for guests of the luxury hotels. If you do find one willing to take you, the fare between Vaitape and Matira is CFP 500, plus CFP 100 for luggage. Taxi fares are high, so check before getting in. If you rent a bicycle, keep an eye on it when you stop to visit the sights.

Avis (tel. 67-70-03, www.avis-tahiti.com) has an office near the wharf in Vaitape and desks at many resorts. A two-seater Bugway vehicle without a roof or doors rents for CFP 14,000 for four hours. The cheapest car is CFP 10,850/12,300/13,500 for 4/8/24 hours. Bicycles are CFP 1,600/1,800/2,000.

Farepiti Rentacar (tel. 67-65-28, farepiticarhire@mail.pf, Mon.–Sat.) is opposite the Centre Artisanal in Vaitape, at the Hôtel Le Maitai Polynesia, and opposite the Sofitel Bora Bora Marara Beach Resort. The smaller cars are usually all taken, and it's likely you'll be asked to take an air-conditioned car. Scooters and bicycles are also available. If you don't have a major credit card, you'll have to leave a deposit of CFP 100,000/50,000/30,000 on the cars/scooters/bicycles.

Bora Bora Tours (tel. 67-70-31, www.boraboratours.com), just south of Vaitape, rents cars starting at CFP 10,200 a day.

If you rent a car and drive at night, watch out for scooters and bicycles without lights. However, to better enjoy the scenery and avoid disturbing the environment, we suggest you dispense with motorized transport here. Little Bora Bora is perfect for cycling. There's an excellent paved road right around the island, only one steep incline (at Fitiiu Point), almost no hills, and lots of scenic bays to shelter you from the wind. Do exercise caution with fast-moving vehicles between Vaitape and Matira Point, however.

Land Tours

Bora Bora Tours (tel. 67-70-31, www.boraboratours.com), just south of Vaitape, offers a two-hour truck tour around Bora Bora (CFP 3,600).

Tupuna Safari (tel. 67-75-06, boraboraisland.com/tupuna) does four-wheel-drive Land Rover island tours that include a drive up a steep ridge opposite Otemanu at CFP 7,100. You can book these trips through The Farm just north of Hôtel Bora Bora.

a Leeward Islands four-wheel-drive safari

Maupiti

Majestic Maupiti (Maurua), 52 kilometers west of Bora Bora, is the least known of the accessible Society Islands. Maupiti's mighty volcanic plug soars above a sapphire lagoon, and the vegetation-draped cliffs complement the magnificent *motu* beaches. Almost every bit of level land on the main island is taken up by fruit trees, while watermelons thrive on the surrounding *motu.* Maupiti abounds in native seabirds, including frigate birds, terns, and others. The absence of Indian mynahs allows you to see native land birds that are almost extinct elsewhere.

The 1,200 people live in the adjacent villages of Vai'ea, Farauru, and Pauma. Tourism is not promoted because there aren't any regular hotels, which is a big advantage. It's sort of like Bora Bora was 30 years ago, before being "discovered" by the world of package tourism.

SIGHTS

It takes only three hours to walk around this 11-square-kilometer island. The nine-kilometer crushed-coral road, lined with breadfruit, mango, banana, and hibiscus, passes crumbling *marae,* freshwater springs, and a beach.

Marae Vaiahu, by the shore a few hundred meters beyond Hotuparaoa Massif, is the largest *marae.* Once a royal landing place opposite the pass into the lagoon, the *marae* still bears the king's throne and ancient burials. Nearby is the sorcerers' rock: Light a fire beside this rock and you will die. Above the road are a few smaller *marae.*

Terei'a Beach, at the west tip of Maupiti, is the only good beach on the main island. At low tide you can wade across from Terei'a's white sands to Motu Auira in waist-deep water.

Marae Vaiorie is a double *marae* with freshwater springs in between. As many as two dozen large *marae* are hidden in Maupiti's mountainous interior, and the island is known for its ghosts. Maupiti is well known among archaeologists for its black basalt stone pounders and fishhooks made from the seven local varieties of mother-of-pearl shell.

It's possible to climb **Mount Teurafaatiu,** the 380-meter summit of Maupiti, from opposite Snack Tarona in Farauru village. The whole trip shouldn't take more than three hours return (take water). The view is unsurpassed.

Activities

Maupiti Nautique (tel. 67-83-80, www.maupiti-nautique.com), at Maupiti Résidence on Tereia Beach, offers scuba diving (CFP 6,500/12,000 one/two tanks), snorkeling trips (CFP 3,500), and whale or dolphin watching (CFP 6,500).

ACCOMMODATIONS

Several of the inhabitants take paying guests, and they usually meet the flights and boats in search of clients. The absence of a regular hotel on Maupiti throws together an odd mix of vacationing French couples, backpackers, and "adventuresome" tourists in the guesthouses (none of which have signs). Agree on the price beforehand, and check your bill when you leave. You could camp on the airport *motu,* but obtaining drinking water would be a problem and there are *no-nos* (insects). Maupiti experiences serious water shortages during the dry season.

US$50-100

Pension Eri (tel. 67-81-29) in Vai'ea village with four rooms in a separate house from that of the family costs CFP 3,000 per person or CFP 5,500 with half board.

Readers have recommended **Maupiti Village** (tel. 67-80-08, maupiti.village@mail.pf) on Motu Tiapa'a, which has two small bungalows at CFP 12,000 per person full board and four rather basic rooms with shared bath at CFP 7,000 full board. The seafood lunches and dinners are excellent. Kayaks are loaned free. Transfers cost CFP 1,500/2,000 to the village/airport.

US$100-150

Pension Tautiare Village (tel. 60-15-90,

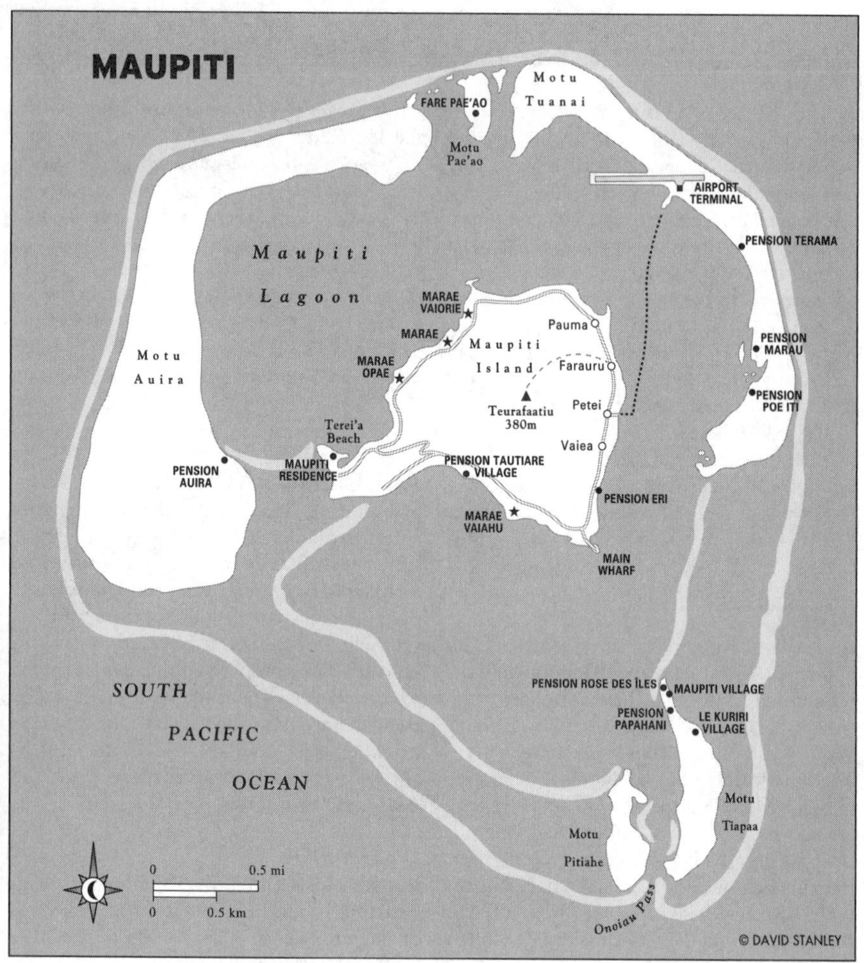

pension-tautiare@mail.pf), near the main wharf two kilometers south of the village, offers four rooms with baths and individual terraces at CFP 8,000/10,500/11,500 single/double/triple. Snorkeling gear and kayaks are loaned free. This appealing pension opened in 2004 just a 15-minute walk from Tereia Beach. Airport transfers are CFP 1,650 per person round-trip.

Maupiti Résidence (tel. 67-82-61, maupiti.residence@mail.pf), nicely situated on Tereia Beach, has two villas at CFP 10,800 double, CFP 14,800 for three or four people, or CFP 15,800 for five people (a 12 percent surcharge is payable for stays of less than three nights). Each of these two-bedroom villas has a kitchen, lounge, and wireless Internet. Meals can be ordered. Sailboats, kayaks, bicycles, and snorkeling gear are loaned free. Residence guests enjoy a 15 percent discount on activities with Maupiti Nautique, which has their base here. Credit cards are accepted.

Pension Auira (tel. 67-80-26) on Motu Auira, the *motu* opposite Terei'a Beach, has six thatched bungalows. The garden bungalows are CFP 7,420 per person per day, including breakfast and dinner; the better-quality beach bungalows are CFP 9,010 per person. Camping may be possible here. The food is good, but the beach and rooms could use a cleaning. At low tide you can wade across the lagoon to Tereia Beach in 20 minutes. Boat transfers from the airport are CFP 2,120 per person return.

Pension Marau (tel. 67-81-19 or 70-56-09, www.pension-marau.com) is on Motu Tuanai, the airport *motu*. The seven simple bungalows are CFP 8,000 single or double, plus CFP 3,500 per person for breakfast and dinner. There's not much to do here. Airport transfers are CFP 500 round-trip.

Also on Motu Tuanai, **Pension Terama** (tel. 67-81-96, http://maupiti.terama.over-blog.com) rents three rooms in a single-story house plus one bungalow at CFP 7,000 per person, including breakfast and dinner. Dining is in a thatched pavilion on the beach. Airport transfers are free.

In addition, there are three small resorts on Motu Tiapaa, one of the islands framing Onoiau Pass. You'll see stingrays while snorkeling. Laid-back **Pension Papahani** (tel. 60-15-35, pensionpapahani@hotmail.fr) has five thatched bungalows with private bath beginning at CFP 9,000 per person, breakfast and a good dinner included. The boat ride to the village is CFP 1,500 round-trip, but to or from the airport it's free.

US$150-250

Pension Poe Iti (tel. 74-58-76, www.maupitipoeiti.com) on Motu Tuanai has four air-conditioned bungalows with private baths, minibars, and TVs at CFP 8,000/9,000/10,000 single/double/triple, plus 5 percent tax. Breakfast and dinner served at a common table are CFP 3,500, plus tax. Kayaks and snorkeling gear are provided, and lagoon tours with a picnic lunch are CFP 3,500. Transfers to the airport or village are free. It's owned by the people who operate the ferry *Maupiti Express 2*.

Maupiti's most luxurious accommodations are at **Le Kuriri Village** (tel. 67-82-23, www.maupiti-kuriri.com) on Motu Tiapaa. The five *fare* with baths are CFP 14,630/25,000 single/double with half board served at a common table. Airport transfers are included.

Also on Motu Tiapaa's lovely white beach is **Pension Rose des Îles** (tel. 67-82-47, www.pension-rose-des-iles.com) with two thatched bungalows at CFP 12,000 per person half board, plus one garden room at CFP 10,000 per person half board. Camping is CFP 2,000 per person. Activities include boat trips around the island (CFP 3,500 per person), mountain climbing, line fishing (CFP 1,500 per person), and sailing. Transfers are CFP 1,150/2,600 per person round-trip to the village/airport.

Fare Pae'ao Chez Janine (tel. 67-81-01, www.maupitilodge.com) on Motu Pae'ao is quiet and offers a superb white beach with some of the finest snorkeling on Maupiti. The six thatched bungalows with baths are CFP 17,852/23,120 single/double, including breakfast and dinner. Reservations are required to ensure an airport pickup (CFP 1,357 per person round-trip). (In 1962 Kenneth Emory and Yosihiko Sinoto excavated a prehistoric cemetery on Pae'ao and found 15 adzes of six different types, providing valuable evidence for the study of Polynesian migrations.)

SERVICES

Banque Socredo (tel. 60-17-00) has a branch on Maupiti, but it's not always operating, so bring sufficient cash and don't count on using your credit cards anywhere. The post office and *mairie* are nearby. The bakery is in the power plant on the edge of town. It's important to check when the baguettes come out of the oven and to be punctual, as they sell out fast. The island youths come here an hour before and hang around waiting. Not all stores sell beer, and the island's supply does run out at times.

GETTING THERE

Maupiti's airport (MAU) is on a *motu*, and you must take a launch to the main island (CFP 500 per person). **Air Tahiti** has flights

© DAVID STANLEY

The barge *Tahiti Nui VI* provides a weekly passenger and freight connection between Papeete and Maupiti.

to Maupiti from Bora Bora (CFP 7,000 one-way) twice a week, Raiatea (CFP 7,400) three times a week, and Papeete (CFP 15,800) five times a week. Reconfirm with the Air Tahiti agent (tel. 60-15-05) near the *mairie.*

The government supply ship *Tahiti Nui VI* connects Maupiti and Papeete once a week, and 12 passengers are accepted. The 140-seat fast ferry *Maupiti Express 2* (www.maupitiexpress.com) arrives from Bora Bora (CFP 4,000/5,000 one-way/round-trip) on Tuesday, Thursday, and Saturday mornings, returning to Bora Bora the same afternoon.

Ships must enter the channel during daylight, thus the compulsory morning arrival, and the boats usually depart from Maupiti on the afternoon of the same day. Onoiau Pass into Maupiti is narrow, and when there's a strong southerly wind it can be dangerous—boats have had to turn back. At low tide a strong current flows out through this pass, and the optimum time for a yacht to enter is around noon.

Other Leeward Islands

TUPAI

Tupai, or Motu Iti (Small Island), 24 kilometers north of Bora Bora, is a tiny coral atoll measuring 1,100 hectares. The opposing horseshoe-shaped *motu* enclose a lagoon that small boats can enter through a pass on the east side. A small airstrip is in the northwest corner of the atoll. In 1860, the king of Bora Bora gave the atoll to a planter named Stackett, and for decades a few dozen people were employed to make copra from coconuts off the 155,000 trees on Tupai. In 1997 the territorial government bought Tupai from its last owner, a Mr. Lejeune, for US$8 million with an eye to resort development. In 2009 Tahiti Nui Travel proposed an 80-room underwater hotel, casino, and two additional hotels for Tupuai. Although there are no permanent inhabitants at the moment, the 1,000 traditional landowners are contesting the title. The scuba operators on Bora Bora often arrange trips here.

MAUPIHAA

Tiny 360-hectare Maupihaa (Mopelia), 185 kilometers southeast of Maupiti, is the only Society Islands atoll that can be entered by

yachts, but to attempt to do so in stormy weather is dangerous. Narrow, unmarked Taihaaru Vahine Pass on Maupihaa's northwest side can only be found by searching for the strong outflow of lagoon water at low tide. Despite this, cruising yachts traveling between Bora Bora and Cook Islands or Samoa often anchor in the atoll's lagoon.

In July 1917 the notorious German raider *Seeadler* was wrecked at Maupihaa after capturing 15 Allied ships. The three-masted schooner was too large to enter the lagoon, and while being careened outside the pass, a freak wave picked the vessel up and threw it onto the reef. Eventually the ship's chivalrous captain, Count Felix von Luckner, was able to carry on to Fiji in a small boat, where he was captured at Wakaya Island. Count von Luckner's journal, *The Sea Devil,* became a best-seller after the war.

About 50 people from Maupiti live on Maupihaa, where they run a nursery to supply oysters to black pearl farms in the Tuamotus. Sea turtles come to Maupihaa to lay their eggs only to be butchered for their flesh by poachers. Large numbers of terns, boobies, and frigate birds nest on the small *motu,* and the seabird fledglings are slaughtered for their meager meat while the unhatched eggs are collected according to need. All of this is supposed to be prohibited, but it's hard to control what goes on in such an isolated place.

MANUAE

Manuae (Scilly), 75 kilometers northwest of Maupihaa, is the westernmost of the Society Islands. This atoll is 15 kilometers in diameter but totals only 400 hectares. Pearl divers once visited Manuae. In 1855 the three-masted schooner *Julia Ann* sank on the Manuae reef. It took the survivors two months to build a small boat, which carried them to safety at Raiatea.

MOTU ONE

Motu One (Bellingshausen), 65 kilometers north of Manuae, got its second name from the Russian explorer Thadeus von Bellingshausen, who visited Tahiti in 1820. Tiny 280-hectare Motu One is circled by a guano-bearing reef, with no pass into the lagoon. Of the 10 people present on Motu One when Hurricane Martin swept through in November 1997, the sole survivor was a woman named Alice Haano who tied herself to a coconut tree. Since 1992, both Manuae and Motu One are protected areas with nine species of seabirds and one endemic land bird.

THE AUSTRAL ISLANDS

The inhabited volcanic islands of Rimatara, Rurutu, Tubuai, Raivavae, and Rapa, plus uninhabited Maria (or Hull) atoll, make up the Austral group. This southernmost island chain in the South Pacific is a 1,280-kilometer extension of the same submerged mountain range as the southern Cook Islands, 900 kilometers northwest. The islands of the Australs seldom exceed elevation of 300 meters, except Rapa, which soars to 650 meters. The southerly location makes these islands notably cooler and drier than Tahiti. Collectively the Australs are known as Tuhaa Pae, the "Fifth Part," or fifth administrative subdivision, of French Polynesia.

The 6,500 mostly Polynesian inhabitants are fishers and farmers who live in attractive villages with homes and churches built of coral limestone. The *himene,* or hymn singing, of the inhabitants of the Australs is among the finest in Polynesia. The rich soil and moderate climate stimulate agriculture, with staple crops such as taro, manioc, Irish potatoes, sweet potatoes, leeks, cabbage, carrots, corn, and coffee. The coconut palm also thrives, except on Rapa. Today, many Austral people live in Papeete.

For visitors, the seldom-visited Austral Islands are a chance to get well off the beaten tourist track. There's good hiking on all the islands, either along the lonely coastal roads or into the interior on tracks and trails used by local residents. In addition to the good views, hidden caves and archaeological sites await the explorer, though these are usually overgrown and hard to find. Most of the pensions can arrange local guides and circle-island tours.

© TAHITI TOURISME

HIGHLIGHTS

Whale-Watching: From July to October, Rurutu offers the best chance of observing humpback whales; you can even snorkel and scuba dive with the giants (page 181).

Lagoon Tours: A boat trip to a *motu* across Tubuai's lagoon allows you to swim and snorkel in an utterly remote location (page 183).

Raivavae: A string of 28 low coral *motu* surround the emerald lagoon of this remote volcanic island and its overgrown archaeological sites (page 186).

Hill Fortresses of Rapa: The terraces, moats, and pyramids high up on the ridges of Rapa offer sweeping views of one of the most isolated islands on earth (page 188).

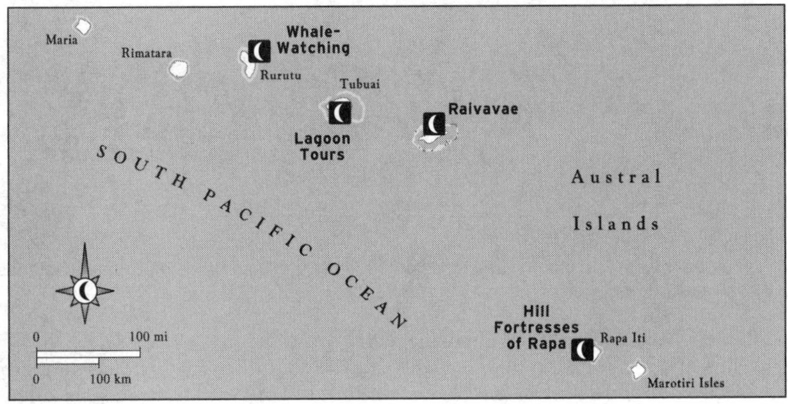

LOOK FOR TO FIND RECOMMENDED SIGHTS, ACTIVITIES, DINING, AND LODGING.

Lagoon tours to small coral *motu* on the reef are offered on Tubuai and Raivavae, with snorkeling and sunbathing the rewards. On Rurutu, there's whale-watching July–October and scuba diving the rest of the year. Tubuai also has a dive shop. Rapa is accessible to most only as part of a cruise package, and a hike up to the old Polynesian hill fortresses is usually arranged. Although Rimatara has flights from Papeete, there are no facilities for visitors. Taken as a whole, the Austral Islands are still a world apart from tourism.

PLANNING YOUR TIME

The supply boat from Tahiti is extremely basic, so most visitors arrive by air. Air Tahiti's "Extension Australes" air pass allows you to visit Rurutu, Tubuai, and Raivavae for a set price. A week to 10 days is ample time to get a feel for the Austral Islands.

Getting There

Air Tahiti has flights to Rurutu and Tubuai 4–5 times per week. Some flights operate Papeete–Tubuai–Rurutu–Papeete, while others go Papeete–Rurutu–Tubuai–Papeete. One-way fares from Tahiti are CFP 20,200 to Rurutu and CFP 22,500 to Tubuai. Rurutu–Tubuai is CFP 10,500. Airports have recently opened on Raivavae and Rimatara. A possible 10-day routing is Papeete–Raivavae on Monday, Raivavae–Tubuai on Wednesday, Tubuai–Rurutu on Sunday, and Rurutu–Papeete on Wednesday.

By Boat

The **Service de Navigation des Australes**

© TAHITI TOURISME

White sand beaches are found on the *motu* (low coral islands) surrounding the main islands of the Australs Group.

(tel. 41-36-06, snathp@mail.pf), in the building marked "Entrepot Tuhaa Pae" at the Tuamotu wharf in Papeete, runs the *Tuhaa Pae III* to the Austral Islands. One-way deck/cabin fares from Papeete are around CFP 6,000/8,500 to Rurutu, Rimatara, or Tubuai, CFP 8,500/12,000 to Raivavae, or CFP 12,000/16,000 to Rapa. Otherwise it's about CFP 35,000 cabin class for the entire 10-day round-trip. Three meals a day cost something like CFP 3,500 per person per day extra at the cafeteria (or bring your own food).

The *Tuhaa Pae III* has nine four-bed, two two-bed, and two one-bed cabins. Some are below the waterline and are very hot with no portholes. The rear deck has a diesely romantic feel for a day or two. For sanitary reasons the seats have been removed from the ship's toilets (you squat). The ship calls at Rimatara, Rurutu, Tubuai, and Raivavae 3–4 times per month. Rapa Iti is visited about once a month, Maria Atoll annually. The schedule changes at a moment's notice, so actually sailing on the *Tuhaa Pae III* requires persistence. Consider going out by boat and returning by plane.

HISTORY

Excavations carried out on the northwest coast of Rurutu uncovered 60 round-ended houses arranged in parallel rows, with 14 *marae* scattered among them, demonstrating the presence of humans here as early as A.D. 900. Ruins of *marae* can also be seen on Rimatara, Tubuai, and Raivavae. Huge stone tikis once graced Raivavae, but most have since been destroyed or removed. The terraced mountain fortifications, or *pa,* on Rapa are unique.

The Australs were one of the great art areas of the Pacific, represented today in many museums. The best-known artifacts are sculpted sharkskin drums, wooden bowls, fly whisks, and tapa cloth. Offerings that could not be touched by human hands were placed on the sacred altars with intricately incised ceremonial ladles. European contact effaced most of these traditions, and the carving done today is crude by comparison.

Rurutu was spotted by Captain James Cook in 1769; he found Tubuai in 1777. In 1789 Fletcher Christian and the *Bounty* mutineers attempted to establish a settlement at the northeast corner of Tubuai. They left after only three months after battles with the islanders in which 66 Polynesians died. The European "discoverer" of Rapa was Captain George Vancouver in 1791. Rimatara wasn't contacted until 1813, by the Australian captain Michael Fodger.

English missionaries converted most of the people to Protestantism in the early 19th century. Whalers and sandalwood ships introduced diseases and firearms, which decimated the Austral islanders. The French didn't complete their annexation of the group until 1901. Since then the Australs have gone their sleepy way.

Rurutu

This island, 565 kilometers south of Papeete, is shaped like a miniature replica of the African continent. Rurutu is estimated to be 11 million years old, and it would normally have eroded to sea level except that 4 million years ago it was uplifted by the movement of tectonic plates. This history accounts for the juxtaposition of coastal coral cliffs with volcanic interior hills. For the hiker, 32-square-kilometer Rurutu is a more varied island to visit than Tubuai. Grassy, fern-covered Taatioe (389 meters) and Manureva (384 meters) are the highest peaks, and coastal cliffs on the southeast side of the island drop 30 meters to the sea. A narrow fringing reef surrounds Rurutu, but there's no lagoon.

The climate of this northernmost Austral island is temperate and dry. The recent history of Rurutu revolves around four important dates: 1821, when the gospel arrived on the island; 1889, when France declared a protectorate over the island; 1970, when Hurricane Emma devastated the three villages; and 1975, when the airport opened.

In January and July Rurutuans practice the ancient art of stone lifting, or *amoraa ofai.* Men get three tries to hoist a 150-kilogram boulder coated with *monoï* (coconut oil) up onto their shoulders, while women attempt a 60-kilogram stone. Dancing and feasting follow the event. The women of Rurutu weave fine pandanus hats, bags, baskets, fans, lamp shades, and mats. A handicraft display is laid out for departing passengers. Rurutu's famous Manureva (Soaring Bird) Dance Group has performed around the world. The main evening entertainment is watching dancers practice in the villages.

an Austral Islands church

Orientation

The pleasant main village, Moerai, boasts a post office, medical center, four small stores, two bakeries, and a bank. An Italian runs a goat cheese factory in Moerai. Two other villages, Avera and Hauti, bring the total island population to about 2,100. Neat fences and flower gardens surround the coral limestone houses. This is the Polynesia of 50 years ago: Though a few pensions and snack bars have

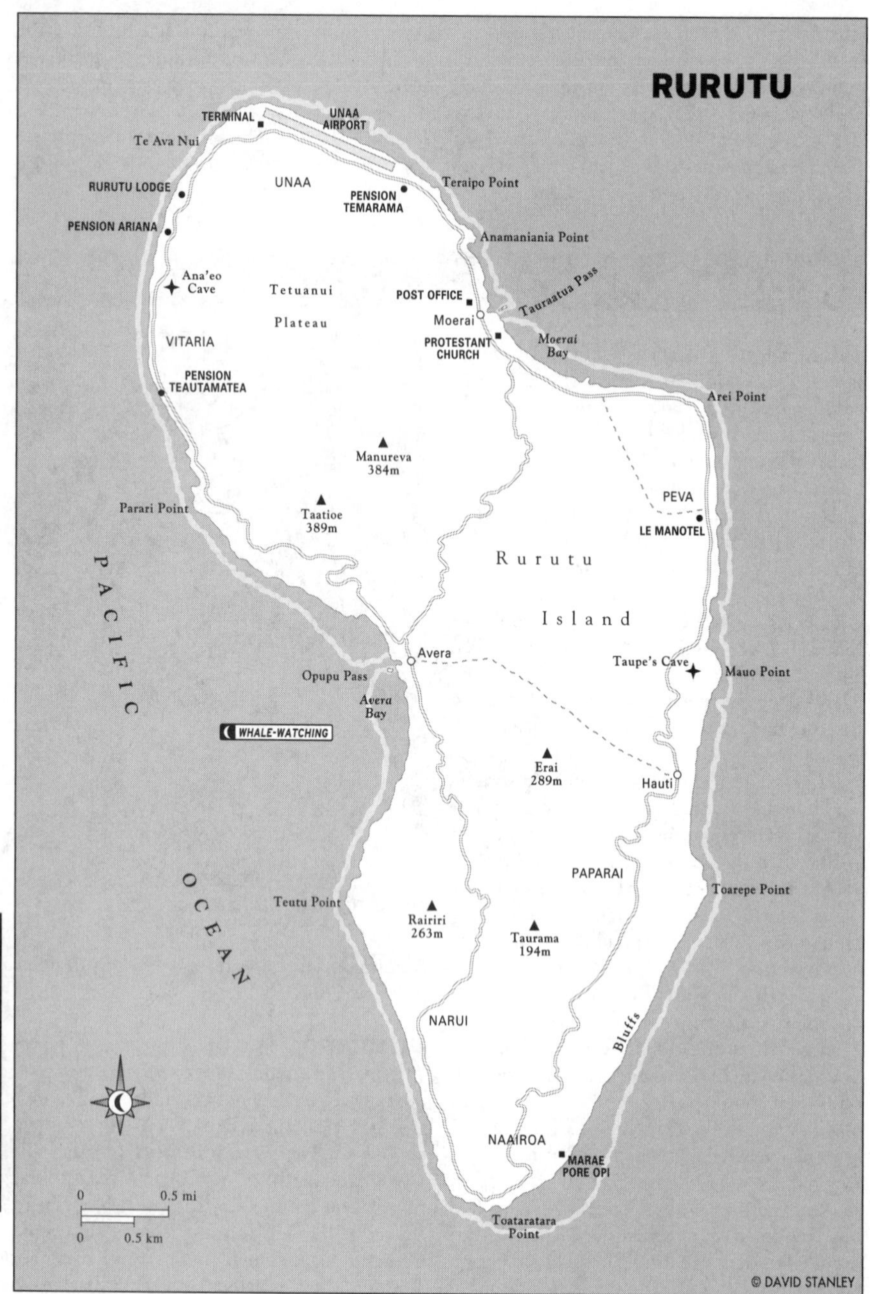
RURUTU
TERMINAL
UNAA AIRPORT
Te Ava Nui
RURUTU LODGE
UNAA
PENSION TEMARAMA
Teraipo Point
PENSION ARIANA
Anamaniania Point
Ana'eo Cave
Tetuanui
Plateau
POST OFFICE
Tauraatua Pass
Moerai
PROTESTANT CHURCH
Moerai Bay
VITARIA
PENSION TEAUTAMATEA
Arei Point
Manureva 384m
Taatioe 389m
Parari Point
PEVA
LE MANOTEL
Rurutu
Island
PACIFIC
Avera
Opupu Pass
Avera Bay
Taupe's Cave
Mauo Point
WHALE-WATCHING
Erai 289m
Hauti
PAPARAI
OCEAN
Teutu Point
Toarepe Point
Rairiri 263m
Taurama 194m
NARUI
Bluffs
NAAIROA
MARAE PORE OPI
0 0.5 mi
0 0.5 km
Toataratara Point
© DAVID STANLEY

ÉRIC DE BISSCHOP

At Moerai village lies the tomb of French navigator Éric de Bisschop, whose exploits equaled, but are not as well known as, those of Thor Heyerdahl. Before World War II de Bisschop sailed a catamaran, the *Kaimiloa*, from Hawaii to the Mediterranean via the Indian Ocean and the tip of Africa. His greatest voyage was aboard the *Tahiti Nui*, a series of three rafts, each of which eventually broke up and sank. In 1956 the *Tahiti Nui* set out from Tahiti to Chile to demonstrate the now-accepted theory that the Polynesians had visited South America in prehistoric times. There, two of his four crewmembers abandoned ship, but de Bisschop doggedly set out to return. After a total of 13 months at sea the expedition's final raft foundered on a reef in the Cook Islands, and its courageous leader, one of the giants of Pacific exploration, was killed.

appeared and electricity functions 24 hours a day, there's almost none of the flashy tourism development you see in the Society Islands nor the pearl farms common in the Tuamotus.

Public transportation is also lacking on the 36-kilometer road around Rurutu, and even by bicycle it can be quite an effort to circle the island, as the route climbs away from the coast on four occasions to avoid high cliffs. South of Avera the road reaches 190 meters, dropping back down to sea level at the southern tip, and then rising again to 124 meters on the way up to Hauti. The direct road from Moerai to Avera also climbs to 168 meters. For hikers a three-kilometer foot trail across the center of the island between Avera and Hauti makes a variety of itineraries possible. Beaches, waterfalls, valleys, bluffs, and around 30 limestone caves beckon the undaunted explorer.

SIGHTS AND RECREATION

One of the nicest spots is near **Toataratara Point** where a side road cuts back up the east coast to **Marae Pore Opi** and a few small beaches. It's quite easy to hike to the TV tower on the summit of **Manureva** from either the 200-meter-high Tetuanui Plateau toward the airport or the saddle of the Moerai–Avera road. Rurutu's highest peak, Taatioe, is nearby. **Teuruarii Marae** behind Pension Teautamatea is a former royal temple excavated in the 1960s. The large **Ana'eo Cave** between Pension Temarama and Pension Ariana is replete with stalactites and stalagmites. Local guides lead hikes along the ridges and to the caves.

Whale-Watching

In June or July, pods of humpback whales swim north from their summer feeding areas in Antarctica. In the warm South Pacific waters the animals mate and bear their young before heading south again in October or November. During their courtship displays, the humpbacks often breach. To see a 14.5-meter male rise from the sea, five-meter flippers flapping at his side, is truly spectacular. A female chaperoning her calf is another favorite sight.

Several companies now operate regular whale-watching trips at Rurutu from July to October. The **Dive Center Raie Manta Club** (tel. 96-84-80, www.raiemantaclub.com), based at Hotel Rurutu Lodge, offers scuba diving with whales at CFP 11,000.

Rurutu Baleines Excursions (tel. 94-07-91) also does half day whale-watching trips. You can even snorkel with the 16-meter beasts. The same company offers four-wheel-drive island tours around Rurutu.

ACCOMMODATIONS AND FOOD

Hotel Rurutu Lodge (tel. 93-03-30, www.hotelrurutulodge.com), on a beach one kilometer southwest of the airport, is the only regular hotel in the Austral Islands. It's a little rundown, with nine tin-roofed bungalows with baths that start at CFP 7,000/9,000 single/double. Add CFP 4,200 per person for breakfast and dinner. Water is extra. Facilities include a restaurant, bar, and derelict swimming pool.

Pension Ariana (tel. 94-06-69, www.pensionariana.pf), just south of Rurutu Lodge, is near a white beach. The four rooms with shared bath are CFP 4,000/5,000 single/double, while the seven bungalows with private baths are CFP 4,500/5,500. The whole place could use a thorough cleaning. Meals, island tours, and bicycle rentals are available. Airport transfers are free.

On the beach a few kilometers south of Rurutu Lodge and six kilometers from Moerai is **Pension Teautamatea** (tel. 93-02-93, www.teautamatea.blogspot.com), with six pleasant rooms with private baths at CFP 8,300/13,000/17,700 single/double/triple, including breakfast and dinner. It rents bicycles, and horseback riding can be arranged.

Pension Temarama (tel. 93-02-80, pensiontemarama@mail.pf), between the airport and Moerai, has eight rooms with private baths in a two-story house from CFP 4,500/5,500. Breakfast and dinner are CFP 4,000 per person per day (no cooking facilities). There's a swimming pool. It provides a good base for visiting the village, and rental cars are available here.

Le Manotel (tel. 93-02-25, www.lemanotel.com) is opposite a sandy beach, six kilometers from the airport on the east side of the island. The four comfortable bungalows in an attractive garden are CFP 11,050/15,578 single/double with half board. A half-day island tour is CFP 3,000 per person. They also rent cars. Round-trip airport transfers are CFP 1,999 per person.

Chambres d'hotes Heiata Nui (tel. 94-05-82, chambresdhotesheiatanui@mail.pf), also known as Chez Louis at Paulette, is near the wharf in Moerai. The six rooms with private baths are CFP 5,000/6,000 single/double. Breakfast is CFP 1,000 per person. Cooking facilities and a lounge are downstairs. Their restaurant, called **Snack Chez Paulette,** serves good local meals and is open to the public.

Restaurant Tiare Hinano (tel. 94-05-00, Tues.–Sun.) in Moerai has Chinese food.

SERVICES AND GETTING THERE

Banque Socredo (tel. 94-04-75) and the post office are at Moerai. The **gendarmerie** (tel. 93-02-05) is at the east end of Moerai.

Unaa Airport (RUR) is at the north tip of Rurutu, three kilometers from Moerai. Some of the hotels offer free transfers to guests who have booked ahead, others charge CFP 1,000 per person round-trip. **Air Tahiti** can be reached at tel. 93-02-50. The supply ship from Papeete ties up at Moerai.

Tubuai

Ten-kilometer-long by five-kilometer-wide Tubuai, largest of the Australs, is 643 kilometers south of Tahiti. Hills on the east and west sides of this oval 45-square-kilometer island are joined by lowland in the middle; when seen from the sea Tubuai looks like two islands. Mount Taitaa (422 meters) is its highest point. Tubuai is surrounded by a barrier reef; a pass on the north side gives access to a wide turquoise lagoon bordered by brilliant white-sand beaches. Surfers are just discovering Tubuai's possibilities.

Tubuai has a mean annual temperature 3°C lower than Tahiti, and it's at its driest and sunniest September–November. The brisk climate permits the cultivation of potatoes, carrots, cabbage, lettuce, oranges, and coffee, but other vegetation is sparse. Several *marae* are on Tubuai, but they're in extremely bad condition, with potatoes growing on the sites. The *Bounty* mutineers unsuccessfully attempted to settle on Tubuai in 1789 (though nothing remains of their Fort George, southeast of Taahuaia). Mormon missionaries arrived as early as 1844, and today there are active branches of the Church of Latter-Day Saints in all the villages. The islanders weave fine pandanus hats, and some wood-carving is done at Mahu.

Most of the 2,000 inhabitants live in

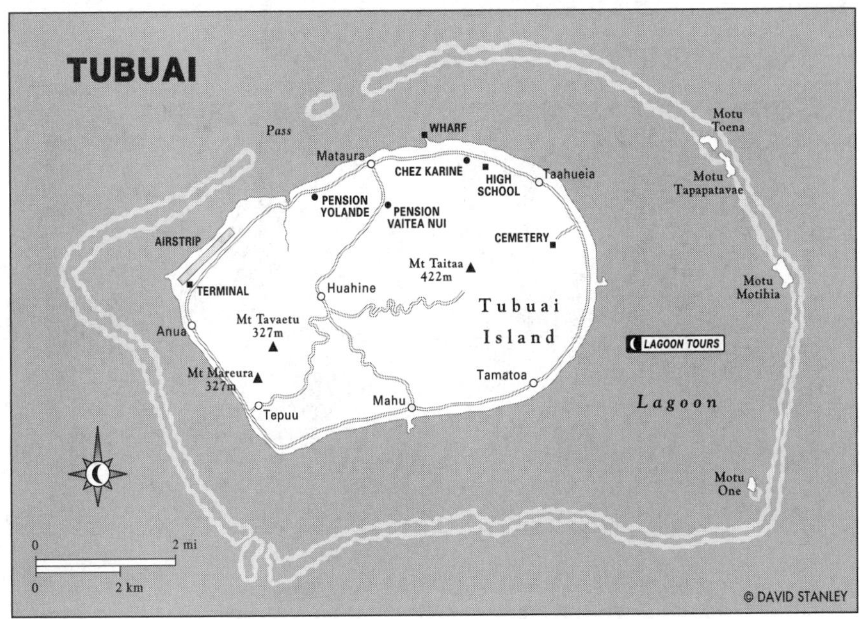

Mataura and Taahuaia, villages on the north coast, though houses and hamlets are found all along the level 24-kilometer road around the island. An eight-kilometer paved road cuts right across the middle of Tubuai to Mahu village on the south coast, but even this presents no challenges for bicyclists (it's an easy hike to the summit of Mount Taitaa from this road). Mataura is the administrative center of the Austral Islands, and the post office, hospital, dental clinic, gendarmerie (tel. 93-22-05), and the branches of two banks are here. The two stores at Mataura bake bread. In early February 2010, Tubuai received a direct hit from Hurricane Oli, damaging or destroying about half the houses on the island.

SPORTS AND RECREATION

La Bonne Bouteille (tel. 95-08-41, www.labonnebouteilleplongee.com) organizes scuba diving (CFP 6,500/11,500 one/two tanks) and *motu* excursions (CFP 5,500) at Tubuai. They also do whale-watching trips (CFP 8,000) mid-July–mid-October.

Tubuai Evasion (tel. 95-01-21, www.tubuai-evasion.com) organizes fishing and snorkeling trips, island tours by four-wheel drive (CFP 4,500) or bicycle (CFP 4,000), and half-day hiking (CFP 4,500). They also rent bicycles at CFP 1,500/5,000 per day/week.

Lagoon Tours

The pensions can help you arrange boat trips to the small reef *motu* just east of Tubuai Island across the lagoon. The snorkeling on the lagoon sides of the *motu* is superb, but one must be aware of deadly currents and undertow when swimming on the ocean side. Avoid the surf and rogue waves by limiting your swimming to the lagoon. It's a great experience to get away from the world and have a shipwreck cartoon island like this all to yourself, but bring adequate drinking water. It's possible to get some very serious sunburn in short order if you're not careful, so sunscreen is also essential. The white sand, coconut trees, views of Tubuai, and sea breezes can be wonderful, provided you take care. Expect to pay around

BREADFRUIT

© DAVID STANLEY

The breadfruit *(uru)* is the plant most often associated with the South Pacific. The theme of a man turning himself into such a tree to save his family during famine often recurs in Polynesian legends. Ancient voyagers brought breadfruit shoots or seeds from Southeast Asia. When baked in an underground oven or roasted over flames, the fruit of the now-seedless Polynesian variety resembles bread. Joseph Banks, botanist on Captain Cook's first voyage, wrote:

> *If a man should in the course of his lifetime plant 10 trees, which if well done might take the labor of an hour or thereabouts, he would completely fulfill his duty to his own as well as future generations.*

The French naturalist Pierre Sonnerat transplanted breadfruit to Réunion in the Indian Ocean as early as 1772, but it's Captain William Bligh who shall always be remembered when the plant is mentioned. In 1787 Bligh set out to collect young shoots in Tahiti for transfer to the West Indies, where they were to be planted to feed slaves. On the way back, his crew mutinied in Tongan waters and cast off both Bligh and the breadfruit. The indomitable captain managed to reach Dutch Timor in a rowboat and in 1792 returned to Tahiti with another ship to complete his task.

The breadfruit *(Artocarpus altilis)*, a tall tree with broad green leaves, provides shade as well as food. A well-watered tree can produce as many as 1,000 pale green breadfruits a year. Robert Lee Eskridge described a breadfruit thus:

> *Its outer rind or skin, very hard, is covered with a golf-ball-like surface of small irregular pits or tiny hollows. An inner rind about a half-inch thick surrounds the fruit itself, which when baked tastes not unlike a doughy potato. Perhaps fresh bread, rolled up until it becomes a semi firm mass, best describes the breadfruit when cooked.*

The starchy, easily digested fruit is rich in vitamin B. When consumed with a protein such as fish or meat it serves as an energy food. The Polynesians learned to preserve breadfruit by pounding it into a paste, which was kept in leaf-lined pits to ferment into *mahi*. Like the coconut, the breadfruit tree itself had many uses, including the provision of wood for outrigger canoes.

MUTINY ON THE *BOUNTY*

In 1788 the HMS *Bounty* sailed from England for the Pacific to collect breadfruit plants to supplement the diet of slaves in the West Indies. Because the *Bounty* arrived at Tahiti at the wrong time of year, it was necessary to spend a long five months there collecting samples, and during this time, part of the crew became overly attached to that isle of pleasure. On April 28, 1789, in Tongan waters, they mutinied against Lieutenant William Bligh under 24-year-old Master's Mate Fletcher Christian. Bligh was set adrift in an open boat with the 18 men who chose to go with him. He then performed the amazing feat of sailing 6,500 kilometers in 41 days, reaching Dutch Timor to give the story to the world.

After the mutiny, the *Bounty* sailed back to Tahiti. Fletcher Christian set out with eight mutineers, 18 Polynesian men and women, and one small girl to find a new home where they would be safe from capture. In 1791 the crewmembers who elected to remain on Tahiti were picked up by the HMS *Pandora* and returned to England for trial. Three were executed. An attempt to colonize Tubuai in the Austral Islands failed, and the *Bounty* sailed through the Cook Islands, Tonga, and Fiji, until Christian remembered the discovery of tiny Pitcairn Island by Captain Carteret of the *Swallow* in 1767. They changed course for Pitcairn and arrived on January 15, 1790. After removing everything of value, the mutineers burned the *Bounty* to avoid detection. For 18 years after the mutiny, the world knew nothing of the fate of the *Bounty* until the American sealer *Topaz* called at Pitcairn for water in 1808 and solved the mystery.

CFP 7,000 per person including a picnic lunch for a trip like this.

ACCOMMODATIONS

Pension Yolande (tel. 95-05-52), lagoon-side in Mataura, two kilometers from the airport, has six rooms at CFP 5,250/6,300 single/double. For CFP 3,000, Yolande will serve you a huge dinner of up to seven courses (duck with tamarind sauce, chicken in lemon sauce, *poisson cru,* spring rolls, baked fish, etc.). Sam is a guitarist who also plays keyboard. An excellent beach is just 50 meters away.

Pension Vaitea Nui (tel. 93-22-40, www.vaiteanui.com), inland a bit from Mataura, has five rooms with baths in a long block at CFP 4,235/6,960 single/double. Cooking facilities are not provided, but there's a restaurant.

Near the college at the west end of Taahueia village, just under three kilometers east of Mataura, is **Chez Karine et Talé** (tel. 93-23-40, charles@mail.pf), with two pleasant self-catering bungalows at CFP 5,000/8,000 single/double, including breakfast.

Pension Toena (tel. 95-04-12, www.toena.pf), also in Taahueia, five kilometers east at Mataura, offers two rooms in the owner's house at CFP 6,500/10,000 single/double with half board. Airport transfers are free.

FOOD

From **Restaurant Te Motu** (tel. 93-24-40) near Taahuaia, you get a good view of the *motu.* Smoked *tazard* (fish), *poisson cru,* mahimahi, and roast lamb are on the menu. You can order drinks.

Snack Vahinerii (tel. 95-03-97, Mon.–Sat.), near the main wharf at Mataura, has grilled fish, grilled chicken, chow mein, *poisson cru,* and grilled beef starting around CFP 1,000. No alcohol is served (but you can bring your own).

GETTING THERE

Tubuai Airport (TUB), in the northwest corner of the island, opened in 1972. The best beach on the main island is beside the five-kilometer road from the airport to Mataura. All the accommodations offer free transfers to guests. **Air Tahiti** (tel. 93-22-75) arrives from Papeete, Rurutu, and Raivavae several times a week.

Ships enter the lagoon through a passage in the barrier reef on the north side and proceed to the wharf a kilometer east of Mataura. Otherwise, the lagoon is too shallow for navigation.

GETTING AROUND

There's no public transportation on Tubuai, but some of the pensions rent bicycles and cars. **Europcar** (tel. 95-02-96) at Mataura rents Fiat Pandas. The only gas station is near the wharf at Mataura.

Other Austral Islands

RIMATARA

Only a narrow fringing reef hugs Rimatara's lagoonless shore; arriving passengers are landed at Amaru or Mutua Ura by whaleboat, and it's customary for newcomers to pass through a cloud of purifying smoke from beachside fires. The women of Rimatara make fine pandanus hats, mats, and bags, and shell necklaces. *Monoï* (skin oil) is prepared from gardenias and coconut oil. As yet without a harbor, wharf, hotels, restaurants, bars, and taxis, Rimatara is still a place to escape the world.

This smallest (nine square kilometers) and lowest (84 meters) of the Australs is home to fewer than 800 people. Dirt roads lead from Amaru, the main village, to Anapoto and Mutua Ura. Water is short in the dry season. The wreck of the interisland ship *Vaeanu II* sits on the reef off Amaru, where it was lost in April 2002. Rimatara began receiving Air Tahiti flights at the new airport in April 2006.

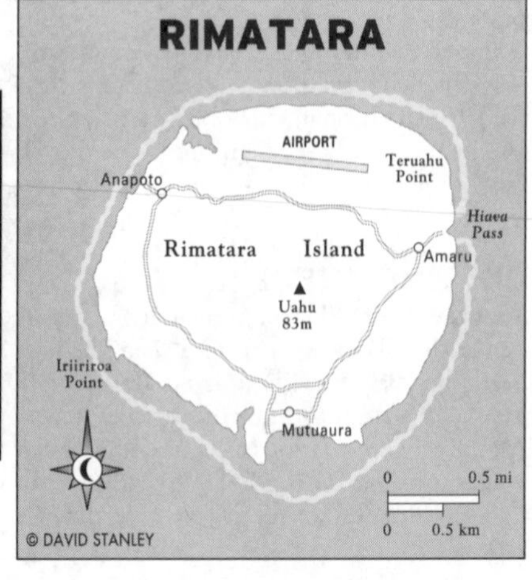

Uninhabited Maria (or Hull) is a four-islet atoll 192 kilometers northwest of Rimatara, visited once or twice a year by men from Rimatara or Rurutu for fishing and copra making. They stay on the atoll two or three months, among seabirds and giant lobsters.

RAIVAVAE

This appealing, nine-kilometer-long and two-kilometer-wide island is just south of the tropic of Capricorn and thus outside the tropics. It's the third most southerly island in the South Pacific (only Rapa and Easter Island are farther south). For archaeology and natural beauty, this is one of the finest islands in Polynesia. Fern-covered Mount Hiro (437 meters) is the highest point on 18-square-kilometer Raivavae. A barrier reef encloses an emerald lagoon, but the 28 small coral *motu* are all on the southern and eastern parts of the reef. The tropical vegetation is rich: Rose and sandalwood are used to make perfumes for local use.

A few years after the arrival of Protestant missionaries in 1822, a malignant fever epidemic reduced the people of Raivavae from 3,000 to a mere 80 in 1834. The present population of around 900 lives in four coastal villages, Rairua, Mahanatoa, Anatonu, and Vaiuru, linked by the 22-kilometer dirt road around the island. A shortcut route direct from Rairua to Vaiuru crosses a 119-meter saddle, with splendid views of the island. The post office is in Rairua.

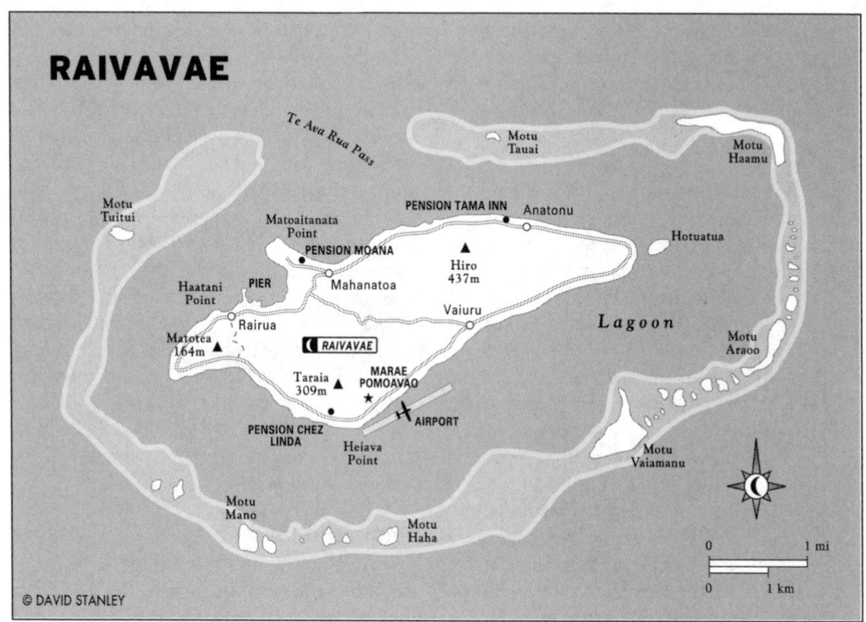

Archaeological Sites

Like the Marquesas and Easter Island, Raivavae was once home to a civilization that erected large stone anthropomorphic figures called tikis. Different teams led by John F. G. Stokes (1921), Frank Stimson (1938), Thor Heyerdahl (1956), Donald Marshall (1957), and Edmundo Edwards (1991) have explored the ancient temples and defensive terraces of Raivavae. Many 2–3-meter-high red stone statues once stood on the island, but most have since been smashed, and two were removed to Tahiti, where they can be seen on the grounds of the Gauguin Museum. One big tiki is still standing in a field by the road just west of Mahanatoa village toward Rairua on Raivavae. Christian converts destroyed most of Raivavae's 92 *marae.* At **Marae Pomoavao** opposite the airport on the south side of the island, huge stone blocks tilt upward among the undergrowth. Several other *marae* remain, but you'd need a guide to find them.

Practicalities

Pension Moana (tel. 95-42-66, moanapension@mail.pf) at Mahanatoa has three rooms with shared bath at CFP 6,000/8,500 per person with half/full board. **Pension Ataha** (tel. 95-43-69, pension.ataha@live.fr) in Rairua charges about the same.

Pension Chez Linda (tel. 95-44-25, www.pensionlindaraivavae.pf) near the airport has four rooms with shared bath at CFP 7,000/10,000 single/double with half board. Bicycles are for rent at CFP 1,000 per day, while picnics on a *motu* are CFP 3,000. Airport transfers are free.

Pension Tama Inn (tel. 95-42-52, www.raivavaetama.com), next to the large church in Anatonu village, has three beach and two garden bungalows, all CFP 8,500/13,000 single/double with half board. Two rooms with shared bath in the main house cost the same. Emmy White is a gracious host who can organize island tours.

In 2002 an airport was constructed on land reclaimed from the lagoon five kilometers southeast of Rairua, and Air Tahiti operates flights from Papeete (CFP 25,100) three times a week. Ships enter the lagoon through a pass on the north side and tie up to the pier at Rairua. A boat calls at the island about every 10–14 days.

RAPA

At 27°38° south latitude, Rapa is the southernmost island in the South Pacific, and one of the most isolated and spectacular. Its nearest neighbor is Raivavae, 600 kilometers away, and Tahiti is 1,244 kilometers north. It's sometimes called Rapa Iti (Little Rapa) to distinguish it from Rapa Nui (Easter Island). Soaring peaks reaching 650 meters form a horseshoe around magnificent Haurei Bay, Rapa's crater harbor, the western section of a drowned volcano. This is only one of 12 deeply indented bays around the island; the absence of reefs allows the sea to cut into the 40-square-kilometer island's outer basalt coasts. Offshore are several sugarloaf-shaped islets. The east slopes of the mountains are bare, while large fern forests are found on the west. Coconut trees cannot grow in the foggy, temperate climate; instead coffee and taro are the main crops.

During the two decades following the arrival of missionaries in 1826, Rapa's population dropped from 2,000 to 300 because of the introduction of European diseases. By 1851 it was down to just 70, and after smallpox and dysentery arrived on a Peruvian ship in 1863, it was a miracle that anyone survived at all. The present population of about 480 lives at Area and Haurei villages on the north and south sides of Rapa's great open bay, connected only by boat. The windy anchorage is around 20 meters deep.

Hill Fortresses of Rapa

Between Haurei and Hiri bays, a timeworn Polynesian fortress with terraces is situated on the crest of a ridge at Morongo Uta, commanding a wide outlook over the steep, rugged hills. Morongo Uta was cleared of vegetation by a party of archaeologists led by William Mulloy in 1956 and is still easily visited. A Norwegian team led by Thor Heyerdahl also studied and restored the earthwork hill fortifications of Rapa. Heyerdahl ended up producing a massive volume with the findings of his expedition. About a dozen of these *pa* (fortresses) are found above Haurei Bay, built to defend the territories of the different tribes of overpopulated ancient Rapa. Today the young men of Rapa organize eight-day bivouacs to hunt wild goats, which range across the island. It's possible to climb to Morongo Uta Pa from Haurei in about an hour on a steep trail for the splendid views.

Accommodations

If you're planning to stay on Rapa, it might be useful to write Le Maire, Rapa, Îles Australes, French Polynesia, well in advance, stating your name, nationality, age, and profession. Information may also be available from the Subdivision Administrative des Îles Australes (tel. 46-86-76), rue des Poilus Tahitiens, Papeete. A number of local residents also rent rooms in their homes. There's no airport on Rapa. The *Tuhaa Pae III* calls at Rapa monthly, so that's how long you'll be there.

Marotiri

Marotiri, or the "Bass Rocks," are nine uninhabited islets totaling just four hectares, 74 kilometers southeast of Rapa. Amazingly enough, some of these pinnacles are crowned with artificially constructed stone platforms and round "towers." One 105-meter-high pinnacle is visible from Rapa in very clear weather. Landing is difficult.

THE TUAMOTU AND GAMBIER ISLANDS

Arrayed in two parallel northwest-southeast chains scattered across an area of ocean 600 kilometers wide and 1,500 kilometers long, the Tuamotus are the largest group of coral atolls in the world. Of the 78 atolls in the group, 21 have one entrance (pass), 10 have two passes, and 47 have no pass at all. Some have an unbroken ring of reef around the lagoon, while others appear as a necklace of islets separated by channels. Although the land area of the Tuamotus is only 726 square kilometers, the lagoons of the atolls total some 6,000 square kilometers of sheltered water.

Variable currents, sudden storms, and poor charts make cruising this group by yacht extremely hazardous—in fact, the Tuamotus are popularly known as the Dangerous Archipelago, or the Labyrinth. Wrecks litter the reefs of many atolls. The breakers become visible only when one is within eight kilometers of the reef, and once in, a yacht must carry on through the group. The usual route is to sail either between Rangiroa and Arutua after a stop at Ahe, or through the Fakarava Pass between Toau and Fakarava. Winds are generally from the east, varying to northeast November–May and southeast June–October.

The Tuamotu people have always lived off seafood, pandanus nuts, and coconuts. They once dove to depths of 30 meters and more, wearing only tiny goggles, to collect mother-of-pearl shells. This activity has largely ceased, as overharvesting has made the oysters rare. Today, cultured-pearl farms operate on Ahe, Aratika, Arutua, Fakarava, Hao, Hikueru, Katiu, Kaukura, Kauehi, Makemo,

HIGHLIGHTS

Tiputa Pass: A fantastic profusion of marine life is seen in this pass in Rangiroa, including sharks and dolphins in abundance. Both scuba diving and organized snorkeling are possible here (page 197).

Garuae Pass: Fakarava boasts French Polynesia's most fabulous drift dive, with a truly amazing variety and abundance of marine life, including numerous sharks and healthy corals (page 206).

Makatea: This atoll is different from every other Tuamotu atoll in that it has been lifted out of the sea. A major phosphate mine operated here until 1966 (page 212).

Rikitea: The most impressive Catholic cathedral in French Polynesia is only one of the relics of 19th century religious fanaticism extant on Mangareva. Attend choir practice for a chance to hear native Mangarevan singing (page 218).

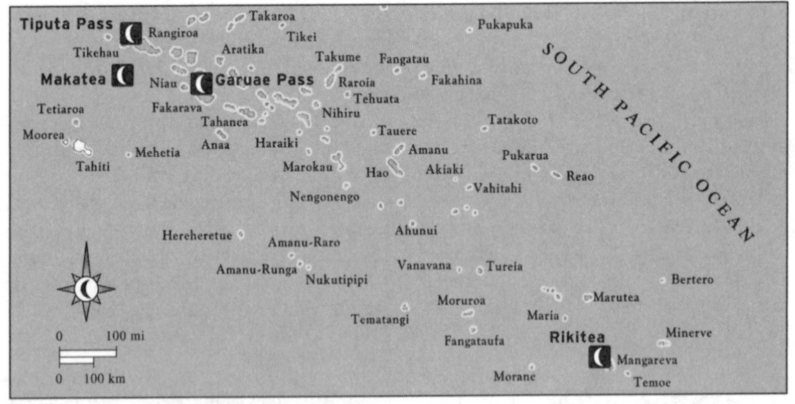

LOOK FOR [icon] TO FIND RECOMMENDED SIGHTS, ACTIVITIES, DINING, AND LODGING.

Manihi, Marutea South, Nengonengo, Raroia, Takapoto, Takaroa, Takume, Taenga, and others. Cultured black pearls *(Pinctada margaritifera)* from the Tuamotus and Gambiers are world-famous. The pearl industry has reversed the depopulation of the atolls and spread prosperity through this remote region.

The scarcity of land and fresh water has always been a major problem. A total of around 17,000 people live on the 48 inhabited islands. Many of these dry, coconut-covered atolls have only a few hundred inhabitants. Although airstrips exist on 26 islands, the isolation has led many Tuamotuans to migrate to Papeete. Deluxe resorts exist on Rangiroa, Tikehau, Manihi, and Fakarava, and homestay accommodations are available on most of the other atolls.

All the Tuamotu atolls offer splendid snorkeling possibilities (bring snorkeling gear), though scuba diving is developed only on Fakarava, Manihi, Rangiroa, and Tikehau. The advantage of atolls other than these is that the people are far less affected by packaged tourism. There it should be easy to hitch rides with the locals across to *le secteur* (uninhabited *motu*) as they go to cut copra or tend the pearl farms. Just don't expect many facilities on these tiny specks of sand scattered in a solitary sea.

Beware of eating poisonous fish all across this archipelago.

© TAHITI TOURISME

A *motu* separates ocean from lagoon in the Tuamotu Islands.

PLANNING YOUR TIME

Air Tahiti has air passes including Ahe, Fakarava, Manihi, Rangiroa, and Tikehau, making them the easiest atolls to visit. Your precise itinerary will depend on flight connections, as the only services that operate daily are those to and from Papeete.

Even serious scuba divers will probably find two or three nights on each atoll sufficient. Rangiroa has the largest selection of hotels, restaurants, and tours, but most activities are water-based. The Tuamotu Islands lack the mountain scenery and archaeological sites found elsewhere in French Polynesia, and those looking for land-based sightseeing, shopping, or organized entertainment will be disappointed. Those who come for the scuba diving and snorkeling will be at home in the Tuamotus.

HISTORY

The Tuamotus were originally settled around A.D. 1000 from the Society and Marquesas Islands, perhaps by political refugees. The inhabitants of the atolls frequently warred among themselves or against those of a Society island, and even King Pomare II was unable to conquer the group despite help from the missionaries and European firearms. Ironically, the Pomare family itself originated on Fakarava.

Magellan's sighting of Pukapuka on the northeast fringe of the Tuamotus in 1521 made it the first South Pacific island ever to be seen by European eyes. Other famous explorers who passed through the Tuamotus include Quirós (1606), Schouten and Le Maire (1616), Roggeveen (1722), Byron (1765), Wallis (1767), Bougainville (1768), Cook (1769), Bligh (1792), Kotzebue (1816), and Bellingshausen (1820), yet it was not until 1835 that all of the islands had been "discovered." Of the 14 European expeditions between 1606 and 1816, only eight bothered to go ashore. Of these, all but Quirós were involved in skirmishes with the islanders. Centuries later, a group of Scandinavians under the leadership of Thor Heyerdahl ran aground on Raroia atoll on August 7, 1947, after having sailed 7,000 kilometers from South America in 101 days on the raft *Kon-Tiki* to prove that Peruvian Indians could have done the same thing centuries before.

Pearl shells and bêche-de-mer were being

THE TUAMOTU AND GAMBIER ISLANDS
Manihi
Ahe
Takaroa
Takapoto
Tikei
Mataiva
TIPUTA PASS
Tikehau
Rangiroa
Arutua
Apataki
Aratika
MAKATEA
Kaukura
Toau
Fakarava Pass
Taiaro
Takume
GARUAE PASS
Kauehi
Raraka
Raroia
Niau
Taenga
Makemo
Katiu
Tehuata
Society Islands
Tuanake
Hiti
Nihiru
Fakarava
Faaite
Tahanea
Tepoto South
Marutea
Motutunga
Tetiaroa
Tekokota
Haraiki
Moorea
Anaa
Hikueru
Tahiti
Reitoru
Mehetia
Marokau
Ravahere
Nengonengo
Hereheretue
Duke of Gloucester Islands
SOUTH
Amanu-Raro
Amanu-Runga
Nukutipipi
PACIFIC
OCEAN
Austral Islands
Tubuai
Tropic Of Capricorn 23.5°S
Raivavae

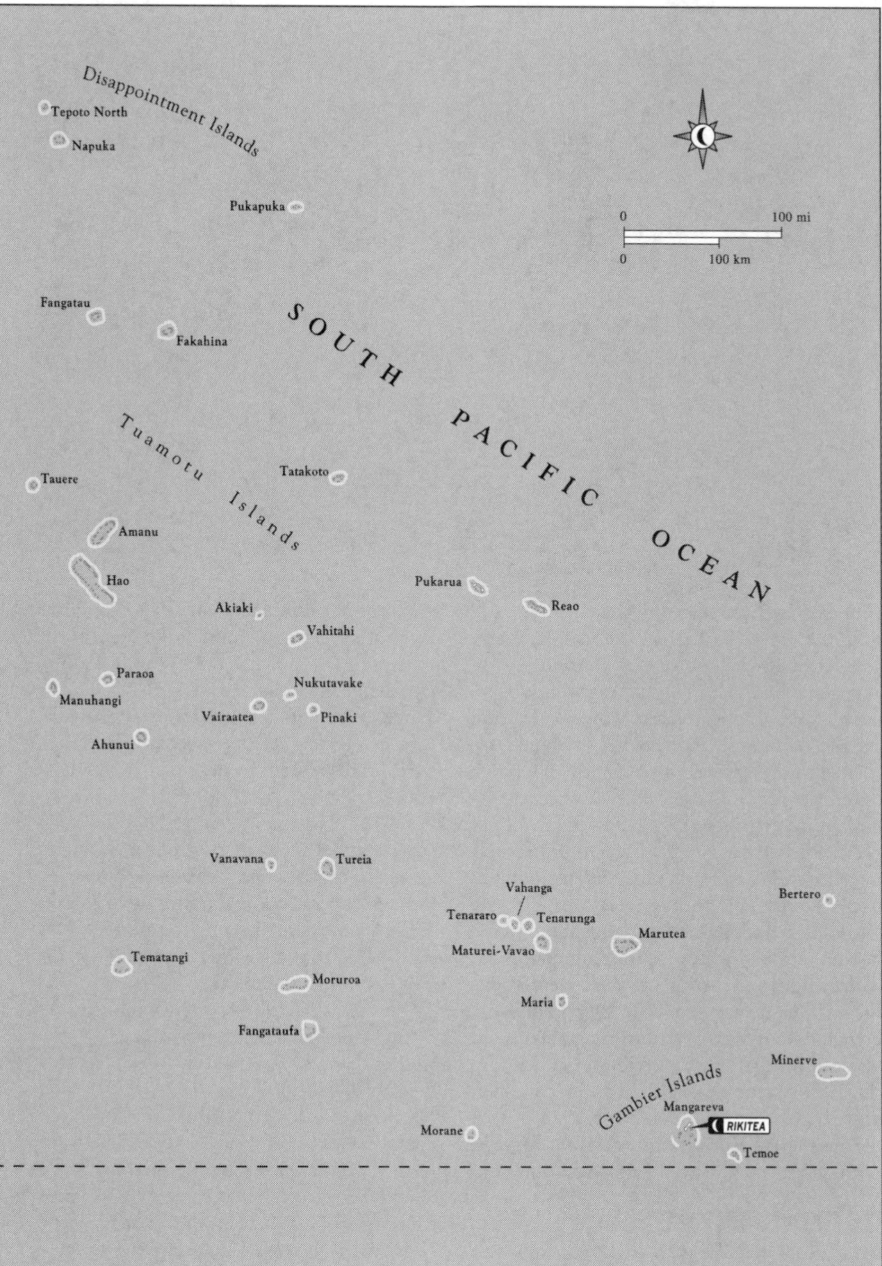
Disappointment Islands
Tepoto North
Napuka
Pukapuka
0
100 mi
0
100 km
Fangatau
Fakahina
SOUTH PACIFIC OCEAN
Tuamotu Islands
Tauere
Tatakoto
Amanu
Hao
Pukarua
Reao
Akiaki
Vahitahi
Paraoa
Manuhangi
Nukutavake
Vairaatea
Pinaki
Ahunui
Vanavana
Tureia
Vahanga
Tenararo
Tenarunga
Bertero
Marutea
Maturei-Vavao
Tematangi
Moruroa
Maria
Fangataufa
Minerve
Gambier Islands
Mangareva
RIKITEA
Morane
Temoe

© TAHITI TOURISME

a white sand beach in the Tuamotu Islands

collected by European trading ships as early as 1809. An American Mormon missionary arrived in 1845, followed by Catholics from Mangareva in 1851, and today two-thirds of the people are Catholic, the rest Mormon. Most of the Mormons are actually Sanitos ("saints") affiliated with the Reorganized Mormon Church of Independence, Missouri, which rejects many of the teachings of the Utah Mormons.

After Tahiti came under French "protection" in 1842, the Tuamotus were gradually brought under French rule through dealings with the local chiefs and Catholic missionary activity. For more than a century, making copra and collecting mother-of-pearl shell were about the only monetary activities. By comparison, French military activity, tourism, and cultured black pearls are recent developments. During the 19th century French naval officers were posted on Anaa and Fakarava, but since 1923 the group has been administered from Papeete. Local government is split into 16 communes.

GETTING THERE

Air Tahiti has flights to Ahe, Apataki, Aratika, Arutua, Fakarava, Katiu, Kauehi, Kaukura, Manihi, Mataiva, Niau, Rangiroa, Takapoto, Takaroa, and Tikehau in the northern Tuamotus, and Anaa, Faaite, Fakahina, Fangatau, Hao, Hikueru, Makemo, Mangareva, Napuka, Nukutavake, Pukapuka, Pukarua, Raroia, Reao, Takume, Tatakoto, Tureia, and Vahitahi in the east.

By Boat

Interisland boats call at most of the Tuamotu atolls about once a week, bringing imported foods and other goods and returning to Papeete with fish. However you come, be aware that it's very difficult to change foreign currency on the atolls, so bring enough cash.

The *Cobia III* runs to the Tuamotus, departing Monday at 1300 for Kaukura (arriving Tuesday 1200), Apataki (2000), Arutua (Wednesday 0500), Aratika (0800), and Fakarava (Thursday 0600), returning to Papeete Friday at 1200. The *Cobia III* has three four-bed cabins at CFP 6,300 one-way. Meals are sold on board. The office (tel. 43-36-43) is on the Tuamotu Wharf at Motu Uta, Papeete.

The *Kura Ora III* leaves Papeete twice a month on a wide-ranging voyage to 23 atolls in the central and eastern Tuamotus. Their office (tel. 45-55-45) is on Papeete's Tuamotu wharf.

Many other copra boats, such as the *Hotu Maru, Mareva Nui,* and *Saint Xavier Maris Stella III* also serve the Tuamotus. Ask about ships of this kind at the large warehouses west of Papeete's Motu Uta interisland wharf. The *Nuku Hau* and *Taporo VIII* go as far as the Gambier Islands. The *Nuku Hau* sails from Papeete to Hao, Tureia, Tenania, Marutea, Rikitea, Tematangi, Nukutepipi, and Hereheretui once a month. Tickets are available at the *Hawaiki-Nui* office (tel. 54-99-54) at Motu Uta.

Rangiroa

Rangiroa, 300 kilometers northeast of Papeete, is the Tuamotus' most populous atoll. Its 1,020-square-kilometer aquamarine lagoon is 78 kilometers long, 24 kilometers wide (too far to see across), and 225 kilometers around—the island of Tahiti would fit inside its reef. The name Rangiroa means "extended sky." Some 240 *motu* sit on this reef. Although Rangiroa is the largest atoll in eastern Polynesia, it's not the biggest in the South Pacific, as all of the brochures claim. Ontong Java in the Solomon Islands encloses 1,400 square kilometers of lagoon. The world's biggest atoll—as the brochures concede—is 2,174-square-kilometer Kwajalein in the Marshall Islands.

Two deep passages through the north side of Rangiroa's coral ring allow a constant exchange of water between the open sea and the lagoon, creating a fertile habitat. While lagoons in the Society Islands are often murky because of runoff from the main volcanic islands and pollution from coastal communities, the waters of the Tuamotus are clean and fresh, with some of the best swimming, snorkeling, and scuba diving in the South Pacific. You've never seen so many fish! However, in 1998 it was revealed that 80 percent of the reefs at Rangiroa had suffered bleaching because of increased water temperatures brought about by the El Niño phenomenon, completing the destruction

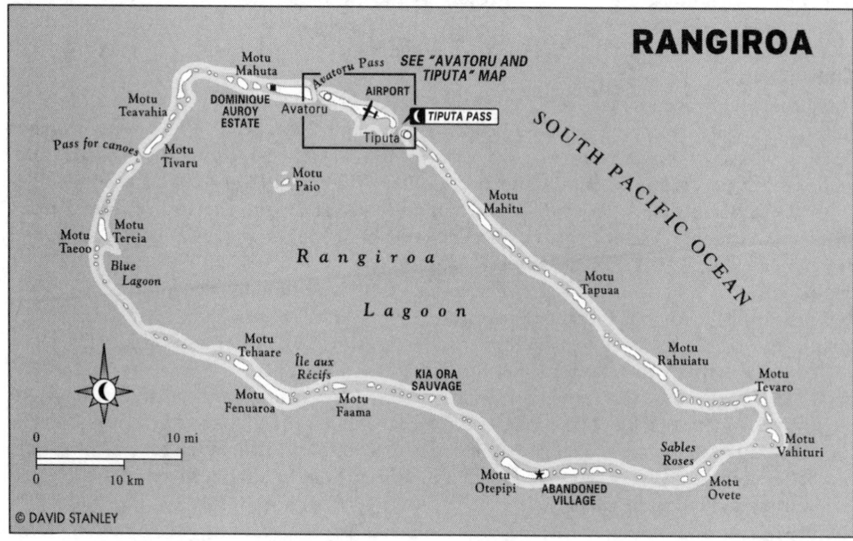

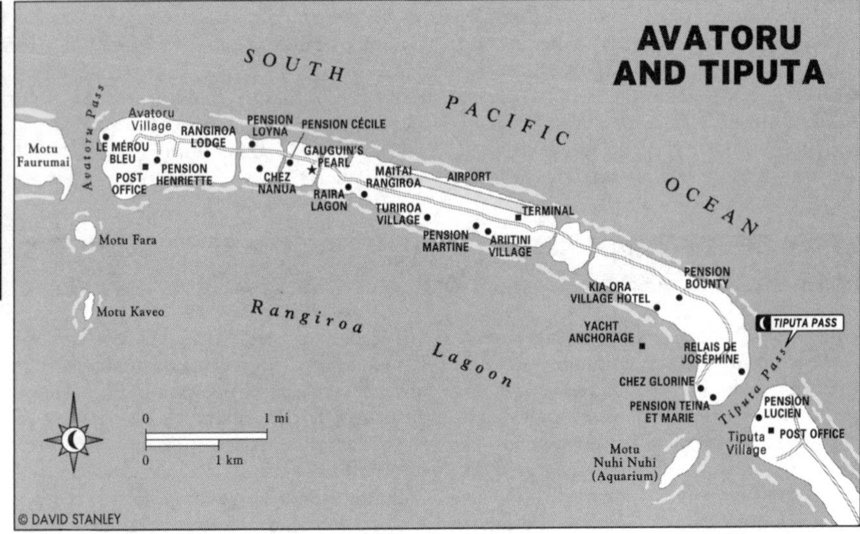

wrought earlier by hurricanes. What draws people to Rangi (as everyone calls it) is the marine life in the lagoon, not the coral. This is one of the prime shark-viewing locales of the world. Most tourists to Rangiroa are French or Italian. The only real beach here is in front of the Kia Ora, and nondivers (and especially honeymooners) may get bored.

Orientation

Rangiroa's twin villages, each facing a passage 500 meters wide, are home to 2,500 people. Avatoru village on Avatoru Pass is at the west end of the airport island, about six kilometers from the airport itself. A paved 10-kilometer road runs east from Avatoru past the airport and the Hôtel Kia Ora Village to Tiputa Pass. Tiputa village is just across the water. The accommodations listings are arranged by category from west to east along this road.

Both villages have small stores; the town hall and hotel school are at Tiputa, and the medical center, gendarmerie (tel. 93-11-55), college, and marine research center are at Avatoru. Avatoru has better commercial facilities, but Tiputa is less touristy and offers the chance to escape by simply walking and wading southeast.

Most of the accommodations face the tranquil lagoon rather than the windy sea, and large ships can enter the lagoon through either pass. For yachts, the sheltered anchorage by the Hôtel Kia Ora Village near Tiputa Pass is recommended (as opposed to the Avatoru anchorage, which is exposed to swells and chop). Far less English is spoken on Rangiroa than in the Society Islands.

SIGHTS

Gauguin's Pearl (tel. 93-11-30, www.gauguinspearl.pf, Mon.–Sat. 0830–1730, Sat and Sun. 0900–1200 and 1500–1700), a pearl farm between Avatoru and the airport, offers a free one-hour tour weekdays at 0830, 1030, and 1400.

Boutique Ikimasho (tel. 96-84-46, www.ikimasho-black-pearls.com), at the entrance to Avatoru, also showcases Tuamotu black pearls.

French Polynesia's only vineyard is on Motu Faurumai, just west of Avatoru Pass. Visits to the **Dominique Auroy Estate** (www.vindetahiti.pf) can be arranged by calling Sébastien (tel. 79-07-45 or 96-04-70). The tour (CFP 8,000) departs Avatoru at 1300 and includes

© DAVID STANLEY

The luxury catamaran *Haumana* cruises the Tuamotu Islands from Rangiroa.

a visit to the vineyards and technical installations along with wine tasting.

SPORTS AND RECREATION

Tiputa Pass

The strong tidal currents *(opape)* through the Tiputa Pass generate flows of three to six knots. It's exciting to shoot this 30-meter-deep pass on an incoming tide, and all the dive shops offer this activity using small motorboats or Zodiacs. Some of the dives tend to be longer and deeper than the norm. The Tiputa Pass current dive begins 45 meters down and is only for advanced divers; even the Tiputa Pass Shark Cave dive to 35 meters calls for some experience. Water temperatures average 27–30°C with visibilities of 30–60 meters.

The marine life seen on drift dives through the pass is fantastic, with humphead wrasses, manta rays, barracudas, turtles, dolphins, and sharks present in abundance. Most of the time the sharks are harmless blacktip or gray reef sharks (but don't risk touching them, even if you see other divers doing so). Big hammerhead sharks frequent Tiputa Pass December–March, while spotted eagle rays are common November–April and manta rays July–October. The dive schedules vary according to the tides, winds, and number of tourists on the atoll, and it's wise to book ahead. All of the operators mentioned below offer free hotel pickups. Many experienced divers rate this as the best dive of their lives.

If you're not a diver, several companies, including **Rangiroa Activités** (tel. 77-65-86, www.rangiroa-snorkeling.com), offer a snorkel through Tiputa Pass at CFP 5,000 per person (don't risk snorkeling in the pass on your own; it can be extremely dangerous due to the strong currents). The dolphin-watching from shore here is also excellent and not to be missed.

Scuba Diving

Rangiroa's original scuba operator is the friendly **Raie Manta Club** (tel. 96-84-80 or 72-31-45, www.raiemantaclub.com), with branches near Rangiroa Lodge in Avatoru village and next to Pension Marie et Teina on Tiputa Pass. Diving costs CFP 6,500 per

TEN SAFETY RULES OF DIVING

1. The most important rule in scuba diving is to **breathe continuously.** If you establish this rule, you won't forget and hold your breath, and overexpansion will never occur.
2. **Come up at a rate of 18 meters per minute or less.** This allows the gas dissolved in your body under pressure to come out of solution safely and also prevents vertigo from fast ascents. Always make a precautionary decompression stop at a depth of five meters.
3. **Never escape to the surface.** Panic is the diver's worst enemy.
4. **Stop, think, and then act.** Always maintain control.
5. **Pace yourself. Know your limitations. A diver should always be able to rest and relax in the water.** Proper use of the buoyancy vest will allow you to rest on the surface and maintain control underwater. Divers who become fatigued in the water are a danger to themselves and their buddies.
6. **Never dive with a cold.** Avoid alcoholic beverages but drink plenty of water. Get a good night's sleep and refrain from strenuous physical activities on the day you dive. Dive conservatively if you are overweight or more than 45 years of age. Make fewer dives the last two days before flying and no dives at all during the final 24 hours.
7. **Plan your dive.** Know your starting point, your diving area, and your exit areas. **Dive your plan.**
8. **Never exceed the safe sport-diving limit of 30 meters.** Make your first dive the deepest of the day.
9. All equipment must be equipped with **quick releases.**
10. **Wear adequate protective clothing against sun and coral.**

person for one tank, including a float through the pass. For the more enthusiastic, a 10-dive package is CFP 61,000 (can be shared by a couple and also used at Tikehau). Every dive is different (falling, pass, cave, undulating bottom, hollow, and night). Snorkelers can go along with the divers when practical; otherwise an introductory dive is CFP 6,900. Divers come from all parts of the world to dive with this highly professional team.

Rangiroa Paradive (tel. 96-05-55, www.rangiroaparadive.com) is next to Chez Glorine at Tiputa Pass. It's CFP 6,400 per dive; the package prices are CFP 30,000/50,100 for 5/10 dives. You can ask for a small price reduction if you haven't booked ahead. Rangiroa Paradive isn't as aggressive about shark feeding as the Raie Manta Club, but it does explore the shark caves, and you'll see legions of sharks on its drift dives. There's no provision for snorkelers here, and divers must show their cards. Without a card you could still do an introductory dive for CFP 7,000.

The Six Passengers (tel. 96-02-60, www.the6passengers.com) is in a hut between Chez Glorine and the Kia Ora. Diving from a Zodiac is CFP 6,600/59,000 for one/10 tanks, night dives CFP 7,800, gear and pickups included. The name refers to the number of people he can take out each time. Snorkelers are not accepted.

TOPdive (tel. 96-05-60, www.topdive.com), on the beach just west of the Kia Ora, offers scuba diving at 0800, 1000, and 1400 (one/10 dives CFP 7,900/67,000). You can also use its 10-dive package at TOPdive centers on Moorea, Bora Bora, Fakarava, and Tahiti.

The **Blue Dolphins Diving Center** (tel. 96-03-01, www.bluedolphinsdiving.com), based at the Hôtel Kia Ora Village, has Japanese-speaking monitors. Diving is at 0730 and 1330 daily with packages of one/10 dives at

CFP 7,700/69,300 including gear. The 10-dive package cannot be shared between two people.

Lagoon Tours

Popular lagoon excursions include picnics to the **Blue Lagoon,** a fish-filled lagoon within a lagoon at Motu Taeoo; the **Île aux Récifs,** a number of uplifted coral formations on the south side of the lagoon; the **Sables Roses,** a stretch of pink sand at the southeast end of the lagoon; and to tiny **Motu Paio,** a mid-lagoon bird sanctuary. **Oviri Excursions** (tel. 96-05-87, oviriexcursions@hotmail.fr) at the Hôtel Kia Ora Village does excellent full-day trips to Sables Roses at CFP 10,000 per person and to Île aux Récifs at CFP 7,500 per person (four-person minimum).

ACCOMMODATIONS

US$50-100

Pension Henriette (tel. 96-84-68), by the lagoon in Avatoru village, rents one bungalow at CFP 5,500 per person with half pension. It can be a little noisy here, but the food is excellent (especially the banana crepes) and it's possible to stop by for lunch even if you're staying elsewhere.

Rangiroa Lodge (tel. 96-82-13, www.rangiroalodge.com) in Avatoru has four rooms at CFP 5,300 double with shared bath or CFP 6,300 with private bath. A bed in one of the two three-bed dorms is CFP 2,300 per person. This is one of the few places with communal cooking facilities, though the proprietors also prepare meals upon request. The snorkeling just off the lodge is outstanding, and they'll loan you gear if you need it. Divers from the adjacent Raie Manta Club often stay here.

Chez Nanua (tel. 96-83-88), between the airport and Avatoru village, allows budget travelers to pitch their tents in a rather poor location at CFP 4,000 per person with two meals. The four simple thatched bungalows with shared bath are CFP 5,500 per person including two meals. You eat with the owners—a little fish and rice every meal. There's no hot water. Airport transfers are free.

Pension Teina et Marie (tel. 96-03-94, rangiroa@mail.pf), behind Pension Glorine at Tiputa Pass, four kilometers east of the airport, has six duplex garden rooms at CFP 6,500 per person and five thatched beach bungalows at CFP 7,500 per person, all including breakfast and dinner. The three three-bed dorms upstairs in a concrete house are CFP 3,500 per person, including breakfast only. When things get crowded, a lounge is converted into another six-bed dorm. You can also camp. Communal cooking facilities are not provided.

Pension Lucien (tel. 96-73-55, http://pensionlucien.free.fr), near the pass in Tiputa village, offers three beach bungalows with private baths at CFP 6,500 per person with half board. Airport transfers are CFP 1,000 per person.

US$100-150

Pension Loyna (tel. 96-82-09), near Avatoru and across the road from the beach, has five rooms with private baths (and hot water) in two buildings at CFP 7,500 per person. The price includes half board (with good food) and airport transfers. Loyna speaks good English.

Near Gauguin's Pearl on the lagoon between the airport and Avatoru is **Pension Cécile** (tel. 93-12-65), where the nine comfortable wooden bungalows with private baths start at CFP 8,000 per person with half board. Lobster is often on the menu, and the fish is very good. Alban does lagoon tours in his boat upon request. The beach in this vicinity is poor.

Pension Tuanake (tel. 96-03-52, www.sitetuanake.fr.st) is by the lagoon next to Gauguin's Pearl, two kilometers west of the airport. The six thatched bungalows with baths (but no cooking facilities) are CFP 6,500/9,700 single/double (or CFP 10,500/15,700 with half board).

Pension Martine (tel. 93-12-25, www.pensionmartine.pf), by the lagoon near the airport terminal, has three fan-cooled bungalows with private baths and terraces (but no cooking) at CFP 9,490/15,900 single/double with half board (lots of fresh fish). It's friendly, clean, and relaxed, and right on a nice, if small,

THE COCONUT PALM

Human life would not be possible on most of the Pacific's far-flung atolls without the all-purpose coconut palm. It reaches maturity in eight years, and then produces about 50 nuts a year for 60 years (the 29-centimeter-wide metal bands around the trunk are for protection against rats). Aside from the tree's aesthetic value and usefulness in providing shade, the water of the green coconut provides a refreshing drink, and the white meat of the young nut is a delicious food. The harder meat of more mature nuts is grated and squeezed, which creates a coconut cream that is used as a sauce in cooking.

The oldest nuts are cracked open and the hard meat removed and then dried to be sold as copra. It takes about 6,000 coconuts to make a tonne of copra. Schooners collect bags of copra, which they carry to a mill beside the interisland wharf at Papeete. Here the copra is pressed into the coconut oil used in making vegetable oil, margarine, candles, soap, cosmetics, and other products. Scented with flowers, the oil nurtures the skin. The world price for copra has been depressed for years, so the government pays a subsidy (more than twice the actual price) to producers to keep them gainfully employed on their home islands.

The juice or sap from the cut flower spathes of the palm provides toddy, a popular drink; the toddy is distilled into a spirit called arrack, the whiskey of the Pacific. Otherwise the sap can be boiled to make candy. Millionaire's salad is made by shredding the growth cut from the heart of the tree. For each salad, a fully mature tree must be sacrificed.

The nut's hard inner shell can be used as a cup and makes excellent firewood. Rope, cordage, brushes, and heavy matting are produced from the coir fiber of the husk. The smoke from burning husks is a most effective mosquito repellent. The leaves of the coconut tree are used to thatch the roofs of the islanders' cottages or are woven into baskets, mats, and fans. The trunk provides timber for building and furniture. Actually, these are only the common uses; there are many others as well.

beach. Ask Corinne to show you around the family pearl farm.

A five-minute walk west of the airport terminal is the **Ariitini Village** (tel. 96-04-41), previously known as Pension Félix, with nine beach bungalows at CFP 8,000 per person, including breakfast and dinner.

A sister of Henriette (of Pension Henriette) runs the popular **Pension Glorine** (tel. 96-04-05, pensionglorine@mail.pf), next to the wharf at Tiputa Pass, four kilometers from the airport. The six spacious thatched bungalows with private baths are CFP 8,000 per person, including two meals (the specialty is fresh lagoon fish). Children under 13 are half price, and bicycle rentals are available. Airport transfers are CFP 800. Nonguests can order meals here (reserve ahead).

US$150-250

Le Mérou Bleu (tel. 96-84-62, www.merou-bleu.com), facing Avatoru Pass, has three thatched bungalows beginning at CFP 13,650/25,200 single/double with half board. For hot water add CFP 2,000. Some of Rangiroa's best surfing is just off its beach.

Pension Henri (tel. 96-82-67, http://henri.sejour-a-rangiroa.com), near Pension Loyna at Avatoru, has five thatched bungalows costing CFP 12,600 single or double (with cold water) or CFP 15,750 (with hot water). Half pension is another CFP 3,675 per person.

Tevahine Dream (tel. 93-12-75, www.tevahinedream.com), near Chez Nanua five kilometers west of the airport, has three thatched bungalows at CFP 12,500 per person per day with half board. Kayaks, bicycles, snorkeling gear, and some activities are free.

The **Hôtel Raira Lagon** (tel. 93-12-30, www.raira-lagon.pf), next to the Maitai Rangiroa, is OK, although the neighboring villagers can be noisy. The 10 small thatched bungalows with private baths and fridges are CFP 13,930/23,000 single/double with half board.

A few well-used bicycles are lent free, and it's right on the beach. The beachfront restaurant is open to the public.

Turiroa Village (tel. 96-04-27, pension .turiroa@mail.pf), less than a kilometer west of the airport terminal, has four bungalows with kitchenettes at CFP 8,000 for 1–4 people. Breakfast is CFP 500 per person. No English is spoken.

Pension Bounty (tel. 96-05-22, www .pension-bounty.com) is near the entrance to Hôtel Kia Ora Village and its beach. The four self-catering studios are CFP 11,500/15,000 single/double including breakfast. Bicycles and airport transfers are free.

US$250 and Up

The **Maitai Rangiroa** (tel. 93-13-50, www .rangiroa.hotelmaitai.com), a bit more than one kilometer west of the airport terminal, dates from 2004 and was previously known as the Novotel Rangiroa Beach Resort. In 2010 the property was acquired by the Tahiti Beachcomber group, which also owns the four InterContinental resorts in the Society Islands and the cruise ship *Paul Gauguin.* The Maitai's 38 air-conditioned bungalows are CFP 26,100/38,500 garden/beach single or double without food, plus 14 percent tax. The hotel restaurant is slow and pricey (even the bottled water costs a lot). There's no real beach here, so this wouldn't be a good place to bring children. However, the snorkeling right offshore is very good. The airport transfers are strangely expensive at CFP 1,800 per person round-trip. In the past, English speakers have been out of place at this hotel, but hopefully some of the old Novotel defects will be corrected by the new management.

Rangiroa's top resort is the **Hôtel Kia Ora Village** (tel. 93-11-11, www.hotelkiaora.com), established in 1973 near Tiputa Pass, a bit more than two kilometers east of the airport by road. It's right on the best beach of this part of the island with reasonable snorkeling offshore. In 2010, the Kia Ora was closed for much needed renovations. The 22 beach bungalows are CFP 45,500 double, the 23 garden bungalows CFP 32,000, while the five larger garden bungalow suites are CFP 38,500, plus 14 percent tax. The 10 over-water units go for CFP 67,000. Meals are extra. Yachties anchored offshore are certainly not welcome to dingy in and use the facilities, but the pricey seafood restaurant is open to all; it has slow service, variable food, and a beautiful view. A wide range of lagoon excursions and activities are offered at higher than usual prices.

In 1991 the Kia Ora Village began offering accommodation in five thatched bungalows at **Kia Ora Sauvage** on Motu Avaerahi on the far south side of the lagoon. It's CFP 41,000 single or double, plus 14 percent tax, plus a compulsory three-meal plan at CFP 9,500 per person, plus CFP 12,600 per person for return boat transfers (two-night minimum stay). The boat leaves at 0900 daily, so you'll probably have to wait one night to go. Kia Ora Sauvage is a Robinson Crusoe experience most people rave about.

Les Relais de Joséphine (tel. 96-02-00, http://relaisjosephine.free.fr), facing directly onto Tiputa Pass, has three deluxe bungalows with four-post beds and terrace at CFP 18,840/29,200 single/double, including continental breakfast and dinner. A third person pays CFP 10,300. Giant trees keep the mosquito-rich compound shady all day, and the tall *fare* with their dysfunctional teak furnishings are consummately romantic. Dolphins frolic just offshore, and the sound of the waves at night is wonderful. There's no beach here, and this place gets varied reviews.

FOOD

The fish dishes (CFP 1,000–2,000) at **Snack de la Marina** (tel. 96-85-64, Tues.–Sat.), Marina de Avatoru, come in large portions.

Snack Chez Auguste and Antionette (tel. 96-85-01, Mon.–Sat.), opposite the Marina de Avatoru, has Chinese food, sandwiches, and ice cream.

Pizzeria Philippo (tel. 73-76-20, Thurs.–Tues.), at the entrance to Avatoru, serves salads and ice cream as well as pizza (CFP 1,000–1,500). Ask about "pizza hour" on Monday night, when all pizzas are just CFP 1,000 (reservations required).

Café Obelix (no phone, CFP 1,000–2,000), next to the Maitai Rangiroa, is an unpretentious roadside restaurant which serves a good portion of mahimahi with fries and cold Hinano beer.

Pizzeria Vaimario (tel. 96-05-96, Tues.–Sun.), near the Maitai Rangiroa, has 10 tables on a tiled outdoor terrace and a couple more inside. There are hamburgers and sandwiches for lunch and a more extensive menu (CFP 2,000–3,000) at dinner. Pizza is around CFP 1,200.

Restaurant Le Kai Kai (tel. 96-03-39, no dinner Wed.), just west of the airport terminal and a 10-minute walk from the Maitai Rangiroa, has a varied meat and seafood menu (main plates CFP 1,500–2,000). *Poisson cru* is a good choice for lunch; there are also great desserts, such as chocolate mousse, crème brûlée, and ice cream. The espressos come with chunks of dark chocolate. You eat on an outdoor terrace, and the staff will switch on a fan to keep you cool. Internet access is available.

The **Rangiroa Lagoon Grill** (tel. 96-04-10, Tues.–Sun., CFP 1,500–5,500), almost opposite the airport terminal, has outdoor seating under the trees. You get a lagoon view with your steak or lobster.

A great place for lunch is **Snack Relley Ohotu** (Mon.–Sat. 0800–1500), next to the wharf at Tiputa Pass on the Avatoru side. There's a nice terrace overlooking the lagoon, good atmosphere, and pleasant music. The menu includes a plat du jour (CFP 1,000), fried fish (CFP 1,000), hamburgers (CFP 500–800), and other choices ranging CFP 800–1,500. Beer is available.

SERVICES

The **Banque de Tahiti** (tel. 96-85-52) has a branch at Avatoru, while **Banque Socredo** (tel. 96-85-63) has branches at the *mairies* in both Avatoru and Tiputa (though only the Avatoru branch changes money). All branches are open limited hours according to a variable timetable (in Tiputa only on Mon., Tues., and Thurs.).

Post offices are found in Avatoru, Tiputa, and the airport.

There is a medical center (tel. 96-83-75) two kilometers east of Avatoru and an infirmary at Tiputa. Dr. Patrick Boutes (tel. 96-85-85) has a private Cabinet Médical at Avatoru. It's prudent to drink bottled water on Rangiroa.

GETTING THERE

Air Tahiti (tel. 93-11-00) flies Tahiti–Rangiroa several times daily (one hour, CFP 16,900 one-way). Five times a week a one-way flight arrives direct from Bora Bora (CFP 24,400), but there are no flights from Rangiroa back to Bora Bora. Raiatea to Rangiroa (CFP 24,400) is weekly. There's service six times a week from Rangiroa to Manihi (CFP 11,100) and four times a week to Tikehau (CFP 6,100) and Fakarava (CFP 6,100). A weekly one-way flight operates from Rangiroa to Nuku Hiva and Hiva Oa in the Marquesas (CFP 28,800). Seats on flights to the Marquesas should be booked well in advance. Many accommodations provide free airport transfers, if you book ahead.

The **airstrip** (RGI) is about six kilometers from Avatoru village by road, accessible to Tiputa village by boat. Most of the Avatoru pensions offer free airport transfers to those who have booked ahead (ask).

Ask about copra boats such as the *Saint Xavier Maris Stella III*. The *Aranui* stops at Rangiroa on the way back to Papeete from the Marquesas, and you could disembark here.

GETTING AROUND

There's no public transportation on Rangiroa, although the scuba operators offer shuttles to their clients. To reach Tiputa village across Tiputa Pass from the airport island, wait for a lift on the dock next to Chez Glorine (watch for dolphins in the pass). A boat ferrying school children across the Tiputa Pass leaves the airport side weekdays at 0600, returning from Tiputa at 1130 and 1600. The usual fee to be taken across is CFP 500 per person each way.

Rangi Rent a Car (tel. 96-03-28), formerly Europcar, with an office near Avatoru and at the Kia Ora, has cars beginning at CFP 7,000/8,500 for four/eight hours, scooters at CFP 4,500/5,500, bicycles CFP 900/1,500. Two-person "fun cars" are slightly cheaper than the regular cars.

Arenahio Location (tel. 96-82-45, carpom@mail.pf), at Carole Pareu between the airport and Avatoru village, also rents bicycles at CFP 1,200 a day, scooters at CFP 4,200 a day, and cars at CFP 7,200 a day. Carole speaks good English. Many of the pensions rent bicycles.

Tikehau

Rangiroa's smaller neighbor, Tikehau (500 inhabitants), is an almost circular atoll 27 kilometers across with the shallow Tuheiava Pass on its west side. Tuherahera village and the airport share an island in the southwest corner of the atoll. Jacques Cousteau led an expedition to Tikehau in 1987 and reported that the atoll was one of the world's richest in marine life. Some of the *motu,* including Motu Puarua, host large seabird colonies. Five pearl farms operate on Tikehau, and tourism is growing fast. There's a far better choice of places to stay than you'll find on Manihi, and it's less developed than Rangiroa. Tikehau's beaches are unsurpassed.

SIGHTS AND RECREATION

All of the pensions organize boat trips to bird islands such as Motu Puarua, picnics on a *motu,* snorkeling in the pass, visits to Eden Point, etc., costing CFP 3,500–8,500 per person.

The **Raie Manta Club** (tel. 96-22-53, www.raiemantaclub.com), based at the Tikehau Village, offers up to four exploration dives a day. Prices (CFP 6,500) are the same as those at the Raie Manta Club on Rangiroa, and the 10-dive packages can be used at both centers. They'll show you huge manta rays (Apr.–Nov.), sea turtles, shark-infested caves, hammerhead sharks (Sept.–Nov.), great schools of barracuda, and fabulous red reefs. Snorkelers are welcome.

Diving is also offered by the **Tikehau Blue Nui Dive Center** (tel. 96-22-40, www.bluenui.com) at the Tikehau Pearl Beach Resort.

ACCOMMODATIONS

US$50-100

A good choice for backpackers is **Pension Panau Lagon** (tel. 96-22-99) on a stunning white beach a few minutes' walk from the airport. The six simple bungalows with baths are CFP 6,500 per person with breakfast and dinner. Camping may be possible here.

US$100-150

The **Pension Tevaihi Village** (tel. 96-23-04), right in Tuherahera village itself, rents four thatched bungalows at CFP 5,000 per person including breakfast. Meals can be ordered.

The **Aito Motel Colette** (tel. 96-23-07) near Tuherahera has five small *fare* at CFP 10,080 single or double. Meals, water, and airport transfers are extra. Although location is nice right on a lovely beach, the surroundings and units could use a cleaning.

In the direction toward the airport and a few minutes beyond Pension Panau Lagon is **Pension Justine** (tel. 96-22-87), with five *fare* at CFP 7,500 per person with half board. Camping is CFP 3,000 per person with breakfast.

Pension Kahaia Beach (tel. 96-22-77), on the pink sands of Motu Kahaia between the village and the Pearl Beach Resort, has five *fare* at CFP 7,500 per person with half board, bicycles, kayaks, and airport transfers. If you like fresh fish, you won't be disappointed here. Camping is CFP 1,250 per person without food. The owner doesn't speak English, but hand gestures will do. The beach and snorkeling are good, and several other deserted *motu* are nearby. It's a good place to relax.

US$150-250

Pension Hotu (tel. 96-22-89, www.pensionhotu.com), on the beach near Tuherahera, rents five *fare* at CFP 6,350 per person without

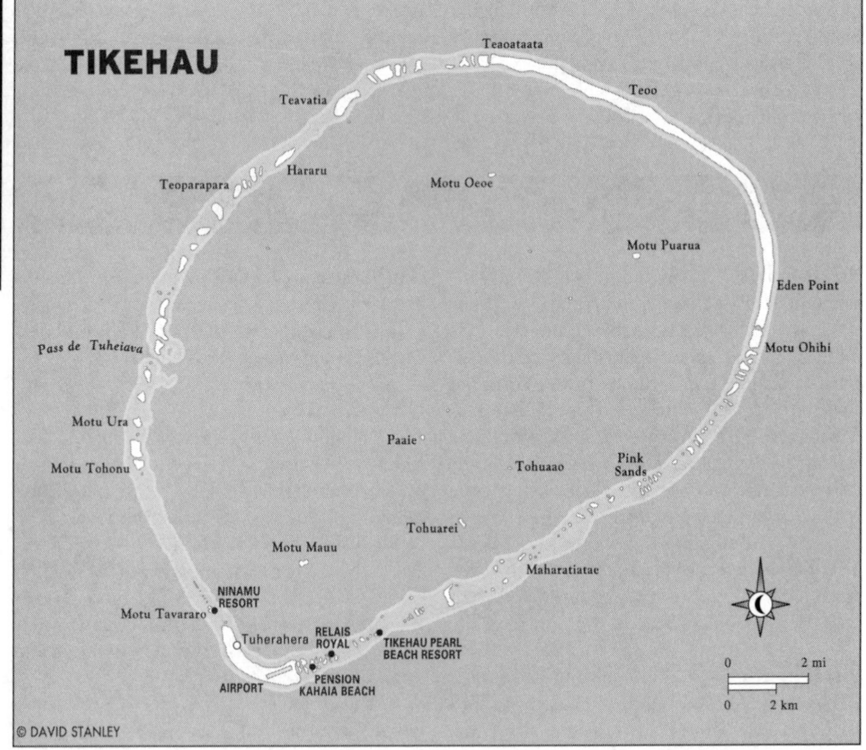

meals. You can cook your own food in a common kitchen or order meals. Airport transfers are free.

The **Tikehau Village** (tel. 96-22-86, tikehau village@mail.pf), on the beach between the airstrip and the village, has nine *fare* with private baths starting at CFP 16,430/20,140 single/double, including two meals (usually fish). Nonguests can order meals here. It's popular among scuba divers as the dive shop is on the premises.

Pension Tematieé (tel. 96-22-65), right next to the airport, has three beach bungalows at CFP 9,450 per person with half board (usually fish).

The **Relais Royal Tikehau** (tel. 96-23-37, www.royaltikehau.com) on a tiny *motu* near the Pearl Beach Resort has seven thatched *fare* on stilts starting at CFP 20,250/30,250 single/double and four rooms with baths at CFP 15,750/23,750. The rates include breakfast, dinner, and tax (minimum stay two nights). Bottled water is expensive here, the food skimpy, and some of the windows cannot be closed. Airport transfers in an open boat are CFP 1,160 per person.

US$250 and Up

In June 2001 the secluded **Tikehau Pearl Beach Resort** (tel. 96-23-00, www.pearl resorts.com) opened on tiny Motu Tiano, a bit east of Motu Kahaia. There are 14 beach bungalows at CFP 40,000 single or double, plus 24 over-water bungalows starting at CFP 49,000, plus 14 percent tax. Add CFP 7,900/10,900 per person for half/full board. Opinions about the food vary. You could always take the free resort shuttle to the village and restock your minibar with groceries and drinks from the store. Some of the rooms are not air-conditioned or screened, and insects can be a problem. If you don't care for the beach of pink and white sand, there's a small swimming pool. One of the bungalows has been converted into a Manea Spa (www.maneaspa.com). Diving is provided by the Tikehau Blue Nui Dive Center (tel. 96-22-40, www.bluenui.com) on the wharf at the resort. Boat transfers from the airport are CFP 5,000 plus tax per person round-trip.

In 2010 the **Ninamu Resort** (www.motuninamu.com) opened on a *motu* near the Tuheiava Pass. The six rustic but comfortable bungalows are available only as part of a one-week package including accommodations, meals, most water sports, and airport transfers for CFP 250,000 per person per week. Scuba diving and deep-sea fishing are extra. The best surfing in the nearby pass is November–March for intermediate to advanced surfers. Bookings are handled by World Surfaris (www.worldsurfaris.com) in San Clemente, California.

GETTING THERE

Air Tahiti flies to Tikehau from Papeete (55 minutes, CFP 16,900) daily and from Rangiroa (CFP 6,100) four times a week. The airstrip is conveniently situated a bit more than one kilometer east of Tuherahera village.

You can also get to Tikehau on ships that tie up to a lagoon-side wharf.

Fakarava

Fakarava is the second-largest Tuamotu atoll, about 250 kilometers southeast of Rangiroa and 435 kilometers northeast of Tahiti. A pass gives access to each end of this rectangular 60-by-25-kilometer lagoon, which is dotted and flanked by 80 coconut-covered *motu*. There's spectacular snorkeling and drift diving in the passes or along the vertical drop-offs. Garuae Pass in the north is almost one kilometer wide, nine meters deep, and the haunt of countless sharks, dolphins, barracuda, and rays. Tumakohua Pass in the south is smaller and accessible to snorkelers. The south pass could be the world's most spectacular shark dive with as many as 1,000 gray reef sharks present when the current in strong. However, if you're not a scuba diver, two nights may be enough on Fakarava.

The French colonial administration for the Tuamotus moved here from Anaa in 1878, and Fakarava's Catholic church is one of the oldest in the group. Robert Louis Stevenson visited Fakarava aboard the yacht *Casco* in 1888 and spent two weeks living in a house near the church in the center of the village, Rotoava. French painter Henri Matisse visited briefly in 1930, and the beauty of the atoll influenced his art for years afterward. The present airstrip, four kilometers from village, opened only in 1995. About 900 people live on the atoll and a number of pearl farms have been established around the lagoon.

Though still in the early stages of being opened to tourism, Fakarava is becoming

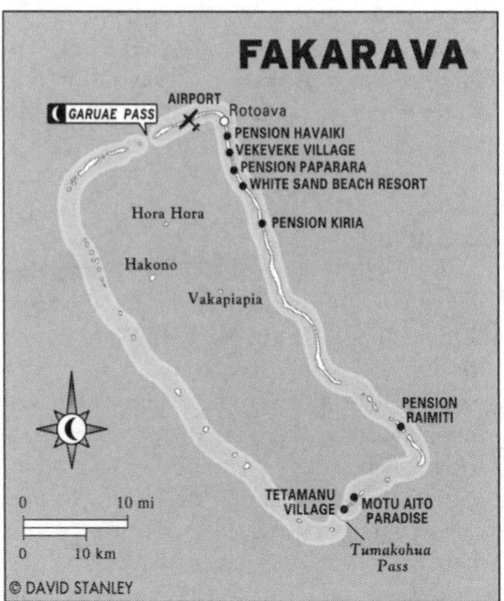

THE LOST TREASURE OF THE TUAMOTUS

During the War of the Pacific (1879-1883) four mercenaries stole 14 tonnes of gold from a church in Pisco, Peru. They buried most of the treasure on Pinaki or Raraka atolls in the Tuamotus before proceeding to Australia, where two were killed by aboriginals and the other two were sentenced to 20 years' imprisonment for murder. Just before his death, the surviving mercenary told prospector Charles Edward Howe the story.

In 1913 Howe began a 13-year search, which finally found part of the treasure on an island near Raraka. He reburied the chests and returned to Australia to organize an expedition that would remove the gold in secret. Before it could set out, however, Howe disappeared. But using Howe's treasure map, diver George Hamilton took over in 1934. Hamilton thought he found the cached gold in a pool but was unable to extract it. After being attacked by a giant octopus and moray eel, Hamilton abandoned the search and the expedition dissolved.

In 1994 a descendant of Hamilton chartered a boat at Fakarava and headed for Tepoto atoll, which had been identified from an old photograph as the site of the treasure. Soon after their arrival at Tepoto, the weather turned nasty and the expedition turned back after narrowly escaping death on the reef.

As far as is known, the US$1.8 million in gold has never been found, but the legend is still very much alive, and traces of old diggings can be seen in a dozen places, mostly around Pinaki's only passage (which is too shallow for even dinghies to enter). Only landowners are allowed to dig for treasure, so a foreigner would have to marry a local first. At night the treasure is guarded by the spirits of three people who were killed after burying the gold.

Some claim the islanders found the gold long ago and, believing it to be cursed, dumped it in the sea. Most scholars say the whole thing is a hoax, yet treasure hunters still dream of finding this elusive treasure.

known. In October 2006, the seven atolls included in the Commune of Fakarava (Aratika, Fakarava, Kauehi, Niau, Raraka, Taiaro, and Toau) became a UNESCO Biosphere Reserve. Fakarava was singled out as the home of rare crustaceans, including squills and sea cicadas. Hopefully this prestigious designation will help promote sustainable development on the atoll.

SCUBA DIVING

Garuae Pass

The incredible Garuae Pass drift dive at Fakarava is for experienced divers only, and shark feeding is unnecessary since the pass is already thick with sharks of many species. If anything, Garuae Pass is more spectacular than the Tiputa Pass at Rangiroa. In fact, it's probably French Polynesia's number-one dive for its combination of profuse marine life, healthy coral, a dramatic drop-off, and sheer adventure. Great schools of barracuda, turtles, sharks, and dolphins are seen in the pass year-round, but some of the other creatures are seasonal: gray sharks (May–June), manta rays (July–Oct.), leopard rays (Nov.–Apr.), and hammerhead sharks (Nov.–Apr.). The moray eel breeding season is in May and June, while huge schools of marbled groupers come here to breed in July. The strong current will sweep you through this huge pass amid a churning sea of life. All of the Fakarava dive shops offer drift dives through Garuae Pass, but it isn't appropriate for snorkelers or novice divers because the tidal flows are too strong.

Dive Shops

Jean-Christophe Lapeyre operates the **Diving Center Te Ava Nui** (tel. 98-43-50, www.divingfakarava.com) at Rotoava, which also dives at Toau Atoll. A one-tank dive is CFP 6,200.

The **Fakarava Diving Center** (tel. 93-40-75, www.fakarava-diving-center.com) at Pension Paparara charges CFP 6,000/55,000 for one/10 dives.

TOPdive (tel. 98-43-76, www.topdive.com) at the White Sand Beach Resort and Pension

motu in the Tuamotu Islands

Raimiti has a 10-dive package costing CFP 70,000 that can also be used at TOPdive centers on Moorea, Bora Bora, Tahiti, and Rangiroa.

ACCOMMODATIONS

US$100-150

The choice of backpackers is friendly **Relais Marama** (tel. 98-42-51, www.relais-marama.com), ocean-side in Rotoava village, four kilometers from the airstrip. It's CFP 5,000/9,000 single/double, including breakfast, for one of the six garden bungalows with shared bath. Cooking facilities are available. Camping is CFP 2,000 per person.

The **Vahitu Dream** (tel. 98-42-63, vahitudream@mail.pf), south of Rotoava on a potholed road, offers five basic rooms with shared bath at CFP 7,500 per person including half board. Loud music is on in the snack bar all day, and the folks here stay up late. It's used mostly by French scuba divers.

Vekeveke Village (tel. 98-42-80, www.pension-fakarava.com), by the lagoon four kilometers beyond the village, has four bungalows at CFP 18,900 per person, including breakfast and dinner.

Pension Paparara (tel. 98-42-66, www.fakarava-divelodge.com), south of Rotoava village on the way to the White Sand Beach Resort Fakarava, rents bungalows at CFP 9,540/16,960/23,850 single/double/triple with half board. Their lagoon excursions by boat are excellent.

US$150-250

Lively **Pension Havaiki** (tel. 93-40-15, www.havaiki.com), on the beach next door to the Vahitu Dream, has eight nice bungalows with cold showers at CFP 12,500/18,900 single/double in the garden or CFP 14,950/23,900 on the beach, including half board. Clotilde's meals are huge and tasty, and nonguests can dine here if they reserve earlier in the day. Some rooms cannot be locked. A long pier points out into the lagoon toward Joachim's pearl-farming shack, and the beach is good. Kayaks and bicycles are lent free, and deep-sea sportfishing can be arranged. ManaSPOT wireless Internet access is available here.

The **Tokerau Village** (tel. 98-41-09, www.tokerau-village.com), 400 meters beyond the White Sand Beach Resort Fakarava, has four sizable bungalows at CFP 12,000/22,000 single/double with half board.

Pension Vaiama Village (tel. 98-41-13, www.fakaravavaiama.com), 7 kilometers south of the village, has four thatched bungalows with private baths at CFP 11,236/19,080 single/double, including half board. Airport transfers are CFP 2,000 per person return.

Pension Kiria (tel. 98-41-83, www.pensionkiriafakarava.com), 9 kilometers south of the village, has three bungalows at CFP CFP 11,000 per person with half board.

US$250 and Up

The three-star **White Sand Beach Resort Fakarava** (tel. 93-41-50, www.whitesandfakarava.com), six kilometers south of Rotoava, formerly known as Le Maitai Dream, opened in 2003. The 30 fan-cooled units range in price from CFP 37,250 double for a garden bungalow to CFP 49,500 for a beach bungalow, plus 14 percent tax. The restaurant-bar has a deck for sunset viewing. Airport transfers are CFP 3,000 per person round-trip for the 15 kilometers.

Pension Raimiti (tel. 71-07-63, www.raimiti.com) is on an idyllic *motu* on the southeast side of the atoll, 90 minutes to three hours from the airport by boat. Its nine bungalows of different sizes start at CFP 49,000/89,000 single/double for two nights including room, board, transfers, and taxes. Lighting in the units is by oil lamp (no electricity). Scuba diving is the main activity here, and two dives cost CFP 15,200 or CFP 65,000 for a 10-dive package. All dives must be booked in advance. Nondivers should bring along a few thick books. Raimiti is gay-friendly, and nudism is accepted.

Near Tumakohua Pass, **Motu Aito Paradise** (tel. 41-29-00, www.fakarava.org) offers rooms in a rustic thatched complex on a tiny coral *motu* at CFP 14,880 per person, including all meals, transfers, and excursions (three-night minimum stay). Airport transfers are CFP 3,000 per person extra. Divers from Te Ava Nui often have lunch here after diving the pass. The sense of remoteness is perfect.

Also at the south end of the atoll is the **Tetamanu Village** (tel. 77-10-06, www.tetamanuvillage.pf). The six simple waterfront *fare* here are CFP 48,500 per person for three nights, including all meals, activities, taxes, and airport transfers (1.5 hours each way by boat). A private bathing pontoon in the adjacent Tumakohua Pass facilitates snorkeling at slack tide. An annex called "Tetamanu Sauvage" on a small *motu* has another six beachfront *fare* at the same rates. Complete facilities are offered for scuba divers. Ask Sané to show you around his pearl farm.

FOOD

Snack Teanuanua (tel. 93-40-65, CFP 1,300–3,000), at the south end of Rotoava, is a picturesque little place with mother of pearl and driftwood decor right at the water's edge. They serve grilled or raw fish plus meat dishes. Call for a free pickup.

GETTING THERE

Air Tahiti flies from Papeete to Fakarava (90 minutes, CFP 18,100) daily, with two flights going on to Rangiroa (CFP 6,100).

The supply ship *Cobia III* calls at Fakarava every Thursday at 0600 (CFP 6,300 couchette to/from Papeete). The passenger-carrying freighter *Aranui* sometimes calls at Fakarava on its way to the Marquesas.

Manihi

Manihi, 175 kilometers northeast of Rangiroa, is also on the package tour circuit, with visions of white-sand beaches and cultured black pearls radiating from its glossy brochures. Unless you have a keen interest in pearl farming, scuba diving is the only reason to come here. The accommodations are isolated and remarkably overpriced. Still, it can be an interesting experience staying on an atoll.

You can see right around Manihi's 6-by-30-kilometer lagoon, and the thousands of resident oysters hanging on underwater racks at the dozen or so pearl farms greatly outnumber the 800 human inhabitants. Because of the pearl industry, the people of Manihi have become more affluent than those on some of the other Tuamotu Islands.

Turipaoa (or Paeua) village and its 50 houses face Tairapa Pass at the west end of a sandy strip just over one kilometer long. The airport island and main resort are just across the pass from Turipaoa, and many of the other *motu* are also inhabited.

SCUBA DIVING

Manihi Blue Nui (tel. 96-42-17, www.bluenui.com) at the Manihi Pearl Beach Resort offers year-round scuba diving on the outer reef walls. They'll also take snorkelers on the boat if space is available. Both PADI and CMAS certification courses are offered.

It's exciting to shoot Tairapa Pass on the incoming tide, and since it's shallower than the passes at Rangiroa, you'll see more. Reef sharks are less common here, but manta and eagle rays are often seen, as are countless Moorish idols. Just inside the lagoon at the mouth of the pass is a site called "The Circus," which is frequented by huge science fiction–like rays with enormous socket eyes. It's a fantastic experience to swim near them (also possible at Rangiroa).

The ocean drop-off abounds in gray sharks, Napoleon fish, giant jack fish, and huge schools of snappers, barracudas, and tuna. Each year around late June or early July, thousands of marbled groupers gather here to breed in one of the most fascinating underwater events in the world. From May to July there are moray eel gatherings. Among other favorite spots are "West Point," with fire, antler, and flower-petal coral in 65-meter visibility, and "The Break," where blacktip, whitetip, gray, and occasionally hammerhead sharks are seen.

ACCOMMODATIONS

US$150-250

Motel Nanihi Paradise (tel. 93-30-40, www.nanihiparadise.com) is on Motu Kamoka, a 30-minute boat ride from the airport. The three two-room self-catering bungalows are CFP 12,000/13,500 per person with half/full board. Airport transfers are CFP 2,500 return per person. Various nautical tours are possible.

The **Pension Hawaiki Pearls** (tel. 96-42-89, www.pensionhawaikipearls.com), formerly known as Pension Vainui, is across the lagoon on Motu Marakorako. A room with shared bath in one of the three two-room bungalows goes for CFP 12,000 per person per day, including all meals. Bring a flashlight to be able to find the outhouse after the electricity is switched off at 2130. A free tour of the owner's pearl farm is offered. Airport transfers are CFP 1,000 per person.

US$250 and Up

The **Manihi Pearl Beach Resort** (tel. 96-42-73, www.pearlresorts.com), by the lagoon near the airport, was known as the Kaina Village until a hurricane blew it away in 1993. Now rebuilt, the five standard beach bungalows are CFP 30,000 single or double, the 17 premium beach bungalows CFP 40,000, the 14 over-water bungalows CFP 52,000, and the five premium over-water bungalows CFP 60,000, all plus 14 percent tax. Add CFP 10,900 per person plus 10 percent tax for full board. The units are well spaced and private but could use an upgrade. There's a large swimming pool facing the rather poor beach (the snorkeling in the pass is excellent, but watch the currents). A Manea Spa (www.maneaspa.com) is available. Tours and activities are minimal, so bring reading material. Almost all guests arrive on prepaid packages. Round-trip airport transfers by golf cart are CFP 2,120 per person. You can easily walk it in five minutes, but the resort staff expect you to use their shuttle. Tourists have been known to ride their bicycles up and down the airport runway just for kicks.

GETTING THERE

Manihi airport (XMH) is on a *motu* 2.5 kilometers north of Turipaoa village by boat (there's no ferry service, and you must arrange with your accommodations to be picked up). The check-in counters at Manihi close 30 minutes before each flight. Most Air Tahiti (tel. 96-42-71) flights are to Manihi from Papeete (75 minutes, CFP 20,200) or Bora Bora (CFP 27,500). Flights between Manihi and Rangiroa are CFP 11,000.

The occasional ship from Papeete enters the lagoon and ties up to a wharf at Turipaoa.

Other Islands and Atolls

AHE

Ahe, 13 kilometers west of Manihi, is often visited by cruising yachts, which are able to enter the 16-kilometer-long lagoon through Tiarero Pass on the northwest side of the atoll. Tenukupara village is south across the lagoon. Facilities include two tiny stores, a post office, and a community center where everyone meets at night. Despite the steady stream of sailing boats, the 566 people are very friendly. All of the houses have solar generating panels supplied after a hurricane in the early 1980s. Only a handful of small children are seen in the village; most are away at school on Rangiroa or Tahiti. Many families follow their children to the main islands while they're at school, so you may even be able to rent a whole house. In addition to being a major producer of pearls, Ahe supplies oysters to the pearl farms on Manihi.

The **Pension Coco Perle Lodge** (tel. 96-44-08, www.cocoperlelodge.com), on Motu Maruaruki on the east side of the atoll, 10 minutes by boat from the airport, has four large bungalows with private baths at CFP 13,000 per person and two bungalows with shared bath for CFP 11,000 per person, both with half board. Excursions to a *motu* are CFP 4,000 per person. Valérie et René at Ahe Plongée offer scuba diving on Ahe.

Chez Raita (tel. 96-44-53, www.ahedream.com), on Motu Kateka, has four bungalows at CFP 9,500 per person with all meals. Ten-minute transfers by boat from the airport are included.

In 1998 the Foreign Legion constructed an airport on Ahe, and Air Tahiti now has three flights a week from Tahiti (CFP 20,200).

ANAA

Anaa is 424 kilometers due east of Tahiti, and it has Air Tahiti flights from Papeete (CFP 18,400) three times a week, one continuing to Makemo (CFP 9,800). Unlike most of the other atolls covered here, Anaa is part of the eastern Tuamotu group that was out-of-bounds to non-French during the nuclear testing era prior to 1996. Devastating hurricanes hit Anaa in 1906 and 1983.

The 463 inhabitants live in five small settlements scattered around Anaa's broken coral ring, and there's no pass into the shallow elongated lagoon. Anaa's tattooed warriors were once widely feared, yet this was the first Tuamotuan atoll to accept Christianity after a local missionary returned from training on Moorea in 1817. In 1845 an American named Benjamin Grouard converted the inhabitants to Mormonism. Catholic missionaries followed in 1851, leading to a mini–religious war and the banning of Mormon missionaries from the colony by the French authorities (they were not allowed to return until 1892). From 1853 to 1878 the French colonial administration of the Tuamotus was based here.

Accommodations are available at **Toku Kaiga** (tel. 98-32-69) in Tokerau village, one kilometer from the airport. The two self-catering bungalows here go for CFP 7,500 per person with half board. **Chez Louise** (tel. 98-32-25) nearby has two rooms at CFP 4,500 per person with half board.

ARUTUA

Numerous black pearl farms grace the 29-kilometer-wide lagoon of this circular atoll between Rangiroa and Apataki. Fifty-seven *motu* border the lagoon. Rautini village near the only pass was rebuilt after devastating hurricanes in 1983, and among the 725 inhabitants are some locally renowned musicians and storytellers. Arutua has Air Tahiti flights from Papeete (CFP 17,400) four times a week. The airstrip is on Motu Purahui, 30 minutes by boat north from the village. The freighter *Cobia III* calls at Arutua every Wednesday at 0500.

HAO

Hao Atoll (population 1,132) was visited by the Spaniard Quirós in 1606. Kaki Pass gives access to the 50-kilometer-long lagoon from the north. The pass has been dredged to a depth of seven meters, and medium-sized ships can enter and proceed eight kilometers to the anchorage off Otepa village on the northeast side of the atoll.

Hao is strategically situated in the heart of French Polynesia, equidistant from Tahiti, Mangareva, and the Marquesas. From 1966 to 1996 a giant French air base on Hao served as the main support base for nuclear testing on Moruroa, 500 kilometers southeast, allowing the French military to fly materials directly into the area without passing through Papeete's Faa'a Airport. Hao's 3,380-meter airport runway is the longest in the South Pacific—long enough to be considered a potential emergency landing site for the NASA space shuttles.

Before 1996 non-French visitors were forbidden to transit the atoll, but with the windup of nuclear testing on Moruroa, the French military base here has closed. Plans are underway to farm tuna commercially in Hao's lagoon. Some current Air Tahiti flights to Mangareva and the eastern Tuamotus are via Hao.

UNINHABITED ISLANDS

Although virtually every island and reef in the Pacific Ocean is claimed by one jurisdiction or another, many islands lack water and other resources needed for permanent inhabitation. Such places are sanctuaries for seabirds, turtles, and other species that coexist poorly with humanity. Aspiring Robinson Crusoes are seldom welcomed by traditional landowners or governments – beachcombers take note.

In the Society Islands, Mehetia, east of Tahiti, and Tupai, north of Bora Bora are visited only occasionally. Numerous atolls in the Tuamotus have no permanent residents, although anglers and copra collectors arrive several times a year. Among these are Ahunui, Akiaki, Anuanuraro, Anuanurunga, Fangataufa, Haraiki, Hiti, Manuhangi, Maria East, Marutea North, Matureivavao, Morane, Motutunga, Paraoa, Pinaki, Ravahere, Reitoru, Rekareka, Tahanea, Tauere, Tekokota, Tenararo, Tenarunga, Tepoto South, Tikei, Tuanake, Vahanga, and Vanavana.

Maria and Marotiri in the Austral Islands are tiny barren islands. Most of the Gambier Islands surrounding Mangareva are uninhabited, including Agakauitai, Akamaru, Kamaka, Makaroa, Manui, and Temoe. Among the desert islands of the Marquesas are Eiao, Fatu Huku, Hatutaa, Mohotani, Motu Iti, Motu One, and Thomasset Rock.

KAUKURA

A narrow pass gives limited access to Kaukura's shallow, 50-kilometer-long lagoon, midway

FRENCH NUCLEAR TESTING

The former French nuclear test site operated until 1996 by the Centre d'Expérimentations du Pacifique is at the southeastern end of the Tuamotu group, 1,200 kilometers from Tahiti. The main site was 30-kilometer-long Moruroa atoll, but Fangataufa atoll, 37 kilometers south of Moruroa, was also used. In 1962 the French nuclear testing facilities in the Algerian Sahara had to be abandoned after that country won its independence, so in 1963 French president Charles de Gaulle officially announced that France was shifting the program to Moruroa and Fangataufa. Between 1966 and 1996 a confirmed 183 nuclear bombs, reaching up to 200 kilotons, were set off in the Tuamotus at the rate of six per year. By 1974 the French had conducted 41 *atmospheric* tests, 36 over or near Moruroa and five over Fangataufa. Five of these were megaton hydrogen bombs.

Way back in 1963, the United States, Britain, and the USSR agreed in the Partial Test Ban Treaty to halt nuclear tests in the atmosphere, but France chose not to sign. In 1974, with opposition mounting in the Territorial Assembly and growing world indignation, French President Valéry Giscard d'Estaing ordered a switch to *underground* tests. Obviously an atoll, with its porous coral cap sitting on a narrow basalt base, is the most dangerous place in the world to stage underground nuclear explosions. This was not the initial intention. Moruroa was chosen for its isolated location, far from major population centers that might be affected by fallout. However, by 1974, when atmospheric testing had to cease, the French military had a huge investment in the area. So rather than move to a more secure location in France or elsewhere, it decided to take a chance. Underground testing was to be carried out in Moruroa's basalt core, 500-1,200 meters below the surface of the atoll.

A serious accident occurred on July 25, 1979, when a nuclear device became stuck halfway down an 800-meter shaft. Since army engineers were unable to move the device, they exploded it where it was, causing a massive chunk of the outer slope of the atoll to break loose. This generated a huge tsunami, which hit Moruroa, overturning cars and injuring seven people. After the blast, a crack 40 centimeters wide and two kilometers long appeared on the surface of the island. As a precaution against further tsunamis and hurricanes, refuge platforms were built at intervals around the atoll. For an hour before and after each test all personnel had to climb up on these platforms.

By 1981 Moruroa was as punctured as Swiss cheese and sinking two centimeters after every test, or a meter and a half between 1976 and 1981. In 1981, with the atoll's 60-kilometer coral rim dangerously fractured by drilling shafts, the French switched to underwater testing in the Moruroa lagoon, in order to be closer to the center of the island's core. The famous French underwater explorer Jacques Cousteau visited Moruroa in 1987 and filmed spectacular cracks and fissures in the atoll as well as submarine slides and subsidence. By 1988 even French officials were acknowledging that the 108 underground blasts had severely weakened the geological formations beneath Moruroa, and it was announced that,

between Rangiroa and Fakarava. Sixty-five *motu* punctuate Kaukura's barrier reef. Fewer than 600 people live in Kaukura's two villages, Raitahiti, one kilometer from the airstrip at the west end of the atoll, and Faro or Paia in the east. A third village, Panau, was destroyed during a hurricane in 1906. Air Tahiti has flights twice a week from Papeete (CFP 17,400). The freighter *Cobia III* calls here every Tuesday at 1200.

MAKATEA

Unlike the low coral atolls of the Tuamotus, Makatea, 230 kilometers northeast of Tahiti, is an uplifted limestone block eight kilometers long and 110 meters high. Gray cliffs plunge 50 meters to the sea. Phosphate was dug up here by workers with shovels from 1908 to 1966 and exported to Japan and New Zealand by the Compagnie Française des Phosphates de

despite the additional cost involved, the largest underground tests would take place henceforth on nearby Fangataufa atoll. The military base remained on Moruroa, and small groups of workers and technicians were sent over to Fangataufa every time a test was performed there.

A 1990 computer model of Moruroa developed by New Zealand scientists suggested that radioactive groundwater with a half-life of several thousand years may be seeping through fractures in the atoll at the rate of 100 meters a year and, according to Professor Manfred Hochstein, head of Auckland University's Geothermal Institute, "in about 30 years the disaster will hit us." In 1999, after years of secrecy and denials, France's Atomic Energy Commission (CEA) finally admitted that fractures exist in the coral cones of Moruroa and Fangataufa.

The last nuclear test in the South Pacific was carried out below Fangataufa on January 27, 1996. Since then the facilities on Moruroa have been demolished and it's unlikely there will ever be another nuclear test in this area. Today computer simulation is used for the testing. After the end of the actual testing, the Tahitian nongovernmental organization Hiti Tau surveyed 737 of the 12,000 Polynesians who worked at Moruroa between 1966 and 1996, and found that many had experienced adverse health effects. Before being employed at the base, all workers at Moruroa had to sign contracts binding them to eternal silence and waiving access to their own medical records or to any right to compensation for future health problems.

Unlike the United States, which has paid millions of dollars in compensation money to the Marshallese victims of its nuclear testing program, France has been slow to acknowledge the effects of its 41 atmospheric nuclear tests. From 1963 to 1983, no public health statistics were published in the territory, and now the rates of thyroid cancer, leukemia, brain tumors, and stillbirths are on the upswing in French Polynesia. The problem of seafood poisoning (ciguatera) in the nearby Gambier Islands is clearly related. No official studies of this impact have been carried out as yet, and the archives are still closed. In July 2001 the Association Moruroa e Tatou was founded, bringing together 1,500 former test site workers, and both they and a parallel group of more than 900 French veterans demanded that their records be released and appropriate action taken. In April 2009 a case was lodged before the Tribunal du Travail in Papeete seeking compensation for the Polynesian workers at the test sites.

Finally, in December 2009, the French National Assembly passed a law providing limited compensation to those with health problems who lived or worked near the test sites in French Polynesia and Algeria. Compensation is to be decided on a case-by-case basis with the recommendations of a government-appointed committee sent to the Ministry of Defense for final approval. The law was rejected as inadequate by veterans groups and on December 19, 2009, some 2,000 people marched to Place Tarahoi in Papeete to demand that the list of 18 illnesses be expanded and coverage extended to the whole of French Polynesia.

l'Océanie. Between the world wars, 115,000 tonnes of raw ore was produced each year, increasing to 300,000 tonnes in the 1960s. During the first half of the 20th century, this operation was the main element of the French Polynesian economy.

At one time 2,000 workers were present, but today just over 60 people live here, hunting coconut crabs, fishing for lobster, and making copra. Five huge concrete pylons remaining from the mining era dominate the L-shaped landing on the west side of the island, and from here, a steep concrete ramp climbs to the central plateau. Half a dozen abandoned locomotives from the phosphate railway rust along the roadsides and near the contemporary villages, Temao, Moumu, and Vaitepau. Across the island at Moumu, a couple of kilometers beyond Vaitepau, is a long white beach. On the way there you'll pass a grotto with steps leading down to a pool. There are no flights to Makatea, but cruise ships call occasionally.

MAKEMO

Makemo is a 64-kilometer-long atoll near the center of the Tuamotu chain. *Motu* with luxuriant green vegetation stretch all along the north side of the atoll, but only sandbars and reefs mark the southern side. Two passes give access to Makemo's lagoon. One is near the main village, Pukeva, about 16 kilometers from the atoll's east end, while the other pass is at the northwest end of Makemo. The main source of income is pearl farming.

Teanuanua Beach Pearl (tel. 98-03-37, teanuanua-pension@mail.pf) provides accommodations in a row of six elevated bungalows with shared bath along a fine white beach. It's CFP 6,500 single or double or CFP 13,000 double for three meals served at a common table. The units share four common bathrooms. Airport transfers and kayaks are free. Activities include fishing, bicycling, visits to a pearl grafting house, and scuba diving with **Scuba Makemo** (tel. 98-03-08, makemodive@mail.pf). Air Tahiti flies from Papeete to Makemo five days a week (CFP 22,500).

MATAIVA

Tiny Mataiva, westernmost of the Tuamotus and 40 kilometers from Tikehau, has three Air Tahiti flights a week from Papeete (CFP 16,900). The airstrip is 400 meters from Pahua village on the west side of the atoll. The village is divided into two parts by a shallow pass crossed by a wooden bridge.

Only 10 kilometers long and five kilometers wide, Mataiva (pop. 204) is worth considering as an off-beat destination. A coral road covers most of the 35 kilometers around the atoll with narrow concrete bridges over the nine shallow channels, or "eyes," that gave the island its name (*mata* means eye, *iva* is nine). Exploratory mining of a 12-million-ton phosphate deposit under the lagoon ended in 1982, and further mining has been strongly opposed by residents aware of the environmental devastation that would be inflicted. Bring cash, as no banks are found here.

Mr. Aroma Huri of Pahua runs a small resort called **Pension Mataiva Super Cool** (tel. 96-32-53) on a white beach south of the pass. To stay in one of the four *fare* is CFP 8,500 per person, including two meals.

Pension Ariiheevai (tel. 76-44-23) at Mahiai has six air-conditioned bungalows with private baths at CFP 8,000/14,000 single/double including all meals. Airport transfers are free.

Another place to stay is the **Mataiva Village** (tel. 96-32-95), on a beach north of the pass, with six bungalows with baths at CFP 6,500/12,000 single/double with half board. Camping is CFP 1,500/2,500 single/double including breakfast. The guesthouses rent bicycles and arrange excursions.

MORUROA

From 1966 to 1996, Moruroa was the main French nuclear test site in the South Pacific. Before 1974, 36 nuclear tests were carried out in the atmosphere above Moruroa, followed by 130 underground tests from 1974 to 1996. Another five atmospheric tests and 10 underground tests were carried out on Fangataufa Atoll, 37 kilometers south of Moruroa. France only halted its testing after worldwide protests, including rioting on Tahiti and an expedition to Moruroa by the Greenpeace ship *Rainbow Warrior II.*

No one is allowed to visit Moruroa or Fangataufa without official approval, and inspections by independent international observers are banned. Initially a detachment of foreign legionnaires kept watch over the abandoned wharf, airstrip, and concrete bunkers at the dismantled Moruroa test site, while Fangataufa was abandoned. In 2000 the troops were withdrawn over fears that a tsunami could be generated if the atoll's external coral cliffs were suddenly to collapse. Such an event would likely release a torrent of radioactivity into the Pacific Ocean, and France's Atomic Energy Commission has installed satellite-controlled seismic sensors at the deserted site to give early warning of a collapse.

NIAU

The shark-free lagoon at Niau, 50 kilometers southeast of Kaukura, is enclosed by an unbroken circle of land eight kilometers in diameter. Low-grade phosphate deposits on the island were judged too poor to mine, and Niau is now a United Nations Environment Programme biosphere reserve. The 171 inhabitants live in Tupuna village, which receives one Air Tahiti flight a week (CFP 17,900).

REAO

No pass gives access to the lagoon of this easternmost inhabited Tuamotu atoll. In 1865 Catholic missionaries from Mangareva arrived on Reao, and in 1901 they established a leper colony here that accepted patients from all over the Tuamotus and Marquesas until it was moved to Tahiti in 1914. About 350 people live on the atoll today. Reao has weekly Air Tahiti flights from Papeete.

TAIARO

In 1972 the private owner of Taiaro, Mr. W. A. Robinson, declared the atoll a nature reserve, and in 1977 it was accepted by the United Nations as a biosphere reserve. Scientific missions studying atoll ecology sometimes visit tiny Taiaro, the only permanent inhabitants of which are a caretaker family. There are no flights to this isolated island northeast of Kauehi and Raraka.

TAKAPOTO

Takapoto and Takaroa atolls are separated by only eight kilometers of open sea, and the airstrip on each is within walking distance of the village. Air Tahiti flies 4–5 times per week from Papeete to Takapoto (CFP 20,200) and Takaroa (CFP 21,800).

There's no pass into the lagoon, but landing by whaleboat at Fakatopatere at the southwest end of the atoll is easy. Jacob Roggeveen lost one of his three ships on Takapoto's reef in 1722. Today the 16-kilometer-long lagoon is a nursery for black pearl oysters. Only 475 people live here.

The **Takapoto Village** (tel. 98-65-44), right on the beach facing the lagoon a short walk from Fakatopatere, has two neat little bungalows with baths and fridges at CFP 6,700/12,400 single/double, including breakfast and dinner.

The **Pension Dina Tikaruga** (tel. 56-10-39, www.pensiondinamoorea.pf/takapoto.htm) is the Takapoto branch of a longstanding pension on Moorea. It has two beach bungalows and one over-water bungalow at the end of a pier at CFP 7,000 per person with half board (children under 12 half price). Canoes, snorkeling gear, and a visit to a pearl farm are included. Airport transfers are free.

TAKAROA

This northeasterly atoll is 24 kilometers long and up to eight kilometers wide. The 30-meter-wide pass is barely three meters deep and the snorkeling here is second to none. On the outer reef near Takaroa's airstrip are two wrecks, one a four-masted sailing ship here since 1906. Pearl farming flourishes in the Takaroa lagoon, which offers good anchorage everywhere. Since the appearance of this industry, visits by cruising yachts have been discouraged because of the danger of boats hitting poorly marked oyster platforms in the lagoon. Most of the 1,100 inhabitants of Teavaroa village belong to the Mormon church, and their village is often called "little America." Tea, coffee, alcohol, and cigarettes are all frowned on, but dog is considered a delicacy. *Marae* remains lurk in the bush. Note that the Poerangi Village pension on Motu Vaimaroro has closed.

TOAU

Yachts can enter the lagoon at Toau, between Kaukura and Fakarava, though the pass is on the windward side. No flights land on Toau.

Gambier Islands

The Gambier (or Mangareva) Islands are just north of the tropic of Capricorn, 1,650 kilometers southeast of Tahiti. The southerly location means a cooler climate. The archipelago, contrasting sharply with the atolls of the Tuamotus, consists of 10 rocky islands enclosed on three sides by a semicircular barrier reef 65 kilometers long. In all, there are 46 square kilometers of dry land. The Polynesian inhabitants named the main and largest island Mangareva, or "Floating Mountain," for 482-meter-high Mount Duff. Unlike the Marquesas, where the mountains are entirely jungle-clad, the Gambiers have hilltops covered with tall *aeho* grass. Black pearls are cultured on numerous platforms on both sides of Mangareva's blue lagoon. A local seabird, the *karako,* crows at dawn like a rooster.

History

Mangareva, which was originally settled from the Marquesas Islands before A.D. 1100, was the jumping-off place for small groups that discovered and occupied Pitcairn and perhaps Easter Island. In 1797 Captain James Wilson of the London Missionary Society's ship *Duff* named the group for English Admiral James Gambier (1756–1833), a hero of the Napoleonic wars who had helped organize the expedition. France made the Gambiers a protectorate in 1871 and annexed the group in 1881.

Mangareva was the area of operations for a fanatical French priest, Father Honoré Laval of the Congregation for the Sacred Hearts. Upon hearing whalers' tales of rampant cannibalism and marvelous pearls, Laval left his monastery in Chile and with another priest reached the Gambiers in 1834. An old Mangarevan prophecy had foretold the coming of two magicians whose god was all-powerful, and Laval himself toppled the dreaded stone effigy of the god Tu on the island's sacred *marae.* He then single-

coastline on Mangareva Island, Gambier Islands

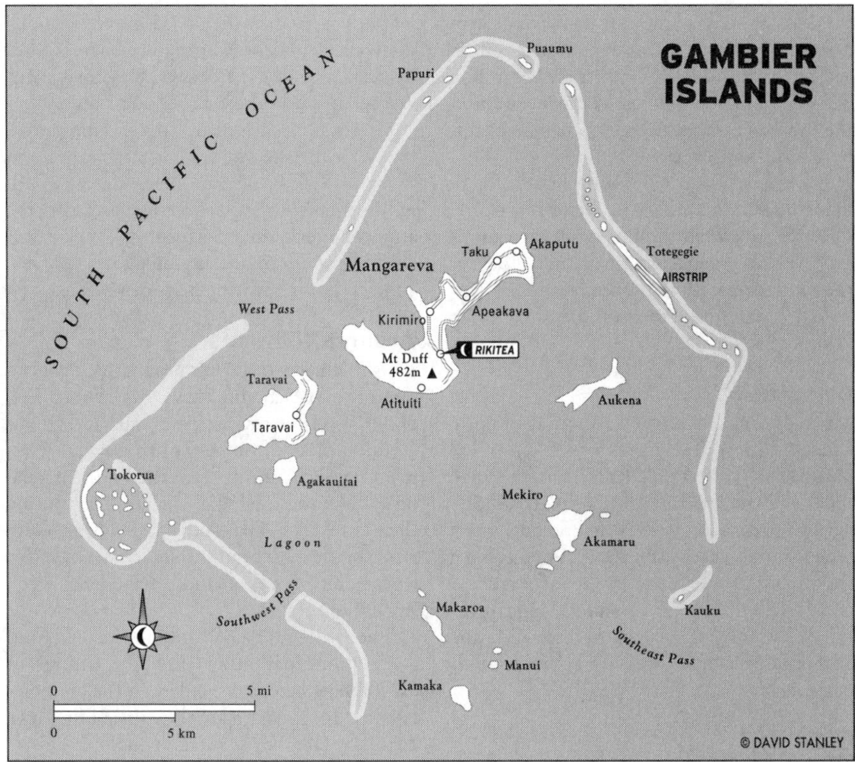

handedly imposed a ruthless and inflexible moral code on the islanders, recruiting them as virtual slaves to build a 1,200-seat cathedral, convents, and triumphal arches—116 stone buildings in all—with the result that he utterly destroyed this once vigorous island culture and practically wiped out its people. During Laval's 37-year reign the population dropped from 9,000 to 500. In 1871 Laval was removed from Mangareva by a French warship, tried for murder on Tahiti, and declared insane.

For a glimpse of the Gambiers half a century ago and a fuller account of Père Laval, read Robert Lee Eskridge's *Manga Reva, The Forgotten Islands.*

The Nuclear Impact

A dramatic intensification of the ciguatera (a kind of seafood poisoning) problem in the Gambiers since the late 1960s is believed to be linked to reef damage or pollution originating at the former nuclear-testing base on Moruroa, 400 kilometers northwest. During the atmospheric testing series (until 1974), the Mangarevans had to take refuge in French-constructed fallout shelters whenever so advised by the military. Before each of the 41 atmospheric tests, French warships would evacuate the 3,000 people from Moruroa, usually to Mangareva, Hao, and Fakarava. Upon arrival the ships were washed down with seawater, spreading radioactive contamination into the lagoons, yet the French never made the slightest attempt to clean up after themselves.

Between 1971 and 1980 the annual incidence of ciguatera remained above 30 percent, peaking at 56 percent in 1975. Each of the inhabitants has suffered 5–7 excruciating attacks of seafood poisoning, and lagoon fish can no longer be eaten. Now, increases in birth defects, kidney problems, and cancer among the inhabitants are allegedly being covered up by the authorities.

It's believed that a deciding reason for the French decision to launch a terrorist attack on Greenpeace's *Rainbow Warrior* at Auckland in 1985 was an intelligence report indicating that the ship intended to proceed to Mangareva with doctors aboard to assess the radiation exposure of residents.

Orientation

Most of the current 1,338 inhabitants of the Gambiers live on 8-by-1.5-kilometer **Mangareva,** of which Rikitea is the main village. A post office, seven small shops, a gendarmerie (tel. 97-82-68), an infirmary, schools, and a cathedral three times as big as the one in Papeete make up the infrastructure of this administrative backwater. Mangareva is the closest inhabited island to Pitcairn Island, and organized tours to Pitcairn occasionally begin here.

SIGHTS

Rikitea

Père Laval's architectural masterpiece is the **Cathedral of St. Michael,** with its twin towers of white coral rock from Kamaka and its altar shining with polished mother-of-pearl—a monument to horror and yet another lost culture. The cathedral was built between 1839 and 1848 on the *ahu* of the island's principal *marae,* and Laval's colleague, Father François Caret, who died in 1844, lies buried in a crypt before the altar. Try to attend choir practice at the Cathedral of St. Michael, if you can. The singing is without musical accompaniment, sometimes in native Mangarevan, a dead language.

The tomb of Grégoire Maputeoa, the 35th and last king of Mangareva (died 1868), is in a small chapel behind the cathedral. Follow the path behind the church to the top of the hill and go through the gate on the left (close it after you, as dogs dig up the graves). Among the walled ruins of Rouru convent in Rikitea one can pick out the chapel, refectory, infirmary, and a dormitory for 60 local nuns.

On the opposite side of Rikitea from the cathedral is the site where a huge nuclear-fallout shelter called the Maison Nucléaire was built by the French to protect the locals during the atmospheric testing at Moruroa. Later it was used by the commune as a shed for heavy machinery, but it has since been demolished.

Around Rikitea

A 28-kilometer road runs around Mangareva, offering ever-changing views. At the north end of the island it passes St. Joseph's Chapel (1836) at Taku, place of worship of the Mangarevan royal family. A sturdy lead-lined nuclear shelter at Taku was used by French officials during their "safe" tests. The south coast of Mangareva is one of the most beautiful in Polynesia, with a tremendous variety of landscapes, plants, trees, smells, and colors.

The white sands of **Aukena** make a good day-trip destination by boat. The Church of St. Raphael here is the oldest in the Gambier Islands. To the south are the ruins of the Rehe Seminary (1840). The Church of Notre-Dame-de-la-Paix (1844) on abandoned **Akamaru** has twin towers added in 1862. Solitary **Makaroa** is a barren, rugged 136-meter-high island.

St. Gabriel Church (1868) on **Taravai** has a neo-Gothic facade decorated with seashells. In a cliff-side cave on the uninhabited island of **Agakauitai** the mummies of 35 generations of cannibal kings are interred.

ACCOMMODATIONS

Pension Bianca et Benoit (tel. 97-83-76, www.chezbiancaetbenoit.pf) is a modern two-story house above the cathedral with three rooms with shared bath at CFP 15,246/21,042 single/double including two meals. Four newer bungalows with private baths are also available. It's just above Rikitea, and the view across to Aukena is lovely.

Five kilometers northeast of the village is **Pension Chez Jojo** (tel. 97-84-69, pensionchezjojo@mail.pf), with two bungalows at CFP 10,345/18,020 single/double including two meals shared with the family. Camping may be possible here.

Chez Tara Etu Kura (tel. 97-83-25, lovinas@mail.pf), by the lagoon at Point Teonekura, charges CFP 11,000 per person, including half board, in a bungalow.

Pension Maro'i (tel. 97-84-62, btqhinarau@hotmail.com), on a beach across the island from Rikitea, has four bungalows with private baths at CFP 9,900 for up to four people, plus CFP 4,200 per person for breakfast and dinner.

GETTING THERE

The airstrip (GMR) is on Totegegie, a long coral island eight kilometers northeast of Rikitea. Arriving passengers pay CFP 500 per person each way for the boat ride to the village. The twice-weekly Air Tahiti flights from Papeete (CFP 32,500 one-way) are either nonstop or via Hao. Coming or going, remember the one-hour time difference between Tahiti and Mangareva.

The supply ships *Nuku Hau* and *Taporo V* from Papeete arrive only monthly. Large vessels can enter the lagoon through passes on the west, southwest, and southeast.

THE MARQUESAS ISLANDS

The Marquesas Islands are the northernmost high islands of the South Pacific, on the same latitude as the Solomon Islands. Though the group was known as Te Henua Enana (The Land of Men) by the Polynesian inhabitants, depopulation during the 19th and 20th centuries has left many of the valleys empty. The 10 main islands form a line 300 kilometers long roughly 1,400 kilometers northeast of Tahiti, but only six are inhabited today: Nuku Hiva, Ua Pou, and Ua Huka in a cluster to the northwest, and Hiva Oa, Tahuata, and Fatu Hiva to the southeast. The administrative centers, Atuona (Hiva Oa), Hakahau (Ua Pou), and Taiohae (Nuku Hiva), are the only places with post offices, banks, gendarmes, and similar services.

These wild, rugged islands feature steep cliffs and valleys leading up to high central ridges, sectioning the islands off into a cartwheel of segments, which creates major transportation difficulties. Large reefs don't form due to the cold south equatorial current, though there are isolated stretches of coral. The absence of protective reefs has prevented the creation of coastal plains, so no roads circle any of the islands. Most of the people live in the narrow, fertile river valleys. The interiors are inhabited only by hundreds of wild horses, cattle, and goats, which have destroyed much of the original vegetation. A Catholic bishop introduced the horses from Chile in 1856, and today they're practically a symbol of the Marquesas. The islands are abundant with lemons, tangerines, oranges, grapefruit, bananas, mangoes, and papayas. Taro and especially breadfruit are the main staples. Birdlife is rich, and the waters

HIGHLIGHTS

Hatiheu Archaeological Sites: Two of the largest and most intriguing archaeological sites in the Marquesas are near Hatiheu on Nuku Hiva's north coast. One has been cleared and is again used for traditional dancing, while a human sacrifice site one kilometer up the road is still partly overgrown (page 231).

Anaho and Haatuatua: These remote beaches on Nuku Hiva are only accessible by boat or on foot. Anaho is one of the finest white sand beaches in the South Pacific, while Haatuatua is wild and deserted, the site of ancient stone platforms (page 231).

Vaipae'e Museum: The Marquesas' finest museum is in a small village on the remote island of Ua Huka. The community museum of Vaipae'e showcases ancient artifacts, quality reproductions of old wood-carvings, and natural history exhibits (page 234).

Atuona: The little town of Atuona on Hiva Oa is notable as the final resting place of the painter Paul Gauguin and the singer Jacques Brel. A cultural center in the town has exhibits on both, and there's an excellent view from their graves on the hillside (page 237).

The Tikis of Puama'u: This evocative archaeological site on the remote north coast of Hiva Oa has the largest tiki in French Polynesia, plus many other ancient statues (page 241).

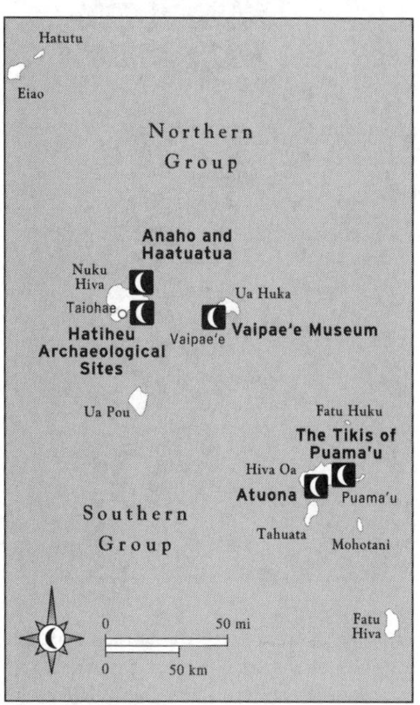

LOOK FOR ☾ TO FIND RECOMMENDED SIGHTS, ACTIVITIES, DINING, AND LODGING.

around the Marquesas teem with lobster, fish, and sharks.

The subtropical climate is hotter and drier than that of Tahiti. July and August are the coolest months. The deep bays on the west sides of the islands are better sheltered for shipping, and the humidity is lower there than on the east sides, which catch the trade winds. The precipitation is uneven, with drought some years, heavy rainfall others. The southern islands of the Marquesas (Hiva Oa, Tahuata, Fatu Hiva) are green and humid; the northern islands (Nuku Hiva, Ua Huka, Ua Pou) are brown and dry.

The difficulty in getting there has kept many potential visitors away. Budget accommodations are scarce, and public transport is nonexistent, which makes getting around a major expense unless you're prepared to rough it. Of the main islands, Hiva Oa has the most colorful recent history, but Nuku Hiva is more varied. Cruising yachts from California often call at the Marquesas on their way to Papeete, and yachties should steer for Hiva Oa first to enjoy the smoothest possible sailing through the rest of the group. For hikers prepared to cope with the humidity, the Marquesas are paradise. A multitude of waterfalls tumbles down

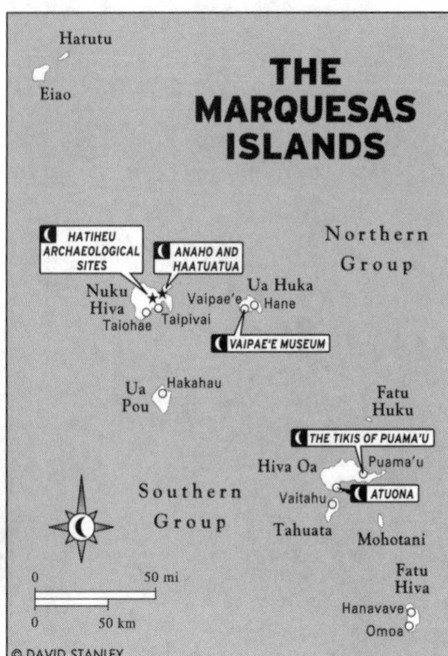

the slopes, and eerie overgrown archaeological remains tell of a golden era long gone. If you enjoy quiet, unspoiled places, you'll like the Marquesas.

PLANNING YOUR TIME

In the *Discover Tahiti and French Polynesia* chapter we've outlined a suggested one-week itinerary, *Tikis and Treks in the Marquesas,* to Hiva Oa and Nuku Hiva. To extend this to Ua Pou and/or Ua Huka, add a couple of days for each. The itinerary is based on Air Tahiti's "Extension Marquises" pass, which allows return flights from Papeete to Nuku Hiva and Hiva Oa for CFP 50,000 when purchased in combination with another Air Tahiti pass. To include Ua Pou and Ua Huka, you'll need a Pass Marqueses (CFP 65,000) that can be bought alone.

Many people visit the Marquesas Islands on a 14-day cruise aboard the passenger-carrying freighter *Aranui.* Those traveling independently by air will want at least two full days on Nuku Hiva, one to explore Taiohae and environs and another for a day trip to Hatiheu and Anaho. Similarly, on Hiva Oa one day can be spent exploring Atuona and another on a day trip to Puama'u. Two days each would be needed to get a feel for Ua Huka and Ua Pou. Thus eight days is the minimum you'd want to spend in the Marquesas, and adding an extra day or two on Nuku Hiva and Hiva Oa is highly recommended.

Events

The Marquesas Islands Festival, or Matava'a o te Henua Enata, is a major cultural event celebrated every four years in December, with dancing, singing, drumming, and sports, plus handicraft displays and feasts. Aside from strengthening and reviving traditional knowledge and skills, numerous archaeological sites have been restored or rebuilt in preparation for these events. Previous festivals have been at Ua Pou (1987), Nuku Hiva (1989), Hiva Oa (1991), Ua Pou (1995), Nuku Hiva (1999), Hiva Oa (2003), and Ua Pou (2007). The next festival will be on Nuku Hiva (2011). A Matava'a Iti Festival, or "mini" festival, is held every other year between the main festivals.

HISTORY

Pre-European Society

Marquesan houses were built on high platforms *(paepae)* scattered through the valleys (and still fairly easy to find). Every tribe had a rectangular ceremonial plaza *(tohua)* where important festivals took place. Archaeologists have been able to trace stone temples (*me'ae,* called *marae* elsewhere in French Polynesia), agricultural terraces, and earthen fortifications *('aka'ua)* half hidden in the jungle, evocative reminders of a vanished civilization. Then as now, the valleys were isolated from one another by high ridges and turbulent seas, yet warfare was vicious and cannibalism an important incentive. An able warrior could attain great power. Local hereditary chiefs exercised authority over commoners.

The Marquesans' artistic style was one of the most powerful and refined in the Pacific. The ironwood war club was their most distinctive symbol, but there were also finely carved wooden bowls, fan handles, and tikis of stone and wood, both miniature and massive. The carvings are noted for the faces: the mouth with lips parted and the bespectacled eyes. Both men and women wore carved ivory earplugs. Men's entire bodies were covered with bold and striking tattoos, a practice banned by the Catholic missionaries. Stilts were used by men in ceremonies and by boys for racing and mock fighting. This was about the only part of Polynesia where polyandry was common. There was a strong cult of the dead: The bodies or skulls of ancestors were carefully preserved. The northern Marquesas Islands may have been inhabited as early as 300 B.C., and both Hawaii (around A.D. 200) and Easter Island (around A.D. 300) were colonized from here.

European Contact

The existence of these islands was long concealed from the world by the Spanish to prevent the English from taking possession of them. The southern group was found by Álvaro de Mendaña in July 1595 during his second voyage of exploration from Peru. He named them Las Marquesas de Mendoza after his benefactor, the Spanish viceroy. The first island sighted (Fatu Hiva) seemed uninhabited, but as Mendaña's *San Jerónimo* sailed nearer, scores of outriggers appeared, paddled by about 400 robust islanders. Their hair was long and loose, and they were naked and tattooed in blue patterns. The natives boarded the ship, but when they became overly curious and bold, Mendaña ordered a gun fired, and they jumped over the side.

Then began one of the most murderous and shameful of all the white explorers' entries into the South Pacific region. As a matter of caution, Mendaña's men began shooting natives on sight, in one instance hanging three bodies in the shore camp on Santa Cristina (Tahuata) as a warning. They left behind three large crosses, the date cut in a tree, syphilis, and more than 200 dead Polynesians. When Captain Cook arrived at Tahuata in 1774 it soon became obvious that knowledge of the earlier Spanish visit had remained alive in oral traditions, and Cook and his crew were shunned.

The northern Marquesas Islands were "discovered" by Joseph Ingraham of the American trading vessel *Hope* on April 19, 1791. After that, slavers, firearms, disease, and alcohol reduced the population. American whalers called frequently from 1800 onward. Although France took possession of the group in 1842, Peruvian slavers kidnapped some Marquesans to South America in 1863 to work the plantations and mines. Those few able to return thanks to diplomatic lobbying by their French protectors brought a catastrophic smallpox epidemic. The Marquesans clung to their warlike cannibalistic ways until 95 percent of their number had died; the remainder adopted Catholicism.

The Marquesans

From 80,000 at the beginning of the 19th century, the population fell to about 15,000 by 1842 when the French "protectors" arrived, and to a devastated 2,000 by 1926. Even today the total population is just 8,658. Though there are some negative attitudes toward the French, the Marquesans realize that without French subsidies their economy would collapse. Hospitalization, drugs, and dental care are provided free by the government.

The Marquesan language, divided into north and south dialects, is only about 50 percent comprehensible to a Tahitian and is actually a bit closer to Rarotongan and Hawaiian. There's a small separatist movement here that believes the Marquesas will receive more benefits as a distinct colony of France, or failing that, as a country independent of Tahiti. And just to complicate matters, twice as many Marquesans live in Papeete as in the Marquesas itself.

GETTING THERE

Direct international flights to Nuku Hiva have been discussed for years, but nothing much has been done, and an expensive round-trip from Tahiti is still required. An **Air Tahiti** ATR flies from Papeete to Nuku Hiva daily (3.5 hours, CFP 29,200) with one of the flights via Rangiroa.

Flights between Nuku Hiva and Ua Huka (CFP 6,900) operate four times a week, connecting with one of the ATR flights from Papeete. From Nuku Hiva to Ua Pou (CFP 6,900) and Hiva Oa (CFP 11,100) the flights are six times a week. Ua Pou to Ua Huka (CFP 6,900) is four times a week. Get a through ticket to your final destination, as flights to Hiva Oa, Ua Pou, and Ua Huka are all the same price from Papeete (CFP 32,500). Tahuata and Fatu Hiva are without air service. All flights are heavily booked. Coming or going, remember the 30-minute time difference between Tahiti and the Marquesas.

By Boat

The passenger-carrying freighter *Aranui* cruises 17 times a year between Papeete and the Marquesas. It calls at all six inhabited Marquesas Islands, plus a couple of the Tuamotus. The routing might be Papeete–Fakarava–Ua Pou–Nuku Hiva–Hiva Oa–Fatu Hiva–Tahuata–Ua Huka–Nuku Hiva–Ua Pou–Rangiroa–Papeete. A vigorous daily program with fairly strenuous but optional hikes is included in the tour price. The only docks in the Marquesas are at Taiohae, Hakahau, Vaipae'e, and Atuona; elsewhere everyone goes ashore in whaleboats, a potential problem for passengers with mobility limitations. In stormy weather, the landings can be dangerous. Still, the *Aranui* is fine for the adventuresome visitor who wants to see a lot in a short time.

This 118-meter freighter had its inaugural sailing in 2002, replacing a smaller German-built boat that had served the Marquesas since 1990. The 200 passengers are accommodated in four classes of accommodations for the 14-day, eight-island cruise. The cheapest cabins start at US$3,675 per person round-trip (double occupancy), all meals included. The best suite is US$5,445 per person, while an intermediate deluxe cabin is US$4,410. Single occupancy costs 50 percent more. There's also an air-conditioned "Class C" dormitory with 30 upper and lower berths that costs US$2,079 per person, and, of course, doesn't involve a single supplement. A US$75 port tax, US$105 cruise tax, and 6 percent value-added tax are extra. Deck passage is intended for local residents only, but it's sometimes possible for tourists to travel interisland within the Marquesas on deck (about CFP 3,000–8,000 a hop). The meals are good but with little choice. The roster of American, French, and German passengers is congenial.

The *Aranui*'s Papeete office (**Compagnie Polynésienne de Transport Maritime,** tel. 42-62-40) is at the interisland wharf at Motu Uta. The CPTM's U.S. office is at 2028 El Camino Real S., Suite B, San Mateo, CA 94403 (tel. 650/574-2575 or 800/972-7268, www.aranui.com). In the United States bookings can be made through **TravLtips** (www.travltips.com). Note that the freighter *Taporo* doesn't accept passengers to the Marquesas.

GETTING AROUND

To island hop within the Marquesas, you can fly with Air Tahiti or try using the *Aranui,* if it happens to be going where you want to go. Ask at local town halls about the supply boat *Ka'oha Nui,* a large luxury yacht owned by the territory that often sails among the islands picking up schoolchildren on holidays, etc. Private boats run from Taiohae to Ua Pou fairly frequently, and there's a municipal boat from Atuona to Tahuata at least once a week. Chartering boats interisland is extremely expensive, and to join a regular trip you just have to be lucky, persistent, and prepared to wait.

Getting around the individual islands can be a challenge, as there's no organized public transportation other than expensive airport transfers, and because of the condition of the roads, rental cars are limited to a few pricey vehicles at Taiohae and Atuona. It's fairly easy to hire a chauffeur-driven vehicle on Hiva Oa, Nuku Hiva, Ua Huka, and Ua Pou, but expect to pay CFP 15,000–25,000 per day. Since this amount can be shared among as many people as can fit inside, you'll want to join or form a group. While making your inquiries, keep your ears open for any mention of boat tours, as these are often no more expensive than land tours.

Hitchhiking is complicated because many of the private vehicles you see out on the roads double as taxis, and drivers who depend on tourists for a large part of their incomes are unlikely to be eager to give rides for free. An option for hardy backpackers is just to count on having to walk the whole way and accept any lifts that happen to be offered. It's too far to walk in one day from Nuku Hiva airport to Taiohae or from Atuona to Puama'u, but many other stretches can be covered on foot. If you're fit you can walk from Taiohae to Taipivai and from Taipivai to Hatiheu on Nuku Hiva, and from Atuona to Ta'aoa or the airport on Hiva Oa. Almost everywhere on Fatu Hiva, Tahuata, Ua Huka, and Ua Pou is accessible on foot, provided you've got the time and strength. If you pack a tent, food, and sufficient water, you'll be self-sufficient and able to see the islands on a shoestring budget.

Nuku Hiva

Nuku Hiva is the largest (339 square kilometers) and most populous (2,650 inhabitants) of the Marquesas. Taiohae (pop. 2,000) on the south coast is the administrative and economic center of the Marquesas. It's a modern little town with a post office, hospital, town hall, bank, grocery stores, street lighting, and several hotels. Winding mountain roads lead northeast from Taiohae to Taipivai and Hatiheu villages or northwest toward the airport. In the center of the island Mount Tekao (1,224 meters) rises above the vast, empty Toovii Plateau.

Taiohae Bay is a flooded volcanic crater guarded by two tiny islands called the Sentinels. Ua Pou is clearly visible across the waters. Though open to the south, Taiohae's deep harbor offers excellent anchorage. Cruising yachts toss in the hock on the east side of the bay, while the *Aranui* ties up to a wharf at the southeast end of town. Take care with the drinking water at Taiohae. Unfortunately, many beaches around Nuku Hiva are infested with sand flies called *no-nos* that give nasty bites (the bugs disappear after dark). Luckily, Hiva Oa is free of these pests.

History

In 1813 Captain David Porter of the American frigate *Essex* annexed Nuku Hiva for the United States, though the act was never ratified by Congress. Britain and the United States had gone to war in 1812, and Porter's mission was to harass British shipping in the Pacific. After capturing a dozen ships off South America, Porter arrived at Nuku Hiva and built a fort at the present site of Taiohae, which he named Madisonville for the U.S. president of his day. Porter allowed himself to be drawn into local conflicts among the Polynesian tribes. A few months later he left to continue his raiding and was defeated by two British warships off Chile. In 1842 the French erected Fort Collet on the site of Porter's fort, above the marina at the east end of Taiohae.

Sandalwood traders followed Porter, then whalers. Herman Melville arrived on the American whaling ship *Acushnet* in 1842, and his book *Typee,* written after a one-month stay in the Taipi Valley, is still the classic narrative of Marquesan life during the 19th century. A half century later, Scottish writer Robert Louis Stevenson visited the island. In 2002 Nuku Hiva was back in the limelight with the filming on the island of the American TV series *Survivor* at a cost of US$100 million.

TAIOHAE

Taiohae's new post office is on a slight plateau in the heart of the official quarter, with the **Residence** of the subdivisional administrator just below toward the beach and the old **Administrative Center** across the street. On a grassy knoll topped by a navigational light above these buildings is the site of **Fort Collet,** which offers a sweeping view of Taiohae Bay. Nothing remains of Porter's original fort

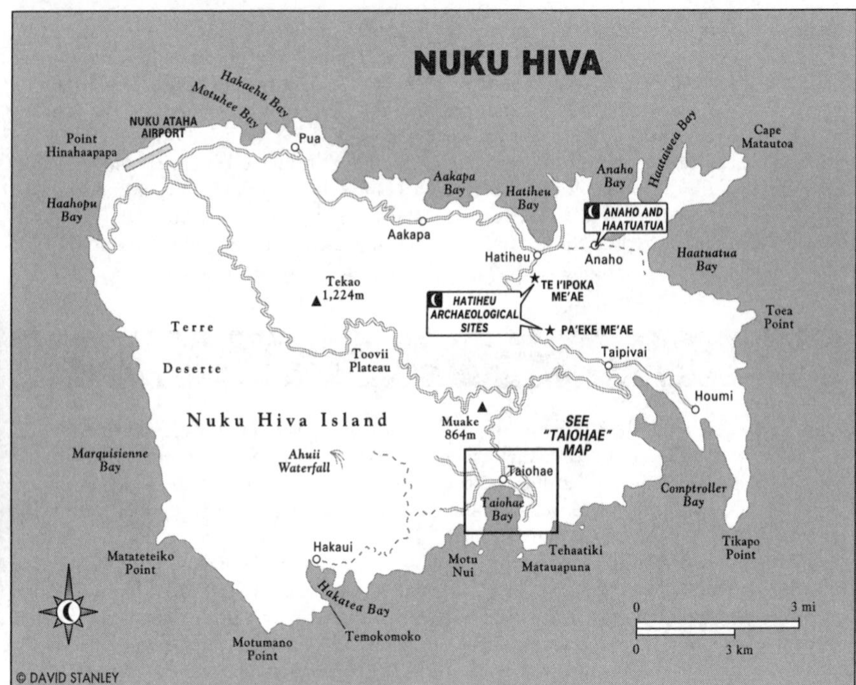

overlooking what he called Massachusetts Bay. Just north of this hill above the old marina is the colonial jail.

The **Monument to the Dead obelisk** (1928), marked by an anchor and cannon, is west along the waterfront past the bank.

Two towers retained from an earlier church give access to the open courtyard of **Notre-Dame Cathedral** (1974) on the west side of central Taiohae. The cathedral's interior is notable for its fine wood carvings, including a massive wooden pulpit bearing the symbols of the four evangelists. The floor behind the pulpit is paved with flower stones from Ua Pou. Among the outstanding wooden Stations of the Cross carved by Damien Haturau, note especially Station No. 1, which depicts Jesus in the Garden of Breadfruit (instead of the Garden of Olives).

Across a small bridge just west of the cathedral is the **Temehea Tohua,** also known as the Tohua Piki Vehine, created for the Marquesas Islands Festival in 1989. Among the modern tikis on this platform are the figures of Temoana and Vaekehu, who were designated king and queen of the island by the French in 1842.

Next to a small cemetery 600 meters farther west along the waterfront is the wooden **Typee Memorial** (1842–1992) by Séverin Kahe'e Taupotini (who also carved the cathedral's pulpit).

At the southwest end of the bay, just before the Keikahanui Pearl Lodge, is the **He'e Tai Inn Art Gallery and Musée** (tel. 92-03-82, Mon.–Sat., by donation) run by American art collector Rose Corser. A good part of her museum collection is on loan from Taiohae's bishop and other local residents. Her gallery displays a tasteful selection of Marquesan artifacts, including Fatu Hiva tapa. Prices are comparable to those at other outlets around town.

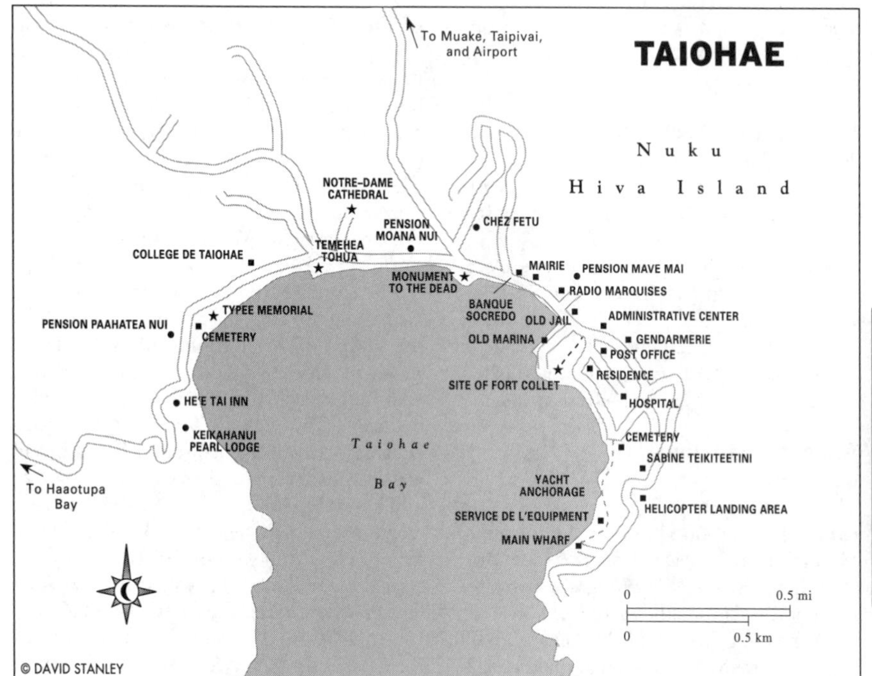

Many stone- and wood-carvers work on Nuku Hiva, and their wooden tikis, bowls, ukuleles, ceremonial war clubs, and paddles are keenly sought after.

The road now leaves the bay and climbs two kilometers over the ridge to secluded **Haaotupa Bay,** also called Colette Bay, a nice picnic spot.

West of Taiohae

At Hakaui, 15 kilometers west of Taiohae, a river runs down a narrow steep-sided valley. Fantastic 350-meter **Ahuii Waterfall** (also known as the Vaipo Waterfall), highest in the territory, drops from the plateau at the far end of the valley, four kilometers from the coast. It's a two-hour walk from Hakaui to the waterfall with a few thigh-high river crossings after rains. The trail passes many crumbling platforms, indicating that the valley was once well populated. Beware of falling pebbles if you swim in the pool at the falls. A boat from Taiohae to Hakaui costs CFP 16,000 and up return, but an overgrown 12-kilometer switchback trail also crosses the 535-meter ridge from above Haaotupa Bay to uninhabited Hakaui. You'll need to be adventurous and good at finding your own way to follow it (allow four hours each way between Taiohae to Hakaui).

Above Taiohae

For a sweeping view of Taiohae Bay, hike up to **Muake** (864 meters) on the ridge due north of town. A steep concrete road zigzags seven kilometers to the point where the airport and Taipivai roads divide. Turn left toward the airport, and then left again into the forest. There was once a Marquesan fort near where the radio tower presently stands. This is a favorite takeoff point for paragliders, and groups from the *Aranui* have a picnic lunch here. Farther west toward the airport is a market gardening area and agricultural station on the 900-meter-high **Toovii Plateau.** Herds of cattle range across the pine-covered plateau.

Sports and Recreation

The dive shop in Taiohae has closed.

Horseback riding is offered by Sabine Teikiteetini (tel. 92-01-56), and rides from Taiohae to Taipivai are possible.

A variety of guided hiking tours are organized by **Marquises Rando** (tel. 92-07-13, www.marquisesrando.com), either for one day or overnight with camping. Prices range CFP 6,600–12,000 per person including transportation to the trailhead and refreshments.

Accommodations

US$25-50

The least expensive place to stay is **Chez Fetu** (tel. 92-03-66), just up the hill from the Monument to the Dead on the waterfront, off Taipivai Road behind Magasin Kamake, a 10-minute walk from the wharf in Taiohae. The three-bed bungalow is CFP 2,000/4,000/6,000 single/double/triple. Communal cooking facilities are available, and there's a terrace facing the valley.

US$50-100

Pension Mave Mai (tel. 92-08-10, pension-mavemai@mail.pf), up the steep road between the old jail and Radio Marquises from near the old marina, has eight air-conditioned rooms in a two-story building at CFP 7,000/8,000/9,000 single/double/triple. The three upstairs rooms have balconies with great views of the bay, while two of the downstairs rooms have kitchens. The owners, Régina and Jean-Claude, can provide meals (CFP 3,000 for half board) and organize a variety of excursions at the usual rates. Four-wheel-drive vehicles are for hire at CFP 12,000 a day.

US$100-150

The friendly two-story **Pension Moana Nui** (tel. 92-03-30, http://pensionmoananui.ifrance.com), on the waterfront in the middle of Taiohae, has seven air-conditioned rooms with private baths (with hot water) above its popular restaurant-bar. Bed, breakfast, and dinner are CFP 9,310/14,790 single/double. Mosquitoes and bar noise are drawbacks, the excellent views from the terrace a definite plus. The Moana Nui rents cars at CFP 11,000, but they're not always available. Boat excursions can be arranged. Airport transfers are CFP 3,500 per person.

Pension Paahatea Nui (tel. 92-00-97, paahateanui@mail.pf) faces the west side of the bay, just up the road running inland from near the small cemetery beside the Typee Memorial. The four neat little bungalows with private baths and TVs are CFP 5,550 per person including breakfast. A common kitchen and washing machine is available.

The **He'e Tai Inn** (tel. 92-03-82, rose.corser@mail.pf), between the Nuku Hiva Village Hôtel and Keikahanui Pearl Lodge, is owned by an American woman named Rose Corser who opened the original Keikahanui Inn in 1979. In 1999 Rose brought in Pearl Resorts, selling her remaining interest in 2006. A year later, she got back into the business with this boutique hotel. The He'e Tai Inn is only open during the sailing boat season, March–July, and caters mostly to cruisers. The six air-conditioned rooms and one suite starting around CFP 10,000 double are in front of Rose's art gallery. As during the good old days, the He'e Tai Inn's snack and coffee shop in the restaurant has happy hours for cruising yachties during the season. Corser is building a new hotel on the site that should be ready by the time you get there.

US$250 AND UP

The **Keikahanui Nuku Hiva Pearl Lodge** (tel. 92-07-10, www.pearlresorts.com), just up the hill from the He'e Tai Inn, was completely rebuilt in 1999 with a small but spectacular cliff-side swimming pool. The 20 air-conditioned bungalows start at CFP 25,000 double, plus 14 percent tax. Cooking facilities are not provided, so for breakfast and dinner add CFP 7,600 plus tax per person. Individual meals in the Lodge restaurant average CFP 1,600 for a starter and CFP 2,600 for a main dish. Bicycles are loaned free. Expect nocturnal rooster noise here. Airport transfers are CFP 9,900 per person round-trip by road. The Keikahanui is named after a tattooed chief.

Food

The **Restaurant Moana Nui** (tel. 92-03-30) on the waterfront is famous for its pizza (CFP 1,600–1,800). It's a popular place to eat and drink.

Roulottes (mobile food wagons) on the pier dish up takeout snacks and meals costing around CFP 1,000.

If you're lucky, you might be able to buy fresh vegetables at the Saturday morning market at the old marina in Taiohae. Be there by 0500, as not much will be left at 0600. The only fresh produce available at the various supermarkets is potatoes and garlic (fresh veggies are easier to find on Hiva Oa).

Information and Services

Tourist information is available from **Comité Tourisme Nuku Hiva** (tel. 92-03-73, www.marquises.pf), at the Subdivision du Service de l'Urbanisme in the old jail (back door) between the *mairie* and the post office. It sells a good topographical map of Nuku Hiva.

Radio Marquises broadcasts from Taiohae over FM 101.3 MHz, with the Réseau France Outre-Mer (RFO) news in French at 0700 and 1230.

Central Taiohae boasts a **Banque Socredo** branch (tel. 91-00-85, weekdays 0730–1130 and 1330–1600). The **post office** on the east side of town sells telephone cards you can use at the public phone outside and at several other locations around the island. The post office also has public computer terminals for Internet access and sells the Tahiti newspapers. The yacht services office at the old marina also provides Internet access plus laundry facilities.

The **gendarmerie** (tel. 91-03-05) is just up the road to the left of the post office, while the public hospital (tel. 91-02-00) is to the right. The Taiohae gendarmes invariably insist on yachties posting their arrival bonds, if they haven't already done so.

THE MIRACULOUS *NONI* FRUIT

In 1996 an American company began promoting the therapeutic proprieties of the knobby green fruit of the endemic *nono* or *noni* tree *(Morinda citrifolia)*, an ingredient in traditional Polynesian medicine. *Noni* pulp has become French Polynesia's largest agricultural export, and the tree is now widely cultivated. The ripe fruit has an unpleasant taste and smell that once made it fit only for pig feed, but mixed with other juices it's quite palatable.

Among the claims made for *noni* juice are that it increases mental clarity and energy levels, supports proper digestion, carries beneficial substances to the skin, enhances the immune system, relieves pain, fights bacteria, retards tumor growth, and promotes longevity.

Miracle cure or spurious elixir, the *noni* juice fad has created a miniboom in producing areas such as the Marquesas. The trees blossom year-round, and a yellow dye is made from the roots. Apart from the juice, *noni* extract is used as an ingredient in many personal hygiene products such as soaps, creams, and shampoos. In the United States, Morinda Inc. has exclusive rights.

Getting There

Nuku Ataha Airport (NHV) is in the arid Terre Déserte at the northwest corner of Nuku Hiva, 32 kilometers from Taiohae along a twisting road over the Toovii Plateau (or 19 kilometers as the crow flies). Upon arrival from Papeete or Rangiroa turn your watch ahead 30 minutes. The main drawback to flying into Nuku Hiva is the cost of airport transfers, which run CFP 4,000 per person each way by four-wheel-drive Toyota Land Cruiser for the 2.5-hour drive. While waiting for your flight it's worth examining the excellent Marquesan low-relief wood carvings made to decorate the airport's bar and shop when the airport was built in 1979. Airport transfers by helicopter are no longer offered.

Air Tahiti (tel. 91-02-25) is in a poorly marked office near the *mairie.*

Information on the *Ka'oha Nui, Meherio,* and other government boats can be obtained from the Service de l'Equipment next to the main wharf at Taiohae.

Getting Around

The only public transportation on Nuku Hiva is the expensive airport transfer. It's possible to walk from Taiohae to Taipivai and Hatiheu in two days if you're fit, camping along the way. The road from Taiohae to Hatiheu is now much improved and concrete most of the way. Another road links Hatiheu to the airport via Aakapa and Pua.

To rent a car without a driver for something approaching normal rates, ask at the Pension Moana Nui (tel. 92-03-30), though its vehicles are often all taken. **Nuku Island Excursions** (tel. 92-04-89), formerly Europcar, on the pier in front of Yacht Service, has four-wheel-drive vehicles with unlimited kilometers. Car rentals often come with a driver and thus cost taxi prices.

Tours

Island tours by Land Rover are the usual way of getting around. **Jocelyne Henua Enana Tours** (tel. 92-00-52, www.marquisesvoyages.com.pf) offers a variety of prearranged tours of Nuku Hiva with extensions to Ua Huka and Ua Pou available. The eight-hour road tour from Taiohae to Hatiheu is CFP 16,000 for two people or CFP 6,500/5,500 each for three/four people. This is about the same price as renting a car, and an English-speaking guide is included. Half-day boat tours to bays on the south side of Nuku Hiva with a chance to see dolphins are CFP 13,000 for the boat for two people or CFP 5,000/4,500 per person for up to four/up to six. Jocelyne also specializes in special tours of anywhere from 1.5 to six hours for cruise ship passengers during their time in port; such activities must be booked in advance by emailing jocelyne@mail.pf.

A boat trip to Hakaui to visit the Ahuii Waterfall is CFP 16,000 for one or two people, CFP 18,000 for three, or CFP 5,000 each for four to six people. This full day trip includes a four-hour round-trip hike to the falls and a picnic lunch. Jocelyne Henua Enana Tours can book this tour with a French-speaking guide. Otherwise try Eric Bastard of **Marquises Plaisance** (tel. 92-08-75).

The catamaran *Moemoea Nui* (tel. 92-01-62, www.marquises-croisiere.com) based at Taiohae is available for cruises of three or six nights around the Marquesas Islands.

TAIPIVAI

Several hundred people live at Taipivai, a five-hour, 16-kilometer walk from Taiohae over the Col Teavanui (576 meters). Vanilla grows wild throughout this valley. At Hooumi, on a fine protected bay near Taipivai, is a truly magical little church. The huge *tohua* of Vahangeku'a at Taipivai is a whopping 170 by 25 meters. Eleven great stone tikis watch over the **Pa'eke Me'ae,** a couple of kilometers up the Taipi Valley toward Hatiheu and then up the slope to the right. Robert Suggs excavated this site in 1957. About two kilometers farther up the road to Hatiheu is a monument to the left of the road marking the spot where Herman Melville spent a month with his tattooed sweetheart Fayaway in 1842. In his novel *Typee* (his spelling for Taipi), he gives a delightful account of the life of the great-grandparents of the present inhabitants.

HATIHEU AND ANAHO

From Taipivai it's another 12 kilometers via the Col Teavaitapuhiva (443 meters) to Hatiheu on the north coast. Some spectacular falls are seen in the distance to the left of the road near the mountain pass. A statue of the Virgin Mary stands on a rocky peak high above Hatiheu Bay and its black sand beach. (Yachts are better off anchoring in protected Anaho Bay than here.) Hatiheu was destroyed by a tsunami in 1946, but 350 people live there today.

© TAHITI TOURISME

aerial view of Hatiheu Bay on the north shore of Nuku Hiva, Marquesas Islands

Hatiheu Archaeological Sites

The restored **Hikoku'a Tohua** is a bit more than one kilometer from Hatiheu back toward Taipivai. Originally built in 1250 and excavated in 1957, the *tohua* consists of two long spectator platforms on opposite sides of a central dance floor. The north end of the dance floor is closed by a stone platform used for ceremonial activities. Several of the tikis on the structure were added during the 1989 Marquesas Islands Festival, while others are old (notice the phallic fertility statue at the entrance on the left).

In the jungle one kilometer farther up the road is the **Te I'ipoka Me'ae,** where many human sacrifices were made to the goddess Te Vana'uau'a. The victims were kept in a pit beneath a huge sacred banyan tree until their turn arrived to be consumed at cannibal feasts. Up the steep wooded slope from here is the overgrown **Kamuihei Tohua** with petroglyphs.

Anaho and Haatuatua

Anaho is two kilometers east of Hatiheu on horseback or foot over a 217-meter pass (no road). It's one of the most beautiful of Nuku Hiva's bays, with a crescent beach of powdery white sand and some of the finest snorkeling in the Marquesas; there is lovely coral and the possibility of seeing turtles or reef sharks. Only a few families reside here, but the two small pensions make it possible to spend a few days in this idyllic location. Robert Louis Stevenson described his joyful stay here in 1888 in *In the South Seas.*

From Anaho it's an easy 45-minute walk east along the south side of the bay and over the low isthmus to uninhabited **Haatuatua Bay,** where you could camp wild. Some of the oldest stone platforms in the Marquesas are hidden in the bush here (go inland on one of the grassy strips near the south end of the beach till you find a southbound trail). No one lives there today, but wild horses are seen.

Accommodations

In Hatiheu village, **Chez Yvonne Katupa** (tel. 92-02-97, hinakonui@mail.pf) offers five bungalows without cooking facilities or hot water at CFP 5,000/7,000 single/double, breakfast included. The bungalows are set in their own garden across a small bridge from Yvonne's restaurant, facing the beach on Hatiheu Bay. Passengers off the *Aranui* enjoy a superb fish and lobster lunch at Yvonne's. Ask to see her collection of artifacts at the *mairie.* It's possible to rent sit-on-top kayaks here or to hire horses. Yvonne arranges transfers from Hatiheu to the airport (75 kilometers) by four-wheel drive at CFP 4,000 per person.

You can also stay at **Te Pua Hinako** (tel. 92-04-14), also known as Chez Juliette, at the northwest end of the beach at Anaho. The two rooms with shared bath are CFP 2,500 per person, or CFP 6,100 per person with all meals. Boat transfers to or from the airport are CFP 7,000 each way for up to six people.

Juliette's son Raymond operates **Pension Kao Tia'e** (tel. 92-00-08) or "Kaoha Tiare" next to Te Pua Hinako. The five bungalows with baths are CFP 6,500 per person, including all meals. Juliette and Raymond hosted TV crews from *Survivor* for several months in late 2001.

Other Northern Islands

UA POU

At 105 square kilometers, Ua Pou is the third-largest Marquesan island. This spectacular, diamond-shaped island lies about 40 kilometers south of Nuku Hiva and is very arid. Ua Pou is the only island in the Marquesas with the sort of towering volcanic plugs seen on Moorea and Bora Bora. One of these sugarloaf-shaped volcanic plugs inspired Jacques Brel's song "La Cathédrale," and the name Ua Pou itself means "the pillars." Mount Oave (1,203 meters), the highest point on Ua Pou, is often cloud-covered.

The island's population of more than 2,158 is larger than that of Hiva Oa. The main village is Hakahau on the northeast coast, with solid concrete streets, government services, and the only port. Five hundred French foreign legionnaires rebuilt the breakwater at Hakahau in 1988, and ships can now tie up to the concrete pier.

Sights

The first stone church in the Marquesas was erected at Hakahau in 1859, and the present **Church of Saint-Etienne** (1981) has a pulpit shaped like a boat carved from a single stump by a group of sculptors. The wooden cross in the church is by Damien Haturau.

The **Tenai Paepae** in the center of the village was restored for the 1995 Marquesas Islands Festival, the same occasion that saw the inauguration of the small **Musée de Ua Pou** at the south end of Hakahau.

Lovely **Anahoa Beach** is a scenic 30-minute walk east of the marina, but unfortunately the beach is infested with *no-nos.* There's a superlative bird's-eye view from the cross overlooking Hakahau on the ridge halfway there.

South of Hakahau

A road leads south from Hakahau to a beach beyond Hohoi. On 88-meter-high **Motu Oa** off the south coast, millions of seabirds nest.

The road from Hohoi to **Hakatao** on the southwest coast crosses a high pass, and the steep descent to Hakatao is only possible in the dry season. The track between Hakatao and **Hakamaii** can be covered only by canoe, hoof, or on foot (a four-hour walk). You can drive the rest of the way around the island.

West of Hakahau

West of Hakahau the road runs to the airport (10 kilometers), Hakahetau (16 kilometers), and Haakuti (22 kilometers). Sea turtles lay their eggs on the white sands of uninhabited **Hakanahi Beach** between the airport and Hakahetau, and large sharks wait offshore to feed on the hatchlings (swimming is not advised). You can often see the sharks from the road above the beach.

Around 200 people live in the charming small village of **Hakahetau.** Local handicrafts are made from the *kea pua* (flower stone), a black volcanic stone with yellow streaks found only on the beaches here.

In Hakahetau, ask for Étienne Hokaupoko (no phone) who lives up on the hillside, a 10-minute walk from the port. His son lives next to the Protestant church in the village and should be able to provide information. Étienne

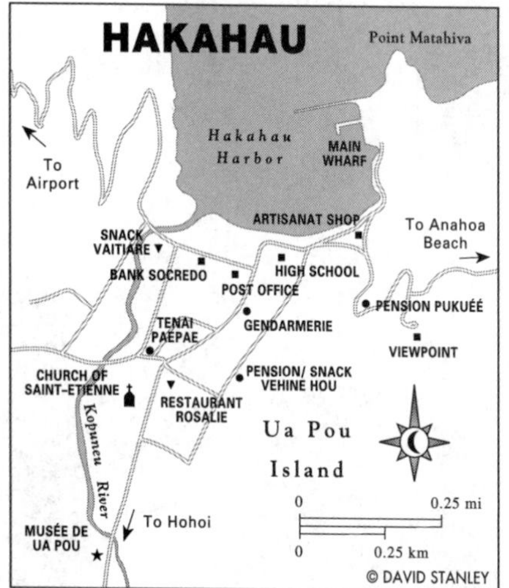

is working on a Marquesan-English dictionary, and he knows many stories he's only too happy to share. Yachties often drop in to sign his guest book.

Shopping

An Artisanat shop near the wharf at Hakahau sells local carvings and shell jewelry. Several wood-carvers work in Hakahau village—just ask for *les sculpteurs.* If you're buying, shop around at the beginning of your stay, as many items are unfinished and you should allow the time to have something completed.

Accommodations

The best established pension in Hakahau is **Pension Pukuéé** (tel. 92-50-83, http://chez.mana.pf/~pukuee), just a few minutes walk from the wharf on the road to Anahoa Beach. Set on a hill overlooking the village, the five shared-bath rooms are CFP 3,000/5,500 single/double. Children under 12 are half price, under age four free. Breakfast/dinner is CFP 500/2,500. Yachties frequently order seafood meals here.

Pension/Snack Vehine Hou (tel. 92-50-63, heato@mail.pf), two blocks east of the Tenai Paepae, has two rooms with shared bath at CFP 4,950/9,350 single/double with breakfast and two garden bungalows with private bath at CFP 7,150/13,200 single/double, including breakfast and dinner. The restaurant (Mon.–Sat.) serves good meals (a specialty is *poisson cru*), and Claire also runs the island's traditional dance group (notice the photos along the bar). Even if you're not staying here, it's the best place to eat and drink on the island.

Pension Chez Dora (tel. 92-53-69), in a quiet location south of town at the top of the hill beyond the museum, has three rooms and two bungalows at CFP 5,300 per person, breakfast included. Dinner is CFP 2,000 per person. The room downstairs has a private bath, while those upstairs share a bath.

Pension Leydj (tel. 92-53-19) at Hakahetau has four rooms with shared bath at CFP 5,830 per person with breakfast and dinner.

Information and Services

Motu Haka (tel. 92-53-21) is a cultural organization that promotes Marquesan language instruction, archaeological projects, and traditional arts while rejecting cultural domination by Tahiti. The Marquesas Islands Festival is one of Motu Haka's projects. You can contact Toti through Pension Chez Dora.

The **Banque Socredo** (tel. 92-53-63), *mairie,* and a post office are all adjacent to each other and opposite the defunct market and not far from the beach. The **gendarmerie** (tel. 91-53-05) is a bit south. Infirmaries are in Hakahau, Hakatao, and Hakamaii. Six or seven stores can be found in Hakahau.

Getting There

Ua Pou's Aneou airstrip (UAP) is on the north coast, 10 kilometers west of Hakahau via a rough road over a ridge. It's in a valley just back from a long black beach between Hakahau and Hakahetau. The pensions in Hakahau offer airport transfers for CFP 2,000 per person. You can reach Air Tahiti in Hakahau at tel. 91-52-25.

UA HUKA

Ua Huka lies 35 kilometers east of Nuku Hiva and 56 kilometers northeast of Ua Pou.

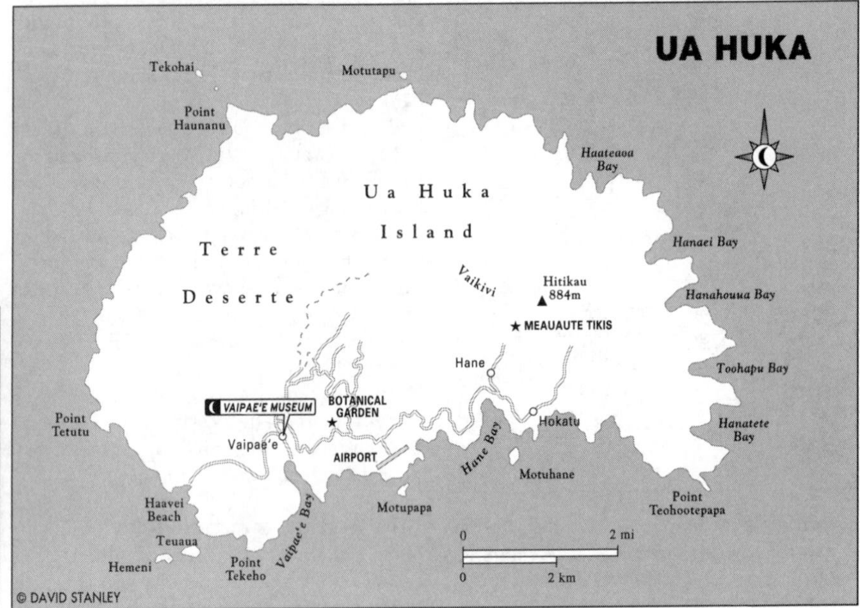

Crescent-shaped Ua Huka is the surviving northern half of an ancient volcano, and its 570 inhabitants live in the truncated crater in the south. Mount Hitikau (884 meters) rises northeast of Hane village. Vaipae'e is the main village of the island, although the hospital is at Hane.

Goats and wild horses range across this arid 83-square-kilometer island, while the tiny islands of Teuaua and Hemeni, off the southwest tip of Ua Huka, are a breeding ground for millions of *kaveka* (sooty terns). Sadly, local residents use these flat islands surrounded by sheer cliffs as a source of eggs.

Archaeological excavations by Professor Y. H. Sinoto in 1965 dated a coastal site on Ua Huka to A.D. 300, which makes it the oldest in French Polynesia; two pottery fragments found here suggest that the island was probably a major dispersal point for the ancient Polynesians. Sinoto believes the migratory paths of Ua Huka's terns may have led the ancient Polynesians on their way to new discoveries.

Vaipae'e Museum

Near the post office in Vaipae'e is a small but admirable Musée Communal (Tel. 91-60-25, weekdays 0700–1400, free) with artifacts donated by local residents at the instigation of former mayor Leon Lichtle. Among the ancient items are pearl fishhooks and octopus lures, plus stone pestles and wooden bowls used for cooking. The seashell collection has a large number of shells from both local and regional waters. Local artist Joseph Tehau Va'atete has created replicas of many lost works from photographs taken on the 1920–1921 Bishop Museum Expedition, including Marquesan tiki, bowls, drums, paddles, and stilts. Copies of some of the old photos hang on the museum walls. Woodcarvers are still very active on Ua Huka, and some examples of their work can be purchased in the craft shop adjacent to the museum, only open when tour groups are present.

Other Sights

Between the airport and Vaipae'e is a plantation that has been converted into a **Botanical**

© TAHITI TOURISME

Marquesan carved coconut shell containers

Garden (tel. 92-61-19, weekdays 0630–1200 and 1430–1630, free) complete with an aviary. Unfortunately the plants are not labeled.

In Hane is a **Centre Artisanal/Musée de la Mer** (tel. 91-60-25), by the beach just below the hospital. The three small **Meaiaute Tikis,** cut from red rock, are in a mango forest up the valley behind Hane, a 25-minute walk from the Auberge Hitikau. There are excellent views from the site.

In October 2003 a **Petroglyph Museum** (tel. 92-60-55) opened by the beach in the center of Hokatu village. The two rooms contain realistic plaster casts of rock carvings from the Vaikivi Valley. The museum opens when groups from cruise ships are in port or when the rare individual tourist tracks down the person with the key.

Accommodations

Chez Alexis (tel. 92-60-19) in Vaipae'e village, a bit toward the wharf from the post office, has three rooms with shared bath is a two-room house at CFP 2,000/4,000 with fan/air-conditioning. Meals can be ordered, or you're welcome to cook your own food. Alexis can arrange horseback riding and boat excursions.

The **Pension Mana Tupuna Village** (tel. 92-60-08, manatupuna@mail.pf) offers three bungalows on the hillside above the road on the north side of Vaipae'e at CFP 7,000/13,000 single/double, including breakfast and dinner. Teiki, or *le petit chef,* is an affable guy who will pick you up at the airport for free.

Also in Vaipae'e is **Chez Christelle** (tel. 92-60-04), a four-room house with shared bath at CFP 2,000 per person. Meals are extra. It's run by the Air Tahiti agent and is down by the river on the north side of town. Christelle rents cars at CFP 10,000 per day.

Le Rêve Marquisien (tel. 92-61-84, revemarquisien@mail.pf) is in the Pahataua Valley, 800 meters from Vaipae'e village. The four comfortable bungalows with baths and TVs are CFP 10,500/12,000 single/double. Meals are CFP 1,500/3,500/3,500 for breakfast/lunch/dinner. Airport transfers are free. It's a good choice for birdwatchers, hikers, and horse riders.

In Hane village, the **Pension Auberge Hitikau** (tel. 92-61-74) offers three rooms with shared bath next to its restaurant at CFP 2,120/3,180 single/double. Lobster is served in the large restaurant at CFP 2,500—*Aranui* passengers often enjoy a meal here.

Also worth checking is **Chez Maurice et Delphine** (tel. 92-60-55) at Hokatu village, 13 kilometers from the airport. The three rooms with shared bath in the family residence above their store in the village are CFP 5,700 per person with breakfast and dinner. They also have three bungalows with private baths and mini-fridges on a hill some distance away at the same price. Airport transfers are CFP 2,000 per person, and Maurice can arrange a rental car.

Getting There

The airstrip (UAH) is on a hilltop between Hane and Vaipae'e, six kilometers from the latter. The pensions generally provide free airport transfers. The Air Tahiti number is tel. 92-60-85. The *Aranui* enters the narrow fjord at

Vaipae'e and anchors. It's quite a show watching the ship trying to turn around.

UNINHABITED ISLANDS

Motane (Mohotani) is an eight-kilometer-long island rising to 520 meters about 18 kilometers southeast of Hiva Oa. The depredations of wild sheep on Motane turned the island into a treeless desert. When the Spaniards "discovered" it in 1595, Motane was well wooded and populated, but today it's uninhabited. Since 1971 Motane has been a protected area with 10 species of seabirds and four endemic land birds.

Uninhabited Eiao and Hatutu islands, 85 kilometers northwest of Nuku Hiva, are the remotest (and oldest) of the Marquesas. **Eiao** is a 40-square-kilometer island, 10 kilometers long and 576 meters high, with rather difficult landings on the northwest and west sides. The French once used Eiao as a site of deportation for criminals or "rebellious" natives. The Queen of Raiatea and 136 Raiateans who had fought against the French were interned here from 1897 to 1900. In 1972 the French Army drilled holes 1,000 meters down into Eiao to check the island's suitability for underground nuclear testing, but deemed the basalt rock too fragile for such use. Wild cattle, sheep, pigs, and donkeys forage across Eiao, ravaging the vegetation and suffering from droughts. In contrast, the profusion of marine life off Eiao is incredible.

Hatutu, the northernmost of the Marquesas, measures 7.5 square kilometers. Seventeen species of seabirds and four endemic land birds nest here.

Hiva Oa

Measuring 40 by 19 kilometers, 315-square-kilometer Hiva Oa (pop. 2,000) is the second-largest of the Marquesas and the main center of the southern cluster of islands. Mount Temetiu (1,276 meters), the highest peak in the Marquesas, towers above Atuona to the west. Steep ridges falling to the coast separate lush valleys on this long crescent-shaped island. Ta'aoa, or "Traitors'" Bay, is a flooded crater presently missing its eastern wall, while Puama'u sits in a younger secondary crater. The administrative headquarters for the Marquesas group has switched back and forth several times: Taiohae was the center until

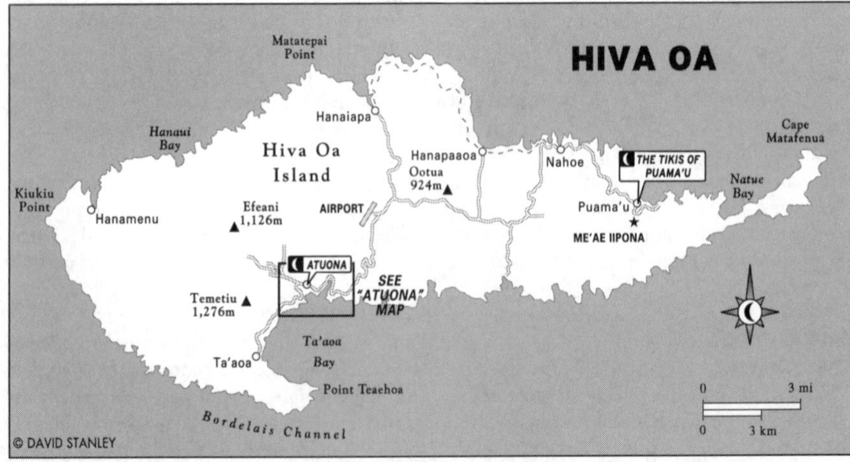

1904, then it was Atuona until 1944, then Taiohae took over once again.

ATUONA

The little town of Atuona is best known for its associations with the painter Paul Gauguin and the singer Jacques Brel, both of whom lived and died here. In 2003 Hiva Oa hosted its second Marquesas Islands Festival and a new **Paul Gauguin Cultural Center** (Mon.–Sat., CFP 600) was erected in the center of town to mark the centenary of Gauguin's death. The center displays 24 colorful reproductions of Gauguin's paintings created in 1997 and 1998 by Alin Marthouret (born 1945). A replica of Gauguin's thatched "Maison du Jouîr" (House of Pleasure) has been built at the center, and a few reproductions of his prints are inside. The original well used by Gauguin during his stay here is also on the grounds. Behind the Cultural Center is the **Jacques Brel Center** (Mon.–Sat., CFP 500) with Brel's aircraft *Jojo.*

Nearby on the main street is **Magasin Gauguin** where Gauguin left an unpaid wine bill when he died. Go up the hill from beside the nearby gendarmerie and take the first fork in the road to the left to reach **Calvary Cemetery,** which hosts the graves of Jacques Brel (1929–1978) and Paul Gauguin (1848–1903). Gauguin's leading detractor, Monseigneur R. J. Martin (1849–1912), is buried under a large white tomb surrounded by a metal fence, higher up in the cemetery than Gauguin. The views of Atuona from here are excellent.

Other sights worth seeking out if you have the time include the **Catholic church,** with its fine carved doors and interior visible through the open walls, and the Salle des Marriages at the **Mairie de Atuona,** which contains another large Gauguin reproduction by Marthouret. The platforms of the *Tohua Pepeu* in central Atuona were built for the Marquesas Islands Festival in December 1991.

Brel Belvédère

Chanson singer Jacques Brel lived at Atuona 1975–1978. He intended to build his home on a ridge overlooking the entire valley, but died before the work could be done. The Brel Belvédère is now accessible off the airport road, about six kilometers out of Atuona. A plaque bears the inscription *Veux-tu que je te dise, gémir n'est pas de mise, Aux Marquises,* the last line in Brel's song *Les Marquises.* The view from here is superb.

Ta'aoa

The beach at Atuona is poor; for better swimming, take the road six kilometers southwest along the bay to the black beach at Ta'aoa. A big restored *tohua* with several *me'ae* platforms and a basalt tiki are found a bit more than one

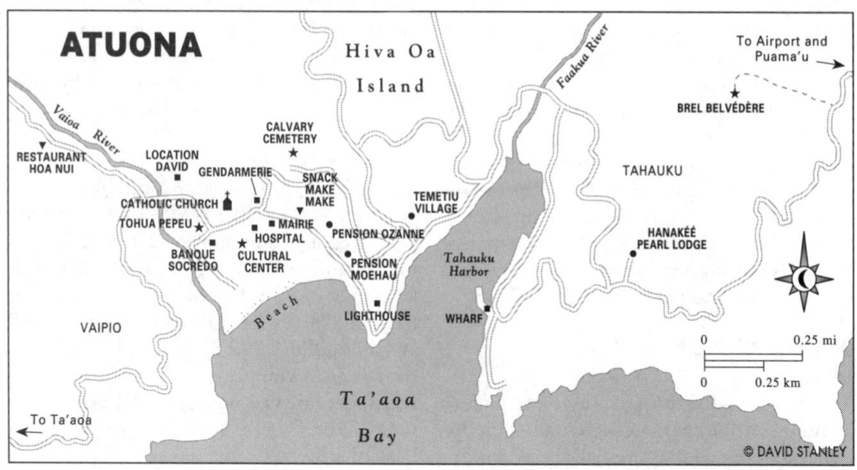

FAMOUS RESIDENTS OF ATUONA

Atuona was made forever famous when Paul Gauguin came to live here in 1901. Despite the attempts of his 14-year-old mistress, Vaeoho, to nurse him back to health, he died of syphilis a year later at age 55 and is buried in the cemetery above the town. When Tioka, Gauguin's neighbor, found him stretched out with one leg hanging over the side of his bed, he bit him on the head as the Marquesans do to see if one really is dead. No, there was no doubt. *Ua mate Koke!* he cried, and disappeared. Gauguin was constantly in conflict with the colonial authorities, who disapproved of his heavy drinking sessions with the locals. Just a week before his death, Gauguin was summarily convicted of "libel of a gendarme in the course of his official duties," fined, and sentenced to three months in prison.

The famous Belgian *chanson* singer Jacques Brel and his companion Maddly Bamy came to the Marquesas aboard his 18-meter yacht, the *Askoy II*, in 1975. Jacques decided to settle at Atuona and sold his boat to an American couple. Maddly, who had been a dancer on her native Guadeloupe, gave dancing lessons to the local girls, while Jacques ran an open-air cinema. His plane, nicknamed *Jojo*, was kept at Hiva Oa airport for trips to Papeete, 1,500 kilometers southwest. The album *Brel 1977* on the Barclay label includes one of his last songs, "Les Marquises." In 1978, Brel died of lung cancer and was buried in Atuona cemetery near Gauguin.

kilometer up the river from here. This intriguing site was also restored for the festival in 2003.

Sports and Recreation

SubAtuona Plongée (tel. 92-70-88, eric.lelyonnais@wanadoo.fr), based at Pension Temetiu Village, offers scuba diving at CFP 7,000/13,000 for one/two tanks (three people minimum). Eric also offers boat transfers from Atuona to Tahuata. A full day excursion to Tahuata will cost CFP 8,000 per person (four people minimum) or CFP 15,000 per person with lunch and scuba diving included.

Alain and Teiva Tricas (tel. 20-40-90 or 20-38-00) guide hikers through the Ta'aoa Valley at CFP 1,000 per hour.

Paco and Patricia at **Hamau Ranch** (tel. 92-70-57, hamauranch@mail.pf) near the airport organize horseback riding on the plateau. Fifteen different riding trails taking from an hour to a full day are available (riders weighing over 90 kilograms not accepted).

Accommodations

US$50-100

The **Mairie de Atuona** (tel. 92-73-32, commune@commune-hivaoa.pf) rents five well-equipped bungalows behind the town hall and post office at CFP 3,000/5,000 single/double. These have cooking facilities and private baths but they can only be booked directly at the *mairie* during business hours (weekdays 0730–1130 and 1300–1600).

Pension John Ozanne (tel. 92-73-43, http://pension-hivaoa.ifrance.com), up the hill from the main street in Atuona, offers a two-story bungalow in the yard at CFP 4,000/5,000 single/double. Cooking facilities are provided. Ozanne's company, Hanamenu Transport, can provide land tours, and he also has a boat he uses for excursions. Ask to see his logbooks, which date to the 1970s and contain dozens of entries by cruisers who have passed this way over the years.

US$100-150

Overlooking Tahauku Bay is the **Pension Temetiu Village** (tel. 91-70-60, www.temetiuvillage.com), also known as Chez Gabi, just up the hill from SMA des Marquises one kilometer east of Atuona on the way to the harbor. The six bungalows with baths start at CFP 7,080/9,000 single/double. The infinity-edge swimming pool has a good view. Nonguests are welcome at the terrace restaurant. Gabriel rents out his eight-passenger boat, the *Pua Ote Tai*.

US$150-250

Relais Moehau (tel. 92-72-69, www.relais moehau.pf) is at the east entrance to Atuona, just up the hill from Snack Make Make on the way to the harbor. It offers eight rooms in a new two-story building on the hillside at CFP 8,005/12,110/16,585 single/double/triple with breakfast. The rooms on the front side of the building are nicer. Airport transfers are CFP 3,600 per person round-trip.

Pension Kanahau (tel. 91-71-31, www .pensionkanahau.com) or "Chez Tania" is Pension Temetiu Village, on the hillside between Atuona and Tahauku Bay. The four bungalows with baths and TV are CFP 10,400/13,300/16,700 single/double/triple with breakfast. The two rooms with cooking facilities are CFP 1,060 extra. Dinner can be ordered and excursions organized.

Pension Kayser Chez Areke (tel. 92-71-11, www.pension-hivaoa.com), on the same hillside as Pension Kanahau and Pension Temetiu Village high above Tahauku Bay, has three rooms at CFP 10,500/21,000 single/double, including half board (minimum two nights). The views are great but it's isolated from town.

Atuona's most upmarket place, the **Hanakéé Hiva Oa Pearl Lodge** (tel. 92-75-87, www .pearlresorts.com), is on the airport road about five kilometers east of Atuona on the hillside overlooking Takauku Bay. There's a swimming pool with a panoramic deck. The 14 stylish bungalows and six suites start at CFP 20,000/25,000 double/triple, plus 14 percent tax. Breakfast and dinner are CFP 7,600 plus tax per person extra, and airport transfers are CFP 4,800 plus tax per person return.

Food

Snack Make Make (tel. 92-74-26, Mon.–Sat.), also called Snack Atuona, 100 meters east of the post office and across the street, has juicy hamburgers, large *poisson cru,* grilled fish, and cold beer. The atmosphere is excellent.

Relais Moehau (tel. 92-72-69, daily 1200–1350 and 1800–2100) has a restaurant specializing in wood-fired pizza.

Restaurant Atuona Hoa Nui (tel. 92-73-63), next to a school on the road up the Vaioa Valley just west of town, serves Chinese and Marquesan dishes nightly at 1900 by reservation only. *Aranui* passengers are often served a meal here.

Information and Services

The **Comité du tourisme de Hiva Oa** (tel. 92-78-93, www.marquises-hivaoa.org.pf) has an information office near the Cultural Center in Atuona.

Banque Socredo (tel. 92-73-54) is next to the Air Tahiti office. The post office, town hall, dental center, and hospital (tel. 92-73-75) are two blocks east, with the gendarmerie (tel. 91-71-05) diagonally opposite.

Getting There

The **airstrip** (AUQ) is on a 441-meter-high plateau, eight kilometers northeast of Atuona. In 1991 the runway was upgraded to allow it to receive direct ATR 42 flights from Papeete. Air Tahiti is at tel. 91-70-90.

It's a two-hour downhill walk from the airport to Atuona. The normal taxi fare from the airport to Atuona is CFP 1,800 per person each way, but the amount collected by the various hotels seems to vary, so check when booking.

A lighthouse on the point between Tahauku Bay and Atuona looks south across Traitors' Bay. Yachts anchor behind the breakwater in Tahauku harbor, two kilometers east of the center of town. The *Aranui* and *Taporo* also tie up here. The gas station at the wharf has a well-stocked grocery store (if you want bread, order it the day before).

In theory, a boat leaves Atuona for Tahuata Monday at noon and Friday at 1600 (CFP 1,000 per person), but it's often laid up with mechanical problems.

Getting Around

Location David (tel. 92-72-87), opposite Magasin Naiki, rents cars at around CFP 12,000 per day all-inclusive. You should reserve two days in advance.

Atuona Rent Car (tel. 92-76-07) has cars at CFP 13,000 per day, and you must call for

LES MARQUISES

BY JACQUES BREL

Ils parlent de la morte
comme tu parles d'un fruit
They speak of death
as you would speak of a fruit

Ils regardent la mer
comme tu regardes un puits
They gaze at the sea
as you look into a well

Les femmes sont lascives
au soleil redouté
The women are enticing
under the dreaded sun

Et s'il n'y a pas d'hiver
cela n'est pas l'été
And if there's no winter,
that doesn't make it summer

La pluie est traversière,
elle bat de grain en grain
The rain sweeps by,
beating heavier and heavier

Quelques vieux chevaux blancs
qui fredonnent Gauguin
On old white horses
that recall Gauguin

Et par manque de brise
le temps s'immobilise
And, without a breeze,
time seems frozen

Aux Marquises.
In the Marquesas.

Du soir montent des feux
et des points de silence
From the darkness rise fires
and silent places

Qui vont s'élargissant
et la lune s'avance
Which widen
as the moon comes up

Et la mer se déchire
infiniment brisée
And the sea breaks,
shattering infinitely

Par des rochers qui prirent
des prénoms affolés
On rocks named
with wild names

Et puis plus loin des chiens
des chants de repentance
And further from the dogs
and penitent songs

Et quelques pas de deux
et quelques pas de danse
And some two-steps
and other dance steps

Et la nuit est soumise
et l'alizé se brise
And the night is subdued
and the trade winds die down

Aux Marquises.

Leur rire est dans le coeur,
le mot dans le regard
Their laughter is from the heart,
and speech with the eyes

Le coeur est voyageur, l'avenir est au hasard
The heart wanders, the future is left to fate

Et passent des cocotiers
qui écrivent des chants d'amour
And then pass collectors
of coconuts who write love songs

Que les soeurs d'alentours ignorent d'ignorer
That the local nuns choose to ignore

Les pirogues s'en vont,
les pirogues s'en viennent
The canoes go out,
the canoes come in

Et mes souvenirs deviennent
ce que les vieux en font
And my memories become
whatever the elders make of them

Veux-tu que je te dise,
gémir n'est pas de mise
May I say to you,
complaining is not the way

Aux Marquises.

a delivery. **Hiva Oa Location** (tel. 91-70-60) is similar.

Before renting a car, ask if the gas station at Tahauku wharf has any fuel available, as it often runs out.

To hire a four-passenger Land Rover with a driver from Atuona to Puama'u will run you CFP 20,000. Taxi companies such as **Taxi Clark** (tel. 72-34-73) should charge CFP 10,000 to Ta'aoa, CFP 12,000 to Hanaiapa, and CFP 20,000 to Puama'u for the whole car round-trip.

PUAMA'U

A second village, Puama'u, is on the northeast coast of Hiva Oa, 30 kilometers from Atuona over a winding mountain road. It's a good eight-hour walk from Atuona to Puama'u, up and down all the way. A few remote descendants of Gauguin are among the 300 people who live there today.

The Tikis of Puama'u

Aside from the village's golden beach, the main reason for coming are the five huge stone tikis to be seen on the **Me'ae Iipona** among the breadfruit trees in the valley behind Puama'u, a 15-minute walk from the village soccer field. One tiki, named Takaii, of a warrior or chief, stands 243 centimeters high—the largest old stone statue in the Marquesas. Nearby is a headless tiki with six fingers on each hand. Also notice the statue of the priestess who died in childbirth, and the sculpted heads of victims of human sacrifice. It's believed the site dates back to the 15th or 16th centuries, with the existing *paepae* constructed in the 18th century. Me'ae Iipona was restored in 1991 for the third Marquesas Islands Festival. A representative selection of native trees and plants grows in and around the site. You may be asked to pay a CFP 300 fee to visit the *me'ae.*

Accommodations

You can stay in Puama'u at **Pension Chez Marie-Antoinette** (tel. 92-75-28, heitaa .etienne@mail.pf), also known as Chez Heitaa, in the upper part of the village not far from the Me'ae Iipona. The three rooms with shared bath are CFP 5,830 per person including half

THE MARQUESAS ISLANDS

© TAHITI TOURISME

The Takaii tiki at Puama'u is said to be the oldest in the Marquesas.

board. The tombs of the last queen of the area and her family are behind the pension.

NORTHWESTERN HIVA OA

At **Hanaiapa** on the north coast, ask for William, who keeps a yachties log. He's happy to have his infrequent visitors sign, and is generous with fresh fruit and vegetables. Barren **Hanamenu Bay** in the northwest corner of Hiva Oa is now uninhabited, but dozens of old stone platforms can still be seen. If you'd like to spend some time as a hermit in the desert, ask for Ozanne in Atuona, who has a house at Hanamenu he might be willing to rent. To the right of Ozanne's house is a small, crystal-clear pool. The trails into this area have become overgrown, and it's now accessible only by boat.

Other Southern Islands

TAHUATA

Tahuata (pop. about 670) is just six kilometers south of Hiva Oa across Bordelais Channel. Fifteen kilometers long by nine kilometers wide, 69-square-kilometer Tahuata is the smallest of the six inhabited islands of the Marquesas. A 17-kilometer track crosses the island from Motopu to Vaitahu, the main village on the west coast. The anchorage at Hana Moe Noa north of Vaitahu is protected from the ocean swells. There's a lovely white beach, and the water here is clear as no rivers run into this bay.

Archaeological sites exist in the Vaitahu Valley, and there's a small collection of artifacts in the school opposite the post office in Vaitahu. Tahuata was the point of first contact between Polynesians and Europeans anywhere in the South Pacific. Mendaña anchored in Vaitahu Bay in 1595, followed by Captain Cook in 1774. Here too, Admiral Abel Dupetit-Thouars took possession of the Marquesas in 1842 and established a fort, despite strong resistance led by Chief Iotete.

Sights

The **Catholic church** at Vaitahu was completed in 1988 to mark the 150th anniversary of the arrival here of missionaries. It has the largest stained glass window in the territory. Local sculptor Damien Haturau carved the huge wooden statue of the Virgin above the church entrance from a 400-year-old *tamanu* tree. There's also a small museum in the village.

Hapatoni village, farther south, is picturesque, with a century-old *tamanu*-bordered road and petroglyphs in the Hanatahau Valley behind. Coral gardens are found offshore, and white-sand beaches skirt the north side of the island.

Accommodations

Pension Amatea (tel. 92-92-84), formerly known as Pension Fara, in Vaitahu has four rooms with shared bath at CFP 4,000 per person, plus CFP 1,000/2,500 for breakfast/dinner. Excursions in four-wheel-drive vehicles or horseback can be arranged.

Getting There

There's no airport on Tahuata. To charter a six-passenger boat to or from Atuona is CFP 15,000–22,000 (one hour). Small boats leave Hiva Oa for Tahuata almost daily, so ask around at the harbor on Takauku Bay near Atuona.

When it's operating, a boat belonging to the Commune of Tahuata (tel. 92-92-19) shuttles between Atuona and Vaitahu on Monday and Friday (one hour, CFP 1,000 per person each way). It leaves Tahuata around dawn, departing Hiva Oa for the return at noon. Southbound, bring groceries with you.

FATU HIVA

Fatu Hiva (84 square kilometers) is the southernmost and youngest of the Marquesas Islands, 56 kilometers southeast of Tahuata. It's far wetter than the northern islands, and the vegetation is lush. Mount Tauaouoho (960 meters) is

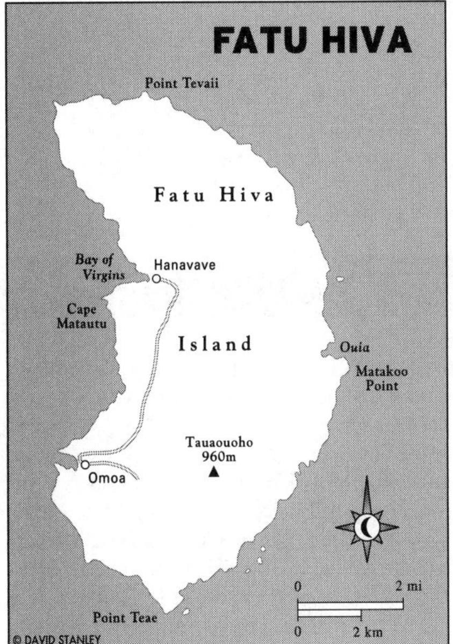

the highest point. Fatu Hiva was the first of the Marquesas to be seen by Europeans (Mendaña passed by in 1595). None landed until 1825, and Catholic missionaries couldn't convert the inhabitants until 1877. In 1937–1938 Thor Heyerdahl spent one year on this island with his young bride, Liv, and wrote a book called *Fatu Hiva* describing their far-from-successful attempt "to return to a simple, natural life."

This is the most remote of the Marquesas, and only a few French officials are present. With 587 inhabitants, Fatu Hiva has only two villages, Omoa and Hanavave, in the former crater on the western side of the island. Surfing off the rocky beach at Omoa can be pretty exciting. Hanavave on the Bay of Virgins offers one of the most fantastic scenic spectacles in all of Polynesia, with tiki-shaped cliffs dotted with goats. Yachts usually anchor here. Horses and canoes are for hire in both villages.

Fatu Hiva is one of the last places in French Polynesia where tapa cloth is still widely made. Until the 1960s, Fatu Hiva tapa bore no designs; instead the human body was decorated with tattoos. Today a revival of the old crafts is taking place, and it's again possible to buy not only wooden sculptures but painted tapa cloth. Hats and mats are woven from pandanus. *Monoï* oils are made from coconut oil, gardenia, jasmine, and sandalwood.

Fatu Hiva doesn't have any *no-nos* but has ample mosquitoes. If you plan on staying longer than four months, get some free antielephantiasis pills, such as Notézine, at any clinic.

Sports and Recreation

It takes about five hours to hike the 17-kilometer dirt road linking Omoa and Hanavave, up and down over the mountains amid breathtaking scenery. It's a long gentle incline from Omoa to a 600-meter pass, followed by a very steep descent into Hanavave. **Vaiéé-Nui Falls** is a pleasant one-hour walk back into the valley from Hanavave. Unfortunately, Hanavave is overrun by skinny half-starved dogs the locals use to hunt pigs.

Omoa is the main center for tapa production in all of French Polynesia. A small private museum with some exquisite wood carvings is behind the *mairie* and handicraft center at Omoa. A bakery and two small stores are also in Omoa.

Accommodations and Food

Several families in Omoa village take paying guests. **Chez Norma** (tel. 92-80-13), also known as Pension Ropati, at Omoa, has four rooms for rent at CFP 1,500 per person, or CFP 4,100 per person with two meals.

Pension Chez Lionel (tel. 92-81-84, chezlionel@mail.pf) at Omoa has one bungalow with cooking facilities at CFP 6,500/8,500 single/double with breakfast. A room with shared bath is CFP 4,500/6,500.

Getting There

There's no airstrip on Fatu Hiva, and the Tuesday catamaran service between Atuona and Omoa operated by the Mairie de Fatu Hiva (tel. 92-80-23) seldom runs. To hire a speedboat, such as the red and yellow *Rautea Nui* owned by Joel Coulon, from Omoa to Tahuata or Hiva Oa will cost around CFP 50,000. The only practical way to visit Hiva Oa is on the *Aranui*.

BACKGROUND

The Land

French Polynesia (or Te Ao Maohi, as it is known to the Polynesians themselves) consists of five great archipelagos, the Society, Austral, Tuamotu, Gambier, and Marquesas Islands, arrayed in chains running from southeast to northwest. The Society Islands are subdivided into the Windward Islands, or Îles du Vent (Tahiti, Moorea, Maiao, Tetiaroa, and Mehetia), and the Leeward Islands, or Îles Sous-le-Vent (Huahine, Raiatea, Taha'a, Bora Bora, Maupiti, Tupai, Maupihaa/Mopelia, Manuae/Scilly, and Motu One/Bellingshausen).

French Polynesia consists of boundless ocean and little land. Together the 35 islands and 83 atolls of French Polynesia total only 3,543 square kilometers in land area, yet they're scattered over a vast area of the southeastern Pacific Ocean, between 7° and 28° south latitude and 131° and 156° west longitude. Papeete (149° west longitude) is actually 8° *east* of Honolulu (157° west longitude). Though French Polynesia is only half the size of Corsica in land area, if Papeete were Paris, then the Gambiers would be in Romania and the Marquesas near Stockholm. At 5,030,000 square kilometers, the territory's 200-nautical-mile exclusive economic zone is by far the largest in the Pacific islands.

There's a wonderful geological diversity to these islands midway between Australia and

© DAVID STANLEY

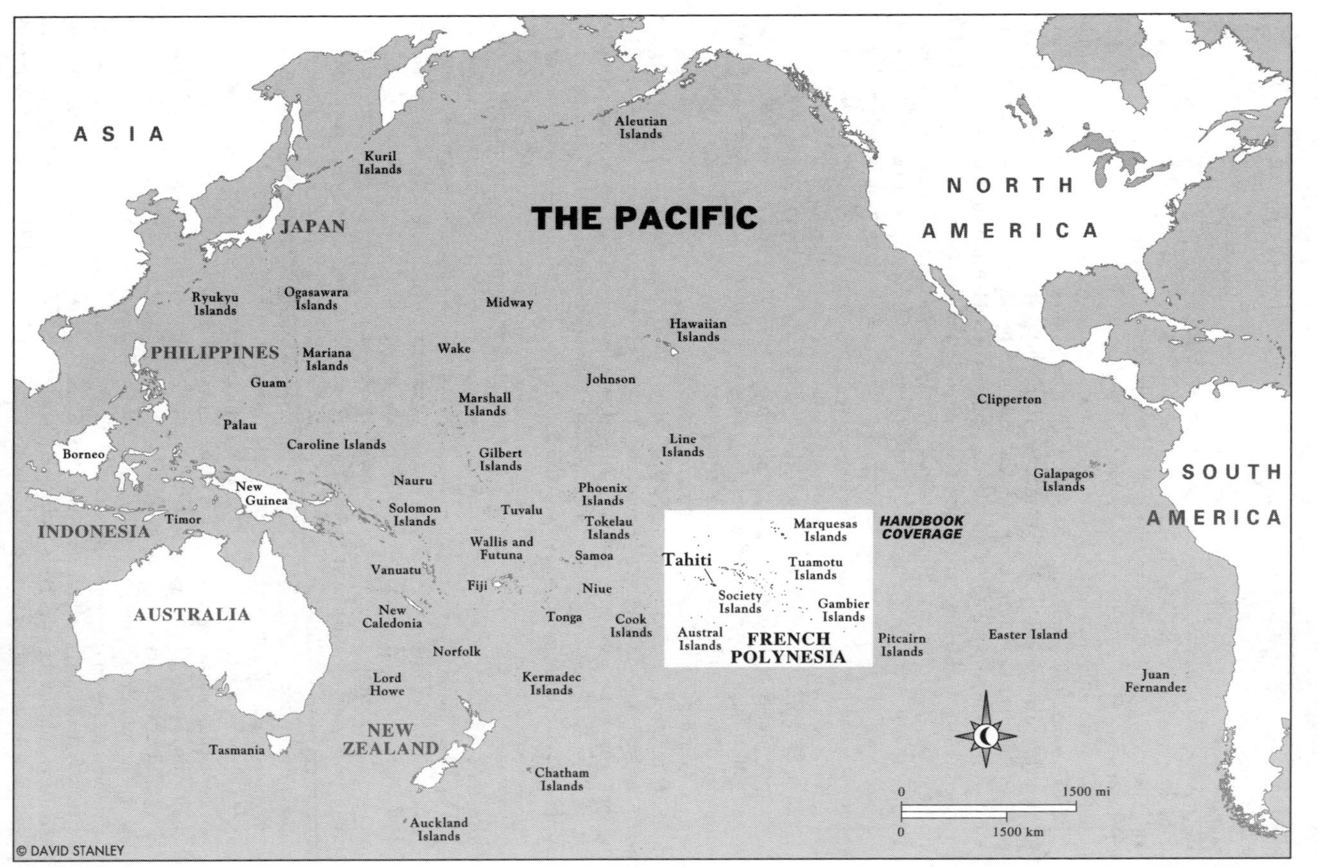
THE PACIFIC
ASIA
NORTH AMERICA
SOUTH AMERICA
Kuril Islands
Aleutian Islands
JAPAN
Ryukyu Islands
Ogasawara Islands
Midway
Hawaiian Islands
PHILIPPINES
Mariana Islands
Wake
Guam
Johnson
Marshall Islands
Clipperton
Palau
Caroline Islands
Borneo
Gilbert Islands
Line Islands
Nauru
Galapagos Islands
New Guinea
Phoenix Islands
Solomon Islands
Tuvalu
Timor
Tokelau Islands
INDONESIA
Marquesas Islands
HANDBOOK COVERAGE
Wallis and Futuna
Samoa
Tahiti
Tuamotu Islands
Vanuatu
Fiji
Niue
Society Islands
Gambier Islands
New Caledonia
AUSTRALIA
Tonga
Cook Islands
Austral Islands
FRENCH POLYNESIA
Pitcairn Islands
Easter Island
Norfolk
Lord Howe
Kermadec Islands
Juan Fernandez
NEW ZEALAND
Tasmania
Chatham Islands
0 1500 mi
0 1500 km
Auckland Islands
© DAVID STANLEY

South America—from the dramatic, jagged volcanic outlines of the Society and Marquesas Islands to the 400-meter-high hills of the Australs and Gambiers to the low coral atolls of the Tuamotus. All of the Marquesas are volcanic islands, while the Tuamotus are all coral islands or atolls. The Societies and Gambiers include both volcanic and coral types.

Tahiti, around 4,000 kilometers from both Auckland and Honolulu or 6,000 kilometers from Los Angeles and Sydney, is not only the best known and most populous of the islands, but also the largest (1,045 square kilometers) and highest (2,241 meters). Bora Bora and Maupiti are noted for their combination of high volcanic peaks framed by low coral rings. Rangiroa is one of the world's largest coral atolls, while Makatea is an uplifted atoll. In the Marquesas, precipitous and sharply crenellated mountains rise hundreds of meters, with craggy peaks, razorback ridges, plummeting waterfalls, deep fertile valleys, and dark broken coastlines pounded by surf. Compare them to the pencil-thin strips of yellow reefs, green vegetation, and white beaches enclosing the transparent Tuamotu lagoons. In all, French Polynesia offers some of the most varied and spectacular scenery in the entire South Pacific.

Darwin's Theory of Atoll Formation

The famous formulator of the theory of natural selection surmised that atolls form as high volcanic islands subside. The original island's fringing reef grows up into a barrier reef as the volcanic part sinks. When the last volcanic material finally disappears below sea level, the coral rim of the reef/atoll remains to indicate how big the island once was.

Of course, all of this takes place over millions of years, but deep below every atoll is the old volcanic core. Darwin's theory is well illustrated at Bora Bora, where a high volcanic island remains inside the rim of Bora Bora's barrier reef; this island's volcanic core is sinking imperceptibly at the rate of one centimeter per century. Return to Bora Bora in 25 million years and all you'll find will be a coral atoll like Rangiroa.

Hot Spots

High or low, most of the islands have a volcanic origin best explained by the "Conveyor Belt Theory." A crack opens in the earth's crust and volcanic magma escapes upward. A submarine volcano builds up slowly until the lava finally breaks the surface, becoming a volcanic island. The Pacific Plate moves northwest approximately 11 centimeters per year; thus over geologic eons the volcano disconnects from the hot spot or crack from which it emerged. As the old volcanoes detach from the crack, new ones develop over the hot spot, and the older islands are carried away from the cleft in the earth's crust from which they were born.

The island then begins to sink as it's carried into deeper water and erosion also cuts into the now-extinct volcano. In the warm, clear waters a living coral reef begins to grow along the shore. As the island subsides, the reef continues to grow upward. In this way a lagoon forms between the reef and shoreline of the slowly sinking island. This barrier reef marks the old margin of the original island.

As the plate moves northwest in an opposite direction from the sliding Pacific Plate, the process is repeated, time and again, until whole chains of islands ride the blue Pacific. Weathering is most advanced on the composite islands and atolls at the northwest ends of the Society, Austral, Tuamotu, and Marquesas chains. Maupiti and Bora Bora, with their exposed volcanic cores, are the oldest of the larger Society Islands. The Tuamotus have eroded almost to sea level; the Gambier Islands originated out of the same hot spot, and their volcanic peaks remain inside a giant atoll reef. The progression of youth, maturity, and old age can be followed throughout French Polynesia. In every case, the islands at the southeast end of the chains are the youngest.

By drilling into the Tuamotu atolls, scientists have proven their point conclusively: The coral formations are about 350 meters thick at the southeast end of the chain, 600 meters

© DAVID STANLEY

Moorea's verdant volcanic peaks soar above Maharepa.

thick at Hao near the center, and 1,000 meters thick at Rangiroa near the northwest end of the Tuamotu Group. Clearly, Rangiroa, where the volcanic rock is now a kilometer below the surface, is many millions of years older than the Gambiers, where a volcanic peak still stands 482 meters above sea level. Geologists estimate that Tahiti is 2–3 million years old, Bora Bora seven million years old, and the Tuamotus 10–40 million years old.

Island-building continues at an active undersea volcano called MacDonald, 50 meters below sea level at the southeast end of the Australs. The crack spews forth about a cubic mile of lava every century, and someday MacDonald too will poke its smoky head above the waves. The theory of plate tectonics, or the sliding crust of the earth, seems proved in the Pacific.

The Life of an Atoll

A circular or horseshoe-shaped coral reef bearing a necklace of sandy, slender islets *(motu)* of debris thrown up by storms, surf, and wind is known as an atoll. Atolls can be up to 100 kilometers across, but the width of dry land is usually only 200–400 meters from inner to outer beach. The central lagoon can measure anywhere from one kilometer to 50 kilometers in diameter; huge Rangiroa Atoll is 77 kilometers long. Entirely landlocked lagoons are rare; passages through the barrier reef are usually found on the leeward side. Most atolls are no higher than four to six meters.

A raised or elevated atoll is one that has been pushed up by some trauma of nature to become a platform of coral rock rising to 70 meters above sea level. Raised atolls are often known for their huge sea caves and steep ocean-side cliffs. The only raised atoll in French Polynesia is crescent-shaped Makatea in the northwestern corner of the Tuamotu group. It is 100 meters high, seven kilometers long, and 4.5 kilometers wide.

Where the volcanic island remains there's often a deep passage between the barrier reef and shore; the reef forms a natural breakwater, which shelters good anchorages. Soil derived from coral is extremely poor in nutrients, while volcanic soil is known for its fertility.

FRENCH POLYNESIA AT A GLANCE

	Population (2007)	Area (hectares)
Windward Islands	194,683	118,580
Leeward Islands	33,165	38,750
Austral Islands	6,304	14,784
Tuamotu Islands	15,558	72,646
Gambier Islands	1,338	4,597
Marquesas Islands	8,658	104,930
FRENCH POLYNESIA	259,706	354,287

Dark-colored beaches are formed from volcanic material; the white beaches of travel brochures are entirely calcareous. The black beaches are cooler and easier on the eyes, and the plant life grows closer and provides patches of shade; the white beaches are generally safer for swimming, as visibility is better.

CORAL REEFS

Coral reefs are the world's oldest ecological system and cover some 200,000 square kilometers worldwide, between 25° north and 25° south latitude. A reef is created by the accumulation of millions of calcareous skeletons left by myriad generations of tiny coral polyps, some no bigger than a pinhead. A small piece of coral is a colony composed of large numbers of polyps. Though the reef's skeleton is usually white, the living polyps are of many different colors. The individual polyps on the surface often live a long time, continuously secreting layers to the skeletal mass beneath the tiny layer of flesh.

Coral polyps thrive in clear salty water where the temperature never drops below 18°C nor goes above 30°C. They require a base not more than 50 meters below the water's surface on which to form. The coral colony grows slowly upward on the consolidated skeletons of its ancestors until it reaches the low-tide mark, after which development extends outward on the edges of the reef. Sunlight is critical for coral growth. Colonies grow quickly on the ocean side, especially the windward side, due to clearer water and a greater abundance of food. A strong, healthy reef can grow 4–5 centimeters per year. Fresh or cloudy water inhibits coral growth, which is why villages and ports all across the Pacific are located at the reef-free mouths of rivers. Hurricanes can kill coral by covering the reef with sand, which prevents light and nutrients from getting through. Erosion caused by logging or urban development can have the same effect.

Polyps extract calcium carbonate from the water and deposit it in their skeletons. All limy reef-building corals also contain microscopic algae within their cells. The algae, like all green plants, obtain energy from the sun and contribute this energy to the growth of the reef's skeleton. As a result, corals behave (and look) more like plants than animals, competing for sunlight just as terrestrial plants do. Many polyps are also carnivorous; they use their minute, stinging tentacles to capture tiny planktonic animals and organic particles at night.

Coral Types

Corals belong to a broad group of stinging creatures, which includes polyps, soft corals, stony corals, sea anemones, sea fans, and jellyfish. Only those types with hard skeletons and a single hollow cavity within the body are considered true corals. Stony corals such as brain, table, staghorn, and mushroom corals have external skeletons and are important reef builders. Soft corals, black corals, and sea fans have internal skeletons. The fire corals are recognized by their smooth, velvety surface and yellowish-brown color. The stinging toxins of this last group can easily penetrate human skin and cause swelling and painful burning that can last up to an hour. The many varieties of soft, colorful anemones gently waving in the current might seem inviting to touch, but beware—many are also poisonous.

The corals, like most other forms of life in the Pacific, colonized the ocean from the fertile seas of Southeast Asia. Thus the number of species declines as you move east. More than 600 species of coral make their home in the Pacific, compared to only 48 in the Caribbean. The diversity of coral colors and forms is endlessly amazing. This is our most unspoiled environment, a world of almost indescribable beauty.

Exploring a Reef

Until you've explored a good coral reef, you haven't experienced one of the greatest joys of nature. While one cannot walk through pristine forests because of a lack of paths, it's quite possible to swim over untouched reefs. Coral reefs are the most densely populated living space on earth—they're the rain forests of the sea. It's wise to bring along a high-quality mask that you've checked thoroughly beforehand, as there's nothing more disheartening than a leaky, ill-fitting mask. Otherwise, dive shops throughout French Polynesia rent or sell snorkeling gear, so do get into the clear warm water around you.

Conservation

Coral reefs are one of the most fragile and complex ecosystems on earth, providing food and shelter for countless species of fish, crustaceans (shrimps, crabs, and lobsters), mollusks (shells), and other animals. The coral reefs of the South Pacific protect shorelines during storms, supply sand to maintain the islands, furnish food for the local population, form a living laboratory for science, and serve as major tourist attractions. Reefs worldwide host more than 2 million species of life. Without coral, the South Pacific would be immeasurably poorer.

Hard corals grow only about 10–25 millimeters per year, and it can take 7,000–10,000 years for a coral reef to form. Though corals look solid, they're easily broken; by standing on them, breaking off pieces, or carelessly dropping anchor you can destroy in a few minutes what took so long to form. Once a piece of coral breaks off, it dies, and it may be years before the coral reestablishes itself and even longer before the broken piece is replaced. The "wound" may become infected by algae, which can multiply and kill the entire coral colony. When this happens over a wide area, the diversity of marine life declines dramatically.

Swim beside or well above the coral. Avoid bumping the coral with your fins, gauges, or other equipment, and don't dive during rough sea conditions. Proper buoyancy control is preferable to excessive weight belts. Snorkelers should check into taking along a float-coat, which will allow equipment adjustments without standing on coral.

Do not remove seashells, coral, plant life, or marine animals from the sea under any circumstances. Doing so upsets the delicate balance of nature, and coral is much more beautiful underwater anyway. This is a particular problem along shorelines frequented by large numbers of tourists, who can completely strip a reef in very little time. If you'd like a souvenir, content yourself with what you find on the beach (although even a seemingly empty shell may be inhabited by a hermit crab). Also think twice about buying jewelry or souvenirs made from coral or seashells. Genuine traditional handicrafts that incorporate shells are one thing, but by buying unmounted seashells or mass-produced coral curios you are contributing to the destruction of the marine environment. The triton shell, for example, keeps in check the reef-destroying crown-of-thorns starfish.

The anchors and anchor chains of private yachts can do serious damage to coral reefs. Pronged anchors are more environmentally friendly than larger, heavier anchors, and plastic tubing over the end of the anchor chain helps minimize damage. If at all possible, anchor in sand. A longer anchor chain makes this easier, and a good windlass is essential for larger boats. A recording depth sounder will help you find sandy areas when none are available in shallow water. If you don't have a depth sounder and can't see the bottom, lower the anchor until it just touches the bottom and feel the anchor line as the boat drifts. If it "grumbles," lift it up, drift a little, and try again. Later, if you notice your chain grumbling, motor over the anchor, lift it out of the coral, and move. Not only do sand and mud hold better, but your anchor

CLIMATE CHANGE

The gravest danger facing the atolls of Oceania is the greenhouse effect, a gradual warming of the earth's environment due to fossil fuel combustion and the widespread clearing of forests. By the year 2030 the concentration of carbon dioxide in the atmosphere will have doubled from pre-industrial levels, and as infrared radiation from the sun is absorbed by the gas, the trapped heat melts mountain glaciers and the polar ice caps. In addition, seawater expands as it warms up, so water levels could rise almost one meter by 2100, destroying shorelines created 5,000 years ago.

A 1982 study demonstrated that sea levels had already risen 12 centimeters in the previous century, and in 1995 the 2,500 scientists from 70 countries involved in the Intergovernmental Panel on Climate Change (IPCC) commissioned by the United Nations completed a two-year study with the warning that over the next century air temperatures may rise as much as 5°C and sea levels could go up 95 centimeters by 2100. Not only will this reduce the growing area for food crops, but rising sea levels will mean salt water intrusion into groundwater supplies – a troubling prospect if accompanied by the increased frequency of droughts that have been predicted. Coastal erosion will force governments to spend vast sums on road repairs and coastline stabilization.

Coral bleaching occurs when an organism's symbiotic algae are expelled in response to environmental stresses, such as when water temperatures rise as little as 1°C above the local maximum for a week or longer. Bleaching is also caused by increased radiation due to ozone degradation, and widespread instances of bleaching and reefs being killed by rising sea temperatures have been confirmed in French Polynesia and the Cook Islands. The earth's surface has warmed 1°C over the past century, and by 2080 water temperatures may have increased 5°C. Acidification of the world's oceans is also gaining pace with sea waters absorbing up to half of the world's carbon dioxide emissions. Corals and shellfish cannot tolerate highly acidic waters. Coral bleaching will become an annual event by 2050, effectively killing all of the region's reefs. Reef destruction will reduce coastal fish stocks and lead to whole shorelines being swept away.

will be less likely to become fouled. Try to arrive before 1500 to be able to see clearly where you're anchoring—Polaroid sunglasses make it easier to distinguish corals. If you scuba dive with an operator who anchors incorrectly, let your concerns be known.

There's an urgent need for stricter government regulation of the marine environment, and in some places coral reefs are already protected. Resort owners can minimize damage to their valuable reefs by providing public mooring buoys so yachts don't have to drop anchor and pontoons so snorkelers aren't tempted to stand on coral. Licensing authorities can make such amenities mandatory whenever appropriate, and in extreme cases, endangered coral gardens should be declared off-limits to private boats. As consumerism spreads, once-remote areas become subject to the problems of pollution and overexploitation: The garbage is visibly piling up on many shores. As a visitor, don't hesitate to practice your conservationist attitudes, for as Marshall McLuhan said, "On Spaceship Earth, there are no passengers, we are all members of the crew."

CLIMATE

The hot and humid summer season runs November–April. The rest of the year the climate is somewhat cooler and drier. The refreshing southeast trade winds, or *alizés,* blow consistently May–August, varying to easterlies September–December. The northeast trades January–April coincide with the hurricane season. The trade winds cool the islands and offer clear sailing for mariners, making May–October the most favorable season to visit.

Rain falls abundantly and frequently in the

Increasing temperatures may already be contributing to the dramatic jump in the number of hurricanes in the South Pacific, and some are now hitting French Polynesia, which is usually missed by such storms. As storm waves wash across the low-lying atolls, eating away the precious land, the entire populations of archipelagos such as the Tuamotu Group may be forced to gradually evacuate long before they're actually flooded. The construction of seawalls to keep out the rising seas would be prohibitively expensive and may even do more harm than good by interfering with natural water flows and sand movement.

Unfortunately, those most responsible for the problem, the industrialized countries led by the United States and including Australia and Canada, have strongly resisted taking any action to significantly cut greenhouse gas emissions, and new industrial polluters such as India and China are making matters much worse. And as if that weren't bad enough, the hydro fluorocarbons (HFCs) being developed by corporate giants such as Du Pont to replace the ozone-destructive chlorofluorocarbons (CFCs) used in cooling systems are far more potent greenhouse gases than carbon dioxide.

In February 2007 the Fourth Assessment Report by the IPCC concluded that

> *warming of the climate system is unequivocal, as is now evident from observations of increases in global average air and ocean temperatures, widespread melting of snow and ice, and rising global average sea level...most of the observed increase in globally averaged temperatures since the mid-20th century is very likely due to the observed increase in anthropogenic greenhouse gas concentrations.*

The word anthropogenic means simply "caused or produced by humans." Climate change deniers, take note.

What to expect? A similar increase in temperature of just 6°C at the end of the Permian Period 250 million years ago eventually wiped out 95 percent of species alive on earth at the time, and it took 100 million years for species diversification to return to previous levels.

islands during the southern summer months (Nov.–Apr.). Rainfall is greatest in the mountains and along the windward shores of the high islands. Winds from the southeast *(maraamu)* are generally drier than those from the northeast or north. The northeast winds often bring rain: Papenoo on the northeast side of Tahiti is twice as wet as rain-shadowed Punaauia.

The Society Islands are far damper than the Marquesas. In fact, the climate of the Marquesas is erratic: Some years the group experiences serious drought, other years it could rain the whole time you're there. The low-lying Tuamotus get the least rainfall of all.

Throughout French Polynesia, the annual rainfall is extremely variable, but the humidity is generally high, reaching 98 percent. Temperatures range from warm to hot year-round; however, the ever-present sea moderates the humidity by bringing continual cooling breezes. In the evening the heat of the Tahiti afternoons is replaced by soft, fragrant mountain breezes called *hupe,* which drift down to the sea.

French Polynesia encompasses such a vast area that latitude is an important factor: at 27° south latitude, Rapa is far cooler than Nuku Hiva (9° south). Areas nearer the equator (the Marquesas) are hotter than those farther south (the Australs).

Hurricanes are relatively rare, although they do hit the Tuamotus and occasionally Tahiti (but almost never the Marquesas). From November 1980 to May 1983 an unusual wave of eight hurricanes and two tropical storms battered the islands because of the El Niño phenomenon. The next hurricane occurred in December 1991. In February 1998 a hurricane passed over the Tuamotus, and another hit Huahine in April 1998, again the fault of El Niño. Hurricane Ollie, which hit Moorea and Tubuai in February 2010, was the most powerful in 35 years. A recent analysis of data shows that in 1977 the belt of storms and winds shifted abruptly eastward, making Tonga and Melanesia drier and French Polynesia wetter. Hurricanes are also striking farther east, and El Niño is expected to recur more frequently. The days immediately following a hurricane are clear and dry.

Tahiti and Moorea have a solar (rather than a lunar) tide, which means that the low tides are at sunrise and sunset, high tides at noon and midnight. Because of this, snorkeling in or near a reef passage will be safest in the morning as the water flows in. Shallow waters are best traversed by yachts around noon when the water is high and slack, and visibility is at its peak. There's almost no twilight in the tropics, which makes Pacific sunsets brief. When the sun begins to go down, you have less than half an hour before darkness.

Currents and Winds

The Pacific Ocean has a greater impact on the world's climate than any other geographical feature on earth. By taking heat away from the equator and toward the poles, it stretches the bounds of the area in which life can exist. Broad circular ocean currents flow from east to west across the tropical Pacific, clockwise in the North Pacific, counterclockwise in the South Pacific. North and south of the "horse latitudes" just outside the tropics, the currents cool and swing east. The prevailing winds move the same way: the southeast trade winds south of the equator, the northeast trade winds north of the equator, and the low-pressure "doldrums" in between. Westerlies blow east above the cool currents north and south of the tropics. This natural air-conditioning system brings warm water to Australia and Japan, cooler water to Peru and California.

The climate of the high islands is closely related to these winds. As air is heated near the equator it rises and flows at high altitudes toward the poles. By the time it reaches about 30° south latitude it will have cooled enough to cause it to fall and flow back toward the equator near sea level. In the southern hemisphere the rotation of the earth deflects the winds to the left to become the southeast trades. When these cool moist trade winds hit a high island, they are warmed by the sun and forced up. Above 500 meters elevation they begin to cool again, and their moisture condenses into clouds. At night the winds do not capture much warmth and are more likely to discharge their moisture as rain. The windward slopes of the high islands catch the trades head-on and are usually wet, while those on the leeward side may be dry. French Polynesia enjoys some of the cleanest air on earth—air that hasn't blown over a continent for weeks.

ENVIRONMENTAL ISSUES

The French nuclear testing program in the Tuamotu Islands 1966–1996 has created the potential for environmental disaster. The Pacific Ocean may be contaminated as radioactive wastes from atmospheric testing before 1974 presently lying in the lagoons of Moruroa and Fangataufa are swept out to sea by rising sea levels. Even worse, large quantities of deadly nuclear waste presently locked in the basalt cores of these same atolls as a result of underground testing after 1974 may eventually leak into the Pacific through crevices and cracks in the coral layer above the basalt. The damage has been done, and there's not much anyone can do about it now.

French Polynesia is especially vulnerable to global warming and climate change. Not only may the low-lying atolls of the Tuamotu and Gambier islands be flooded over the next century, but coastal areas throughout the territory will be subject to severe erosion. And most of the population lives beside the sea. Hurricanes and droughts could also become more severe and prolonged over the next few decades. The people of the Pacific may have to pay the price of greenhouse gases emitted in Asia, Australia, Europe, and the Americas.

Tourism-related construction can cause

TROPICAL HURRICANES

The official hurricane (or tropical cyclone) season south of the equator is November-April, although hurricanes have also occurred in May and October. Since the ocean provides the energy, these low-pressure systems can form only over water with a surface temperature above 27°C; during years when water temperatures are high (such as during the recent El Niño) their frequency increases. The rotation of the earth must give the storm its initial spin, and this occurs mostly between latitudes 5° and 20° on either side of the equator.

As rainfall increases and the seas rise, the winds are drawn into a spiral that reaches its maximum speed in a ring around the center. In the South Pacific a cyclone develops as these circular winds, rotating clockwise, increase in velocity: Force 8-9 winds blowing at 34-47 knots are called a gale; force 10-11 at 48-63 knots are a storm; force 12 winds revolving at 64 knots or more are a hurricane. Wind speeds can go as high as 100 knots with gusts to 140 on the left side of the storm's path in the direction it's moving.

The eye of the hurricane can be 10-30 kilometers wide and surprisingly clear and calm, although at sea, contradictory wave patterns continue to wreak havoc. In the South Pacific most hurricanes move south at speeds of 5-20 knots. As water is sucked into the low-pressure eye of the hurricane and waves reach 14 meters in height, coastlines can receive a surge of up to four meters of water, especially if the storm enters a narrowing bay or occurs at high tide.

unsightly beach erosion through the clearing of vegetation and the extraction of sand. Resort sewage causes lagoon pollution, while the reefs are blasted to provide passes for tourist craft and stripped of corals or shells by visitors. Locally scarce water supplies are diverted to hotels and golf courses, and prices for foods such as fruit and fish can be artificially inflated. Access to the ocean can be blocked by wall-to-wall restaurants and resorts. "Ecotourism" can lead to the destruction of natural areas if not conducted with sensitivity.

Flora and Fauna

FLORA

The variety of floral species encountered in the Pacific islands declines as you move away from the Asian mainland. Although some species may have spread across the islands by means of floating seeds or fruit, wind and birds were probably more effective. The microscopic spores of ferns, for example, can be carried vast distances by the wind.

The high islands of French Polynesia support a great variety of plant life, while the low islands are restricted to a few hardy, drought-resistant species such as coconuts and pandanus. Rain forests fill the valleys and damp windward slopes of the high islands, while brush and thickets grow in more exposed locations. Hillsides in the drier areas are covered with coarse grasses. The absence of leaf-eating animals has allowed the vegetation to develop largely without the protective spines and thorns found elsewhere.

In the coastal areas of Tahiti most of the plants now seen have been introduced by humans. Avocado, banana, custard apple, guava, grapefruit, lime, lychee, mango, orange, papaya, pineapple, watermelon, and a hundred more are cultivated. Mountain bananas *(fei)* grow wild in the high country. *Mape* (Tahitian chestnut) grows along the streams, and other trees you'll encounter include almond, candlenut, casuarina (ironwood), flamboyant, barringtonia, *purau* (wild hibiscus), pistachio, and rosewood. A South American tree, *Miconia calvescens,* was planted at the botanical garden next to the Gauguin Museum in 1937, from which it spread across much of central Tahiti, supplanting the native vegetation.

Mangroves are often found along some high-island coastal lagoons. The cable roots of the saltwater-tolerant red mangrove anchor in the shallow upper layer of oxygenated mud, avoiding the layers of hydrogen sulfide below. The tree provides shade for tiny organisms dwelling in the tidal mudflats—a place for birds to nest and for fish or shellfish to feed and spawn. The mangroves also perform the same task as land-building coral colonies along the reefs. As sediments are trapped between the roots, the trees extend farther into the lagoon, creating a unique natural environment. The past two decades have seen widespread destruction of the mangroves.

Distance, drought, and poor soil have made atoll vegetation among the most unvaried on earth. Though a tropical atoll might seem "lush," no more than 15 native species may be present. On the atolls, taro, a root vegetable with broad heart-shaped leaves, must be cultivated in deep organic pits. The vegetation of a raised atoll is apt to be far denser, with many more species, yet it's also likely that fewer than half will be native.

Flowers

In French Polynesia the air is sweet with the bouquet of tropical blossoms such as bursting bougainvillea, camellia, frangipani, ginger, orchids, poinsettia, and *pitate* jasmine. The fragrant flowers of the Polynesian hibiscus *(purau)* are yellow, not red or pink as on the Chinese hibiscus. A useful tree, the hibiscus has a soft wood used for house and canoe construction, and bast fiber used to make cordage and mats.

The national flower, the delicate, heavily scented *tiare Tahiti (Gardenia taitensis),* can have anywhere from six to nine white petals. It blooms year-round, but especially

© DAVID STANLEY

This massive banyan tree stands in the botanical garden behind the Territorial Assembly in Papeete.

September–April. In his *Plants and Flowers of Tahiti* Jean-Claude Belhay writes, "The tiare is to Polynesia what the lotus is to India: a veritable symbol." Follow local custom by wearing this blossom or a hibiscus behind your left ear if you're happily taken, behind your right ear if you're still available.

FAUNA

Few land animals reached the eastern Pacific without the help of humans. Ancient Polynesian navigators introduced pigs, dogs, and chickens; they also deliberately brought along rats, both for their delicate bones used in tattooing and for food. Captain Cook contributed cattle, horses, and goats; Captain Wallis left behind cats. More goats were dropped off by whalers in the Marquesas. Giant African snails *(Achatina fulica)* were brought to Tahiti from Hawaii in the 1960s by a local policeman fond of fancy French food. He tried to set up a snail farm with the result that some escaped, multiplied, and now crawl wild, destroying the vegetation.

Birds

Of the 104 species of birds in French Polynesia, half of the 30 species of native land birds are found only here. Among the 48 species of seabirds are the white-tailed tropic birds, brown and black noddies, white and crested terns, petrels, and boobies. The *itatae* (white tern), often seen flying about with its mate far from land, lays a single egg in the fork of a tree without any nest. The baby terns can fly soon after hatching. Its call is a sharp ke-ke-yek-yek. The *oio* (black noddy) nests in colonies, preferably in palm trees, building a flat nest of dead leaves, sticks, and stems. It calls a deep cra-cra-cra. Thirteen species of North American or Siberian land birds visit occasionally, and another 13 species of introduced birds are always here. The most notorious among them is the hopping common mynah bird *(Acridotheres tristis)* with its yellow beak and feet, which was introduced from Indonesia at the turn of the last century to control insects. Today these noisy, aggressive birds are ubiquitous—feeding on fruit trees and forcing the native finches and blue-tinged doves out of their habitat.

Bird-watching is a highly recommended pursuit for the serious Pacific traveler; you'll find it opens unexpected doors. Good field guides are few but a determined interest will bring you into contact with fascinating people and lead to great adventures. The best time to observe forest birds is in the very early morning—they move around a lot less in the heat of the day.

Fish

The South Pacific's richest store of life is found in the silent underwater world of the pelagic and lagoon fishes. Fishes are the most diverse group of vertebrates, accounting for 20,000 of 30,000 existing species, and it's estimated that half the fish remaining on our globe are swimming in this great ocean. Coral pinnacles on the lagoon floor provide a safe haven for angelfish, butterfly fish, damselfish, groupers, soldierfish, surgeonfish, triggerfish, trumpet fish, and countless more. These fish seldom venture more than a few meters away from the protective coral, but larger fish such as barracuda, jackfish, parrot fish, pike, stingrays, and small sharks range across lagoon waters that are seldom deeper than 30 meters. The external side of the reef is also home to many of these fish, but the open ocean is reserved for bonito, mahimahi, swordfish, tuna, wrasses, and the larger sharks. Passes between ocean and lagoon can be crowded with fish in transit, offering a favorite hunting ground for predators.

In the open sea the food chain begins with phytoplankton, which flourish wherever ocean up-swellings bring nutrients such as nitrates and phosphates to the surface. In the western Pacific this occurs near the equator, where massive currents draw water away toward Japan and Australia. Large schools of fast-moving tuna ply these waters feeding on smaller fish, which consume tiny phytoplankton drifting near the sunlit surface. The phytoplankton also exist in tropical lagoons where mangrove leaves, sea grasses, and other plant material are consumed by far more varied populations of reef fish, mollusks, and crustaceans.

It's believed that most Pacific marine organisms evolved in the triangular area bounded by New Guinea, the Philippines, and the Malay Peninsula. This "cradle of Indo-Pacific marine life" includes a wide variety of habitats and has remained stable through several geological ages. From this cradle the rest of the Pacific was colonized.

It should be noted here that the feeding of sharks, rays, eels, and other fish is widely practiced in French Polynesia, but it's a controversial activity. Supplying food to wild creatures of any kind destroys their natural feeding habits and makes them vulnerable to human predators, and handling marine life can have unpredictable consequences. More study is required to determine whether shark feeding by tourism operators tends to attract sharks to lagoons and beaches used for public recreation.

Marine Mammals

Porpoises don't exist in French Polynesia, but dolphins come in a variety of species. Spinner dolphins leap from the water and spin like ballerinas. Many legends tell of dolphins saving humans, especially children, from drowning (the most famous concerns Telemachus, son of Odysseus). Dolphins often try to race in front of ferries and large ships. The commercialization of dolphins in enclosures, such as the one on Moorea, is a questionable activity.

Whales generally visit French Polynesia August–November. Humpbacks arrive about this time to give birth in the warm waters. As the weather grows warmer they return to the summer feeding areas around Antarctica. Sadly, Japanese whalers continue to hunt the animals in the Antarctic for "scientific purposes," and endangered fin and humpback whales are usually hidden among the 400 minke whale kills reported each year. Thanks to the efforts of Dr. Michael Poole and others, French Polynesia's large exclusive economic zone was declared a marine mammal sanctuary in 2002. Whale-watching trips are offered in season at Moorea and Rurutu.

Sharks

The danger from sharks (*mao* in Tahitian, *requin* in French) to swimmers has been greatly exaggerated. Of some 300 different species, only 28 are known to have attacked humans. Most dangerous are the white, tiger, and bull sharks. Fortunately, all of these usually frequent deep water far from the coasts. An average of 70–100 shark attacks a year occur worldwide with 10 fatalities, so considering the number of people who swim in the sea, your chances of being involved are about one in 10 million. In the South Pacific, shark attacks on snorkelers or scuba divers are extremely rare, and the tiny mosquito is a far more dangerous predator.

You're always safer if you keep your head underwater (with a mask and snorkel), and don't panic if you see a shark—you might attract it. Even if you do, they're usually only curious, so keep your eye on the shark and slowly back off. The swimming techniques of humans must seem very clumsy to fish, so it's not surprising they want a closer look. Sharks are attracted by shiny objects (a knife or jewelry), bright colors (especially yellow and red), urine, blood, spearfishing, and splashing.

Sharks normally stay outside the reef, but get local advice. White beaches are safer than dark, and clear water safer than murky. Avoid swimming in locations where sewage or edible wastes enter the water, or where fish have just been cleaned. You should also exercise care in places where local residents have been fishing with spears or even a hook and line that day.

Never swim alone if you suspect the presence of sharks. If you see one, even a supposedly harmless nurse shark lying on the bottom, get out of the water calmly and quickly, and go elsewhere. Studies indicate that sharks, like most other creatures, have a "personal space" around them that they will defend. Thus an attack could be a shark's way of warning someone to keep a distance, and it's a fact that more than half of the victims of these incidents are not eaten but merely bitten. Sharks are much less of a problem in the South Pacific than in colder waters, where small marine mammals are commonly hunted by sharks. You won't be mistaken for a seal or an otter here.

Let common sense be your guide, not irrational fear or carelessness. Many snorkelers and scuba divers actually come *looking* for reef sharks, and local dive masters and guides are able to hand-feed chunks of tuna to them with impunity. If you're in the market for some shark action, dive shops at Bora Bora, Moorea, and Rangiroa can easily provide it. Just be aware that getting into the water with feeding sharks always entails some danger. Never snorkel on your own (without the services of an experienced guide) near a spot where shark feeding is practiced, as you never know how the sharks will react to a surface swimmer without any food for them. Like all wild animals, the shark deserves to be approached with respect.

Sea Urchins

Sea urchins (living pincushions) are common in tropical waters. The black variety is the most dangerous: Its long, sharp quills can go right through a snorkeler's fins. Even the small ones, which you can easily pick up in your hand, can pinch you if you're careless. They're found on rocky shores and reefs, never on clear, sandy beaches where the surf rolls in.

Most sea urchins are not poisonous, though quill punctures are painful and can become infected if not treated. The pain is caused by an injected protein, which you can eliminate by holding the injured area in a pail of very hot water for about 15 minutes. This will coagulate the protein, eliminating the pain for good. If you can't heat water, soak the area in vinegar or urine for 15 minutes. Remove the quills if possible, but being made of calcium, they'll decompose in a couple of weeks anyway—not much of a consolation as you limp along in the meantime. In some places sea urchins are considered a delicacy: The orange or yellow urchin gonads are delicious with lemon and salt.

Other Hazardous Creatures

Although jellyfish, stonefish, crown-of-thorns starfish, cone shells, eels, and poisonous sea snakes are dangerous, injuries resulting from any of these are rare. Gently apply methylated spirits, alcohol, or urine (but not water, kerosene, or gasoline) to areas stung by jellyfish. Inoffensive sea cucumbers (bêche-de-mer) punctuate the lagoon shallows, but stonefish also rest on the bottom and are hard to see because of camouflaging; if you happen to step on one, its dorsal fins inject a painful poison, which burns like fire in the blood. Avoid them by dragging your feet. Fortunately, stonefish are not common.

It's worth knowing that the venom produced by most marine animals is destroyed by heat, so your first move should be to soak the injured part in very hot water for 30 minutes. (Also hold an opposite foot or hand in the same water to prevent scalding due to numbness.) Other authorities claim the best first aid is to squeeze blood from a sea cucumber scraped raw on coral directly onto the stonefish wound. If a hospital or clinic is nearby, go there immediately.

Never pick up a live cone shell; some varieties have a deadly stinger dart coming out from the pointed end. The tiny blue-ring octopus is only five centimeters long but packs a poison that can kill a human. Eels hide in reef crevices by day; most are harmful only if you inadvertently poke your hand or foot in at them. Of course, never tempt fate by approaching them (fun-loving dive masters sometimes feed the big ones by hand and stroke their backs).

Reptiles

Land snakes don't exist in French Polynesia, and the sea snakes are shy and inoffensive. This, and the relative absence of leeches, poisonous plants, thorns, and dangerous wild animals, makes the South Pacific a paradise for hikers. One creature to watch out for is the centipede, which often hides under stones or anything else lying around. It's a long, flat, fast-moving insect not to be confused with the round, slow, and harmless millipede. The centipede's bite, though painful, is not lethal to a healthy adult.

Geckos and skinks are small lizards often seen on the islands. The skink hunts insects by day; its tail breaks off if you catch it, but a new one quickly grows. The gecko is nocturnal

© TAHITI TOURISME
sea turtles

and has no eyelids. Adhesive toe pads enable it to pass along vertical surfaces, and it changes color to avoid detection. Unlike the skink, which avoids humans, geckos often live in people's homes, where they eat insects attracted by electric lights. Its loud clicking call may be a territorial warning to other geckos. Two species of geckos are asexual: In these, males do not exist, and the unfertilized eggs hatch into females identical to the mother. Geckos are the most advanced members of the animal world where this phenomenon takes place. During the 1970s a sexual species of house gecko was introduced to Samoa and Vanuatu, and in 1988 it arrived on Tahiti. These larger, more aggressive geckos have drastically reduced the population of the endemic asexual species.

Five of the seven species of sea turtles are present in Polynesia (the green, hawksbill, leatherback, loggerhead, and olive ridley turtles). These magnificent creatures are sometimes erroneously referred to as "tortoises," which are land turtles. All species of sea turtles now face extinction through ruthless hunting, egg harvesting, and beach destruction. Sea turtles come ashore November–February to lay their eggs on the beach from which they themselves originally hatched, but the female turtles don't commence this activity until they are 20 years old. Thus a drop in numbers today has irreversible consequences a generation later, and it's estimated that breeding females already number in the hundreds or low thousands. Turtles often choke on floating plastic bags they mistake for food, or they drown in fishing nets.

History and Government

THE ERA OF DISCOVERY AND SETTLEMENT

Prehistory

Oceania is the site of many "lasts." It was the last area on earth to be settled by humans, the last to be discovered by Europeans, and the last to be both colonized and decolonized. Sometime after 2000 B.C., Austronesian peoples entered the Pacific from Indonesia or the Philippines. The Austronesians had pottery and advanced outrigger canoes. Their distinctive *lapita* pottery, decorated in horizontal geometric bands and dated from 1500 to 500 B.C., has been found at sites ranging from New Britain to New Caledonia, Tonga, and Samoa. *Lapita* pottery has allowed archaeologists to trace the migrations of an Austronesian-speaking race, the Polynesians, with some precision, and recent comparisons of DNA samples have confirmed that they traveled from the south China coast to Taiwan, the Philippines, Indonesia, New Guinea, Santa Cruz, Fiji, and Samoa.

The colorful theory that Oceania was colonized from the Americas is no longer entertained. The Austronesian languages are today spoken from Madagascar through Indonesia all the way to Easter Island and Hawaii—half the circumference of the world! All of the introduced plants of old Polynesia, except the sweet potato, originated in Southeast Asia. The endemic diseases of Oceania, leprosy and the filaria parasite (which causes elephantiasis), were unknown in the Americas. The amazing continuity of Polynesian culture is illustrated by motifs in contemporary tattooing and tapa, which are very similar to those on ancient *lapita* pottery.

The Colonization of Polynesia

The early Polynesians set out from Southeast Asia 3,500 years ago on a migratory trek that would lead them to make the "many islands" of Polynesia their home. Great voyagers, they sailed their huge double-hulled canoes far and wide, steering with huge paddles and pandanus sails. To navigate they read the sun, stars, currents, swells, winds, clouds, and birds. For instance, the brown noddy returns to roost on an island at night, and a sighting at sea would be a sure sign of land nearby.

Sailing purposefully, against the prevailing winds and currents, the *Lapita* peoples reached the Bismarck Archipelago by 1500 B.C., Tonga (via Fiji) by 1300 B.C., and Samoa by 1000 B.C. Around the first century A.D. they pushed out from this primeval area, remembered as Havaiki, into the eastern half of the Pacific.

The islands of French Polynesia were colonized at uncertain dates around the start of the first millennium A.D. Perhaps because of overpopulation in Samoa, by 300 B.C. groups of Polynesians had pressed on to the Marquesas. Hawaii (A.D. 200) and Easter Island (A.D. 300) were both discovered by Polynesians from the Marquesas. The Society Islands were reached by the Marquesans around A.D. 600, and from there or from the Marquesas the migrants continued to the Cook Islands (A.D. 800), the Tuamotus (A.D. 900), and New Zealand (before A.D. 1100). The Polynesians carried with them all the plants and animals needed to continue their way of life.

These were not chance landfalls but planned voyages of colonization: The Polynesians could (and often did) return the way they came. That one could deliberately sail such distances against the trade winds and currents without the help of modern navigational equipment was proved in 1976 when the *Hokule'a,* a reconstructed oceangoing canoe, sailed 5,000 kilometers south from Hawaii to Tahiti. The expedition's Micronesian navigator, Mau Piailug, succeeded in setting a course by the ocean swells and relative positions of the stars alone, which guided the group very precisely along its way. Other signs used to find an island were clouds (which hang over peaks and remain stationary), seabirds (boobies fly up to 50 kilometers offshore, frigate birds up to 80 kilometers), and mysterious *te lapa* (underwater streaks of light radiating 120–150 kilometers from an island, disappearing closer in).

Since 1976 the *Hokule'a* has made several additional return trips to Tahiti; during 1985–1987 Hawaiian navigator Nainoa Thompson used traditional methods to guide the *Hokule'a* on a 27-month "Voyage of Rediscovery" that included a return west–east journey between Samoa and Tahiti. To date the vessel has logged well over 100,000 kilometers using traditional methods, introducing Polynesian voyaging to countless thousands. In 1992 the canoe *Te Aurere* sailed from New Zealand to Rarotonga for the Festival of Pacific Arts—the first such voyage in 1,000 years—where it joined the *Hokule'a* and a fleet of other canoes in a dramatic demonstration of the current revival of traditional Polynesian navigation. In 1995 the *Hokule'a* led a three-canoe flotilla from Hawaii to Tahiti, returning in May with another three double-hulled canoes, which joined them in the Marquesas. In 1999 the vessel reached Easter Island, and in 2007 it set sail for Satawal in Micronesia. (For more information on the *Hokule'a,* visit http://pvs.kcc.hawaii.edu.)

The Polynesians were the real discoverers of the Pacific, completing all their major voyages long before Europeans even dreamed this ocean existed. In double canoes lashed together to form rafts, carrying their plants and animals with them, they penetrated as close to Antarctica as the South Island of New Zealand,

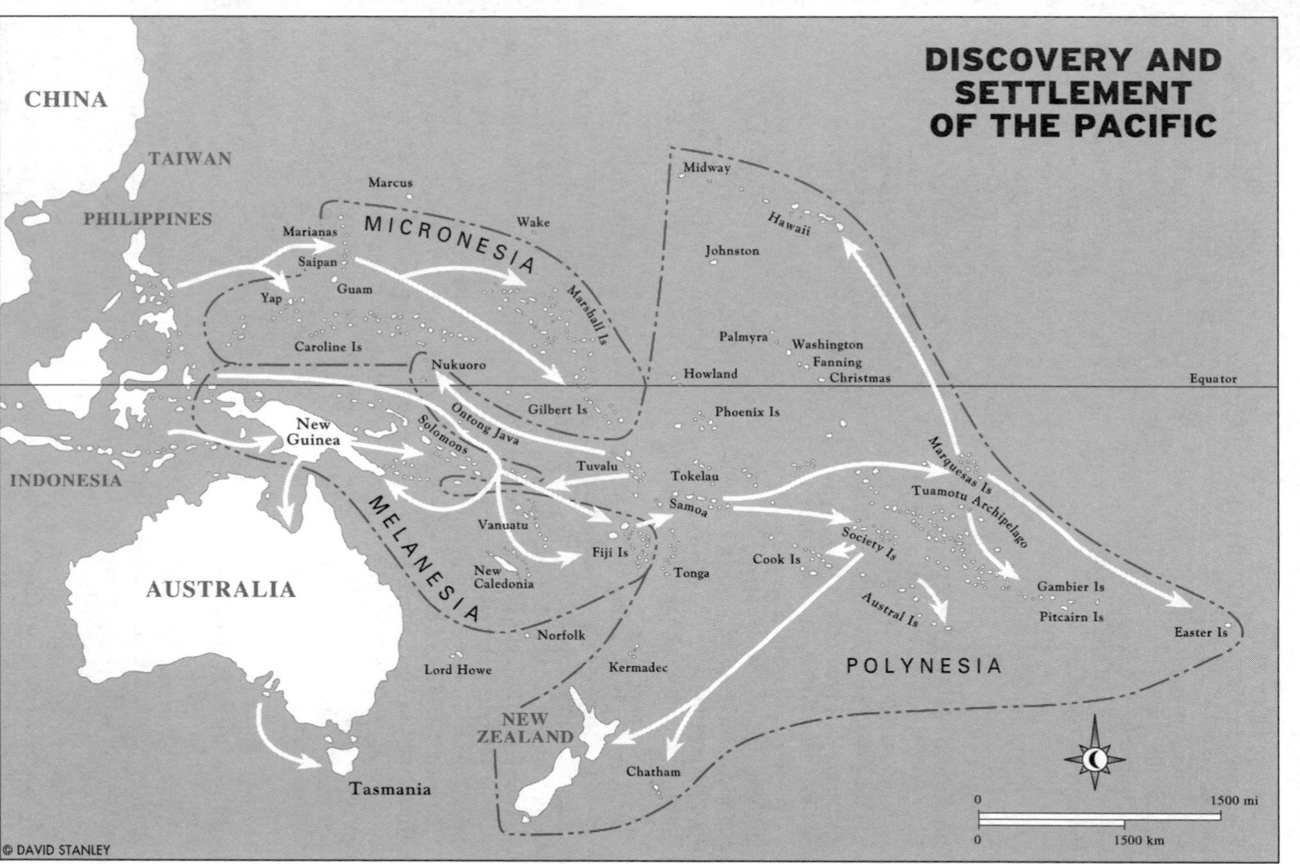
DISCOVERY AND SETTLEMENT OF THE PACIFIC
CHINA
TAIWAN
PHILIPPINES
INDONESIA
AUSTRALIA
Tasmania
MICRONESIA
MELANESIA
POLYNESIA
NEW ZEALAND
Marcus
Marianas
Saipan
Guam
Yap
Wake
Marshall Is
Caroline Is
Nukuoro
Gilbert Is
New Guinea
Solomons
Ontong Java
Tuvalu
Vanuatu
New Caledonia
Fiji Is
Norfolk
Lord Howe
Kermadec
Midway
Hawaii
Johnston
Palmyra
Washington
Fanning
Christmas
Howland
Equator
Phoenix Is
Tokelau
Samoa
Tonga
Cook Is
Society Is
Austral Is
Marquesas Is
Tuamotu Archipelago
Gambier Is
Pitcairn Is
Easter Is
Chatham
0
1500 mi
0
1500 km
© DAVID STANLEY

as far north as Hawaii, and as far east as Easter Island—a full 13,000 kilometers from where it's presumed they first entered the Pacific.

Neolithic Society

The Polynesians lived from fishing and agriculture, using tools made from stone, bone, shell, and wood. The men were responsible for planting, harvesting, fishing, cooking, and house and canoe building; the women tended the fields and animals, gathered food and fuel, prepared food, and made tapa clothes and household items. Both men and women worked together in family or community groups, not as individuals.

The Polynesians lost the art of pottery-making during their long stay in Havaiki (possibly Samoa) and had to cook their food in underground ovens *(umu).* It was sometimes *tapu* (taboo) for men and women to eat together. Breadfruit, taro, yams, sweet potatoes, bananas, and coconuts were cultivated (the Polynesians had no cereals). Taro was grown in organic pits; breadfruit was preserved by fermentation through burial (still a rare delicacy). Pigs, chickens, and dogs were also kept for food, but the surrounding sea yielded the most important source of protein. Stone fishponds and fish traps were built in the lagoons.

Canoes were made of planks stitched together with sennit and caulked with gum from breadfruit trees. Pandanus and coconut fronds were woven into handicrafts. Clothing consisted of tapa (bark cloth). Both men and women wore belts of pandanus leaves or tapa when at work, and during leisure, a skirt that reached to their knees. Ornaments were of feathers, whale or dolphin teeth, and flowers. Both sexes were artfully tattooed using candlenut oil and soot.

For weapons there were clubs, spears, and slings. Archery was practiced only as a game to determine who could shoot farthest. Spear throwing, wrestling, boxing, kite flying, surfing, and canoe racing were popular sports. Polynesian music was made with nasal flutes and cylindrical sharkskin or hollow slit drums. Their dancing is still appreciated today.

The Polynesians used no masks and few colors, usually leaving their artworks unpainted. Art forms were very traditional, and there was a defined class of artists producing works of remarkable delicacy and deftness. The museums of the world possess many fine stone and wood tikis in human form from the Marquesas Islands, where the decorative sense was highly developed. Sculpture in the Australs was more naturalistic, and only here were female tikis common. The Tahitians showed less interest in the plastic arts but excelled in the social arts of poetry, oratory, theater, music, song, and dance. Life on the Tuamotus was a struggle for existence, and objects had utilitarian functions. Countless Polynesian cult objects were destroyed in the early 19th century by overzealous missionaries.

The larger islands produced a surplus, which allowed the emergence of a powerful ruling class. The common people lived in fear of their gods and chiefs. Prior to European contact three hereditary classes structured the Society Islands: high chiefs *(ari'i),* lesser chiefs *(raatira),* and commoners *(manahune).* A small slave class *(titi)* also existed. The various *ari'i* tribes controlled wedge-shaped valleys, and their authority was balanced. None managed to gain permanent supremacy over the rest. In this rigid hierarchical system, where high chiefs had more mana than commoners, marriage or even physical contact between people of unequal mana was forbidden. Children resulting from sexual relations between the classes were killed.

Religion centered around an open-air temple, called a *marae,* with a stone altar. Here priests prayed to the ancestors or gods and conducted all the significant ceremonies of Polynesian life. An individual's social position was determined by his or her family connections, and the recitation of one's genealogy confirmed it. Human sacrifices took place on important occasions on a high chief's *marae.*

The Polynesians were cannibals, although the intensity of the practice varied from group to group: Cannibalism was rife in the Marquesas but relatively rare on Tahiti. It was believed that the mana or spiritual power of an enemy would be transferred to the consumer;

DATELINE: FRENCH POLYNESIA

300 B.C.:	Polynesians reach the Marquesas
A.D. 600:	Polynesians reach the Society Islands
1521	Magellan sights Pukapuka in the Tuamotus
1595	Mendaña contacts the Marquesas
1606	Quirós passes through the Tuamotus
1722	Roggeveen sights Bora Bora
1767	Englishman Samuel Wallis contacts Tahiti
1768	Frenchman Bougainville visits Tahiti
1769	Captain Cook observes transit of Venus at Tahiti
1774	Spanish priests spend one year on Tahiti
1777	last of Captain Cook's four visits to Tahiti
1788	Bligh's HMS *Bounty* at Tahiti
1793	founding of the Pomare dynasty
1797	arrival on Tahiti of first Protestant missionaries
1803	Pomare II flees to Moorea
1812	Pomare's subjects convert to Protestantism
1815	Pomare II reconquers Tahiti
1818	foundation of Papeete by Reverend Crook
1827	50-year reign of Queen Pomare IV begins
1834	French Catholic missionaries arrive at Mangareva
1836	French Catholic priests are expelled from Tahiti
1838	French gunboat demands compensation
1839	Britain rejects Tahitian request for a protectorate
1842	French protectorate is declared over Tahiti and the Marquesas
1842	Herman Melville visits French Polynesia
1844	Mormon missionaries arrive on Tubuai, Austral Islands
1844-1847	Tahitian War of Independence
1847	Queen Pomare accepts French protectorate
1854	one-seventh of Tahitians die during smallpox epidemic
1865-1866	1,010 Chinese laborers arrive on Tahiti
1877	death of Queen Pomare IV
1880	French protectorate changes into a colony
1884	a fire destroys much of Papeete
1885	ban on Tahitian singing and dancing lifted
1887	France annexes the Leeward Islands
1889	French protectorate declared over Austral Islands

to eat the body of one who was greatly despised was the ultimate revenge.

Members of the Raiatea-based Arioi Society traveled through the islands performing ritual copulation and religious rites. The fertility god Oro had descended on a rainbow to Bora Bora's Mount Pahia, where he found a beautiful *vahine.* Their child was the first Arioi. In their pursuit of absolute *free* love, the Arioi shared spouses and killed their own children.

But the Arioi were not the only practitioners of infanticide in French Polynesia. The whole social structure could be threatened by a surplus of children among the chiefly class. Such children might demand arable land from commoners who supplied the chiefs with food. And a struggle between too many potential heirs could create strife. Thus the *ari'i* often did away with unwanted infants after birth. The Arioi Society itself may have been a partial

1890	British missionaries depart Leeward Islands
1891	Paul Gauguin arrives at Tahiti
1900	Austral Islands annexed by France
1903	Paul Gauguin dies on Hiva Oa
1908	phosphate mining begins at Makatea
1914	German cruisers shell Papeete
1916	1,000 Polynesians join Bataillon du Pacifique
1918	influenza pandemic kills 20 percent of population of Tahiti
1942	American military base on Bora Bora
1945	Tahitians become French citizens
1946	French Polynesia becomes an "overseas territory"
1946	territorial assembly created
1958	Pouvanaa a Oopa is arrested
1961	opening of Faa'a Airport on Tahiti
1962	French halt nuclear testing in Algeria
1963	French nuclear testing moves to Polynesia
1965	phosphate mine closes on Makatea
1966	first atmospheric nuclear explosion in the Tuamotus
1974	French nuclear testing moves underground
1977	French Polynesia is granted partial internal autonomy
1984	internal autonomy increases slightly in Polynesia
1985	South Pacific Nuclear-Free Zone Treaty signed
1987	Université Française du Pacifique is established
1992	President Mitterrand suspends nuclear testing
1994	income tax introduced in French Polynesia
1995	President Chirac restarts nuclear testing
1996	nuclear testing ends and site is dismantled
1998	Value Added Tax imposed in French Polynesia
1998	Air Tahiti Nui launches flights to Los Angeles
2002	whale and dolphin sanctuary declared
2004	French Polynesia becomes an "overseas country"
2004	Oscar Temaru elected president
2006	Gaston Tong Sang becomes president
2009	Gaston Flosse indicted for corruption
2010	Tahiti Hilton closes due to tourism slump

solution, as unwanted *ari'i* children were assigned a benign role as Arioi with the assurance that they themselves would never produce any offspring.

Jean-Jacques Rousseau and the 18th-century French rationalists created the romantic image of the "noble savage." Their vision of an ideal state of existence in harmony with nature disregarded the inequalities, cannibalism, and warfare that were a central part of island life, just as much of today's travel literature ignores the poverty and political/economic exploitation many Pacific peoples now face. Still, the legend of the South Pacific maintains its magical hold.

EUROPEAN CONTACT

European Exploration

While the Polynesian history of the islands goes back two millennia, the European period began only in the 16th century when the Magellan expedition sailed past the Tuamotus. In 1595, on his second trip from Peru to the Solomon Islands, Álvaro de Mendaña sighted the southern Marquesas Islands. Eleven years later another Spanish expedition led by Pedro Fernandez de Quirós found a few of the Tuamotu atolls, but these visitors stayed only a few days, and their discoveries were deliberately concealed by the Spanish authorities to avoid attracting rival powers to the area.

The systematic European exploration of the Pacific in the 18th century was actually a search for *terra australis incognita,* a mythical southern continent believed to balance the continents of the north. Dutchman Jacob Roggeveen's 1722 voyage failed to discover the unknown continent, but he did find Easter Island and narrowed the area of conjecture considerably. On June 18, 1767, that Captain Samuel Wallis on the HMS *Dolphin* "discovered" Tahiti (which was already well populated at the time).

At first the Tahitians attacked the ship, but after experiencing European gunfire they decided to be friendly. Eager to trade, they loaded the Englishmen down with pigs, fowl, and fruit. Iron was in the highest demand, and Tahitian women lured the sailors to exchange nails for love. Consequently, to prevent the ship's timbers from being torn asunder for the nails, no man was allowed onshore except in parties strictly for food and water. Wallis sent ashore a landing party, which named Tahiti "King George III Island," turned some sod, and hoisted the Union Jack. A year later the French explorer Louis-Antoine de Bougainville arrived on the east coast, unaware of Wallis's discovery, and claimed Tahiti for the king of France.

Wallis and Bougainville visited only briefly, leaving it to Captain James Cook to really describe Polynesia to Europeans. Cook visited "Otaheite" four times, in 1769, 1773, 1774, and 1777. His first three-month visit was to observe the transit of the planet Venus across the face of the sun. The second and third were in search of the southern continent, while the fourth was to find a northwest passage between the Pacific and Atlantic Oceans. Some of the finest artists and scientists of the day accompanied Captain Cook. Their explorations added the Leeward Islands, two Austral islands, and a dozen Tuamotu islands to European knowledge. On Tahiti Cook met a high priest from Raiatea named Tupaia, who had an astonishing knowledge of the Pacific and could name dozens of islands. He drew Cook a map that included the Cook Islands, the Marquesas, and perhaps also some Samoan islands.

In 1788 Tahiti was visited for five months by the HMS *Bounty,* commanded by Lieutenant William Bligh with orders to collect young breadfruit plants for transportation to the West Indies. However, the famous mutiny did not take place at Tahiti but in Tongan waters, and from there Bligh and loyal members of his crew managed to escape by navigating an open boat 6,500 kilometers to Dutch Timor. In 1791, the HMS *Pandora* came to Tahiti in search of the *Bounty* mutineers, intending to take them to England for trial. They captured 14 survivors of the 16 who had elected to stay on Tahiti when Fletcher Christian and eight others left for Pitcairn. Although glamorized by Hollywood, the mutineers helped destroy traditional Tahitian society by acting as mercenaries for rival chiefs. In 1792 Bligh returned to Tahiti in another ship and completed his original mission.

By the early 19th century, ruffian British and American whalers were fanning out over the Pacific. Other ships traded with the islanders for sandalwood, bêche-de-mer, and mother-of-pearl, as well as the usual supplies. These early contacts with Europeans had a hugely disintegrating effect on native cultures. When introduced into the South Pacific, European sicknesses—mere discomforts to them—devastated whole populations. Measles, influenza, tuberculosis, scarlet fever, dysentery, smallpox, typhus, typhoid, and whooping cough were deadly because the islanders had never developed resistance to them. The Europeans' alcohol, weapons, and venereal disease further accelerated the process.

Kings and Missionaries

In March 1797 the ship *Duff* dropped off on Tahiti 18 Protestant missionaries and their wives after a 207-day journey from England. By this time Pomare, chief of the area adjoining Matavai Bay, had become powerful through the use of European tools, firearms, and mercenaries. He welcomed the missionaries but would not be converted; infanticide, sexual freedom, and human sacrifices continued. By 1800 all but five of the original 18 had left Tahiti disappointed.

In 1803 Pomare I died and his despotic son, Pomare II, attempted to conquer the entire island. After initial success he was forced to flee to Moorea in 1808. Missionary Henry Nott went with him, and in 1812 Pomare II turned to him for help in regaining his lost power. Though the missionaries refused to baptize Pomare II himself because of his heathen and drunken habits, his subjects on Moorea became nominal Christians. In 1815 this "Christian king" managed to regain Tahiti and overthrow paganism. Instead of being punished, the defeated clans were forgiven and allowed to become Christians. The persistent missionaries then enforced the 10 Commandments and dressed the Tahitian women in "Mother Hubbard" costumes—dresses that covered their bodies from head to toe. Henceforth singing anything but hymns was banned, dancing proscribed, and all customs that offended puritanical sensibilities wiped away. Morality police terrorized the confused Tahitians in an eternal crusade against sin. Even the wearing of flowers in the hair was prohibited.

In *Omoo* (1847), Herman Melville comments:

> *Doubtless, in thus denationalizing the Tahitians, as it were, the missionaries were prompted by a sincere desire for good; but the effect has been lamentable. Supplied with no amusements, in place of those forbidden, the Tahitians, who require more recreation than other people, have sunk into a listlessness, or indulge in sensualities, a hundred times more pernicious than all the games ever celebrated in the Temple of Tanee.*

The Rape of Polynesia

Upon Pomare II's death from drink at age 40 in 1821, the crown passed to his infant son, Pomare III, but he died in 1827. At this juncture the most remarkable Tahitian of the 19th century, Aimata, half-sister of Pomare II, became Queen Pomare Vahine IV. She was to rule Tahiti, Moorea, and part of the Austral and Tuamotu groups for half a century until her death in 1877, a barefoot Tahitian Queen Victoria. She allied herself closely with the London Missionary Society (LMS), and when two fanatical French-Catholic priests, Honoré Laval and François Caret, arrived on Tahiti in 1836 from their stronghold at Mangareva (Gambier Islands), she expelled them promptly.

This affront brought a French frigate to Papeete in 1838, demanding 2,000 piastres compensation and a salute to the French flag. Although the conditions were met, the queen and her chiefs wrote to England appealing for help, but none came. A Belgian named Moerenhout who had formerly served as the U.S. consul was appointed French consul to Queen Pomare in 1838, and in 1839 a second French gunboat arrived and threatened to bombard Tahiti unless 2,000 Spanish dollars were paid and Catholic missionaries given free entry. Back in Mangareva, Laval pushed forward a grandiose building program that wiped out 80 percent of the population of the Gambiers from overwork.

In September 1842, while the queen and George Pritchard, the English consul, were away, Moerenhout tricked four local chiefs into signing a petition asking to be brought under French "protection." This demand was immediately accepted by French Admiral Abel Dupetit-Thouars, who was in league with Moerenhout, and on September 9, 1842, they forced Queen Pomare to accept a French protectorate. When the queen tried to maintain her power and keep her red-and-white royal flag, Dupetit-Thouars deposed the queen on November 8, 1843, and occupied her kingdom, an arbitrary act that was rejected by the French king, who reestablished the protectorate in 1844. Queen Pomare fled to Raiatea, and Pritchard was deported to England in March 1844, bringing Britain and France to the brink of war. The Tahitians resisted for three years: Old French forts and war memorials recall the struggle.

THE COLONIAL ERA

A French Protectorate

At the beginning of 1847, when Queen Pomare realized that no British assistance was forthcoming, she and her people reluctantly accepted the French protectorate. As a compromise, the British elicited a promise from the French not to annex the Leeward Islands, so Huahine, Raiatea, and Bora Bora remained independent until 1887. The French had taken possession of the Marquesas in 1842, even before imposing a protectorate on Tahiti. The Austral Islands were added in 1900, and only prior British action prevented the annexation of the Cook Islands. French missionaries attempted to convert the Tahitians to Catholicism, but only in the Marquesas were they fully successful.

Queen Pomare tried to defend the interests of her people as best she could, but much of her nation was dying: Between the 18th century and 1926 the population of the Marquesas fell from 80,000 to only 2,000. In April 1774 Captain Cook had tried to estimate the population of Tahiti by counting the number of men he saw in a fleet of war canoes and ascribing three members to each one's family. Cook's figure was 204,000, but according to anthropologist Bengt Danielsson, the correct number at the time of discovery was about 150,000. By 1829 it had dropped to 8,568, and a low of 7,169 was reached in 1865.

Pomare V, the final, degenerate member of the line, was more interested in earthly pleasures than the traditions upheld by his mother. In 1880, with French interests at work on the Panama Canal, a smart colonial administrator convinced him to sign away his kingdom for a 5,000-franc-a-month pension. Thus, on June 29, 1880, the protectorate became the full French colony it is today, the Établissements Français de l'Océanie. In 1957 the name was changed to Polynésie Française. Right up until the 1970s the colony was run by governors appointed in Paris who implemented the policies of the French government. There was no system of indirect rule through local chiefs as was the case in the British colonies: Here French officials decided everything, and their authority could not be questioned. Even the 18-member Conseil Générale created in 1885 to oversee certain financial matters had its powers reduced in 1899 and was replaced in 1903 by an impotent advisory council composed of French civil servants. The only elected official with any authority (and a budget) was the mayor of Papeete.

The most earthshaking event between 1880 and 1960 was a visit by two German cruisers, the *Scharnhorst* and *Gneisenau,* which shelled Papeete, destroying the marketplace on September 22, 1914. (Two months later both were sunk by the British at the Battle of the Falkland Islands.) A thousand Tahitian volunteers subsequently served in Europe, 300 of them becoming casualties. On September 2, 1940, the colony declared its support for the Free French, and soon after Pearl Harbor the Americans arrived to establish a base on Bora Bora. Polynesia remained cut off from occupied metropolitan France until the end of the war, although several hundred Tahitians served with the Pacific battalion in North Africa and Italy. In 1946 the colony was made an overseas territory, or *territoire d'outre-mer* (TOM), endowed with an elected territorial assembly. Representation in the French parliament was also granted.

The economy of the early colonial period had been based on cotton growing (1865–1900), vanilla cultivation (1870–1960), pearl shell collecting (1870–1960), copra making, and phosphate mining (1908–1966). These were to be replaced by nuclear testing (1963–1996), tourism (1961–present), and cultured pearls (1968–present).

The Nuclear Era

The early 1960s were momentous times for French Polynesia. Within a few years, an international airport opened on Tahiti, MGM filmed *Mutiny on the Bounty,* and the French began testing their atomic bombs. After Algeria became independent in July 1962, the French decided to move their Sahara nuclear testing facilities to Moruroa atoll in the Tuamotu Islands, 1,200 kilometers southeast of Tahiti. In 1963, when all local political parties protested the invasion of Polynesia by thousands of French troops and technicians sent to establish a nuclear testing center, President Charles de Gaulle simply outlawed political parties. The French set off their first atmospheric nuclear explosion at Moruroa on July 2, 1966, spreading contamination as far as Peru and New Zealand. In 1974 international protests forced the French to switch to the underground tests that continued until 1996. During those three decades of infamy, 181 nuclear explosions, 41 of them in the atmosphere, rocked the Tuamotus.

In the 1960s and 1970s, as independence blossomed across the South Pacific, France tightened its strategic grip on French Polynesia. The spirit of the time is best summed up in the life of one man, Pouvanaa a Oopa, an outspoken World War I hero from Huahine. In 1949 he became the first Polynesian to occupy a seat in the French Chamber of Deputies. His party gained control of the territorial assembly in 1953, and in 1957 he was elected vice president of the newly formed Government Council. In 1958 Pouvanaa campaigned for independence in a referendum vote, but when this failed because of a controversy over the imposition of an income tax, the French government reestablished central control and had Pouvanaa arrested on trumped-up charges of arson. He was eventually sentenced to an eight-year prison term and exiled to France for 15 years. De Gaulle wanted Pouvanaa out of the way until French nuclear testing facilities could be established in Polynesia, and he was not freed until 1968. In 1971 he won the French Polynesian seat in the French Senate, a post he held until his death in early 1977. Tahitians refer to the man as *metua* (father), and his statue stands in front of Papeete's Territorial Assembly.

Pouvanaa's successors, John Teariki and Francis Sanford, were also defenders of Polynesian autonomy and opponents of nuclear testing. Their combined efforts convinced the French government to grant Polynesia a new statute with slightly increased autonomy in 1977. A year later, Faa'a mayor Oscar Temaru formed Tavini Huiraatira, the Polynesian Liberation Front, the leading antinuclear, pro-independence party in the territory. The 1982 territorial elections were won by the neo-Gaullist Tahoeraa Huiraatira (Popular Union), led by the pronuclear, anti-independence mayor of Pirae, Gaston Flosse. To stem growing support for independence, Flosse negotiated enhanced autonomy for the territory in 1984 and 1996.

The independence cause was given impetus by France's last fling at nuclear testing. In April 1992, President Mitterrand halted the testing program at Moruroa, but in June 1995, newly elected President Jacques Chirac ordered a resumption of underground nuclear testing in the Tuamotus, and despite worldwide protests the first test was carried out on September 5, 1995. Early the next morning nonviolent demonstrators blocked the runway of Faa'a Airport after it was reported that Gaston Flosse was attempting to escape to France. When police charged the protesters to clear the runway, the demonstration turned into a riot in which the airport and Papeete were ransacked.

Meanwhile, at the Moruroa test site, two large Greenpeace protest vessels had been boarded by tear gas–firing French commandos and impounded (the ships were not released until six months later). Worldwide condemnation of the test series reached unprecedented levels, and in January 1996 the French announced that the testing had been completed. The facilities on Moruroa have since been decommissioned, and it's highly unlikely the testing will ever resume, yet deadly radiation may already be leaking into the sea through cracks in the atoll's porous coral cap. A mantle of secrecy hangs over France's former nuclear playground in the South Pacific, and many of the 15,000 workers exposed to contamination during the 30 years of testing are now demanding an independent medical inquiry and compensation from France.

After 1996 Flosse and party attempted to enhance the illusion of autonomy by developing the concept of Tahiti Nui, or "Greater Tahiti." Tens of millions of euros were spent to build a new waterfront promenade and presidential palace in Papeete and an immense town hall and six-story general hospital at Pirae (Flosse's hometown). Raiatea has been given a new cruise ship terminal, and five-star resorts have been erected on half a dozen islands thanks to generous tax concessions. The government-sponsored airline, Air Tahiti Nui, was granted landing rights in Paris, thereby forcing two privately-owned French airlines (Air Lib and Corsair) to drop the route, and a territorial TV station, Tahiti Nui TV, has been launched. In March 2004 a Flosse-backed constitutional amendment had French Polynesia declared a *pays d'outre-mer* (overseas country) with a right to maintain overseas missions.

In May 2004 a stunning upset occurred in elections for an expanded 57-seat Territorial Assembly. Flosse's party lost its majority for the first time in decades, and the pro-independence leader Oscar Temaru became president of French Polynesia. Temaru declared his willingness to negotiate with France and warned his followers that a referendum on independence might be 10–15 years away. This change of leadership has facilitated the territory's integration into the South Pacific as a whole, and French Polynesia was granted observer status by the Pacific Islands Forum, an influential regional grouping. Since 2004 the presidency has alternated between Temaru, Flosse, and Bora Bora mayor Gaston Tong Sang nearly a dozen times as assembly members are lured to rival coalitions by offers of power positions. In November 2009, Gaston Flosse was sent to Tahiti's Nuutania Prison after being indicted for taking bribes and destroying evidence during his term in office.

GOVERNMENT

In 1885 an organic decree created the colonial system of government, which remained in effect

The colonial-style Palais Présidentiel de Papeete is the seat of the president of French Polynesia.

WHAT'S IN A NAME?

Over the years, that part of eastern Polynesia controlled by France has been called many things. After 1880 it was the Établissements Français de l'Océanie, becoming Polynésie Française, or French Polynesia, in 1957, the designation still officially recognized by the authorities. French-occupied Polynesia better reflects the political reality, but variations such as (French) Polynesia, "French" Polynesia, and Tahiti-Polynesia are also seen. In recent years the pro-French faction in the Territorial Assembly has adopted Tahiti Nui, or "Greater Tahiti," to give the impression that it enjoys more autonomy than is actually the case, whereas the pro-independence camp seems to favor Te Ao Maohi, which translates to Land of the Maohi. Maohinui is also heard. Tourism officials on Tahiti often use Tahiti and Its Islands. When in doubt, "Tahiti" will get you by, although there's a lot more to this colorful region than just its largest and best-known island.

until the proclamation of a new statute in 1958. In 1977 the French granted the territory partial internal self-government, and Francis Sanford was elected premier of "autonomous" Polynesia. A new local-government statute, passed by the French parliament and promulgated on September 6, 1984, gave slightly more powers to the Polynesians, and in 1996 additional powers were transferred to the territory to slow the momentum toward full independence. Yet the constitution of the Republic of France remains the supreme law of the land, and local laws can be overturned by a Constitutional Council comprising French judges.

A Territorial Assembly elects the president of the government, who chooses 15 cabinet ministers (before 1984 the French high commissioner was the chief executive). The 57 assembly members are elected every five years from separate districts. The territory is represented in Paris by two elected deputies: a senator as well as a social and economic counselor. The French government, through its high commissioner (called "governor" until 1977), retains control over foreign relations, immigration, defense, justice, the police, the municipalities, higher education, and the currency.

French Polynesia is divided into 48 communes, each with an elected Municipal Council, which chooses a mayor from its ranks. Every main town on an island has its *mairie* or hôtel de ville (town hall). These elected municipal bodies, however, are controlled by appointed French civil servants, who run the five administrative subdivisions. The administrators of the Windward, Tuamotu-Gambier, and Austral subdivisions are based at Papeete, while the headquarters of the Leeward Islands administration is at Uturoa (Raiatea), and that of the Marquesas Islands is at Taiohae (Nuku Hiva).

The territorial flag consists of three horizontal bands—red, white, and red with a double-hulled Polynesian sailing canoe superimposed on the white band. On the canoe are five figures representing the five archipelagos.

Economy

The inflow of people and money since the early 1960s has stimulated consumerism, and except for tourism and cultured pearls, the economy of French Polynesia is now dominated by French government spending. The nuclear testing program provoked an influx of 30,000 French settlers, plus a massive infusion of capital, which distorted the formerly self-supporting economy into one totally dependent on France.

French Polynesia has the highest per capita gross domestic product (GDP) in the South Pacific, about CFP 2,090,000 (17,514 euros) per person in 2006, nearly seven times as much as Fiji. Paris contributes little to the territorial budget, but it finances the many departments and services under the direct control of the high commissioner, spending an average of 1.6 billion euros per year in the territory, or nearly a third of the GDP. Much of it goes to the military and to the 2,200 expatriate French civil servants who earn salaries 84 percent higher than those doing the same work in France. Of the total workforce of 68,000, about 40 percent work for some level of government while the other 60 percent are privately employed. Four out of every five jobs are in services. Unemployment is almost 12 percent.

In 1994 the territorial government introduced an income tax of 2 percent on earnings over CFP 150,000 a month, plus new taxes on gasoline, wine, telecommunications, and unearned income. Indirect taxes, such as licensing fees and customs duties, long accounted for more than half of territorial government revenue. In 1998 it was announced that customs duties would be reduced and the lost revenue replaced by a *taxe sur la valeur ajoutée* (TVA), or value-added tax (VAT), added to the price of most goods and services. The TVA is currently 5 percent on groceries, drugs, transportation, tourist activities, admissions, rentals, prepaid meal plans, and accommodations, 10

coconuts drying into copra

percent on other services, and 16 percent on other goods. For decades the price of imported goods has been doubled by taxation, and this consumption tax has further increased the cost of living. Imports are still taxed at the rate of 16 percent (compared to 30 percent in 1999).

With pearl exports falling and tourism in a steep decline, French Polynesia is currently facing a severe economic crisis. In 2009 the gross domestic product fell three percent after 10 years of growth. Unemployment is on the rise, leading to a drop in consumption. In 2010, the territorial government faced a serious tax shortfall.

TRADE

Before the start of nuclear testing, trade was balanced. Only 42 years later, 2008 imports stood at CFP 178,146 million while exports amounted to just CFP 22,239 million, one of the highest disparities in the world. Much of the imbalance is consumed by the French administration itself. Foreign currency spent by tourists on imported goods and services also helps steady the situation.

© DAVID STANLEY

A mill at Motu Uta, Papeete, on Tahiti, crushes French Polynesia's copra into coconut oil and animal feed.

More than 30 percent of the imports come from France, which has imposed a series of self-favoring restrictions. Imports include food, fuel, building material, consumer goods, and automobiles. The main exports are pearls, coconut oil, jewelry, and *noni.* The main agricultural export from the outer islands is copra; copra production has been heavily subsidized by the government since 1967 to discourage migration to Tahiti. The copra is crushed into coconut oil and animal feed at the Motu Uta mill in Papeete. Cultured pearls from farms in the Tuamotus are the largest export, accounting for 38 percent of the total.

AGRICULTURE AND FISHING

Labor recruiting for the nuclear testing program caused local agriculture to collapse in the mid-1960s. Between 1962 and 1988 the percentage of the workforce employed in agriculture dropped from 46 percent to 10 percent, and today agriculture accounts for just over 3 percent of salaried employment. Vanilla and coconut oil combined now account for less than 5 percent of exports, and the export of *noni* pulp to the United States for the making of juice is equally important.

About 80 percent of all food consumed locally is imported. Bread and rice are heavily subsidized by the government. Local vegetables supply half of local needs, while Tahitian coffee covers 20 percent of consumption. French Polynesia does manage, however, to cover three-quarters of its own fruit requirements, and the local pineapple and grapefruit crop goes to the fruit-juice factory on Moorea. Most industry is related to food processing (fruit-juice factory, brewery, soft drinks, etc.) or coconut products. It's rumored that marijuana *(pakalolo)* is now the leading cash crop, although you won't be aware of it. Officially, milk, copra, fruit, vegetables, and eggs are the main agricultural products, in that order. Large areas have been planted in Caribbean pine to provide for future timber needs. Considerable livestock is kept in the Marquesas.

Aquaculture is being developed, with tanks for freshwater shrimp, prawns, live bait, and green mussels. Deep-water fishing within the territory's huge exclusive economic zone is done by about 100 local boats. Most of the fish are consumed locally, but catches have fallen in recent years due to declining fish stocks.

MINING

One of the few potential sources of real wealth is the undersea mineral nodules within the huge exclusive economic zone (EEZ) of French Polynesia. The potato-sized nodules contain manganese, cobalt, nickel, and copper; total deposits are valued at US$3 trillion, enough to supply the world for thousands of years. In the past two decades Japan has spent US$100 million on seabed surveys in preparation for eventual mining, although that's still decades away.

In 1976 the French government passed legislation that gave it control of this zone, not only along France's coastal waters but also around all her overseas territories and departments. The National Marine Research Center and private firms have already drawn up plans to recover nickel, cobalt, manganese, and copper nodules from depths of more than 4,000 meters. The French government has adamantly refused to give the Territorial Assembly any jurisdiction over this tremendous resource, an important indicator as to why it is determined to hold onto its colony at any price.

CULTURED PEARLS

According to myth, the Polynesian god Oro descended to earth on a rainbow to present a Bora Bora princess with a black pearl. Later pearls appeared in the mourning costumes of Tahitian priests at the funerals of important chiefs. The commercial quest for pearls began around 1870 as island divers wearing only tiny goggles plunged effortlessly to depths of 25–30 meters in the Tuamotu lagoons to collect oysters. Finding a pearl this way was one chance in 15,000, and the real objective was the shell, which could be made into mother-of-pearl buttons. By 1960, overharvesting had depleted the slow-growing oyster beds, and today live oysters are collected only to supply cultured-pearl farms. The shell is now a mere by-product, made into decorative items.

French Polynesia's cultured-pearl industry is now second only to tourism as a money earner, providing around 10,000 jobs. It all began in 1963 when an experimental farm was established on Hikueru atoll in the Tuamotus. The first commercial farm opened on Manihi in 1968, but the real boom began only in the late 1980s, and today hundreds of cooperative and private pearl farms operate on 26 atolls, employing thousands of people. Although small companies and family operations are still able to participate in the industry, pearl production is becoming increasingly concentrated in a few hands because of the vertical integration of farming, wholesaling, and retailing. Robert Wan's Tahiti Perles now controls more than half the industry, and the next four companies account for another quarter of production.

The industry is drawing many people back to ancestral islands they abandoned after

pearl diving in the Tuamotus

devastating hurricanes in 1983. Pearl farming relieves pressure on natural stocks and creates an incentive to protect marine environments. Pollution from fertilizer runoff or sewage can make a lagoon unsuitable for pearl farming, which is why the farms are concentrated on lightly populated atolls where other forms of agriculture are scarcely practiced. On the downside, the pearl farm workers often feed themselves with fish they catch in the lagoons, leading to a big decline in marine life.

Another source of conflict are sea turtles, which crack open the oyster shells to get one of their preferred foods. To prevent this, wire netting must be erected around the farms, although it's far easier to simply harvest the endangered turtles.

The strings of oysters must be monitored constantly and lowered or raised if there are variations in water temperature. The larger farms use high-pressure hoses to clean the shells, while smaller family operations often employ the traditional method of manually removing fouling organisms from the shells with a knife. Overcrowding can create hotspots that spread infections to other farms, and more research and government supervision will be required if this industry is to flourish in the long term.

Unlike the Japanese cultured white pearl, the Polynesian black pearl is created only by the giant black-lip oyster *(Pinctada margaritifera),* which thrives in the Tuamotu lagoons. Beginning in the 19th century, the oysters were collected by Polynesian divers who could dive up to 40 meters. It takes around three years for a pearl to form in a seeded oyster. A spherical pearl is formed when a Mississippi River mussel graft from Tennessee is introduced inside the coat; the oyster creates only a hemispherical half pearl if the graft goes between the coat and the shell. Half pearls are much cheaper than real pearls and make outstanding rings and pendants. Some of the grafts used are surprisingly large and the layer of nacre around such pearls may be relatively thin, but only an X-ray can tell. Thin coating on a pearl greatly reduces its value.

The cooperatives sell their production at Papeete auctions held twice a year. Private producers sell their pearls through independent dealers or plush retail outlets in Papeete. Every year about a million black pearls are exported to Japan, Hong Kong, the United States, and Thailand, making the territory the world's second-largest source of loose pearls (after Australia, which produces the smaller yellow pearls). To control quality and pricing, the export of loose reject pearls is prohibited, although finished jewelry is exempt. Pearl prices have fallen in recent years due to overproduction and smuggling to avoid the export tax. The value of cultured pearl exports has fallen from 93 million euros in 2006 to 89 million euros in 2007 and 71 million euros in 2008.

TOURISM

French Polynesia is second only to Fiji as a South Pacific destination, with 134,597 visitors in 2009, 28 percent of them from North America, 25 percent from France, 22 percent from other European countries, 12 percent from Asia, and 10 percent from Australia and New Zealand. Yet tourism is far less developed here than it is in Hawaii. A single Waikiki hotel could have more rooms than the entire island of Tahiti; Hawaii gets more visitors in 10 days than French Polynesia gets in a year. The "tyranny of distance" has thus far prevented most of the islands from being spoiled.

The number of visitors has steadily declined in recent years due to the perception that French Polynesia is expensive. From 2008 to 2009 tourist arrivals dropped by almost a third, and a few large resorts (including the Tahiti Hilton) closed their doors. In 2009 French Polynesia got around half as many North American tourists as it did in 2007. Japanese tourists stay mostly in luxury resorts, while French visitors are more likely to seek out small pensions. Thirty-six percent of French Polynesia's North American visitors come to take a cruise. A significant proportion of the Americans arrive on once-in-a-lifetime honeymoons and never return. On average, French tourists stay twice as long as any other group.

Almost all tourists visit Tahiti and Moorea, and over half also go to Bora Bora. About 10 percent reach Rangiroa, but the other islands are far less visited.

Money generated by tourism covers a third of French Polynesia's import bill and provides around 10,000 jobs, but 80 percent of the things tourists buy are also imported. Many of the luxury resorts are foreign-owned and operated, and in many cases resort development has been at the expense of the environment. Tourism development was responsible for the 35 percent increase in the population of Bora Bora between the 1996 and 2007 censuses.

People and Culture

French Polynesia's population of 260,000 is around 63 percent Polynesian, 12 percent European, 17 percent Polynesian-European, 5 percent Chinese, and 3 percent Polynesian-Chinese. These are only estimates because the last census that provided an ethnic breakdown took place in 1988 and it is now forbidden to collect this type of information. About 69 percent of the total population lives on Tahiti (compared to only 25 percent before the nuclear-testing boom began in the 1960s), but a total of 76 far-flung islands are inhabited. People from the Australs, Tuamotus, and Marquesas migrate to Tahiti, and Tahitians to New Caledonia, creating the problem of idled land and abandoned homes. The rapid growth of Papeete has led to unemployment and social problems such as alcoholism, petty crime, and domestic violence.

The indigenous people of French Polynesia are the Maohi or Eastern Polynesians (as opposed to the Western Polynesians in Samoa and Tonga), and some local nationalists refer to their country as Te Ao Maohi. The word *colon* formerly applied to French men who arrived long before the bomb and made a living as planters or traders, and practically all of them married Polynesian women. Most of these *colons* have already died. Their descendants are termed *demis* or *afa,* and they now dominate politics and the local bureaucracy. The present Europeans *(popa'a)* are mostly recently arrived metropolitan French *(faranis).* Their numbers increased dramatically in the 1960s and 1970s, and most live in urban areas where they're involved in the administration, military, or professions. In contrast, very few Polynesians have migrated to France, although 7,000 live in New Caledonia.

Local Chinese *(tinito)* dominate business throughout the territory. In Papeete and Uturoa, entire streets are lined with Chinese stores, and individual Chinese merchants are found on almost every island. They're also prominent in pearl farming and tourism. During the U.S. Civil War, when the supply of cotton to Europe was disrupted, Scotsman William Stewart decided to set up a cotton plantation on the south side of Tahiti. Unable to convince Tahitians to do the heavy work, Stewart brought in a contingent of 1,010 Chinese laborers from Canton in 1865–1866. When the war ended the enterprise went bankrupt, but many of the Chinese stayed on as market gardeners, hawkers, and opium dealers. Things began changing in 1964 when France recognized the People's Republic of China and granted French citizenship to the territory's Chinese (most other Tahitians had become French citizens right after World War II). The French government tried to assimilate the Chinese by requiring that they adopt French-sounding names and by closing all Chinese schools. Despite this, the Chinese community has remained distinct.

From 1976 to 1983 about 18,000 people migrated to the territory, 77 percent of them from France and another 13 percent from New Caledonia. Nearly 1,000 new settlers continue to arrive each year. About 40,000 Europeans are now present in the territory, plus 8,000 soldiers, police officers, and transient officials.

dock workers of Motu Uta, Papeete, Tahiti

Most Tahitians would like to see this immigration restricted, as it is in virtually every other Pacific state. French citizens even have a tax incentive to come, since they become legal residents after six months and one day in the territory, and are thus exempt from French income tax (in French Polynesia the tax rate is only 2 percent). There's an undercurrent of anti-French sentiment; English speakers are better liked by the Tahitians.

Tahitian Life

For the French, lunch is the main meal of the day, followed by a siesta. Dinner may consist of leftovers from lunch. Tahitians traditionally eat their main meal of fish and native vegetables in the evening, when the day's work is over. People at home often take a shower before or after a meal and put flowers in their hair.

Tahitians often observe with amusement or disdain the efforts of individuals to rise above the group. In a society where sharing and reciprocal generosity have traditionally been important qualities, the deliberate accumulation of personal wealth has always been viewed as a vice. Now with the influx of government and tourist money, Tahitian life is changing, quickly in Papeete, more slowly in the outer islands. To prevent the Polynesians from being made paupers in their own country, foreigners other than French are not usually permitted to buy land here, and 85 percent of the land is still owned by Polynesians.

The educational curriculum is entirely French. Children enter school at age three and for 12 years study the French language, literature, culture, history, and geography, but not much about Polynesia. About 80 percent of the population speaks Tahitian at home, but there is little formal training in it (teaching in Tahitian has been allowed only since 1984). The failure rate ranges 40–60 percent, and most of the rest of the children are behind schedule. About a quarter of the schools are privately run by the churches, but these must teach exactly the same curriculum or lose their subsidies. The whole aim is to transform the Polynesians into Pacific French. In 1989 the

Université de la Polynésie Française (www.upf.pf) opened on Tahiti, specializing in law, humanities, social sciences, languages, and science. As yet, few doctors and lawyers are Polynesian, and most professionals practicing in the territory are expatriate French.

Most Tahitians live along the coast because the interior is too rugged. A traditional Tahitian residence consists of several separate buildings: the *fare tutu* (kitchen), the *fare tamaa* (dining area), the *fare taoto* (bedrooms), plus bathing and sanitary outhouses. Often several generations live together, and young children are sent to live with their grandparents. Adoption is commonplace and family relationships complex. Young Tahitians generally go out as groups, rather than on individual "dates."

The lifestyle may be summed up in the words *aita e peapea* (no problem) and *fiu* (fed up, bored). About the only time the normally languid Tahitians go really wild is when they're dancing or behind the wheel of a car.

Sexuality and Gender Roles

Since the days of Wallis and Bougainville, Tahitian women have had a reputation for promiscuity. Well, for better or worse, this is largely a thing of the past, if it ever existed at all. As a short-term visitor your liaisons with Tahitians are likely to remain polite. Westerners' obsession with the sexuality of Polynesians usually reflects their own frustrations, and the view that Tahitian morality is loose is rather ironic considering that Polynesians have always shared whatever they have, cared for their old and young, and refrained from ostracizing unwed mothers or attaching shame to their offspring.

Polynesia's *mahus,* or "third sex," bears little of the stigma attached to female impersonators in the West. A young boy may adopt the female role by his own choice or that of his parents, performing female tasks at home and eventually finding a job usually performed by women, such as serving in a restaurant or hotel. Generally only one *mahu* exists in each village or community, proof that this type of individual serves a certain sociological function. George Mortimer of the British ship *Mercury* recorded an encounter with a *mahu* in 1789. Though Tahitians may poke fun at a *mahu,* they're fully accepted in society, for example teaching Sunday school. Many, but not all, *mahus* are also gay. Today, with money all-important, a few transvestites have involved themselves in male prostitution, and the term *raerae* has been coined for this category. Now there are even Miss Tane (Miss Male) beauty contests.

THE POLYNESIANS

The ancient Polynesians developed a rigid social system with hereditary chiefs; descent was usually through the father. In most of Polynesia there were only two classes, chiefs and commoners, but in the Hawaiian Islands, Tahiti, and Tonga an intermediate class existed. Slaves were outside the class system entirely, but slavery was practiced only in New Zealand, the Cook Islands, and Mangareva. People lived in scattered dwellings rather than villages, although there were groupings around the major temples and chiefs' residences. Their economy centered on fishing and agriculture. Land was collectively owned by families and tribes. Though the land was worked collectively by commoners, the chiefly families controlled and distributed its produce by well-defined customs. Large numbers of people could be mobilized for public works or war.

Two related forces governed Polynesian life: mana and *tapu.* Our word *taboo* originated from the Polynesian *tapu.* Numerous taboos regulated Polynesian life, such as prohibitions against taking certain plants or fish that were intended for chiefly use. Mana was a spiritual power—gods and high chiefs had the most, and commoners had the least. Early missionaries would often publicly violate the taboos and smash the images of the gods to show that their mana had vanished.

Gods

The Polynesians worshiped a pantheon of gods, who had more mana than any human. The most important were Tangaroa (the creator and god of the oceans), and Oro, or Tu (the god of war), who demanded human sacrifices. The most fascinating figure in Polynesian mythology was Maui, a Krishna- or Prometheus-like figure who caught the sun with a cord to give its fire to the world. He lifted the firmament to prevent it from crushing mankind, fished the islands out of the ocean with a hook, and was killed trying to gain the prize of immortality for humanity. Also worth noting is Hina, the heroine who fled to the moon to avoid incest with her brother and so that the sound of her tapa beater wouldn't bother anyone. Tane (the god of light) and Rongo (the god of agriculture and peace) were other important gods. This polytheism, which may have disseminated from Raiatea in the Society Islands, was most important in eastern Polynesia. The *Arioi* confraternity, centered in Raiatea and thought to be possessed by the gods, traveled about putting on dramatic representations of the myths.

The Eastern Polynesians were enthusiastic temple builders, evidenced today by widespread ruins. Known by the Polynesian names *marae, me'ae,* or *ahu,* these platform and courtyard structures of coral and basalt blocks often had low surrounding walls and internal arrangements of upright wooden slabs. Once temples for religious cults, they were used for seating the gods and for presenting fruits and other foods to them at ritual feasts. Sometimes, but rarely, human sacrifices took place on the *marae.* Religion in western Polynesia was very low-key, with few priests or cult images. No temples have been found in Tonga and very few in Samoa. The gods of eastern Polynesia were represented in human form. The ancestors were more important as a source of descent for social ranking, and genealogies were carefully preserved. Surviving elements of the old religion are the still-widespread belief in spirits *(aitu),* the continuing use of traditional medicine, and the influence of myth. More than 150 years after conversion by early missionaries, most Polynesians maintain their early Christian piety and fervid devotion.

RELIGION

Though the old Polynesian religion died out in the early 19th century, the Tahitians are still a strongly religious people. Protestant missionaries arrived on Tahiti 39 years before the Catholics and 47 years before the Mormons, so 45 percent of the people now belong to the Evangelical Church, which is strongest in the Austral and Leeward Islands. Until the middle of the 20th century this church was one of the only democratic institutions in the colony, and it continues to exert strong influence on social matters (for example, it resolutely opposed nuclear testing).

Of the 34 percent of the total population who are Catholic, half are Polynesians from the Tuamotus and Marquesas, and the other half are French. Another 5 percent are Seventh-Day Adventists, and 10 percent are Mormons. A Mormon group called Sanitos, which rejects Brigham Young as a second prophet, has had a strong following in the Tuamotus since the 19th century. Several other Christian sects are also represented, and some Chinese are Buddhists. It's not unusual to see two or three different churches in a village of 100 people. All the main denominations operate their own schools. Local ministers and priests are powerful figures in the outer-island communities. One vestige of the pre-Christian religion is a widespread belief in ghosts *(tupapau).*

Of course, the optimum way to experience religion in French Polynesia is to go to church on Sunday. Protestant church services are conducted mostly in Tahitian; Catholic services are in French. Sitting through a service (1–2 hours) is often worthwhile just to hear the singing and to observe the women's hats. If you decide to go, don't get up and walk out in the middle—see it through. You'll be rewarded by the joyous singing and fellowship, and you'll encounter the islanders on a different level. After church, people gather for a family meal or picnic and spend the rest of the day relaxing and socializing. If you're a guest in an island home, you'll be invited to accompany them to church. Never wear a pareu to church—you'll be asked to leave.

© DAVID STANLEY

the Evangelical Church in Papeete: A majority of the people of French Polynesia are Protestants.

LANGUAGE

French is spoken throughout the territory, and visitors who stray off the usual tourist trail will sometimes have difficulty making themselves understood in English. However, almost everyone involved in the tourist industry speaks good English. Young Polynesians often become curious and friendly when they hear you speaking English, and if you know a few words in Tahitian, you'll impress everyone.

Contemporary Tahitian is the chiefly or royal dialect used in the translation of the Bible by early Protestant missionaries, and today, as communications improve, the outer-island dialects are becoming mingled with the predominant Tahitian. Tahitian or Maohi is one of a family of Austronesian languages spoken from Madagascar through Indonesia, all the way to Easter Island and Hawaii. The related languages of eastern Polynesia (Hawaiian, Tahitian, Tuamotuan, Mangarevan, Marquesan, Rarotongan, and Maori) are quite different from those of western Polynesia (Samoan and Tongan). Among the Polynesian languages, the consonants did the changing rather than the vowels. The *k* and *l* in Hawaiian are generally rendered as a *t* and *r* in Tahitian.

Instead of attempting to speak French to the Tahitians, turn to the Tahitian vocabulary at the end of this guide and give it a try. Remember to pronounce each vowel separately, *a* as the *ah* in "far," *e* as the *ai* in "day," *i* as the *ee* in "see," *o* as the *oh* in "go," and *u* as the *oo* in "lulu"—similar to Latin or Spanish. Written Tahitian has only eight consonants: *f, h, m, n, p, r, t,* and *v.* Two consonants never follow one another, and all words end in a vowel. No silent letters exist in Tahitian, but there is a glottal stop, often marked with an apostrophe. A slight variation in pronunciation or vowel length can change the meaning of a word completely, so don't be surprised if your efforts produce some unexpected results!

Tahitian is rhetorical and poetical but not scientific. Soft and flowing, it's a musical language whose accent lies mostly on the vowels. To adapt to modern life, many words have been borrowed from European languages; these too are infused with vowels to make them more melodious to the Polynesian ear: *faraipani* (frying pan), *manua* (man of war), *matete* (market), *mati* (match), *moni* (money), *oniani* (onion), *painapo* (pineapple), *pani* (pan), *pata* (butter), *pipi* (peas), *poti* (boat), *taiete* (society), *tapitana* (captain), *tauera* (towel), and *tavana* (governor).

Writer Pierre Loti was impressed by the mystical vocabulary of Tahitian:

> *The sad, weird, mysterious utterances of nature: the scarcely articulate stirrings of fancy.... Faa-fano: the departure of the soul at death. Aa: happiness, earth, sky, paradise. Mahoi: essence or soul of God. Tapetape: the line where the sea grows deep. Tutai: red clouds on the horizon. Ari: depth, emptiness, a wave of the sea. Po: night, unknown dark world, Hell.*

Arts and Entertainment

The big hotels on Tahiti, Moorea, Huahine, and Bora Bora offer exciting dance shows several nights a week. They're generally accompanied by a barbecue or traditional feast, but if the price asked for the meal is too steep, settle for a drink at the bar and enjoy the show (usually no cover charge). Many of the regular performances are listed in this guide, but be sure to confirm the times and dates as these do change to accommodate tour groups.

On most islands Friday night is the time to let it all hang out; on Saturday many people are preparing for a family get-together or church on Sunday. The nonhotel disco bar scene is limited mostly to Papeete and Uturoa. The drinking age in French Polynesia is officially 18, but it's not strictly enforced. Consuming alcohol on the street and smoking in restaurants and bars are not allowed.

MUSIC AND DANCE

Protestant missionaries banned dancing in the 1820s, and the 19th-century French colonial administration forbade performances that disturbed Victorian decorum. Dancing began to reappear as early as 1853, but only after 1908 were the restrictions fully removed. Traditional Tahitian dancing experienced a revival in the 1950s with the formation of Madeleine Moua's Pupu Heiva dance troupe, followed in the 1960s by Coco Hotahota's Temaeva and Gilles Hollande's Ora Tahiti. Yves Roche founded the Tahiti ma ensemble in 1962. These groups rediscovered the near-forgotten myths of old Polynesia and popularized them with exciting music, dance, song, and costumes. During major festivals, several dozen troupes consisting of 20–50 dancers and 6–10 musicians participate in thrilling competitions.

The Tahitian *tamure* or *'ori Tahiti* is a fast, provocative, erotic dance done by rapidly shifting the weight from one foot to the other. The rubber-legged men are almost acrobatic, though their movements tend to follow those of the women closely. The tossing, shell-decorated fiber skirts *(mores),* the hand-held pandanus wands, and the tall headdresses add to the drama.

Dances such as the *aparima, 'ote'a,* and *hivinau* reenact Polynesian legends, and each movement tells part of a story. The *aparima,* or "kiss of the hands," is a slow dance resembling the Hawaiian hula or Samoan *siva* executed mainly with the hands in a standing or sitting position. The hand movements repeat the story told in the accompanying song. The *'ote'a* is a theme dance executed to the accompaniment of drums with great precision and admirable timing by a group of men wearing tall headdresses and/or women with wide belts arrayed in two lines. The *ute* is a restrained dance based on ancient refrains.

The slit-log gong beaten with a wooden stick is now a common instrument throughout Polynesia, even though the eastern Polynesians originally had only skin drums. The *to'ere* slit drum was introduced to Tahiti from western

© TAHITI TOURISME

A Polynesian dance troupe performs on island night.

Polynesia after 1915, and it's marvelous the way the Tahitians have made it their own. Each of these slit rosewood drums, hit with a stick, is slightly different in size and pitch. The *to'ere*'s staccato beat is electrifying. A split-bamboo drum *(ofe)* hit against the ground often provides a contrasting sound. The *pahu* is a more conventional bass drum made from a hollowed coconut tree trunk with a sharkskin cover. Its sound resembles the human heartbeat. The smallest *pahu* is the *fa'atete,* which is hit with sticks.

Another traditional Polynesian musical instrument is the bamboo nose flute *(vivo),* which sounds rather like the call of a bird, though today guitars and ukuleles are more often seen. The ukulele was originally the *braguinha,* brought to Hawaii by Portuguese immigrants a century ago. Homemade ukuleles with the half-shells of coconuts as sound boxes emit pleasant tones, while those sporting empty tins give a more metallic sound. The hollow, piercing note produced by the conch shell or *pu* once accompanied pagan ceremonies on the *marae.*

In the early 19th century, missionaries replaced the old chants of Polynesia with the harmonious gospel singing heard in the islands today, yet even the hymns were transformed into an original Oceanic medium. Prior to the arrival of Europeans, traditional Tahitian vocal music was limited to polyphonic chants conveying oral history and customs, and the contrapuntal *himene,* or hymns, sung by large choirs today are based on those ancient chants. As the singers sway to the tempo, the spiritual quality of the *himene* can be extremely moving, so for the musical experience of a lifetime, attend church any Sunday.

String bands have made European instruments such as the guitar and ukulele an integral part of Tahitian music. The contemporary popular music favored by the island youth is heavily influenced by reggae and localized Anglo-American pop.

HANDICRAFTS AND SHOPPING

Some of French Polynesia's finest wood-carving is from the Marquesas Islands. However, the traditional handicrafts that have survived best are the practical arts done by women (weaving, basket-making, pareu painting). In cases where the items still perform their original function, they remain as vital as ever. Contemporary Tahitian pareu designs reflect the esthetic judgments of the lost art of tapa making. Among the European-derived items are the patchwork quilts *(tifaifai)* of Tahiti.

Whenever possible, buy handicrafts from local women's committee shops, church groups, local markets, or from the craftspeople themselves, but avoid objects made from turtle shell or leather, clam shell, or marine mammal ivory, which are prohibited entry into many countries under endangered species laws. Failure to declare such items to customs officers can lead to heavy fines. Also resist the temptation to buy jewelry or other items made from seashells and coral, the collection of which damages the reefs. Souvenirs made from straw or seeds may be held for fumigation or confiscated upon arrival. The shiny Polynesian-style wood carvings sold in the airport and at resorts are often imported from Indonesia.

Hustling and bargaining are not practiced in French Polynesia: It's expensive for everyone. Haggling may even be considered insulting, so just pay the price asked or keep looking. Black pearl jewelry is an exception: Because the markups are so high, discounts are often available.

Wood Carving

Most local souvenir shops sell "tikis" carved from wood or stone in the Marquesas Islands. The original Tiki was a god of fertility, and really old tikis are still shrouded in superstition. Today they're viewed mainly as good-luck charms and often come decorated with mother-of-pearl. Other items carved from wood include mallets (to beat tapa cloth), *umete* bowls, and slit *to'ere* drums.

Weaving

Woven articles are the most widespread handicrafts. Pandanus fiber is the most common,

© DAVID STANLEY

shell jewelry, baskets, and pareus for sale at an open-air market in Papeete

TAHITI IN LITERATURE

Through the years, European writers have traveled to Polynesia in search of Bougainville's Nouvelle Cythère or Rousseau's noble savage. Brought to the stage and silver screen, their stories entered the popular imagination alongside Gauguin's rich images, creating the romantic myth of the South Seas paradise now cultivated by the travel industry. An enjoyable way to get a feel for the region is to read a couple of the books mentioned below before you come.

Herman Melville, author of the whaling classic *Moby Dick* (1851), deserted his New Bedford whaler at Nuku Hiva in 1842 and *Typee* (1846) describes his experiences there. An Australian whaling ship carried Melville on to Tahiti, but he joined a mutiny on board, which landed him in the Papeete *calabooza* (prison). His second Polynesian book, *Omoo* (1847), was a result. In both, Melville decries the ruin of Polynesian culture by Western influence.

Pierre Loti's *The Marriage of Loti* (1880) is a sentimental tale of the love of a young French midshipman for a Polynesian girl named Rarahu. Loti's naïveté is rather absurd, but his friendship with Queen Pomare IV and his fine imagery make the book worth reading. Loti's writings moved Paul Gauguin to come to Tahiti.

In 1888-1890 Robert Louis Stevenson, famous author of *Treasure Island* and *Kidnapped,* cruised the Pacific in his schooner, the *Casco.* His book *In the South Seas* describes his visits to the Marquesas and Tuamotus. Stevenson settled at Tautira on Tahiti-iti for a time, but he eventually retired at Apia in Samoa, which offered the author better mail service. In 1890 Stevenson and his family bought a large tract of land just outside Apia and built a large framed house he called Vailima. In 1894 he was buried on Mount Vaea, just above his home.

Jack London and his wife Charmian cruised the Pacific aboard their yacht, the *Snark,* in 1907-1909. A longtime admirer of Melville, London found only a wretched swamp at Taipivai in the Marquesas. His *South Sea Tales* (1911) was the first of the 10 books that he wrote on the Pacific. London's story "The House of Mapuhi," about a Jewish pearl buyer, earned him a costly lawsuit. London was a product of his

but coconut leaf and husk, vine tendril, banana stem, tree and shrub bark, and the stems and leaves of water weeds are all used. On some islands the fibers are passed through a fire, boiled, and then bleached in the sun. Vegetable dyes of very lovely mellow tones are sometimes used, but gaudier store dyes are much more prevalent. Shells are occasionally used to cut, curl, or make the fibers pliable. Polynesian woven arts are characterized by colorful, skillful patterns. Carefully woven pandanus hats and mats come from the Austral Islands.

Tifaifai Quilts

Early missionaries introduced the Tahitians to quilting, and two-layer patchwork *tifaifai* have now taken the place of tapa (bark cloth). Used as bed covers and pillows by tourists, *tifaifai* is still used by Tahitians to cloak newlyweds and to cover coffins. To be wrapped in a *tifaifai* is the highest honor. Each woman has individual quilt patterns that are her trademarks, and bold floral designs are popular, with contrasting colors drawn from nature. A complicated *tifaifai* can take up to six months to complete and cost more than US$1,000.

The French artist Henri Matisse, who in 1930 spent several weeks at the former Hôtel Stuart on Papeete's boulevard Pomare, was so impressed by the Tahitian *tifaifai* that he applied the same technique and adopted many designs for his *"gouaches découpées."* You can see full-size reproductions of several Matisse paintings from his Papeete period just inside the Immeuble Matisse, boulevard Pomare 415, adjacent to Hôtel Tiare Tahiti.

Clothing and Accessories

As this is a French colony, it's not surprising

time, and the modern reader is often shocked by his insensitive portrayal of the islanders.

In 1913–1914 the youthful poet Rupert Brooke visited Tahiti, where he fell in love with Mamua, a girl from Mataiea whom he immortalized in his poem *Tiare Tahiti.* Later Brooke fought in World War I and wrote five famous war sonnets. He died of blood poisoning on a French hospital ship in the Mediterranean in 1915.

W. Somerset Maugham toured Polynesia in 1916–1917 to research his novel *The Moon and Sixpence* (1919), a fictional life of Paul Gauguin. Maugham's *A Writer's Notebook,* published in 1984, nineteen years after his death, describes his travels in the Pacific. On Tahiti, Maugham discovered not only material for his books but by chance found a glass door pane with a female figure painted by Gauguin himself, which he bought for 200 francs. In 1962 it sold at Sotheby's in London for US$37,400.

American writers Charles Nordhoff and James Norman Hall came to Tahiti after World War I, married Tahitian women, and collaborated on 11 books. Their most famous was the *Bounty Trilogy* (1934), which tells of Fletcher Christian's *Mutiny on the Bounty,* the escape to Dutch Timor of Captain Bligh and his crew in *Men Against the Sea,* and the mutineer's fate in *Pitcairn's Island.* Three generations of filmmakers have selected this saga as their way of presenting paradise.

Hall remained on Tahiti until his death in 1951, and he was buried on the hill behind his home at Arue. His last book, *The Forgotten One,* is a collection of true stories about expatriate intellectuals and writers lost in the South Seas. Hall's account of the 28-year correspondence with his American friend Robert Dean Frisbie, who settled on Pukapuka in the Cook Islands during the 1920s, is touching.

James A. Michener joined the U.S. Navy in 1942 and ended up visiting about 50 South Sea islands, among them Bora Bora. His *Tales of the South Pacific* (1947) tells of the impact of World War II on the South Pacific and the Pacific's impact on those who served. It was later made into the long-running Broadway musical, *South Pacific.* Michener's *Return to Paradise* (1951) is a readable collection of essays and short stories.

that many of the best buys are related to fashion. A tropical shirt, sundress, or T-shirt is a purchase of immediate usefulness. The pareu is a typically Tahitian leisure garment consisting of a brightly colored hand-blocked or painted local fabric about two meters long and a meter wide. There are dozens of ways both men and women can wear a pareu. It's the most common apparel for local women throughout the territory, including Papeete, so pick one up!

Local cosmetics such as Monoï Tiare Tahiti, a fragrant coconut-oil skin moisturizer, and coconut-oil soap will put you in form. Jasmine shampoo, cologne, and perfume are also made locally from the *tiare Tahiti* flower. Vanilla is used to flavor coffee. Other curios to buy include hand-carved mother-of-pearl shell, shark's-tooth pendants, hematite (black stone) carvings, and bamboo fishhooks.

Black Pearls

Black-pearl jewelry is widely available throughout French Polynesia. The color, shape, weight, and size of the pearl are important. The darkest pearls are the most valuable. Prices vary considerably, so shop around before buying pearls. Be aware that the export of more than 10 unset pearls per person is prohibited without a license and that the folks operating the X-ray machines at the airport are on the lookout. To avoid having to pay an export tax when leaving French Polynesia, don't lose the proof of purchase and export tax-exemption form you'll be given by the merchant. One copy must be given to the customs officer; otherwise the tax may be charged to your credit card later. Black pearl prices have fallen considerably since 2001 because of oversupply and poor quality control.

Music Recordings

Those who have been thrilled by hypnotic Tahitian music and dance will want to take some Polynesian music home with them on compact disc, available at hotels and souvenir shops throughout the islands. The largest local company producing these CDs is Éditions Manuiti (www.manuiti.pf) or Tamure Records. Among the well-known local singers and musicians appearing on Manuiti are Bimbo, Charley Manu, Guy Roche, Yves Roche, Emma Terangi, Andy Tupaia, and Henriette Winkler. Small Tahitian groups such as the Moorea Lagon Kaina Boys, the Barefoot Boys, and Tamarii Punaruu, as well as large folkloric ensembles such as Maeva Tahiti, Tiare Tahiti, and Coco's Temaeva (often recorded at major festivals) are also well represented. The Tahitian recordings of the Hawaiian artist Bobby Holcomb are highly recommended. Visit www.southpacific.org/music.html for specific CD listings.

HOLIDAYS AND FESTIVALS

Public Holidays

Public holidays in French Polynesia include New Year's Day (January 1), Gospel Day (March 5), Good Friday and Easter Monday (March/April), Labor Day (May 1), Victory Day (May 8), Ascension Day (May), Pentecost or Whitmonday (May/June), Bastille Day (July 14), Assumption Day (August 15), All Saints' Day (November 1), Armistice Day (November 11), and Christmas Day (December 25).

Ironically, Internal Autonomy Day really commemorates June 29, 1880, when King Pomare V was deposed and French Polynesia became a full French colony, not September 6, 1984, when the territory achieved a degree of internal autonomy. On **All Saints' Day** (November 1) the locals illuminate the cemeteries at Papeete, Arue, Punaauia, and elsewhere with candles. On **New Year's Eve** the Papeete waterfront is beautifully illuminated, and there's a seven-kilometer foot race. *Everything* will be closed on these holidays (and maybe also the days before and after—ask).

Festivals and Other Events

The big event of the year is the two-week-long **Heiva i Tahiti** (www.tahiti-heiva.org), which runs from the end of June to Bastille Day (July

© DAVID STANLEY

The Heiva i Tahiti Festival includes a canoe race around Moorea from the starting point in Papeete.

a performance by a traditional dance troupe during the Heiva i Tahiti Festival in Papeete

14). Formerly known as La Fête du Juillet or the Tiurai Festival (the Tahitian word *tiurai* comes from the English *July*), the Heiva originated way back in 1881. Long before that, a pagan festival was held around this time to mark the southern hemisphere solstice. Today it brings contestants and participants to Tahiti from all over the territory to take part in elaborate processions, competitive dancing and singing, feasting, and partying. There are bicycle, car, horse, and outrigger-canoe races, *pétanque,* archery, and javelin-throwing contests, fire walking, stone lifting, sidewalk bazaars, arts and crafts exhibitions, tattooing, games, and joyous carnivals. **Bastille Day** itself, which marks the fall of the Bastille in Paris on July 14, 1789, at the height of the French Revolution, features a military parade in the capital. Ask at the Office du Tourisme in Papeete about when to see the canoe races along Papeete waterfront and around Moorea, horse racing at the Pirae track, and the Taupiti nui dance competitions at the Tahua To'ata, an open-air stadium next to the Cultural Center. Tickets to most Heiva events are sold at the Cultural Center in Papeete or at the gate. As happens during carnival in Rio de Janeiro, you must pay to sit in the stands to watch the performances (CFP 1,000–3,000), but you get three hours or more of unforgettable nonstop entertainment. (If an event is canceled due to weather conditions, your advance ticket will be valid for the rescheduled event, but there are usually no refunds.)

The July celebrations on Bora Bora are as good as those on Tahiti, and festivals are also held on Huahine, Raiatea, and Taha'a at that time. Note that all ships, planes, and hotels are fully booked around July 14, so be in the right place beforehand or get firm reservations, especially if you want to be on Bora Bora that day. At this time of year, races, games, and dance competitions take place on many different islands, and the older women often prove themselves graceful dancers and excellent singers.

Chinese New Year in January or February is celebrated with dances and fireworks. **World Environment Day** (June 5) is marked by guided excursions to Tahiti's interior, and on the following weekend special activities are arranged at tourist sites around the island. The **Agricultural Fair** on Tahiti in mid-August involves the construction of a Tahitian village. Papeete's **Carnival de Tahiti** at the end of October features dancing contests (waltz, foxtrot, rock), nightly parades along boulevard Pomare, and several gala evenings. Since 1987 a Marquesas Islands Festival has been held about every four years.

Major Sporting Events

The 42-kilometer **Tahiti Moorea Marathon** (www.mooreaevents.org) has been held on northern Moorea every February since 1988. In 1997 Patrick Muturi of Kenya set the record time for men of two hours, 21 minutes, and 31 seconds. The women's record is held by Gitte Karlshoj of Denmark, who logged two hours, 50 minutes, and 23 seconds in 1999. A major surfing event (www.surf.pf) is the **Billabong Pro** surfing competition at Teahupoo on Tahiti-iti in May. The **Tahiti**

Open at the Atimaono golf course on Tahiti is in June or July.

The **Te Aito** individual outrigger canoe race is held on Tahiti around the end of July. The **Hawaiki Nui Va'a** outrigger canoe race (www.hawaikinuivaa.pf) in October or November is a stirring three-day event with almost 100 canoe teams crossing from Huahine to Raiatea (44.5 kilometers) the first day, Raiatea to Taha'a (26 kilometers) the second, and Taha'a to Bora Bora (58 kilometers) the third. The **Va'a Hine,** a women-only canoe race from Raiatea to Taha'a and back (40 kilometers), occurs a day or two before the men's race. **L'Aitoman de Moorea** or "Iron Man" triathlon (www.mooreaevents.org) combines swimming (3.8 kilometers), bicycle riding (180 kilometers), and running (41 kilometers).

ESSENTIALS

Getting There

French Polynesia is well connected by air to the United States, Chile, New Zealand, Australia, and Japan, but poorly linked to the other Pacific islands. **Air Tahiti Nui** only began service from Papeete in 1998, yet it now delivers a majority of arrivals to the territory. It flies to Los Angeles five times a week, to Paris four times a week, to Auckland three times a week, and to Tokyo twice a week, plus a code share to Sydney three times a week. The Government of French Polynesia is Air Tahiti Nui's major shareholder, and the carrier's political clout has allowed it to muscle in on routes previously served by other French carriers.

Qantas lists flights to Papeete in its timetable, but these are code shares with Air Tahiti Nui. Air New Zealand also code-shares with Air Tahiti Nui between Los Angeles and Papeete. So even if you have a ticket issued by these other companies, you'll still fly on an Air Tahiti Nui plane (unless you're arriving from Auckland on Air New Zealand). Aircalin, Air France, Hawaiian, and LAN Chile fly their own planes to Tahiti.

BOOKING TIPS

Preparations

First decide where and when you're going and how long you wish to stay. Most North Americans and Europeans will pass through

© DAVID STANLEY

Los Angeles International Airport (LAX) on their way to Tahiti, although it's also possible to arrive via Honolulu. Many people think of Tahiti as somewhere far away on the other side of the globe, but it's only 8.5 hours from Los Angeles; since it takes about five hours to fly from Los Angeles to Hawaii, the flight to Tahiti is only 3.5 hours longer.

Your plane ticket will be your biggest single expense, so spend some time considering the possibilities. If you're online, your first step should be to check the Internet sites of the airlines. The sites of Air Tahiti Nui and Air New Zealand often list "airfare specials," which will give you an idea of how much you'll have to spend. Then call the airlines on their toll-free 800 numbers to hear the sort of fare information they're providing. The following international airlines have flights to Tahiti:

- **Aircalin:** tel. 800/254-7251, www.aircalin.nc, flights from Nouméa
- **Air France:** tel. 800/237-2747, www.airfrance.us, flights from Los Angeles and Paris
- **Air New Zealand:** tel. 800/262-1234, tel. 800/663-5494 in Canada, www.airnewzealand.com, a flight from Auckland and code shares from Los Angeles
- **Air Tahiti Nui:** tel. 877/824-4846, www.airtahitinui.com, flights from Auckland, Los Angeles, Paris, and Tokyo
- **Hawaiian Airlines:** tel. 800/367-5320, www.hawaiianair.com, flights from Honolulu
- **LAN Chile Airlines:** tel. 866/435-9526, www.lan.com, flights from Santiago and Easter Island
- **Qantas Airways:** tel. 800/227-4500, www.qantas.com.au, code-share flights from Auckland, Los Angeles, and Sydney

Occasionally Canada and parts of the United States have different toll-free numbers, so if the number given above doesn't work, dial 800 information at 800/555-1212 (all 800, 866, and 888 numbers are free).

Call all of the carriers and say you want the *lowest possible fare.* The excursion fares are cheapest, but these often have limitations and restrictions, so be sure to ask. Some have an advance-purchase deadline, which means it's wise to begin shopping early. Also check the fare seasons.

If you're not happy with the answers you get, call the number back later and try again. Many different operators take calls on these lines, and some are more knowledgeable than others. The numbers are often busy during peak business hours, so call first thing in the morning, after dinner, or on the weekend. *Be persistent.*

Cheaper Fares

You can sometimes get a better deal from a "consolidator," a specialist travel agency that deals in bulk and sells seats and rooms at wholesale prices. Many airlines have more seats than they can market through normal channels, so they sell their unused long-haul capacity to "discounters" or "bucket shops" at discounts of 40–50 percent off the official tariffs. The discounters buy tickets on this gray market and pass the savings along to you.

Despite their occasionally shady appearance, most discounters and consolidators are perfectly legitimate, and your ticket will probably be issued by the airline itself. Most discounted tickets look and are exactly the same as regular full-fare tickets, but they're usually nonrefundable. There may also be other restrictions not associated with the more expensive tickets, as well as penalties if you wish to change your routing or reservations. Such tickets may not qualify for frequent-flier miles.

With ongoing changes in the ticket distribution system, it's not uncommon for the airlines to offer fares directly on their website rivaling those previously available only via consolidators or contracted rates. Like consolidator tickets, the "Web specials" of the airlines carry many restrictions that you should review carefully. In any case, some consumer protection is obtained by paying by credit card.

Internet Bookings

For an exact fare quote that you can book

instantly online, simply access an online travel agency. You type in your destination and travel dates, and then watch as the site's system searches its database for the lowest fare. You may be offered complicated routings at odd hours, but you'll certainly get useful information.

Try a couple of sites for comparison, such as **Air Tickets Direct** (www.airticketsdirect.com), **Cheap Flights** (www.cheapflights.com), **Cheap Tickets** (www.cheaptickets.com), **Flights.com** (www.flights.com), **Hotwire.com** (www.hotwire.com), **Lowestfare.com** (www.lowestfare.com), **Expedia** (www.expedia.com), **OneTravel.com** (www.onetravel.com), **Orbitz** (www.orbitz.com), **Priceline** (www.priceline.com), and **Travelocity** (www.travelocity.com). **SideStep** (www.sidestep.com) searches over 200 travel websites for the best deals.

All these companies are aimed at the U.S. market, and a credit card with a billing address outside the United States may not be accepted. The agency will also decline your business if you give a name or address that is different from the one on your card. So, despite the global reach of the Internet, you'll probably have to use a website based in your own country.

Flight Network (www.flightnetwork.com) in Canada allows you to search for specials online. **Travelocity.ca** (www.travelocity.ca) is also based in Canada, and there are branches in 22 other countries. **Expedia.ca** (www.expedia.ca) is in Canada, and **Expedia.co.uk** (www.expedia.co.uk) is in the United Kingdom. Other Expedia sites are in over a dozen countries.

In Australia, it's **Travel.com.au** (www.travel.com.au) and **Flightcentre.com** (www.flightcentre.com.au). Flightcentre.com links to similar sites in Canada, Hong Kong, India, New Zealand, South Africa, the United Kingdom, and the United States.

If you live in Europe, turn to **Flightbookers** (www.ebookers.com) in the United Kingdom and 11 other European countries. **Cheapestflights.co.uk** (www.cheapestflights.co.uk), **Priceline.co.uk** (www.priceline.co.uk), and **Travel Bag** (www.travelbag.co.uk) are also in Britain. **Opodo** (www.opodo.com) operates in 11 European countries. **Travel Overland** (www.travel-overland.de) is in Munich.

When comparing prices, note whether taxes, processing fees, fuel or security surcharges, and shipping are charged extra. Check beforehand if you're allowed to change your reservations or refund the ticket. After booking, print out your confirmation. If you're reluctant to place an order on an unfamiliar site, look for their contact telephone number and give them a call to hear how they sound (a listing here is not a recommendation). At all of these sites, you'll be asked to pay by credit card over their secure server.

Student Fares

Students and people under 26 years old can sometimes benefit from lower student fares by booking through **STA Travel** (www.statravel.com), with branches around the world. In the United States, call their toll-free number (tel. 800/781-4040) for information. **Student Universe** (230 3rd Ave., Waltham, MA 02451, USA, tel. 617/321-3100 or 800/272-9676, www.studentuniverse.com) allows you to get quotes and purchase student tickets online. Canada's largest student travel organization is **Travel Cuts** (www.travelcuts.com).

Circle-Pacific and Round-the-World

The Star Alliance's Circle-Pacific Fare provides a trip around the Pacific (including Asia) on Air New Zealand and other Star Alliance carriers. You get 22,000 or 26,000 miles with all the stops you want (minimum of three). Travel must begin in Honolulu, Los Angeles, San Francisco, Seattle, or Vancouver (no add-ons). It's valid for six months, but you must travel in a continuous circle without any backtracking. No date changes are allowed for the outbound sector, but subsequent changes are free. To reissue the ticket (for example, to add additional stops after departure) costs extra, so plan your trip carefully. Qantas also has a Circle-Pacific fare, so compare.

Similar is the Star Alliance's Round-the-World Fare valid on flights operated by the Star Alliance. You're allowed 29,000, 34,000, or 39,000 miles with a minimum of three and a maximum of 15 stops. One transatlantic and one transpacific journey must be included, but the ticket is valid for one year, and backtracking is allowed. Call Air New Zealand to check the cost of this ticket as prices vary considerably from country to country.

For circle-Pacific or round-the-world fares, try **Airtreks** (tel. 877/247-8735, www.airtreks.com) or **Air Brokers International** (tel. 800/883-3273, www.airbrokers.com), both based in San Francisco, or **JustFares.com** (tel. 800/766-3601, www.justfares.com) in Seattle. In Canada, there's **Long Haul Travel** (www.longhaultravel.ca) in Toronto. The **World Travelers' Club** (237 Estudillo Ave., Suite 205, San Leandro, CA 94577, USA, tel. 510/895-8495 or 800/693-0411, www.around-the-world.com) is very good on circle-the-Pacific fares.

AIR SERVICES

From North America

Air Tahiti Nui is the only carrier actually flying to Tahiti from North America (services on Air New Zealand and Qantas are code shares with Air Tahiti Nui). The airline flies nonstop from Papeete to Los Angeles with connections to many other cities. For current fares, visit www.airtahitinui.com. Passengers originating in Canada must change planes in Los Angeles and go through U.S. immigration and security controls. The Air Tahiti Nui flights to New York, which operated from 2005 to 2008, have been discontinued.

From Los Angeles, Delta Air Lines codeshares with Air France to Papeete, which is worth knowing if you have Delta frequent-flier miles.

The only U.S. airline serving Tahiti is Hawaiian Airlines, which offers flights to Papeete via its base in Honolulu with connections to and from 10 western U.S. mainland cities. Fare seasons to Tahiti are complicated, so call well ahead. A free stop in Honolulu is available on Hawaiian Airlines tickets (a good idea on the way down as flight misconnections are common here).

North American Ticket Agents

Two companies worth calling for discounted tickets to Tahiti are the **Adventure Center** (1311 63rd St., Suite 200, Emeryville, CA 94608, USA, tel. 510/654-1879 or 800/228-8747, www.adventurecenter.com) and **Fiji Travel** (15727 S. Western Ave., Suite C, Gardena, CA 90247, USA, tel. 310/512-6430 or 800/500-3454, www.fijitravel.com).

A leading Canadian specialist travel agency is **Pacesetter Travel** (1070 Douglas St., Suite 350, Victoria, BC V8W 2C4, Canada, tel. 250/361-4887 or 877/895-3160, www.pacesettertravel.com), with offices in Calgary, Ottawa, Toronto, Vancouver, and Victoria.

From Australia

In recent years the airlines have struggled to remain profitable without cutting services, and one method they've used is code sharing with other airlines. All Qantas flights between Auckland and Papeete are now code shares with Air Tahiti Nui. Air Tahiti Nui advertises three flights a week to Sydney, but between Auckland and Sydney these are code shares with Qantas, and Australian passengers must change planes at Auckland. For details and specials on Air Tahiti Nui, check www.airtahitinui.com.au.

You can sometimes get a better price by working through a travel agent specializing in bargain airfares, such as Flight Centres International (www.flightcentre.com.au). If you're looking for a more complicated ticket involving a number of stops, try **Trailfinders** (8 Spring St., Sydney, NSW 2000, Australia, tel. 02/9276-4200, www.trailfinders.com.au).

The cheapest tickets must be bought 14 days in advance, and heavy cancellation penalties apply. Shop around, as you can often find much better deals than the published fares, especially during the off months.

From New Zealand

Air New Zealand and Air Tahiti Nui (www.airtahitinui.co.nz) both fly from Auckland to Tahiti with add-ons from Wellington and Christchurch available. Cancellation and date-change fees apply.

Some tickets have advance-purchase requirements, so start shopping well ahead. It's sometimes almost as cheap to buy a package tour to French Polynesia with airfare, accommodations, and transfers included, but these are usually limited to seven nights and you're stuck in a boring tourist-oriented environment. Ask if you can extend your return date and still get the tour price. Agents to call include STA Travel and Flight Centre International (www.flightcentre.co.nz).

From South America

LAN Chile Airlines flies from Santiago, Chile, to Tahiti via Easter Island twice a week, with additional flights during the southern summer high season December–March. On all flights to Easter Island, low-season fares are available March–November.

LAN Chile's Tahiti service is heavily booked between Easter Island and Santiago but seldom full between Easter Island and Tahiti.

From Europe

From Paris, Air France and Air Tahiti Nui fly direct to Papeete via Los Angeles. Also call Air New Zealand and Qantas to ask what prices they are charging to Tahiti.

The British specialist in South Pacific itineraries is **Trailfinders** (1 Threadneedle St., London EC2R 8JX, UK, tel. 020/7628-7628, www.trailfinders.com), in business since 1970. Its 24 offices around the United Kingdom and Ireland offer a variety of discounted round-the-world tickets through the South Pacific, which are often much cheaper than the published fares. If you're in the United Kingdom, it's easy to order a free copy of their magazine *Trailfinder* and brochures online.

Western Air Travel (Bickham, Totnes, Devon TQ9 7NJ, UK, tel. 0845/680-1298, www.westernair.co.uk) is also good on round-the-world tickets. Check the ads in the London entertainment magazines for other such companies. **Roundtheworldflights.com** (102 Islington High St., Islington, London N1 8EG, UK, tel. 020/7704-5700, www.roundtheworldflights.com) allows you to build your own flights online.

In Switzerland try **Globetrotter Travel Service** (Neuengasse 30, 3001 Bern, Switzerland, tel. 031/313-0032, www.globetrotter.ch).

In Germany, one of the most efficient travel agencies selling tickets to Tahiti is **Jet-Travel e.K.** (Buchholzstr. 35, D-53127 Bonn, Germany, tel. 0228/28-4315, www.jet-travel.de). The website of **Travel Overland** (Barerstr. 73, D-80799 Munich, Germany, tel. 089/2727-6100, www.travel-overland.de), with offices in five German cities, quotes exact fares on flights to Papeete.

From Other Pacific Islands

French Polynesia is poorly connected to its South Pacific neighbors. LAN Chile Airlines operates a Boeing 767 service from Santiago to Papeete via Easter Island twice a week. Flights on Aircalin to Nouméa, New Caledonia, are weekly. Twice a week, Air Tahiti and Air Rarotonga operate a joint code-share service between Papeete and Rarotonga using a 60-seater Air Tahiti ATR-72 aircraft. At US$460 one way, it takes about two hours and 45 minutes. Unfortunately, there's no way to go from Tahiti to Tonga, Samoa, or Fiji without passing through Auckland or Hawaii.

These flights cannot be combined in a round-the-world ticket because LAN Chile belongs to the Oneworld group, while Air New Zealand is part of the Star Alliance, and Aircalin, Air Tahiti, and Air Rarotonga don't belong to either.

Side Trip to Easter Island

From Tahiti it's cheaper to make a side trip to Easter Island than to go to the Marquesas. Most Papeete travel agencies sell three- and seven-night packages designed for Tahiti residents that include airfare, accommodations, transfers, and often sightseeing tours. There's usually no single supplement. Check several agencies, as prices vary considerably, and inquire about the price of a return air ticket alone at the LAN Chile office in the Vaima Center (low off-season fares available Mar.–Nov.).

You'll probably need only a passport (no visa) to visit Easter Island. Be aware that an entry tax or *cobro por reciprocidad* will be collected upon arrival in Santiago if you go on to South America, with the amount varying according to nationality (U.S. passports US$131, Canada US$132, Australia US$61, Mexico US$23). This tax also applies to each child in your party.

Tahiti Nui Travel (tel. 46-42-00, www.tahiti-nui.com), off boulevard Pomare below the Vaima Center in Papeete, can book a one-week package to Easter Island at CFP 39,000 single, excluding airfare. Also check **Manureva Tours** (tel. 50-91-00), on boulevard Pomare next to the Banque de Tahiti just west of the Vaima Center; **Tekura Tahiti Travel** (tel. 43-12-00, www.tahiti-tekuratravel.com), on rue Jaussen behind the cathedral; and **eTahiti Travel** (tel. 83-51-60, www.etahititravel.com), in the Vaima Center, 4th floor, suite 124. Visit them all, as prices do vary, and check the vouchers carefully after you've booked. Airfare Papeete–Easter Island is around CFP 54,000 round-trip.

AIRLINE DELAYS AND CANCELLATIONS

When planning your trip, allow a minimum two-hour stopover between connecting flights at U.S. airports, although with airport delays on the increase, even this may not be enough. In the islands, allow at least a day between flights. Try to avoid flying on weekends and holidays, when the congestion is at its worst.

If your flight is canceled due to mechanical problems with the aircraft, the airline will cover your hotel bill and meals. If they reschedule the flight on short notice for reasons of their own or you're bumped off an overbooked flight, they should also pay. They may not feel obligated to pay, however, if the delay is due to weather conditions, a strike by another company, security alerts, and so on.

To compensate for no-shows, most airlines overbook their flights. To avoid being bumped, ask for your seat assignment when booking, check in early, and go to the departure area well before flight time. Of course, if you *are* bumped by a reputable international airline at a major airport, you'll be regaled with free meals and lodging, and sometimes even free flight vouchers (don't expect anything like this from Air Tahiti). Some airlines require you to reconfirm your onward reservations whenever you break your journey for more than 72 hours, while others (such as Air New Zealand) don't. Whatever; it's always best to reconfirm and leave a local contact number to ensure that you're still in the system.

BAGGAGE

International airlines generally allow economy-class passengers 20 kilos of baggage. However, if any United States airport is included in your ticket, the allowance is two pieces not over 32 kilos each for all your flights on that carrier. Under the piece system, neither bag must have a combined length, width, and height of more than 158 centimeters (62 inches), and the two pieces together must not exceed 272 centimeters (107 inches). On most long-haul tickets to and from North America or Europe, the piece system should apply to all sectors, but check this with the airline and look on your ticket. The frequent-flier programs of some airlines allow participants to carry up to 10 kilos of excess baggage free of charge. On Air Tahiti flights within French Polynesia, you may be restricted to as little as 10 kilos total, so it's better to pack according to the lowest common denominator. Overweight luggage costs 1 percent of the full business-class fare per kilogram—watch out, this can be a lot!

Air Tahiti will accept a bicycle, folding kayak, golf bag, or surfboard as one of your two pieces of checked luggage so long as it doesn't weigh over 23 kilograms. Additional pieces or overweight items attract excess baggage charges. Surfboards over 1.8 meters in length may not be accepted on domestic Air Tahiti flights. Sailboards sometimes raise questions, so if you travel with a sailboard, call it a surfboard at check-in.

Tag your bags with your name, address, and phone number inside and out. Stow anything that could conceivably be considered a weapon (scissors, sewing needles, razor blades, nail clippers, etc.) in your checked luggage. Metal objects, such as flashlights and umbrellas, that might require a visual inspection should also be packed away. If in doubt, ask the person at the check-in counter or security personnel if you'll be allowed to carry a certain item aboard the plane. As you're checking in, look to see if the three-letter city codes on your baggage tag receipt and boarding pass are the same. If you're headed to Papeete, the tag should read "PPT."

Check your bag straight through to your final destination; otherwise the airline staff may disclaim responsibility if it's lost or delayed at an intermediate stop. If your baggage is damaged or doesn't arrive at your destination, inform the airline officials *immediately* and have them fill out a written report; otherwise future claims for compensation will be compromised. Keep receipts for any money you're forced to spend to replace missing items.

On flights touching the United States, you'll be told to leave your baggage unlocked. In that case, consider loosely fastening the zippers together with nylon cable ties available at any hardware store. Upon arrival, if you notice that the ties have been cut or that the bag has been mysteriously patched up with tape, carefully examine the contents right away. This could be a sign that baggage handlers have pilfered items, and you must report the theft before leaving the customs hall in order to be eligible for compensation.

Claims for lost luggage can take weeks to process. Keep in touch with the airline to show your concern, and hang on to your baggage tag until the matter is resolved. If you feel you did not receive the attention you deserved, write the airline an objective letter outlining the case. Get the names of the employees you're dealing with, so you can mention them in the letter. On domestic Air Tahiti flights, if your checked luggage is delayed more than 24 hours, you are entitled to compensation.

ORGANIZED TOURS

Packaged Holidays

Any travel agent worth their commission would rather sell you a package tour instead of only a plane ticket, and it's a fact that some vacation packages actually cost less than regular round-trip airfare. While packaged travel certainly isn't for everyone, reduced group airfares and discounted hotel rates make some tours an excellent value. For two people with limited time and a desire to stay at first-class hotels, this is the cheapest way to go.

The "wholesalers" who put these packages together get their rooms at bulk rates far lower than what individuals pay, and the airlines also give them deals. If they'll let you extend your return date to give you some time to yourself, this can be a great deal, especially with the hotel thrown in for "free." Special-interest tours are very popular among sportspeople who want to be sure they'll get to participate in the various activities they enjoy.

The main drawback to the tours is that you're on a fixed itinerary in a tourist-oriented environment, out of touch with local life. You may not like the hotel or meals you get, and singles pay a healthy supplement. You'll probably get prepaid vouchers to turn in as you go along and won't be escorted by a tour conductor. Do check all the restrictions.

What follows is a list of North American companies that make individualized travel arrangements and offer package tours to French Polynesia. Spend some time surfing through their websites, and cross-check the resorts they offer using the listings in this guide.

- **Blue Pacific Vacations,** 21625 Prairie St., Suite 202, Chatsworth, CA 91311-5833, USA, tel. 866/662-5057, www.bluepacificvacations.com
- **eTravelBound,** 2312 Ryan Way, Bullhead City, AZ 86442, USA, tel. 928/763-8255, www.etravelbound.com
- **Fiji Travel,** 15727 S. Western Ave., Suite C, Gardena, CA. 90247, USA, tel. 310/512-6430 or 800/500-3454, www.fijitravel.com
- **Fly Tahiti,** 5200 Warner Ave., Suite 110, Huntington Beach, CA 92649, USA, tel. 714/274-0379 or 866/982-4484, www.flytahiti.com

- **Goway Travel,** 5757 W. Century Blvd., Suite 807, Los Angeles, CA 90045, USA, tel. 800/387-8850, www.goway.com
- **Islands in the Sun,** 300 Continental Blvd., Suite 350, El Segundo, California 90245, USA, tel. 310/536-0051 or 888/828-6877, www.islandsinthesun.com
- **Jetabout Island Vacations,** 300 Continental Blvd., Suite 350, El Segundo, CA 90245, USA, tel. 800/548-7509, www.jetabouttahiti vacations.com
- **Journey Pacific,** 5660 N. Fort Apache Rd., Las Vegas, NV 89149, USA, tel. 800/704-7094, www.journeypacific.com
- **Manuia Tours,** 127 Stevenson St., San Francisco, CA 94105, USA, tel. 415/495-4500, www.manuiatours.com
- **Pacific Destination Center,** 18685-A Main St., Suite 622, Huntington Beach, CA 92648, USA, tel. 714/960-4011 or 800/227-5317, www.pacific-destinations.com
- **Pacific for Less,** 1993 S. Kihei Rd., Suite 21-130, Kihei, HI 96753, USA, tel. 808/875-7589 or 800/915-2776, www.pacific-for-less.com
- **Pleasant Holidays,** 2404 Townsgate Rd., Westlake Village, CA 91361, USA, tel. 800/742-9244, www.pleasantholidays.com
- **See ANZ,** 215 W. Superior St., Suite 200, Chicago, IL 60610, USA, tel. 312/202-6919 or 800/934-8391, www.seeanz.com
- **South Seas Adventures,** 7171 N. 63rd St., Longmont, CO 80503, USA, tel. 800/576-7327, www.south-seas-adventures.com
- **Swain Tours,** 6 W. Lancaster Ave., Ardmore, PA 19003, USA, tel. 800/227-9246, www .swaintours.com
- **Sunspots International,** 1918 NE 181st, Portland, OR 97230, USA, tel. 800/266-6115, www.sunspotsintl.com
- **Travel2,** 300 Continental Blvd., Suite 350, El Segundo, California 90245, USA, tel. 888/410-5770, www.travel2-us.com
- **Tahiti Discount Travel,** 4500 Campus Dr., Suite 510, Newport Beach, CA 92660, USA, tel. 949/250-9122, www.tahiti-discount travel.com
- **Tahiti Legends,** 19891 Beach Blvd., Suite 107, Huntington Beach, CA 92648, USA, tel. 714/374-5656 or 800/200-1213, www .tahitilegends.com
- **Tahiti Travel,** 6535 Wilshire Blvd., Suite 253, Los Angeles, CA 90048, USA, tel. 323/655-2181 or 800/747-9997, www .tahititravel.com
- **Tahiti Travel Planners,** New Millennium Tours, 559 West Diversey Pkwy., Suite 346, Chicago, IL 60614, USA, tel. 773/935-4707 or 800/772-9231, www.gotahiti.com
- **Travel Wizard,** 100 Smith Ranch Rd., Suite 110, San Rafael, CA, 94903, USA, tel. 415/446-5252 or 800/330-8820, www.travel wizard.com

Tahiti Vacations (21625 Prairie St., Chatsworth, CA 91311-5833, USA, tel. 800/553-3477, www.tahitivacations.net) is the only tour operator in North America to concentrate exclusively on Tahiti. **True Tahiti Vacation** (tel. 310/464-1490, www.true tahitivacation.com) is a honeymoon planning specialist run by an American woman named Laurel Samuela who lives on Moorea. Laurel offers personal service to readers of this guide. **Easy Tahiti** (www.easytahiti.com), **eTahiti Travel** (www.etahititravel.com), **Tahiti Cruise and Vacation** (www.tahiti-and-vacation .com), and **Tahiti Nui Travel** (www.tahiti-nui .com), all based in Papeete, also take direct bookings.

Rob Jenneve of **Island Adventures** (225-C N. Fairway, Goleta, CA 93117, USA, tel. 805/683-0488 or 800/289-4957, www.island adventures.com) puts together customized flight and accommodation packages, which are only slightly more expensive than regular round-trip airfare. Rob can steer you toward deluxe resorts, which offer value for money, and he's willing to spend the time to help you find what you really want in planning your trip. According to him, "It's no problem to vary your nights, extend your return, or leave some free time in the middle for spontaneous adventure."

Rascals in Paradise (500 Sansome St., Suite 601, San Francisco, CA. 94111, USA, tel. 415/273-2224, www.rascalsinparadise.com) has been organizing personalized tours to French Polynesia for families since 1987. Since then, the company has been instrumental in initiating numerous children's programs.

From Australia

Hideaway Holidays (Val Gavriloff, Newington Technology Park, Unit 14A/8 Avenue of Americas, Newington, NSW 2127, Australia, tel. 02/8799-2500, www.hideawayholidays.com.au) specializes in packages to every part of the South Pacific. It has been in the business for many years.

Other Australian wholesalers and tour operators involved in French Polynesia include:

- **Adventure World,** Level 20, 141 Walker St., North Sydney, NSW 2060, Australia, tel. 02/8913-0755, www.adventureworld.com.au
- **Coral Seas Travel,** 141 Walker St., North Sydney, NSW 2060, Australia, tel. 1800/641-803, www.coralseas.com.au
- **Goway Travel,** 350 Kent St., 8th Floor, Sydney, NSW 2000, Australia, tel. 02/9262-4755, www.goway.com
- **Talpacific Holidays,** Level 5, 11 Finchley St., Milton, QLD 4064, Australia, tel. 1300/137-727, www.talpacific.com
- **Wotif,** 13 Railway Terrace, Milton, QLD 4064, Australia, tel. 1300/887-979, www.wotif.com

From New Zealand

Ginz Travel (Level 1, 538 Wairakei Rd., Christchurch, NZ, tel. 03/357-0010, www.ginz.com) arranges flights, accommodations, rental cars, and package deals to French Polynesia.

Go Holidays (Gen-I Tower, Level 4, 66 Wyndham St., Auckland, NZ, tel. 09/914-4000 or 0800/464646, www.goholidays.co.nz) also has packaged tours and cruises to French Polynesia.

From Europe

Austravel (3 Barton Arcade, Deansgate, Manchester M3 2BB, UK, tel. 0800/988-4676, www.austravel.com), with a second office in Edinburgh, is a South Pacific–oriented tour company owned by the Thomson Travel Group.

Audley Travel (New Mill, New Mill Lane, Witney, Oxon OX29 9SX, UK, tel. 01993/838-830, www.audleytravel.com) plans tailor-made trips to French Polynesia of 14–18 days.

All Ways Pacific Travel (7 Whielden St., Old Amersham, Bucks HP7 0HT, UK, tel. 01494/432-747, www.all-ways.co.uk) sells packages to French Polynesia for senior or retired travelers.

In Germany, **Pacific Travel House** (Bayerstr. 95, D-80335 München, tel. 089/543-2180, www.pacific-travel-house.com), **Polynesia Tours** (Torstr. 11, D-10119 Berlin, tel. 030/4030-3085, www.polynesia-tours.de), and **Adventure Holidays** (Brüsselerstr. 37, 50674 Köln, tel. 0221/530-3590, www.adventure-holidays.com) offer a variety of package tours.

In Sweden, there's **Tour Pacific** (Sundstorget 3, SE-25110 Helsingborg, Sweden, tel. 042/179500, www.tourpacific.se).

In Austria, the South Pacific specialist is **Coco Weltweit Reisen** (Eduard-Bodem-Gasse 8, A-6020 Innsbruck, tel. 0512/365-791, www.coco-tours.at).

Scuba Tours

The South Pacific is one of the world's prime scuba locales, and most of the islands have excellent facilities for divers. Although it's not that difficult to make your own arrangements as you go, you should consider joining an organized scuba tour if you want to cram in as much diving as possible. To stay in business, the dive travel specialists mentioned below are forced to charge prices similar to what you'd pay on the beach, and the convenience of having everything prearranged is often worth it. Before booking, find out exactly where you'll be staying and ask if daily transfers and meals are provided. Of course, diver certification is mandatory.

Before deciding, consider booking a cabin on a "liveaboard" dive boat. **Aqua Polynesie** (www.aquatiki.com), based at Fakarava, operates scuba diving cruises around the Tuamotu and Marquesas islands on the 14-meter catamaran *Aquatiki*. The boat anchors right above the dive sites, so no time is wasted commuting back and forth, and this is about the only way to dive on remote atolls like Toau, Aratika, Kauehi, Raraka, and Tahanea. Three double cabins are available, costing 2,840/3,550/4,260 euros per person for 8/10/12 nights. Nondivers and children under 16 receive a discount.

Companies specializing in dive tours to French Polynesia include:

- **Caradonna Dive Adventures,** 2101 W. State Rd. 434, Suite 221, Longwood, FL 32779, USA, tel. 407/774-9000 or 800/328-2288, www.caradonna.com
- **Dive Discovery,** 77 Mark Dr., Suite 18, San Rafael, CA, 94903, USA, tel. 415/444-5100 or 800/886-7321, www.divediscovery.com
- **South Pacific Island Travel,** 10701 Aurora Ave. N., Seattle, WA 98133, USA, tel. 206/367-0956 or 877/773-4846, www.spislandtravel.com
- **World of Diving,** 215 Pier Ave., Suite C, Hermosa Beach, CA 90254, USA, tel. 800/463-4846, www.worldofdiving.com

In Australia, try **Allways Dive Expeditions** (168 High St., Ashburton, Melbourne, VIC 3147, Australia, tel. 03/9885-8863, www.allwaysdive.com.au).

Dive, Fish, Snow Travel (39A, Apollo Dr., Mairangi Bay, Auckland, NZ, tel. 09/479-2210, www.divefishsnow.co.nz) arranges scuba tours to French Polynesia at competitive rates.

In Europe, there's **Schöner Tauchen** (Hastedter Heerstr. 211, D-28207 Bremen, Germany, tel. 0421/450-010, www.schoener-tauchen.com).

Alternatively, you can make your own arrangements directly with island dive shops.

Surfing Tours

Tahitian Surf Travel (www.tahitisurftravel.com) has loads of information on surfing travel throughout French Polynesia.

Waterways Surf Adventures (1828 Broadway, Suite D, Santa Monica, CA 90404, USA, tel. 310/584-9900, www.waterwaystravel.com) has surfing tours to Tahiti and Moorea.

In New Zealand there's **Island Holidays** (2 Northcroft St., Takapuna, Auckland 9, NZ, tel. 09/486-1625, www.islandholidays.co.nz).

Tours for Naturalists

Reef and Rainforest Adventure Travel (400 Harbor Dr., Suite D, Sausalito, CA 94965, USA, tel. 415/289-1760 or 800/794-9767, www.reefrainforest.com) books diving, cruises, and other adventure tours to French Polynesia.

Cox and Kings (25 Davis Blvd., Tampa, FL 33606-3499, USA, tel. 813/258-3323 or 800/999-1758, www.coxandkingsusa.com) schedules upscale nature-oriented trips several times a year.

Tahiti Expeditions (www.tahitiexpeditions.com) is a Moorea-based company led by botanist Frank Murphy. Their expeditions and day excursions are unique experiences.

CRUISES AND CHARTERS

Tourist Cruises

Several cruise ships ply the Society Islands from Tahiti to Bora Bora on one-week trips. The main market is the U.S. West Coast, which is almost as close to Tahiti as it is to the better-known cruising grounds in the Caribbean. When evaluating cruise costs, check whether gratuities, port taxes, transfers, shore excursions, alcoholic drinks, and airfare are included. The companies and ships operating here tend to vary from year to year.

The best established vessel is the 332-passenger *Paul Gauguin,* which has operated in French

© DAVID STANLEY

Large cruise ships on round-the-world voyages can tie up at the wharf in downtown Papeete.

Polynesia continuously since its construction at Saint-Nazaire, France, in 1997. Originally operated by Radisson Seven Seas Cruises, the *Paul Gauguin* was acquired by the Pacific Beachcomber Group (www.pgcruises.com) in 2009 to prevent a move away from Papeete. This ship does seven-night cruises from Papeete to Taha'a, Bora Bora, Raiatea, and Moorea year-round starting at US$2,248 per person double occupancy (airfare, fees, taxes, and surcharges are extra). Exact prices vary, but with meals and interisland travel included, a cruise could actually cost you less than a resort-based holiday.

Princess Cruises (www.princess.com) operates 684-passenger Princess-class cruise ships on 10-day cruises out of Papeete. Several different itineraries are available on these huge love boats, including Papeete to Rarotonga and Papeete to Hawaii.

For information on the highly recommended adventure cruises to the Marquesas Islands aboard the passenger-carrying freighter *Aranui* (www.aranui.com), turn to *The Marquesas Islands* chapter.

Smaller Vessels

The 67-meter, 37-cabin mini–cruise ships *Tu Moana* and *Tia Moana* do seven-day cruises around Huahine, Raiatea, Taha'a, and Bora Bora starting at 5,950 euros per person. They're run by **Nomade Yachting Bora Bora** (www.boraboracruises.com), formerly Bora Bora Cruises.

Haumana Cruises (tel. 50-06-74, www.tahiti-haumana-cruises.com) operates the 36-meter, 12-cabin catamaran *Haumana* from Rangiroa in the Tuamotu Islands. Cruises of three, four, and seven nights are offered. The *Haumana* caters well to people interested in fishing, surfing, and scuba diving in remote locations.

Dream Yacht Charter (tel. 56-36-39, www.dreamyachtcharter.com), formerly Archipels Croisières and based on Moorea and Raiatea, operates all-inclusive cruises on its six 17-meter, eight-passenger catamarans. It offers six-night cruises from Fakarava to Rangiroa or around the Leeward Islands, beginning every Saturday, or three nights cruising the Rangiroa lagoon.

Shore excursions and almost everything other than interisland airfare and alcohol is included. For couples it's much cheaper than chartering a yacht, and your crew does all the work. Just don't expect a luxury trip with gourmet cuisine, even though the website may suggest it. Hopefully your fellow passengers will be agreeable.

Also consider yacht cruises in the same areas on lesser-known vessels, such as the yacht *Coup de Coeur* (http://chez.mana.pf/trinidad), the yacht *Wanda* (www.charterwanda.com), and the catamaran *Tane* (www.raiatea.com/tane), all based at Raiatea; the yacht *Bisou Futé* (www.bisoufute.com), based at Taha'a; the *Eden Martin* (www.sailing-huahine.com), based at Huahine; or the catamaran *Margouillat* (www.tahiticruise.pf), at Tahiti.

Polynésie Croisière (tel. 28-60-06, www.polynesie-croisiere.com) offers 3–13-day cruises from Raiatea on the 14.5-meter, six-cabin catamaran *Motu-One.* Scuba diving is their specialty.

Tall ships on South Pacific voyages are regular visitors to Papeete.

Motor Yacht Charters (tel. 66-17-74, www.motoryachtchartertahiti.com) offers day or longer charters around the Windward Islands on the power boat MV *Atara Royal,* based at Raiatea.

Le Vie en Bleu (tel. 77-90-99, www.tahiti-whales.com) does yacht and catamaran charters at Rangiroa in the Tuamotu Islands. An 11-meter monohull is CFP 47,000 a day for up to four people including meals, a skipper, and transfers (scuba diving is extra). Whale watching is possible from August to November.

Aqua Polynésie (tel. 73-47-31, www.aquatiki.com) operates dive cruises on the catamaran *Aqua Tiki* based at Fakarava in the Tuamotu Islands.

The catamaran *Moemoea Nui* (www.marquises-croisiere.com) does one-week cruises around the Marquesas Islands.

Yacht Charters

If you were planning to spend a substantial amount to stay at a luxury resort, consider chartering a yacht instead. Divided among the members of your party, the per-person charter price will be about the same, but you'll experience much more of the Pacific's beauty on a boat than you would staying in a hotel room. Charterers visit isolated lagoons and thus receive insights into island life unspoiled by normal tourist trappings. Of course, activities such as sailing, snorkeling, and general exploring by sea and land are included in the price.

Yacht charters are available either "bareboat" (for those with the skill to sail on their own) or "crewed" (in which case charterers pay a daily fee for a skipper).

Tahiti Yacht Charter (tel. 45-04-00, www.tahitiyachtcharter.com) has 15 charter yachts available at Tahiti and Raiatea. It's based at the Marina Apooiti, one kilometer west of Raiatea Airport. Prices begin at 3,150 euros per week for a four-cabin yacht in the low season (Nov–Mar.) and increase to 8,500 euros for a large catamaran in the high season (July–Aug.). A skipper costs 155 euros per day, a cook 130 euros. This may seem like a lot, but split among a nautical-minded group, it's comparable to a deluxe hotel room.

The South Pacific's largest bareboat yacht charter operation is **The Moorings Ltd.,** a Florida company with several dozen yachts based at Raiatea's Marina Apooiti. Prices are steeper during the April–September high season, and provisioning, security insurance, and local tax are extra. If you're new to sailing, a skipper must be hired, plus a cook (if required). Charterers are given a complete briefing on channels and anchorages, and provided with a detailed set of charts. All boats are radio-equipped, and a voice from The Moorings is available to talk nervous skippers in and out. Travel by night is forbidden, but by day it's easy sailing. All charters are from noon to noon. Contact The Moorings Ltd. (93 North Park Place Blvd., Clearwater, FL 33759, USA, tel. 888/952-8420, www.moorings.com) and ask about specials when calling.

A third yacht charter operation, **Sunsail Tahiti** (tel. 60-04-85, www.sunsailtahiti.com), is based at Raiatea's Faaroa Bay. Prices are similar with substantial reductions for periods longer than 8 or 15 days. The high season is July–August, intermediate April–June and September–November. Those without the required sailing skills will have to hire a skipper.

A few private brokers arranging bareboat or crewed yacht charters are listed below:

- **Charter World Pty. Ltd.,** 23 Passchendaele St., Hampton, Melbourne, VIC 3188, Australia, tel. 03/9521-0033 or 800/335-039, www.charterworld.com.au
- **Luxury Yacht Charters,** Box 939, Main Beach, QLD 4217, Australia, tel. 1800/218-049, www.luxurychartergroup.com
- **Paradise Adventures and Cruises,** Heidi Gavriloff, Newington Technology Park, Unit 14A/8 Ave. of Americas, Newington, NSW 2127, Australia, tel. 02/8799-2500, www.paradiseadventures.com.au
- **Sail Connections Ltd.,** Unit 26, 8 Madden St., Auckland 1, NZ, tel. 09/358-0556, www.sailconnections.com
- **The Windward Islands Cruising Company,** San Francisco, CA, USA, tel. 650/343-0717, www.pacific-adventure.com
- **Yachting Partners International,** 28-29 Richmond Pl., Brighton, East Sussex, BN2 9NA, UK, tel. 44-1273/571-722, www.ypi.co.uk

One of the most experienced brokers arranging such charters is **Ocean Voyages** (1709 Bridgeway, Sausalito, CA 94965, USA, tel. 415/332-4681 or 800/299-4444, www.oceanvoyages.com). For groups of four or six people, Ocean Voyages books charter vessels such as the catamaran *Fai Manu,* based at Taha'a, or the sloop *Coup de Coeur.* The Taha'a-based sloop *Bisou Futé* accommodates eight, while two couples are as many as can be accommodated on the cabin cruiser *Danae IV* at Raiatea. Ocean Voyages also organizes yacht trips from Mangareva to Pitcairn, one of the few practicable ways of actually spending a few days there.

BY SHIP

Even as much Pacific shipping was being sunk during World War II, airstrips were springing up on all the main islands. This hastened the inevitable replacement of the old steamships with modern aircraft, and it's now extremely rare to arrive in the South Pacific by boat (private yachts excepted). Most islands export similar products, and there's little interregional trade; large container ships headed for Australia, New Zealand, and the United States don't usually accept passengers.

Those bitten by nostalgia for the slower prewar ways may like to know that a couple of passenger-carrying freighters do still call at the islands, though their fares are much higher than those charged by the airlines. A specialized agency booking such passages is **TravLtips** (P.O. Box 580188, Flushing, NY 11358, USA, tel. 800/872-8584, www.travltips.com). Also try **Freighter World Cruises** (180 S. Lake Ave., Suite 340, Pasadena, CA 91101, USA, tel. 626/449-3106 or 800/531-7774, www.freighterworld.com).

BY SAILING YACHT

Getting Aboard

It's possible to hitch rides into the Pacific on yachts from California, Panama, New Zealand, and Australia, or around the yachting triangle Papeete–Suva–Honolulu. If you've never crewed before, consider looking for a yacht already in the islands. In Tahiti, for example, after a month on the open sea, some of the original crew may have flown home or onward, opening a place for you. Cruising yachts are recognizable by their foreign flags, wind-vane steering gear, sturdy appearance, and laundry hung out to dry. Good captains evaluate crew on personality, attitude, and a willingness to learn more than experience, so don't lie. Be honest and open when interviewing with a skipper—a deception will soon become apparent.

It's also good to know what a captain's *really* like before you commit yourself to an isolated month with her or him. To determine what might happen should the electronic gadgetry break down, find out if there's a sextant aboard and whether he or she knows how to use it. A boat that looks run-down may often be mechanically unsound too. Also be concerned about a skipper who doesn't do a careful safety briefing early on, or who seems to have a hard time hanging onto crew. If the previous crew has left the boat at an unlikely place such as the Marquesas, there must have been a reason. Once you're on a boat and part of the yachtie community, things are easy.

Time of Year

The weather and seasons play a deciding role in any South Pacific trip by sailboat, and you'll have to pull out of many beautiful places, or be unable to stop there, because of bad weather. The prime season for rides in the South Pacific is May–October; sometimes you'll even have to turn one down. Be aware of the hurricane season (Nov.–Mar. in the South Pacific), as few yachts will be cruising at that time.

Also, know which way the winds are blowing; the prevailing trade winds in the tropics south of the equator are from the southeast. South of the tropic of Capricorn the winds are out of the west. Because of the action of prevailing southeast trade winds, boat trips are smoother from east to west than west to east throughout the South Pacific, so that's the way to go.

Yachting Routes

The common yachting route, or "Coconut Milk Run," across the South Pacific uses the northeast and southeast trades: from California to Tahiti via the Marquesas or Hawaii, then Rarotonga, Niue, Vava'u, Suva, and New Zealand. Some yachts continue west from Fiji to Port Vila. In the other direction, you'll sail on the westerlies from New Zealand to a point south of the Australs, then north on the trades to Tahiti.

About 300 yachts leave the U.S. West Coast for Tahiti every year, almost always crewed by couples or men only. Most stay in the South Seas about a year before returning to North America, while a few continue around the world. Cruising yachts average about 150 kilometers a day, so it takes about a month to get from the U.S. West Coast to Hawaii, then another month from Hawaii to Tahiti.

To enjoy the finest weather conditions, many yachts clear the Panama Canal or depart California in February to arrive in the Marquesas in March. From Hawaii, yachts often leave for Tahiti in April or May. Many stay on for the *Heiva i Tahiti* festival, which ends on July 14, at which time they sail west to Tonga or Fiji, where you'll find them in July and August. By late October the bulk of the yachting community is sailing south via New Caledonia to New Zealand or Australia to spend the southern summer there. Jimmy Cornell's www.noonsite.com provides lots of valuable information for cruising yachties.

Life Aboard

To crew on a yacht you must be willing to wash and iron clothes, cook, steer, keep watch at night, and help with engine work. Other jobs might include changing and resetting sails, cleaning the boat, scraping the bottom, pulling up the anchor, and climbing the main mast to watch for reefs. Do more than is expected of you. A safety harness must be worn in rough weather. As a guest in someone else's home, you'll want to wash your dishes promptly after use and put them, and all other gear, back where you found it. Tampons must not be thrown in the toilet bowl. Smoking is usually prohibited as a safety hazard.

Anybody who wants to get on well under sail must be flexible and tolerant, both physically and emotionally. Expense-sharing crew members pay US$50 per person a week or more. After 30 days you'll be happy to hit land for a freshwater shower. Give adequate notice when you're ready to leave the boat, but *do* disembark when your journey's up. Boat people have few enough opportunities for privacy as it is. If you've had a good trip, ask the captain to write you a letter of recommendation; it'll help you hitch another ride.

Food for Thought

When you consider the big investment, depreciation, cost of maintenance, operating expenses, and considerable risk (most cruising yachts are not insured), travel by sailing yacht is quite a luxury. The huge cost can be surmised from charter fees (US$650 per day and up for a 10-meter yacht). International law makes a clear distinction between passengers and crew. Crew members paying only for their own food, cooking gas, and part of the diesel are very different from charterers who do nothing and pay full costs. The crew is there to help operate the boat, adding safety, but like passengers, they're very much under the control of the captain. Crew has no say in where the yacht will go.

The skipper is personally responsible for crew coming into foreign ports: He's entitled to hold their passports and to see that they have onward tickets and sufficient funds for further traveling. Otherwise the skipper might have to pay their hotel bills and even return airfares to the crew's country of origin. Crew may be asked to pay a share of third-party liability insurance. Possession of drugs would probably result in seizure of the yacht. Because of such considerations, skippers often hesitate to accept crew. Crew members should remember that at no cost to themselves they can learn a bit of sailing and visit places nearly inaccessible by other means. Although not for everyone, it's *the* way to see the real South Pacific, and folks who arrive by *vaa* (sailing canoe) are treated differently from other tourists.

INTERNATIONAL AIRPORT

Faa'a International Airport (PPT, www.tahiti-aeroport.pf) is conveniently situated 5.5 kilometers southwest of Papeete. The runway was created in 1959–1961, using material dredged from the lagoon or trucked in from the Punaruu Valley. A taxi into town is CFP 1,500, or CFP 2,500 after 2000, plus CFP 100 per piece of luggage. (The driver will *always* want CFP 2,500 if you don't verify the price beforehand. Some drivers even try to get CFP 2,500 per person!) Buses up on the main highway will take you to the same place for only CFP 130 (CFP 200 after 1800) and operate from 0400 to 2000 daily. The large resorts are not allowed to have airport shuttles due to lobbying by the taxi drivers. The tour buses at the airport are strictly for people on prepaid packages.

Many flights to Tahiti arrive in the middle of the night. If you're not willing to spend a lot of money for the possibility of a few hours of sleep, it's possible to sit in the terminal (open 24 hours a day) until dawn. Luggage carts in the baggage claim area cost a refundable CFP 100 coin.

The **Banque de Polynésie** (tel. 86-60-56), to the left as you come out of customs, opens one hour before and after the arrival and departure of all international flights. It charges a commission of CFP 474 on all transactions. Euros are changed at a standard rate, but for other currencies the rate is 1 percent better for traveler's checks than it is for cash. There's also a **Banque Socredo** branch (tel. 50-08-04) next to the Air Tahiti ticket office facing the parking lot at the far right (west) end of the airport. It's open weekdays 0800–1145 and 1400–1700

© DAVID STANLEY

All international flights to French Polynesia arrive at Faa'a International Airport.

(no exchanges after 1630). Both banks have ATMs accessible 24 hours, but they usually don't accept U.S. bank cards. Visa cards from countries other than France may be rejected.

Air Tahiti has a ticket office in the terminal open daily 0600–1630. The following car rental companies have counters at the airport: Avis, Daniel, Europcar, Hertz, and Pierrot et Jacqueline. Car rentals at the airport incur a special CFP 700 tax. Tahiti Nui Travel operates a full-service travel agency (weekdays 0800–1200 and 1300–1700, Sat. 0700–1100) next to the car rental offices.

Self-service Air Tahiti check-in kiosks allow you to avoid the lineups for domestic flights by printing your own boarding card. A separate baggage drop-off aisle is nearby. For all international flights, you must check in manually at counters at the other end of the terminal.

The airport post office (weekdays 0800–1200 and 1330–1630) in front of the Air Tahiti security controls sells a Carte ManaSPOT, which provides Wi-Fi Internet access at the restaurants and bars in the airport plus other hotspots throughout French Polynesia. The post office sells a different card for dial-up Internet access that also allows you to use the public telephones at the airport. The Airport Business Center next to McDonald's offers Internet access on their computers at CFP 300 for 15 minutes. The Bar Manureva snack bar with its nice terrace is open 24 hours and is surprisingly reasonable (draft beer CFP 330, baguette sandwich CFP 400). Public toilets are near the snack bar.

The airport luggage-storage office *(consigne a bagages)* is open daily 0500–2300, and two hours before international departures. It charges CFP 395 per day for a handbag, CFP 755 for a suitcase, backpack, or golf bags, CFP 950 for a bicycle, and CFP 1,600–2,700 for surfboards. This left-luggage office is poorly marked; it's behind the Fare Hei flower market in the middle of the parking lot. (Your own hotel may be willing to hold your bags at no cost.)

There's no bank in the departure lounge, but you can spend your leftover Pacific francs at the duty-free shops or at the surprisingly reasonable Bar Revanui. The Fare Hei, just outside the terminal, sells inexpensive shell and flower leis, which the locals give to arriving or departing friends.

Upon arrival, fresh fruits, vegetables, and flowers are prohibited entry. The airport tax of 10 euros will have been included in your ticket price. The airport information number is tel. 86-60-60.

Getting Around

BY AIR

The domestic carrier **Air Tahiti** (www.airtahiti.aero) flies to 47 airstrips in every corner of French Polynesia, with important hubs at Papeete (Windward Islands), Bora Bora (Leeward Islands), Rangiroa (northern Tuamotus), Hao (eastern Tuamotus), and Nuku Hiva (Marquesas). Its fleet consists of five 66-seat ATR 72s, four 48-seat ATR 42s, a 19-seat Twin-Otter, and a nine-seat Beechcraft King Air 200. The Twin-Otter is used only in the Marquesas, and the Beechcraft in the Tuamotus. The French-made ATRs (Avions de Transport Regional) are economical in fuel consumption and maintenance requirements, and they perform well under island conditions. The high-winged design makes them perfect for aerial sightseeing along the way.

Round-trip tickets are about 10 percent cheaper than two one-ways. Air Tahiti doesn't allow stopovers on its tickets, so if you're flying round-trip from Tahiti to Bora Bora and want to stop at Raiatea on the way out and Huahine on the way back, you'll have to buy four separate tickets (total CFP 39,600). Ask about the "Pass Bleu," which allows you to visit these islands plus Moorea for CFP 28,400 (certain restrictions apply).

No student discounts are available, but people under 25 and over 59 can get discounts of up to 50 percent on certain flights by paying CFP 1,000 for a Carte Jeune or Carte Marama discount card. Family reduction cards (CFP 2,000) provide a potential 50 percent reduction for the parents and 75 percent off for children under 12. Identification and one photo are required. The full discount is given only on off-peak flights. These *cartes de réduction* must be purchased at Air Tahiti's downtown Papeete office, not at the airport office. If you apply for the card on an outer island, there's a 10-day wait as the application is forwarded to Tahiti for processing. Even if you have such a card from a previous trip, discount card bookings can be made only from within French Polynesia.

Better than point-to-point fares are the six Air Tahiti **Air Passes.** These are valid for 28 days, but only one stopover can be made on each island included in the package. For example, you can go Papeete–Moorea–Huahine–Raiatea–Maupiti–Bora Bora–Papeete for CFP 37,100. Otherwise pay CFP 52,600 for Papeete–Moorea–Huahine–Raiatea–Maupiti–Bora Bora–Tikehau–Rangiroa–Fakarava–Papeete. This compares with an individual ticket price of CFP 53,700 to do the first circuit or CFP 93,000 for the second, which makes the air passes good value. The Society Islands Air Passes can be extended to include the Austral Islands for another CFP 29,200. To add Nuku Huva and Hiva Oa to a pass is CFP 50,000 extra. All flights must be booked in advance, but date changes are possible (reroutings are not). Air Tahiti's agent in North America, Tahiti Vacations (tel. 800/553-3477, www.tahitivacations.net), will have current information. The passes are nonrefundable once travel has begun.

Air Tahiti also offers packages *(Séjours dans les îles)* to almost all its destinations, including airfare, transfers, hotel rooms (double occupancy), and the occasional breakfast or excursion. Outside the main Society Islands, dinner is usually included. Air Tahiti's packages are much cheaper than what you'd pay if

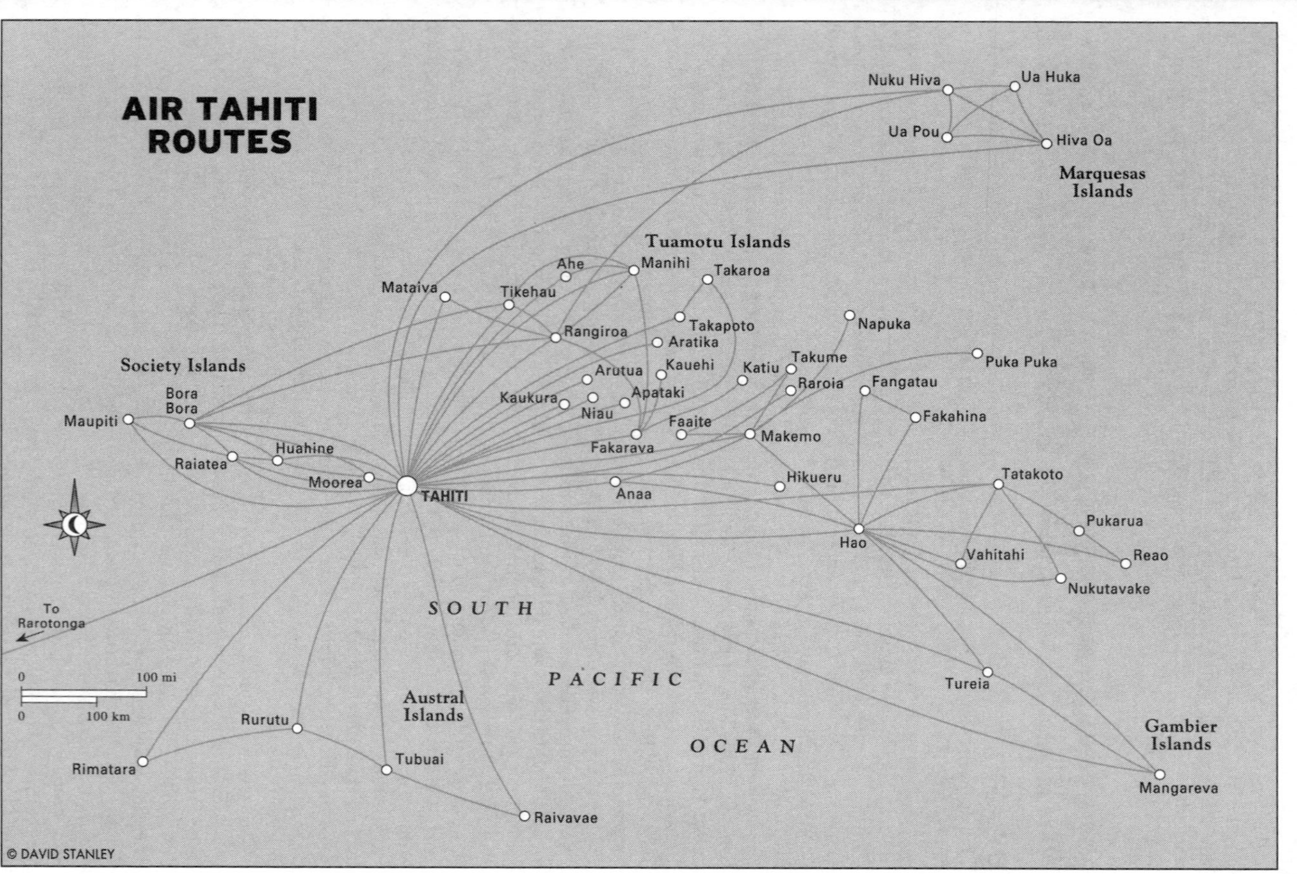
AIR TAHITI ROUTES
Nuku Hiva
Ua Huka
Ua Pou
Hiva Oa
Marquesas Islands
Tuamotu Islands
Ahe
Manihi
Takaroa
Mataiva
Tikehau
Takapoto
Napuka
Rangiroa
Aratika
Puka Puka
Society Islands
Takume
Arutua
Kauehi
Katiu
Bora Bora
Raroia
Fangatau
Maupiti
Kaukura
Apataki
Niau
Fakahina
Faaite
Makemo
Huahine
Fakarava
Raiatea
Moorea
Hikueru
Tatakoto
TAHITI
Anaa
Pukarua
Hao
Vahitahi
Reao
Nukutavake
To Rarotonga
SOUTH
0 100 mi
0 100 km
PACIFIC
Tureia
Austral Islands
Rururu
Gambier Islands
Tubuai
OCEAN
Rimatara
Mangareva
Raivavae
© DAVID STANLEY

© DAVID STANLEY

one of Air Tahiti's 66-seat ATR 72 aircraft

you booked each component separately. Cruise packages are also offered. Many of the possibilities are outlined on www.islandsadventures.com, or consult the listings in the back of Air Tahiti's well-designed timetable.

Air Tahiti tickets are refundable at the place of purchase, less a fee of CFP 1,000 per coupon, but you must cancel your reservations 24 hours before flight time to avoid a CFP 2,000 penalty. Do this in person and have your flight coupon amended, as no-shows are charged CFP 4,000 to make a new reservation (all existing reservations will be automatically canceled). Standby passengers are given any unclaimed seats 20 minutes before each flight. On the other hand, you'll be offered CFP 10,000 compensation if you're bumped from an overbooked flight.

If you're told a flight you want is full, keep checking back, as local passengers often change their minds and seats may become available (except around major public holidays). It's not necessary to reconfirm reservations for flights between Tahiti, Moorea, Huahine, Raiatea, Bora Bora, Rangiroa, and Manihi, but elsewhere it's essential to reconfirm. (If your bookings were made from abroad, do reconfirm *everything* upon arrival in Papeete, as mixups in communications between foreign travel agencies and Air Tahiti are routine.) Beware of planes leaving 20 minutes early.

If you buy your ticket locally, the baggage allowance on domestic flights is 10 kilograms, but if your Air Tahiti flight tickets were purchased seven days before your arrival in French Polynesia, the allowance is 20 kilograms. With the air passes you can increase your baggage allowance to 50 kilograms by paying a surcharge at the time of ticketing. Scuba divers are allowed an extra five kilograms for their diving equipment (scuba certification card required). All baggage above those limits is charged at the rate of the full fare for that sector divided by 80 per kilogram (surfboards over 1.8 meters long or items weighing over 32 kilograms are not accepted). Hand luggage is limited to three kilos. A discount is available if you prepay all your excess baggage fees at the first check-in.

Fresh fruit and vegetables cannot be carried from Tahiti to the Austral, Tuamotu, Gambier, or Marquesas Islands.

On Bora Bora, Maupiti, and Mangareva passengers are transferred from the airport to town by boat. This ride is included in the airfare at Bora Bora but costs CFP 500 per person each way at Maupiti and Mangareva. Smoking aboard the aircraft is prohibited, and all flights are free seating. On flights over 30 minutes, in-flight service consists of a coffee or juice. A meal is served on flights to the Marquesas or Mangareva only.

The main Air Tahiti office (tel. 86-42-42) in Papeete is at the corner of rue Maréchal Foch and rue Edouard Ahnne. It's closed on Sunday. Check carefully to make sure all the flights listed in the published timetable are actually operating. Any travel agency in Papeete can book Air Tahiti flights for the same price as the Air Tahiti office.

Air Tahiti Services

Air Tahiti flies from Papeete to Huahine (CFP 11,400), Raiatea (CFP 13,000), and Bora Bora (CFP 15,400) 4–10 times per day. Five times a week there's a direct connection from Moorea to Huahine (CFP 13,900), Raiatea (CFP 13,900), and Bora Bora (CFP 19,500); Raiatea to Maupiti (CFP 7,400) is three days a week. The daily transversal flights from Bora Bora to Rangiroa and Tikehau (CFP 24,400) eliminate the need to backtrack to Papeete. An Air Tahiti subsidiary, Air Moorea, links Papeete to Moorea (CFP 3,900) almost every hour.

Flights between Papeete and Rangiroa (CFP 16,900) operate 2–4 times per day, continuing from Rangiroa to Tikehau (CFP 6,100), Fakarava (CFP 6,100), and Manihi (CFP 11,100) 4–6 times per week. Air Tahiti also has flights to the East Tuamotu atolls and Mangareva. Many flights between outer islands of the Tuamotus operate in one direction only. All flights from the Leeward Islands to the Tuamotus and from the Tuamotus to the Marquesas are one-way only.

Flights bound for the Marquesas are the longest and most expensive of Air Tahiti's services. The ATR service from Papeete to Nuku Hiva (CFP 29,200) operates daily. Once or twice a week these flights call at Hiva Oa on their way to or from Nuku Hiva, and one weekly ATR flight calls at Rangiroa. At Nuku Hiva the Papeete flights connect for Ua Pou (CFP 6,900), Hiva Oa (CFP 11,000), and Ua Huka (CFP 6,900). If you know you'll be going on to Hiva Oa, Ua Huka, or Ua Pou, get a through ticket from Papeete; the fare is only CFP 3,300 more than a ticket as far as Nuku Hiva.

The Austral group is well connected to Papeete, with flights to Rurutu (CFP 20,200) and Tubuai (CFP 22,500) 4–5 days a week with alternating Papeete–Rurutu–Tubuai–Papeete or Papeete–Tubuai–Rurutu–Papeete routings. The twice-weekly Rurutu–Tubuai leg costs CFP 10,500. When you add up these fares it becomes clear that a visit to the Australs is only cost-effective as an add-on to an air pass—obviously, they're your best bet if you really want to get around.

During July and August, the peak holiday season, extra flights are scheduled. Most runways are unlighted, so few flights operate at night. Air Tahiti is fairly reliable; still, you should avoid scheduling a flight back to Papeete on the same day that your international flight leaves Tahiti. It's always wise to allow some leeway in case there's a problem with the air service. Save that ride around Tahiti until the end.

BY BOAT

To save money, some budget travelers tour French Polynesia by cargo boat. There's a certain adventure and romance to taking an interisland freighter, and you can go anywhere by copra boat, including islands without airstrips and resorts. Ships leave Papeete regularly for the different island groups. You'll meet local people and receive a gentle introduction to the island of your choice. Problems about overweight baggage, tight reservations, and airport transport are eliminated, and thanks to government subsidies, travel by ferry or passenger-carrying freighter is much cheaper than the plane. Seasickness, cockroaches, diesel fumes, and the heavy scent of copra are all part of the experience. You'll find specific information on the main interisland boats in the chapter introductions.

For the cheapest ride and the most local color, travel deck class. There's usually an awning in case of rain, and you'll be surrounded by Tahitians, but don't count on getting a lot of sleep if you go this way. Lay your mat pointed to one side of the boat, because if you lie parallel to the length of the boat you'll roll from side to side. Don't step over other peoples' mats, but if you must, first remove your shoes and excuse yourself. Otherwise take a cabin, which you'll share with three or four other passengers, still cheaper than an airplane seat. Food is included only on really long trips (ask), but snacks may be sold on board. On most trips you're better off taking all your own food rather than buying a meal plan.

For any boat trip farther than Moorea, check the schedule and pick up tickets at the company office as far in advance as possible. Take along your passport, as the staff may insist on checking the expiration date of your visa before selling you a ticket to a point outside the Society Islands. Except on the tourist-class *Aranui,* it's usually not possible to book your passage before arriving on Tahiti. If you really want to go, there'll be something leaving around the date you want. On an outer island, be wary when someone, even a member of the crew, tells you the departure time of a ship: They're as apt to leave early as late.

Boat trips are always smoother northwest-bound than southeast-bound because you go with the prevailing winds. If you plan to fly one-way, you'll have more certainty of getting where you want to go when you want to go if you fly out from Papeete and come back by boat. (Of course, this doesn't apply on trips to Moorea.) *Bon voyage.*

BY BUS

On Huahine and Raiatea folkloric *le truck* still provide an entertaining unscheduled passenger service. Passengers sit on long wooden benches in back, and there's no problem with luggage. On Tahiti and Moorea, unfortunately, most of these colorful vehicles have been replaced with air-conditioned buses that stop only at official stops and issue printed tickets. Still, Tahiti bus fares are fairly low and are usually posted inside the vehicle. You pay through the driver as you enter on Tahiti, as you leave on Moorea. The drivers are generally friendly and will stop to pick you up anywhere if you wave.

On Tahiti buses leave Papeete for the outlying districts periodically throughout the day until 1700; they continue running to Faa'a Airport and the Sofitel Tahiti Maeva Beach Resort until 2000. On Huahine and Raiatea service is usually limited to a trip into the main town in the morning and a return to the villages in the afternoon. On Moorea and Bora Bora public buses meet the ferries from Papeete. No public transportation is available on the roads of the Austral, Tuamotu, Gambier, or Marquesas Islands.

CAR RENTALS

Car rentals in the Society Islands are generally overpriced. Although the locally operated companies may offer slightly cheaper rates than the franchises, it's also true that Avis, Europcar, and Hertz are required to meet international standards of service, and they have head offices where you can complain if something goes seriously wrong. Always find out if insurance, mileage, and tax are included, and check for restrictions on where you'll be allowed to take the car. If in doubt, ask to see a copy of the standard rental contract before making reservations.

Car rentals are available at most of the airports served by Air Tahiti. On Tahiti there's sometimes a mileage charge, whereas on Moorea, Huahine, Raiatea, and Bora Bora all rentals come with unlimited mileage. Public liability insurance is included by law, but collision damage waiver (CDW) insurance is extra. The insurance policies don't cover a flat tire, stolen radios or accessories, broken keys, or towing charges if the renter is found to be responsible. If you can get a small group together, consider renting a minibus for a do-it-yourself island tour. The smallest cars can be uncomfortable if there are more than two of you, and impossible for a group of four with luggage. Unfortunately, the selection of cars is limited, and they may not have the model you reserved.

Unless you have a major credit card you'll have to put a large cash deposit down on the car. Your home driver's license will be accepted, although you must have had your driver's license for at least a year. Some companies rent to people aged 18–24, but those under 25 must show a major credit card, and the deductible amount not covered by the CDW insurance will be much higher.

Except on Tahiti, rental scooters are usually available, and a strictly enforced local regulation requires you to wear a helmet *(casque)* at all times (CFP 5,000 fine for failure to comply). On some outer islands you can rent an open two-seater "fun car" or "Bugway" slightly bigger than a golf cart, and no helmet or driver's license is required for these. These and the bicycles carry no insurance.

One potential hassle with renting cars on the outer islands is that the agency sometimes gives you a car with the fuel tank only one-quarter full, so immediately after renting you must go to a gas station and tank up. Try to avoid putting in more gas than you can use by calculating how many kilometers you might drive, then dividing that by 10 for the number of liters of gasoline you might need. Don't put in more than CFP 2,000 (just under 15 liters) in any case or you'll be giving a nice gift to the rental agency (which, of course, is its hope in giving you a car that's not full). Gas stations are usually only in the main towns and open only on weekdays during business hours, plus perhaps a couple of hours on weekend mornings. Expect to pay around CFP 140 per liter for gas, which works out to just over US$6.50 per U.S. gallon—the South Pacific's highest-priced gasoline to drive the region's most expensive rental cars.

As in continental Europe and North America, driving is on the right-hand side of the road. Two traffic signs to know: A white line across a red background indicates a one-way street, while a slanting blue line on a white background means no parking. At unmarked intersections in Papeete, the driver on the right has priority. At traffic circles, the car already in the circle has priority over those entering. The seldom-observed speed limit is 40 km/h in Papeete, 60 km/h around the island, and 90 km/h on the RDO expressway.

Drive with extreme care in congested areas—traffic accidents are frequent (43 percent of fatal accidents involve alcohol and another 26 percent speeding). People aged 18–25 account for 57 percent of the dead and injured in accidents here. Remember those sudden tropical downpours and don't leave the windows open. Also avoid parking under coconut trees (a falling nut might break the window), and never go off and leave the keys in the ignition. Lock the doors as you would at home.

A good alternative to renting a car are the four-wheel-drive jeep safaris offered on Tahiti, Moorea, Huahine, Raiatea, Taha'a, and Bora Bora. These take you along rough interior roads inaccessible to most rental vehicles, and the guides know all the best spots. Prices vary CFP 4,000–10,000 per person depending on how far you go.

BY BICYCLE

Bicycling in the South Pacific? Sure, why not? It's cheap, convenient, healthy, quick, environmentally sound, safe, and, above all, *fun*. You'll be able to go where and when you please, stop easily and often to meet people and take photos, save money on taxi fares—really *see* the country. Most roads are flat along the coast, but be careful on coral roads, especially inclines: If you slip and fall, you could hurt yourself badly. On the high islands, interior roads tend to be very steep. Never ride your bike through mud.

You can rent bicycles almost anywhere except on Tahiti. If you bring your own, a sturdy, single-speed mountain bike with wide wheels, safety chain, and good brakes will be ideal. Thick tires and a plastic liner between tube and tire will reduce punctures. Know how to fix your own bike. Take along a good repair kit (pump, puncture kit, freewheel tool, spare spokes, cables, chain links, assorted nuts and bolts, etc.) and a repair manual. A couple of good bicycle shops do exist in Papeete, but that's it. Don't try riding with a backpack: Sturdy, waterproof panniers (bike bags) are required; you'll also want a good lock. Refuse to lend your bike to *anyone.*

Air Tahiti Nui will carry a bicycle as checked luggage for free so long as it weighs under 23 kilograms. If you're using another carrier, verify their policy before booking. Take off the pedals and panniers, turn the handlebars sideways and tie them down, deflate the tires, and clean off the dirt before checking in (or use a special bike-carrying bag) and arrive at the airport early. On domestic Air Tahiti flights, checked baggage cannot have a combined length, width, and height of over 150 centimeters. Larger items being sent as freight must be delivered 1.5 hours before the flight. Interisland boats sometimes charge a token amount to carry a bike; other times it's free.

Bicycling on the island of Tahiti is risky because of devil-may-care motorists, but most of the outer islands have excellent, uncrowded roads. It's wiser to use buses on Tahiti, though a bike would come in handy on the other islands where buses are rare. The distances are just made for cycling.

BY OCEAN KAYAK AND CANOE

Ocean kayaking has caught on in the South Pacific, and you can now rent kayaks on Tahiti, Moorea, Huahine, and Bora Bora. Almost every island has a sheltered lagoon ready-made for the excitement of kayak touring, so you can be a real independent 21st-century explorer. Many international airlines accept folding kayaks as checked baggage at no charge.

For a better introduction to ocean kayaking than is possible here, visit your local public library for sea kayaking manuals. Noted author Paul Theroux toured the entire South Pacific by kayak, and his experiences are recounted in *The Happy Isles of Oceania: Paddling the Pacific.*

If you get off the beaten track, you might have a chance to borrow an outrigger canoe. Never attempt to take a dugout canoe through even light surf: You'll be swamped. Don't try to pull or lift a canoe by its outrigger: It will break. Drag the canoe by holding the solid main body. A bailer is *essential* equipment.

TAXIS AND HITCHHIKING

French Polynesia has some of the most expensive taxis in the world, and they're best avoided. If you must take one, always verify the fare before getting in. Hitching around Tahiti is easy and only a matter of time.

Visas and Officialdom

Everyone needs a passport valid six months beyond the departure date. French are admitted freely for an unlimited stay, and citizens of the European Union countries, Australia, Norway, and Switzerland get three months without a visa. Citizens of the United States, Canada, New Zealand, Japan, and 13 other countries are granted a one-month stay free upon arrival at Papeete. If you need a visa for France, you'll also need one for French Polynesia. If in doubt, call your airline beforehand to verify visa requirements. If you do require a visa, make sure the words *valable pour la Polynésie Française* are endorsed on the visa, as visas for France are not accepted. Transit passengers only changing planes in Papeete also require a visa unless they fall into one of the categories above (this applies especially to South American passengers arriving from Chile in transit to New Zealand).

Extensions of stay are possible after you arrive, but they cost CFP 3,500 and you'll have to go to the post office to buy a stamp. You'll also need to show "sufficient funds" and your

FRENCH CONSULATES GENERAL

- **Australia:** St. Martin's Tower, 31 Market St., Sydney, NSW 2000, tel. 02/9268-2400; 6 Perth Ave., Yarralumla, Canberra, ACT 2600, tel. 02/6216-0100, www.ambafrance-au.org
- **Canada:** French consulates general are found in Moncton, Montreal, Ottawa, Quebec, Toronto, and Vancouver.
- **Chile:** Ave. Condell 65, Providencia, Santiago, tel. 02/470-8000
- **Fiji:** Dominion House, 7th floor, Scott St., Suva, tel. 679/331-0526
- **Japan:** 1-11-44 Minami-Azabu, Minato-ku, Tokyo 106-8514, tel. 03/5798-6000; 8 Izumidono-cho, Yoshida Sakyo-ku, Kyoto 606-8301, tel. 075/761-2988
- **New Zealand:** Rural Bank Bldg., 13th floor, 34/42 Manners St., Wellington, tel. 04/384-2579
- **Singapore:** 101/103 Cluny Park Rd., Singapore 259595, tel. 65/6880-7800
- **United States:** French consulates general exist in Atlanta, Boston, Chicago, Houston, Los Angeles, Miami, New Orleans, New York, San Francisco, and Washington. To get the address of the one nearest you, visit www.info-france-usa.org.

ticket to leave French Polynesia and provide one photo. The two immigration offices are in Papeete. People from countries outside the European Union are limited to three months total; if you know you'll be staying longer than a month, it's much better to get a three-month visa at a French consulate before arrival, making this formality unnecessary.

French Polynesia requires an onward or return ticket of everyone (including nonresident French citizens). Although the immigration officials don't always check it, the airlines usually do. If you happen to arrive without one, you could be refused entry or required to post a cash bond equivalent to the value of a full-fare ticket back to your home country. To avoid problems along the way, make sure the name on your passport is the same as the name on your plane ticket (no nicknames or married names).

If you hold a passport from a country other than Canada or the United States and will be passing through Los Angeles on your way to Tahiti, you must visit the Electronic System for Travel Authorization website at https://esta.cbp.dhs.gov not less than 72 hours prior to departure to complete an online application form requesting authorization to transit the United States. This applies even if you will not be leaving the airport.

Yacht Entry

The main port of entry for cruising yachts is Papeete. Upon application to the local gendarmerie, entry may also be allowed at Bora Bora, Hiva Oa, Huahine, Mangareva, Moorea, Nuku Hiva, Raiatea, Raivavae, Rangiroa, Rurutu, Tubuai, and Ua Pou. Have an accurate inventory list for your vessel ready. It's also best to have a French courtesy flag with you, as they're not always available in places such as the Marquesas. Even after clearance, you must continue to report your arrival at each respective office every time you visit any of the islands just mentioned. The well-paid gendarmes are usually friendly and courteous if you are. Boats arriving from Tonga, Fiji, and the Samoas must be fumigated (also those which have called at ports in Central or South America during the previous 21 days).

Anyone arriving by yacht without an onward ticket must post a bond or *caution* at a local bank equivalent to the airfare back to his or her country of origin. This is refundable upon departure at any Banque Socredo branch, less a 3 percent administrative fee. Make sure the receipt shows the currency in which the original deposit was made and get an assurance that it will be refunded in kind. To reclaim the bond you'll need a letter from Immigration verifying that you've been officially checked out. If any individual on the yacht doesn't have the bond money, the captain is responsible. The bond can be charged to a credit card.

Once the bond is posted, a "temporary" three-month visa (CFP 3,500) is issued. The French authorities sometimes refuse extensions beyond the initial three months, so ask about this while checking in. Boats can be left at Raiatea Carenage if you have to leave temporarily, but yachts staying in French Polynesia longer than a total of one year in any two-year period are charged full customs duty on the vessel. Failure to comply can result in confiscation of the boat until any outstanding fees are paid. Actually, the rules are not hard and fast, and everyone has a different experience. Crew changes should be made at Papeete. Visiting yachts cannot be chartered to third parties without permission.

After clearing customs in Papeete, outbound yachts may spend the duration of their period of stay cruising the outer islands. Make sure every island where you *might* stop is listed on your clearance. You may buy duty-free fuel immediately after clearance. The officials want all transient boats out of the country by October 31, the onset of the hurricane season.

GETTING MARRIED IN FRENCH POLYNESIA

In 2009 French laws were changed to allow nonresident foreigners the possibility of getting legally married in French Polynesia without the former 30-day residency waiting period. It's now possible to arrange a binding Polynesian wedding provided both parties are 18 or older, not already married, not closely related, of different sexes, and not of French nationality or a resident of a French jurisdiction. Both parties must be present at the ceremony and each must have a witness over 18 years of age. An interpreter must be present.

The couple must submit a number of legal documents to the communal authorities at least one month and 10 days prior to the ceremony. These include a written request signed by both parties, an application form, passport and birth certificate copies, the death certificate of any previous spouse, proof of residence, and a copy of any prenuptial agreement. French translations of these documents may be required, and a personal interview at a French consulate can be requested at the discretion of the mayor.

Marriages cannot take place on Sundays or public holidays. After the ceremony the couple will receive a French Family Record Book *(Livret de Famille)* for which a charge may apply. The couple will be responsible for registering the marriage in their own country, if necessary.

These requirements may appear onerous, but most resorts in French Polynesia will gladly assist in making all the arrangements, for a price. Those interested should contact their resort of choice and the Tahiti Tourisme office in their country of residence for advice on how to get started. Additional information is at www.tahiti-tourisme.com/weddings.

Accommodations

Hotel prices range from CFP 1,200 for a dormitory bed all the way up to CFP 449,000 double (3,762 euros) plus 14 percent tax for a royal villa at Bora Bora. Price wars sometimes erupt between rival resorts, and at times you'll be charged less than the prices quoted in this guide. At the luxury hotels, always check their websites for specials before booking. If your hotel can't provide running water, electricity, air-conditioning, or something similar because of a hurricane or otherwise, ask for a price reduction. You might get 10 percent off.

The 14 percent hotel tax consists of a 5 percent room tax used to finance "tourism promotions," the 5 percent value added tax (VAT), and a 4 percent service charge. This 14 percent tax is on top of the rack room rates at "classified hotels" (seldom included in the quoted price), and some hotels such as the Four Seasons Bora Bora add an additional 6 percent "resort fee" to these charges. The 5 percent tourist development tax and 4 percent service charge don't apply to pensions and small family-operated accommodations, but they must still collect the 5 percent VAT on accommodations (often included in the basic rate). Most municipalities in the Society Islands add a *taxe de séjour* (sojourn tax) to accommodation bills to cover municipal services. This varies from CFP 150 per person per day at the large hotels to CFP 50 at the pensions, and it's almost always charged extra.

Be aware that most large hotels tack a CFP 1,000 or 10 percent commission onto any rental cars, lagoon excursions, and scuba diving booked through their front desks. Many small hotels add a surcharge to your bill if you stay only one night, and some charge a supplement during the high seasons (June–Oct. and mid-Dec.–mid-Jan.). Discounts may be offered during the low months of February–March.

A wise government regulation prohibiting buildings higher than a coconut tree outside Papeete means that many of the hotels are low-rise affairs or consist of small Tahitian *fare.*

ACCOMMODATIONS PRICE RANGES

Throughout this guide, accommodations are generally grouped in the price categories that follow. In French Polynesia many pensions have a compulsory meal plan, and to determine the category at these, the food portion has been valued at CFP 6,000/8,000 for half/full board in a double room. The exchange rate employed below is only indicative.

- US$25-50 CFP 2,000-4,000
- US$50-100 CFP 4,000-8,000
- US$100-150 CFP 8,000-12,000
- US$150-250 CFP 12,000-20,000
- US$250 and up CFP 20,000 and up

A room with cooking facilities can save you a lot on restaurant meals. Resort meal plans are often grossly overpriced and can be dispensed with entirely if you're staying somewhere with nonhotel restaurants nearby. At CFP 3,000 per person, deluxe hotel breakfasts are a rip-off. Even at isolated offshore resorts, you can often avoid them by ordering breakfast from room service rather than taking the pricey buffet. If you have to choose a meal plan, take only breakfast and dinner (Modified American Plan, or *demi-pension*) and have fruit for lunch.

When selecting a hotel, bear in mind that although a thatched bungalow may be cooler and infinitely more attractive than a concrete box, it's also more likely to have insect problems. If in doubt, check the window screens and carry mosquito coils and/or repellent. If you're lucky, there'll be a resident lizard or two to eat the bugs. Always turn on a light before getting out of bed to use the facilities at night, as even the finest hotels in the tropics have cockroaches.

As you check into your room, note the nearest fire exits. And don't automatically take the first room offered; if you're paying good money, look at several, then choose. Needless to say, always ask the price of your accommodations before accepting them. In cases where there's a local and a tourist price, you'll pay the higher tariff if you don't check beforehand.

Hotel Chains

Of the large hotels, Sofitel, InterContinental, and Le Méridien are represented on several islands. Amanresorts and Orient Express each have one upscale property on Bora Bora. In 2009 the former Sheraton resorts on Moorea and Bora Bora owned by local businessman Louis Wane began using the Hilton name, although they're actually managed by a local company.

French Polynesia's homegrown hotel chain, Pearl Resorts (www.pearlresorts.com), offers nine tasteful hotels in the top-end price range. Most of the Pearl Resorts properties are owned by Air Tahiti, Banque Socredo, and other local investors. Another local company, Pacific Beachcomber SA, owns the four InterContinental resorts plus the 330-passenger cruise ship *Paul Gauguin*.

We don't solicit freebies from the hotel chains; our only income derives from the price you paid for this guide. So we don't mind telling you that most of these luxury hotels are just not worth the exorbitant prices they charge. Many simply recreate Hawaii at several times the cost, offering far more luxury than you need. Even worse, they tend to isolate you in a French or American environment, away from the South Pacific you came to experience. The flashy resorts are worth visiting as sightseeing attractions, watering holes, or sources of entertainment, but unless you're a millionaire, sleep elsewhere. There are always middle-level hotels that charge half what the top-end places want while providing adequate comfort. And if you really *can* afford US$800 per night and up, you might do better chartering a skippered or bareboat yacht.

Over-Water Bungalows

The over-water bungalow was invented in

thatched over-water bungalows at the Moorea Pearl Resort, part of French Polynesia's homegrown hotel chain

French Polynesia in the 1960s, and you'll now find them on Tahiti, Moorea, Huahine, Raiatea, Taha'a, Bora Bora, Rangiroa, Tikehau, and Manihi. They range in price from CFP 18,000 double plus tax at Club Bali Hai on Moorea to CFP 284,600 at the Hilton Bora Bora Nui Resort.

There's little doubt that this type of accommodation is environmentally harmful. The coral formations are inevitably affected during construction, and unconcerned guests do further damage by touching the living corals while snorkeling around their rooms. Much of the coral near the existing bungalows is dead, and fish are present only because they are fed. We've even heard reports of improper sewage disposal at over-water bungalows.

The lagoons of French Polynesia are in the public domain, and the resort owners are clearly profiting by using them as building sites. To boot, some resorts have employed huge dredges to suck sand from the lagoon floors for the construction of artificial beaches, thereby destroying the spawning areas of fishes and further damaging the coral.

Pensions

A unique accommodation option is the well-established network of homestays, in which you get a private room or bungalow provided by a local family. *Logement chez l'habitant* is available on all the outer islands, and even in Papeete itself. The main clientele of these establishments is local residents and Europeans, but they're an excellent alternative to the large hotels for all but the most demanding tourist.

Most travel agents abroad won't book the pensions or lodgings with the inhabitants because no commissions are paid, but you can make reservations directly with the owners themselves either by email or by phone. Calling ahead works best, as not all pensions have email, and even those that do are often unprepared to respond to messages in English.

One Papeete travel agency specializing in such bookings is **Tekura Tahiti Travel** (www.tahiti-tekuratravel.com), on rue Jaussen behind the cathedral, although it tends to work with the more upmarket places. Air Tahiti's "Séjours dans les îles" packages (www.islandsadventures.com) are built largely around pensions, and their website provides photos and much useful information. Most pensions don't accept credit cards, even if their website or brochure says they will. Many have a two-night minimum stay or charge extra if you leave after one night. Refunds may not be given if you discover upon arrival that you don't like a pension and decide to check out early. English may not be spoken.

These private bed-and-breakfast–style guesthouses can be hard to locate. There's usually no sign outside, and some don't cater to walk-in clients who show up unexpectedly. Also, the limited number of beds in each may be taken (most pensions have less than 10 rooms). Sometimes you'll get airport transfers at no additional charge if you book ahead. Other times you'll be charged for a short transfer you could easily have covered on foot.

Conditions at the pensions vary a lot. Blankets and especially towels may not be provided, and the room won't be cleaned every day. Don't expect hot water in the shower or a lot of privacy. Mosquitoes are a problem almost everywhere, and you should arrive armed with repellent and coils. Be prepared for rooster noise in the middle of the night. You're often required to take meals (typically fish and root vegetables), often because there are no other eating options, and this can make these places pricey. If you're on a tight budget or don't like fish, look for a place with cooking facilities and prepare your own food. Many pensions provide free drinking water, while others have only expensive bottled water. The family may lend or rent you a bicycle and can be generally helpful in arranging tours, etc. It's a great way to meet the people while finding a place to stay for much less than you'd pay at an international resort.

Backpacker Accommodations

French Polynesia is one of the few South Pacific destinations where camping is a practical option and a tent can prove very convenient to fall back on. Regular campgrounds exist on

Moorea, Huahine, Raiatea, and Bora Bora. On Rangiroa it's possible to camp at certain small hotels (listed in this guide). On the outer islands camping should be no problem, but ask permission of the landowner, or pitch your tent well out of sight of the road. Ensure this hospitality for the next traveler by not leaving a mess. Make sure your tent is water- and mosquito-proof, and try to find a spot swept by the trades. Never camp under a coconut tree, as falling coconuts hurt (actually, coconuts have two eyes, so they strike only the wicked).

Dormitory accommodations are available on many of the main islands, with communal cooking facilities usually provided. If you're traveling alone, these are excellent since you get to meet other travelers. Couples can usually get a double room for a price only slightly above two dorm beds. The dormitories are safe enough if you take standard precautions with your valuables. Far fewer backpackers tour French Polynesia than was the case a decade ago, and many of those you meet now at the cheaper places are "flashpackers" who don't mind spending large sums on scuba diving and similar activities while cutting corners on accommodations.

Reserving Rooms

Booking accommodations from abroad often works to your disadvantage because full-service travel agents will begin by trying to sell you their most expensive properties (which pay them the highest commissions) and work down from there. The quite-adequate middle and budget places included in this guide often aren't on their screens or are sold at highly inflated prices. We provide the rates here for direct local bookings, and if you book through a travel agent abroad, you could end up paying considerably more as multiple commissions are tacked on. Nowadays the Internet has made booking direct infinitely easier. Most medium and all upscale hotels now accept Internet and email bookings at normal or even sharply reduced rates.

Although it's usually not to your advantage to reserve rooms in the lowest price range, you can often obtain substantial discounts at the luxury hotels by including them as part of a package tour. At places like the Hôtel Hilton Moorea Lagoon, guests on prepaid packages may have been charged less than half of the accommodations price quoted in this guide. Thus if you intend to spend most of your time at a specific first-class hotel, you'll benefit from bulk rates by taking a package tour instead of paying the higher "rack rate" that the hotels charge to individuals who just walk in off the street.

Food

Restaurant meals are subject to a 10 percent value added tax (VAT) and four percent service charge. These fees are usually included in the menu price, although resort restaurants often add them on later. The restaurants are often exorbitant, but you can bring the price down by ordering only a single main dish. Fresh bread should come with the meal. Avoid appetizers, alcohol, and desserts. No service charges are tacked on, and tipping is unnecessary, so it's not as expensive as it looks. US$25 will usually see you through an excellent no-frills lunch of fried fish at a small French restaurant. The same thing in a deluxe hotel dining room will be about 50 percent more. Even the finest places are affordable if you order this way.

Some restaurants post the menu in the window, but most do not. In that case, have a look at it before sitting down. Check the main plates, as that's all you'll need to take. If the price is right, the ambience congenial, and local French are at the tables, sit right down. Sure, food at a snack bar would be half as much, but your Coke will be extra, and in the end it's smart to pay a little more to enjoy excellent cuisine once in a while. A large plastic bottle

THE POLYNESIAN PALATE

The traditional diet of the Pacific Islanders consists of root crops and fruit, plus lagoon fish and the occasional pig. The vegetables include taro, yams, cassava (manioc), breadfruit, and sweet potatoes. The sweet potato is something of an anomaly – it's the only Pacific food plant with a South American origin. How it got to the islands is not known.

Taro is an elephant-eared plant cultivated in freshwater swamps. Papaya (pawpaw) is nourishing: One-third of a cup contains as much vitamin C as 18 apples. To ripen a green papaya overnight, puncture it a few times with a knife. Don't overeat papaya – unless you *need* an effective laxative.

Raw fish (*poisson cru* or *ia ota*) is an appetizing dish enjoyed in many Pacific countries. To prepare it, clean and skin the fish, then dice the fillet. Squeeze lemon or lime juice over it, and store in a cool place about 10 hours. When it's ready to serve, add chopped onions, garlic, green peppers, tomatoes, and coconut cream to taste. Local fishmongers know which species make the best raw fish, but know what you're doing before you join them – island stomachs are probably stronger than yours. Cautious health experts recommend eating only well-cooked foods and peeling your own fruit, but the islanders swear by raw fish.

of Eau Royale mineral water will add CFP 300 to your bill, but in Papeete you can ask for free *eau ordinaire* (tap water). Elsewhere you may be told it's not potable. Beware of set meals designed for tourists, as these usually cost double the average entrée. If you can't order à la carte, walk back out the door.

Local restaurants offer French, Chinese, Vietnamese, Italian, and, of course, Tahitian dishes. The *nouvelle cuisine Tahitienne* is a combination of European and Asian recipes, with local seafood and vegetables, plus the classic *ma'a Tahiti* (Tahitian food). The French are famous for their sauces, so try something exotic. Lunch is the main meal of the day in French Polynesia, and many restaurants offer a plat du jour designed for regular customers. This is often displayed on a blackboard near the entrance and is usually good value. Most restaurants serve lunch 1130–1400 and dinner 1800–2100. Don't expect snappy service.

If it's all too expensive, groceries are a good alternative. There are lots of nice places to picnic, and at CFP 50 a loaf, that crisp French white bread is incredibly cheap and good. French *baguettes* are subsidized by the government, unlike that awful sliced white bread in a plastic package, which is CFP 430 per loaf! Cheap red wines such as Selection Faragui are imported from France in bulk and bottled locally in plastic bottles. Add a nice piece of French cheese and you're ready for a budget traveler's banquet. *Casse-croûtes* are big healthy sandwiches made with those long French baguettes, and at about CFP 300 they're a rare bargain.

There's also Martinique rum and Hinano beer (CFP 200 in grocery stores), brewed locally by the Brasserie de Tahiti. Founded in 1914, this company's first beer was called Aorai, and today it produces Heineken as well as Hinano. Remember the deposit on Hinano beer bottles (CFP 60 on large bottles), which makes beer cheap to buy cold and carry out. Supermarkets aren't allowed to sell alcohol after 1000 on Sundays or holidays (stock your fridge on Saturday).

The *maitai* is a cocktail made with rum, liqueur, and fruit juice. Moorea's famous Rotui fruit drinks are sold in tall liter containers in a variety of types. The tastiest is perhaps *pamplemousse* (grapefruit), produced from local Moorea fruit, but the pineapple juice is also outstanding. At about CFP 262 a carton, they're excellent value. Also watch for the Sun Wave fruit drinks at CFP 180 for a one-liter carton in grocery stores. At CFP 110 in supermarkets, bottled Eau Royale mineral water is also quite cheap (the tap water isn't safe outside Papeete and Bora Bora).

If you're going to the outer islands, take as many edibles with you as possible; it's always more expensive there. Keep in mind that virtually every food plant you see growing on the islands is cultivated by someone. Even fishing floats or seashells washed up on a beach, or fish in the lagoon near someone's home, may be considered private property.

Tahitian Specialties

If you can spare the cash, attend a Tahitian *tamaaraa* (feast) at a big hotel and try some Polynesian specialties roasted in an *ahimaa* (underground oven). Basalt stones are preheated with a wood fire in a meter-deep pit, and then covered with leaves. Each type of food is wrapped separately in banana leaves to retain its own flavor and then lowered in. The oven is then covered with more banana leaves, wet sacking, and sand, and left 1–3 hours to bake: suckling pig, mahimahi, taro, *umara* (sweet potato), *uru* (breadfruit), and *fafa* (a spinach-like cooked vegetable made from taro tops).

Also sample the gamy flavor of *fei,* the red cooking banana that flourishes in Tahiti's uninhabited interior. The Tahitian chestnut tree *(mape)* grows near streams, and you can often buy the delicious cooked nuts at markets. *Miti hue* is a coconut-milk sauce fermented with the juice of river shrimp. Traditionally *ma'a Tahiti* is eaten with the fingers.

Poisson cru (ia ota), small pieces of raw bonito (skipjack) or yellowfin tuna marinated with lime juice and soaked in coconut milk, is enjoyable, as is *fafaru* ("smelly fish"), prepared by marinating pieces of fish in seawater in an airtight coconut-shell container. As with the durian, although the smell is repugnant, the first bite can be addicting. Other typical Tahitian plates are chicken and pork casserole with *fafa,* pork and cabbage casserole *(pua'a chou),* and goat cooked in ginger.

Po'e is a sticky sweet pudding made of starchy banana, papaya, taro, or pumpkin flour, flavored with vanilla and topped with

fruit display

coconut-milk sauce. Many varieties of this treat are made throughout Polynesia. *Faraoa ipo* is Tuamotu coconut bread. The local coffee is flavored with vanilla bean and served with sugar and coconut cream.

Polynesian Cooking

The ancient Polynesians lost the art of pottery making more than a millennium ago and instead developed an ingenious way of cooking in an underground earth oven known as an *ahimaa*. First, a stack of dry coconut husks is burned in a pit. Once the fire is going well, coral stones are heaped on top, and when most of the husks have burned away, the food is wrapped in banana leaves and placed on the hot stones—fish and meat below, vegetables above. A whole pig may be cleaned and then stuffed with banana leaves and hot stones. This cooks the beast from inside out as well as outside in, and the leaves create steam. The food is then covered with more leaves and stones, and after about 2.5 hours everything is cooked. Many resorts stage an island night when this fare is served to the accompaniment of Polynesian dancing.

Conduct and Customs

Foreign travel is an exceptional experience enjoyed by a privileged few. Too often, tourists try to transfer their lifestyles to tropical islands, thereby missing out on what is unique to the region. Travel can be a learning experience if approached openly and with a positive attitude, so read up on the local culture before you arrive, and become aware of the social and environmental problems of the area. A wise traveler soon graduates from hearing and seeing to listening and observing. It's not for nothing that we have two eyes but only one mouth.

The path is primed with packaged pleasures, but pierce the bubble of tourism and you'll encounter something far from the schedules and organized efficiency: a time to learn how other people live. Walk gently, for human qualities are as fragile and responsive to abuse as the brilliant reefs. The islanders are by nature softspoken and reserved. Consider that you're only one of thousands of visitors to their islands, so don't expect to be treated better than anyone else. Respect is one of the most important things in life and humility is also greatly appreciated.

Keep your time values to yourself; the islanders lead an unstressful lifestyle and assume you are there to share it.

This is no tourist's paradise, and local residents are not exhibits or paid performers. They have just as many problems as you, and if you see them as real people, you're less likely to be viewed as a stereotypical tourist. You may have come to escape civilization, but keep in mind that you're just a guest.

Most important of all, try to see things their way. Take an interest in local customs, values, languages, challenges, and successes. If things work differently than they do back home, give thanks—that's why you've come. Reflect on what you've experienced and you'll return home with a better understanding of how much we all have in common, outwardly different as we may seem. Do that and your trip won't have been wasted.

Dress

The dress code in French Polynesia is very casual—you can even go around barefoot. Cleanliness *is* important, however. Formal wear or jacket and tie are unnecessary (unless you're to be received by the high commissioner). One exception is downtown Papeete, where scanty dress would be out of place.

People usually shake hands when meeting; visitors are expected to shake hands with everyone present. If a Polynesian man's hand is dirty, he'll extend his wrist or elbow. Women kiss each other on the cheeks. When entering a private residence it's polite to remove your shoes.

All the beaches of French Polynesia are public to one meter above the high-tide mark, although some trained guard dogs don't recognize this. Topless sunbathing is legal in French Polynesia and commonly practiced at resorts by European tourists, though total nudity is permissible only on offshore *motu* and floating pontoons. Some resorts have a policy that female guests are welcome to practice topless sunbathing outside their bungalows or on the beach but not at the resort swimming pool.

Tips for Travelers

RESIDENCE AND EMPLOYMENT OPPORTUNITIES

Tourists are prohibited from accepting paid employment in French Polynesia. Work and residence permits are difficult to obtain and can take several months to process. Applications for residence permits must be sent to the French consular office in the country of origin. An employer can request a work permit for a foreign employee through the Service de l'Emploi in Papeete. The Service des Affairs Administratives in Papeete needs 2–4 months to process applications to establish professional practices in French Polynesia. Information on the formalities involved in acquiring a residence permit and the taxes to be paid is available on the website of the Investment Promotion Authority (www.tahiti-invest.com).

OPPORTUNITIES FOR STUDY

International students are accepted at the Université de la Polynésie Française (www.upf.pf). Individuals must apply through the cultural section of the French Embassy in their home country November 15–January 15. Some foreign universities have student exchange programs with the UPF. In all cases, academic transcripts and a good knowledge of French will be required. Once a student has been accepted, a long-term visa must be obtained from a French consulate.

The most common form of study practiced by visitors (including children) is scuba-diving training. Most resort dive shops offer three-day CMAS, NAUI, or PADI open water certification courses at around CFP 45,000 per person. The programs combine theory with practice sessions in a swimming pool and the ocean. Numerous advanced courses are also available, and there are introductory resort courses to those who only want a taste of scuba diving. If you take a scuba certification course, make sure it's PADI accredited, as the French CMAS certification may not be recognized elsewhere. Of course, no special visas are required for this type of study, but you may be asked to show a medical certificate. Scuba training will enhance your understanding and enjoyment of the sea.

TRAVELERS WITH DISABILITIES

French disability rights legislation has not been fully implemented in French Polynesia, and very few facilities are provided for travelers with disabilities. The top resorts generally have a couple of rooms equipped for disabled guests. For example, the 270-room InterContinental Resort Tahiti has two garden rooms adapted for the disabled, with the resort's restaurants, bars, and swimming pools accessible by elevator. The InterContinental Resort Moorea is similar, and the Sofitel and Hilton resorts on Moorea each have two or three disabled-friendly rooms. The disabled are also catered for at the Sofitel and Hilton Bora Bora Nui on Bora Bora. Needless to say, these rooms are often in high demand and must be reserved well in advance. You should also mention any special needs to your airline when booking. Most public transportation in French Polynesia is not wheelchair-friendly.

TRAVELING WITH CHILDREN

Unlike Fiji and the Cook Islands, there are no strictly "adults only" resorts in French Polynesia, and families with small children are welcome almost everywhere. Many upscale resorts provide free accommodations for children as long as they're sharing a room with their parents. The Le Méridien, Radisson, and Pearl resorts offer free accommodations for children under 16 years old and give kids 50 percent off their meals. The InterContinental Resort Tahiti, InterContinental Resort Moorea, and InterContinental Le Moana Resort Bora Bora all accommodate children under 15 for free and provide meals for children under 12 at half price. On Moorea, Hotel Residence Les Tipaniers on Moorea has thatched bungalows with cooking facilities that are ideal for families, and children under 10 stay free. On Raiatea, the Sunset Beach Motel charges children under 13 only CFP 500 each. The Sofitel chain allows children under 12 to share their parent's room for free and provides a 50 percent discount on their meals. Pearl Resorts provides a cartoon TV channel and DVDs for kids.

Babies under the age of two are seldom charged for anything, although most of the cheaper accommodations do not supply a baby cot. Take along a tent-like baby travel cot if this might affect you. Also, very few restaurants have high chairs for children, and a small travel high chair that can be attached to restaurant tables will come in handy. Similarly, life vests for infants are generally not supplied during boat transfers or on nautical tours, and it would be a good idea to bring your own.

Air Tahiti's family reduction cards (CFP 2,000) provide a potential 50 percent reduction for the parents and 75 percent off for children under 12. Identification and one photo are required. The full discount is given only on off-peak flights. This *cartes de réduction* must be purchased at Air Tahiti's downtown Papeete office, not at the airport office.

WOMEN TRAVELING ALONE

Despite the laissez-faire attitude promoted in the travel brochures, female travelers should take care: There have been sexual assaults on foreign women by Polynesian men. In many Polynesian cultures there's a custom known as "sleep crawling," in which a boy silently enters a girl's home at night and lies beside her to prove his bravery. Visiting women sometimes become objects of this type of unwanted attention, even in well-known resorts such as on Bora Bora and Moorea. Women should avoid staying alone in isolated tourist bungalows or camping outside organized campgrounds.

In many traditional island cultures a woman seen wandering aimlessly along a remote beach was thought to be in search of male companionship, and "no" meant "yes." Single women hiking, camping, sunbathing, and simply traveling alone may be seen in the same light, an impression strongly reinforced by the type of videos available in the islands. Two women together will have less to worry about, especially if they're well covered and look purposeful. Peeping Toms can be a nuisance in both budget accommodations and on beaches away from the main resorts.

GAY AND LESBIAN TRAVELERS

Homosexuality is legal and accepted in French Polynesia, and gay and lesbian visitors do not need to behave any differently here than they would at home. Homophobia is rare. On Moorea, Tiki Theater Village offers nonbinding marriage ceremonies for same sex couples. A well-known gay venue in Papeete is the Tiki Soft Café, on rue des Remparts, especially Fridays after 1700.

WHAT TO TAKE

For maximum mobility, bring only a small wheeled suitcase or a soft medium-size backpack with an internal frame. Try to keep your weight (bag and contents) down to 20 kilograms, or 10 kilograms if you plan to use interisland flights and haven't booked ahead. For clothing, take loose-fitting cotton washables, light in color and weight, for the humid tropical climate. Dress is casual in the islands. The pareu (par-RAY-o) is a bright two-meter piece of cloth that serves as an all-purpose wrap garment for both men and women. They're widely sold in the islands, so you can easily pick one up. Stick to clothes you can rinse in your room sink, and don't bring more than two outfits. If you'll be taking a cruise or traveling by boat, a light sweater or windbreaker may come in handy, as it can be cool at night. You'll also need a sun hat or visor, and maybe a small umbrella.

A mask and snorkel are essential equipment—you'll be missing half of French Polynesia's beauty without them. Reef shoes can also be very handy. The waters are warm, varying less than 1°C between the surface and 100 meters, so a wetsuit is not essential for scuba divers (although it will protect you from coral cuts). Some dive shops tack on an extra US$10 or more for "equipment rental" (regulator, buoyancy compensator, and gauges) and serious divers will want to bring their own gear.

If you bring a tent, don't bother bringing a foam pad, as the ground is rarely cold here. You'll seldom need a sleeping bag in the tropics, so that's another item you can easily cut. Other things to consider taking include a small portable radio, a compass, a pocket flashlight, a plastic cup, a can and bottle opener, a spoon, and a water bottle. Also bring adequate reading material, as very little is available in English here. It's nice to have along postcards from your hometown and snapshots of your family to use as conversation pieces.

Bring an adequate supply of any personal medications, plus your prescriptions (in generic terminology). Aside from the obvious toiletries, you might want to bring wax earplugs, insect repellent, sunscreen, lip balm, a motion-sickness remedy, a diarrhea remedy, a cold remedy, Alka-Seltzer, aspirin, antibacterial ointment, and antiseptic cream. Baby powder prevents and treats prickly heat rash.

Everyone needs a passport to enter French Polynesia, but don't bother getting an international driver's license; your regular license is all you need to drive here. Traveler's checks are recommended, and in French Polynesia, American Express is the most efficient company when it comes to providing refunds for lost checks. The best plastic to have is Visa and MasterCard. Be aware, French Polynesia's ATMs are not entirely reliable.

Carry your valuables in a money belt worn around your waist or neck under your clothing; most camping stores have these. Make several photocopies of the information page of your passport, personal identification, driver's license, scuba certification card, credit cards, airline tickets, receipts for purchase of travelers checks, etc.—you should be able to get them all on both sides of one sheet. On the side of the photocopies, write the phone numbers you'd need to call to report lost documents.

The digital revolution has made bulky film cameras a thing of the past. The memory cards of digital cameras are unaffected by airport X-ray machines and you can use them over and over again. Camera stores in Papeete and some other towns can burn your photos onto CDs, although it's much easier to simply carry a couple of spare memory cards. You'll need a 240-volt-compatible battery charger, plus an adapter with two circular pins. A spare battery could come in handy if you'll be staying somewhere without easily accessible electrical plugs.

Health and Safety

For a tropical area, French Polynesia is a healthy place. The sea and air are clear and usually pollution-free. The humidity nourishes the skin, and the local fruit is brimming with vitamins. If you take a few precautions, you'll never have a sick day. Malaria and cholera don't exist here. The information provided below is intended to make you knowledgeable, not fearful. If you have access to the Internet, check wwwnc.cdc.gov/travel for up-to-the-minute information.

Public hospitals are found in Papeete (Tahiti), Taravao (Tahiti), Afareaitu (Moorea), Uturoa (Raiatea), Mataura (Tubuai), Taiohae (Nuku Hiva), and Atuona (Hiva Oa). Other islands have only infirmaries or dispensaries. Private clinics are found throughout the Society Islands, but there are none in the eastern outer islands (over there, ask for the *infirmerie*).

The government-run medical facilities typically provide subsidized medical treatment to local residents but have much higher rates for foreigners. It's usually no more expensive to visit a private doctor or clinic, and often it's actually cheaper. Private doctors can afford to provide faster service because everyone is paying, and we've tried to list local doctors and dentists throughout this guide. In emergencies and outside clinic hours, you can always turn to the government-run facilities.

American-made medications may by unobtainable in the islands, so bring along a supply of whatever you think you'll need. If you have to replace anything, quote the generic name at the pharmacy rather than the brand name. Otherwise go to any Chinese general store and ask the owner to recommend a good Chinese patent medicine for what ails you. The cost will be a third of what European medicines or herbs cost, and the Chinese medicine is often as effective or more so. You should be aware that French Polynesia has one of the highest HIV infection rates in the South Pacific, partly due to the transient military population in Papeete.

Travel Insurance

Medical costs in French Polynesia are rather high although still lower than those in North America. If you have a serious accident, travel insurance could save you from having to pay a stiff bill. Check to see if your regular group health insurance covers you while you're traveling abroad. Some travel policies pay only the amount above and beyond what your national or group health insurance will pay and are invalid if you don't have any health insurance at all.

If you decide to buy travel insurance, make sure emergency medical evacuations are covered. Some policies are invalid if you engage in any "dangerous activities," such as scuba diving, parasailing, surfing, or even riding a motor scooter, so be sure to read the fine print. Scuba divers should know that there's a large recompression chamber *(caisson hyperbare)* at the Centre Hospitalier in Papeete, but an emergency medical evacuation will still be costly, and there isn't any point buying a policy that doesn't cover it. Medical insurance especially designed for scuba divers is available from **Divers Alert Network** (6 W. Colony Pl., Durham, NC 27705, USA, tel. 919/684-2948 or 800/446-2671, www.diversalertnetwork.org).

Some companies will pay your bills directly while others require you to pay and collect receipts that may be reimbursed later. Ask if travel delays, lost baggage, and theft are included. Theft insurance never covers items left on the beach while you're swimming. All this said, you should weigh the advantages and decide for yourself if you want a policy. Just don't be influenced by what your travel agent says, as he or she will only want to sell you coverage in order to earn another commission. An annual plan purchased through your bank or automobile club may work out better.

Acclimatizing

Don't go from winter weather into the steaming tropics without a rest before and after.

Minimize jet lag by setting your watch to local time at your destination as soon as you board the aircraft. Westbound flights into the South Pacific from North America or Europe are less jolting since you follow the sun and your body gets a few hours of extra sleep. On the way home you're moving against the sun and the hours of sleep your body loses cause jet lag. Airplane cabins have low humidity, so drink lots of juice or water instead of carbonated drinks, and don't overeat in-flight. It's also wise to forgo coffee, as it will only keep you awake, and alcohol, which will dehydrate you.

Scuba diving on departure day can give you a severe case of the bends. Before flying there should be a minimum of 12 hours' surface interval after a no-decompression dive and a minimum of 24 hours after a decompression dive. Factors contributing to decompression sickness include a lack of sleep or the excessive consumption of alcohol before diving.

If you start feeling seasick onboard a ship, stare at the horizon, which is always steady, and stop thinking about it. Anti–motion sickness pills are useful to have along; otherwise, ginger helps alleviate seasickness. Travel stores sell Acubands that find a pressure point on the wrist and create a stable flow of blood to the head, thus miraculously preventing seasickness.

The tap water is safe to drink in downtown Papeete and on Bora Bora, but ask first elsewhere. If in doubt, boil it or use purification pills. Tap water that is uncomfortably hot to touch is usually safe. Allow it to cool in a clean container. Bottled mineral water is cheap at supermarkets. Don't forget that if the tap water is contaminated, the local ice will be too. Avoid brushing your teeth with water unfit to drink, and wash or peel fruit and vegetables if you can. Cooked food is less subject to contamination than raw.

Sunburn

Though you may think a tan will make you look healthier and more attractive, it's actually very damaging to the skin, which becomes dry, rigid, and prematurely old and wrinkled, especially on the face. Begin with short exposures to the sun, perhaps half an hour at a time, followed by an equal time in the shade. Avoid the sun 1000–1500, the most dangerous time. Clouds and beach umbrellas will not protect you fully. Wear a T-shirt while snorkeling to protect your back. Drink plenty of liquids to keep your pores open. Sunbathing is the main cause of cataracts to the eyes, so wear sunglasses and a wide-brimmed hat, and beware of reflected sunlight.

Use a sunscreen lotion containing PABA rather than oil, and don't forget to apply it to your nose, lips, forehead, neck, hands, and feet. Sunscreens protect you from ultraviolet rays (a leading cause of cancer), while oils magnify the sun's effect. A 15-factor sunscreen provides 93 percent protection (a more expensive 30-factor sunscreen is only slightly better at 97 percent protection). Apply the lotion *before* going to the beach to avoid being burned on the way, and reapply every couple of hours to replace sunscreen washed away by perspiration. Swimming also washes away your protection. After sunbathing take a tepid shower rather than a hot one, which would wash away your natural skin oils. Stay moist and use a vitamin E evening cream to preserve the youth of your skin. Calamine ointment soothes skin already burned, as does coconut oil. Pharmacists recommend Solarcaine to soothe burned skin. Rinsing off with a vinegar solution reduces peeling, and aspirin relieves some of the pain and irritation. Vitamin A and calcium counteract overdoses of vitamin D received from the sun. The fairer your skin, the more essential it is to take care.

As earth's ozone layer is depleted through the commercial use of chlorofluorocarbons (CFCs) and other factors, the need to protect oneself from ultraviolet radiation is becoming more urgent. Deaths from skin cancer are on the increase. Previously the cancers didn't develop until age 50 or 60, but now much younger people are affected.

Ailments

Cuts and scratches infect easily in the tropics

and take a long time to heal. Prevent infection from coral cuts by immediately washing wounds with soap and fresh water, then rubbing in vinegar, lemon juice, or alcohol (whiskey will do)—it's painful but effective. Use an antiseptic such as hydrogen peroxide and an antibacterial ointment such as Neosporin if you have them. Islanders usually dab coral cuts with lime juice. All cuts turn septic quickly in the tropics, so try to keep them clean and covered.

For bites, burns, and cuts, an antiseptic such as Solarcaine speeds healing and helps prevent infection. Pure aloe vera is good for sunburn, scratches, and even coral cuts. Bites by *no-no* sand flies itch for days and can become infected. Not everyone is affected by insect bites in the same way. Some people are practically immune to insects, while their traveling companions experiencing exactly the same conditions are soon covered with bites. You'll soon know which type you are.

Prickly heat, an intensely irritating rash, is caused by wearing heavy clothing that is inappropriate for the climate. When sweat glands are blocked and the sweat is unable to evaporate, the skin becomes soggy and small red blisters appear. Synthetic fabrics such as nylon are especially bad in this regard. Take a cold shower, apply calamine lotion, dust with talcum powder, and take off those clothes! Until things improve, avoid alcohol, tea, coffee, and any physical activity that makes you sweat. If you're sweating profusely, increase your intake of salt slightly to avoid fatigue, but not without concurrently drinking more water.

Use antidiarrheal medications such as Lomotil or Imodium sparingly. Rather than taking drugs to plug yourself up, drink plenty of unsweetened liquids such as green coconut or fresh fruit juice to help flush you out. Egg yolk mixed with nutmeg helps diarrhea, or have a rice and tea day. Avoid dairy products. Most cases of diarrhea are self-limiting and require only simple replacement of the fluids and salts lost in diarrheal stools. If the diarrhea is persistent or you experience high fever, drowsiness, or blood in the stool, stop traveling, rest, and consider seeing a doctor. For constipation eat pineapple or any peeled fruit.

Toxic Fish

More than 400 species of tropical reef fish, including wrasses, snappers, groupers, jacks, moray eels, surgeonfish, shellfish, and especially barracudas are known to cause seafood poisoning (ciguatera). There's no way of telling whether a fish will cause ciguatera: A species can be poisonous on one side of an island but not on the other.

In 1976 French and Japanese scientists working in the Gambier Islands determined that a one-celled dinoflagellate or plankton called *Gambierdiscus toxicus* was the cause. Normally these microalgae are found only in the ocean depths, but when a reef ecosystem is disturbed by natural or human causes they can multiply dramatically in a lagoon. The dinoflagellates are consumed by tiny herbivorous fish, and the toxin passes up through the food chain to larger fish, where it becomes concentrated in the head and guts. The toxins have no effect on the fish that feed on them.

French Polynesia's 700–800 cases of ciguatera per year are more than in the rest of the South Pacific combined, leading to suspicions that the former French nuclear testing program is responsible. Ciguatera didn't exist on Hao atoll in the Tuamotus until military dredging for a 3,380-meter runway began in 1965. By mid-1968, 43 percent of the population had been affected. Between 1971 and 1980 more than 30 percent of the population of Mangareva near the Moruroa nuclear test site suffered from seafood poisoning. The symptoms (numbness and tingling around the mouth and extremities, reversal of hot and cold sensations, prickling, itching, nausea, vomiting, erratic heartbeat, joint and muscle pains) usually subside in a few days. Induce vomiting, take castor oil as a laxative, and avoid alcohol if you're unlucky. Symptoms can recur for up to a year, and victims may become allergic to all seafood.

Avoid biointoxication by cleaning fish as soon as they're caught, discarding the head and organs, and taking special care with oversized fish caught in shallow water. Small fish are generally safer. Whether the fish is consumed cooked or raw has no bearing on this problem. Local residents often know from experience which species may be eaten.

Dengue Fever

Dengue fever is a mosquito-transmitted disease endemic in Polynesia. Symptoms such as headaches, sore throat, pain in the joints, fever, chills, nausea, and rash only appear one or two weeks after the bite. This painful illness, also known as "breakbone fever," can last anywhere from 5 to 15 days. Although you can relieve the symptoms somewhat, the only real cure is to stay in bed, drink lots of water, and wait it out. Avoid aspirin, as it can lead to complications. No vaccine exists, so just try to avoid getting bitten (the *Aedes aegypti* mosquito bites only during the day). Dengue fever can kill children under 13, so extra care must be taken to protect them if an outbreak is in progress.

During the 2001 dengue fever epidemic in French Polynesia—the worst in the territory's history—there were an estimated 30,000 cases with 10,000 requiring some form of hospital treatment. Of these, 4,000 cases were considered severe, and six deaths occurred among children aged 6–12. Fumigations and a clean-up campaign eventually overcame the disease. A new outbreak in 2006 was far less severe due to a local immunity left by the 2001 epidemic.

Swine Flu

The global swine flu pandemic reached French Polynesia in 2008, and by 2009 several thousand cases of influenza A (H1N1) had been confirmed. The territorial health authorities activated crisis management teams to respond to the disease, and among the emergency measures taken were the stricter monitoring of air and sea borders, the tracing of cases, the shipment of samples to Australia for testing, the preparation of emergency plans, the acquisition of needed supplies, and the creation of an operations center. The Ministry of Health claims they will be ready to intervene quickly should another outbreak occur.

Vaccinations

Most visitors are not required to get any vaccinations at all before coming to French Polynesia. Tetanus, diphtheria, and typhoid fever shots are not mandatory, but they're worth considering if you're going far off the beaten track. Tetanus and diphtheria shots are given together, and a booster is required every 10 years. The typhoid fever shot is every three years. Polio is believed to have been eradicated from the region.

A yellow-fever vaccination is required if you've been in an infected area within six days before arrival. Yellow fever is a mosquito-borne disease that occurs only in Central Africa and northern South America (excluding Chile), places you're not likely to have been just before arriving in French Polynesia. Since the vaccination is valid 10 years, get one if you're an inveterate globe-trotter.

Immune globulin (IG) and the Havrix vaccine aren't 100 percent effective against hepatitis A, but they do increase your general resistance to infections. IG prophylaxis must be repeated every five months. Hepatitis B vaccination involves three doses in a six-month period (duration of protection unknown) and is recommended mostly for people planning extended stays in the region.

Information and Services

MONEY

The French Pacific franc, or CFP (for *cour de franc Pacifique),* is legal tender in French Polynesia, Wallis and Futuna, and New Caledonia (there is no difference between the banknotes circulating in those French territories). There are beautifully colored big banknotes of CFP 500, 1,000, 5,000, and 10,000, and coins of CFP 1, 2, 5, 10, 20, 50, and 100. The 10,000 note is confusingly similar in color and design to CFP 1,000, so when changing money, ask the clerk to give you CFP 5,000 notes instead.

The best currency to carry to French Polynesia is the euro, as it's pegged at exactly one euro to CFP 119.33 buying or selling. You can easily determine how many CFP you'll get for your dollar or pound by finding out how many euros it's worth, then multiplying by 119.33. You'll find the rates for most currencies at www.xe.com/ucc/full.

There have been calls to adopt the euro as the currency in French Polynesia, but it hasn't happened yet over fears that the European Commission might gain the power to intervene in the local taxation system. If the euro is adopted during the life of this edition, simply divide all prices herein by 100 to get the euro rates (local businesses will probably take the opportunity to round up their prices, as happened in Europe in 2002).

All banks levy a stiff commission on foreign currency transactions (including euro transactions). The Banque de Polynésie (www.sg-bdp.pf) deducts CFP 474 commission, the Banque Socredo (www.websoc.pf) CFP 581, and the Banque de Tahiti (www.banque-tahiti.pf) a rip-off CFP 1,306. Traveler's checks attract a rate of exchange about 1.5 percent higher than cash dollars, but a passport is required for identification. The easiest way to avoid the high commissions and long bank lines is to

Banque Socredo has more branches than any other bank in French Polynesia.

EXCHANGE RATES

(approximate figures for orientation only)

- One euro = 119.331 Pacific francs
- One U.S. dollar = 92 Pacific francs
- One Canadian dollar = 89 Pacific francs
- One Australian dollar = 83 Pacific francs
- One New Zealand dollar = 65 Pacific francs
- One pound sterling = 145 Pacific francs
- One Swiss franc = 89 Pacific francs
- 100 Japanese yen = 108 Pacific francs

change money infrequently. When changing a large amount, it might be worth comparing the rates at all three banks, as they do differ slightly. Even with the commissions, you'll still get more CFP for your dollars after arriving in French Polynesia than you would from a bank or airport exchange office back home.

The bulk of your travel funds should be in traveler's checks, preferably American Express, which is represented by Tahiti Tours (15 rue Jeanne d'Arc, Papeete, tel. 46-90-00, www.americanexpress.pf, Mon. 1330–1600, Tues.–Fri. 1230–1600) near the Vaima Center in Papeete. To claim a refund for lost or stolen American Express traveler's checks, contact Tahiti Tours (hotline number tel. 46-90-09) or call the Sydney American Express office collect (tel. 02/9271-8664). It'll also cancel lost credit cards as long as you know the numbers.

Many banks in French Polynesia have automated teller machines (ATMs) outside their offices, and these should provide local currency against checking-account Visa and MasterCard at a rate slightly better than traveler's checks, without commission. Banque Socredo has ATMs at their branches throughout the territory (including at Faa'a airport). Be sure to select the English instructions, although the translations aren't always reliable. Despite advertised links to international services such as Cirrus and Maestro, American checking account ATM cards may not work in French Polynesia. Numerous travelers have reported problems with ATMs that produced "amount too high" messages instead of banknotes. Other times, only French Cirrus and Maestro were accepted. The ATMs at the international airport are notorious in this regard! If the machine doesn't work the first time, don't try again, as you could be charged for each attempt without receiving any cash. Go inside the bank and complain (if it's open). Also, ask your bank what fees it'll charge if you use an ATM abroad, as they can be unexpectedly high. Get your special personal identification number (PIN) while you're there, as most ATMs require it. Be aware that there are weekly limits on ATM withdrawals, and if you think you might run short, you should have several different cards. To avoid emergencies, don't be 100 percent dependent on ATMs and bring some cash or traveler's checks as well.

Credit cards are accepted in many places on the main islands, but Pacific francs in cash are easier to use at restaurants, shops, etc. If you want to use a credit card, always ask beforehand, even if the business has a sign, brochure, or website that says it's possible. Visa and MasterCard are universally accepted in the Society Islands, but American Express and Diner's Club are not. Visa and MasterCard can be used to obtain cash advances at most banks, but remember that cash advances accrue interest from the moment you receive the money—ask your bank if it has a debit card that allows the charges to be deducted from your checking account automatically. Occasionally you'll be charged 5 percent extra to pay by credit card. MasterCard and Visa levy surcharges of around 2.5 percent on foreign currency conversions associated with their cards. If you need to have money wired to you from abroad, the Banque

THE FRENCH PACIFIC FRANC

The *cour de franc Pacifique*, or CFP, grew out of the dark days of World War II when France was under German occupation. During this period, the French franc (FF) lost two-thirds of its prewar value while prices remained stable in the Pacific. When the French colonies reestablished contact with metropolitan France after the war, a new currency was needed to avoid economic chaos. Thus the French Pacific franc was created in 1945 at the rate of 2.4 FF to one CFP. Over the next few years the French franc was devalued three times, and each time the CFP was devalued against it, lowering the rate to 5.5 FF to one CFP by 1949. That year, 100 old FF became one new FF, thus 5.5 new FF equaled 100 old CFP, a relationship that remained in place for more than half a century. In 2002 France adopted the euro, but the CFP remained legal tender in France's three Pacific territories at the fixed rate of one euro to CFP 119.331. Until 1967 the Banque de l'Indochine was responsible for issuing the Pacific franc, a function now carried out by the French government. There has been talk of adopting the euro in French Polynesia, but many locals are opposed out of fears of inflation and a loss of autonomy.

de Polynésie has a connection with Western Union.

On many outer islands, credit cards, traveler's checks, and foreign banknotes other than euros won't be accepted, so it's essential to change enough money before leaving Papeete. Apart from Tahiti, there are banks on Bora Bora, Huahine, Hiva Oa, Moorea, Nuku Hiva, Raiatea, Rangiroa, Rurutu, Taha'a, Tubuai, and Ua Pou. All of these islands have Banque Socredo branches, and the Banque de Tahiti is represented on eight of them, the Banque de Polynésie on four. Bora Bora, Moorea, and Raiatea each have three different banks. If you're headed for any island other than these, take along enough CFP in cash to see you through. Euros in cash are widely accepted, even on remote atolls.

Controlling Costs

French Polynesia is easily the most expensive corner of the South Pacific, with an inflation rate of 3.4 percent in 2008. For American visitors, the rising prices really bite when combined with the declining U.S. dollar. The high price structure is directly related to the strength of the euro and the extremely high salaries paid to government employees who pay zero income tax. The minimum wage here is CFP 859 per hour or over US$1,750 a month, 30 percent higher than the federal minimum wage in the United States. You'll have a much better time in French Polynesia if you accept this and lower your value-for-money expectations while doubling your budget.

In 1998 a value-added tax (VAT) or *taxe sur la valeur ajoutée* (TVA) came into effect on many items. Currently, the TVA is 5 percent on groceries, rooms, and prepaid meals, 10 percent on services (including restaurants, bars, car rentals, and excursions), and 16 percent on store purchases. Large "classified hotels" are taxed 10 percent, whereas small hotels and pensions charge 5 percent. Bus and public ferry fares are free of tax. The TVA is usually hidden in the basic price, but the hotel taxes are charged extra.

Fortunately, facilities for budget travelers are available throughout the Society Islands, often with cooking facilities that allow you to save on meals. Bread (and indirectly the ubiquitous baguette sandwiches) is heavily subsidized and a real bargain. Beer, fruit juice, and mineral water from grocery stores are reasonable. Cheap transportation is available by interisland boat, and on Tahiti there's the bus. Bicycles can be hired in many places.

Time is what you need the most of to see French Polynesia inexpensively, along with the wisdom to avoid trying to see and do too much. There are countless organized tours and activities designed to separate you from your money, but none are really essential, and the beautiful scenery, spectacular beaches, challenging hikes, and exotic atmosphere are free. Bargaining is not common in French Polynesia, and no one will try to cheat you (with the exception of the odd taxi driver). There's *no tipping.*

COMMUNICATIONS

Post

The 63 post offices (www.opt.pf) throughout French Polynesia are open weekdays 0730–1500. Main branches sell ready-made padded envelopes and boxes. Parcels with an aggregate length, width, and height of over 90 centimeters or weighing more than 20 kilograms cannot be mailed. Rolls (posters, calendars, etc.) longer than 90 centimeters are also not accepted. Letters cannot weigh over two kilograms, and when mailing parcels it's much cheaper to keep the weight under two kilograms. Registration *(recommandation)* is extra, and insurance *(envois avec valeur déclarée)* is also possible. Always use airmail *(poste aérienne)* when posting a letter; surface mail takes months to arrive. Postcards can still take up to two weeks to reach the United States.

To pick up poste restante (general delivery) mail, you must show your passport and pay a fee per piece. Incoming mail is often delayed or lost.

There's no residential mail delivery in French Polynesia, and what appear to be mail boxes along rural roads are actually bread delivery boxes. Since there are usually no street addresses, almost everyone has a post office box or B.P. *(boîte postale).* French Polynesia issues its own colorful postage stamps—available at local post offices. They make nice souvenirs.

Telecommunications

Public telephones are found almost everywhere in the territory, but they accept local telephone cards only (no coins). Thus anyone planning on using the phone will have to pick up a telephone card or OPTcard, sold at all post offices. They're valid for both local and international calls, and are available in denominations of CFP 1,000, 2,000, and 5,000. With the card, calls cost CFP 17 per minute within one island, CFP 22 interisland, CFP 28 to a cell phone, or CFP 31 international. Dial 44-10-00 then the secret code on your card.

For long-distance calls, using a card is cheaper than paying cash, and you don't get hit with stiff three-minute minimum charges for operator-assisted calls. By using a telephone card to call long distance you limit the amount the call can possibly cost and won't end up overspending should you forget to keep track of the time.

To dial overseas direct from Tahiti, listen for the dial tone, and then push 00 (Tahiti's international access code). When you hear another dial tone, press the country code of your party (Canada and the United States are both 1), the city or area code, and the number. For information (in French), dial 3612 (a paid call); to get the operator, dial 19. All the main islands have direct dialing via satellite.

Operator-assisted long-distance calls are best placed at post offices, which also handle fax *(télécopie)* services. Calls made from hotel rooms are charged double or triple—you could be presented a truly astronomical bill. Collect calls overseas are possible to Australia, Canada, France, New Zealand, Vanuatu, and the United States (but not to the United Kingdom): dial 19 and say you want a *conversation payable à l'arrivée.*

If calling from abroad, French Polynesia's telephone code is **689.** To call direct from the United States or Canada, one must dial 011-689 and the six-digit telephone number (there are no area codes). International access codes do vary, so always check in the front of your local telephone book.

Throughout this guide we've tried to supply the local telephone numbers you'll need. Many tourist-oriented businesses will have someone handy who speaks English, so don't hesitate to call ahead. You'll get current information, be able to check prices and perhaps make a reservation, and often save yourself a lot of time and worry. If you need to consult the French Polynesia phone book, ask to see the *annuaire* at any post office. You can also search online for numbers at www.annuaireopt.pf.

Mobile Phones

Many activities operators on the move and small pensions in remote areas have mobile telephone numbers, which always begin with a 7. Visitors can also connect to the local Vini network (www.vini.pf) provided their cell phone operates on a 900 Mhz frequency and they have set up "roaming" service before leaving home. Vini has working agreements with Cingular and T-Mobile in the United States and FIDO and Rogers Wireless in Canada. Another option is to purchase a rechargeable Vinicard to replace an existing SIM card. Vinicards can be purchased at any post office (although outer islands sometimes run out of cards).

Email

Email and the Internet were introduced to French Polynesia in 1995, and they've really caught on in recent years. An increasing number of tourism-related businesses in the islands now have websites and email addresses, which makes communicating with them from abroad a lot easier. We've included websites in the listings throughout this guide. The sites usually provide the company's email address, and you should visit the site before emailing in any case, as your questions may be answered there. Many resorts now have Facebook pages, which are excellent sources of photos and insider tips.

Internet cafés are found on all the main islands, allowing you to check your Web-based email at around CFP 10 per minute. In French Polynesia the computers usually have French keyboards, which vary slightly from English keyboards, leading to annoying typing problems. Ask the operator if he or she has a machine with an English keyboard or to explain the quirks of the French keyboard.

Of course, to receive email online, you'll need a Web-based electronic mailbox. Many providers now provide these to their clients; otherwise you should open a Yahoo or Hotmail account before leaving home. To do so, simply click "Sign Up" at www.yahoo.com or www.hotmail.com. You must check your mail at least once a month; otherwise your free account may be canceled. Communicating has never been so easy.

If you want to use your own laptop, you'll need to buy an access card from Mana (tel. 47-99-99, www.mana.pf), French Polynesia's only ISP. Their MiPASS, available at most post offices or at the Mana Agency just off Pont de l'Est in Papeete, costs CFP 3,300/4,950/9,900 for 10/25/75 hours of slow dial-up Internet access. A toll-free number is provided, but the price some resorts charge for local telephone calls can be surprisingly high. For wireless Internet access, you'll need a Carte ManaSPOT costing CFP 990/1,980/5,280 for 1/3/10 hours of Wi-Fi access. A list of "Zones ManaSPOT" throughout French Polynesia where the ManaSPOT card can be used is on www.manaspot.pf. Outside Papeete, most Wi-Fi hotspots are at post offices. Most of the restaurants and hotels with ManaSPOT Wi-Fi access also sell the cards.

MEDIA

Two morning papers are published in Papeete. *Les Nouvelles de Tahiti* (tel. 47-52-00, www.lesnouvelles.pf) was founded in 1957 and has a circulation of 6,500 copies daily except Sunday. In 1964 *La Dépêche de Tahiti* (tel. 46-43-43, www.ladepeche.pf) merged with an existing paper, and 18,500 copies a day are sold at present. Both are part of the Groupe Hersant publishing empire.

The free monthly *Tahiti Beach Press* (tel. 42-68-50, www.tahitibeachpress.com), edited by Jan Prince, includes tourist information and interesting stories about French Polynesia.

If you read French, the monthly magazine *Tahiti Pacifique* (www.tahiti-pacifique.com) is a lively observer of political and economic affairs, founded in 1991 (single copies CFP 700, airmail subscription CFP 9,000).

Television was introduced to Tahiti in 1965, and state-owned Réseau France Outre-Mer (RFO, www.rfo.fr) broadcasts on two channels in French and (occasionally) in Tahitian. A territorial station (Tahiti Nui TV, www.tntv.pf) and two cable companies (Canal+ and Tahiti Nui Satellite) also operate.

Radio

A great way to connect with the local scene is to take along a small AM/FM/shortwave portable radio. Your only expense will be the radio itself and batteries. Almost a dozen FM radio stations broadcast around Papeete.

- **Radio Polynésie** (RFO, polynesie.rfo.fr) is a government-run station that presents the main news of the day (in French) at 0500, 0600, 0700, 0800, and 1800.
- **Radio 1** (www.radio1.pf) gives a news and weather report at 0630 and plays mostly French and Anglo-American music.
- **Tiare FM** (www.tiarefm.pf), Radio 1's sister station, plays more Tahitian music. Both are owned by the powerful Groupe Aline.
- **NRJ** (www.nrj.pf), Radio 1's competitor, owned by the newspaper *La Dépêche,* offers French and Anglo-American music.
- **Radio Maohi,** based at Pirae, plays Tahitian music during the day but at night competes with NRJ for listeners.
- **Radio Tefana** is a Tahitian-language station based at Faa'a that features Tahitian music.

In Papeete, you'll find these stations at the following frequencies:

- 88.2 MHz—Radio Maohi
- 91.8 MHz—Radio Polynésie
- 92.8 MHz—Radio Tefana
- 94.3 MHz—RFO
- 95.2 MHz—Radio Polynésie
- 95.6 MHz—Radio LVDL
- 98.7 MHz—Radio 1
- 100.5 MHz—Radio Fara
- 103.0 MHz—NRJ
- 103.8 MHz—Radio 1
- 104.2 MHz—Tiare FM
- 106.0 MHz—Tiare FM
- 107.3 MHz—Taui FM

Outside Papeete the frequencies used by these stations vary. At Taravao, look for Radio Polynésie at 89.0 MHz, Radio 1 at 90.9 MHz, Radio Maohi at 94.8 MHz, Tiare FM at 98.3 MHz, and Star FM at 100.8 MHz. Radio Marquises uses 101.3 MHz at Nuku Hiva and 95 MHz at Hiva Oa. Radio Polynésie broadcasts throughout the territory over **738 kHz AM.** None of the local AM/FM stations broadcast in English. You can also try picking up the BBC World Service and Radio Australia. Their frequencies vary according to the time of day and work best at night. Set your tuning buttons to some of these stations as soon as you arrive.

TOURIST INFORMATION

French Polynesia's tourism promotion office, Tahiti Tourisme (www.tahiti-tourisme.com), has overseas branches in many countries. Within French Polynesia the same organization operates tourist information offices on Tahiti, Moorea, Huahine, Raiatea, and Bora Bora. If open, these offices can provide free brochures and answer questions, but they're not travel agencies, so you must make your own hotel and transportation bookings (they won't make phone calls for you). They're financed by the 5 percent room tax you're charged every time you stay at a hotel in French Polynesia.

TIME AND MEASUREMENTS

Time

The sun rises at 0600 and sets at 1800 in French Polynesia throughout the year. Businesses open early in the morning but often close for a two-hour siesta at midday. Normal office hours are weekdays 0730–1130 and 1330–1630. Many shops keep the same schedule but remain open until 1730 and Saturday 0730–1200. A few shops remain open at lunchtime, and small convenience stores are often open Saturday afternoon until 1800 and Sunday 0600–0800. Banking hours are variable, either 0800–1530 or 0800–1100 and 1400–1700 weekdays. A few banks in Papeete open Saturday morning (check the sign on the door). Most businesses are closed on Sunday.

INFORMATION OFFICES

- **Australia:** Tahiti Tourisme, Suite 3, Level 8, 25 Bligh St., Sydney, NSW 2000, tel. 02/9233-4920, www.tahitinow.com.au
- **Chile:** Oficina de Turismo de Tahiti, Av. 11 de Septiembre 2214, Oficina 116, Providencia, Santiago, tel. 02/251-2826, www.tahiti-tourisme.cl
- **China:** Tahiti Tourisme, Room 1612A, Kuntai International Maison, Chaowai Dajie, 100020, Beijing, tel. 01/5879-7849, www.tahiti-tourisme.cn
- **France:** Office du Tourisme de Tahiti, 28 Boulevard Saint-Germain, 75005 Paris, tel. 08/1146-4680, www.tahiti-tourisme.fr
- **French Polynesia:** Tahiti Tourisme, B.P. 65, Papeete, 98713 Tahiti, tel. 50-57-00, www.tahiti-tourisme.pf
- **Germany:** Tahiti Tourisme, Paul-Ehrlich-Str. 27, 60596 Frankfurt, tel. 069/1753-7100, www.tahiti-tourisme.de
- **Italy:** Tahiti Tourisme, Piazza Caiazzo 3, 20124 Milano, tel. 02/6698-0317, www.tahiti-tourisme.it
- **Japan:** Tahiti Tourisme, Kokusai Building 1F, 3-1-1 Marunouchi, Chiyoda-ku, Tokyo 100-0005, tel. 03/5220-3877, www.tahiti-tourisme.jp
- **New Zealand:** Tahiti Tourisme, Unit A, 246 Hobson St., Auckland, tel. 09/368-5262, www.tahiti-tourisme.co.nz
- **Spain:** Tahiti Tourisme, Calle Serrano 93, 28006 Madrid, tel. 091/411-0167, www.tahiti-tourisme.es
- **United Kingdom:** Tahiti Tourisme, 3rd floor, Colechurch House, 1 London Bridge Walk, London SE1 2SX, tel. 020/7367-0933, www.tahiti-tourisme.co.uk
- **United States:** Tahiti Tourisme, 300 North Continental Blvd., Suite 160, El Segundo, CA 90245, tel. 310/414-8484, www.tahiti-tourisme.com

French Polynesia is in the same time zone as Hawaii, 10 hours behind Greenwich Mean Time (GMT) or two hours behind California (except mid-Mar.–mid-Nov., when it's three hours). The Marquesas are 30 minutes ahead of Tahiti, and the Gambier Islands are an hour ahead of Tahiti. Standard time is used year-round in French Polynesia. French Polynesia is east of the International Date Line, so the day is the same as that of the United States but a day behind Fiji, New Zealand, and Australia.

You're better off calling from North America to French Polynesia in the evening, as it will be mid-afternoon in the islands (plus you'll probably benefit from off-peak telephone rates). From Europe, call very late at night. In the other direction, if you're calling from the islands to North America or Europe, do so in the early morning, as it will already be afternoon in North America and evening in Europe.

In this guide all clock times are rendered according to the 24-hour airline timetable system, i.e. 0100 is 1 A.M., 1300 is 1 P.M., and 2330 is 11:30 P.M. The islanders operate on "coconut time"—the nut will fall when it is ripe. In the languid air of the South Seas, punctuality takes on a new meaning. Appointments are approximate and service relaxed. Even the seasons are fuzzy: sometimes wetter, sometimes drier, but almost always hot. Slow down to the island pace and get in step with where you are. You may not get as much done, but you'll enjoy life a lot more.

Measurements

The metric system is used here. Study the conversion table in the back of this guide if you're not used to thinking metric. Most distances herein are quoted in kilometers—they become easy to comprehend when you know than one kilometer is the distance a normal person walks in 10 minutes. A meter is slightly more than a yard, and a liter is just over a quart. Unless otherwise indicated, north is at the top of all maps in this guide.

Electrical Currents

If you're taking along a plug-in razor, radio, computer, electric immersion coil, camera battery charger, or other electrical appliance, be aware that 220 volts AC is commonly used in French Polynesia. Take care, however, as some luxury hotel rooms provide 110-volt outlets as a convenience to North American visitors. A 220-volt appliance will run too slowly in a 110-volt outlet, but a 110-volt appliance will quickly burn out and be destroyed in a 220-volt outlet.

Most appliances require a converter to change from one voltage to another. You'll also need an adapter to cope with sockets that take two round-pronged plugs in French Polynesia. Pick up both items before you leave home, as they're hard to find in the islands. Some sockets have a switch that must be turned on. Remember voltages if you buy duty-free appliances: dual voltage (110/220 V) items are best.

Videos

Commercial travel videotapes make nice souvenirs, but always keep in mind that there are three incompatible video formats loose in the world: NTSC (used in North America), PAL (used in Britain, Germany, Japan, Australia, and New Zealand), and SECAM (used in France, French Polynesia, and Russia). Don't buy prerecorded tapes abroad unless they're of the system used in your country.

RESOURCES

Glossary

afa a *demi*, or person of mixed Polynesian and European blood

ahimaa an underground, earthen oven. After A.D. 500, the Polynesians had lost the art of making pottery, so they were compelled to bake their food rather than boil it.

aito ironwood

anse cove (French)

aparima a Tahitian dance that tells a story with the hands

archipelago a group of islands

ari'i a Tahitian high chief; the traditional head of a clan or tribe

Arioi a pre-European religious society that traveled among the Society Islands presenting ceremonies and entertainments

atoll a low-lying, ring-shaped coral reef enclosing a lagoon

bareboat charter chartering a yacht without crew or provisions

bark cloth see *tapa*

barrier reef a coral reef separated from the adjacent shore by a lagoon

bêche-de-mer sea cucumber; an edible sea slug; in Tahitian, *rori;* in French, *trépang*

B.P. *boîte postale;* post office box

breadfruit a large, round fruit with starchy flesh grown on an *uru* tree *(Artocarpus altilis)*

C Celsius

caldera a wide crater formed through the collapse or explosion of a volcano

cassava manioc; the starchy edible root of the tapioca plant

casse-croûte a large sandwich made with a baguette

CFP *cour de franc Pacifique;* the currency in French Polynesia

chain an archaic unit of length equivalent to 20 meters

ciguatera a form of fish poisoning caused by microscopic algae

CMAS Confédération Mondiale des Activités Subaquatiques; the French counterpart of PADI

code share a system whereby two or more airlines own seats on a single flight

coir coconut husk sennit used to make rope, etc.

copra dried coconut meat used in the manufacture of coconut oil, cosmetics, soap, and margarine

coral a hard, calcareous substance of various shapes, composed of the skeletons of tiny marine animals called polyps

coral bank a coral formation over 150 meters long

coral bleaching the expulsion of symbiotic algae by corals

coral head a coral formation a few meters across

coral patch a coral formation up to 150 meters long

cyclone Also known as a hurricane (in the Caribbean) or typhoon (in Japan). A tropical storm that rotates around a center of low atmospheric pressure; it becomes a cyclone when its winds reach force 12, or 64 knots. At sea the air will be filled with foam and driving spray, the water surface completely white with 14-meter-high waves. In the Northern Hemisphere, cyclones spin counterclockwise, while south of the equator they move clockwise. The winds of cyclonic storms are deflected toward a low-pressure area at the center, although the "eye" of the cyclone may be calm.

demi-pension a breakfast and dinner meal plan, also called the Modified American Plan (MAP) or half board; *pension complète* means three meals, the American Plan (AP) or full board

desiccated coconut the shredded meat of dehydrated fresh coconut

DOM-TOM Départements et Territoires d'Outre-Mer; the French colonial bureaucratic structure

EEZ Exclusive Economic Zone; a 200-nautical-mile offshore belt of an island nation or seacoast state that controls the mineral exploitation and fishing rights

endemic native to a particular area and existing only there

fafa a "spinach" of cooked taro leaves

farani French; *français*

fare Tahitian house

filaria parasitic worms transmitted by biting insects to the blood or tissues of mammals. The obstruction of the lymphatic glands by the worms can cause an enlargement of the legs or other parts, a disease known as elephantiasis.

fissure a narrow crack or chasm of some length and depth

FIT foreign independent travel; a custom-designed, prepaid tour composed of many individualized arrangements

fringing reef a reef along the shore of an island

gendarme a French police officer on duty only in rural areas in France and French overseas territories

GPS Global Positioning System, the space-age successor of the sextant

guano manure of seabirds, used as a fertilizer

guyot a submerged atoll, the coral of which couldn't keep up with rising water levels

Havai'i legendary homeland of the Polynesians

Hiro the Polynesian god of thieves

hoa a shallow channel between *motu*

hurricane see cyclone

kaina country; *kaina* music is Tahitian country music, usually a string band

knot about three kilometers per hour

lagoon an expanse of water bounded by a reef

lapita pottery made by the ancient Polynesians from 1600 to 500 B.C.

lava tube a conduit formed as molten rock continues to flow below a cooled surface during the growth of a lava field. When the eruption ends, a tunnel is left with a flat floor where the last lava hardened.

LDS Latter-day Saints; the Mormons

leeward downwind; the shore (or side) sheltered from the wind; as opposed to windward

lei a garland, often of fresh flowers, but sometimes of paper, shells, etc., hung about the neck of a person being welcomed or feted

le truck a truck with seats in back, used for public transportation on Tahiti

liveaboard a tour boat with cabin accommodation for scuba divers

LMS London Missionary Society; a Protestant group that spread Christianity from Tahiti (1797) across the Pacific

ma'a Tahiti Tahitian food

ma'a Tinito Chinese food

mahimahi dorado, Pacific dolphinfish (no relation to the mammal)

mahu a male Tahitian transvestite, sometimes also gay

mairie town hall

makatea an uplifted reef around the coast of an elevated atoll

mama ruau literally "grandmother," but also used for the Mother Hubbard long dress introduced to Tahiti by missionaries

mana authority, prestige, virtue, "face," psychic power, a positive force

manahune a commoner or member of the lower class in pre-Christian Tahitian society

mangrove a tropical shrub with branches that send down roots forming dense thickets along tidal shores

manioc cassava, tapioca, a starchy root crop

maohi a native of French Polynesia

mape Tahitian chestnut tree

maraamu southeast trade winds, or *alizés*

marae a Tahitian temple or open-air religious place, called *me'ae* in the Marquesas

marara flying fish

matrilineal a system of tracing descent through the mother's familial line

Melanesia the high island groups of the western Pacific (Fiji, New Caledonia, Vanuatu, Solomon Islands, Papua New Guinea); from *melas* (black)

Micronesia chains of high and low islands mostly north of the Equator (the Carolines, Gilberts, Marianas, Marshalls); from *micro* (small)

monoï perfumed coconut oil

motu a flat reef islet

mynah an Indian starling-like bird

NAUI National Association of Underwater Instructors

noanoa perfume

noni the knobby green tree fruit of the *noni* or *nono* tree *(Morinda citrifolia)*

no-nos sand flies

Oro the Polynesian god of war

ote'a a Tahitian ceremonial dance performed by men and women in two lines

pa ancient Polynesian stone fortress

Pacific rim the continental landmasses and large countries around the fringe of the Pacific

PADI Professional Association of Dive Instructors

pandanus screw pine with slender stem and prop roots. The sword-shaped leaves are used for plaiting mats and hats. In Tahitian, *fara*

papa'a a Tahitian word used to refer to Europeans

parasailing a sport in which participants are carried aloft by a parachute pulled behind a speedboat

pareu a Tahitian sarong-like wraparound skirt or loincloth

pass a channel through a barrier reef, usually with an outward flow of water

passage an inside passage between an island and a barrier reef

patrilineal a system of tracing descent through the father's familial line

pawpaw papaya

pelagic relating to the open sea, away from land

peretane Britain, British in Tahitian

pétanque French lawn bowling in which small metal balls are thrown

pirogue outrigger canoe (French), in Tahitian *vaa*

PK *pointe kilométrique,* a system of marking kilometers along highways in French Polynesia

poe a sticky pudding made from bananas, papaya, pumpkin, or taro mixed with starch, baked in an oven, and served with coconut milk; in Rapanui *po'i*

poisson cru (French) raw fish marinated in lime; in Tahitian *ia ota*

Polynesia divided into western Polynesia (Tonga and Samoa) and eastern Polynesia (French Polynesia, Cook Islands, Hawaii, Easter Island, and New Zealand); from *poly* (many)

pp per person

punt a flat-bottomed boat

pupu traditional Tahitian dance group

raatira Tahitian chief, dance leader

rain shadow the dry side of a mountain, sheltered from the windward side

reef a coral ridge near the ocean surface

roulotte a mobile food van or truck

scuba self-contained underwater breathing apparatus

self-catering see self-contained

self-contained a room with private facilities (a toilet and shower not shared with other guests); the brochure term "en-suite" means the same thing; as opposed to a "self-catering" unit with cooking facilities

sennit braided coconut-fiber rope

shareboat charter a yacht tour for individuals or couples who join a small group on a fixed itinerary

shoal a shallow sandbar or mud bank

shoulder season a travel period between high/peak and low/off-peak seasons

subduction the action of one tectonic plate wedging under another

subsidence geological sinking or settling

symbiosis a mutually advantageous relationship between unlike organisms

tahua in the old days a skilled Tahitian artisan or priest; today a sorcerer or healer

tamaaraa a Tahitian feast

tamure a new name for Ori Tahiti, a very fast erotic dance

tapa a cloth made from the pounded bark of the paper mulberry tree *(Broussonetia papyrifera).* It's soaked and beaten with a mallet to flatten and intertwine the fibers, then painted with geometric designs.

tapu taboo, sacred, set apart, forbidden, a negative force

taro a starchy elephant-eared tuber *(Colocasia esculenta),* a staple food of the Pacific islanders

tatau the Tahitian original of the adopted English word *tattoo*

tavana the elected mayor of a Tahitian commune (from the English *governor*)

tifaifai a Tahitian patchwork quilt based on either European or Polynesian motifs

tiki a humanlike sculpture representing an anonymous ancestor used for protection in the days of religious rites and sorcery

timeshare part ownership of a residential unit with the right to occupy the premises for a certain period each year in exchange for payment of an annual maintenance fee

tinito Tahitian for Chinese

TNC transnational corporation (also referred to as a multinational corporation)

to'ere a hollow wooden drum hit with a stick

trade wind a steady wind blowing toward the equator from either northeast or southeast

trench the section at the bottom of the ocean where one tectonic plate wedges under another

tridacna clam eaten everywhere in the Pacific, its size varies between 10 centimeters and one meter

tropical storm a cyclonic storm with winds of 35-64 knots

truck see *le truck*

tsunami a fast-moving wave caused by an undersea earthquake; sometimes erroneously called a tidal wave

tu'i (Polynesian) king, ruler

umara sweet potato *(Ipomoea batatas)*

US$ United States dollar

vigia a mark on a nautical chart indicating a dangerous rock or shoal

VTT vélo à tout terrain; mountain bike

windward the point or side from which the wind blows, as opposed to leeward

zoreille a recent arrival from France; from *les oreilles* (the ears); also called a *métro*

zories rubber shower sandals, thongs, flip-flops

ALTERNATIVE PLACE NAMES

- **Bass Islands** Marotiri Islands
- **Bellingshausen** Motu One
- **Hatutaa** Hatutu
- **Hatutu** Hatutaa
- **Hull** Maria
- **Maiao** Tapuaemanu
- **Maria** Hull
- **Marotiri Islands** Bass Islands
- **Maupihaa** Mopelia
- **Maupiti** Maurau
- **Maurau** Maupiti
- **Mohotani** Motane
- **Mopelia** Maupihaa
- **Moruroa** Mururoa
- **Motane** Mohotani
- **Motu Iti** Tupai
- **Motu One** Bellingshausen
- **Mururoa** Moruroa
- **Puamotu** Tuamotu
- **Scilly** Manuae
- **Taha'a** Uporu
- **Tapuaemanu** Maiao
- **Temoe** Timoe
- **Timoe** Temoe
- **Tuamotu** Puamotu
- **Tupai** Motu Iti
- **Uporu** Taha'a

Phrasebook

BASIC TAHITIAN

ahiahi evening
ahimaa earth oven
aita no
aita e peapea no problem
aita maitai no good
aito ironwood
amu eat
ananahi tomorrow
arearea fun, to have fun
atea far away
atua god
avae moon, month
avatea midday (1000-1500)
e yes
eaha te huru? How are you?
e haere oe ihea? Where are you going?
e hia? How much?
faraoa bread
fare house
fare iti toilet
fare moni bank
fare niau thatched house
fare punu tin-roofed house
fare pure church
fare rata post office
fare toa shop
fenua land
fetii parent, family
fiu fed up, bored
haari coconut
haere goodbye (to a person leaving)
haere mai io nei come here
haere maru go easy, take it easy
hauti play, make love
hei flower garland, lei
here hoe number-one sweetheart
himene song, from the English "hymn"
hoa friend
ia orana good day, may you live, prosper
i nanahi yesterday
ino bad
inu drink
ioa name
ite know
ma'a food
maeva welcome
mahana sun, light, day
mahanahana warm
maitai good, I'm fine; also a cocktail
maitai roa very good
manava welcome
manu bird
manuia to your health!
manureva airplane
mao shark
mauruuru thank you
mauruuru roa thank you very much
meka swordfish
miti salt water
moana deep ocean
moemoea dream
moni money
nana goodbye
naonao mosquito
nehenehe beautiful
niau coconut-palm frond
oa oa happy
ohipa work
oia yes
ora life, health
ori dance
oromatua the spirits of the dead
otaa bundle, luggage
oti finished
pahi boat, ship
painapo pineapple
pape water, juice
parahi goodbye (to a person staying)
pareu sarong
pia beer
pohe death
poipoi morning
popaa foreigner, European
poti'i teenage girl, young woman
raerae effeminate
roto lake
taapapu understand
taata human being, man
tabu forbidden

tahatai beach
tama'a lunch
tama'a maitai bon appétit
tamaaraa Tahitian feast
tamarii child
tane man, husband
taofe coffee
taote doctor
taravana crazy
tiare flower
to'e to'e cold
tupapau ghost
ua rain
uaina wine
uteute red
vahine woman, wife
vai freshwater
veavea hot

Numbers

hoe 1
piti 2
toru 3
maha 4
pae 5
ono 6
hitu 7
vau 8
iva 9
ahuru 10
ahuru ma hoe 11
ahuru ma piti 12
ahuru ma toru 13
ahuru ma maha 14
ahuru ma pae 15
ahuru ma ono 16
ahuru ma hitu 17
ahuru ma vau 18
ahuru ma iva 19
piti ahuru 20
piti ahuru ma hoe 21
piti ahuru ma piti 22
piti ahuru ma toru 23
toru ahuru 30
maha ahuru 40
pae ahuru 50
ono ahuru 60
hitu ahuru 70
vau ahuru 80
iva ahuru 90
hanere 100
tauatini 1,000
ahuru tauatini 10,000
mirioni 1,000,000

BASIC FRENCH

bonjour hello
bonsoir good evening
salut hi
Je vais à . . . I am going to . . .
Où allez-vous? Where are you going?
Jusqu'où allez-vous? How far are you going?
Où se trouve . . . ? Where is . . . ?
C'est loin d'ici? Is it far from here?
À quelle heure? At what time?
un horaire timetable
hier yesterday
aujourd'hui today
demain tomorrow
Je désire, je voudrais . . . I want . . .
J'aime . . . I like . . .
Je ne comprends pas. I don't understand.
une chambre a room
Vous êtes très gentil. You are very kind.
Où habitez-vous? Where do you live?
Il fait mauvais temps. It's bad weather.
le gendarmerie police station
Quel travail faites-vous? What work do you do?
le chômage, les chômeurs unemployment, the unemployed
Je t'aime. I love you.
une boutique, un magasin a store
le pain bread
le lait milk
le vin wine
le casse-croûte snack
les conserves canned foods
les fruits de mer seafood
un café très chaud hot coffee
l'eau water
le plat du jour set meal
Combien ça fait?, Combien ça coûte?, Combien?, Quel prix? How much does it cost?

la clef the key
la route, la piste the road
la plage the beach
la falaise cliff
la cascade waterfall
les grottes caves
Est-ce que je peux camper ici? May I camp here?
Je voudrais camper. I would like to camp.
le terrain de camping campsite
Devrais-je demander la permission? Should I ask permission?
s'il vous plaît please
oui yes
merci thank you
cher expensive
bon marché cheap

Numbers

un 1
deux 2
trois 3
quatre 4
cinq 5
six 6
sept 7
huit 8
neuf 9
dix 10
onze 11
douze 12
treize 13
quatorze 14
quinze 15
seize 16
dix-sept 17
dix-huit 18
dix-neuf 19
vingt 20
vingt-et-un 21
vingt-deux 22
vingt-trois 23
trente 30
quarante 40
cinquante 50
soixante 60
soixante-dix 70
quatre-vingts 80
quatre-vingt-dix 90
cent 100
mille 1,000
dix mille 10,000
million 1,000,000

Suggested Reading

GUIDEBOOKS

Amsler, Kurt. *The French Polynesia Dive Guide.* New York: Abbeville Press, 2001. Describes and maps the territory's 27 top dive sites.

Bier, James A. *Reference Map of Oceania.* Honolulu: University of Hawaii Press, 2007. A fully indexed map of the Pacific Islands with 51 detailed inset maps of individual islands. Useful details such as time zones are included.

Bondurant, Richard. *Cocktails in Tahiti.* Tahiti Publishing Company, 2006. The best cocktails from the world's most beautiful islands.

Chester, Sharon, et al. *Mave Mai, The Marquesas Islands.* San Mateo, CA: Wandering Albatross, 1998. A useful 137-page guide by a team of authors, several of whom have worked aboard the freighter *Aranui.* Each island is described in detail, and the natural history sections are complete and well illustrated. Practical listings of accommodations, restaurants, and transport are not included.

Cornell, Jimmy. *World Cruising Routes.* Camden, ME: International Marine, 2002. Details more than 500 cruising routes worldwide.

Davock, Marcia. *Cruising Guide to Tahiti and the French Society Islands.* Stamford, CT: Wescott Cove Publishing, 1985. Though researched nearly three decades ago, this large-format, spiral-bound guide is still a must for anyone intending to sail around Tahiti and Moorea. The coverage of islands other than these two is sketchy.

DESCRIPTION AND TRAVEL

Ellis, William. *Polynesian Researches.* Rutland, VT: Charles E. Tuttle, 1969. An early missionary's detailed observations of Tahiti during the years 1817–1825.

Finney, Ben. *Voyage of Discovery: A Cultural Odyssey through Polynesia.* Berkeley, CA: University of California Press, 1994. A complete account of the 1985 journey of the traditional sailing canoe *Hokule'a* through Polynesia.

Hendrie, Peter. *Pacific Journeys.* Honolulu: University of Hawaii Press, 2003. Includes 300 color photos of the islands of Polynesia and Melanesia, from Papua New Guinea to Easter Island.

Heyerdahl, Thor. *Fatu Hiva: Back to Nature.* New York: Doubleday, 1974. In 1936 Heyerdahl and his wife, Liv, went to live on Fatu Hiva. This book describes their year there.

Horwitz, Tony. *Blue Latitudes: Boldly Going Where Captain Cook Has Gone Before.* New York: Henry Holt, 2003. A Pulitzer Prize–winning author journeys in the wake of the greatest of all Pacific explorers.

Lee, Georgia. *Te Moana Nui.* Los Osos, CA: Cloud Mountain, 2001. A noted archaeologist explores lost isles of the South Pacific from French Polynesia to Easter Island.

Stevenson, Robert Louis. *In the South Seas.* New York: Scribner's, 1901. The author's memoir of his travels through the Marquesas, Tuamotus, and Gilberts by yacht in the years 1888–1890.

Sylvain, Adolphe. *Sylvain's Tahiti.* Los Angeles, CA: Taschen America, 2001. Timeless black-and-white images of Tahiti by a romantic photographer who spent 45 years in the islands.

Theroux, Paul. *The Happy Isles of Oceania.* London: Hamish Hamilton, 1992. The master of railway travelogues sets out with kayak and tent to tour the Pacific.

NATURAL SCIENCE

Allen, Gerald R., and Roger Steene. *Indo-Pacific Coral Reef Field Guide.* El Cajon, CA: Odyssey Publishing, 1998. Essential for identifying the creatures of the reefs.

Harrison, Peter. *Seabirds of the World.* Princeton, NJ: Princeton University Press, 1996. An ideal field guide to carry aboard a yacht or ship.

Morris, Rod, and Alison Balance. *South Sea Islands: A Natural History.* Toronto: Firefly Books, 2003. A celebration of the exotic ecosystems of the South Sea Islands, featuring spectacular color photography.

Myers, Robert F., and Ewald Lieske. *Coral Reef Fishes.* Princeton, NJ: Princeton University Press, 2001. An inexpensive field guide to the marine life of the tropical Pacific.

Safina, Carl. *Song for the Blue Ocean.* New York: Owl Books, 1999. Safina chronicles the decline of the world's marine resources due to human activities—an enthralling and alarming read.

Veron, J. E. N. *Corals of Australia and the Indo-Pacific.* Honolulu: University of Hawaii Press, 1993. An authoritative, illustrated work.

Wheatley, Nigel. *Where to Watch Birds in Australasia and Oceania.* Princeton, NJ: Princeton University Press, 1998. The descriptions of nature reserves and forested areas will interest any ecotourist.

Whistler, W. Arthur. *Wayside Plants of the Islands.* Honolulu: University of Hawaii Press, 1995. A guide to the lowland flora of the Pacific islands.

HISTORY

Aldrich, Robert. *France and the South Pacific since 1940.* Honolulu: University of Hawaii Press, 1993. A lively view of the French presence in the islands.

Alexander, Caroline. *The Bounty: The True Story of the Mutiny on the Bounty.* New York: Viking Adult, 2003. A new examination of William Bligh and the famous mutiny.

Denoon, Donald, et al. *The Cambridge History of the Pacific Islanders.* Port Melbourne, Australia: Cambridge University Press, 1997. A team of scholars examines the history of the inhabitants of Oceania from first colonization to the nuclear era. While acknowledging the great diversity of Pacific peoples, cultures, and experiences, the book looks for common patterns and related themes, presenting them in an insightful and innovative way.

Edwards, Edmundo. *Archaeological Survey of Raivavae.* Los Osos, CA: Easter Island Foundation, 2003. Covers the history and legends of this Austral Island.

Howarth, David. *Tahiti: A Paradise Lost.* New York: Penguin Books, 1985. A readable history of European exploration in the Society Islands until the French takeover in 1842.

Howe, K. R. *Nature, Culture, and History.* Honolulu: University of Hawaii Press, 2000. A wide range of contemporary Pacific issues are examined in this timely book.

Irwin, Geoffrey. *The Prehistoric Exploration and Colonization of the Pacific.* Cambridge, UK: Cambridge University Press, 1992. Geoffrey Irwin uses an innovative model to establish a detailed theory of prehistoric navigation.

Kirch, Patrick Vinton. *On the Road of the Winds.* Berkeley, CA: University of California Press, 2000. This archaeological history of the Pacific islands before European contact is easily the most important of its kind in two decades.

McEvedy, Colin. *The Penguin Historical Atlas of the Pacific.* New York: Penguin USA, 1998. Through stories and maps, McEvedy brings Pacific history into sharp focus—a truly unique book.

Oliver, Douglas L. *Polynesia: In Early Historic Times.* Honolulu: Bess Press, 2002. A new account of Polynesian life and culture at the time of first European contact.

Thomas, Nicholas. *Cook: The Extraordinary Voyages of Captain James Cook.* New York: Walker & Company, 2004. An opinionated anthropological history of Cook's three voyages and their impact on the region.

SOCIAL SCIENCE

Danielsson, Bengt. *Work and Life on Raroia.* London: George Allen & Unwin, 1956. Danielsson spent 18 months on this atoll observing Tuamotu life, and this book, published in 1956, is still the only detailed history of the Tuamotu Islands.

Levy, Robert. *Tahitians: Mind and Experience in the Society Islands.* Chicago: University of Chicago Press, 1973. Levy's study, based on several years of fieldwork on Tahiti and Huahine in the 1960s, includes an intriguing examination of the *mahu* (transvestite) phenomenon.

Marshall, Don. *Raivavae.* New York: Doubleday and Co., 1961. The author, who is a professional anthropologist, did fieldwork on this high island in the Austral group in 1957–1958 to find out what was left of the old orgiastic pagan religion and sexual rites.

Oliver, Douglas L. *Oceania: The Native Cultures of Australia and the Pacific Islands.* Honolulu: University of Hawaii Press, 1988. A massive, two-volume, 1,275-page anthropological survey of the precontact anthropology, history, economy, and politics of the entire region.

LITERATURE

Briand, Paul L., Jr. *In Search of Paradise.* Honolulu: Mutual Publishing, 1987. A joint biography of Charles Nordhoff and James Norman Hall.

Day, A. Grove, and Carl Stroven, eds. *Best South Sea Stories.* Honolulu: Mutual Publishing, 1985. Fifteen extracts from the writings of famous European authors.

Day, A. Grove. *The Lure of Tahiti.* Honolulu: Mutual Publishing, 1986. Fifteen choice extracts from the rich literature of "the most romantic island in the world."

Hall, James Norman. *The Forgotten One and Other True Tales of the South Seas.* Honolulu: Mutual Publishing, 1987. A book about expatriate writers and intellectuals who sought refuge on the out-of-the-world islands of the Pacific.

Hall, James Norman, and Charles Bernard Nordhoff. *The Bounty Trilogy.* Retells in fictional form the famous mutiny, Bligh's escape to Timor, and the mutineers' fate on Pitcairn.

London, Jack. *South Sea Tales.* Honolulu: Mutual Publishing, 1985. Stories based on London's visit to Tahiti, Samoa, Fiji, and the Solomons in the early 20th century.

Loti, Pierre. *The Marriage of Loti.* London: Kegan Paul International, 1987. This tale of Loti's visits to Tahiti in 1872 helped foster the romantic myth of Polynesia in Europe.

Maugham, W. Somerset. *The Moon and Sixpence.* London: Penguin Classics, 1993. Story of a London stockbroker who leaves his job for Tahiti and ends up leading an artist's primitive life that isn't as romantic as he had hoped.

Maugham, W. Somerset. *The Trembling of a Leaf.* Honolulu: Mutual Publishing, 1985. The responses of a varied mix of white males—colonial administrator, trader, sea captain, bank manager, and missionary—to the peoples and environment of the South Pacific. Maugham is a masterful storyteller, and his journey to Samoa and Tahiti in 1916–1917 supplied him with poignant material.

Melville, Herman. *Typee, A Peep at Polynesian Life.* London: Penguin Classics, 1996. In 1842 Melville deserted from an American whaler at Nuku Hiva, Marquesas Islands. This semifictional account of Melville's four months among the Typee people was followed by *Omoo,* in which Melville gives his impressions of Tahiti at the time of the French takeover.

Michener, James A. *Tales of the South Pacific.* Greenwich, CT: Fawcett Books, 1989. Short stories based on Michener's wartime experiences in the islands.

Michener, James A. *Return to Paradise.* Greenwich, CT: Fawcett Books, 1974. Michener takes a second look at his wartime haunts in this collection of stories.

Stevenson, Robert Louis. *South Sea Tales.* New York: Oxford Paperbacks, 1999. A collection of Stevenson's best stories about the islands.

Stewart, Frank, ed. *Varua Tupu.* Honolulu: University of Hawaii Press, 2006. A 216-page anthology of French Polynesian art and writing in translation.

THE ARTS

Barbieri, Gian Paolo. *Tahiti Tattoo*. Los Angeles: Taschen America, 1998. An outstanding reference on the Polynesian art of tattooing.

Cachin, Francoise. *The Quest for Paradise*. New York: Harry N. Abrams, 1992. An illustrated biography of Gauguin.

Danielsson, Bengt. *Gauguin in the South Seas*. New York: Doubleday, 1966. Danielsson's fascinating account of Gauguin's 10 years in Polynesia.

Kaeppler, Adrienne, C. Kaufmann, and Douglas Newton. *Oceanic Art*. New York: Abrams, 1997. The first major survey of the arts of Polynesia, Melanesia, and Micronesia in over three decades, this admirable volume brings the reader up to date on recent scholarship in the field. Of the 900 illustrations, more than a third are new.

Meyer, Anthony J. P. *Oceanic Art*. London: Konemann, 2000. This two-volume work provides 800 stunning color photos of art objects from all across the Pacific.

Thomas, Nicholas. *Oceanic Art*. London: Thames and Hudson, 1995. Almost 200 illustrations grace the pages of this readable survey.

LANGUAGE

Anisson du Perron, Jacques, and Mai-Arii Cadousteau. *Dictionaire Moderne, Tahitien-Français et Français-Tahitien*. Papeete: Stepolde, 1973.

Lynch, John. *Pacific Languages: An Introduction*. Honolulu: University of Hawaii Press, 1998. The grammatical features of the Oceanic, Papuan, and Australian languages.

Tryon, Darrell T. *Say It in Tahitian*. Sydney: Pacific Publications, 1977. For lovers of Polynesia, an instant introduction to spoken Tahitian.

REFERENCE BOOKS

Atlas de la Polynésie Française. Paris: Editions de l'ORSTOM, 1993. A major thematic atlas summarizing the geography, population, and history of the territory.

Craig, Robert D. *Dictionary of Polynesian Mythology*. Westport, CT: Greenwood Press, 1989. Aside from hundreds of alphabetical entries listing the legends, stories, gods, goddesses, and heroes of the Polynesians, this book charts the evolution of 30 Polynesian languages.

Jackson, Miles M., ed. *Pacific Island Studies: A Survey of the Literature*. Westport, CT: Greenwood Press, 1986. In addition to comprehensive listings, there are extensive essays that put the most important works in perspective.

Lal, Brig V., and Kate Fortune, eds. *The Pacific Islands: An Encyclopedia*. Honolulu: University of Hawaii Press, 2000. This important book combines the writings of 200 acknowledged experts on the physical environment, peoples, history, politics, economics, society, and culture of the South Pacific. The accompanying CD-ROM provides a wealth of maps, graphs, photos, biographies, and more.

BOOKSELLERS AND PUBLISHERS

Some of the titles listed above are out of print and not available in bookstores. Major research libraries should have a few; otherwise try the specialized antiquarian booksellers or regional publishers that follow. Many of these titles can be ordered online through www.southpacific.org/books.html.

Bibliophile, 103 Adelaide Parade, Woollahra, Sydney, NSW 2025, Australia, tel. 02/9387-1154, www.bibliophile.com.au. An antiquarian bookstore specializing in books about Oceania. View their extensive catalog online.

Bluewater Books & Charts, 1811 Cordova Rd., Fort Lauderdale, FL 33316, USA, tel. 954/763-6533 or 800/942-2583, www.bluewaterweb.com. An outstanding source of navigational charts of the Pacific.

Book Bin, 215 SW Fourth St., Corvallis, OR 97333, USA, tel. 541/752-0040, www.bookbin.com. Their searchable catalog of books on the Pacific Islands at Abe Books lists hundreds of rare titles.

Jean-Louis Boglio, P.O. Box 72, Currumbin, Queensland 4223, Australia, tel. 07/5534-9349, www.maritimebooks.com.au. An excellent source of new and used books on the French territories in the Pacific.

Mutual Publishing Company, 1215 Center St., Suite 210, Honolulu, HI 96816, USA, tel. 808/732-1709, www.mutualpublishing.com. The classics of expatriate Pacific literature, available in cheap paperback editions.

Pacific Island Books, 2802 E. 132nd Circle, Thornton, CO 80241, USA, tel. 303/920-8338, www.pacificislandbooks.com. One of the best U.S. sources of books about the Pacific. It stocks many titles published by the USP Press.

Serendipity Books, 256 Railway Parade, West Leederville, WA 6007, Australia, tel. 08/9382-2246, www.serendipitybooks.com.au. The largest stock of antiquarian, second-hand, and out-of-print books on the Pacific in Western Australia.

University of Hawaii Press, 2840 Kolowalu St., Honolulu, HI 96822-1888, USA, tel. 808/956-8255, www.uhpress.hawaii.edu. Their *Hawaii and the Pacific* catalog is well worth requesting if you're trying to build a Pacific library.

PERIODICALS

Commodores' Bulletin, Seven Seas Cruising Association, 2501 East Commercial Blvd., Suite 203, Fort Lauderdale, FL 33308, USA, tel. 954/771-5660, www.ssca.org, US$75 per year worldwide by airmail. This monthly bulletin is chock-full of useful information for anyone wishing to tour the Pacific by sailing boat. All Pacific yachties and friends should be Seven Seas members.

The Contemporary Pacific, University of Hawaii Press, 2840 Kolowalu St., Honolulu, HI 96822, USA, www.uhpress.hawaii.edu, published twice a year, US$35 per year. Publishes a good mix of articles of interest to both scholars and general readers; the country-by-country "Political Review" in each number is a concise summary of events during the preceding year. The "Dialogue" section offers informed comment on the more controversial issues in the region, while recent publications on the islands are examined through book reviews. Those interested in current topics in Pacific island affairs should check recent volumes for background information.

Islands Business, P.O. Box 12718, Suva, Fiji Islands, tel. 330-3108, www.islandsbusiness.com, annual airmailed subscription A$45 to Australia, NZ$65 to New Zealand, US$52 to North America, US$62 to Europe. A monthly newsmagazine with in-depth coverage of political and economic trends around the Pacific. Travel and aviation news gets some prominence.

Rapa Nui Journal, P.O. Box 6774, Los Osos, CA 93412-6774, USA, www.islandheritage.org, biannually, US$40 per year in North America, US$50 elsewhere. Though primarily about Easter Island, this outstanding journal publishes many scholarly reports on archaeology in French Polynesia.

Surfer Travel Reports, P.O. Box 1028, Dana Point, CA 92629, USA, www.surfermag.com/travel/pacific. These reports provide a detailed analysis of surfing conditions at different destinations. Back issues on specific countries are available at US$7 each (the last issue on Tahiti was No. 6.4 and on Tubuai No. 15.5). This is by far your best source of surfing information.

Tahiti Beach Press, Jan Prince, B.P. 887, 98713 Papeete, Tahiti, French Polynesia, www.tahitibeachpress.com, subscription US$20 a year. Established in 1980, this is Tahiti's only English-language magazine.

Tahiti Pacifique, Alex W. du Prel, B.P. 368, 98728 Moorea, www.tahiti-pacifique.com, annual subscription 75 euros. For those who read French, this monthly magazine offers a style of informed and critical commentary quite unlike that seen in the daily press of the French territories.

Undercurrent, 3020 Bridgeway, Suite 102, Sausalito, CA 94965, USA, tel. 415/289-0501 or 800/326-1896, www.undercurrent.org, US$35 per year. A monthly consumer protection–oriented newsletter for serious scuba divers. Unlike virtually every other diving publication, *Undercurrent* accepts no advertising or free trips, which allows its writers to tell it as it is. In January 2010, the print edition was discontinued and *Undercurrent* is now only available online.

DISCOGRAPHY

Music lovers will be pleased to know that authentic Pacific music is readily available on compact disc. In compiling this selection, we've tried to list noncommercial recordings that are faithful to the traditional music of the islands as it exists today. Island music based on Western pop has been avoided. You can buy many of these CDs at music shops in Papeete, or order them online through www.southpacific.org/music.html.

Air Mail Music: Tahiti, Manuiti/Playasound, 1998. A great collection of old-fashioned string band music by several artists.

A Journey to Tahiti, Manuiti/Playasound, 1994. A collection of songs by Bimbo, Emma, Tahiti ma, Poline, Heikura, and Charley Manu.

Coco's Temaeva, Manuiti/Playasound. Founded by Coco Hotahota in 1962, Temaeva has won more prizes at the annual Heiva i Tahiti festivals than any other professional dance troupe. These recordings are from 1966–1972.

Echo des Îles Tuamotu et Bora Bora, Manuiti/Playasound. Classic songs recorded 1954–1969 by the late Marie Mariteragi, queen of Tuamotu kaina music.

Fanshawe, David, ed. *South Pacific: Island Music.* New York: Nonesuch Records, 2003. Originally released in 1981, this recording takes you from Tahiti to the Cook Islands, Tonga, Samoa, Fiji, Kiribati, and the Solomon Islands.

Fanshawe, David, ed. *Spirit of Polynesia.* Saydisc Records. An anthology of the music of 12 Pacific countries recorded between 1978 and 1988. Many of the pieces are from French Polynesia.

Heart of Tahiti. GNP Crescendo Records, 1999. Twenty top Tahitian tunes by stars like Charley Manu, Yves Roche, and Eddie Lund.

Magic of the South Seas. New York: Arc Music, 2000. An anthology of music from Tahiti, the Marquesas Islands, Tonga, and Fiji.

Melodies des Atolls, Manuiti/Playasound, 2001. Twenty outstanding Tahitian songs from the 1950s in the Tahiti Belle Epoque series.

Rapa Iti, Vol. II. Shanachie Records, 1994. Choral singing and chanting from the Austral Group.

Royal Folkloric Troupe, Manuiti/Playasound, 1994. Volume 2 of Coco's Temaeva featuring Coco Hotahota's Royal Folkloric Troupe of Tahiti, renowned for its original choreography.

South Pacific Drums, Manuiti/Playasound, 1994. A compilation of 39 of the best percussion recordings in Manuiti's archives—an excellent introduction to the traditional music of Polynesia.

Tahiti Belle Epoque, Vol. 7, Manuiti/Playasound, 2000. Classics from the years 1971–1977 by the great vocalist Emma Terangi (1938–2000) from Hikueru atoll in the Tuamotus.

Tahiti, The Gauguin Years: Songs and Dances. Nonesuch, 2003. A classic collection of old Polynesian songs.

Internet Resources

Air Tahiti
www.airtahiti.aero
Peruse the illustrated articles in Air Tahiti's inflight magazine while checking flight schedules and fares.

Air Tahiti Nui
www.airtahitinui-usa.com
The site of the main air carrier, with details on flights and packages to French Polynesia plus destination information.

e-Tahiti Travel
www.etahititravel.com
An online travel agency with clear information on packages, hotels, cruises, flights, excursions, and car rentals. The trip planner allows you to price your visit, and the island guide provides useful information on 13 islands.

Haere Mai
www.haere-mai.pf
The home page of the federation of guesthouses and family accommodations in French Polynesia provides listings in all five archipelagoes. Photos, descriptions, and prices are supplied.

Map South Pacific
www.mapsouthpacific.com
South Pacific maps and travel guides to Tahiti, Fiji, Samoa, Vanuatu, Easter Island, and more.

Pacific Pictures
www.pacific-pictures.com
Author David Stanley's personal collection of photos of French Polynesia and 14 other Pacific countries and territories.

Philatelic Center of French Polynesia
www.tahitiphilatelie.com
The Philatelic Bureau's site is appealing for the varied background information provided on local stamp issues and telephone cards. If you're curious about the arrival of the gospel in Polynesia, Tahitian music, seashells of Polynesia, the return of the Pacific Battalion, etc., look here.

Polynesia Diving
www.polynesia-diving.com
The listings of dive sites, scuba operators, lodgings, and cruises will help scuba divers plan their trips.

Tahiti1.com
www.tahiti1.com
A news and information portal where you can sample Tahitian cooking and cocktails, view the flowers, check boat timetables to the outer islands, read the legends of old Polynesia, learn about tattooing, and much more.

Tahiti Black Pearls
www.perlesdetahiti.net
The site of GIE Perles de Tahiti is about the best primer you'll find on the subject—a must for anyone in the market for a black pearl.

Tahiti Diving Guide
www.diving-tahiti.com
A dozen diving destinations are briefly described and mapped on this attractive site.

Tahiti Explorer
www.tahitiexplorer.com
Get clued in on black pearls, cruises, diving, flights, hotels, the weather, people, geography, etc. The photo albums and trip reports are a huge resource, and there's a travel forum.

Tahiti Guide
www.tahitiguide.com
French Polynesia's most complete Web guide with accommodations listings, activities, attractions, and more than 30 maps.

Tahiti Presse
http://en.tahitipresse.pf
The website of this Tahitian news agency posts daily reports on a wide variety of topics.

Tahiti Sun Travel
www.tahitisun.com
Provides detailed travel information on Tahiti, Moorea, Huahine, Raiatea, Taha'a, Bora Bora, and the Tuamotu Islands. There's also a page about Marlon Brando's island, Tetiaroa.

Tahiti Tatou
www.tahititatou.com
Learn about the designs, meanings, and origins of Polynesian tattooing here.

Tahiti Tourisme
www.tahiti-tourisme.com
This official tourism site provides another useful introduction to French Polynesia. The many outside links allow you to access additional information, and there's an events calendar. Many of Tahiti Tourisme's overseas offices have sites of their own.

The Tahiti Traveler
www.thetahititraveler.com
An online travel guide with background information, island guides, hotel listings, a photo gallery, and screensavers.

Travelmaxia
www.travelmaxia.com
This Internet portal provides a vast amount of information on accommodations in French Polynesia. You're able to email the properties directly using the online forms—this is not a tour company.

True Tahiti Vacations
www.truetahitivacation.com
A good source of ideas for romantic vacations and honeymoons. There are sections on spa escapes, island activities, and specials.

The Islands at a Glance

ISLAND GROUP	LAND AREA (SQ KM)	HIGHEST POINT (M)	POPULATION	LATITUDE	LONGITUDE
Society Islands					
Bora Bora	29.3	727	8,930	16.45°S	151.87°W
Huahine	74.8	669	5,986	16.72°S	151.10°W
Maiao	8.3	180	299	17.67°S	150.63°W
Manuae	4.0	4	24	16.52°S	154.72°W
Maupihaa	3.6	4	9	16.87°S	154.00°W
Maupiti	11.4	380	1,197	16.45°S	152.25°W
Moorea	125.2	1,207	16,208	17.57°S	150.00°W
Motu One	2.8	4	0	15.80°S	154.55°W
Raiatea	171.4	1,017	12,008	16.82°S	151.43°W
Tahaa	90.2	590	5,011	16.62°S	151.49°W
Tahiti	1,045.1	2,241	178,173	17.32°S	149.35°W
Tetiaroa	4.9	3	3	17.00°S	149.57°W
Austral Islands					
Raivavae	17.9	437	905	23.92°S	147.80°W
Rapa	40.5	650	480	26.60°S	144.37°W
Rimatara	8.6	84	786	22.67°S	153.42°W
Rurutu	32.3	389	2,089	22.48°S	151.33°W
Tubuai	45.0	422	2,044	23.35°S	149.58°W
Tuamotu Islands					
Ahe	12.2	4	566	14.50°S	146.33°W
Amanu	25.0	4	156	17.72°S	140.65°W
Anaa	37.7	4	463	17.50°S	145.50°W
Apataki	20.0	4	495	15.50°S	146.33°W
Aratika	8.3	4	233	15.55°S	146.65°W
Arutua	15.0	4	725	15.17°S	146.67°W

ISLAND GROUP	LAND AREA (SQ KM)	HIGHEST POINT (M)	POPULATION	LATITUDE	LONGITUDE
Tuamotu Islands (continued)					
Faaite	8.8	4	362	16.75°S	145.17°W
Fakahina	8.3	4	131	16.00°S	140.08°W
Fakarava	13.8	4	797	16.17°S	145.58°W
Fangatau	5.9	4	121	15.75°S	140.83°W
Hao	18.5	4	1,132	18.25°S	140.92°W
Hereheretue	3.4	4	58	19.87°S	144.97°W
Hikueru	2.8	4	169	17.53°S	142.53°W
Katiu	10.0	4	285	16.52°S	144.20°W
Kauehi	15.0	4	243	15.98°S	145.15°W
Kaukura	11.0	4	541	15.72°S	146.83°W
Makatea	29.5	111	61	16.17°S	148.23°W
Makemo	13.1	4	728	16.43°S	143.93°W
Manihi	13.0	4	816	14.50°S	145.92°W
Marokau	4.5	4	99	18.00°S	142.25°W
Marutea South	4.0	4	240	21.09°S	135.06°W
Mataiva	15.0	4	204	14.88°S	148.72°W
Moruroa	10.5	6	0	21.82°S	138.80°W
Napuka	8.1	4	272	14.17°S	141.20°W
Nengonengo	0.7	4	9	18.70°S	141.77°W
Niau	21.6	5	171	16.18°S	146.37°W
Nihiru	2.0	4	6	16.68°S	142.88°W
Nukutavake	3.6	4	165	19.18°S	138.70°W
Nukutipipi	0.8	4	0	20.67°S	142.50°W
Pukapuka	5.4	4	164	14.80°S	138.82°W
Pukarua	6.5	4	206	18.27°S	137.00°W
Rangiroa	79.2	4	2,473	15.80°S	147.97°W

ISLAND GROUP	LAND AREA (SQ KM)	HIGHEST POINT (M)	POPULATION	LATITUDE	LONGITUDE
Tuamotu Islands (continued)					
Raraka	7.0	4	72	16.13°S	145.00°W
Raroia	7.5	2	197	15.93°S	142.37°W
Reao	9.4	4	362	18.47°S	136.47°W
Taenga	4.9	4	90	16.30°S	143.80°W
Taiaro	3.3	5	4	15.77°S	144.62°W
Takapoto	15.0	4	475	14.53°S	145.23°W
Takaroa	16.5	4	1,104	14.37°S	144.97°W
Takume	4.5	4	105	15.65°S	142.10°W
Tatakoto	7.3	4	228	17.28°S	138.33°W
Tematangi	5.5	4	56	21.64°S	140.62°W
Tepoto North	1.8	4	44	14.00°S	141.33°W
Tikehau	20.0	4	507	14.87°S	148.25°W
Toau	12.0	4	55	15.97°S	145.82°W
Tureia	8.3	4	255	20.78°S	138.50°W
Vahitahi	2.5	4	81	18.58°S	138.83°W
Vairaatea	3.0	4	65	19.23°S	139.32°W
Gambier Islands					
Aukena	1.3	198	40	23.13°S	134.90°W
Mangareva	15.4	482	1,030	23.13°S	134.92°W
Taravai	5.7	255	7	23.13°S	135.03°W
Marquesas Islands					
Fatu Hiva	83.8	960	587	10.40°S	138.67°W
Hiva Oa	315.5	1,276	2,009	9.78°S	138.78°W
Nuku Hiva	339.5	1,224	2,664	8.95°S	140.25°W
Tahuata	69.3	1,040	670	9.93°S	139.10°W
Ua Huka	83.4	884	570	8.92°S	139.56°W
Ua Pou	105.3	1,203	2,158	9.40°S	140.08°W

Index

A

B

C

G

H

IJK

QR

S

T

UV

WXYZ

List of Maps

Acknowledgments

Special thanks to Madame Jacques Brel for kind permission to reproduce *Les Marquises* and to Rike Grotmaack and Malte Peter for tips on traveling with children.

Thanks too to the following readers who took the trouble to write us about their trips: Dominick Derosa, Nicos Hadjicostis, Lille Kollar, Jean-Marie Libeau, John McQueen, Francis Mortimer, and Laurel Samuela.

To have your own name included here in the next edition, write: David Stanley, *Moon Tahiti,* Avalon Travel, 1700 Fourth St., Berkeley, CA 94710, USA, feedback@moon.com.

A Note From the Author

While out researching my books I find it cheaper to pay my own way, and you can rest assured that nothing in this book is designed to repay freebies from hotels, restaurants, tour operators, or airlines. I prefer to arrive unexpected and uninvited, and to experience things as they really are. On the road I seldom identify myself to anyone. Unlike many other travel writers, I don't allow myself to be chaperoned by local tourist offices or leave out justified criticism that might have an impact on book sales. The essential difference between this book and the myriad travel brochures free for the taking in airports and tourist offices all across the Pacific is that this book represents you, the traveler, while the brochures represent the travel industry. The companies and organizations included herein are there for information purposes only, and a mention in no way implies an endorsement.

www.moon.com

DESTINATIONS | ACTIVITIES | BLOGS | MAPS | BOOKS

MOON.COM is ready to help plan your next trip! Filled with fresh trip ideas and strategies, author interviews, informative travel blogs, a detailed map library, and descriptions of all the Moon guidebooks, Moon.com is all you need to get out and explore the world—or even places in your own backyard. While at Moon.com, sign up for our monthly e-newsletter for updates on new releases, travel tips, and expert advice from our on-the-go Moon authors. As always, when you travel with Moon, expect an experience that is uncommon and truly unique.

MOON IS ON FACEBOOK—BECOME A FAN!

JOIN THE MOON PHOTO GROUP ON FLICKR

MAP SYMBOLS

Expressway	Highlight	Airfield	Golf Course
Primary Road	City/Town	Airport	Parking Area
Secondary Road	State Capital	Mountain	Archaeological Site
Unpaved Road	National Capital	Unique Natural Feature	Church
Trail	Point of Interest	Waterfall	Gas Station
Ferry	Accommodation	Park	Glacier
Railroad	Restaurant/Bar	Trailhead	Mangrove
Pedestrian Walkway	Other Location	Skiing Area	Reef
Stairs	Campground		Swamp

CONVERSION TABLES

°C = (°F - 32) / 1.8
°F = (°C x 1.8) + 32
1 inch = 2.54 centimeters (cm)
1 foot = 0.304 meters (m)
1 yard = 0.914 meters
1 mile = 1.6093 kilometers (km)
1 km = 0.6214 miles
1 fathom = 1.8288 m
1 chain = 20.1168 m
1 furlong = 201.168 m
1 acre = 0.4047 hectares
1 sq km = 100 hectares
1 sq mile = 2.59 square km
1 ounce = 28.35 grams
1 pound = 0.4536 kilograms
1 short ton = 0.90718 metric ton
1 short ton = 2,000 pounds
1 long ton = 1.016 metric tons
1 long ton = 2,240 pounds
1 metric ton = 1,000 kilograms
1 quart = 0.94635 liters
1 US gallon = 3.7854 liters
1 Imperial gallon = 4.5459 liters
1 nautical mile = 1.852 km

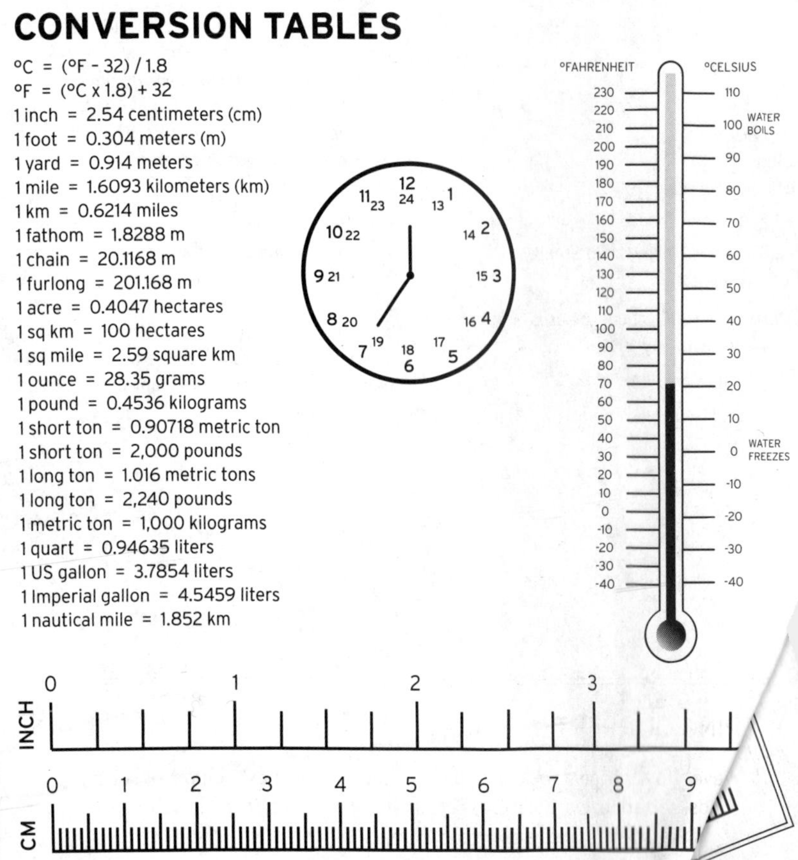

MOON TAHITI
Avalon Travel
a member of the Perseus Books Group
1700 Fourth Street
Berkeley, CA 94710, USA
www.moon.com

Editor and Series Manager: Kathryn Ettinger
Copy Editor: Christopher Church
Graphics Coordinator: Darren Alessi
Production Coordinator: Darren Alessi
Cover Designer: Darren Alessi
Map Editor: Mike Morgenfeld
Cartographers: Allison Rawley, Chris Henrick, Mike Morgenfeld
Indexer: Deana Shields

ISBN: 978-1-59880-738-7
ISSN: 1544-0842

Printing History
1st Edition – 1989
7th Edition – February 2011
5 4

Front cover photo: © Photo Resource Hawaii / Alamy
Title page photo: © David Stanley
Color interior photos: All © David Stanley except pages 6 (bottom), 7 (bottom right), 9 (top), 14, 20, and 24 © Tahiti Tourisme

Printed in Canada by Friesens

All recommendations, including those for sights, activities, hotels, restaurants, and shops, are based on each author's individual judgment. We do not accept payment for inclusion in our travel guides, and our authors don't accept free goods or services in exchange for positive coverage.

NG CURRENT

If y
that a favorite gem you'd like to see included in the next edition, or see anything
comme updating, clarification, or correction, please drop us a line. Send your
via email to feedback@moon.com, or use the address above.

MAP SYMBOLS

Expressway
Primary Road
Secondary Road
Unpaved Road
Trail
Ferry
Railroad
Pedestrian Walkway
Stairs

Highlight
City/Town
State Capital
National Capital
Point of Interest
Accommodation
Restaurant/Bar
Other Location
Campground

Airfield
Airport
Mountain
Unique Natural Feature
Waterfall
Park
Trailhead
Skiing Area

Golf Course
Parking Area
Archaeological Site
Church
Gas Station
Glacier
Mangrove
Reef
Swamp

CONVERSION TABLES

°C = (°F - 32) / 1.8
°F = (°C x 1.8) + 32
1 inch = 2.54 centimeters (cm)
1 foot = 0.304 meters (m)
1 yard = 0.914 meters
1 mile = 1.6093 kilometers (km)
1 km = 0.6214 miles
1 fathom = 1.8288 m
1 chain = 20.1168 m
1 furlong = 201.168 m
1 acre = 0.4047 hectares
1 sq km = 100 hectares
1 sq mile = 2.59 square km
1 ounce = 28.35 grams
1 pound = 0.4536 kilograms
1 short ton = 0.90718 metric ton
1 short ton = 2,000 pounds
1 long ton = 1.016 metric tons
1 long ton = 2,240 pounds
1 metric ton = 1,000 kilograms
1 quart = 0.94635 liters
1 US gallon = 3.7854 liters
1 Imperial gallon = 4.5459 liters
1 nautical mile = 1.852 km

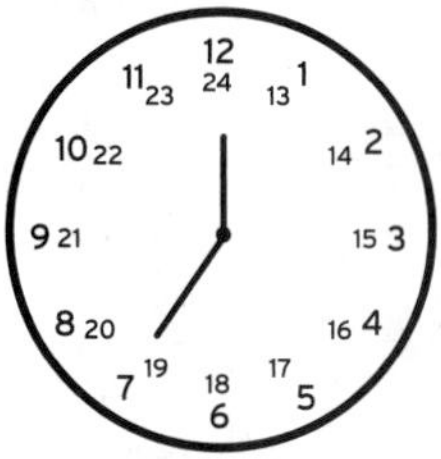

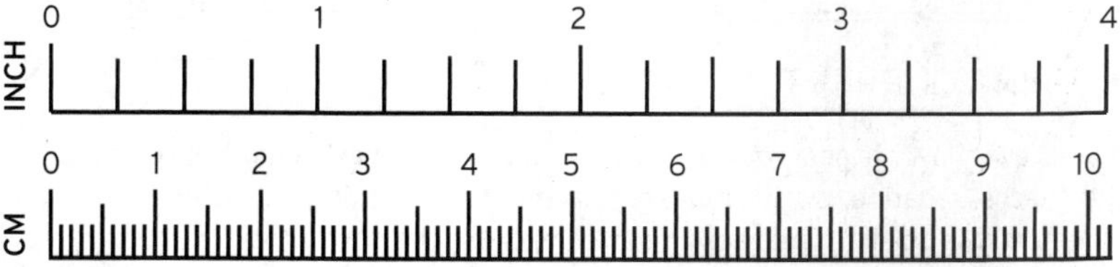

12 24 1 13 2 14 3 15 4 16 5 17 6 18 7 19 8 20 9 21 10 22 11 23

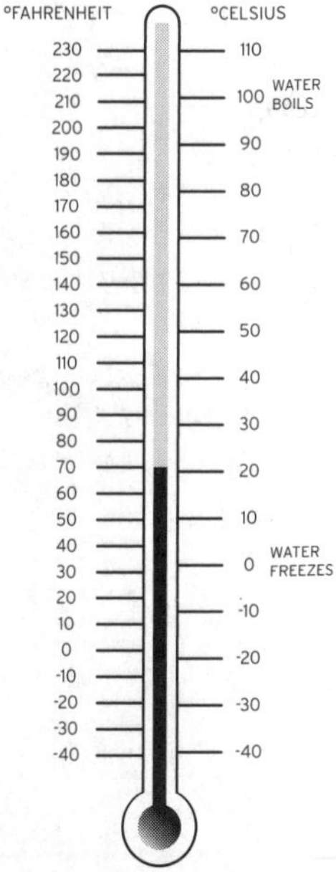

°FAHRENHEIT
°CELSIUS
230 220 210 200 190 180 170 160 150 140 130 120 110 100 90 80 70 60 50 40 30 20 10 0 -10 -20 -30 -40
110 100 WATER BOILS 90 80 70 60 50 40 30 20 10 0 WATER FREEZES -10 -20 -30 -40

INCH
0 1 2 3 4

CM
0 1 2 3 4 5 6 7 8 9 10

MOON TAHITI
Avalon Travel
a member of the Perseus Books Group
1700 Fourth Street
Berkeley, CA 94710, USA
www.moon.com

Editor and Series Manager: Kathryn Ettinger
Copy Editor: Christopher Church
Graphics Coordinator: Darren Alessi
Production Coordinator: Darren Alessi
Cover Designer: Darren Alessi
Map Editor: Mike Morgenfeld
Cartographers: Allison Rawley, Chris Henrick, Mike Morgenfeld
Indexer: Deana Shields

ISBN: 978-1-59880-738-7
ISSN: 1544-0842

Printing History
1st Edition – 1989
7th Edition – February 2011
5 4

Front cover photo: © Photo Resource Hawaii / Alamy
Title page photo: © David Stanley
Color interior photos: All © David Stanley except pages 6 (bottom), 7 (bottom right), 9 (top), 14, 20, and 24 © Tahiti Tourisme

Printed in Canada by Friesens

KEEPING CURRENT

If you have a favorite gem you'd like to see included in the next edition, or see anything that needs updating, clarification, or correction, please drop us a line. Send your comments via email to feedback@moon.com, or use the address above.